The Unofficial Guide

DISNEY
Cruise Line 2025

Tammy Whiting with Len Testa and Erin Foster

The *Disney Wish* docked at Castaway Cay

Tendering to shore in Grand Cayman from the *Disney Fantasy*

The Disney Cruise Line terminal in Port Canaveral

The Disney Cruise Line terminal in Fort Lauderdale

The AquaLab water-play area and Twist 'n' Spout slide on the *Disney Magic*

One of many pools on the *Disney Wish*

Adult pool on the *Disney Dream*

Adult pool on the *Disney Magic*

The atrium of the *Disney Wonder*

The atrium of the *Disney Dream*

The Bayou lounge on the *Disney Wish*

Cove Café adults-only lounge and coffee bar on the *Disney Magic*

The Rose lounge on the *Disney Wish*

Star Wars: Hyperspace Lounge on the *Disney Wish*

Concierge lounge on the *Disney Magic*

Concierge lounge on the *Disney Wish*

The Grand Cabana on Castaway Cay

Serenity Bay on Castaway Cay

Snorkeling on Castaway Cay

Spring-a-Leak water-play area
on Castaway Cay

The Family Beach on Lookout Cay

A family cabana on Lookout Cay

Rush Out Gush Out family water-play
area on Lookout Cay

Goombay Cultural Center
on Lookout Cay

1923 dining room on the *Disney Wish*

Enchanted Garden dining room
on the *Disney Fantasy*

Animator's Palate dining room
on the *Disney Fantasy*

Royal Palace dining room
on the *Disney Dream*

Tiana's Place dining room
on the *Disney Wonder*

Cabanas buffet restaurant
on the *Disney Magic*

Palo adult dining on the *Disney Wonder*

Enchanté adult dining
on the *Disney Wish*

Andy's Room in the *Disney Magic*'s Oceaneer Club

Oceaneer Club on the *Disney Wish*

Oceaneer Club on the *Disney Dream*

Oceaneer Lab on the *Disney Dream*

Vibe teen club on the *Disney Wonder*

The Hideaway, part of Vibe teen club on the *Disney Wish*

"It's A Small World" Nursery! on the *Disney Magic*

Minigolf on the *Disney Dream*

Concierge 2-Story Royal Suite
with Verandah on the *Disney Wish*

Deluxe Family Oceanview Stateroom
on the *Disney Fantasy*

Standard Inside Stateroom
on the *Disney Wish*

Concierge 1-Bedroom Suite
on the *Disney Fantasy*

Deluxe Oceanview Stateroom
with Verandah on the *Disney Magic*

Concierge 1-Story Royal Suite with
Verandah on the *Disney Wish*

Concierge *Wish* Tower Suite
on the *Disney Wish*

Deluxe Family Oceanview Stateroom with
Verandah on the *Disney Dream*

Fitness Center on the *Disney Dream*

The Rainforest in Senses Spa on the *Disney Wish*

Luna family nightclub and lounge on the *Disney Wish*

Buena Vista Theatre on the *Disney Dream*

Bibbidi Bobbidi Boutique on the *Disney Wish*

Sweet On You on the *Disney Fantasy*

The *Disney Dream* decorated for Halloween on the High Seas

The Grand Hall of the *Disney Wish* on a Very Merrytime Cruise

THE *unofficial* GUIDE®

TO Disney Cruise Line

2025

TAMMY WHITING
with LEN TESTA and ERIN FOSTER

Every effort has been made to ensure the accuracy of this book, and its contents are believed to be correct at the time of publication. Nevertheless, please be aware that these contents are subject to change after publication, owing to numerous factors that influence the cruise industry. The publisher therefore cannot accept responsibility for errors or omissions; for changes in prices, itineraries, and other information presented in this guide; or for the consequences of relying on this information. We strongly suggest that you write or call ahead for confirmation when making your travel plans.

The authors' assessments of restaurants, shows, port adventures, and the like are subjective—they may not reflect the publisher's opinion or align with a reader's own experience. Readers are invited to write the publisher with ideas, comments, and suggestions for future editions.

The Unofficial Guides
An imprint of AdventureKEEN
2204 First Ave. S., Ste. 102
Birmingham, AL 35233

Editor: Kate Johnson
Cover and color-insert design: Scott McGrew
Photos: Tammy Whiting
Text design: Vertigo Design, with updates by Annie Long
Maps and illustrations: Steve Jones
Proofreader: Emily Beaumont
Indexer: Potomac Indexing

Cover photo: The *Disney Wonder* in Alaska

To contact us from within the United States, please call 800-678-7006 or fax 877-374-9016. You may also reach us at info@theunofficialguides.com; TheUnofficialGuides on Facebook, Instagram, Threads, and Pinterest; TheUGSeries on X (formerly Twitter); and TheUnofficialGuideSeries on YouTube.

AdventureKEEN also publishes its books in a variety of electronic formats. Some content that appears in print may not be available in electronic formats.

ISBN 978-1-62809-162-5 (pbk.), ISBN 978-1-62809-163-2 (e-book)

Distributed by Publishers Group West

Manufactured in the United States of America

5 4 3 2 1

COME CHECK US OUT!

Supplement your valuable guidebook with tips, news, and deals by visiting our websites:

theunofficialguides.com
touringplans.com

Sign up for the Unofficial Guide newsletter for even more travel tips and special offers.

Join the conversation on social media:

 TheUGSeries

 TheUnofficialGuides

 TheUnofficialGuides

 TheUnofficialGuides

 TheUnofficialGuideSeries

 TheUnofficialGuides

Other Unofficial Guides

The Disneyland Story: The Unofficial Guide to the Evolution of Walt Disney's Dream

Universal vs. Disney: The Unofficial Guide to American Theme Parks' Greatest Rivalry

The Unofficial Guide to Walt Disney World

The Unofficial Guide to Disneyland

The Unofficial Guide to Las Vegas

The Unofficial Guide to Universal Orlando

The Unofficial Guide to Washington, D.C.

CONTENTS

LIST *of* DIAGRAMS *and* MAPS

ABOUT *the* AUTHORS

TAMMY WHITING is an avid cruiser who has sailed all over the world on over 75 cruises, more than 50 of those on Disney Cruise Line. She's worked in the travel industry for over 17 years and owns Storybook Destinations. While Tammy's favorite way to travel is on a cruise ship, she's never turned her nose up at a vacation. She has enjoyed amazing trips to Tokyo Disney, Disneyland Paris, Antarctica, the Galapagos, European river cruises, and guided tours with Adventures by Disney. Tammy lived in Europe for five years as a military brat and has been a military spouse for over 30 years, living in almost every corner of the United States. When she isn't traveling, you can find her enjoying her family, buying camera equipment, and planning her next trip.

LEN TESTA is coauthor of the *Unofficial Guides* series, covering Walt Disney World, Disneyland, Las Vegas, Universal Orlando, and Washington, D.C. While Len has published works in travel, computer science, and endocrinology, it's widely acknowledged that he's just the pretty face for a group of people way more talented than he is (and "pretty face" is a stretch at best). Len sends love to his daughter, Hannah.

ERIN FOSTER was a charter member of the Disney Parks Moms Panel (now the planDisney panel). She has been on many sailings of the *Magic, Wonder, Dream, Fantasy,* and *Wish,* including the *Wish*'s maiden voyage in 2022. Erin is a regular contributor to the blog at TouringPlans.

ACKNOWLEDGMENTS

THE FIRST THANKS go to Erin Foster, who helmed this guide for 10 years and whose words are throughout, and Scott Sanders, who selflessly contributes his vast knowledge of all things Disney Cruise Line. Thank you to the Ladies of Leisure and other dear friends who continue to sail with me through the years to keep me up-to-date. Thank you to my family, who are my number one supporters, and my husband, who is my number one fan. Lastly, thank you to Luke, the greatest little human on the planet.

—*Tammy Whiting*

IT TOOK A LIFEBOAT full of people to produce this book and its companion web content. David Davies created our website for DCL information. Thanks to Bill Hirsch, Larissa Tapigliani, and Matt Hochberg for answering my incessant questions about the cruise industry.

—*Len Testa*

INTRODUCTION

ABOUT *this* GUIDE

WHY "UNOFFICIAL"?

THE MATERIAL IN THIS BOOK is original and has not been reviewed or approved by the Walt Disney Company Inc. or Disney Cruise Line. To the contrary, we represent and serve you, the consumer: If a ship serves mediocre food or has subpar entertainment, we say so. Through our independence, we hope to make selecting a cruise efficient and economical and to help make your cruise experience on-target and fun.

To that end, our *unofficial* guide offers the following:

- A planning timeline for your Disney cruise (see page 11)
- Tips on saving money on your cruise (see page 20)
- Details about what makes each DCL ship unique and what they have in common (see page 37)
- Updated deck plans for the ships (see page 51)
- What to expect on the newest ships, the *Disney Treasure* and *Disney Destiny* (see pages 46 and 48)
- What to consider when choosing a stateroom, along with recommendations for specific staterooms (see page 103)
- Updated stateroom floor plans (see page 89)
- A link to stateroom video tours from across the DCL fleet (see page 89)
- Advice on when and how to book your cruise (see page 110)
- What life on board is like (see page 130)
- Firsthand reviews and experiences from Lookout Cay at Lighthouse Point (see page 333)
- What to expect in ports of call (see page 343)
- Comparisons between DCL and other cruise lines (see page 373)
- Our thoughts on what's next for DCL (see page 385)

DISNEY CRUISE LINE:
An Overview

THE WALT DISNEY COMPANY launched its cruise line In 1998, with the 2,400-passenger **Disney Magic,** forever changing the cruise industry. An almost identical ship, the **Disney Wonder,** entered service in 1999. Two larger ships, the **Disney Dream** and **Disney Fantasy,** joined the fleet in 2011 and 2012, respectively. In 2016, DCL announced it would be building two additional ships. A year later, this was amended to include a third new ship: The **Disney Wish,** the first of this new generation of ships, now known as the **Wish class,** set sail during the summer of 2022. The second *Wish*-class ship, the **Disney Treasure,** launched Christmas week of 2024. The third *Wish*-class ship, the **Disney Destiny,** is scheduled to set sail in 2025.

In late 2022, Disney confirmed the purchase of a partially built megaship initially known as the **Global Dream,** which became available when its builder, Genting Hong Kong, collapsed during the pandemic. Now known as the **Disney Adventure,** this ship will be based in Singapore and will sail to exciting new destinations for DCL. It is expected to debut in 2025.

In starting a cruise line, Disney put together a team of industry veterans, dozens of the world's best-known ship designers, and its own unrivaled creative talent. Together, they created the DCL ships, recognizing that the smallest detail would be critical to the line's success.

The result? The team succeeded, starting with the ships' design aesthetic, which is simultaneously classic and innovative. Exteriors are traditional, reminiscent of the great ocean liners of the past but with some quintessentially Disney twists. Inside, the ships feature up-to-the-minute technology and brim with novel ideas for dining, entertainment, and cabin design. Even DCL's exclusive cruise terminal at Port Canaveral, Florida, is part of the overall strategy.

Disney was the first cruise line to feature **split bathrooms** in the majority of their staterooms, which means there are two separate bathroom areas, one with a sink and toilet and the other with a sink and shower/tub combo, allowing two people to get ready at the same time. Disney is still the only major cruise line with tubs in most of their staterooms.

Disney pioneered another cruise industry first: *Fireworks at Sea*. Featured on almost every itinerary, fireworks at sea was a huge hit with cruisers and, to this day, draws big crowds up on the top decks.

Since 1998, Disney has used its first private island, **Castaway Cay** (see page 321), as an exclusive destination for Bahamian cruises. In summer 2024, Disney debuted a second private getaway, **Disney Lookout Cay at Lighthouse Point** on the island of Eleuthera.

As for dining, Disney practically reinvented the concept for cruises when it introduced rotational dining (see page 198), where not only do you dine in a different restaurant with a different motif each

THE DISNEY CRUISE LINE FLEET

	Disney Magic	Disney Wonder	Disney Dream	Disney Fantasy	Disney Wish	Disney Treasure	Disney Destiny
YEAR LAUNCHED	1998	1999	2011	2012	2022	2024	2025
GODMOTHER	Patricia Disney	Tinker Bell	Jennifer Hudson	Mariah Carey	Make-A-Wish children	TBD	TBD
CAPACITY							
PASSENGERS	2,713	2,713	4,000	4,000	4,000	4,000	4,000
CREW	950	950	1,458	1,458	1,555	1,555	1,555
PASSENGER DECKS	11	11	14	14	15	15	15
STATEROOMS							
INSIDE	256	256	150	150	121	123	123
OCEANVIEW	362	362	199	199	185	185	185
OUTSIDE VERANDAH	259	259	901	901	948	948	948
TOTAL STATEROOMS	877	877	1,250	1,250	1,254	1,256	1,256
DESIGN/ DECOR	Art Deco	Art Nouveau	Art Deco	Art Nouveau	Enchantment*	Adventure**	Heroes and Villains

* Gothic, Baroque, and French Rococo
** Gilded palace with Asian and African artistic influences

evening, but your servers and dining companions also move with you. Rotational dining was incredibly well received, and other cruise lines quickly followed suit.

The foundation of DCL's business is built on **Bahamian** and **Caribbean** cruises out of Port Canaveral, which is a little over an hour from Walt Disney World. DCL has expanded its Florida footprint with a dedicated terminal in Port Everglades in Fort Lauderdale, which is about 3 hours from Disney World. Disney has committed to one ship sailing out of Port Everglades year-round, with an additional seasonal ship beginning in 2025.

Disney also offers **Alaskan, Bermudan, Canadian, European, Hawaiian, Pacific Coast, Panama Canal, South Pacific,** and **transatlantic** cruises. Other departure ports in 2025 and early 2026 include Barcelona, Spain; Civitavecchia (Rome), Italy; Southampton, England; Galveston, Texas; San Diego; San Juan, Puerto Rico; Vancouver, Canada; and Sydney, Australia.

Bahamian cruises originating in Port Canaveral and Fort Lauderdale stop at least once at Castaway Cay or Lookout Cay at Lighthouse Point. Alaskan and European itineraries are well conceived and engaging. By comparison, DCL's Bahamian and Caribbean itineraries are comparable to other cruise lines'; however, they're still good for first-time cruisers or repeat cruisers looking to experience one of the new ships or ports of call.

THE NEXT GENERATION OF DISNEY SHIPS

DCL'S FIRST NEW SHIP in more than a decade, the *Disney Wish,* made a splashy debut in 2022. When DCL's third wave of ships (the *Wish* class) was announced, there was speculation that the new vessels would be substantially different from their older sisters. As it turns out, the *Disney Wish* adheres to the model of the first four ships, both in outward appearance and in the interior spaces, albeit with a more modern, high-tech feel and an even greater reliance on Disney imagery in its theming. The sixth ship, the *Disney Treasure,* is similarly appointed, and the *Disney Destiny* will be as well.

Questions remain about how the introduction of additional ships will affect Disney's original fleet long-term. We've already seen some changes: The *Disney Magic,* which once spent summers in Europe, now sails in the Caribbean and the Bahamas out of Florida and Galveston and will head through the Panama Canal to the West Coast of the United States in 2026. The *Dream* and *Fantasy,* which were based almost exclusively in the Bahamas and the Caribbean for a decade, have now taken over European routes formerly plied by the *Magic.* The *Wonder,* which used to winter in the Caribbean, has been on the US West Coast and then in the South Pacific and Australia for much of the year since 2023.

The *Global Dream* megaship, now known as the *Disney Adventure,* is set to be based out of Singapore for at least five years following its projected debut in 2025. Disney has also announced a fourth *Wish*-class ship that will begin sailing year-round from Japan in 2029.

Newer ships tend to take on more traditional routes to encourage repeat guests to come back, and DCL's first two ships are now more than 25 years old—an age at which many cruise ships tend to be retired, repurposed, or sold to a smaller line. Disney found a way to increase interest in the *Wonder* by sending it to the far Pacific in 2023, and the *Magic* has gotten a boost by initially being the primary ship assigned to Disney's new island destination, Lookout Cay at Lighthouse Point. These itinerary shifts should keep the *Magic* and *Wonder* viable for a few more years, but we continue to ponder whether more drastic changes lie ahead for Disney's oldest vessels. Will they be substantially rethemed at some point, or will they even be retired by the end of the decade?

As Disney's newest ships edge closer to completion, check **disney cruise.disney.go.com** and the ***Disney Parks Blog*** (disneyparks.disney .go.com/blog) for official announcements, and visit the ***Unofficial Guide* blog** (theunofficialguides.com) for our takes on these announcements.

DCL'S TARGET MARKET

DISNEY CRUISES ARE tailored to families who are new to cruising. However, like the theme parks, the cruise line is a Disney product for kids of all ages. Each ship has at least one adults-only restaurant, swimming pool, and nightclub. Initially, cruise experts questioned whether

DCL could fill its ships when kids are in school. Disney determined that the ships would sell out if 1%–2% of the estimated 40 million annual visitors to its resorts and parks bought a Disney cruise vacation. Disney was right, and after 25 years of success, no one is questioning.

Missy, an *Unofficial Guide* reader from Pennsylvania, describes her onboard experience:

> *When you are on a Disney Cruise Line vacation, your stateroom becomes your home away from home. Whether I've spent the day enjoying onboard activities or adventuring on a shore excursion, the most refreshing part of the day to me is returning to my stateroom after dinner to find all the comforts provided by our stateroom host. The nightly turndown service provides a tidy room, a turned-down bed, fluffed pillows, and fresh towels. It's an added bonus to see what unique designs of towel art and nighttime chocolates we receive as well!*

AWARDS AND ACCOLADES

DISNEY OFFERS EXCELLENT SERVICE, has some of the most attractive ships sailing, and goes out of its way to make sure everyone has a great time. While other cruise lines may be better in some areas, travel and general media outlets give DCL consistently strong marks across all categories. Among its most recent accolades are the following:

- **U.S. News & World Report Best Cruise Lines 2024** Best Cruise Line for Families (for the 10th consecutive year)
- **Cruise Critic's Editors' Picks Awards 2023** Best for Families
- **The Points Guy Awards 2023** Best Family Cruise Line
- **Travel & Leisure's World's Best Awards 2022** No. 1 Large-Ship Ocean Cruise Line
- **Newsweek 2024** One of America's best companies for customer service (No. 2, below Viking, out of the five cruise operators that were ranked)

CASTAWAY CLUB

DISNEY CALLS REPEAT CRUISERS Castaway Club members. Like most loyalty programs, the more loyal you are, the more perks you get. There are four Castaway Club levels (listed from highest to lowest): Pearl, Platinum, Gold, and Silver. Whereas some other cruise lines reward repeat cruisers based on the number of nights they've spent on board or give bonus points for more expensive cabins, Disney assigns your level based on the number of Disney cruises you've completed, no matter how short or how much money you've spent. While we would prefer a per-night model, it doesn't seem like Disney will move to that anytime soon. Here's how the levels break down:

- **Pearl** Guests who have completed 25 or more cruises with Disney
- **Platinum** Guests who have completed 10-24 cruises with Disney
- **Gold** Guests who have completed 5-9 cruises with Disney
- **Silver** Guests who have completed 1-4 cruises with Disney

WHEN BOOKING WINDOW OPENS FOR ONBOARD ACTIVITIES
Concierge guests: 130 days before sailing
Pearl Castaway Club members: 123 days before sailing
Platinum Castaway Club members: 120 days before sailing
Gold Castaway Club members: 105 days before sailing
Silver Castaway Club members: 90 days before sailing
All other guests: 75 days before sailing

WHEN BOOKING WINDOW OPENS FOR ONLINE CHECK-IN AND PORT-ARRIVAL TIME SELECTION
Concierge guests and Pearl Castaway Club members: Port-arrival time not required; may check in online **40 days** before sailing
Platinum Castaway Club members: 38 days before sailing
Gold Castaway Club members: 35 days before sailing
Silver Castaway Club members: 33 days before sailing
All other guests: 30 days before sailing

After your first sailing, you'll be assigned a unique Castaway Club number. The perks start before boarding, with a dedicated phone number to call DCL, but one of the best perks occurs when new itineraries or ships are released. Disney usually begins the booking in tiers, with Pearl members booking the first day, then Platinum members, and so on down the line. That may not seem like a big deal, but it's actually a great perk. Coveted staterooms (like the Oceanview Staterooms with obstructions, which sell for the price of Inside Staterooms on the classic ships) are the first to fill up. Prices for popular itineraries can go up every day on those release days, and some new itineraries have filled up before they were even available for first-time guests to book. Maiden voyages are especially popular, and while the maiden voyage of the *Treasure* was unfortunately timed and did not sell out early, the maiden voyage of the *Wish* was booked solid before it even made it to the Gold-level members.

Castaway Club members also book **onboard activities** in tiers, which gives them a better chance to enjoy the best dining times at specialty restaurants or popular excursions. **Online check-in** is also done in tiers, which means the higher tiers can get earlier arrival times at the port before those times fill up. (Concierge guests and Pearl members don't have to pick a port-arrival time; they can arrive whenever they like.) See the tables above to find out when the booking window opens for each level for onboard activities and online check-in.

Each port has a special check-in line for Castaway Club members and Concierge guests. On board, the perks range from good to very good. All Castaway Club members receive a welcome-back gift in their stateroom; currently, the higher your level, the more gifts you receive. Pearl, Platinum, and Gold members also get 10% off most merchandise on board, and on sailings of eight nights or longer, they may be invited to a special reception with crew members. Pearl and Platinum cruisers, along with their guests age 18 and older staying in the same stateroom, get a free prix fixe dinner at Palo or Palo Steakhouse, or they can take the value of the prix fixe dinner and apply it to the à la carte menu. Pearl members also get an unlimited digital photo package every time they sail.

While Pearl is the highest official Castaway Club status, Disney has recently begun recognizing its most loyal guests in additional ways. In 2023, it built a colorful fence near the Castaway Cay pier that recognizes guests who have sailed Disney Cruise Line more than 50 times by displaying their names. Some special gifts have also been mailed to guests who have sailed more than 75 and even 100 times.

The benefits of being the highest-level Castaway Club member in the stateroom apply to everyone in the stateroom. That means if Tammy is sailing with a friend who has never sailed, that friend still takes advantage of Tammy's perks, like early booking and the free meal at Palo Steakhouse. This applies only to friends or family staying in the stateroom; it does not apply to friends or family traveling in a separate stateroom.

*un**official* **TIP** Castaway Club status usually only matters when it comes to booking—once you're on the ship, the cast members don't care who sleeps in which stateroom. Guest Services will issue you keys to both staterooms.

In 2023, Disney announced that to keep your Castaway Club status active, you must book a cruise or sail at least once every five years.

WHERE *to* FIND MORE INFORMATION

AT DISNEY CRUISE LINE'S WEBSITE (disneycruise.disney.go.com), you can see which itineraries each ship serves; search for cruises by destination, month, length, departure port, and ship; and check stateroom prices. After your sailing is booked and paid for, you'll make reservations for port adventures, restaurants, and kids' activities here or in the DCL Navigator app.

Free trip-planning videos for DCL, Walt Disney World, Adventures by Disney (river and expedition cruises), and other Disney destinations are available at disneycruise.disney.go.com/cruise-planning-tools. (*Note:* You must complete a short survey before watching the videos.) Besides being a good planning tool, the video is an excellent way to prepare kids who have never cruised.

The ***Disney Parks Blog*** (disneyparks.disney.go.com/blog) is the official public source for news about the Disney theme parks worldwide, DCL, Adventures by Disney, Disney's Aulani resort in Hawaii, and more. To find DCL posts, click "Destinations" at the top of the page, then scroll down to "Disney Cruise Line."

If you are considering sailing on the *Disney Wish* and are a Disney+ subscriber, you may be interested in the hour-long program ***Making the***

Wish: Disney's Newest Cruise Ship, which details many aspects of the ship's design and construction, including interviews with engineers, Imagineers, and crew members.

DCLNews.com posts official news and press releases about Disney Cruise Line. Though intended for the media, most of the site is open to the public. The resources include fact sheets, press releases, photos, and videos of the ships.

Scott Sanders's *Disney Cruise Line Blog* (disneycruiselineblog.com) posts almost daily updates, including everything from rumors about new itineraries to the skinny on new merchandise. The website also has a cool feature that lets you see the current location and itinerary of every ship in the Disney fleet. You'll find tips and advice from Scott throughout this book. His X account, **@TheDCLBlog,** is also a terrific resource for up-to-the-minute DCL news.

The **planDisney** panel (plandisney.disney.go.com) is staffed by veterans of many DCL voyages. Trained by Disney cast members, the planDisney team can answer virtually any DCL planning question, big or small. The site also hosts short videos on Disney trip planning, including content specific to DCL (see plandisney.disney.go.com/plan disney-video-library).

If you enjoy listening to podcasts, three that focus specifically on Disney cruising are *The DCL Dude Podcast* (thedcldudepodcast.libsyn .com), the *DCL Podcast* (dclpodcast.com), and *DCL Duo* (dclduo.com). Our friend Matt Hochberg hosts the *Royal Caribbean Blog Podcast* (royalcaribbeanblog.com/podcast), which offers valuable tips about cruising in general and insights about some of the ports that DCL visits. Want the inside scoop on all things Disney? Check out *The Disney Dish,* hosted by Len Testa, the coauthor of this book, and Jim Hill, an entertainment writer and Disney historian. (Go to podcasts.jimhill media.com and click on "Disney Dish Podcast.")

MouseSavers (mousesavers.com) offers discounts and money-saving tips for all Disney trip planning, shopping, and entertainment. Click the "Disney Cruise Line" tab for the latest information about DCL promotions and special offers. Regarding deals and discounts, online travel guru **The Points Guy** (Brian Kelly) has a DCL section on his website (thepointsguy.com/cruise/disney-cruise-line).

The **US government** offers many online resources for citizens traveling to other countries. For example, the **Department of State's travel website** (travel.state.gov) features weather and safety advisories, advice on what to do if you lose your passport, information on visa requirements, and more.

The **World Travel Guide**'s country reports (worldtravelguide.net /country-guides) are an easy-to-read source of information about foreign ports. Though the site is geared primarily to British and European travelers, Americans will also find it helpful.

If you're flying to your cruise's embarkation point, check your airline's website and that of the **Transportation Security Administration** (tsa.gov) to ensure you know the latest air travel rules and procedures.

The list of prohibited items is beneficial (theugseries.com/tsa-allowed). Be aware, however, that acceptable items for air travel and for DCL boarding may be different (see page 141).

Did you know you can directly text the TSA with travel questions? To start a chat, text the word "travel" to the AskTSA number (☎ 275-872). You'll receive a message explaining that automated responses are available 24/7, though for questions the algorithm cannot answer, live employees staff the line from 8 a.m. to 6 p.m. Eastern time. Guests with medical concerns or other special circumstances may get extra assistance at TSA checkpoints by completing the form at tsa.gov/contact-center/form/cares 72 hours before travel.

If you're interested in the legal nuances of cruising, maritime attorney Jim Walker's *Cruise Law News* blog (cruiselawnews.com) discusses issues related to the rights of passengers and crew on most major cruise lines.

To learn more about the types of jobs available on DCL and other cruise lines, look at the **Florida-Caribbean Cruise Association**'s *Cruise Industry Onboard Employment Overview* booklet (theugseries.com/fcca-guide).

Finally, try searching **Facebook** for a group specific to your DCL sailing. Many cruise-specific groups share tips on excursion booking, pricing changes, and other information and may organize get-togethers and gift exchanges. It's a great way to meet new friends before you sail. The DCL board on **Reddit** (reddit.com/r/dcl) is another excellent source of up-to-the-minute news and advice.

HOW *to* CONTACT
the AUTHORS

MANY OF OUR READERS write to us with questions, comments, or their own travel strategies. Reader comments are frequently incorporated into revised editions and have contributed immeasurably to their improvement. If you'd like to get in touch, you can write or email us at the following addresses:

Tammy and Len
The Unofficial Guide to Disney Cruise Line
2204 First Ave. S., Ste. 102
Birmingham, AL 35233
info@theunofficialguides.com

You can also look us up on social media: **TheUnofficialGuideSeries** on YouTube; **@TheUnofficialGuides** on Facebook; and **@TheUGSeries** on X, Instagram, and Pinterest.

STAY UPDATED

WHEN IT COMES TO Disney Cruise Line, the only constant is change, so it's essential to stay abreast of the latest developments even after this

CONTACTING DISNEY CRUISE LINE BY PHONE
General Information, Booking, and Managing Your Reservation ☎ 800-951-3532
Embarkation Information Line ☎ 407-566-4040
Contacting Someone On Board ☎ 888-322-8732
Lost and Found After Your Cruise ☎ 407-566-3734
Global Assistance with Disney's Vacation Protection Plan ☎ 877-303-5909

book goes to press. The *Unofficial Guide* **blog** (theunofficialguides.com) posts regular updates on DCL itineraries and policy changes; we'll also aggregate this information and post updates and corrections for this edition of the print book at theugseries.com/dcl-updates-2025.

READER SURVEY

TOURINGPLANS.COM HOSTS a questionnaire that you can use to express opinions about your Disney cruise: touringplans.com/disney -cruise-line/survey. The questionnaire lets every member of your party, regardless of age, tell us what they think about attractions, restaurants, and more. If you'd rather print the survey and mail it to us, send it to **Reader Survey** using the street address above.

YOUR CRUISE-PLANNING TIMELINE

12–18 MONTHS BEFORE SAILING

- **Choose an itinerary and book your cruise.** Disney usually releases itineraries 12–18 months before the sailing dates. We recommend booking early if possible.

BEFORE FINAL PAYMENT OR AT THE TIME OF DEPOSIT

- **Buy trip insurance.** If using Disney's Vacation Protection Plan, you must purchase before making your final payment or, for Concierge guests, when you make your deposit.
- **If flying, book your flight.** Don't forget to take our advice and arrive at least one day before you sail.
- **Book your hotel for the night before your cruise.** See our hotel recommendations for departure ports in Part 8.
- **Download and set up the DCL Navigator app** and link your reservation.
- **Check your passports and proof of citizenship.** Check the expiration date on everyone's passport and ensure they do not expire for at least six months after the sailing ends. If you are using another acceptable proof of citizenship, locate those documents and put them in a safe place.
- **Find and join the Facebook group for your sailing** if you would like to meet other guests and register for any guest-led activities.
- **Link to other staterooms.** Link to the staterooms of other members of your party.

75–150 DAYS BEFORE SAILING

- **Make your final payment.** Your due date will be based on the length of your cruise or, for Concierge guests, your stateroom type.
- **Book excursions and activities.** Your activities and excursions booking date will be based on the number of times you have sailed with Disney or, for Concierge guests, your stateroom type.

45 DAYS BEFORE SAILING

- **Order your DisneyBand+.** If purchasing DisneyBand+, order 11–45 days before your sailing. The earlier, the better.

30–40 DAYS BEFORE SAILING

- **Check in online.** Your online check-in date is based on the number of times you have sailed with Disney or, for Concierge guests, your stateroom type.

10 DAYS BEFORE SAILING

- **Check the weather** of your departure port and ports of call.
- **Pack for your cruise.**

5 DAYS BEFORE SAILING

- **Stop mail and newspapers.** Hold any deliveries to your home.
- **Let your credit card company know you are traveling** so that it doesn't place a hold on your credit card when it detects unusual charges.

2 DAYS BEFORE SAILING

- **Check in for your flight** 24 hours beforehand.

DAY OF SAILING

- **Fill out the health questionnaire** that will arrive in your inbox the morning of sailing.

DOLLARS *and* SENSE

WHAT IS *and* ISN'T INCLUDED *in your* CRUISE FARE

YOU'LL GET NO ARGUMENT FROM US—a Disney cruise isn't cheap. Given the cost, you might wonder what other expenses you'll encounter on board. Here's a quick rundown of what is and isn't included in your cruise fare.

FOOD

INCLUDED: LOTS OF FOOD All meals, including snacks, in the dining rooms, at most pool deck windows, and at buffets are included. You won't go hungry!

NOT INCLUDED: ADULT DINING Remy and **Enchanté** cost at least $135 per person for dinner and at least $80 for brunch. **Palo** and **Palo Steakhouse** cost at least $50 per person for brunch and dinner. Dinner is fixed price, but be aware that many popular dishes are not offered on the prix fixe menu; they're à la carte only. Keeping that in mind, you may pay considerably more than the prix fixe minimum. Alcohol and tips are always extra.

INCLUDED: MOST ROOM-SERVICE FOOD Except for some drinks and prepackaged snacks, which are clearly marked, your fare includes all room service. Just be prepared to tip the crew member who delivers it. Room service is an excellent option if you are in the mood for breakfast on your verandah, need a snack to tide you over until the next meal, or don't feel like going out for dinner.

INCLUDED: ALL-YOU-WANT SOFT DRINKS AND ICE CREAM Soda, juices, coffee, water, cocoa, and hot and iced tea are included and unlimited at meals, as are beverages served from the drink dispensers on the pool deck. Unlimited soft-serve ice cream is also included.

NOT INCLUDED: The specialty ice creams sold at **Vanellope's Sweets & Treats** on the *Dream*, **Sweet on You** on the *Fantasy*, **Inside Out: Joyful Sweets** on the *Wish*, **Jambeaux's Sweets** on the *Treasure*, and **Edna À La Mode** on the *Destiny* cost extra, as do the specialty smoothies at the pool deck windows and in the spas.

NOT INCLUDED: BOTTLED DRINKS, PACKAGED SNACKS, ALCOHOL, AND FANCY COFFEES Bottled water, soda not served as part of meal service or on the pool deck, and alcoholic beverages cost extra, as do packaged snacks such as popcorn and peanuts. You'll also pay for specialty coffees, espresso drinks, and teas from bars and cafés (such as **Cove Café**). Adults age 21 and older may bring a limited amount of beer and wine aboard in their carry-on luggage; a $29 corkage fee applies if you bring your own bottle of wine to a full-service restaurant on board.

unofficial **TIP**
You won't be charged a corkage fee if you open your wine in your room and bring a glass to dinner.

NOT INCLUDED: THEATER SNACKS Kiosks outside the movie theaters and live-production venues sell soft drinks, beer and wine, packaged snacks like M&M's, and fresh popcorn before showtimes. The prices are a smidge less than you'd pay at your local Cineplex—but you can always grab a soda and a plate of chicken nuggets and fries from the top deck to nosh on free of charge. Concierge guests can pick up popcorn anytime it's available at no extra charge.

NOT INCLUDED: SOME BAR SNACKS Some onboard bars offer free nighttime nibbles, such as chips and salsa, cut veggies, or mini hot dogs. If you want more-substantial or themed bar food, the sports-themed bars offer hearty snackage at various times, such as soft pretzels with cheese sauce, Buffalo wings, bangers and mash, loaded potato tots, or a trio of sliders. Expect to pay $8–$12 per item. These light bites can be a decent dinner replacement if you're not in the mood for the hullabaloo in the main dining room.

ENTERTAINMENT AND ACTIVITIES

INCLUDED: LOTS OF ENTERTAINMENT There's no extra charge for live shows, movies, or character greetings.

NOT INCLUDED: BINGO The only form of gambling offered on DCL is bingo, which is super popular! Games range from $25 for a three-pack of paper cards to $75 for a family pack of two 24-chance electronic handsets, plus bonus paper-card packs. Note that prices go up during bingo sessions later in the cruise.

INCLUDED: SOME CLASSES AND ACTIVITIES Towel-folding classes and some cooking demonstrations, which you usually find on longer sailings, are offered free of charge.

THE BEST BANGS FOR YOUR BUCK ON A DCL CRUISE

1. **Porters for your bags.** The $2–$5 per bag you'll tip your porter both boarding and returning home is money well spent. When you're boarding, not having to handle your bags is one less hassle in a hectic process. When you debark, it helps you end your cruise on a high note.

2. **Oceanview Staterooms.** There's a huge price jump from Oceanview to Verandah on some itineraries, so if the prospect of having no natural light in your stateroom is more than you can bear but a Verandah Stateroom is beyond your budget, we recommend a stateroom with a porthole. Oceanview Staterooms don't sell as quickly as Inside Staterooms (the least expensive rooms) or Verandah Staterooms (often in the highest demand) and frequently have easy access to the main dining rooms, Guest Services, and the adult lounge areas.

3. **Cabanas at Castaway Cay or Lookout Cay.** Hold up! How can something that costs at least $500 be a bang for your buck? Here's the thing: The amenities that come with a cabana equal more than the sum of their parts. If you have enough people to fill a cabana or can find someone to share with, the free equipment rentals, shelter from the sun, dedicated beach, and personalized service make this worth checking out. Our only qualm in including the cabanas here is that they're notoriously difficult to book because they are so popular.

4. **Brunch at Palo or Palo Steakhouse.** A quiet, no-rush brunch or dinner for adults with excellent service and fantastic food for just $50 plus tip? *Yeah, baby!*

5. **Room service.** Most items on the room-service menu are free. For the price of a tip, you can get a cheese plate to stave off the afternoon munchies, fresh coffee and pastries in the morning, or warm cookies and milk in your stateroom before bed, among other treats. That's our idea of pampering!

6. **Castaway Ray's Stingray Adventure.** It's a winner with kids and adults. Because it's on Castaway Cay, there's no time wasted getting to and from your port adventure—just show up at your appointed time and have fun interacting with the rays. See page 330 for more info.

7. **Coffee.** The swill at the beverage stations can best be described as a tepid, vaguely coffee-flavored substance that could sap you of your will to live. Pony up for the good stuff at **Cove Café** or one of the other coffee bars on board. Sure, it's around $3–$6 plus tip, but that's less than you'd pay at Starbucks. Ask for a **Café Fanatic** rewards card and get every sixth coffee drink free. (For some of us, that's sometime early in day two.)

8. **Castaway Cay 5K.** This port adventure is free, and you can take pride in knowing that you've gotten your exercise in for the day. Every participant gets a plastic medal, regardless of how fast they run. To keep it real, try to beat your personal best every time you come to the island.

9. **Gratuities.** DCL ships are full of enthusiastic cast members who work hard to make your trip magical. Please give generous tips to your servers, stateroom attendants, baristas, and bartenders. And don't forget to name these folks when you're filling out the surveys at the end of the cruise.

10. **Plastic popcorn buckets.** Buy a plastic popcorn bucket outside the DCL theaters for less than $10 and you can get it refilled at any show throughout your voyage for less than $2. If you're a big movie snacker, you can reap big savings.

NOT INCLUDED: SOME ONBOARD SEMINARS The most notable examples of fee-based seminars are the many adult-beverage tastings. Costs usually range from $40 to $50 per person, with a few in the $100 range.

INCLUDED: GYM FACILITIES Covered in your fare is the use of the fitness center, which has weights, cardio machines, and floor equipment along with changing rooms with showers and a sauna.

NOT INCLUDED: PERSONAL TRAINING AND SOME FITNESS CLASSES
Body Sculpt Boot Camp packages, for example, consist of two 30-minute sessions for $69 or four 30-minute sessions for $119. Personal training is offered at $89 for a 45-minute session. An 18% gratuity may apply depending on the class.

NOT INCLUDED: SPA AND SALON SERVICES Spa treatments (including massages, facials, steam rooms, and upscale showers) range in cost from $118 to more than $500 per person, per treatment. Salon services range from $50 to $70 for manicures and pedicures and from about $35 to $75 for hairstyling, depending on hair length.

INCLUDED: POOLS AND MOST SPORTS Pools, waterslides, and hot tubs are included, as are activities such as miniature golf (depending on the ship), basketball, and shuffleboard.

NOT INCLUDED: SPORTS SIMULATORS These can be booked on the *Dream* and *Fantasy* for an additional charge.

INCLUDED: BEACHES AND RESTAURANTS ON CASTAWAY CAY AND LOOKOUT CAY Food, nonalcoholic beverages, lounge chairs, towels, and beach umbrellas are included. The 5K on Castaway Cay is also free.

NOT INCLUDED: RECREATION, ALCOHOL, AND CABANAS ON CASTAWAY CAY AND LOOKOUT CAY DCL charges for bike rentals, floats, snorkeling, and watercraft use. Private cabanas are also available for a fee (see pages 327 and 334). Alcohol pricing is comparable to that on the ships, with a possible slight increase for island taxes.

KIDS' STUFF

INCLUDED: KIDS' CLUBS These include the **Oceaneer Club/Lab** for ages 3–10, **Edge** for ages 11–14, and **Vibe** for ages 14–17.

NOT INCLUDED: CHILDCARE FOR KIDS UNDER 3 "It's a Small World" **Nursery!** charges $9 per hour for the first child and $8 per hour for a second child in the same family.

NOT INCLUDED: MAKEOVERS AT BIBBIDI BOBBIDI BOUTIQUE Kids' salon services start at about $100 for the Deluxe Carriage Package, which includes basic hairstyling, makeup, and nail polish. Packages top out at **more than $1,000** for multinight experiences with several costumes. (We love our kids, but perhaps not *this* much.)

NOT INCLUDED: TEA PARTIES AND SUCH Some unique dining experiences for children can be booked on board for a substantial additional charge. **Olaf's Royal Picnic** is on the *Disney Wish,* and The **Royal Court Royal Tea Party** can be found on the *Magic, Wonder, Dream,* and *Fantasy.* See page 275 for details.

MISCELLANEOUS

NOT INCLUDED: INTERNET Except for accessing the Navigator app, you must pay to use your ship's Wi-Fi network. See Part 6 (page 134) for pricing information and tech tips.

NOT INCLUDED: SHIP-TO-SHORE CALLS Each stateroom has a landline-style phone (remember those?) with voicemail; ship-to-shore calls from these phones cost an astronomical $7–$9.50 a minute. Don't do that! See Part 6 (page 134) for advice on using your cell phone on board.

NOT INCLUDED: PHOTOS Similar to the Memory Maker packages at Walt Disney World, DCL offers packages of photos taken by onboard photographers. Most packages are expensive, and none are included in the price of your cruise (except for Pearl Castaway Club members, who get a photo package as a perk). See page 271 for details.

NOT INCLUDED: SHORE EXCURSIONS Known in DCL-speak as **port adventures,** these cost anywhere from about $15 for a 1-hour bike rental on Castaway Cay to $5,999 for the **Cruising on a Private Motor Yacht** excursion in Tortola. Be aware that shore excursions often have extra-cost options such as photo packages, and meals may not be included. Bring cash to tip your guides and drivers.

NOT INCLUDED: LAUNDRY It costs $3 to wash and $3 to dry a load of clothes in the onboard laundry rooms. Detergent, fabric softener, and dryer sheets are available for $1 each, per load. Dry-cleaning is also available for an additional fee; typical pricing is about $6 for a men's shirt. Garment pressing is available for roughly half the price of dry-cleaning.

SCOTT'S MONEY-SAVING STRATEGIES
by Scott Sanders of the Disney Cruise Line Blog

IT'S COMPLETELY POSSIBLE to go on a Disney cruise and not spend a dime aside from gratuities. The ships offer everything you need and more while you're on board. However, there are plenty of opportunities to enhance your vacation, and I highly recommend budgeting for some onboard spending—it is a vacation, after all.

My favorite money-saving strategy is to book shore excursions via third parties. You'll just need to make sure the one you book will return you to the ship by the all-aboard time. If that sounds too stressful, you can also explore on your own where it's safe to do so—a good number of the ports of call have things to see and do within walking distance from the ship.

Not picky about where you sleep? Book an Inside Stateroom. If you're just using your stateroom for sleeping, showering, and changing clothes, why spend more?

My last tip is a way to save on your next cruise. You can purchase a "placeholder" for a future cruise (which is really simple with the DCL Navigator app), allowing you to save 10% off the prevailing rate. The placeholder not only saves you money on the overall price of your cruise but also lets you pay a reduced deposit for voyages of seven nights or longer (see page 30 for more details).

We consider the prices of dry-cleaning and pressing on board to be a pretty good deal compared to the same services on land.

NOT INCLUDED: TIPS Disney automatically adds daily gratuities of $14.50 per guest ($15.50 per Concierge guest) to your onboard account if you did not choose to prepay gratuities. An 18% gratuity is automatically added to spa services and bar and beverage tabs. See the section starting on page 144 for our tipping guidelines.

NOT INCLUDED: TRANSPORTATION TO THE PORT Round-trip service between Walt Disney World and Port Canaveral runs $90 per person; transportation costs between any city's cruise terminal and airport will vary. See the section starting on page 177 for details.

IS IT WORTH IT?

AS YOU PLAN YOUR CRUISE, you may find yourself asking questions along these lines:

- Is it worth paying a higher price for Disney versus another cruise line?
- Is splurging on a cabana worth the (considerable) expense?
- My child wants to go to the princess tea. Is it worth it?
- Is the food at Palo Steakhouse worth the high price?
- Is that seaplane excursion really worth $5,400?
- Should I spring for a second stateroom for my family with teens?

The dirty little secret most travel writers won't tell you is that our answer to these questions is "We don't know"—and we say that even after having asked ourselves about all these things and paid for them out of our pockets.

Here's what we do know: We can tell you what the charge on your credit card will be. We can tell you our (and other guests') personal perceptions of the quality of the food, service, and attention to detail. We can tell you what the views are like, how long waits are likely to be, and which experiences were worth it to us, but we can't tell you whether they'll be worth it to you. (Even the coauthors of this book disagree about the worth of some activities and expenses.)

unofficial **TIP**
In general, worth is achieved when benefits exceed costs.

Because vacation time and money are scarce commodities, you want to be reassured that the benefits you'll gain from your experiences will be greater than your investment in terms of both money and time. You want to be reassured that your investment will be worth it. But we can't tell you if a Disney cruise will be worth it to you because we don't know you.

As an example, consider the upcharge for Concierge Staterooms. Tammy will split the cost of a Concierge Stateroom with a friend faster than you can whip out a credit card, but Scott Sanders from the *Disney Cruise Line Blog* would rather cruise multiple times in an Inside Stateroom than pay the price to sail once in Concierge. Scott says, "The lounge is awesome, but I can't drink enough espresso and sparkling water to make it worth it." In this case, what's worth it to Tammy is not worth it to Scott.

So, how do you determine whether any Disney cruise experience will be worth it to you? Here are more questions to consider:

1. **What is your income or vacation budget?** If you make $50,000 a year, spending 10% (or more than 10%) of your annual income on a cruise vacation would be a significant expense. Making $500,000 a year would take far less of a bite out of your bottom line.

2. **What is the financial opportunity cost of the experience?** Will spending money on a cabana mean you'll have less money to spend on things like port adventures and adult dining? Which would you rather have?

3. **What is the time opportunity cost of the experience?** Is going on that 8-hour port adventure more important to you than experiencing the ship's amenities to their fullest?

4. **What are the actual financial costs of the experience?** Have you researched the options for promotions and discounts? What are the hidden taxes, gratuities, and other fees that would make the experience more costly? How could you make the experience less costly?

5. **Will you have the opportunity to do this again?** Suppose Christmas is the only time that your extended family, including your aging parents, is available to travel. In that case, the extra expense of a holiday cruise might be well worth it.

6. **Are there aspects of your personality that will affect the experience?** If you detest dressing up for dinner, then Remy might not be worth it to you, no matter how good the food is. (For us, it's 1,000% worth it.)

7. **Are there aspects of other family members' personalities that will affect the experience?** What would you do if your child didn't want to go to the kids' clubs? Would your vacation be affected (positively or negatively) if you had less opportunity for adult time?

8. **Is a comparable experience available elsewhere?** If you've experienced a cool zip-line course before, you can probably skip the zip-line excursion in port.

9. **Why do you want to cruise?** Do you value relaxation? Convenience? Novelty? Adventure? Indulgence? Quality or quantity of food? Ease of planning? Family time? Private time? Are you interested in the destination or the journey? If the cruise won't meet one or more of your needs, then it's probably not worth it.

10. **Will you feel frustrated if you must do without something you're used to?** If, for instance, you dread having to sleep in the same stateroom with your kids, then the extra expense of a second stateroom may well be worth it.

11. **Will these experiences make for great memories down the road?** A princess or pirate makeover for your kids at Bibbidi Bobbidi Boutique might seem unnecessary. But if you know your Disney princess–obsessed 5-year-old will be overjoyed to get the royal treatment and will talk about it for months afterward, then it could be worth the expense.

12. **How disappointed would you be if the cruise didn't go as planned?** Let's face it—things don't always happen as we expect them to. The weather doesn't cooperate, kids get sick, and so on. If you think the experience will be a total bust if it's not perfect, a cruise may not be for you.

13. **Would you do it even if it were free?** We have friends who are deathly afraid of heights. Even if they were offered a free parasailing excursion at Castaway Cay, they wouldn't take it.

14. **Will you feel regretful or foolish if you spend your time or money on the experience?** Guests often wait over an hour for the AquaDuck waterslides on the *Dream* and *Fantasy.* Coauthor Erin said that if it was her favorite slide in the world, she had nothing but time on her hands, and she knew she'd never get to do it again, she'd still hate that she waited that long for a water ride that lasted just a few minutes. Likewise, we have family members who'd regret spending $200 to eat at Remy, even if it was the best food they'd ever tasted.

By asking yourself these and similar questions, you may determine whether a particular DCL experience will be worth it to you. If you still have questions, try getting advice from someone in a similar situation. Choose thoughtfully: If you have three kids who love Disney princesses and you're trying to decide whether to shell out hundreds of dollars for makeovers at Bibbidi Bobbidi Boutique, a parent whose kids are obsessed with football and Marvel superheroes probably wouldn't be much help. Likewise, if you have a taste for luxury, chances are that someone who travels as frugally as possible would have a different opinion about the value of a Concierge-level suite.

Someone with circumstances similar to yours will likely have the most valuable perspectives. Finding someone you can relate to is particularly important when lurking on message boards, reading reviews on travel sites, and scanning social media posts.

If you're seeking DCL advice from someone you don't know, ask that person for a benchmark: Try to get their opinion on something you're both familiar with. If you both like restaurants X and Y, chances are good that you'll agree with their assessment of restaurant Z.

We asked some readers why Disney is worth it to them. The responses included the following:

I have sailed on several cruise lines, and Disney is often the most costly up front, but when sailing on a competitor, you often feel nickel-and-dimed for seemingly basic amenities, like something as simple as soda, which is included in a Disney cruise. The level of luxury and attention to detail is unmatched, which is something I've come to expect from the brand. From the elaborate Broadway-style shows to the fireworks at sea to the deluxe staterooms with split baths, I feel the money spent is worth it on every level. There are also those Disney touches you simply can't get anywhere else, such as more intimate character meet and greets than theme park meet and greets.

— Chris from Pennsylvania

I love that there are magical opportunities for children of all ages. You can do as much or as little as you want, as it is truly your vacation to experience. Want to relax overlooking the ocean? Want to battle your family in the Incredi-Games course? Does your family like a healthy battle of trivia? Or maybe you're adults looking to unwind with piano music and a glass of wine while the kids play in the Oceaneer Club. I could go on all day about the activities. I truly enjoy the multigenerational family in which grandparents can see the grandkids soak in the Disney magic while they relax and

enjoy some pampering too. A Disney Cruise is truly the vacation for
everyone, with a level of service that cannot be found on other lines!

— Jen from Massachusetts

A pure bottom-line analysis is essential when planning any expenditure, such as a vacation—you can afford only what your budget allows. Still, you should also consider your vacation goals. Do you want your children to be fully occupied during your trip, or do you want to travel without kids? Do you want a particular type of food on the ship, or do you not care as long as it's there when you get hungry? Do you want to go on port adventures, or do you just want to relax, sip fruity cocktails, and stare at the ocean? Depending on your answers to these questions and more, the extra cost of cruising with Disney might well be worth it to you . . . or it might not.

DON'T RELY SOLELY ON ONLINE REVIEWS. We thank Matt Hochberg of *The Royal Caribbean Blog* for pointing us to a 2018 *New York Times* article titled "Why You Can't Really Trust Negative Online Reviews." It starts with a bemusing fact: "The Great Wall of China has more than 9,000 Google reviews, with an average of 4.2 stars. Not bad for one of the most astonishing achievements in human history."

The point here, however strange, is that you can't please everyone when it comes to online comments. The *Times* also notes, "Reviews are subjective [even ours], and the tiny subset of people who leave reviews aren't average." So, if you see extremely biased comments about DCL online, know that they're not necessarily the last word, and weigh them against other, more balanced commentary.

SAVING MONEY

SO, HOW CAN YOU SAVE MONEY on that expensive cruise? First, let's look at prices in general. We analyzed more than 60,000 cruise fares for this edition. Cruise demand continued to be strong in 2024, which meant few last-minute discounts on any DCL sailing. For four-night Bahamian cruises on the *Wish,* Disney's newest ship for most of 2024, virtually all of the lowest fares were offered more than a year before the sail date. Things were slightly better on the older *Dream,* where the best fares were offered three to six months in advance.

The chart on the opposite page shows the average price per night for the *Disney Fantasy*'s 2025 itineraries. The *Fantasy* was only sailing seven-night cruises back when we first started tracking its year-round pricing, making it easy to identify high and low seasons. These days, the *Fantasy* is offering everything from 3-night cruises in the Bahamas to 3-night cruises around Belgium and 12-night Mediterranean sailings, plus the transatlantic voyages to get there. This year's version reflects the average nightly cost of those cruises, regardless of itinerary.

It's fair to point out that the cost of a cruise around Belgium or France would naturally be more expensive than a cruise out of

DCL Year-Round Per-Night Pricing

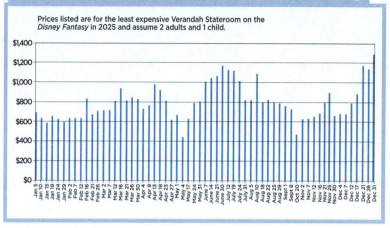

Prices listed are for the least expensive Verandah Stateroom on the *Disney Fantasy* in 2025 and assume 2 adults and 1 child.

Florida. But that only reflects the fact that a ship is a movable asset, and Disney is going to sail it from whatever ports earn it the highest profits. If you're planning to be on the ship more than on the shore, this chart tells you when to book.

PRICE TRENDS BY SHIP AND ITINERARY

YOU'LL NOTICE ON PAGE 27 that we suggest booking early *and* booking late. These are complementary suggestions—if you can't do one, do the other. In this section, we show how these strategies work for different ships in the Disney fleet on some of DCL's most popular itineraries. The charts on pages 22–25 represent our analysis of more than a million cruise fares gathered from DCL's website for every combination of party size, stateroom category, ship, and itinerary. To simplify this discussion, we show the pricing trends for two-adult, two-child families in Verandah Staterooms for sailings in 2024, from about a year out to a few days in advance, as follows:

- Four-night **Bahamian** cruises on the *Dream*
- Four-night **Bahamian** cruises on the *Wish*
- Seven-night **Caribbean** cruises on the *Fantasy*
- Seven-night **Alaskan** cruises on the *Wonder*

The charts show trends for the highest and lowest prices for Verandah Staterooms on all decks. They use a 30-day rolling average for the prices to smooth out tiny variations.

Bahamian Cruises

In 2024, booking a four-night Bahamian sailing on the *Dream* out of Fort Lauderdale on the day itineraries were released would get you a

Disney Dream 4-Night Bahamian Cruises: 2024 Price Trends

good price, but there was another large dip in pricing just under six months out, when average fares were more than $1,000 (around 30%) less than the high point.

The *Wish* offers four-night Bahamian cruises from Port Canaveral and sees higher demand and higher price points. The average fare was cheapest on opening day. There was a slight dip around seven months out, but for all but the cheapest rooms, the opening-day prices were better. Our advice for the *Wish* is to book sooner rather than later.

Caribbean Cruises

Pricing for seven-night Caribbean sailings was harder to predict. While prices for the most expensive staterooms only went up, pricing for the least expensive staterooms started a steady decline around nine months out and, after one or two small increases, hit rock bottom around 30 days before sailing. With the *Treasure* taking over the traditional seven-night Caribbean sailings from Port Canaveral in 2025, we expect that to change. The popularity of a new ship will probably cause a steady increase as the sailing gets closer. We recommend booking early.

Alaskan and Mediterranean Cruises

Alaskan cruises are very popular and are priced accordingly. In 2024, the price on the day itineraries were released was the cheapest they ever were. The average fare increased more than 35% between opening day and sailing day. The obvious advice here is to book as early as possible.

Disney Wish 4-Night Bahamian Cruises: 2024 Price Trends

CRUISE FARE (2 adults and 2 children)

- High Fare
- Average Fare
- Low Fare

PURCHASED THIS MANY DAYS IN ADVANCE

CRUISE COSTS FROM A DIFFERENT PERSPECTIVE

WHILE RESEARCHING PRICE TRENDS during summer 2024, we found that among the least expensive single-stateroom choices for 2025 was a **3-night Bahamian cruise** in an Inside Stateroom on the *Dream* in mid-September for **$2,869,** or about $239 per person, per night, for two adults and two children. Among the most expensive choices? A jaw-dropping **$136,290** for that same family, or about $2,839 per person, per night, for a **12-night Mediterranean with Greek Isles cruise from Civitavecchia (Rome) ending in Barcelona** in a Concierge Royal Suite with Verandah on the *Fantasy* in July.

Right about now, you're probably contemplating the myriad things you could spend $136K on besides a vacation—a down payment on a large house or a couple of years of college, for instance. But be aware that total costs aren't always the most helpful gauge of whether a particular cruise is a good value. Instead, think about the cost per person per night. As noted above, that low-priced Bahamian cruise for four works out to about $239 per person per night—not a bad price for a cruise. But in many port cities that DCL visits, you could book a land-based vacation with a decent hotel, several nice meals, and a few extras for that same per-person, per-night price, whereas on the cruise, most of your money would be going toward a small stateroom. And you'll have, at a minimum, extra expenses in gratuities, port excursions, and other activities you might choose. Granted, that may be exactly what you want, but it's worth weighing the pros and cons.

Disney Fantasy 7-Night Caribbean Cruises: 2024 Price Trends

DO THE MATH. It's possible to have a perfectly lovely cruise without paying for a thing beyond the cost of your stateroom, plus customary tips and the costs of traveling to and from the port—and we have done that several times. More likely, however, you'll incur added costs for extras like port adventures, adult dining, childcare, and souvenirs, so factor at least some of these into your budget. (See page 12 for what is and is not included in the price of your cruise.)

To use a personal example from summer 2024, Tammy took a four-night cruise with a friend on the *Magic*. The base price for two adults, including the prepayment of baseline tips, was about $3,816 for an Oceanview Stateroom. Their onboard spending was relatively restrained—or so they thought.

- Just under $100 in purchases at the gift shop
- One brunch at Palo
- One port excursion (Blue Lagoon in Nassau)
- Additional tips for our stateroom host and our server in the main dining room
- A few sodas in the lounges
- Premium internet for four nights for one device

All those extras totaled around $700 in stateroom charges—or about an 18% bump in the cruise cost.

LAST-MINUTE SAVINGS

AS MENTIONED IN our general tips to save money on page 27, last-minute deals are often offered when a ship or a particular category

Disney Wonder 7-Night Alaskan Cruises: Summer 2024 Price Trends

is not filling up. These deals are highly restricted: There are no cancellations or changes, and they must be paid in full at the time of booking. You also do not get to choose a specific stateroom; you only get to select a general stateroom type: **VGT** (**Verandah Guarantee**), **OGT** (**Oceanview Guarantee**), and **IGT** (**Inside Guarantee**).

VGT, OGT, and IGT rates don't typically appear on the DCL website until about three months before the sailing date, so if you're booking far in advance, you won't see these prices listed. You are most likely to benefit from them if you have more flexibility. In March 2024, for example, we spot-checked prices for a **7-Night Western Caribbean cruise** on the *Fantasy* in May 2024, about eight weeks before the sailing. The lowest available price for a Deluxe Oceanview Stateroom with Verandah for a party of two adults in a specific location was **$4,537.** The VGT rate for the same sailing and party was **$3,753**—a **savings of almost $800** right off the bat. The least expensive Oceanview Stateroom was $4,033, so you could upgrade your stateroom and still save. If you're OK with Disney picking your stateroom for you and with the restrictions, it's a great savings.

Note: Don't confuse VGT, OGT, and IGT rates with the similarly named **GTY.** GTY is used when a category is almost full (not almost empty like the rates above) and is *not* a discounted rate. Disney wants some flexibility when assigning those last few staterooms in a category, so when guests pick their stateroom, they cannot select a specific one, only a guarantee of that category (or, rarely, a better one).

continued on page 29

10 TIPS FOR SAVING MONEY ON A DISNEY CRUISE

1. BOOK EARLY. Generally, the price stated on the day new itineraries come out is the cheapest it will get. There are exceptions, and I'll talk about those below, but this is still a good rule of thumb. If you are looking at peak times like summer, Thanksgiving, Christmas, or Easter, I can almost guarantee that the price won't go down and will continue to rise over time. When a sailing starts filling up, the prices go up. I've seen prices jump hundreds of dollars overnight. If you know what you want, book it as soon as possible, then sit back and watch the prices soar as you pat yourself on the back.

2. BOOK LATE. That may seem to contradict point No. 1, but here are the exceptions. Last-minute deals are offered if a particular sailing is not filling up. These are highly restricted fares known as IGT, OGT, and VGT rates. **IGT** means you are guaranteed an Inside Stateroom or better, **OGT** guarantees you an Oceanview Stateroom or better, and **VGT** guarantees you a Verandah Stateroom or better. These rates enable you to pick a general category but not a specific category or stateroom. They are nonrefundable and must be paid in full when booked, and no changes can be made. If you're flexible during the offseason and are not wedded to a particular sailing date or stateroom location, you may want to risk waiting until your time frame gets close to book. These rates aren't usually lower than opening day, but they'll save you money compared to current prices. See page 24 for more details.

3. KNOW WHAT DISCOUNTS YOU QUALIFY FOR. Disney periodically offers discounts for Florida residents, military personnel, and Canadians. US Department of Defense civilian employees also qualify for military rates when available. Disney generally releases Florida-resident and military discounts on Monday mornings. The *Disney Cruise Line Blog* does a great job of listing all the available specials every Monday. In 2023, Disney released a great special for Disney+ subscribers. Let your travel agent know what you qualify for so they can watch for applicable deals.

4. BOOK TWO STATEROOMS. This one sounds backward, but it's true. Sometimes booking two staterooms is less expensive than booking one. On the classic ships especially, it's almost always less for a family of five to book two Inside Staterooms than the only option for a single stateroom for five—one Verandah Stateroom. Sometimes, it's also cheaper for a family of four to get two Inside Staterooms rather than a Verandah Stateroom. That's because sometimes the cost for the third and fourth person in a Verandah Stateroom is more than the cost for two people in an Inside Stateroom. You may value a second bathroom more than a verandah.

5. TIME YOUR VACATION CAREFULLY. Timing is everything on a Disney cruise. Summer and holiday cruises are expensive. You can save a fortune if you have the flexibility to go during the school year.

September is historically the least expensive month because of hurricane season and school starting. If you are tied down during the school year, try the week before school starts or the week after it ends. Schools nationwide are on different schedules, and sometimes you can snag a deal because yours ends earlier or starts later.

6. DON'T COUNT OUT THE CLASSIC SHIPS. The classic (older) ships tend to have more specials, which are still amazing. I wouldn't, and don't, hesitate to sail on either one. With the *Wish* taking over the typical *Dream* itineraries, you can find some fantastic deals on the *Dream*, and the same will be true of the *Fantasy* as the *Treasure* takes over the seven-night Caribbean sailings.

7. LOOK FOR ONBOARD CREDITS. One way to save some money is onboard credits. DCL doesn't allow their cruises to be discounted (the price should be the same everywhere), so many travel agencies instead offer onboard credits as a thank-you for booking with them. These credits are applied to your account on board and can generally be used for anything you purchase on the ship, including excursions, tips, alcohol, and merchandise. One word of caution: Don't sacrifice good service for the biggest onboard credit. Most agencies that offer onboard credits will have them listed on their website.

8. PAY WITH GIFT CARDS. Sometimes you can find Disney gift cards at a discount. Paying $95 for a $100 gift card doesn't sound like much of a savings, but it does add up.

9. BOOK YOUR NEXT CRUISE WHILE ON BOARD. Seriously! If you think there is any chance under heaven that you will get on another cruise in the next two years, book a placeholder on board. You can book up to two staterooms to be used on the same future sailing for $250 each. After you or your travel agent converts it to a specific itinerary and date, you'll save 10% on that cruise, as long as it's within two years of the placeholder-booking date and non-Concierge. You'll also pay a reduced deposit on sailings of seven nights or longer. If you don't use that placeholder, you get the $250 back. It's a no-lose situation. See page 30 for more details.

10. USE A TRAVEL AGENT. Using a travel agent for a cruise isn't just for convenience and possible onboard credits. In addition to all the knowledge they bring, travel agents can save you money. A good agent knows all the points above and can guide you to the best prices. They can steer you toward things like secret porthole staterooms, which are Oceanview Staterooms with an Inside Stateroom price. They can put a stateroom on hold for you the second a big special is announced, before the rooms disappear. They will also remind you when to book activities and ensure you're prepared for online check-in. A good travel agent will ensure your cruise is the one you've been dreaming about.

ONBOARD-BOOKING BLACKOUT DATES FOR 2025 AND EARLY 2026

DISNEY MAGIC SAILINGS

November 24, 2025	4-Night Western Caribbean Cruise from Galveston
November 28, 2025	5-Night Western Caribbean Cruise from Galveston
December 24, 2025	4-Night Western Caribbean Cruise from Galveston
December 28, 2025	5-Night Western Caribbean Cruise from Galveston

DISNEY WONDER SAILINGS

March 27, 2026	3-Night Baja Cruise from San Diego
March 30, 2026	4-Night Baja Cruise from San Diego
April 3, 2026	3-Night Baja Cruise from San Diego

DISNEY DREAM SAILINGS

November 22, 2025	4-Night Bahamian Cruise from Fort Lauderdale
November 26, 2025	5-Night Bahamian Cruise from Fort Lauderdale
December 19, 2025	3-Night Bahamian Cruise from Fort Lauderdale
December 22, 2025	4-Night Bahamian Cruise from Fort Lauderdale
December 26, 2025	3-Night Bahamian Cruise from Fort Lauderdale
March 30, 2026	4-Night Bahamian Cruise from Fort Lauderdale
April 3, 2026	3-Night Bahamian Cruise from Fort Lauderdale
April 6, 2026	4-Night Bahamian Cruise from Fort Lauderdale

DISNEY FANTASY SAILINGS

November 21, 2025	4-Night Bahamian Cruise from Port Canaveral
November 25, 2025	5-Night Bahamian Cruise from Port Canaveral
December 21, 2025	5-Night Bahamian Cruise from Port Canaveral
December 26, 2025	5-Night Bahamian Cruise from Port Canaveral
December 31, 2025	4-Night Bahamian Cruise from Port Canaveral
March 29, 2026	5-Night Bahamian Cruise from Port Canaveral
April 3, 2026	5-Night Bahamian Cruise from Port Canaveral

DISNEY WISH SAILINGS

April 14, 2025	4-Night Bahamian Cruise from Port Canaveral
April 18, 2025	3-Night Bahamian Cruise from Port Canaveral
April 21, 2025	4-Night Bahamian Cruise from Port Canaveral
November 24, 2025	4-Night Bahamian Cruise from Port Canaveral
November 28, 2025	3-Night Bahamian Cruise from Port Canaveral
December 22, 2025	4-Night Bahamian Cruise from Port Canaveral
December 26, 2025	3-Night Bahamian Cruise from Port Canaveral
December 29, 2025	4-Night Bahamian Cruise from Port Canaveral
March 30, 2026	4-Night Bahamian Cruise from Port Canaveral
April 3, 2026	3-Night Bahamian Cruise from Port Canaveral
April 6, 2026	4-Night Bahamian Cruise from Port Canaveral

DISNEY TREASURE SAILINGS

November 22, 2025	7-Night Eastern Caribbean Cruise from Port Canaveral
December 20, 2025	7-Night Eastern Caribbean Cruise from Port Canaveral
December 27, 2025	7-Night Western Caribbean Cruise from Port Canaveral
March 28, 2026	7-Night Eastern Caribbean Cruise from Port Canaveral

continued from page 25

UPGRADING AT THE PORT

SOMETIMES THERE ARE SAVINGS to be had on the day you sail. If the ship is not full, there will be substantial discounts on the remaining staterooms. In our experience, it's about one-third to half of the price you would pay to upgrade if you did it before embarkation day. We have scored some pretty awesome staterooms doing it this way. You must also be one of the first people in the port because these deals go fast. If you're interested, go to the supervisor's desk as soon as you finish checking in. They can tell you what, if anything, is available. When nothing is left, they usually put up a sign saying they are full.

While we love these savings, we highly recommend you book the category you want. If you are sailing to Alaska, for example, and booked an Oceanview Stateroom in hopes of upgrading at the port to a Verandah Stateroom, that's fine—if you will be happy in an Oceanview Stateroom. If you will ultimately not be happy without a verandah, don't risk it. Book the Verandah Stateroom. These savings are great but not reliable enough to risk it.

MILITARY OR RESIDENT SAVINGS

SAVINGS MAY BE AVAILABLE for military personnel and residents of Florida and Canada. These savings don't usually come out until about two months before the sailing, but sometimes they are released earlier. Scott from the *Disney Cruise Line Blog* lists all the current rates on his website every Monday. Military rates are available in the following categories:

- **Retired and active-duty US military personnel** (and their spouses) from all branches
- **National Guard and U.S. Army Reserve members** (must show active-duty orders dated January 1 of the previous year)
- **U.S. Department of Defense civilian personnel**

Military rates apply only to new bookings. These savings can be significant. If a military rate is released and the guest is already booked, they can often still save by canceling and rebooking even if they are within the penalty period.

Florida-resident rates can also provide significant savings, and they can be applied to existing bookings for even more savings. Proof of residency must be submitted for at least one adult in the stateroom.

Canada-resident rates may not be quite the savings that miliary and Florida-resident rates are, but they are good. These can also be applied to existing bookings. Proof of residency is required at check-in.

We aren't sure why Disney will apply resident rates, but not military rates, to existing bookings. It seems a little stingy, given Disney's usually very generous support of our military members.

REPEAT CRUISER SAVINGS

BOOKING YOUR NEXT CRUISE while on your current cruise is a great way to save money, but you need to understand the process.

HOW TO BOOK There used to be desks on board to handle rebooking, but these days, you'll book right in the app while on board. Disney doesn't want you to miss this opportunity, of course, so it's right at the top of your app's home screen and titled "10% Off a Future Cruise." Follow the directions and book up to two staterooms for the same future sailing. Each reservation is called a placeholder. After they process, you can see the confirmation numbers in the same app section, and you should get a follow-up email.

THE BENEFITS When you book a placeholder on board, you get a 10% discount on the future cruise fare. In addition, onboard booking enables you to put down a 10% deposit on cruises of seven or more nights instead of the standard 20%. These benefits are available only if you book on board; there are no equivalent deals for booking at home. You can book up to two staterooms on one sail date per household, regardless of the number of adults in the household. Having two staterooms booked means you can invite some friends or family to join you on your next sailing, and they will save 10% as well. You have **exactly two years** (from the date you booked) to sail. If you book a placeholder but end up not sailing within the two-year window, your $250 will automatically be refunded. If you realize after booking that you will not sail within the next two years or need that $250, you can cancel the placeholder and get it back. It's a low-risk situation!

> *unofficial* **TIP**
> If you're on a long sailing, book your placeholders on one of the last days of your cruise. This could give you a week or more on the back end to take advantage of the two-year use window.

THE EXCEPTIONS If you're booking a Concierge Stateroom or want to book a cruise during a period when blackout dates are in effect (see page 28), you don't get any price breaks other than a small onboard credit. In addition, if you use a travel agent who offers onboard credits, you will almost certainly get a bigger credit from them if you do *not* rebook on board, as onboard bookings significantly reduce their commission. Also, onboard discounts can't be combined with other discounts, such as military; Florida-resident; and IGT, OGT, or VGT rates.

CASTAWAY CLUB WELCOME OFFER If you rebook within 60 days after debarking your first Disney cruise, you may be eligible for special savings on select sailings. Save $50 per stateroom, per night (up to $350), on a Verandah Stateroom; $40 per stateroom, per night (up to $280), on an Oceanview Stateroom; and $30 per stateroom, per night, on an Inside Stateroom (up to $210).

A LITTLE HELP FROM YOUR FRIEND You can book on board directly with Disney or use a travel agent. If you'd like to add a travel agent who did not book your current cruise or use a different agent from the one who booked your current cruise, you can choose to book directly with

Disney. You have precisely 30 days from the day you booked to transfer your booking to a new travel agent if you like.

Tip: If you already have a cruise booked and are wondering if you should book an additional cruise now or wait until you get on board, the answer is now. Prices may increase between now and then, negating that 10% savings. Book now, and if the price stays the same or goes up less than 10%, book that placeholder on board and move the money over to it. If you booked with a travel agent, they could help ensure you keep the same stateroom; otherwise, call DCL and tell the representative you want the same stateroom.

WALT DISNEY WORLD *or a* DISNEY CRUISE?

DISNEY FANS OFTEN ASK if they should take a Disney cruise or visit Walt Disney World. It used to be pretty clear-cut: Walt Disney World can be done for much less than a Disney cruise. However, as prices for WDW rise and you consider all that's included in a cruise, you may find the price difference is considerably smaller nowadays. There's more to consider than just price, too. Here are some other factors to consider as you make your decision:

- **Travel to the vacation.** Disney World is in Florida, but you can hop on a Disney cruise in many locations. If you live near a DCL departure port, the savings in time and money compared with traveling to Orlando for your vacation could be substantial. You'll also be able to take less time off from work if you board the cruise near your home.

- **Weather.** Some vacationers are leery of sailing during hurricane season (see page 148), making Walt Disney World potentially more attractive during that time. However, if you're not concerned about the weather, some of the lowest prices you'll find on a Disney cruise are during these months.

- **Motion sickness.** While most folks find that they have minimal motion-sickness issues on a Disney cruise, any cruising may be too much for severe sufferers. Disney World (with a focus on the tamer rides) or an Adventures by Disney river cruise (see Part 16) would make more sense for you.

- **Mobility issues.** The average Disney World visitor walks 7–12 miles per day. You could rent a wheelchair or a scooter, but that's still a lot of miles to cover each day. On the other hand, the ships are large but contained. DCL could be a convenient solution if you have difficulty walking long distances or transferring in and out of mobility devices.

- **Access to healthcare.** DCL ships have basic medical facilities (see page 132), but if you have complicated medical needs, you may find that ready access to hospitals on land makes Disney World a safer option.

- **Access to childcare.** Here's where DCL has a clear advantage: Group childcare is unavailable at WDW, and hiring a babysitter can get pricey fast. On a Disney cruise, however, high-quality group childcare is included in the price of your trip and is available throughout the day and evening for kids ages 3–17. (Infant and toddler care is available for a small extra fee.) This may be particularly appealing for a single parent who needs occasional downtime to recharge during vacation or for the parent(s) of an only child who might benefit from interacting with other children, rather than just adults, during the vacation.

- **Variety of accommodations.** There are many stateroom categories, but nearly all are variations on a box, with the notable exception of Concierge Staterooms. Suppose you want to stay with extended family in one unit or have access to residential-style amenities like full kitchens or private communal living spaces. In that case, you're out of luck in a standard stateroom. With a Disney World vacation, however, you can choose from hundreds of thousands of hotel rooms, villas, rental homes, and accommodations to meet every need. One thing to note: Some of the larger villas on-site will approach the price of larger Concierge Staterooms on board, so be sure to compare.

- **Pace of vacation.** It's a near cliché to come home from Disney World saying you need a vacation from your vacation, especially with kids in tow. Disney World trips involve lots of running around to enjoy the countless attractions and entertainment. This is much less true on a Disney cruise, where sleeping in and lounging around are much more acceptable daily plans.

- **Variety of dining.** The food on DCL is plentiful, all-inclusive, and available anytime, but your choices are more limited. Disney World may be the better choice if you like exploring various cuisines.

- **Need for planning.** Planning a Disney World trip is complicated due in part to the need for ride and dining reservations, some of which need to be made far in advance. With DCL, there's much less of a need to map out your time beforehand. You can decide on most shipboard activities at the spur of the moment. And it's perfectly fine to wing it and wander around in most ports. If you prefer a primarily spontaneous vacation, DCL may be the way to go.

- **Shorter lines.** We're professionals at avoiding lines at Disney World, but even we encounter lengthy waits from time to time. The only times you might wait in line on a ship are for the occasional photo op or for a turn on the waterslides.

- **Family togetherness.** Because DCL is a smaller-scale proposition than Disney World, family members are less likely to be pulled in different directions due to competing interests. On the other hand, if you want to separate from your traveling companions, it would be hard to avoid someone for an entire cruise.

- **Children's age considerations.** Families will find plenty to enjoy together on the ships, but most kids will want to spend at least some time in the onboard kids' clubs. This is great, but the clubs are strict about age requirements, particularly in the older groups. This could be a challenge if the kids in your party can't go to the same club. If, for example, you have an 8- and 12-year-old or a 13- and 18-year-old who want to hang out together on vacation, Disney World will provide more opportunities.

- **Pregnancy and babies.** DCL is off-limits if you're more than 24 weeks pregnant or have a baby under 6 months old, but you might have a great time at Disney World. Also, consider the sleeping (or not-sleeping) arrangements in a small stateroom with a toddler on an erratic sleep schedule or feeding arrangements with a baby who's not eating much solid food. The pros and cons of potty training on a cruise ship are also worth considering.

- **Connectivity.** Internet access on the ships can be pricey depending on the level of access you want (see page 134), and service can be spotty. If you must have 100% reliable service 24-7, then a Disney cruise may not be for you.

- **Disney overload.** If you want your kids to have a Disney experience but want to limit your own exposure to the Mouse, then DCL is the better choice. If you skip the musical shows and character greetings, your Disney exposure on a cruise is relatively minimal.

• **Price.** There are bare-bones and ultra-luxury versions of Disney World and DCL vacations. When researching costs, compare apples to apples (budget DCL vs. budget Disney World, not budget DCL vs. luxury Disney World). Also, consider the extra costs you might incur, such as Park Hopper add-ons and Lightning Lanes at Disney World or port adventures on DCL, and whether those are needs or wants for you.

If you choose Disney World over a cruise, check out our sibling publication, *The Unofficial Guide to Walt Disney World,* by Becky Gandillon with Bob Sehlinger and Len Testa, along with **TouringPlans .com.** These resources can give you the complete scoop on planning a Walt Disney World trip with minimum hassle and maximum fun.

COMPARING PRICES

WHILE WE KNOW that a DCL vacation is traditionally more expensive than a WDW vacation, we also know that the price difference between the two is getting smaller and smaller. We weren't sure by how much, so we did some comparison shopping to find out. (We did our research in the summer of 2024; naturally, pricing will vary depending on when you check.)

EXAMPLE 1 (SEVEN NIGHTS, TWO ADULTS AND TWO KIDS): We priced the September 21–28, 2024, **seven-night Western Caribbean** sailing of the *Fantasy* for two adults and two children, ages 9 and 14, in one stateroom. The lowest rate we found was **$5,718** for an Inside Stateroom. Since that could make for a cramped experience for four people, we also priced an Oceanview Stateroom ($6,485) and a Verandah Stateroom ($6,628).

For Walt Disney World, we priced a standard-view room for four people at the Moderate-tier **Port Orleans Resort–French Quarter** for seven nights, starting September 21, 2024. To approximate the cruise's onboard activities, we also included seven-day theme park tickets, plus the seven-day Park Hopper add-on, for everyone in the family. At this point, the total WDW price is $5,509, about $1,119 less than the Verandah Stateroom and only about $200 less than an Inside Stateroom. A savings of $1,100 is nothing to sneeze at, but that price doesn't include food. If we added the Disney Quick-Service Dining Plan at WDW, we would be at **$6,873**—more expensive than a Verandah Stateroom, which includes unlimited food. And we still haven't added Lightning Lane purchases (Disney World's ride reservation system) to our visit.

Of course, that's not a perfect comparison. Maybe you saved money on your cruise by booking early or on board. Maybe you saved money at WDW because you managed to get the dining plan free. Maybe you decided to do some expensive port adventures on your cruise. Either way, you'll see that the price difference isn't huge; it's definitely a lot closer than in previous years.

Overall winner on price: DCL, but it's close.

EXAMPLE 2 (FOUR NIGHTS, TWO ADULTS, SPLURGE): We priced the December 23, 2024, **four-night Bahamian cruise** on the *Wish* for two adults. This is a holiday splurge, so we priced a Concierge Family Oceanview Stateroom with Verandah at **$13,633**. For WDW, we chose a Theme Park View–Club Level room at Disney's Deluxe-tier **Grand Floridian Resort & Spa.** A four-night stay for two adults, plus five-day park tickets, a five-day Park Hopper add-on, and the Disney Dining Plan would be **$13,344.** That's before five days of Lightning Lanes, which would run a minimum of $100 a day at that time of year.

Overall winner on price: DCL by a hair.

EXAMPLE 3 (FOUR NIGHTS, TWO ADULTS, BUDGET): We priced the February 6, 2025, **four-night Bahamian cruise** on the *Dream* for two adults. In this case, we wanted a budget getaway, so we chose an Inside Stateroom (**$2,312**). At Walt Disney World, comparable digs would be a non-Preferred room at the Value-tier **Pop Century Resort.** A four-night stay for two, plus four-day park tickets and a four-day Park Hopper add-on, came to **$2,633,** not including food.

Overall winner on price: DCL.

EXAMPLE 4 (THREE NIGHTS, ONE ADULT): We priced the May 9, 2025, **three-night Bahamian cruise** on the *Wish* for one adult at **$1,973** in an Inside Stateroom. If our solo traveler went to Walt Disney World in a standard room at the Value-tier **Pop Century** and purchased four-day park tickets, a four-day Park Hopper add-on, and the Quick-Service Dining Plan, it would be **$1,734.**

Overall winner on price: WDW.

In Examples 3 and 4, note that DCL's stateroom rate for one guest is only slightly less than the rate for two guests. (The rates are technically the same, but the stateroom for two includes some additional taxes and port fees.) That means our solo traveler effectively pays for the food and entertainment of a nonexistent roommate. With Walt Disney World, on the other hand, solo travelers pay only for their own food and entertainment.

In the same examples, the price difference between cruising on the older *Dream* and the much newer *Wish* is obvious. If you want to relax in the Bahamas, the *Dream* is the affordable way to go. These differences become more pronounced when you look at DCL's itineraries outside of the Bahamas and the Caribbean. Compared with the prices of European cruises, even a higher-end Walt Disney World vacation looks downright thrifty. But as with all things Disney, it makes sense to sit down with a spreadsheet and a calculator to examine the cost comparisons as they apply to your family's circumstances and vacation priorities.

PART 2

THE SHIPS *at a* GLANCE

KEY QUESTIONS ANSWERED IN THIS CHAPTER

- What are the differences between the ships? *(see below)*
- What is the right ship for me? *(see page 38)*

OVERVIEW *and*
OUR RECOMMENDATIONS

THE FIRST DISNEY SHIP, the **Disney Magic,** was launched in 1998 with a capacity of roughly 2,700 passengers and 950 crew members. The **Disney Wonder,** with the same capacity, was launched a year later. The **Disney Dream** and **Disney Fantasy,** which took their maiden voyages a little over a decade later, each hold up to 4,000 passengers and 1,450 crew. The **Disney Wish**'s inaugural season began in 2022, and its first sister ship, the **Disney Treasure,** begins sailing at the end of 2024. Their guest capacities are identical to those of the *Dream* and *Fantasy,* with a slightly higher crew count of 1,555. The **Disney Destiny** and **Disney Adventure** are both scheduled to sail in 2025. The *Destiny* will have the same guest and crew counts as the *Wish* and *Treasure,* while the *Adventure* will be significantly (and by that we mean massively) bigger than the other ships, with around 6,700 passengers and 2,500 crew members.

All of the ships have sleek lines, red smokestacks, and nautical styling that calls to mind classic ocean liners but with instantly recognizable Disney signatures. The colors—dark blue, white, red, and yellow—and the famous face-and-ears silhouette on the smokestacks are clearly those of Mickey Mouse. Look closely at the *Magic*'s stern ornamentation, for example, and you'll see a 15-foot Goofy hanging by his overalls. (It's Donald and his nephew Huey on the *Wonder,* Mickey on the *Dream,* Dumbo on the *Fantasy,* Rapunzel on the *Wish,* Peter Pan and Captain Hook on the *Treasure,* and Spider-Man and his Spider-Bots on the *Destiny.*)

Although the *Disney Adventure* will keep those same colors, it took the typical Disney-ship mold and broke it. While it was initially designed to carry 9,000 passengers, Disney has lowered that to around 6,700. That's still over 50% more than Disney's biggest ships. We think this ship will be full of surprises and differences from the others, and we can't wait to try it out.

Conor from Florida offers this tip for getting up to speed on the design of the ships:

> The **Art of the Ship** *tour is a must-do. Not only is it a great way to understand the layout of the ship, but you'll also discover incredible interior details, hear fantastic stories around the building of the ship, and get to interact with a great crew member giving the tour.*

The ships' interiors combine nautical themes with additional design styles, including Art Nouveau and Art Deco. Art Nouveau, popular at the turn of the 20th century, incorporates natural shapes, such as plants and animals, into its geometric designs; Art Deco has the geometry without the nature—think sleek, streamlined interiors like those found in 1930s movies.

The *Wish* is inspired by Gothic, French Baroque, and Rococo styles. Disney describes its hybrid aesthetic as "Enchantment." The *Treasure* has an "Adventure" theme, with Asian and African influences, and the *Destiny* has a "Heroes and Villains" theme.

Disney images are tastefully interwoven throughout the ships, from Mickey's profile in the wrought-iron railings to the bronze statue of Helmsman Mickey featured prominently in the *Magic*'s atrium, Ariel on the *Wonder*, Admiral Donald on the *Dream*, Mademoiselle Minnie decked out in full 1920s flapper style on the *Fantasy*, regal Cinderella on the *Wish*, Jasmine and Aladdin riding the Magic Carpet on the *Treasure*, and T'Challa (the Black Panther), on the *Destiny*. Disney art is on every wall and in every stairwell and corridor. A grand staircase

FEATURES FOUND ON EVERY DCL SHIP	
• Adult pool and deck areas	• Bars, lounges, and cafés
• Buffet restaurant	• Family pools and water-play areas
• Fitness center	• Full-service spa and salon, with sauna
• Guest Services desk	• Health Center
• Infant, child, tween, and teen clubs	• Venues for live shows and movies
• Basketball court, shuffleboard, and other sports areas	• Outdoor LED screen for movies, concerts, and videos
• One or two upscale restaurants exclusively for adults (age 18 and up)	• Opportunities to buy digital photos taken by onboard photographers
• Included, unlimited soft-serve ice cream "on tap"	• Three main dining rooms for guests to rotate through during dinners on board
• Onboard Wi-Fi (free to use with the DCL Navigator app)	• A Bibbidi Bobbidi Boutique for princess and pirate makeovers
• Concierge lounge and sundeck	• Retail shopping

on each ship sweeps from the atrium lobby to shops offering DCL-themed clothing, collectibles, jewelry, and more.

The first six ships and the *Destiny* have one or two lower decks with staterooms; three decks with public areas such as theaters, lounges, and shops; and then three or five upper decks of staterooms. Two or three sports and sundecks offer separate pools and facilities for families with and without children. Signs point toward lounges and facilities, and all elevators are clearly marked FORWARD, AFT, or MIDSHIP.

Deck 4 of most of the ships is where you will find quiet, lovely lounge chairs with an ocean view—shaded and relatively well protected from wind so you can sit back and enjoy the sea.

DCL CHEAT SHEET

CAN'T REMEMBER, SAY, which ship has the AquaDunk and which has the AquaDuck without looking it up? Neither can we from time to time. The handy table on pages 39–41 displays the ships' similarities and differences at a glance.

All Disney Cruise Line ships have amenities in common, including those listed in the box on the opposite page. The *Wish*, *Treasure*, and *Destiny* have some not found on any other DCL vessel:

FEATURES UNIQUE TO THE *WISH, TREASURE,* AND *DESTINY*	
• **AquaMouse** water coaster	• Oceanview Concierge Staterooms above the bridge
• Adult-dining restaurants **Enchanté** and **Palo Steakhouse**	• Two movie theaters (smaller than the single theater on the other ships)
• **The Hideaway,** a dedicated lounge area for guests ages 18–20	• **The Outdoor Oasis,** a retreat attached to Senses Spa, with plush loungers and space for yoga
• The **Hero Zone** play area for kids of all ages	• The interactive mobile game **Disney Uncharted Adventure**
• Access to the bow of the ship	• A slide to enter the kids' clubs
• **Star Wars: Hyperspace Lounge** (*Wish*) and **The Haunted Mansion Parlor** (*Treasure* and *Destiny*) bars, themed to the movie series and ride, respectively	

The *Dream* and *Fantasy* share the following exclusive features:

FEATURES UNIQUE TO THE *DREAM* AND *FANTASY*	
• The **AquaDuck** water coaster	• Electronic sports simulators
• **Meridian,** a martini bar	• A minigolf course
• **Remy,** an upscale French restaurant for adults only	• **Satellite Falls,** an adults-only area with a splash pool and sundeck
• **Skyline,** a smart craft-cocktail bar with changing virtual cityscapes	• A Champagne bar (**Pink** on the *Dream*, **Ooh La La** on the *Fantasy*)

Finally, despite being the oldest DCL ship, the *Magic* boasts something singular, the **AquaDunk,** a vertical waterslide. (The **AquaDuck** on the *Dream* and *Fantasy* sounds similar, but it's a horizontal coaster.)

DECK PLANS

SEE PAGES 51–53 for shared deck plans for the *Magic* and *Wonder*, followed by shared deck plans for the *Dream* and *Fantasy* on pages 54–57. *Wish, Treasure,* and *Destiny* deck plans are found on pages 58–61.

RANKING THE SHIPS

IGNORING THE DIFFERENT itineraries each ship serves, here's how we rank the Disney ships:

1. Fantasy **2.** Treasure **3.** Dream **4.** Wish **5.** Wonder **6.** Magic

At press time, we hadn't been on the *Destiny,* but we expect it to be substantially like the *Wish* and *Treasure,* with minor improvements based on guest and crew feedback. The *Treasure,* of course, is the newest ship in the DCL fleet, and we expect the *Destiny* to be great and the *Adventure* to be a fun change. Nevertheless, we think Disney made a few missteps on the *Wish*-class ships. While a walking track is not the norm on other lines, it was a staple on the first four Disney ships, and it is missed. The adult infinity pool is beautiful but nowhere near big enough. There are also a few barriers to accessibility (see page 164).

Given the premium prices you pay to cruise on the *Wish* and *Treasure,* we think you'll have just as lovely a time on the **Dream** and **Fantasy,** which offer significantly better value. These two ships are still in great condition. They have better restaurants, bars, and pools than the two oldest ships, along with more on-deck activities, more space for kids' activities, more deck space for sunbathing, better spas, and more interactive games. These advantages make up for the ships' slightly smaller staterooms: Non-Concierge staterooms on the *Dream* and *Fantasy,* for example, are 2%–9% (or 5–22 square feet) smaller than corresponding staterooms on the *Magic* and *Wonder.*

Of course, most non-Caribbean itineraries have just one ship as an option, and we're happy to be on any of the DCL vessels when we want to visit places like Alaska, Europe, or Australia.

The **Disney Magic**

STRENGTHS	WEAKNESSES
• There are some great deals to be had.	• As the fleet's oldest ship, it sometimes shows its age.
• Regularly visits Lookout Cay at Lighthouse Point and will sail through the Panama Canal in 2026	

DCL'S FIRST SHIP has undergone several rounds of renovations since its launch in 1998. The first, in 2013, was an extensive renovation

continued on page 42

WHAT'S DIFFERENT ACROSS THE SHIPS

FEATURE/CATEGORY	Magic	Wonder	Dream	Fantasy	Wish	Treasure	Destiny
DINING (Adult) *(Eating at these restaurants costs extra.)*							
	Palo	Palo	Palo, Remy	Palo, Remy	Palo Steakhouse, Enchanté	Palo Steakhouse, Enchanté	Palo Steakhouse, Enchanté
DINING (Counter Service) *(* Indicates that menu items cost extra.)*							
	Daisy's De-Lites, Duck-in Diner, Eye Scream Treats, Frozone Treats*, Pinocchio's Pizzeria	Daisy's De-Lites, Eye Scream Treats, Pete's Boiler Bites, Pinocchio's Pizzeria, Sulley's Sips*	Eye Scream Treats, Flo's Cafe, Frozone Treats*, Senses Juice Bar*, Vanellope's Sweets & Treats*	Eye Scream Treats, Flo's Cafe, Frozone Treats*, Senses Juice Bar*, Sweet on You*	Daisy's Pizza Pies, Donald's Cantina, Goofy's Grill, Mickey's Smokestack Barbecue, Sweet Minnie's Ice Cream, Inside Out: Joyful Sweets*	Daisy's Pizza Pies, Donald's Cantina, Goofy's Grill, Mickey's Smokestack Barbecue, Sweet Minnie's Ice Cream, Jambeaux's Sweets*	Daisy's Pizza Pies, Donald's Cantina, Goofy's Grill, Mickey's Smokestack Barbecue, Sweet Minnie's Ice Cream, Edna À La Mode*
DINING (Rotational)							
	Animator's Palate, Lumiere's, Rapunzel's Royal Table	Animator's Palate, Tiana's Place, Triton's	Animator's Palate, Enchanted Garden, Royal Palace	Animator's Palate, Enchanted Garden, Royal Court	Arendelle, 1923, Worlds of Marvel	Plaza del Coco, 1923, Worlds of Marvel	Pride Lands: Feast of the Lion King, 1923, Worlds of Marvel
FAMILY ENTERTAINMENT (Live Stage Shows)							
	Disney Dreams, Tangled: The Musical, Twice Charmed	Disney Dreams, Frozen: A Musical Spectacular, The Golden Mickeys	Beauty and the Beast, Disney's Believe, The Golden Mickeys	Disney's Aladdin, Disney's Believe, Frozen: A Musical Spectacular	Disney's Aladdin, Disney Seas the Adventure, The Little Mermaid	Beauty and the Beast, Disney Seas the Adventure, Disney The Tale of Moana	Frozen, A Musical Spectacular; Disney Seas the Adventure; Disney Hercules
NIGHTLIFE AND BARS (Adult Nightlife Area)							
	After Hours	After Hours	The District	Europa	None—the bars and lounges are scattered around the ship.	None—the bars and lounges are scattered around the ship	None—the bars and lounges are scattered around the ship
NIGHTLIFE AND BARS (Champagne Bar)							
	None	None	Pink	Ooh La La	None	None	None

continued on next page

WHAT'S DIFFERENT ACROSS THE SHIPS (continued)

FEATURE/CATEGORY	Magic	Wonder	Dream	Fantasy	Wish	Treasure	Destiny
NIGHTLIFE AND BARS (Dance Club)							
	Fathoms	Azure	Evolution	The Tube	Luna	Sarabi	Saga
NIGHTLIFE AND BARS (Live-Music Venue)							
	Keys, Soul Cat Lounge	Cadillac Lounge, French Quarter Lounge	District Lounge	La Piazza	The Bayou,, Nightingale's	Scat Cat Lounge, Skipper Society	De Vil's, The Sanctum
NIGHTLIFE AND BARS (Martini Bar)							
	None	None	Meridian	Meridian	None	None	None
NIGHTLIFE AND BARS (Pool Bars)							
	Signals (21+)	Signals (21+)	Cove Bar, Currents, Waves (all ages)	Cove Bar, Currents, Waves (all ages)	Cove Bar (21+) Currents, The Lookout (all ages)	Cove Bar (21+) Currents, The Lookout (all ages)	Cove Bar (21+) Currents, The Lookout (all ages)
NIGHTLIFE AND BARS (Pub/Sports Bar)							
	O'Gills Pub	Crown & Fin Pub	Pub 687	O'Gills Pub	Keg & Compass	Periscope Pub	Cask and Cannon
NIGHTLIFE AND BARS (Craft Cocktail Bar)							
	None	None	Skyline	Skyline	The Rose	The Rose	The Rose
NIGHTLIFE AND BARS (Themed Lounge)							
	None	None	None	None	Star Wars: Hyperspace Lounge	The Haunted Mansion Parlor	The Haunted Mansion Parlor
POOLS AND WATER PLAY AREAS (Adult Pools)							
	Quiet Cove Pool	Quiet Cove Pool	Quiet Cove Pool, Satellite Falls	Quiet Cove Pool, Satellite Falls	Quiet Cove Pool, Quiet Cove Hot Tub	Quiet Cove Pool, Quiet Cove Hot Tub	Quiet Cove Pool, Quiet Cove Hot Tub
POOLS AND WATER PLAY AREAS (Concierge Pools)							
	None	Hot tub	Hot tub	Hot tub	Two hot tubs and a water feature	Two hot tubs and a water feature	Two hot tubs and a water feature

POOLS AND WATER PLAY AREAS (Family Pool)							
	Goofy's Pool	Goofy's Pool	Donald's Pool, Funnel Puddle	Donald's Pool, Funnel Puddle	Chip 'n Dale's Pool, Mickey's Pool	Chip 'n Dale's Pool, Mickey's Pool	Chip 'n Dale's Pool, Mickey's Pool
POOLS AND WATER PLAY AREAS (Kids' Pools and Splash Areas)							
	AquaLab, Nephews' Splash Zone	AquaLab, Dory's Reef	Mickey's Pool, Nemo's Reef	AquaLab, Mickey's Pool, Nemo's Reef	Daisy's Pool, Donald's Pool, Goofy's Pool, Minnie's Pool, Pluto's Pool, Trixie's Falls, Toy Story Splash Zone	Daisy's Pool, Donald's Pool, Goofy's Pool, Minnie's Pool, Pluto's Pool, Trixie's Falls, Toy Story Splash Zone	Daisy's Pool, Donald's Pool, Goofy's Pool, Minnie's Pool, Pluto's Pool, Trixie's Falls, Toy Story Splash Zone
POOLS AND WATER PLAY AREAS (Teen Splash Pool)							
	None	None	Vibe	Vibe	None	None	None
POOLS AND WATER PLAY AREAS (Water Rides)							
	AquaDunk (vertical waterslide), Twist 'n' Spout (kids' waterslide)	Twist 'n' Spout (kids' waterslide)	AquaDuck (water coaster), Mickey's Slide	AquaDuck (water coaster), Mickey's Slide	AquaMouse, Slide-a-saurus Rex	AquaMouse, Slide-a-saurus Rex	AquaMouse, Slide-a-saurus Rex
SPORTS AND RECREATION							
	Basketball, Foosball, shuffleboard, table tennis	Basketball, Foosball, shuffleboard, table tennis	Basketball, Foosball, shuffleboard, table tennis, minigolf	Basketball, Foosball, shuffleboard, table tennis, minigolf	Basketball, Foosball, shuffleboard, table tennis, air hockey, Incredi-Games racecourse	Basketball, Foosball, shuffleboard, table tennis, air hockey, Incredi-Games racecourse	Basketball, Foosball, shuffleboard, table tennis, air hockey, Incredi-Games racecourse
MISCELLANEOUS (Interactive Enchanted Art)							
	None	None	Yes	Yes	Yes	Yes	Yes
MISCELLANEOUS (Interactive Game Played Around the Ship)							
	None	None	Midship Detective Agency	Midship Detective Agency	Disney Uncharted Adventure	Disney Uncharted Adventure	Disney Uncharted Adventure
MISCELLANEOUS (Shutters Photo Studio)							
	Yes	Yes	Yes	Yes	Yes	Yes	Yes
MISCELLANEOUS (Virtual Porthole in Inside Staterooms)							
	None	None	Yes	Yes	None	None	None

continued from page 38

during a two-month dry dock in Cádiz, Spain. This makeover included cosmetic updates to the lobby atrium; **Keys**, the piano bar; **Palo,** the adults-only, fine-dining Italian restaurant; and **Fathoms,** the dance club. The kids' clubs underwent extensive reimagining and reopened with the more vibrant and interactive *Toy Story* and Marvel additions. In addition, Vista Spa became **Senses Spa,** Topsiders Buffet became **Cabanas,** and the dining room Parrot Cay became **Carioca's.** Two years later, the *Magic* underwent an additional dry dock, during which a **Bibbidi Bobbidi Boutique** kids' makeover salon was added and the **Edge** tween club received a location update. The ship got yet another refresh in 2018, when teen club **Vibe** received updated decor; the **Cove Café** coffee bar was spruced up; and, most significantly, Carioca's was again rethemed (this time much more successfully) as **Rapunzel's Royal Table,** featuring elements from *Tangled,* live music, and singing. The most recent dry dock, in 2023, saw the conversion of some standard staterooms to Concierge Staterooms, a significant update to the Concierge lounge, and the transformation of the Promenade Lounge to the **Soul Cat Lounge,** themed to look like the Half Note Lounge, Joe Gardner's favorite music spot from the Disney and Pixar film *Soul.*

 # *The* **Disney Wonder**

STRENGTHS	WEAKNESSES
• Has some of Disney's newest and most exciting itineraries, including Alaska, Hawaii, and Australia	• Does not have a headliner-type slide, as every other ship does
• Tiana's Place is one of our favorite dining rooms across the fleet.	

LAUNCHED IN 1999 as the second of DCL's ships, the *Wonder* was beginning to show its age by 2016, with visible wear and tear and dated decor in many guest areas. In late 2016, the ship underwent a dry dock with significant updating and retheming, emerging in much better condition and with amenities, entertainment, and fittings on par with the rest of the fleet.

The *Wonder* continues to have the most in common with its sister the *Magic,* but with slightly different theming. When you board the ship at Deck 3, you're greeted by Ariel instead of Mickey, and an Art Nouveau–style atrium rather than Art Deco. In keeping with the *Little Mermaid* theme, one of the main dining rooms on the *Wonder* is **Triton's,** named for Ariel's dad (its counterpart on the *Magic* is the *Beauty and the Beast*–themed **Lumiere's**).

The 2016 dry dock introduced **Cabanas** buffet and **Tiana's Place,** a unique restaurant inspired by *The Princess and the Frog* that serves New Orleans–style cuisine accompanied by live jazz. Additionally, the *Wonder*'s antiquated version of **Animator's Palate** was retrofitted with an interactive show to match its counterparts on the other ships. The *Wonder*'s dining is now on par with that of the rest of the DCL fleet.

Len, a cynic whose capacity for scorn would make Ebenezer Scrooge exclaim, "Dude, lighten up!," thinks ***Frozen: A Musical Spectacular*** (presented on both the *Wonder* and the *Fantasy*) is the best stage show in the DCL fleet. In addition to catchy songs, solid stage design, and a snappy pace, it has special effects that had him saying, "Wow!" out loud.

The kids' clubs were also reimagined. The **Oceaneer Club** now features **Marvel Super Hero Academy,** where young guests train to become superheroes (with help from Spider-Man during live character appearances), and ***Frozen* Adventures,** where a digital Olaf leads kids in games and songs.

A 2019 *Wonder* dry dock saw the addition of a New Orleans–themed family nightclub, the **French Quarter Lounge,** designed to complement Tiana's Place. Also freshened up during this refurb were **Cove Café** coffee bar, **Signals** pool bar, and **Vibe** teen club. A 2023 dry dock finally upgraded the internet to keep pace with the rest of the fleet.

From a bells-and-whistles standpoint, the *Wonder* continues to lag behind its newer sisters. You won't find a headliner waterslide like the AquaDunk (*Magic*) or a water coaster like the AquaDuck (*Dream, Fantasy*) or AquaMouse (*Wish, Treasure, Destiny*). And Inside Staterooms lack the "virtual portholes" found on the *Dream* and *Fantasy*.

Nevertheless, the *Wonder* is a great ship. The smaller capacity means fewer people jockeying for space in ports of call, and the older ships have a cozier, homier atmosphere. By the end of a long sailing, the cast members feel like family.

The **Disney Dream**

STRENGTHS	WEAKNESSES
• Virtual portholes add some fun to Inside Staterooms.	• There are more guests on the *Dream*-class ships, making for bigger crowds in ports.
• Pricing is quite reasonable compared to similar itineraries on other ships.	

FOLLOWING THE SUCCESSES of the *Magic* and *Wonder*, DCL ordered two new ships that almost doubled the number of guests it could serve, allowed it to expand the number of itineraries offered, and brought several first-evers to a cruise ship. The new *Dream*-class vessels (the *Dream* and *Fantasy*) were built by Meyer Werft in Germany rather than Italy's Fincantieri, creator of the *Magic* and *Wonder*.

The *Disney Dream*, the first of these new ships, set sail in 2011. It's 151 feet longer, 35 feet taller, and 15 feet wider than the *Magic* and *Wonder*. With three additional decks, the ship can hold 50% more passengers and crew than its predecessors.

Disney Imagineering had great fun designing the second-generation ships. Inside Staterooms were given **"virtual portholes,"** which show the view from the bridge on a round screen, with Disney characters popping by on-screen occasionally. This feature proved so popular with kids that on many cruises Inside Staterooms had fares higher than those of Oceanview Staterooms. On the top deck, the **AquaDuck**, a waterslide that circles the ship, was added to the usual pools. Between the pool deck and your stateroom, you'll find interactive art that reacts when you pass it, along with the **Midship Detective Agency**, a scavenger hunt game that sends families all over the ship collecting clues.

When it came to dining, the buffet in **Cabanas** improved traffic flow and food quality compared with the dated Beach Blanket Buffet on the *Wonder* and Topsiders on the *Magic* (thankfully, both eventually became Cabanas as well). As for the *Dream*'s three main dining rooms, **Animator's Palate** was improved with new technology as part of the dinner show, **Enchanted Garden** took its place as the prettiest of the three, and **Royal Palace** is a tribute to all things Disney princess (but mostly Cinderella).

Both adults and kids scored big with improvements to the new ship. In addition to the adults-only Palo, **Remy** was added as another upscale-dining option for the 18-and-up crowd. With a subtle *Ratatouille* theme and not one but two celebrated chefs creating the menus, Remy initially shocked cruisers with its prices—a minimum of $135 plus alcohol per dinner, among the highest in the industry—but diners were pleased nonetheless. The adult lounges, in the area called **The District** on Deck 4, provide more-intimate, better-themed spaces to take the edge off than **After Hours,** the comparable space on the *Magic* and *Wonder*. **Skyline,** one of The District's bars, showcases a great use of technology, with a virtual cityscape display that changes every 15 minutes. It's mesmerizing and one of our favorite spaces across the fleet.

Kids got greatly expanded club areas with a Pixar theme. The teen area got a pool and a makeover that made it one of the most stylish spaces on board. Teens also got their own pampering spot, **Chill Spa**.

Though the *Dream* still feels contemporary, Disney continues to improve the ship. A 2015 dry-dock refresh added a **Bibbidi Bobbidi Boutique** makeover salon for children, on Deck 5; **Vanellope's Sweets & Treats,** a premium-ice-cream shop, on Deck 11; and a *Star Wars*–themed area of the Oceaneer Club where children "pilot" a simulated *Millennium Falcon*. This dry dock also included the adults-only pool, **Satellite Falls,** which had proven very popular on the *Disney Fantasy* when it began sailing a few years prior.

After 10 years of being based in Port Canaveral, the *Dream* moved to southern Florida in 2022 to make room for the *Wish* at Port Canaveral. The *Dream* sailed out of Miami in 2022 and part of 2023 before making Fort Lauderdale's Port Everglades its permanent home.

In 2024, the *Dream* underwent a 35-night dry dock in Southampton, during which several staterooms were converted to Concierge, a Tower Suite was added, and the spa and Concierge lounge were refreshed and expanded. In addition, a cantina was added to the pool deck; the **Oceaneer Club** got a new Marvel workshop; and **Edge** moved to Deck 5 next door to Vibe, where it has access to an outdoor space for the first time. The new Concierge lounge has a *Hercules* theme, with light, airy colors and gold accents. The new *Dream* Tower Suite, located in the funnel, sleeps eight guests.

The **Disney Fantasy**

STRENGTHS	WEAKNESSES
• The AquaDuck coaster is fun for all ages.	• Aft staterooms have vibration issues from time to time.
• Satellite Falls is one of the best adult pool areas in the fleet.	

DCL'S FOURTH SHIP first sailed in 2012, one year after the *Dream* came into service. The *Fantasy* is nearly identical to its sister but got some unique tweaks due to guest and cast-member feedback. The ship is based in Port Canaveral and sails primarily four- and five-night Bahamian itineraries in the Caribbean in 2025, although it's spending that summer in Europe.

Walking into the atrium of the *Fantasy,* you see a bronze statue of Minnie Mouse and a striking peacock-inspired carpet, an indication of the ship's Art Nouveau style as opposed to the *Dream*'s Deco look.

The *Dream*'s technology package got some enhancements on the *Fantasy.* The **Midship Detective Agency** has three different storylines (including the Muppets), surpassing the version on the *Dream,* and the show at **Animator's Palate** got a very cool audience-interaction element that we won't spoil here. Besides this addition, the restaurants are identical to the *Dream*'s, with one subtle name change: Royal Palace is **Royal Court** and includes even more princessy goodness. **Cabanas, Enchanted Garden, Palo,** and **Remy** are the same. In addition to the **AquaDuck,** the pool deck includes the **AquaLab** splash area.

The *Fantasy*'s nightlife area is **Europa.** The one constant between the two bar/nightclub areas on the *Dream* and *Fantasy* is **Skyline,** though it displays different cityscapes in this rendition (we still love it). **The Tube**'s *Austin Powers*–style decor makes it a fun place to hang out, but **Ooh La La** is either too high-concept or low-concept for our tastes; we prefer the whimsical look of the *Dream*'s **Pink** for our Champagne needs. **O'Gills Pub** is a neat, lightly themed Irish bar that was later added to the *Magic,* although we prefer **Pub 687,** the sports bar on the *Dream.*

The **Disney Wish**

STRENGTHS	WEAKNESSES
• The ship is stunning.	• The adult lounges are spread throughout the ship rather than in one area.
• Hero Zone is an innovative space with great activities for families.	• The ship lacks a walking track, a popular feature on the previous four ships.
• There are several impressive new Concierge Stateroom types not found on any previous ships.	

HAVING ENTERED SERVICE in 2022, a decade after the *Fantasy*, the *Wish* is the first in the third generation, or *Wish* class, of DCL ships. It debuted to near frenzied levels of excitement, with the first sailing selling out before it became available to the general public—and during a global pandemic at that.

The *Wish* has a gorgeous exterior that harmonizes with the rest of the fleet's. Inside, it has opulent furnishings and visually appealing color schemes. Of note, the *Wish* has an even more Disney feel than the other ships. We're not always sure that's a good thing. What we mean here isn't theming so much as aggressive branding. For example, the upscale bars on the *Dream* and *Fantasy* are not Disney-themed, but the *Wish* has the ultrathemed **Star Wars: Hyperspace Lounge.** Similarly, the other ships have spas and beauty salons that are tastefully appointed but not specifically Disneyfied. On the *Wish*, however, the women's beauty salon is the **Untangled Salon,** with Rapunzel and *Tangled* imagery throughout, and the barber shop is **Hook's Barbery,** with "narrative details inspired by Captain Hook." And that's just the adult spaces.

Don't get us wrong—we love Disney. But there comes a point where theming becomes all-consuming. While monitoring guest reports and media accounts of the *Wish*'s first few months of service, we lost count of the number of times we read variations on the phrase "theme park at sea." For many (if not most) people, the raison d'etre of a cruise vacation is relaxation. "Theme park at sea" is the opposite of relaxation. Yes, it's entertaining—and indeed, it could be precisely what your family wants—but serene it is not. And while there are a few places on the *Wish* where you can get away from "all Disney, all the time," there are fewer than on DCL's four original vessels.

The *Wish* does have some big wins for us, like **Luna,** a two-story lounge that hosts family activities during the day and turns into the adult nightlife area at night. We were also excited to see some lovely specialty coffee shops spread throughout the ship and not confined to the adult area. **Hero Zone** is a spectacular space for sports, games, the Disney Silent DJ Party, and our favorite—Jack Jack's Diaper Dash. On one day of the cruise, it's also where Disney sets up an inflatable *Incredibles*-themed racecourse for the very popular Incredi-Games.

The *Wish* sails primarily three- and four-night Bahamian cruises out of Port Canaveral.

The *Disney Treasure*

STRENGTHS	WEAKNESSES
• As one of Disney's newest ships, it has all the latest bells and whistles.	• There is no dedicated adult lounge area, so you will often encounter children outside the lounges.
• The Grand Hall has rich, deep colors, unlike any of the previous ships.	

THE MAIDEN VOYAGE for the highly anticipated *Disney Treasure* was scheduled for Christmas week of 2024, which had many Disney fans saying, "Huh?" Nevertheless, despite a slow-selling maiden voyage, future dates for the *Treasure* sold briskly. During its inaugural season, the *Treasure* will sail seven-night Eastern and Western Caribbean itineraries, routes formerly traveled by the *Fantasy*.

The theme of the *Treasure* is "Adventure," with design elements drawn from real-world locales in Asia and Africa and from Disney films like *Aladdin*. The Grand Hall atrium features a statue of Aladdin and Jasmine riding the Magic Carpet, sitting atop a larger deep-blue carpet. Above, the ceiling is filled with a gold light fixture with Moroccan-inspired design.

Except for theming elements, the *Treasure* emulates the *Wish* in many regards. The overall layout, stateroom configurations, youth spaces, theaters, pools and slides, spa and salons, pool deck buffet restaurant (**Marceline Market**), quick-service restaurants, Pirate Night party (**Pirate's Rockin' Parlay Party**), and **Hero Zone** play area are all virtually identical to the *Wish*'s.

Also like the *Wish* are the two adult-dining venues, **Palo Steakhouse** and **Enchanté** (and their connected bar, **The Rose**), and two of the rotational-dining restaurants, **1923** and **Worlds of Marvel.**

Plaza de Coco, a theatrical dining experience themed to the film *Coco*, is new to the DCL rotational-restaurant lineup. Dinner includes performances by a live mariachi band. There are two distinct shows at dinner, shown on separate nights. In the first, Miguel and the town mariachis entertain with lively songs and dances. The second time you visit, the plaza is transformed into a fun-filled Día de los Muertos celebration with Mamá Coco, Abuelita, and the rest of the Rivera family.

In addition to **Avengers: Quantum Encounter,** found on the *Wish*, Worlds of Marvel on the *Treasure* features a second show with characters from *Guardians of the Galaxy*. Called **Marvel Celebration of Heroes: Groot Remix,** the show follows Groot as he plans a surprise party for his friend Rocket while diners enjoy trivia and an "awesome mix" of songs.

The pool-deck sweets shop, **Jumbeaux's Sweets,** is themed to the film *Zootopia*. Like similar shops on the *Wish, Dream,* and *Fantasy,* Jumbeaux's serves ice cream and gelato, with a selection of toppings and sauces, as well as an array of pastries and candies.

New bars and cafés include:

HEI HEI CAFÉ Named for Moana's sidekick chicken, this casual café off the Grand Hall serves a selection of coffee, tea, specialty beverages, and snacks. It has furniture styled with construction techniques used by the Polynesian people to craft sea vessels.

JADE CRICKET CAFÉ Named for Mulan's sidekick cricket, Cri-Kee, and also located off the Grand Hall, this café has offerings similar to those at Hei Hei Café. Still, it has plum-blossom decor with metallic counters reminiscent of Mulan's armor.

PERISCOPE PUB This sports bar is themed to the film *20,000 Leagues Under the Sea*. While sipping craft brews or specialty cocktails, look through the "glass" ceiling to the watery world above. Or stay up-to-date with what's happening on land with the surrounding "scientific" monitors displaying news and live sports coverage.

SARABI Named for the lioness matriarch in *The Lion King*, this two-story space, like the *Wish*'s **Luna,** hosts family activities and adult nightlife.

SCAT CAT LOUNGE Diving deep into the Disney catalog, Scat Cat is themed to *The Aristocats*. A pianist on a baby grand piano covered in paw prints plays tunes while guests enjoy upscale cocktails.

SKIPPER SOCIETY Located near the Grand Hall, this lounge has a Jungle Cruise theme. Your beverages will have adventurous names, and your servers will be well versed in puns and corny jokes.

Live entertainment includes a brand-new show called **Disney The Tale of Moana,** along with **Beauty and the Beast** from the *Dream* and **Disney Seas the Adventure** from the *Wish*.

Overall, if you liked the *Wish* and wished it had longer sailings, you'll be delighted with the *Treasure*. Likewise, if the *Wish* was not your cup of tea, then the *Treasure* will likely also leave you wanting.

The **Disney Destiny**

STRENGTHS	WEAKNESSES
• It has one of our favorite themes yet: "Heroes and Villains."	• We expect the pricing to be quite high for the first few years.
• Pride Lands: The Feast of the Lion King could be the best main dining room yet.	• If you aren't a Marvel fan, the Marvel theming may be lost on you—and there's a lot of it.

WE DIDN'T HAVE all the details for the *Disney Destiny* at press time, but here's what we do know. It is scheduled to set sail on four- and five-night sailings to the Bahamas and the Western Caribbean beginning in late 2025 from Fort Lauderdale. It will be very similar to its sister ships, the *Wish* and *Treasure*, and should have an almost identical layout. Many elements from those ships were kept, such as **Hero Zone, Marceline Market,** adult-dining restaurants **Palo Steakhouse** and **Enchanté,** and the **1923** and **Worlds of Marvel** dining rooms, as well as the quick-service restaurants, the kids' clubs, and more.

The theming is "Heroes and Villains," and heroic Minnie makes an appearance on the bow. The Grand Hall went all in on Marvel, with a statue of T'Challa, the Black Panther, and the vibrant colors of the *Black Panther* films. The metalwork on the pillars is inspired by the banded armor and stacked jewelry found in the Kingdom of Wakanda.

There's a new live-entertainment dining room called **Pride Lands: Feast of the Lion King,** where favorites from *The Lion King*, such as "Circle of Life," will be performed during dinner.

Edna À La Mode, the ice-cream and sweets shop, is themed after *The Incredibles,* with statues of Edna and Jack-Jack welcoming guests inside to purchase sweet treats.

We're also thrilled they are bringing **Disney Hercules** back to the stage in the Walt Disney Theatre. It appears to be a different version than the one that previously played on the *Wonder* and *Magic,* but we are excited all the same.

Some of the new bars and cafés include:

CAFÉ MEGARA AND CAFÉ MERIDA These two coffee bars off the Grand Hall are named after the heroines Megara from *Hercules* and Merida from *Brave.*

CASK AND CANNON is the *Pirates of the Caribbean*-themed sports bar.

DE VIL'S will be a highlight here. It's a *101 Dalmatians*–inspired lounge complete with a black-and-white spotted piano.

SAGA Similar to **Luna** on the *Wish* and **Sarabi** on the *Treasure,* this two-story entertainment space, inspired by Wakanda, is home to family activities during the day and adult nightlife in the evenings.

THE SANCTUM is a mystical lounge on Deck 3 patterned after the world of *Doctor Strange.*

The Haunted Mansion Parlor, first seen on the *Treasure,* will also be on board. If you like the *Wish*-class ships and Marvel, you'll undoubtedly love the newest version.

The **Disney Adventure**

STRENGTHS	WEAKNESSES
• The *Disney Adventure* is totally different from the other DCL ships.	• Singapore is a long way away for US guests.
• Concierge level will offer more amenities than any on other DCL ship.	• Much higher passenger count than the rest of the fleet
• There are more waterslides and water-play areas than on any other DCL ship.	

THE *DISNEY ADVENTURE* is scheduled to begin sailing three- and four-night itineraries in 2025, so we had not been on board at press time. The *Adventure* is a huge departure from the rest of the DCL fleet. While it still sports the classic colors with the signature red smokestacks and dark-blue hull, the *Adventure* is much larger—208,000 gross tons compared to the *Wish*-class ships, which are 144,000 gross tons. The *Wish*-class ships can accommodate 4,000 passengers, while the *Adventure* has a capacity of 6,700. This is a much bigger ship than DCL fans are used to. Singapore will be the ship's home port for at least five years, and Captain Mickey adorns the bow. See Part 17 for more on the *Disney Adventure.*

CONCIERGE LOUNGES

WHEN THE *MAGIC* AND *WONDER* were built, the Concierge level almost seemed like an afterthought. There were only 20 Concierge Staterooms and no dedicated lounge. The *Dream* and *Fantasy* more than doubled the number of Concierge Staterooms to 41 and put a lounge smack-dab in the middle. Concierge on the *Dream* and *Fantasy* was incredibly popular, and eventually Disney added more Concierge Staterooms and created lounge space on both the *Magic* and the *Wonder*. By the time the *Wish*-class ships were built, Disney had doubled down on Concierge. The *Wish*-class ships have 76 Concierge Staterooms and the largest Concierge lounge yet.

The ***Magic***'s lounge on Deck 10 was added in 2015 and expanded in 2022. It's a much larger space now, with floor-to-ceiling windows and great views. There's an outdoor space with additional seating and tables. It's covered and open-air, so we'd have to use the word *sundeck* liberally for this one.

In 2016, Disney converted the Outlook Café on Deck 10 of the ***Wonder*** (added in 2009 with Alaska sailings in mind) into a Concierge lounge. After further enhancements and expansions, it's now a bright, open space with a wonderful sundeck above Deck 11 that's accessed through outdoor stairs and has some of the best views on the ship.

Until 2024, the ***Dream*** and ***Fantasy*** had identical lounges and sundecks. Located on Deck 12, the lounge has no exterior views, but a large round skylight lets in lots of natural light. It's a nicely appointed space, with plenty of room for the number of Concierge guests on board. A door inside opens to stairs to the Concierge sundeck on Deck 13. The sundeck has lots of seating and a hot tub. In 2024, the lounge on the *Dream* was expanded to accommodate the additional Concierge Staterooms and was rethemed with subtle *Hercules* touches. It's a bright space with light colors and touches of gold. We expect a similar update to the *Fantasy*'s lounge in the fall of 2025.

Not surprisingly, the newest ships, the ***Wish*** and ***Treasure*** (and presumably the ***Destiny***), have the most impressive lounges and sundecks. The lounge is located on Deck 12, and it is absolutely huge. It's also the first to have a dedicated kitchen, which means you can order hot meals. That's an excellent perk for Concierge guests. There's a small sundeck right outside, and interior and exterior stairs lead up to another beautiful sundeck on Deck 13 with two hot tubs, an abundance of lounge chairs, and an outdoor bar with self-serve smoothie machines. You read that right: Dole Whips on demand.

Magic/Wonder DECK PLANS

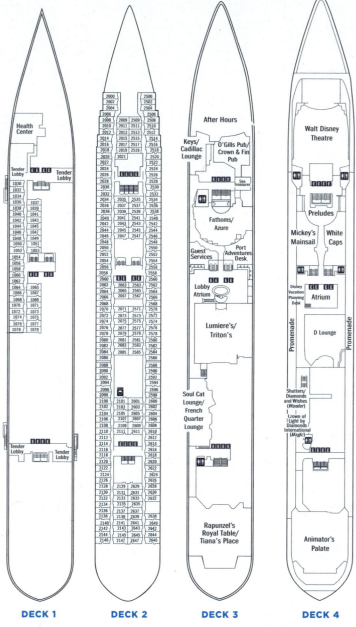

DECK 1

Health Center

Tender Lobby

Tender Lobby

1030	
1032	
1034	
1036	1037
1038	1039
1040	1041
1042	1043
1044	1045
1046	1047
1048	1049
1050	1051
1052	1053
1054	
1056	
1058	
1060	
1062	
1064	1065
1066	1067
1068	1069
1070	1071
1072	1073
1074	1075
1076	1077
1078	1079

Tender Lobby

Tender Lobby

DECK 2

2000		2500
2002		2502
2004		2504
2006		2506
2008	2009	2509	2508
2010	2011	2511	2510
2012	2013	2513	2512
2014	2015	2515	2514
2016	2017	2517	2516
2018	2019	2519	2518
2020	2021		2520
2022			2522
2024			2524
2026			2526
2028			2528
2030			2530
2032			2532
2034	2035	2535	2534
2036	2037	2537	2536
2038	2039	2539	2538
2040	2041	2541	2540
2042	2043	2543	2542
2044	2045	2545	2544
2046	2047	2547	2546
2048			2548
2050			2550
2052			2552
2054			2554
2056			2556
2058			2558
2060			2560
2062	2063	2563	2562
2064	2065	2565	2564
2066	2067	2567	2566
2068			2568
2070	2071	2571	2570
2072	2073	2573	2572
2074	2075	2575	2574
2076	2077	2577	2576
2078	2079	2579	2578
2080	2081	2581	2580
2082	2083	2583	2582
2084	2085	2585	2584
2086			2586
2088			2588
2090			2590
2092			2592
2094			2594
2096			2596
2098			2598
2100	2101	2601	2600
2102	2103	2603	2602
2104	2105	2605	2604
2106	2107	2607	2606
2108	2109	2609	2608
2110	2111	2611	2610
2112			2612
2114			2614
2116			2616
2118			2618
2120			2620
2122			2622
2124			2624
2126			2626
2128	2129	2629	2628
2130	2131	2631	2630
2132	2133	2633	2632
2134	2135	2635	
2136	2137	2637	
2138	2139	2639	2638
2140	2141	2641	2640
2142	2143	2643	2642
2144	2145	2645	2644
2146	2147	2647	2646

DECK 3

After Hours

Keys/ Cadillac Lounge

O'Gills Pub/ Crown & Fin Pub

Sea Treasures

Fathoms/ Azure

Guest Services

Port Adventures Desk

Lobby Atrium

Lumiere's/ Triton's

Soul Cat Lounge/ French Quarter Lounge

Rapunzel's Royal Table/ Tiana's Place

DECK 4

Walt Disney Theatre

Preludes

Mickey's Mainsail

White Caps

Disney Vacation Planning Desk

Atrium

Promenade

D Lounge

Promenade

Shutters/ Diamonds and Wishes (*Wonder*)

Crown of Light by Diamonds International (*Magic*)

Animator's Palate

continued on next page

Magic / Wonder DECK PLANS

continued from previous page

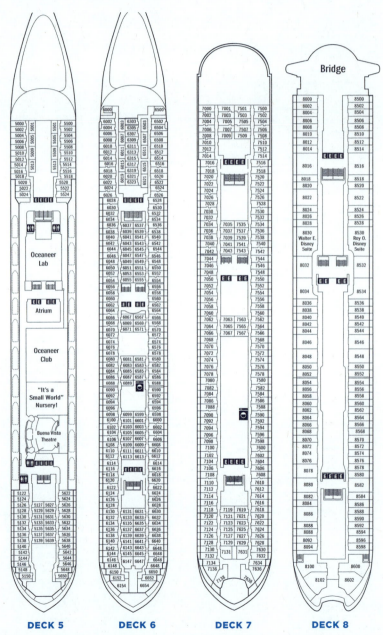

DECK 5   **DECK 6**   **DECK 7**   **DECK 8**

Magic/Wonder **DECK PLANS**

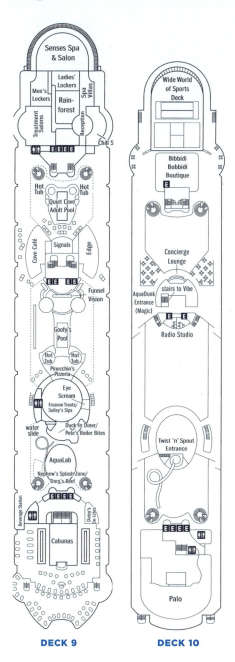

Senses Spa & Salon

Ladies' Lockers

Men's Lockers

Rain-forest

Spa Villas

Treatment Salons

Reception

Chill S

Hot Tub

Hot Tub

Quiet Cove Adult Pool

Cove Café

Signals

Edge

Funnel Vision

Goofy's Pool

Hot Tub

Hot Tub

Pinocchio's Pizzeria

Eye Scream

Frozone Treats/ Sulley's Sips

water slide

Duck In Diner/ Pete's Boiler Bites

AquaLab

Nephew's Splash Zone/ Dory's Reef

Beverage Station

Daisy's De-Lites

Cabanas

DECK 9

Wide World of Sports Deck

Bibbidi Bobbidi Boutique

Concierge Lounge

AquaDunk Entrance (Magic)

stairs to Vibe

Radio Studio

Twist 'n' Spout Entrance

Palo

DECK 10

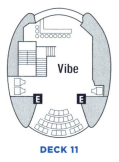

Vibe

DECK 11

Dream/Fantasy **DECK PLANS**

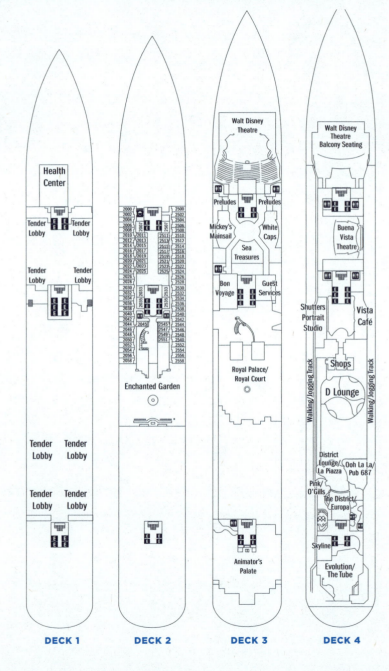

DECK 1

Health Center

Tender Lobby — Tender Lobby

Tender Lobby — Tender Lobby

Tender Lobby — Tender Lobby

Tender Lobby — Tender Lobby

DECK 2

2000
2002
2004
2006 2007
2008
2010 2011 2500
2012 2013 2502
2014 2015 2504
2016 2017 2506
2018 2019 2508
2020 2021 2510
2022 2023 2511 2512
2024 2025 2513 2514
2026   2515 2516
2028   2517 2518
2030   2519 2520
2032   2521 2522
2034   2523 2524
2035 2033 2525 2526
2036 2535 2533 2528
2038   2530
2040   2532
2042   2534
2044 2045 2535 2536
2046   2538
2048 2047 2540
2050   2542
2052 2545 2544
2054 2547 2546
2056 2549 2548
2058 2551 2540
                 2550
                 2552
                 2554
                 2556
                 2558

Enchanted Garden

DECK 3

Walt Disney Theatre

Preludes   Preludes

Mickey's Mainsail   White Caps

Sea Treasures

Bon Voyage   Guest Services

Royal Palace/ Royal Court

Animator's Palate

DECK 4

Walt Disney Theatre Balcony Seating

Buena Vista Theatre

Shutters Portrait Studio   Vista Café

Walking/Jogging Track   Walking/Jogging Track

Shops

D Lounge

District Lounge/ La Piazza   Ooh La La/ Pub 687

Pink/ O'Gills

The District/ Europa

Skyline

Evolution/ The Tube

Dream/Fantasy DECK PLANS

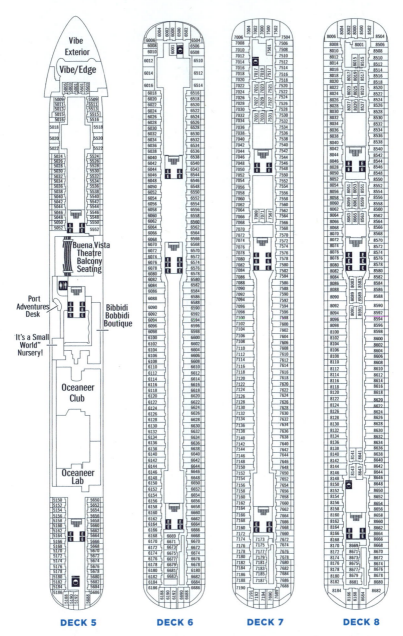

DECK 5

Vibe
Exterior
Vibe/Edge

Buena Vista
Theatre
Balcony
Seating

Port
Adventures
Desk

It's a Small
World"
Nursery!

Oceaneer
Club

Oceaneer
Lab

DECK 6

Bibbidi
Bobbidi
Boutique

DECK 7

DECK 8

continued on next page

Dream/Fantasy DECK PLANS

continued from previous page

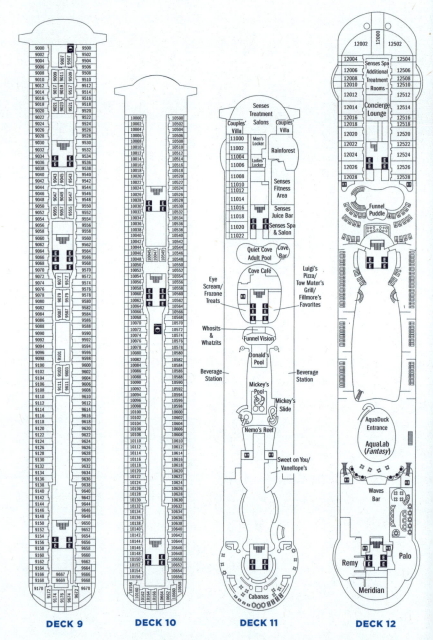

DECK 9   **DECK 10**   **DECK 11**   **DECK 12**

Dream/Fantasy DECK PLANS

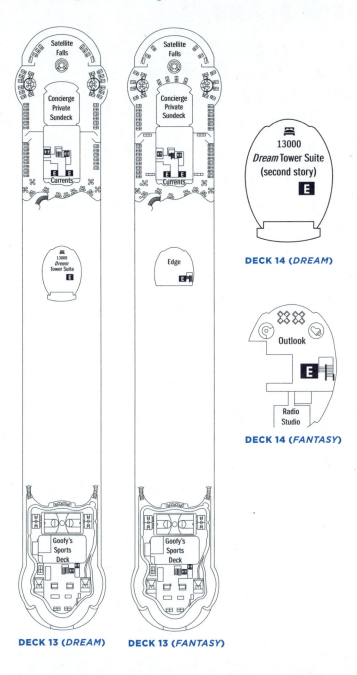

DECK 13 (*DREAM*)

DECK 13 (*FANTASY*)

DECK 14 (*DREAM*)

DECK 14 (*FANTASY*)

Wish/Treasure/Destiny
DECK PLANS

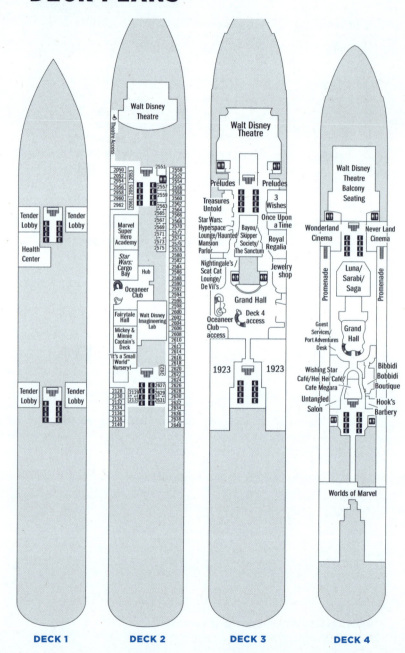

DECK 1

Tender Lobby

Tender Lobby

Health Center

Tender Lobby

Tender Lobby

DECK 2

Walt Disney Theatre

Theatre Access

2050
2052
2954
2956
2958
2960
2962

2051
2055
2061

2551
2557
2559

2563
2565
2567
2569
2571
2573
2575

2550
2552
2554
2556
2558
2560
2562
2564
2566
2568
2570
2572
2574
2576
2578
2580
2582
2584
2586
2588
2590
2592
2594
2596
2598
2600
2602
2604
2606
2608
2610
2612
2614
2616
2618
2620
2622
2624
2626
2628
2630
2632
2634
2636
2638
2640

Marvel Super Hero Academy

Star Wars: Cargo Bay

Hub

Oceaneer Club

Fairytale Hall

Walt Disney Imagineering Lab

Mickey & Minnie Captain's Deck

"It's a Small World" Nursery!

2623

2128
2130
2132
2134
2136
2138
2140

2129
2131

2627
2629
2631

DECK 3

Walt Disney Theatre

Préludes

Preludes

Treasures Untold

3 Wishes

Star Wars: Hyperspace Lounge/Haunted Mansion Parlor

Bayou/ Skipper Society/ The Sanctum

Once Upon a Time

Royal Regalia

Nightingale's / Scat Cat Lounge/ De Vil's

Jewelry shop

Grand Hall

Oceaneer Club access

Deck 4 access

1923

1923

DECK 4

Walt Disney Theatre Balcony Seating

Wonderland Cinema

Never Land Cinema

Luna/ Sarabi/ Saga

Promenade

Promenade

Guest Services/ Port Adventures Desk

Grand Hall

Wishing Star Café/Hei Hei Café/ Cafe Megara

Bibbidi Bobbidi Boutique

Untangled Salon

Hook's Barbery

Worlds of Marvel

Wish/Treasure/Destiny
DECK PLANS *continued on next page*

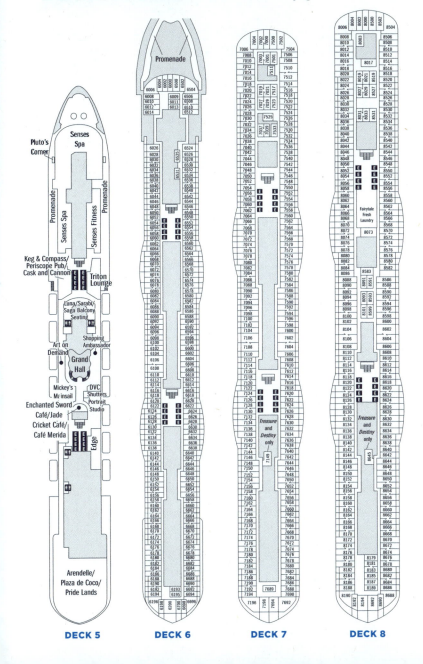

DECK 5 **DECK 6** **DECK 7** **DECK 8**

Wish/Treasure/Destiny
DECK PLANS *continued from previous page*

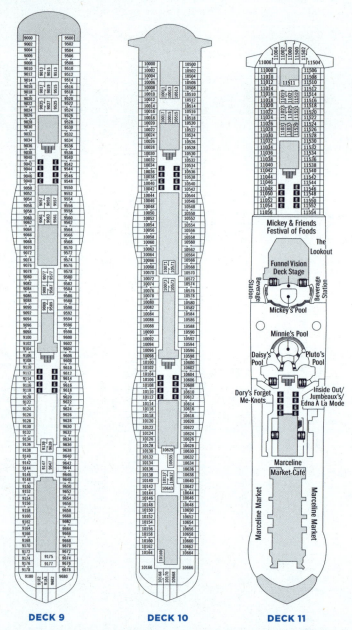

DECK 9   **DECK 10**   **DECK 11**

Wish/Treasure/Destiny
DECK PLANS

Concierge
Tower
Suite
14000

DECK 15

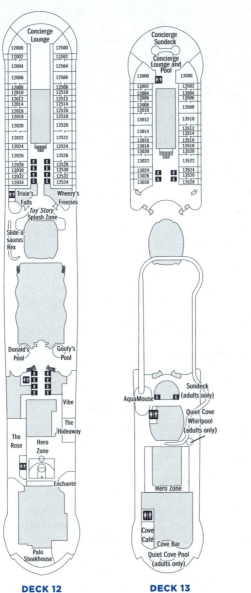

Concierge Lounge

12000	12500
12002	12502
12004	12504
12006	12506
12008	12508
12010	12510
12012	12512
12014	12514
12016	12516
12018	12518
12020	12520
12022	12522
12024	12524
12026	12526
12028	12528
12030	12530
12032	12532
12034	12534

Trixie's Falls
Wheezy's Freezies
Toy Story Splash Zone
Slide-a-saurus Rex

Donald's Pool
Goofy's Pool

Vibe
The Hideaway
The Rose
Hero Zone
Enchanté

Palo Steakhouse

DECK 12

Concierge Sundeck
Concierge Lounge and Pool

13000	13500
13002	13502
13004	13504
13006	13506
13008	13508
13010	
13012	13510
13014	13512
13016	13514
13018	13516
13020	13518
13022	13520
13024	13522
13026	13524
13028	13526
	13528

AquaMouse
Sundeck (adults only)
Quiet Cove Whirlpool (adults only)

Hero Zone

Cove Café
Cove Bar
Quiet Cove Pool (adults only)

DECK 13

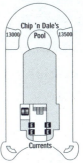

Chip 'n Dale's Pool
13000   13500

Currents

Concierge Tower Suite (14000)

Sundeck (adults only)

DECK 14

CHOOSING *an* ITINERARY

OVERVIEW

DCL OFFERS MORE THAN 50 itineraries that cover 11 geographic regions or major routes, classified as follows: **Alaska, Bahamas, Caribbean, Europe, Hawaii, Mexico, New Zealand** and **Australia, Pacific Coast, Panama Canal, South Pacific,** and **transatlantic.**

However, these cruises don't fit neatly into their assigned geographic categories as defined by Disney. For example, both Bahamian and Caribbean cruises stop at Disney's island destinations in the Bahamas; the sailings that DCL classifies as Canadian stop only along the Atlantic Coast; and its Alaska cruises include Vancouver, Canada, as a port of call. Further muddying the waters, so to speak, Disney breaks out a number of these cruise regions into subcategories. For instance, Caribbean cruises encompass Eastern, Southern, and Western Caribbean itineraries. In contrast, European cruises include British Isles, Mediterranean, Northern European, Norwegian Fjords, and Western European itineraries—which are sometimes subdivided even further into trips with names such as "Mediterranean with Greek Isles" and "Norwegian Fjords with Iceland."

DCL uses **repositioning cruises** whenever it needs to move a ship between the US and Europe, between the Atlantic and the Pacific, or from one base port to another within a geographic area (say, from San Juan, Puerto Rico, to Port Canaveral, Florida). Any cruise that starts at one port and ends at another is a repositioning cruise, the most notable being **South Pacific, transatlantic,** and **Panama Canal** cruises.

Disney cruises vary in length (and price) within each geographic area to appeal to as wide an audience as possible. For instance, guests interested in visiting the Bahamas can choose from three-, four-, five-, or even seven-night cruises.

To help fit its ships into the ports' schedules, DCL offers multiple versions of many itineraries, each of which visits the same ports but in a different order. Consider the many four-night Bahamian cruises out of Port Canaveral on the *Wish:* All visit Nassau and Castaway Cay and include a day at sea, but at the time of this writing, they can be configured in the following six ways:

4-NIGHT BAHAMIAN CRUISE ITINERARIES (*DISNEY WISH*)				
ITINERARY	**NIGHT 1**	**NIGHT 2**	**NIGHT 3**	**NIGHT 4**
Version 1	Port Canaveral	Nassau	Castaway Cay	At sea
Version 2	Port Canaveral	Nassau	At sea	Castaway Cay
Version 3	Port Canaveral	At sea	Nassau	Castaway Cay
Version 4	Port Canaveral	At sea	Castaway Cay	Nassau
Version 5	Port Canaveral	Castaway Cay	Nassau	At sea
Version 6	Port Canaveral	Castaway Cay	At sea	Nassau

As long as the itinerary offers the ports you want, there's little need to worry about the order in which you experience them. Simply choose your cruise based on the dates and pricing that make the most sense for you and your family.

ITINERARY RELEASE DATES

KNOWING WHEN NEW ITINERARIES are released is helpful if you want the lowest price for a specific cruise. It's also beneficial if you want to book a particular type of stateroom that's in high demand or a popular sailing like a Christmas cruise.

New itineraries are especially popular. When Disney announced the first sailings to and from Australia, they sold out almost immediately. A similarly rapid sellout happened when Disney announced its first sailings out of New Orleans.

Disney usually announces its ships' schedules in seasonal blocks (spring, summer, and so on) about 12–15 months ahead of the first sailings of that season. New ships historically get their own separate release date, but they follow the same pattern.

Disney doesn't give more than a few days' notice when releases happen, but we can look at historical release dates and get a general time frame. Scott Sanders from *The Disney Cruise Line Blog* has a list of release dates on his website (disneycruiselineblog.com). See his current list on the next page and check his website for updates.

As discussed on page 5, booking usually begins in tiers by Castaway Club status, with Pearl members booking first, then Platinum, Gold, and Silver, followed by new cruisers. Residents of Disney Golden Oak (Disney's swanky neighborhood on Walt Disney World property) also often get an early crack with Platinum members. Disney Vacation Club members and Adventures by Disney Insiders (guests who have traveled on Adventures by Disney) often get to book with Silver cruisers, assuming they don't have their own higher status.

HISTORICAL ITINERARY-RELEASE DATES			
YEAR OF SAILINGS	**WHEN ITINERARIES WERE RELEASED, BY SEASON**		
	JANUARY–MAY	**SUMMER**	**FALL**
2018	Tuesday October 25, 2016	Tuesday February 21, 2017	Thursday May 11, 2017
2019	Thursday October 26, 2017	Thursday March 1, 2018	Thursday May 17, 2018
2020	Thursday September 27, 2018	Thursday February 28, 2019	Thursday June 6, 2019
2021	Thursday September 26, 2019	Monday February 24, 2020	Thursday July 23, 2020
2022	Thursday October 15, 2020	Thursday March 18, 2021	Thursday June 17, 2021
2023	Tuesday October 12, 2021	Wednesday April 27, 2022	Thursday July 21, 2022
2024	Wednesday December 7, 2022	Thursday March 23, 2023	Thursday June 15, 2023
2025	Thursday October 26, 2023	Thursday March 14, 2024	Tuesday June 18, 2024
2026	Tuesday, June 18, 2024	TBA	TBA

NEW ITINERARIES

ARE YOU SOMEONE who likes to be first? As for Tammy, she enjoys being on first-of-their-kind cruises above all else. Above price, above better itineraries, you name it. It's good to know yourself, right?

New itineraries and ships offer the chance to be first. Often, new ports are excited to welcome Disney Cruise Line to the city, and they hold welcome ceremonies or have welcome parties in the port. Tammy was on the first visit to Liverpool for DCL several years ago, and there was a welcome festival within walking distance of the ship. That night, it felt like the whole town came out to see the fireworks show that the city held in the ship's honor as the *Magic* pulled away from the dock. Sometimes, you'll find unique gifts (like a commemorative print) in your stateroom as well.

New itineraries may also mean rocky sailing, so to speak. When a new ship starts sailing, Disney does its best to schedule a reasonable launch date, but they haven't always been able to stick to that date. The *Fantasy* and *Wish* were both late for different reasons, and the fully booked maiden voyages (and a few sailings scheduled for right afterward) were rescheduled. Disney offered compensation for those guests, but it was disappointing for those who couldn't switch to the new date.

When the *Wish* finally sailed, the first few voyages still had hiccups. A little cosmetic work was still happening, and some kinks were still being worked out. Combine that with the number of bloggers and social media influencers posting and trying to find a way for their content to stand out over the first few sailings, along with guests buying as much inaugural merchandise as their arms could carry, and it was a bit hectic at times. It did settle down after a month or two, but that's probably the new norm for inaugural sailings. If you don't care about being first and want a more reliable experience, or your schedule can't handle a last-minute delay, you may want to skip the first few months on a new ship.

ITINERARY CHANGES

ITINERARIES CAN CHANGE for many reasons. Fortunately, these changes don't happen often. When they do, it can be frustrating and disappointing—particularly if they occur on a cruise you've been planning for years—but understand that in nearly every case, Disney makes these changes with your safety and well-being in mind.

unofficial **TIP**
If your preferred itinerary is fully booked, check back often to see if other guests have canceled or ask your travel agent to check for you. Cancellations happen as plans change.

Occasionally, DCL has altered itineraries just hours in advance because of weather conditions or issues in a foreign country (for example, unrest in the region caused DCL to reschedule visits to Turkey during the 2024 Mediterranean sailing on the *Dream*). We've also been on cruises where the itinerary changed midtrip due to the weather: On our Norway cruise, a highly anticipated stop in Geiranger became a sea day when it was too windy to dock.

Less common are cancellations or reschedulings of entire sailings. When they happen, Disney usually does what it can to soften the blow. For example, a few published sail dates for 2015 were canceled and rescheduled due to problems with a planned regular-maintenance dry dock of the *Dream*. Guests whose travel plans had been affected by the cancellations were helped with rescheduling and given a $250 onboard credit. A similar situation happened in 2022, when the *Wish*'s first sailings were postponed by six weeks: Guests whose cruises were affected by the delay were generously compensated with 50% off any rebooked sailing.

The 2017 hurricane season was particularly troublesome for the cruise industry in general, with Hurricanes Franklin, Irma, and Maria all necessitating ship rerouting and the latter two storms causing substantial damage to popular ports. Some storm-related DCL itinerary changes in 2017 included a canceled stop in Cozumel, some *Dream* and *Fantasy* sailings returning early to Port Canaveral, and other *Dream* and *Fantasy* sailings being scrapped altogether. Eastern Caribbean sailings on the *Fantasy* were subject to itinerary changes well into 2018. Due to 2022's Hurricane Ian, DCL extended a sailing of the *Wish* by several days to keep it in safe waters, necessitating the cancellation of the next *Wish* sailing.

Even when changing the whole itinerary can be avoided, changes to some parts of a sailing may still be necessary. For example, during the middle of a March 2018 sailing of the *Fantasy*, several planned port adventures in Cozumel, including a popular excursion to the Mayan ruins in Tulum, had to be canceled due to travel-safety warnings issued by the US Embassy in Mexico. In summer 2019, the *Fantasy* swapped a scheduled stop in San Juan to visit St. Thomas due to events in Puerto Rico. After Russia invaded Ukraine in February 2022, port stops in St. Petersburg and several countries adjacent to the conflict were dropped from European sailings for the foreseeable future.

Somewhat more common are changes to arrival and departure times. We hear several stories a year about ships docking late due to bad weather or other factors. For example, heavy fog caused a December 2018 sailing of the *Wonder* to arrive at Galveston several hours behind schedule, causing many passengers to miss their early-afternoon flights. Hurricane Ian (2022) caused a multihour delay in the *Fantasy*'s return to Port Canaveral. Subtropical Storm Nicole (2022) saw sailings of the *Dream* and *Wish* modified, with Bahamian ports swapped for Caribbean ports. Also in 2022, a sailing of the *Fantasy* was changed from an Eastern Caribbean cruise to a Western Caribbean cruise due to Tropical Storm Fiona. In 2019, Hurricane Dorian forced the cancellation of one sailing of the *Dream,* while a different sailing that started as a three-night trip ended up as a six-night trip to keep the ship out of harm's way. And in August 2022, a sailing of the *Wonder* left Vancouver about 8 hours late due to a tugboat-workers strike.

unofficial **TIP**
No ports are guaranteed, even the most popular ports like Castaway Cay. In her many cruises, Tammy has missed Castaway Cay a few times.

Again, such itinerary disruptions are rare, typically affecting just a few sailings each year. They're unlikely to happen on your cruise. Still, we mention them here because they may affect your decisions about booking excursions through Disney or another vendor (see page 347), buying travel insurance (see page 113), packing additional required medications, or adding some buffer time to your scheduled flight home.

THEMED ITINERARIES
and HOLIDAYS

MARVEL DAY AT SEA

DCL BEGAN HOSTING Marvel-themed sailings in 2017. In 2025, they take place on select five-night sailings of the *Dream* from Fort Lauderdale. Disney changes up activities from time to time, but you can probably expect featured activities to include photo ops with Marvel stars such as Black Panther, Captain Marvel, Iron Man, Spider-Man, and Thor; an excellent superhero-filled stunt show on deck; a new show in the Walt Disney Theatre featuring Doctor Strange; an interactive show where Doctor Strange tutors guests in the Mystic Arts; Disney characters like Mickey and Minnie dressed up in their own superhero costumes; near-constant showings of Marvel films; trivia games; and character-drawing lessons. The menu items offered are standard DCL fare, with suggestions matched to specific characters—Thor, for example, likes roasted cod or pasta with meatballs, while Scarlet Witch prefers gingered soba noodles or ricotta gnocchi. Who knew? Before you sail, you will get a chance to sign up for special meet-and-greet times. There will be one "Marvel Day" when most activities happen, but you'll probably see Marvel-themed characters throughout the sailing.

EASTER

EASTER IS CELEBRATED on the ships, but in a much more low-key fashion than many other holidays. There are no Easter decorations, and the festivities last for only one day rather than throughout the sailing. Religious services are offered, typically including a sunrise service, a Catholic Mass, and an interdenominational Protestant service. When we sailed on the *Fantasy* during a recent Easter, secular observations of the holiday included appearances by the White Rabbit from *Alice in Wonderland* (standing in for the Easter Bunny) and Mickey and Minnie wearing what was supposed to be their pastel Easter finery but looked to us like what they'd be sporting on the golf course. Other events include themed craft activities, face painting for children, and candy and cookies handed out in the lobby atrium.

INDEPENDENCE DAY

DEPENDING ON YOUR ship's itinerary, you'll likely see some special onboard activities on July 4. We recently spent Independence Day on the *Magic*. There was a lobby party that started with a genuinely inspiring rendition of "The Star-Spangled Banner" sung by a Walt Disney Theatre performer and concluded with a dance party featuring Mickey in an Uncle Sam hat, Minnie dressed like Betsy Ross, and Chip 'n Dale in tricorne caps, bopping to songs like "Party in the USA" and "American Pie."

Other activities included themed crafts, American-history trivia contests, and face painting. The breakfast and lunch buffets at Cabanas were heavy on red, white, and blue desserts.

HALLOWEEN ON THE HIGH SEAS

ONE OF THE BEST places to celebrate Halloween is on a Disney cruise. Halloween celebrations begin in September and run through October 31. In 2025, the first sailing begins on September 5. Expect to see pumpkins, black cats, and other decorations on every ship. Halloween on the High Seas sailings offer Halloween-themed movies, trick-or-treating by the pool, deck parties, crafts, and more. The crew and officers dress up and join in the dance parties.

Expect that one afternoon activity will be **Mickey's Mouse-querade Party,** with music and dancing; Halloween parties will be held in all the kids' clubs, with a costume contest for adults that night. There are rules about costumes on board. From Disney:

During themed cruises and onboard celebrations like Pirate Night, Guests are invited to dress in costume. We value safety and good judgment and ask guests to choose costumes that are family-friendly, not obstructive, objectionable, offensive, or violent. To avoid any disappointment or delay in the boarding process, please refrain from bringing toys or props that resemble guns, knives, or other related implements. Masks that completely cover a person's face may only be worn when standing still at character photo locations and must be carried [not worn] when moving around the ship. Guests may dress as their favorite character but may not pose for pictures or sign autographs. Guests that fail to comply with these guidelines may be removed from events unless their costume can be modified.

THANKSGIVING

IF YOUR CRUISE DATES include the fourth Thursday in November, you'll celebrate Thanksgiving on board. Expect to see Mickey, Minnie, Goofy, and Donald in Pilgrim costumes, plus many other Disney characters in seasonal outfits. (Don't be surprised to see the rest of the ship already decked out for Christmas.) The main dining rooms will serve a traditional Thanksgiving menu. And it wouldn't be Turkey Day without (American) football. Games are broadcast on each ship's big Funnel Vision LED screen near the family pool, as well as at the sports bars.

CHRISTMAS, HANUKKAH, AND KWANZAA

DCL BEGINS DECORATING its ships for the winter holidays in early to mid-November. Dates vary from year to year: In 2025, the first **Very Merrytime Cruise** begins on November 7. (*Merrytime* is a Disneyfied play on the word *maritime*.) Expect to see the ship's atrium decked out with a massive Christmas tree, a Hanukkah menorah, and a Kwanzaa kinara, in addition to the many other decorative elements on board. A tree-lighting ceremony is typically held on the first night of each Very Merrytime Cruise.

Family activities include making greeting cards, drawing Disney characters in holiday outfits, listening to carolers, attending holiday-themed deck parties, and decorating cookies or gingerbread houses (always one of our family's favorite activities). Each ship will have storytellers scheduled throughout the day, and you can expect to see lots of holiday-themed merchandise for sale. Mickey, Minnie, Goofy, and other characters will be dressed in their winter finery, and there should be plenty of holiday movies on your stateroom TV.

Even **Castaway Cay** and **Lookout Cay** will be in the holiday spirit, with some palm trees decorated with garlands and lights and plastic sandy snowmen providing an amusing photo op. Disney characters wear holiday-themed island outfits, and the shuttle bus from the dock on Castaway Cay is decorated with reindeer antlers.

Jewish religious services are typically conducted during each night of Hanukkah. A Catholic Mass is held at midnight on December 24;

another Mass and an interdenominational Protestant service are held on December 25. Santa Claus sometimes hands out small gifts to children in the atrium on Christmas morning, along with milk and cookies.

Finally, the ships' onboard music, piped into the hallways and public areas, switches from standard Disney tunes to Christmas-themed tracks. Some people enjoy it; others prefer the regular Disney music.

What If I Don't Celebrate Christmas or Halloween?

You're by no means obligated to participate in anything. That said, if you're an observant Jew who isn't comfortable with Christmas festivities or you have religious reservations about Halloween, then you may want to avoid cruises themed to these holidays, as the theming permeates every aspect of the ships, from decor to music to activities. Granted, we have non-Christian friends and family who love the Very Merrytime Cruises—but during late November and December, it's all Christmas all the time, with a barely audible whisper of "How do you spell *Hanukkah*?"

Is It Weird Celebrating a Major Holiday Aboard a Ship?

If you have deeply entrenched holiday traditions at home, moving the festivities to an ocean liner can be disorienting. Here are some tips to help things go smoothly. And remember, if you're on a ship, you're not doing the cooking and cleaning often associated with holidays—that could be a priceless gift.

- **Invite your extended family to join you on the ship.** We've celebrated Christmas and Thanksgiving on board with extended family and had some of our most memorable holidays. Tammy's son even decided to propose to his future wife when we had the whole family on board for a Thanksgiving cruise celebrating Tammy's parents' 50th anniversary! If being together is the most important thing for your holiday celebration, what could be better than having everyone on a Disney cruise?

- **Make a clean break.** Sometimes your immediate family needs a holiday alone. A holiday cruise may be the perfect solution.

- **Plan an alternative celebration.** Because of work and travel schedules, *many* folks celebrate the secular aspects of Christmas on a day other than December 25. When on board for Christmas, we open our gifts to each other before or after we sail. (OK, it's before. Who are we kidding? We can't wait.)

- **Bring small decorations to liven up your stateroom.** We've found tiny folding artificial trees at Target, or you could string garland on your stateroom ceiling. (*Note:* String lights are not permitted.) Disney also sells some in-room holiday decorations, although they are not cheap. If that's what you need to feel festive, go for it.

- **Consider whether you want to dress festively.** If matching PJs are a thing for your family, rest assured you won't be the only ones wearing them.

NEW YEAR'S EVE

DURING THE DAY, video screens on each ship's pool deck display a clock counting the hours, minutes, and seconds until midnight. The pool deck is also the site of a big family-themed party in the evening, with DJs and live entertainment continuing through midnight. Each ship's dance club also hosts a party at midnight, complete with a DJ, hats, noisemakers, confetti, and bubbly drinks. Families will want to see the special fireworks display and the atrium's balloon drop at midnight. The kids' clubs host parties early in the evening, allowing the little ones to get to bed at a reasonable hour.

A warning if you're traveling with teenagers: Just before midnight, servers pass out flutes of Champagne on deck. They check IDs (offering underage guests something like sparkling cider instead), but be aware that many grown-ups take just a sip or two of their drinks and then set down their glasses on a table or ledge before retiring for the night. On different New Year's Eve sailings, we've seen more than a few teens polishing off the abandoned bubbly—so keep a watchful eye out if your holiday travel party includes young people under 21.

OTHER SPECIAL CRUISE SAILINGS

TCM CLASSIC MOVIE CRUISES These cruises aren't themed days per se but rather buyouts of a DCL ship by Turner Classic Movies (TCM), typically once a year. In 2024, the TCM Classic Cruise was the *Magic*'s October 26–31 sailing from Fort Lauderdale. See tcmcruise .com for information about 2025 sailings.

DVC MEMBER CRUISES Booked through and open exclusively to members of the Disney Vacation Club (DVC), Disney's time-share program, these cruises also take over a ship for an entire sailing. Perks include special stateroom gifts, discussions led by Imagineers and Disney executives, and previews of Disney films that haven't been released yet. These sailings, typically one or two per year, often sell out quickly. For more information, go to disneyvacationclub.disney.go.com.

 # BEST ITINERARIES *for* . . .

SO, HOW DO YOU PICK? With so many options, it may seem overwhelming to choose. Let us reassure you. After dozens and dozens of cruises, we have never debarked and said, "I wish I hadn't done that." Cruises are great vacations, and you'll probably enjoy whichever itinerary you choose. However, you do have to choose, and we have some recommendations that may help you make that decision.

BEST ITINERARIES FOR FIRST-TIMERS

IF YOU'VE NEVER cruised before, consider the following:

- We don't recommend three-night sailings. They are just too short. You'll be so rushed seeing and experiencing everything that you won't have time to relax.
- Having said that, as much as we love European itineraries, you probably don't need to fly to Europe for your first cruise. You'll spend so much time off the ship that you'll barely have time to enjoy the ship itself.
- Alaska sailings are some of our favorites! But the cold weather makes them very different than a "normal" warm-weather cruise.
- We love the *Wish* and *Treasure*, but they have a premium price tag.

We recommend an itinerary of four or five nights on the *Dream* for your first cruise. Four or five nights is a great amount of time for newbies, and the *Dream* is a larger ship with good restaurants and bars, a spa, ample space for kids' activities, and plentiful areas for pools and lounging. The price tag is better than the newest ships, and Fort Lauderdale is easy to navigate. The *Treasure* will probably impress you if you're looking for a longer cruise and don't mind the price. If you want to sail from Port Canaveral, the *Wish* is a beautiful ship with a significant wow factor, and the *Fantasy* is a great option when it's not in Europe during the summer.

BEST ITINERARIES FOR REPEAT GUESTS

IF YOU HAVE cruised before, here are our recommendations:

- If you started with a short cruise, you should go longer next time. But you probably already knew that. If you were on the *Wish* and loved it, try the *Treasure*.

- If you started with a traditional itinerary like the Bahamas or the Caribbean, and the beaches were your favorite part, try a longer cruise with different beach ports. The longer Southern Caribbean cruises may be perfect with their beautiful towns and striking blue waters.

- If you started with a traditional itinerary and loved being on a ship as much as you loved the beautiful beaches, try something with different kinds of ports like Alaska or Europe.

- If you started on the *Wish* or *Treasure* and want a different class of ship, try the *Dream* or *Fantasy*. It's not as big of a shock to the system as the smaller, classic ships may be.

For your next cruise, decide what you loved and didn't love about your first one. That should make it much easier to pick the next one.

BEST ITINERARIES FOR ADULTS

GIVEN THAT DISNEY is synonymous with family-friendly, it's natural for those who travel without children to wonder if DCL is a good choice for them. Happily, just as with the Disney parks, there's something for folks of all ages to enjoy on a Disney cruise. All the ships have an adults-only pool and coffeehouse. Some entertainment districts are adults-only after 9 p.m., and the spas are limited to age 18 and up (except for teens in the Chill Spa). Likewise, every ship has restaurants that don't allow kids. Castaway Cay and Lookout Cay have adult beaches with their own dining, bar, and cabanas (cabanas must be reserved in advance).

If your idea of a fun cruise is a party barge, then DCL probably isn't for you—there's no casino, and the nightlife is more mild than wild. If, on the other hand, raucous exploits aren't your thing, then the more sedate nature of Disney cruising could be just what you're looking for. Spend some time at the spa, skip the stage

unofficial **TIP**
If you are sailing to Alaska, you will travel through Canada and need to be aware of its entry requirements. Canada does not allow anyone with a felony conviction to enter their country, and they consider a DUI a felony—even a very old DUI.

shows, dine at adult restaurants, and enjoy some downtime. We've traveled several times with just adults and had a fantastic time.

- Avoid summer and holidays when kids are out of school, if possible.
- Choose a longer itinerary.
- Pick an itinerary that includes your dream destination. It's a great way to preview the place and see if you want to plan a longer trip there.

Parents are always hesitant to pull their kids out of school, so cruises during the school year (and not near a school holiday) will have fewer children. Longer sailings are even more challenging for families with school-age children, so if you can do a long sailing during the school year, you've hit the bull's-eye. Historically, repositioning cruises, like Hawaii to Australia or the United States to Europe, have very few children. If you can't do those longer sailings during the school year, you can still maximize your adult time by taking advantage of the adults-only spaces on board and at the island destinations. That's the strategy Tammy employs when she travels every September with a group of women who have and love children but want to enjoy a few days of adult conversation and activities. The kids never bothered them anyway!

BEST ITINERARIES FOR KIDS

LET US START BY SAYING that your kids will almost certainly have a blast on a DCL cruise. As parents, we know that one of the most challenging parts of planning a vacation with kids is ensuring they stay entertained. For us, this usually means making sure that every travel day has at least a couple of things specifically designed to appeal to our kids and their friends—things that we'd prefer didn't involve shopping or sitting passively in front of a screen.

It can be exhausting to plan this way (and we're professionals!). It's one of the main reasons a trip to Disney World is so appealing to parents: Disney's theme parks provide near constant, wide-ranging entertainment options for both kids and adults. A family that hasn't planned a thing beyond making a park reservation can show up and find something fun to do. Disney cruises work the same way: Family activities, including trivia contests, scavenger hunts, and shuffleboard, are scheduled throughout the day on virtually every day of every sailing.

DCL provides nearly nonstop organized activities for kids ages 3–17. Some activities for younger children start as early as 7 a.m., while activities for older teens can run until 2 a.m. on some sailings. Off the ships, Castaway Cay and Lookout Cay (see Part 14) have designated recreation areas for families, teens, tweens, and tiny tikes. There are also shore excursions created just for families; some port stops include teen-only excursions and sightseeing events.

While the youth clubs on the *Magic* and *Wonder* are substantially smaller than those on the *Dream, Fantasy, Wish,* and *Treasure,* note that DCL often runs concurrent, age-appropriate activities within the same club. For example, the Oceaneer Club accepts children ages 3–10; however, the younger kids may gather for a game with marsh-mallows in one area of the club while the older kids sing karaoke in another.

Our own children have found Disney's kids' activities much more fun than hanging around with us on the ship. It may be a cliché, but it's true: we saw the kids only during meals, at bedtime, or when we specifically scheduled things to do as a family. Thanks to the internet, our kids are still in contact with friends they've made on cruises, even though some are an ocean away.

On the other hand, if your kids aren't interested in the clubs, or if you're determined to make your cruise a time for family together-ness, there are still plenty of activities you can enjoy as a family. These include structured activities like family game shows and trivia contests and unstructured ones like board games and scavenger hunts.

- If you're looking for sailings with many other children and potential friends for the kids, sail during the summer or on school holidays.

- Check the list of port adventures for the itineraries you're considering, and make sure you see something your children would enjoy. Check the age requirements to make sure they are old enough as well.

- Consider travel time. Traveling to a foreign country to start your cruise may cause little ones to get off on the wrong foot. Pick something closer to home if you don't think they'd handle long travel times well.

We think seven-night sailings on the *Treasure* are perfect for most families, but if peak pricing for summer sailings is out of your budget, check pricing early or late in the summer when pricing won't be as high. Otherwise, look at the 5-night or longer sailings on the *Dream* or *Fantasy* out of Florida, which will be more reasonably priced and offer plenty for kids and families to enjoy.

OTHER RECOMMENDATIONS

HERE ARE SOME ADDITIONAL QUESTIONS to ask yourself, along with our advice for each situation.

- **Do you want a long, relaxing vacation?** Choose a sailing with multiple consec-utive sea days, such as a Panama Canal or transatlantic crossing.

- **Do you want to do lots of sightseeing?** Choose a longer Mediterranean or Northern European cruise.

- **Do you want to lie on the beach as much as possible?** Choose a seven-night cruise on the *Treasure*.

- **Don't like hot weather?** Choose an Alaskan, Canadian Coastline, or Northern European cruise.

- **Do you want to sail in a new part of the world?** Choose a South Pacific cruise or an Australia and New Zealand cruise.

- **Do you like museums and the city scene?** Choose a Mediterranean DCL cruise.

- **Are you prone to motion sickness?** Consider a three-night cruise on the *Dream* or *Wish* with no sea days or an Alaskan cruise, as these tend to be very smooth.

- **Do you really like Castaway Cay or Lookout Cay?** Choose a "double dip" sailing with two stops on Castaway Cay or Lookout Cay. There are even sailings that stop at both.

- **Don't have a passport and don't want to get one?** Choose a closed-loop cruise (see page 116).

- **Looking for the experience of a lifetime?** Choose a Concierge Stateroom on an extended European cruise. Or book the *Treasure* Tower Suite, the largest Concierge Stateroom on the *Treasure* at 1,966 square feet, for a family reunion over the holidays.

▌ BACK-*to*-BACK CRUISING

HAVE YOU EVER ended a cruise and thought, "*Waaah*, I don't want to go home! Can't I stay on board forever?" That's almost exactly what you do when you book back-to-back cruises—cruises on the same ship where the second cruise begins on the day the first cruise ends. And we think it's *glorious*. The only thing that may beat it is a back-to-back-to-back, which Tammy has tried and can attest to.

Here are some other reasons you might consider a back-to-back cruise, besides not wanting to leave.

1. **The ship you like doesn't offer longer cruises.** Our first back-to-back cruises were three and four nights on the *Dream*. Back-to-back bookings on the *Wish* are quickly becoming popular with veteran DCL cruisers who want more time to explore the new ship.

2. **You want to see more ports.** Do you want to see both the Eastern and Western Caribbean? Book two consecutive cruises on the *Treasure*. How about the Baltic *and* the Mediterranean? The *Dream* has you covered; check the summer European itineraries.

3. **You want to save on transportation costs.** Combining two itineraries can be less expensive (assuming you plan to do both in the first place). For instance, it's much more economical to fly to Vancouver, British Columbia; do a 7-night Alaskan cruise, immediately followed by a 10-night cruise to Hawaii; and then fly home from Oahu than to book round-trip airfare to Canada *and* round-trip airfare to Honolulu.

4. **You're amassing Castaway Club credits.** We're not saying that one of our researchers booked a back-to-back cruise just because the second cruise was the one that pushed her into Platinum Castaway Club status. But we're not saying she didn't, either.

5. **You *really* love a port like Castaway Cay.** If you're a Castaway Cay devotee and the few itineraries with "double dips" (two stops at Castaway Cay on one sailing) don't align with your vacation schedule, then you can cobble together your own double-dip vacation by scheduling a four-night and three-night sailing on the *Dream* or the *Wish* back-to-back.

How does it work? First a caveat: Not every consecutive cruise can be booked back-to-back due to the Passenger Vessel Services Act. It applies to ships registered outside of the United States, including the DCL ships (and almost every other ocean cruise ship), which are registered in the Bahamas. If your first cruise leaves from a US port, your next cruise ends in another US port, *and* you haven't visited "a distant foreign port" along the way, you cannot do a back-to-back cruise.

Oddly, the DCL website lets you book back-to-back cruises that violate the law, but once Disney catches your mistake, you'll be forced to choose one cruise or the other.

Here's a back-to-back that works: an Alaskan cruise starting in Vancouver, followed by a Pacific Coast cruise from Vancouver to San Diego—you're good to go because you start in Canada.

One that does not work: Honolulu to Vancouver, followed by Vancouver to San Diego—you start in one US city and end in another; plus, Vancouver, despite being in Canada, is too close to the United States to be considered a *distant* foreign port.

Note that when booking back-to-back, it's great if you can keep the same stateroom for both cruises. If you are changing staterooms, you must pack your bags and a crew member will move them to your new stateroom. If you stay in the same stateroom, you can leave everything as is! That gets harder to do the later you book the cruise, so we recommend booking early.

You will have to debark, clear customs, and show your documents and IDs again. There will be a short wait to get back on board, but it won't take long, and you'll be back on board before anyone else. The empty ship once prompted Len to do carpet angels in the atrium.

unofficial **TIP**
Back-to-back cruisers must settle their accounts at the end of their first sailing. Your internet package will not carry over, though we've had good luck continuing to use our specialty coffee card punches on the second sailing.

SURF *and* TURF, DISNEY-STYLE

COMBINING YOUR CRUISE WITH A WALT DISNEY WORLD VACATION

DISNEY SELLS PACKAGES that combine a Disney cruise with a trip to Walt Disney World for cruises departing from Port Canaveral called **Land and Sea** packages.

Land and Sea packages include lodging at a Disney resort. Theme park admission, the Disney Dining Plan, and other components can be added to the Disney World portion of the trip. For more information, see disneycruise.disney.go.com/featured/packages/land-sea.

Because you don't have much flexibility when you book a Land and Sea package through DCL and often save money when you book individual components à la carte, we recommend making separate reservations for each part of a theme park/cruise vacation. Whether you book Land and Sea together or individually, you can arrange bus transportation between Port Canaveral and your Walt Disney World resort for a fee.

The most frequently asked question about combining a theme park vacation with a cruise is whether to visit Walt Disney World before or after the cruise. We have found that most people who did both preferred to relax on the cruise after the more-hectic park visit. Mukta from California said the following:

> *I am coming from out of state, so I love to visit WDW before a Disney cruise. I visit the parks from open to close and walk so much I am exhausted at the end of each day. Enjoying a cruise after that feels even more relaxing. On the cruise, I can sleep in without guilt, build my own itinerary, and schedule as much leisure time as I like.*

UPCOMING DRY DOCKS

IT'S A GOOD IDEA to keep track of when a ship will be dry-docked when choosing an itinerary. If you choose to sail immediately before a dry dock, you may encounter a ship in need of some updates and maintenance. If you choose to sail immediately after a dry dock, you'll get a nice spruced-up ship. But there is a chance that delays can happen, and your sailing could have ongoing maintenance, or worse, be canceled. The latter is rare, and Disney certainly does everything it can to make sure that doesn't happen, but it's a risk. For Tammy, it's worth the risk—she loves new/redone ships. There is one dry dock scheduled for 2025: The *Disney Fantasy* will be dry-docked from September 15 to October 20.

ITINERARY ADD-ONS

DISNEY OFFERS A FEW THINGS that can be added to your cruise to enhance or expand your itinerary.

WEDDINGS AND VOW RENEWALS

IF YOU'VE ALWAYS DREAMED of getting married on a Disney cruise, you can make that happen—for a price, of course. If you missed your chance to get married on board, it's not too late! Disney also does vow renewals.

These prices can change at peak times, but at press time, weddings and vow renewals start at $4,000 on board, which includes up to 16 guests plus the happy couple. Ceremonies on Castaway Cay start at $6,000. Additional guests can be added for $20 per person, age three and up. Wedding and vow renewal packages include a location, an officiant, flowers, chairs, microphones, a commemorative certificate, cake, and Champagne.

For both weddings and vow renewals, Disney can only do a limited number on each sailing, so book earlier rather than later. They are added right to your cruise reservation, and you'll pay the 20% deposit when you book and pay in full when you pay your cruise in full. Tammy's been a guest at a wedding on board and has seen many others take place, and she can vouch for how beautiful they are. When the new couple is announced, and the entire atrium applauds? Chills.

ADVENTURES BY DISNEY

A GREAT WAY TO TURN YOUR CRUISE into a land-and-sea vacation in another country is by adding a short **Adventures by Disney** (**ABD**) vacation to your cruise. The dates of many of these adventures, called **Escapes,** coincide with the beginning or end of a Disney cruise.

In 2025, you can visit Sydney, Barcelona, London, and Rome with ABD in conjunction with your cruise. If you are looking for more time in a spectacular city or just want to plus-up your vacation, it's a great way to do it. ABD is not cheap, but it is a fantastic way to travel if it fits your budget. ABD cruises are more about the level of service you'll receive than about Mickey following you through Barcelona. In our opinion, these high-end, luxury tours are worth every penny. Tammy has done a few adventures and cannot recommend them enough.

CHOOSING *a* STATEROOM

▌ STATEROOMS *at a* GLANCE

DCL'S SHIPS BOAST some of the largest staterooms in the industry, which partially explains why its fares are correspondingly high. An Inside Stateroom, generally the least expensive stateroom on any ship, is 169–184 square feet on Disney's ships, compared with 114–165 square feet on Royal Caribbean and 160–185 on Carnival. Disney's Oceanview and Verandah (balcony) Staterooms are also larger than Royal Caribbean's and Carnival's.

Besides being more spacious, DCL's bathroom layout is superior to that in staterooms on other cruise lines. All except Category 11 staterooms (the smallest Inside Staterooms) and some accessible staterooms have a split-bath design, in which the shower and toilet each have their own door and sink. The advantage is that two people can get ready at the same time. Except for accessible staterooms, all bathrooms also have bathtubs, something you don't usually find on other cruise lines until you get to the suite categories.

The clever incorporation of storage space is another plus. Most DCL staterooms have two closets, each big enough to store one large suitcase or two small ones; under-bed storage for carry-on or soft-sided luggage; and several drawers built into the desk area. Additional nooks and crannies are scattered throughout each stateroom.

But while Disney staterooms are generally larger than those on other cruise lines,

> *unofficial* **TIP**
> *Wish*-class staterooms have plenty of closet space, but they have shelves instead of drawers, making it more challenging to contain and separate smaller items. Packing cubes will help.

they're still smaller than the typical hotel room. For example, a room at a Walt Disney World Value-tier hotel, such as Pop Century Resort, is about 260 square feet—about 40% larger than a DCL Inside Stateroom. Even a well-appointed Family Oceanview Stateroom with Verandah tops out at 304 square feet, a little smaller than a room at a Disney Moderate resort, such as Caribbean Beach Resort.

STATEROOM TITLES DECODED

YOU MAY BE WONDERING what the different stateroom titles mean. Here are some different terms you will encounter.

INSIDE STATEROOM These staterooms have no views of the outside and are usually found on the interior of the ship's decks.

OCEANVIEW STATEROOM These staterooms have a view of the outside through one or two portholes, or through the door to your verandah if it's an Oceanview Stateroom with Verandah.

> *unofficial* **TIP**
> On the *Dream* and *Fantasy,* Inside Staterooms have virtual portholes, or video screens that combine real-time views from outside the ship with animated snippets of Disney characters.

VERANDAH STATEROOM These staterooms have a sliding glass door to access your private verandah (or balcony).

CONCIERGE STATEROOM These staterooms include additional amenities inside the stateroom and aboard the ship.

NAVIGATOR'S VERANDAH This type of verandah has an obstructed view of some kind (see page 102 for more on verandahs).

STANDARD The bathroom is not split.

DELUXE The bathrooms are split.

FAMILY The stateroom sleeps up to five guests.

HOW STATEROOM CATEGORY AFFECTS *your* CRUISE PRICE

ALONG WITH YOUR departure date and how far in advance you book, the type of stateroom you choose is one of the significant factors in determining your cruise's cost.

The chart on the next page shows how much a fare increases, based on the stateroom category, for a typical seven-night cruise on the *Fantasy* for two adults and two children.

A Category 4A stateroom—the most expensive non-Concierge category—costs, on average, about $2,000 (30%) more than the least expensive stateroom. With that higher cost you get another 130 square feet of space and a better view.

What's remarkable is the steady upward movement of the lines until you reach Concierge level. This shows that Disney is very consistent in its pricing across stateroom categories. That's interesting because there aren't the same number of staterooms in each category—the vast majority are Verandah Staterooms, but a larger supply doesn't equal a lower price in this case. Disney seems to have just the right amount of each type of stateroom to meet guest demand.

SHOULD YOU UPGRADE?

FOR MANY DCL CRUISERS, the stateroom decision is ultimately between a small Inside Stateroom and a larger Oceanview or Verandah Stateroom. Depending on the ship, itinerary, and time of year, the price difference can be a little or a lot.

For this edition, we spot-checked the costs of Disney cruises in different stateroom categories for a family of four (two adults and two children, ages 9 and 14). The fares in our examples are for spring or summer 2025; prices will vary depending on when you check.

For our first example, we priced a **3-Night Bahamian Cruise from Port Canaveral** on the *Wish*. For the May 2, 2025, sailing, an Inside Stateroom cost **$3,602,** an Oceanview Stateroom was **$3,811,** and a Verandah Stateroom was **$4,081.** Choosing the Oceanview Stateroom over the Inside Stateroom seems like a no-brainer: For $252 more, you get a bigger stateroom, a split bath, and a view of the ocean. The $479 bump from Inside to Verandah gives you even more space, plus a balcony.

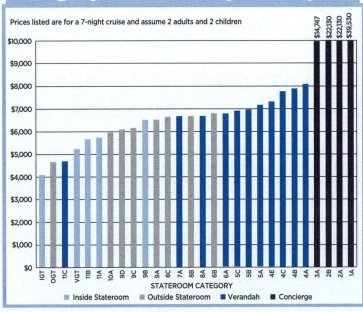

Average Cruise Fares by Stateroom Category on the *Disney Fantasy*

Prices listed are for a 7-night cruise and assume 2 adults and 2 children

3A $14,747 2B $22,130 2A $22,130 1A $39,530

STATEROOM CATEGORY

■ Inside Stateroom   ■ Outside Stateroom   ■ Verandah   ■ Concierge

On some longer sailings, however, the cost of jumping from Inside to Verandah is significant. For the July 7, 2025, **9-Night Alaskan Cruise from Vancouver** on the *Wonder,* our hypothetical family of four would pay a whopping **$10,264** for an Inside Stateroom. To upgrade to an Oceanview Stateroom, they'd need to spend at least **$12,659,** or $2,395 more than the Inside rate; to get a Verandah Stateroom, they'd need to spend at least **$17,927,** or $7,633 more. (For that same sailing, the cheapest Concierge Stateroom still available was **$34,689,** more than three times the price of the Inside Stateroom.)

Not only are there price differences among stateroom types, but there are often differences within the same macro type as well. For some 2025 **four-night Bahamian sailings** on the *Dream,* for instance, the cheapest Verandah Staterooms (Category 7A, Deck 7 Aft) for our family of four cost **$3,644,** while the most expensive non-Concierge Verandah Staterooms (Category 4A, Deck 10 Midship) are **$4,125**— a $481 difference. For the June 30, 2025, **12-Night Mediterranean Cruise with Greek Isles** on the *Fantasy,* the least expensive Verandah Stateroom is **$20,623,** while the highest-priced non-Concierge Verandah Stateroom is **$23,335,** or $2,712 more.

WILL A CHEAPER STATEROOM DETRACT FROM YOUR EXPERIENCE? To repeat a familiar phrase, it depends. If you're just happy to be on a Disney cruise and consider your stateroom merely a place to lay your head, then you'll have a great time no matter what room you choose. If, on the other hand, you consider an outside view to be non-negotiable, then an Oceanview Stateroom would be worth the bump in price over an Inside Stateroom— you'd just need to figure out how much you'd be willing to pay.

 unofficial **TIP**

On many shorter sailings, you'll find the price jump between Inside and Oceanview, and sometimes from Oceanview to Verandah, is minimal. Always check!

IS CONCIERGE WORTH IT?

A DISNEY CRUISE is already a relatively luxe vacation, but what if you want to plus it up even more? Booking a Concierge Stateroom is one option. The amenities offered to Concierge guests are substantial, as is the price. Not surprisingly, this is one of the areas of cruising where we are most often asked, "Is it worth it?" At the risk of repeating ourselves, it depends.

CONCIERGE LEVELS ACROSS THE SHIPS

THE CONCIERGE LEVELS on the *Dream* and *Fantasy* were nearly identical until the *Dream*'s dry dock in 2024, when the lounge was expanded to accommodate the addition of more Concierge Staterooms. We expect the *Fantasy* to undergo a similar upgrade in fall 2025. The staterooms are on Decks 11 and 12, with an exclusive Concierge lounge on Deck 12. The lounge has stairs to a private sundeck with a hot tub on Deck 13 right by Satellite Falls. On the *Magic* and *Wonder,* Concierge

Staterooms are on Deck 8, while the Concierge lounges and staff are on Deck 10. The lounges on the *Magic* and *Wonder* are slightly different from each other, but both have been expanded and are beautiful, bright spaces now, with sundecks. We have a more detailed breakdown of the lounges on page 50. On the *Wish, Treasure,* and *Destiny,* the Concierge Staterooms are on Decks 10–15, with the majority grouped on Decks 12 and 13. The lounge is on Deck 12, and the Concierge pool and private sundeck are on Deck 13.

Prepare to be wowed upon entering these staterooms, particularly those in Categories 1 and 2. We already think Disney has great staterooms, but the finishing touches in Concierge are beyond our expectations. In fact, if you're considering booking here, we think you'd do well to choose it for an itinerary and ship you've already taken so you're not torn between exploring the ship and port and just hanging out in your stateroom and the Concierge lounge.

THE BENEFITS

THE BENEFITS OF BOOKING this level are not only quantifiable—more space, lounge access, and early booking opportunities for specialty dining and port excursions (notably the private cabanas at Castaway Cay and Lookout Cay)—but they're also intangible when it comes to the added level of service. Also quantifiable is the cost: For an apples-to-apples comparison, plan to pay around 50% more for a Category 3 (Concierge) versus a Category 4 (non-Concierge) stateroom.

Concierge-level perks range from "really useful" to "just OK." The pampering begins before you board: The Concierge team will contact you before your booking window for port excursions and dining to ask for your requests. While adult-dining reservations usually aren't difficult to get no matter where you're booked, Concierge can secure your top choices. One of the most significant benefits is early access to the private cabanas on Castaway Cay or Lookout Cay. There are more Concierge guests than cabanas, so getting a cabana is in no way guaranteed, but you have a shot. It's nearly impossible if you're not in Concierge.

On boarding day, Concierge guests have a separate check-in line and then wait in a private lounge in the terminal until boarding begins. Concierge guests are the first to board after Family of the Day and back-to-back cruisers. After boarding, they can immediately go to the Concierge lunch offered in one of the main dining rooms or visit the Concierge lounge. Concierge Staterooms are ready very soon after boarding, unlike other staterooms, which won't be ready until 1:30 p.m. or later.

Once on board, in addition to lounge access with alcohol in the evenings, specialty coffee anytime, and food and snacks all day, Concierge guests also get free popcorn at the theaters, a character meet and greet, early entry into the nightly shows, and Concierge hosts ready to help with anything they need. No more standing in line at Guest Services; the Concierge hosts will handle it.

The Basic Surf internet plan is included for 24 hours for guests in Category 3 staterooms. Guests staying in Category 2 staterooms will receive the Basic Surf internet plan for the length of their cruise, while guests in Category 1 staterooms will receive the Premium Surf plan for their entire sailing.

Guests in Concierge Staterooms with a dining table (Category 2 and up) can order hot meals, including breakfast, from one of the main dining rooms delivered to their suites.

The Royal Suites (Category 1A on the *Magic* and *Wonder;* Categories 1A and 1B on the *Dream;* Category 1A on the *Fantasy;* and Categories 1A, 1B, and 1C on the *Wish, Treasure,* and *Destiny*) come with even more. Royal Suite guests have a freezer full of complementary Mickey ice-cream bars and a wine fridge full of Champagne and wine that you can purchase. On the *Wish*-class ships, that wine fridge is included in your price and will be restocked daily. The *Wish*-class ships also have a special room service menu only for Royal Suite guests.

On debarkation day, Concierge guests have one last little perk: They are escorted to the front of the line to debark.

Tammy is a massive fan of Concierge. Some of the staterooms are absolutely spectacular, but the Concierge staff is why she loves it. They are the best of the best at what they do. The *Wish, Treasure,* and *Destiny* have more Concierge Staterooms than the first four ships. When the *Wish* first sailed, the Concierge lounge was woefully understaffed, and the Concierge hosts were overworked. After a few tough months, Disney added more hosts, and the service is back to the standard we expect from Disney.

THE COST

A REASONABLE RATE for a Concierge Family Oceanview Stateroom with Verandah in 2024–25 is less than $750 per person, per night; for comparison, a reasonable rate for a non-Concierge Deluxe Family Oceanview Stateroom with Verandah is around $350 per night. (From another perspective, if you spent the same amount on a Royal Caribbean Concierge Club Stateroom as on a DCL Concierge Stateroom, you'd sometimes get a suite rather than a one-room stateroom.)

In short, the lowest level of DCL Concierge access costs several hundred dollars more per person, per night, than a similar non-Concierge Stateroom, but if you're taking this leap, you're not cruising because it's economical; you're doing so because you enjoy the theming, service, and entertainment.

SO . . . IS IT WORTH IT?

BEING LOGICAL TYPES, we like to approach the question methodically. If you accept that (1) a Disney cruise is worth the surcharge you pay over other cruise lines, (2) a Verandah Stateroom is worth what you pay over an Inside Stateroom, (3) the expense will neither kill your overall bottom line nor negatively affect other aspects of your vacation, and (4) you enjoy personal attention, then the next linear progression is that, yes, the extra space of a (one-bedroom) Concierge Stateroom could be worth the price Disney charges. Basically, Concierge means not just upgraded accommodations but also avoiding all the little annoyances of a cruise vacation—lines, noise, masses of fellow cruisers—by waving them away with a magic wand made of money.

Even Tammy, who loves Concierge and would permanently take up residence in a Concierge Stateroom if her wallet and husband would agree, can't sail Concierge *every* time. But she finds the splurge worth it if she splits the cost or is celebrating something special. Tammy cruises frequently, jumps between standard staterooms and Concierge, and has a great time in any stateroom type. She can assure you that while Concierge makes you feel like royalty, non-Concierge does not feel like steerage class.

STATEROOM DEEP DIVE

AT 169–184 SQUARE FEET, an **Inside Stateroom** has enough room for two adults, or two adults and one small child. Granted, it's not exactly spacious, but a family of this size shouldn't have much competition for the bathroom. If you're a family of three or four and you have two tweens or teens, you'll appreciate the extra space of a **Deluxe Oceanview Stateroom with Verandah** (218–268 square feet, depending on the ship and the stateroom's location on that ship) or a **Deluxe Family Oceanview Stateroom with Verandah** (284–304 square feet).

Alternatively, you could book two staterooms: either two connecting Inside Staterooms or Inside and Oceanview Staterooms across the hall from each other. The advantage of two staterooms, besides the extra space and extra bathroom, is that the kids can sleep late if they want. Additionally, putting the kids in a different stateroom allows parents to access the verandah (usually on the kids' side of the stateroom) more easily when the beds are pulled down and the TV (on the kids' side of the stateroom on all ships except the *Wish, Treasure,* and presumably *Destiny*) without disturbing anyone

STATEROOM APPOINTMENTS

EVERY DCL STATEROOM is outfitted with the items listed in the table on the opposite page: Staterooms with exterior windows have blackout curtains that do an amazing job of blocking the sun. If you need light to wake up in the morning, don't close the curtains unless you want to sleep until the crack of noon.

Bathrooms are stocked with large pump bottles of shampoo, conditioner, body wash, and lotion; your stateroom host will refill these as needed. DCL introduced the big bottles in 2019 in an effort to reduce waste and plastic use, but not everybody likes them: Some guests say they don't squeeze out enough product per pump, others don't like the

DCL STATEROOM AMENITIES	
• **Bedside lamps**	• **Ice bucket** and glasses
• **Closet**	• **In-room phone** with voicemail
• **Coffee table**	• **In-room thermostat**
• **Custom artwork** Usually depicts Disney characters and themes relevant to the cruise line, ships, islands, or travel	• **Life jackets**
	• **Minifridge**
• **Desk with chair and dedicated lighting** You'll have enough room to get actual work done.	• **Privacy curtain** This separates the sleeping area from the sofa.
	• **Private bath** with sink, toilet, and shower
• **Electronic safe** It's just big enough for storing passports, wallets, and other small valuables.	• **Room-service breakfast menus**
	• **Satellite TV** with remote
	• **Sleeper sofa**
• **Hair dryer**	• **Toiletries** Soap, shampoo, conditioner, body wash, and body lotion
• **Hooks** (for towels) and **hangers**	

space they take up in the bathroom, and still others miss being able to take home mini soaps and shampoos as souvenirs.

KEEPING YOUR COOL Some cruisers report that the minifridges don't get very cold. Our first suggestion would be to adjust the fridge's temperature control. We've also read that propping the door open slightly with a towel clip or a specially made "refrigerator airing card" (available online) can help it cool better by increasing air circulation inside. Disney says the minifridges should work well enough to properly store temperature-sensitive medications, such as insulin; if you're not sure the fridge in your stateroom is up to the job, check with Guest Services.

unofficial **TIP**
On the *Dream, Fantasy, Wish, Treasure,* and *Destiny,* your stateroom lights will work only if you insert a plastic card into a slot on the wall by the door. You're supposed to use your Key to the World Card, but any similar card will do.

Special Features on the *Wish, Treasure,* and *Destiny*

Functional updates and fresh design touches distinguish the *Wish, Treasure,* and (presumably) *Destiny*'s staterooms from those of their four older sisters, but there's still no mistaking that you're on a Disney ship. Here's a rundown of what's new:

- Instead of a dorm-size minifridge hidden in a cabinet, there's a small refrigerator hidden in a desk drawer.
- Stateroom TVs are full-size flat-screens versus the computer-monitor-size TVs on the other ships.
- The stateroom phone is mounted on the wall near the storage shelves.
- Bathrooms have a night-light switch and under-counter lighting. The night-light is bright enough that you won't need to bring your own.
- The artwork in each stateroom is uniformly themed to a Disney animated film, such as *Frozen, Cinderella, Sleeping Beauty, Moana, The Lion King, Aladdin, Encanto,* or *Up.*
- Dedicated USB and USB-C outlets are on each side of the primary bed.

- As on the *Dream* and *Fantasy,* the bed linens are by Frette, but the *Wish*-class ships have tiny Mickey Mouse images woven into the fabric.
- Buttons on the shower nozzle control the water pressure and temperature. Push and turn the left button to adjust the pressure; push and turn the right button to adjust the temperature.
- Bathrobes are provided in all *Wish, Treasure,* and (presumably) *Destiny* staterooms. On the other ships, they're provided only for Concierge guests (and are for sale in the gift shops).

While most of these changes are welcome, a couple are not. First of all, the plastic dividers in the desk-drawer fridge eat up storage space. If you want to chill that plate of leftover Key lime pie you ordered from room service, you'll have to take out some of the dividers to get it to fit.

Second, the new TV setup strikes us as poorly thought out, to put it mildly. Yes, the stateroom TVs on the other ships are old and dinky, but they're also mounted on a swivel arm attached to the dresser. On the *Dream, Fantasy, Magic,* and *Wonder,* if you want to watch TV on the sofa after your partner has gone to bed, or your kids are using the foldout bed and want to watch TV while they fall asleep, you can point the set whichever way you want. On the *Wish, Treasure,* and (presumably) *Destiny,* however, the TVs are firmly mounted on the wall opposite the foot of the main bed—or, in inside staterooms, the wall *beside* the bed.

Enough guests complained about the *Wish*'s TV situation that in early 2023, DCL created a Bring Your Own Device (BYOD) system specifically for the *Wish.* With BYOD, you can stream the in-stateroom television content directly to your personal smartphone or tablet. You can, for example, watch the stateroom TV content on your iPad in bed without disturbing your stateroom mates. To be clear, you can't stream services like Netflix, Hulu, or even Disney+ to your device, just the content that's available via the in-room televisions.

To access this service, you'll need to connect to the DCL-guest Wi-Fi network, but you are not required to have a paid internet connection. To access the TV content, open the DCL Navigator app, click the "More" tab, then click on "Stateroom TV Streaming." You can also stream to a laptop by typing mxms.dcl.disney.go.com in your browser window. Again, this only works if you're on the *Wish, Treasure,* or (presumably) *Destiny* and are connected to the ship's guest Wi-Fi network.

WHAT YOU *WON'T* FIND Staterooms don't have minibars, coffee makers, microwaves, teakettles, steam irons, or ironing boards. Irons are provided in the onboard laundry rooms; you can also have your clothes sent out for pressing (see page 142).

DCL has removed alarm clocks from most staterooms. If you prefer to use a dedicated alarm clock instead of your phone, you may be able to borrow one from Guest Services, but bring your own to be safe. Alternatively, you can request a wake-up call.

BED CONFIGURATIONS Note that the primary beds in the majority of DCL staterooms are standard queen-size beds, not the split twins that you might find on some other cruise lines. In addition, all staterooms have a foldout sofa bed; some staterooms have extra beds that pull down from the ceiling or the wall.

If you have more than two adults in the stateroom, it's likely that two of them will be sharing a bed. This usually isn't a problem for couples or some siblings, but there are other situations in which people who are comfortable traveling together, even sharing a stateroom, might not want to sleep in the same bed. As you make your decisions about what type of stateroom you need, consider the number and type of beds, as well as the stated sleeping capacity of the stateroom.

*un*official **TIP**

There are weight limits for DCL upper bunks. These range from 220 to 265 pounds, depending on the ship. Any guest approaching 200 pounds would likely be too large to be comfortable on the upper bunk.

If you want to ensure that you have the maximum number of separate beds in your stateroom, you'll have to do some sleuthing. Not all staterooms in a category accommodate the maximum occupancy listed for that category. Several do not have a pull-down bed. If you want to be sure your stateroom has one, ask your travel agent or call DCL. Alternatively, when searching online, if you change your party size to the maximum number allowed in that stateroom type and that stateroom comes up as an option, it does have the pull-down.

DOOR DECOR The door to your stateroom is made of metal and is magnetic (except some Concierge Stateroom doors that are metal topped with a wood veneer, making them decidedly less magnetic). Many repeat cruisers are fond of decorating their doors with magnets related to family celebrations, the cruise destination, a holiday, or something Disney-related in general. The longer your cruise, the more likely you are to see doors festooned with magnets, sometimes quite elaborately. We like to take a different route to our stateroom to see all the door decorations as often as possible.

Of course, you're under no obligation to decorate your door, but if you choose to do so, be aware that you can't tack or stick anything to it—no tape or adhesive wall hangers. Any damage to your door will result in a charge to your folio (room account).

FISH EXTENDERS Mounted in a nook beside every DCL stateroom door is a small metal sculpture in the shape of a fish, starfish, shell, crown, or other object fitting the theme of the ship. They're cute, but they're not just for decoration; set away from the wall by a few millimeters, they also function as tiny shelves. You'll find your Key to the World Card here on embarkation day, and you may also receive notes and reminders here over the course of your cruise.

*un*official **TIP**

Even if you're not gung ho about decorating your door, some guests bring at least one or two door magnets to help them easily spot their stateroom in a seemingly endless corridor.

A **fish extender**—a uniquely DCL gadget—is a vertical strip of fabric with pockets (like an over-the-door shoe organizer) that you

can hang from your doorside sculpture to extend its functionality. (The idea originated on DISboards.com, where user EpcotKilter Fan posted this ingenious storage solution, created for a 2005 DCL cruise.) You can make your own extender or buy one from a website such as Etsy. Some repeat cruisers use theirs to participate in Secret Santa–style gift exchanges arranged in Facebook groups before their trip. Despite the *Wish*-

unofficial **TIP**
We don't recommend participating in gift exchanges on your first sailing. It's more to keep track of—and you booked a cruise to relax, not stress unnecessarily. Get the lay of the land—well, sea—the first time.

class ships launching with nary a fish in sight next to stateroom doors, groups still refer to them as fish extenders.

UNDERSTANDING STATEROOM CLASSIFICATIONS

DCL USES AN alphanumeric system to indicate different types of staterooms. You might have heard your travel agent say something like, "I could put you in a 6B for this price, or I could book you in a 4C for that price." What do these codes mean?

There are 23 stateroom classifications on the *Wonder* and *Magic;* 27 on the *Dream* and *Fantasy;* and 26 on the *Wish, Treasure,* and *Destiny.* These can be confusing to veteran cruisers and novices alike.

To demystify the system, here are the key points you need to know:

- In general, **the least expensive staterooms** are designated with the highest category number: **11.**
- The cost and quality of a stateroom generally increase as its category number decreases. For example, a **Category 4** stateroom is typically more expensive than a **Category 5** stateroom.
- When a letter modifies a numeric classification—**Category 4A,** for instance—the letter indicates **the stateroom's location on the ship.** In general, A staterooms are on higher decks than Bs, which are on higher decks than Cs, and so on. An A stateroom isn't necessarily better than a B or C stateroom, however.
- **Midship staterooms,** in the center of the ship on any deck, tend to be more expensive and desirable—and thus tend to have lower category numbers—than other staterooms. This is because (1) the staterooms are generally larger and (2) this location is both more convenient to other parts of the ship and less conducive to motion sickness (see page 132) than other locations.
- **Concierge Staterooms** start with the numbers **1, 2,** or **3.**
- Even within the same stateroom classification, you may find as many as **four or five different verandah configurations** (see page 102).

STATEROOM FLOOR PLANS

Note: *Due to the shape of the ships, there are minor variations in floor plans even within stateroom categories. In addition to the floor-plan art included in this section, video tours are available on our YouTube channel (scan the QR code at right and search for the specific stateroom name and ship). Staterooms on other ships in the same class will be almost identical in layout.*

• CATEGORIES 11A–11C (all ships):
Standard Inside Stateroom

MAXIMUM OCCUPANCY 3 or 4 people

SQUARE FOOTAGE 184 (*Magic/Wonder*), 169 (all other ships)

FEATURES One queen-size bed, one sleeper sofa, combined bath with tub and shower. Some have a pull-down upper berth.

LOCATION Decks 2 and 5–7 (*Magic/Wonder*), Decks 2 and 5–10 (*Dream/Fantasy*), Decks 2 and 6–11 (*Wish/Treasure/Destiny*)

• CATEGORIES 10A (*Magic/Wonder/Dream/Fantasy*)
AND 10B AND 10C (*Magic/Wonder*): Deluxe Inside Stateroom

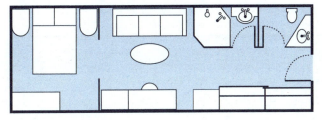

MAXIMUM OCCUPANCY 3 or 4 people

SQUARE FOOTAGE 214 (*Magic/Wonder*), 204 (*Dream/Fantasy*)

FEATURES One queen-size bed, one sleeper sofa, split bath. Some have a pull-down upper berth.

LOCATION **Category 10A:** Decks 5 and 7 (*Magic/Wonder*), Decks 5–9 (*Dream/Fantasy*) **Category 10B:** Deck 2 Midship (*Magic/Wonder*) **Category 10C:** Deck 1 Midship and Deck 2 Aft (*Magic/Wonder*)

• CATEGORIES 9A–9D (all ships):
Deluxe Oceanview Stateroom

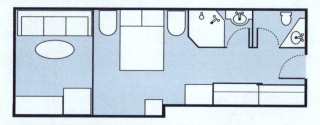

MAXIMUM OCCUPANCY 3 or 4 people

SQUARE FOOTAGE 214 (*Magic/Wonder*), 204 (*Dream/Fantasy*), 218 (*Wish/Treasure/Destiny*)

FEATURES Same as a Category 10, plus a window view of the ocean. Category 9D staterooms have two small portholes instead of one larger one. The 9A staterooms on Decks 6–8 of the *Dream* and *Fantasy* and Decks 2 and 6–8 of the *Wish, Treasure,* and *Destiny* are interesting because they're at the ships' extreme forward and aft ends, affording them unique views at a relatively low cost. The far-forward Category 9 staterooms on Decks 6–8 of the *Wish, Treasure,* and *Destiny* have unique slanted walls and slanted portholes that follow the curvature of the ship.

LOCATION Category 9A: Decks 5–7 Forward (*Magic/Wonder*), Decks 5–8 Forward (*Dream/Fantasy*), Decks 7 and 8 (*Wish/Treasure/Destiny*) **Categories 9B and 9C:** Deck 2 (*Magic/Wonder*), Decks 2 and 6–8 (all other ships) **Category 9D:** Deck 1 (*Magic/Wonder*), Decks 2 and 6–8 (all other ships)

• CATEGORIES 8B AND 8C
(*Dream/Fantasy/Wish/Treasure/Destiny*):
Deluxe Family Oceanview Stateroom

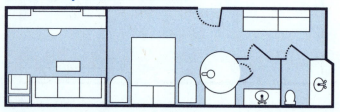

MAXIMUM OCCUPANCY 3, 4, or 5 people

SQUARE FOOTAGE 241 (*Dream/Fantasy*), 237 (*Wish/Treasure/Destiny*)

FEATURES One queen-size bed and a one-person sleeper sofa. Most also have a one-person pull-down bed in the wall; a few have a one-person pull-down bed in the ceiling. Tubs and showers are round on the *Dream* and *Fantasy* and rectangular on the *Wish, Treasure,* and *Destiny*.

LOCATION Decks 5–9 (*Dream/Fantasy*), Decks 6–9 (*Wish/Treasure/Destiny*)

- **CATEGORY 8A** (*Dream/Fantasy*): **Deluxe Family Oceanview Stateroom**

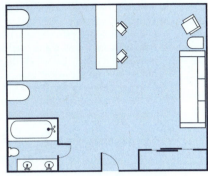

MAXIMUM OCCUPANCY 3 or 4 people

SQUARE FOOTAGE 241 (according to Disney; we think they are probably closer to 300)

FEATURES One queen-size bed, a one-person sleeper sofa; no split bath. They usually have two large portholes instead of one and a divider wall of some type between the bed and sofa.

LOCATION Deck 5 or 6

- **CATEGORY 7A** (all ships): **Deluxe Oceanview Stateroom with Navigator's Verandah**

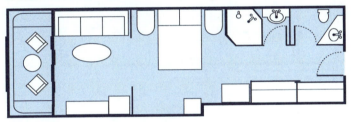

MAXIMUM OCCUPANCY 3 or 4 people

SQUARE FOOTAGE (including verandah) 268 (*Magic/Wonder*), 246 (*Dream/ Fantasy*), 243 (*Wish/Treasure/Destiny*)

FEATURES One queen-size bed, a one-person sleeper sofa, split bath. Some also have an upper-berth pull-down bed. On the *Magic* and *Wonder,* the **Navigator's Verandahs** have a small, semienclosed, teak-floored deck attached to the stateroom and feature a large window cut into the metal. On the *Dream, Fantasy, Wish, Treasure,* and *Destiny,* these staterooms have Undersize or Obstructed-View Verandahs.

LOCATION Decks 5–7 (*Magic/Wonder*), Decks 5 and 9 (*Dream/Fantasy*), Decks 6–9 (*Wish/Treasure/Destiny*)

- **CATEGORIES 6A** (all ships) **AND 6B** (*Dream/Fantasy/Wish/ Treasure/Destiny*): **Deluxe Oceanview Stateroom with Verandah**

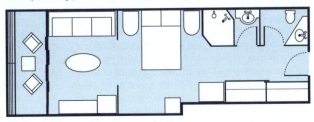

MAXIMUM OCCUPANCY 3 or 4 people

SQUARE FOOTAGE (including verandah) 268 (*Magic/Wonder*), 246 (*Dream/Fantasy*), 243 (*Wish/Treasure/Destiny*)

FEATURES One queen-size bed; a one-person sleeper sofa; a one-person pull-down bed, typically above the sofa; split bath. Category 6 staterooms have what DCL calls **White-Wall Verandahs,** or verandahs with a solid wall instead of a plexiglass railing. The walls on the *Magic* and *Wonder* come up higher than on the newer ships.

LOCATION Category 6A: Decks 5–7 Aft (*Magic/Wonder*), Decks 8 and 9 Aft (*Dream/Fantasy*), Decks 8 and 9 (*Wish/Treasure/Destiny*) **Category 6B:** Decks 5–7 (*Dream/Fantasy*), Decks 6 and 7 (*Wish/Treasure/Destiny*)

• CATEGORIES 5A–5C (all ships):
Deluxe Oceanview Stateroom with Verandah

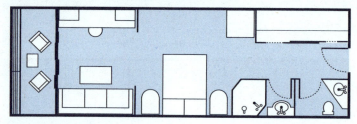

MAXIMUM OCCUPANCY 3 or 4 people

SQUARE FOOTAGE (including verandah) 268 (*Magic/Wonder*), 246 (*Dream/Fantasy*), 243 (*Wish/Treasure/Destiny*)

FEATURES One queen-size bed; a one-person sleeper sofa; some have a one-person pull-down bed, typically above the sofa; split bath.

LOCATION Decks 5–7 (*Magic* and *Wonder*), Decks 6–10 (all other ships)

• CATEGORIES 4A, 4B, AND 4E (all ships)
AND CATEGORY 4C (*Dream/Fantasy/Wish/Treasure/Destiny*):
Deluxe Family Oceanview Stateroom with Verandah

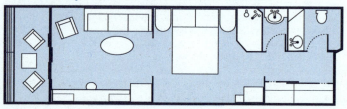

MAXIMUM OCCUPANCY 4 or 5 people

SQUARE FOOTAGE (including verandah) 304 (*Magic/Wonder*), 299 (*Dream/Fantasy;* see comment about 4Es below), 284 (*Wlsh/Treasure/Destiny*)

FEATURES One queen-size bed, a one-person sleeper sofa, split bath; most have a one-person pull-down wall bed, and some also have a pull-down upper-berth bed. Category 4A, 4B, and 4C staterooms on the *Dream* and *Fantasy* have round tubs. **Category 4E** staterooms on the *Dream* and

Fantasy are only 246 square feet but have much larger verandahs than the other Category 4 staterooms. If selecting a Category 4C stateroom (Decks 6 and 7) on the *Wish, Treasure,* or *Destiny,* consider your deck plan: Some staterooms on the "bumpout" (convex) portion of these ships have significantly larger verandahs than their neighbors.

LOCATION Deck 8 (*Magic/Wonder*), Decks 5–10 (*Dream/Fantasy*), Decks 6–11 (*Wish/Treasure/Destiny*)

• CATEGORY 3B *(Wish/Treasure/Destiny)*:
Concierge Family Oceanview Stateroom

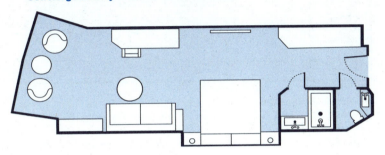

MAXIMUM OCCUPANCY 4 or 5 people
SQUARE FOOTAGE 357
FEATURES King-size bed, sleeper sofa for two, one-person upper-berth pull-down bed. This is the lowest price point for access to Concierge amenities. While these staterooms do not have verandahs, they are significantly larger than the 3As and feature floor-to-ceiling windows with stunning ocean views.
LOCATION Deck 11 Forward

• CATEGORY 3A (all ships):
Concierge Family Oceanview Stateroom with Verandah

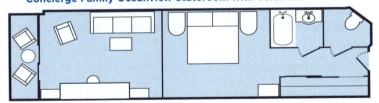

MAXIMUM OCCUPANCY 4 or 5 people
SQUARE FOOTAGE (including verandah) 304 (*Magic/Wonder*), 306 (*Dream/ Fantasy*), 296 (*Wish/Treasure/Destiny*)
FEATURES One king-size bed (*Wish/Treasure/Destiny*) or queen-size bed (*Magic/Wonder/Dream/Fantasy*), a two-person sleeper sofa, and a one-person upper-berth pull-down bed.
LOCATION Deck 8 (*Magic/Wonder*), Decks 11 and 12 (*Dream/Fantasy*), Decks 12 and 13 (*Wish/Treasure/Destiny*)

- **CATEGORY 2B** (all ships):
  Concierge 1-Bedroom Suite with Verandah

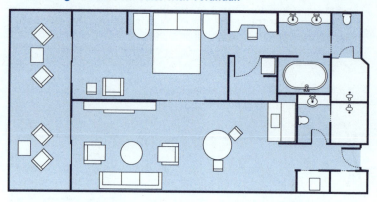

MAXIMUM OCCUPANCY 5 people

SQUARE FOOTAGE (including verandah) 614 (*Magic/Wonder*), 622 (*Dream/ Fantasy*), 608 (*Wish/Treasure/Destiny*)

FEATURES Layouts vary slightly among ships, but they all feature a separate bedroom with queen-size bed (king-size on the *Wish, Treasure,* and *Destiny*) and a bathroom with a large tub and separate shower. The second bathroom has just a shower. The living room has a two-person sleeper sofa and a one-person pull-down bed (the pull-down is in the bedroom on the *Magic* and *Wonder*).

LOCATION Deck 8 (*Magic/Wonder*), Decks 11 and 12 Forward (*Dream/Fantasy*), Decks 12 and 13 Forward (*Wish/Treasure/Destiny*)

- **CATEGORY 2A** (*all ships*): Concierge 1-Bedroom Suite with Verandah
MAXIMUM OCCUPANCY 5 people

SQUARE FOOTAGE (including verandah) 614 (*Magic/Wonder*), 622 (*Dream/ Fantasy*), 1,031 (*Wish/Treasure/Destiny*)

FEATURES See Category 2B features (above). There are four 2As on the *Magic* and *Wonder,* and they have more of a sideways design than the 2Bs, with a larger living room area. On the *Dream, Fantasy, Wish, Treasure,* and *Destiny,* the 2A and 2B staterooms are identical on the inside, but the verandahs on the 2As are huge.

LOCATION Deck 8 (*Magic/Wonder*), Deck 12 Forward (all other ships)

- **CATEGORY 1C** (*Wish/Treasure/Destiny*):
Concierge 1-Story Royal Suite with Verandah

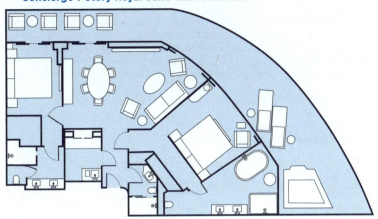

MAXIMUM OCCUPANCY 6 people
SQUARE FOOTAGE (including verandah) 1,507
FEATURES Two bedrooms with king-size beds and walk-in closets; three full
  bathrooms; large corner verandah with a private hot tub; living room; din-
  ing room with a six-seat table; and pantry.
LOCATION Deck 10 Aft.

- **CATEGORY 1B** (*Magic/Wonder*):
Concierge 2-Bedroom Suite with Verandah

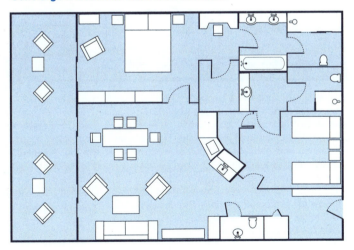

MAXIMUM OCCUPANCY 7 people

SQUARE FOOTAGE (including verandah) 945

FEATURES The main bedroom has a queen-size bed; a walk-in closet; and a bath with a double vanity, tub, and walk-in shower. The other bedroom has twin beds, a pull-down bed, a bath with shower and vanity, and a walk-in closet. Two others can sleep on the convertible sofa in the living room. In addition, the suite features a large living room with seating for 10 people, a large private verandah suitable for entertaining a few guests, and another half bath.

LOCATION Deck 8 Forward

• CATEGORIES 1B *(Dream)* AND 1A *(Fantasy)*: Concierge Royal Suite with Verandah

MAXIMUM OCCUPANCY 5 people

SQUARE FOOTAGE (including verandah) 1,781

FEATURES Royal Suites on the *Dream* and *Fantasy* have one long room separated into dining and living areas. The main bedroom features a queen-size bed and bath with a double vanity, shower, and tub. A pull-down double bed and a single pull-down bed in the living room complete the sleeping arrangements. The most impressive feature of these suites on the *Dream* and *Fantasy* may be the verandah, which curves around the suite to follow the contour of the deck. Besides being large enough to land aircraft on, it includes a private hot tub.

LOCATION Deck 12 Forward

• CATEGORY 1B (*Wish/Treasure/Destiny*):
Concierge 2-Story Royal Suite with Verandah

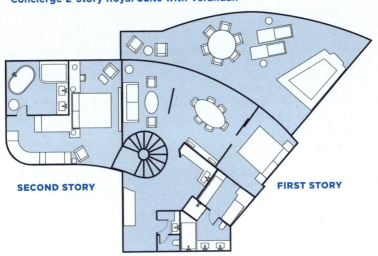

SECOND STORY   **FIRST STORY**

MAXIMUM OCCUPANCY 6 people

SQUARE FOOTAGE (including verandah) 1,759

FEATURES Two bedrooms with king-size beds and walk-in closets, three full bathrooms, a verandah with a private hot tub, a living room, a dining room with a six-seat table, and a kitchen. A spiral staircase connects the two floors in these suites.

LOCATION Decks 13 and 14 Forward

• CATEGORY 1A (*Magic/Wonder*):
Concierge Royal Suite with Verandah

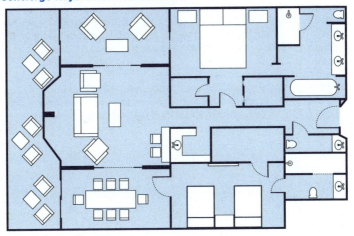

MAXIMUM OCCUPANCY 7 people
SQUARE FOOTAGE (including verandah) 1,029
FEATURES Main bedroom: queen-size (*Magic*) or king-size (*Wonder*) bed, walk-in closet, double vanity, walk-in shower. Second bedroom: twin beds, two pull-down beds, bath with tub and sink, and walk-in closet. There is also a pull-down bed in the living room, a separate dining room, a living room, a media room, a long private verandah, and a half bath.
LOCATION Deck 8

• CATEGORY 1A (*Wish/Treasure/Destiny*): Concierge Tower Suite

MAXIMUM OCCUPANCY 8 people
SQUARE FOOTAGE 1,966
FEATURES With subtle *Moana* theming in the *Wish* Tower Suite and EPCOT theming in the *Treasure*'s Tomorrow Tower Suite, these massive suites feature two main bedrooms, a kids' room with built-in bunk beds, and a library with a queen-size pull-down bed; four and a half bathrooms; an eight-seat dining table; and a kitchen with dishwasher, refrigerator, and coffee maker. The living room affords views across the ship's upper decks through a two-story wall of windows. The main bedrooms, on the upper level, have walk-in closets, king-size beds, and floor-to-ceiling windows overlooking the living area and the ship's upper decks. The main bathrooms have rainfall showerheads, double vanities, and spa tubs. All fixtures and finishes are top-of-the-line.
LOCATION Inside the ship's forward funnel stack on Decks 14 and 15 (this is the only area designated as Deck 15 on the entire ship).

• CATEGORY 1A (*Dream*): *Dream* Tower Suite

MAXIMUM OCCUPANCY 8 people
SQUARE FOOTAGE (including verandah) 2,030
FEATURES The Tower Suite on the *Dream* is inspired by the Sorcerer's Apprentice scene in *Fantasia* and is the biggest stateroom in the fleet. It has two main bedrooms with king-size beds, a kids' room with built-in bunk beds, and a library with a queen-size pull-down bed. There are four and a half bathrooms, a dining salon, and a pantry with refrigerator and coffee maker. The living room has a two-story wall of windows. The main bathrooms have rainfall showerheads, double vanities, and spa tubs. All fixtures and finishes are top-of-the-line.
LOCATION Inside the ship's forward funnel stack on Decks 13 and 14
COMMENT A floor plan for the *Dream* tower Suite was not available at press time, but it will be comparable to that of the *Wish* Tower Suite.

WISH TOWER SUITE

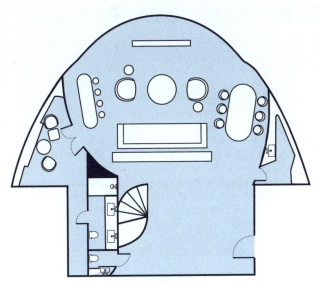

FIRST STORY

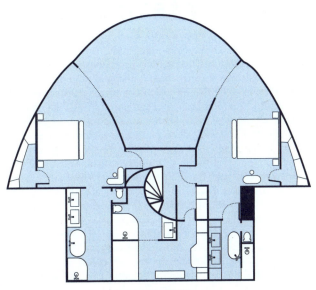

SECOND STORY

BOOKING *a* CRUISE *without* SELECTING *a* STATEROOM

UNLIKE BOOKING A HOTEL, where you typically don't find out your exact stateroom until you arrive, most guests booking a Disney cruise choose a specific stateroom when they make their reservation. When a preferred stateroom category is nearly full, however, DCL offers what's known as a **GTY reservation.** *GTY* stands for "guarantee," meaning you're guaranteed to be in a particular stateroom category or higher, though you may not know exactly which stateroom you're in until immediately before you depart. There are no discounts associated with GTY reservations; it's just a way for Disney to keep some flexibility when assigning them.

These are often confused with another set of similar acronyms, discussed on page 24. Called **VGT** (Verandah Guarantee), **OGT** (Oceanview Guarantee), and **IGT** (Inside Guarantee) rates, these are highly restrictive, nonrefundable fares that do not allow you to select a specific stateroom but can save you money if you are OK with the restrictions and letting Disney select your stateroom for you.

STATEROOM SELECTION *for* LARGER PARTIES

GUESTS TRAVELING WITH four or fewer people are often fine staying in one stateroom. DCL offers many options for ship location and stateroom size at various price points—just choose where you want to be and how much you want to spend, and you're good to go. Guests traveling with parties of five or more people, and guests traveling with extended family, blended families, or unrelated friends may have more-complicated decisions to make when choosing their staterooms.

A quick glance at DCL's deck plans and stateroom classifications shows that on the *Magic,* for example, the lowest stateroom category that will sleep a party of five is a **Category 4 Deluxe Family Oceanview Stateroom with Verandah** on an upper deck. Let's look, then, at pricing for a hypothetical family of five—two adults and three kids ages 16, 13, and 9—for the **4-Night Bahamian Cruise** on the *Magic* on May 7, 2025. At the time of our search, the lowest price to put this family in one stateroom was **$6,372** for a **Category 4E.** If, however, we tried to book that same family of five into two **Category 11C Standard Inside Staterooms,** with one adult and the two older kids in one stateroom and one adult and the 9-year-old in the other, the total price would be **$4,835** ($2,813 for the stateroom with three people and $2,022 for the stateroom with two), for a savings of $1,537.

Of course, you have some trade-offs to consider—the most obvious in this case is that the family gives up access to a verandah. On the other hand, they gain more than 100 square feet of living space and an additional shower and toilet. For many families, the advantages of saving about $1,500 and gaining a bathroom would far outweigh the loss of a stateroom with a view.

Making things even more complicated, the pricing is different if you book the same family of five into the same two Inside Staterooms but in a slightly different combination. If you book one adult, one teen, and the 9-year-old in the first stateroom, their cost is $2,786, and the price for the second adult and the second teen is $2,022, for a total of **$4,808.** This slight difference in booking strategy saves $27. (The second person in a stateroom is always charged an adult rate, regardless of age. If the 9-year-old is booked into a stateroom with just one other person, he's priced at the adult rate, but if he's the third person in a stateroom, he's priced at the children's rate.) In summary, always book the oldest guests as the first and second guests in a stateroom.

Granted, a $27 savings is a drop in the bucket for a cruise vacation that costs many thousands of dollars, but if you're traveling with a very large party (a family reunion, for example), such small tweaks can add up in your favor. Again, though, be aware that the Castaway Club status of the travelers also has ramifications for stateroom assignments; if members of your party have different statuses, it may be worth a few dollars to choose a different booking configuration. (See pages 5–7 for more information.) Also note that once you're on board, it's easy to tinker with who actually sleeps where, regardless of how the booking was made.

Consider the following questions when booking staterooms for larger parties:

- **Do we need connecting staterooms?** Guests traveling with small children may prefer them, while guests traveling with well-behaved teens or other adults may find that non-connecting staterooms next to each other or nonadjacent staterooms near each other are enough.

- **Does it matter if all members of the party have the same stateroom type?** Is parity needed to keep the peace among family members? Are we willing to have an Oceanview Stateroom and an Inside Stateroom, or a Verandah Stateroom and an Oceanview or Inside Stateroom? Is it sufficient if only one stateroom has a verandah that everyone can use?

TO VERANDAH *or not to* VERANDAH?

A VERANDAH (note the tasteful *H* at the end) is analogous to a balcony at a hotel. Some cruise lines have verandahs that face toward the center of the ship, often toward a pool or open deck stage, but those on most DCL ships face out toward the ocean. The *Disney Adventure* will be the first Disney ship to have inward-facing verandahs.

TYPES OF VERANDAHS

ALL VERANDAHS ARE NOT CREATED EQUAL, and DCL uses a variety of terms to describe theirs. For example:

- **Standard (Family) Verandah** Has a transparent acrylic wall from the deck to the railing between you and the ocean. You can see the ocean from anywhere, sitting or standing.

- **White-Wall Verandah** Has a solid white wall from the deck to the railing. You can see the ocean if you're standing up, but you're not likely to if you're sitting down. Most of these staterooms are located in the aft portion of the ship.

- **Navigator's Verandah** On the *Magic* and *Wonder,* the verandah has both a solid wall from the deck to the railing and some enclosure above the railing. Picture a balcony with a large porthole opening to a view of the ocean. You can see the ocean if you're standing up but not if you're sitting down. Most have one chair and one fixed bench built into the wall rather than two regular chairs. On the other ships, a Navigator's Verandah is only partially obstructed.

- **Obstructed-View Verandah** A significant portion of the view is blocked by ship walls or something like the lifeboats.

- **Undersize Verandah** Smaller than is typical on DCL ships.

- **Extended Verandah** Larger than is typical on DCL ships. There may be room for lounge chairs or four regular chairs instead of just two.

Some staterooms have combinations of these verandah types. For example, many far-aft staterooms on Decks 7, 8, 9, and 10 of the *Dream* and *Fantasy* have Extended Verandahs with white walls.

COST CONSIDERATIONS

THE TYPE OF VERANDAH you select can have cost implications. For example, we spot-checked the July 16, 2025, **4-Night Bahamian Cruise** on the *Magic* for a party of two adults in a Deluxe Oceanview Stateroom with Verandah. Within seven consecutive staterooms on Deck 7 Aft, there are three verandah configurations available, each incrementally more expensive than the other:

- **Obstructed-View Verandah:** $4,073
- **White-Wall Verandah:** $4,185
- **Standard Verandah:** $4,729

The same party on the February 2024 **4-Night Bahamian Cruise** from Fort Lauderdale on the *Dream* could choose among five variants of the Deluxe Oceanview Stateroom with Verandah on Deck 6:

- **Undersize Verandah:** $2,285
- **Obstructed-View Verandah:** $2,301
- **Standard Verandah:** $2,341
- **Extended Verandah:** $2,445
- **Family Verandah:** $2,629

In this situation, you can get a stateroom with seating for four (Extended Verandah) for just $104 more than a stateroom with seating for two (Standard Verandah). It's a modest tweak that could make a big difference for some families, although you could be sacrificing other factors, such as the stateroom's location on the ship. *Family Verandah* is somewhat misleading: It's the most expensive option not because of the verandah type (which is Standard) but because of the stateroom type.

If you dream of sitting with a glass of wine and staring at the sea, be sure you're getting a verandah configuration that will allow you to do this. It may well be worth it to spend a few dollars, or even a few hundred dollars, more for better sight lines. Or, if you don't particularly care, you can save yourself a few bucks by choosing a different verandah configuration.

Also note that if your party is staying in two adjacent Verandah Staterooms, you may be able to open the divider separating the outdoor space between them, effectively creating one extra-large verandah. Not all Verandah Staterooms offer this option, so check with your stateroom host to see if the divider is removable.

WEATHER AND SAFETY CONCERNS

IF YOU'RE SAILING to a cold-weather destination, you may find that a verandah is less of an imperative than if you're traveling to tropical locales. While it might be nice to stand out on your balcony to view the trees, wildlife, or glaciers for a few minutes, it probably won't be comfortable to read or dine outdoors for very long. We do recommend at least an Oceanview Stateroom. The highlight of an Alaskan itinerary is those views!

Some guests with small children may have safety concerns. Verandah doors have a lock that's above adult shoulder height. It is theoretically possible for an enterprising grade-schooler to climb on a chair or coffee table to reach the lock, though it would take some real ingenuity and strength to open the door. If you're concerned that you may have a late-night escape artist on your hands, then you may want to save verandah lodging for when Junior is a bit older.

VERANDAH ETIQUETTE

ALTHOUGH YOUR VERANDAH is your private outdoor space, please keep in mind the following rules and courtesies:

- **No smoking.** Cigarette/cigar smoke inevitably drifts to neighboring verandahs, so please smoke only in designated areas of the ship (see page 169). The same rule applies to vaping and e-cigarettes.

- **No drying wet clothing or towels.** They are almost guaranteed to blow away.

- *No nudity!* Verandahs are private, but not *that* private. Your naked glory may be visible from other ships, port locations, or nearby verandahs.

- **No loud music or conversation.** You will be heard in nearby staterooms.

OUR RECOMMENDATIONS *for* STATEROOMS

THE BEST STATEROOM TYPE is the one that meets your individual needs. Here are some things to think about as you make your decision. A Disney-specialist travel agent can give you advice here as well.

continued on page 107

TAMMY'S STATEROOM SCOOP

• CATEGORY 1 *(see pages 95–99)*

Magic **class:** I recommend stateroom **8530** for Castaway Cay views and **8030** for possible Lookout Cay views; you'll be thrilled with either.

Dream **class:** The **Royal Suites** are two of my favorites on any ship. You've misunderstood the assignment if you don't spend at least 50% of your time on the verandah. If you don't care about the island views, decide whether you prefer a bright and sunny bathroom or a bright and sunny main bedroom. The floor-to-ceiling windows are in the bathroom in 12002 and in the bedroom in 12502. The *Dream* just introduced a new category for the *Dream*-class ships: the *Dream* **Tower Suite,** which is located in the funnel. At 2,030 square feet, it's the biggest stateroom on any ship. There is no verandah, but there are floor-to-ceiling windows in the two-story living room, four bedrooms, and four and a half bathrooms.

Wish **class:** These staterooms are simply spectacular. The *Wish* **Tower Suite** on the *Wish,* the **Tomorrow Tower Suite** on the *Treasure,* and the *Destiny* **Tower Suite** on the *Destiny* are located in the funnel. They sleep up to eight guests and are ginormous at 1,966 square feet. They're perfect for large groups who are willing to pay the cost. The one- and two-story **Royal Suites** are likewise some of the most luxurious accommodations I've ever been in, on land or sea. If you need an outdoor space, these staterooms are smaller than the Tower Suites but have a private hot tub and huge verandahs. The one-story Royal Suites are all the way aft on **Deck 10,** so they aren't quite as convenient to the Concierge lounge or sundeck as the two-story suites, which are forward on **Deck 13,** but that doesn't matter much because the Concierge hosts bring you almost anything you want.

• CATEGORY 2 *(see page 94)*

Magic **class:** On the *Magic*-class ships, I recommend **8032, 8034, 8532,** or **8534** because the twin pull-down bed is in the living room instead of the main bedroom, giving the latter its own closed-off space. The living room also feels huge compared to the other Category 2s on the *Magic.*

Dream **class:** On the *Dream* class ships, six suites have bigger verandahs because they are on the ships' bumpouts (outward curves): **12006, 12012, 12506, 12512, 11006,** and **11002.** For the best view of Castaway Cay, book 12512. The Concierge Staterooms on **Deck 12** have easier access to the Concierge lounge and sundeck than the ones on Deck 11. Most of these are in Category 2B, and there is only one stateroom in Category 2A: **12000.** It's located between the two Royal Suites at the front and center of the ship. A private hallway connects them if you happen to be booking one of those as well. 12000 has a huge verandah and incredible views. It costs more, but it's worth it!

Wish **class:** The Category 2 staterooms on **Deck 13** are convenient to the sundeck, though a staircase inside the Concierge lounge makes both the lounge on Deck 12 and the sundeck on Deck 13 easy to get to. The Category 2A staterooms with Extended Verandahs have incredible outdoor space. For these, I recommend starboard-side staterooms, and **12500** would be my first pick, with 12000 still being a close second because of that giant verandah; **12504** is a particularly lovely Category 2B.

• CATEGORY 3 *(see page 93)*

Magic **class:** Category 3 staterooms are essentially Category 4s with Concierge furnishings and service. On the *Magic*-class ships, I prefer a stateroom on the starboard side if visiting Castaway Cay and usually the port side for Lookout Cay.

Dream **class:** On the *Dream*-class ships, I likewise prefer a starboard stateroom; I also recommend one of the staterooms on the bumpouts (outward curves), on each

---

* *Magic* **class:** *Magic/Wonder*   *Dream* **class:** *Dream/Fantasy*
  Wish **class:** *Wish/Treasure/Destiny*

• CATEGORY 3 *(continued)*

side of the ship: **12008, 12010, 12508, 12510,** and **11004.** If you need to split a group between two staterooms, book **12512** with **12510** to open the verandah partition between the two staterooms for amazing Castaway Cay views, or choose the port side option for Lookout Cay.

Wish class: 3Bs are the only Concierge Staterooms without a verandah. What they lack in balconies, though, they make up for in floor-to-ceiling windows. Category 3B has two corner staterooms I call **Secret Suites;** each has a separate bedroom with a door. My pick would be **11006,** which is stunning. If you don't absolutely need a verandah, I highly recommend the 3Bs over the 3As—these staterooms are so nice, I have a feeling they'll be recategorized at some point. They already cost more than the 3As!

• CATEGORY 4 *(see page 92)*

Magic class: Category 4 (Family) staterooms are the biggest non-Concierge State-rooms on these ships. (*Family* means the stateroom is slightly longer and may sleep up to five.) The A, B, C, and D versions have similar features. I gravitate toward the starboard side for the views when on Castaway Cay and usually the port side when on Lookout Cay. The 4Es do have White-Wall Verandahs.

Dream class: Category 4E on *Dream*-class ships lack the round tubs of the other Category 4s. The *Dream*-class 4Es have spacious verandahs, and if you don't mind possible vibrations on the aft end of the ship, these staterooms have fantastic views as well, although they sleep only four. If you need a stateroom that sleeps five or want a round tub, choose starboard and midship for Castaway Cay, and port and midship for Lookout Cay.

Wish class: Like the *Dream*-class ships, the *Wish*-class ships have bumpouts on each side, but the *Wish*-class ships have non-Concierge Staterooms on theirs. Category 4's bumpout staterooms, particularly those in the center of each bump, have large Extended Verandahs. Like Category 3 on the *Wish* class, corner-aft staterooms **6196** and **6696** are Secret Suites—my top picks in Category 4. Unlike the Secret Suites in Category 3, however, these have verandahs. Other good aft options are **6700, 9182, 9184, 10168, 10170,** and **10668;** all afford great views from spacious verandahs.

• CATEGORY 5 *(see page 92)*

Magic and *Dream* classes: These are all standard-size staterooms with unobstructed verandahs. There are no wrong choices.

Wish class: The hidden gems in Category 5 are the staterooms at the edges of the bumpouts; these have bigger verandahs than other Category 5 staterooms on these ships. On **Deck 10,** for example, my picks are **10044, 10046, 10544,** and **10546.** The staterooms toward the front of each bumpout have somewhat better views facing forward, while the staterooms facing toward the back of each bumpout have slightly better views facing aft, which means better views of Castaway Cay in particular. Facing all the way aft are **6198** or **6698.** With their large verandahs and excellent views, these staterooms are my top two picks in Category 5.

• CATEGORY 6 *(see page 91)*

Magic class: Category 6 staterooms are like Category 5 staterooms, but on the *Magic*-class ships they all have White-Wall Verandahs. Staterooms on **Deck 6** have slightly larger verandahs. Staterooms **6652, 6650,** and **6648** are my picks, in that order.

Dream class: Category 6 Staterooms on the *Dream*-class ships all have short White-Wall, Undersize, or Obstructed-View Verandahs. Some of these differences are minor, so if you want to save a little over a Category 5, I'd choose **6188** and **6688** because I love those aft Extended Verandahs.

* *Magic* class: Magic/Wonder   *Dream* class: Dream/Fantasy
  Wish class: Wish/Treasure/Destiny

TAMMY'S STATEROOM SCOOP *(continued)*

• CATEGORY 6 *(continued)*

Wish class: Category 6A staterooms **8192** and **8690** are on the far-aft side of the ship. They have huge verandahs with stellar views, but be aware that the staterooms themselves are quite small. Neither has a couch—only a foldout chair—so keep this in mind when booking your stateroom.

• CATEGORY 7 *(see page 91)*

Magic class: There's a big difference between the *Dream*- and *Magic*-class Category 7s. Most Navigator's Verandahs on the *Magic*-class ships are enclosed, with a large round or oval windowlike opening. The *Magic* class has four Category 7 staterooms whose verandahs are not fully enclosed: **6134, 6634, 7120,** and **7620.**

Dream class: These Category 7 verandahs have views that are slightly more obstructed than the views from Category 6 verandahs. There are two aft, **5188** or **5688,** with large verandahs—I'd pick those.

Wish class: Verandahs in **Deck 6's** 7As are less obstructed than 7As on higher decks.

• CATEGORY 8 *(see pages 90–91)*

Magic class: There are no Category 8 staterooms on the *Magic*-class ships.

Dream class: Category 8 (Family) staterooms have very large portholes with seating. (*Family* means these are bigger staterooms that sleep up to five and have round tubs.) Category 8As, which are more like suites than staterooms, have two large portholes and lots of space; many have a divider between the bed and seating area. Not all have tubs, though. **5020, 5022, 5520,** and **5522** have a great dividing wall, plus tubs.

Wish class: There are no Category 8A staterooms on the *Wish*-class ships, and that's sad news for those who love the *Dream* class's 8As, which are known for their massive size and double portholes. As for Category 8B and 8C, I'd be cautious of booking a Category 8 stateroom that's on **Deck 6 Aft**—these staterooms are directly above the Arendelle restaurant, where the show can get slightly loud.

• CATEGORY 9 *(see page 90)*

Magic class: On the *Magic* class, I would avoid **Deck 1** if I were staying in a Category 9 stateroom—this is a short deck with no access to the aft elevators. The Oceanview Staterooms on **Deck 1** also have two small portholes instead of one large porthole, which significantly limits your view. The 9C staterooms that are all the way forward, like **2504** and **2510,** have a bit more space due to the curvature of the ship.

Dream class: On the *Dream* class, the 9Bs on **Deck 2** are conveniently located outside Enchanted Garden. The *Dream* class also has some large corner staterooms that are 9Ds: **7006, 7504, 8006,** and **8504.**

Wish class: Because of the angle of the ship, 9D staterooms have slanted portholes and terrific views. The largest of these staterooms—and thus the ones I recommend first in this category—are **7006, 7504, 8006,** and **8504.**

• CATEGORY 10 *(see page 89)*

Magic class: These Inside Staterooms are the same size and have the same setup as Category 9s, but they have no outside views. The *Magic* class has its own exciting unofficial category: **"secret porthole" staterooms.** These are Inside Staterooms that actually have a window, albeit with an obstructed view. If you want some natural light for the price of an Inside Stateroom, these are the staterooms for you—book **5020, 5022, 5024, 5520, 5522,** or **5524** on the *Magic*-class ships. *Warning:* These staterooms are more popular than a Dole Whip on a sweltering day, so book early.

---

* *Magic* class: *Magic/Wonder*   *Dream* class: *Dream/Fantasy*
  Wish class: *Wish/Treasure/Destiny*

- **CATEGORY 10** *(continued)*

Dream **class:** On the *Dream*-class ships, these staterooms have so-called virtual portholes, which give a view (via camera) of what's happening outside, with some occasional Disney magic thrown in. I'd probably avoid 5015 and 5515 due to their proximity to Vibe and the Walt Disney Theatre.

Wish **class:** *Wish*-class ships have no Category 10 staterooms.

- **CATEGORY 11** *(see page 89)*

Magic **class:** There are no split baths—standard in all other categories—in the *Magic*-class Category 11 staterooms. While I highly recommend split baths for families, some people prefer having one large bathroom instead of two smaller ones. Additionally, on the *Magic*-class ships, some 11Bs located on Decks 5 and 6 Forward have a **"sideways" layout.** These staterooms are pretty popular because they feel a bit roomier than the typical Inside Stateroom layout.

Dream **class:** Category 11 staterooms on **Deck 2** are surprisingly convenient. I would recommend them.

Wish **class:** Some *Wish*-class staterooms on the starboard side of **Deck 2** have an interesting shape. There are also some, like **7689,** where the entrance is in its own little nook. If you're looking for quiet, those staterooms are good bets.

continued from page 103

- **What is your budget?** If the sky's the limit, then a Verandah Stateroom or Concierge Stateroom will likely appeal to you, if only for the extra square footage. If you're watching your pennies, an Inside Stateroom will leave you more funds for excursions or fine dining.

- **What is the price difference between category types?** On some sailings it can be thousands of dollars, but on other cruises it's minimal (see page 80).

- **How long is your voyage?** You might be able to cope with an Inside Stateroom for a few days, but you might find it oppressive over a week or more. DCL's new South Pacific sailings between Hawaii and Australia in 2024–25 can have *nine or more straight days* at sea. In this case, we'd recommend booking at least an Oceanview Stateroom for your sanity's sake.

- **Where are you sailing?** The scenery on your cruise—Caribbean ports, glaciers in Alaska, fjords in Norway—might influence your choice of an Inside Stateroom versus one with a view. Additionally, consider what it costs to go on port adventures at your destination. Many beach destinations have fun things to do close by that are inexpensive or even free, but on an Alaskan cruise the most appealing excursions—such as helicoptering to a dogsled run—cost hundreds of dollars per person. If you're sticking to a budget but still want to participate in some off-ship activities, you may want to economize on your stateroom.

- **How many people are in your party?** If you're traveling with a large group, you'll probably be splitting up into several staterooms. A family may be able to economize by having one group get a Verandah Stateroom while the other gets an Inside or Oceanview Stateroom, giving you the best of both worlds. If your group is all in one stateroom, then the per-person square footage may be the deciding factor. (See page 100 for more on stateroom selection for larger parties.)

- **Do you have claustrophobia?** If you don't like compact spaces, you may want to avoid Inside Staterooms, particularly those without a virtual porthole.

- **Do you love the ocean?** If so, you may prefer an Oceanview or Verandah Stateroom over an Inside Stateroom.

- **How old are the members of your party?** If you have little ones, you'll likely be spending a good bit of time in your stateroom while they nap or you get them ready for an early bedtime. In this case, you may find that a verandah gives you a more appealing place to chat with your partner, order room service, or read a book than an Inside or Oceanview Stateroom.

- **Is this your first cruise?** If you're a regular cruiser, then you might not need a view or verandah on every trip. If you're a first-timer, depending on your budget and your affinity for cruising, you may be looking for a once-in-a-decade experience on this cruise or an upgraded experience on a trip a year or two from now.

- **Do you want to do everything the ship has to offer, or do you want to just chill in your stateroom?** If your stateroom isn't going to be central to your cruise experience because you know you'll always be out and about meeting characters, watching shows, playing bingo, and singing karaoke, then an Inside Stateroom will likely meet your needs. But if you want to spend your vacation reading novels and doing lots of nothing, then a stateroom with a verandah might be just the thing you need.

- **How many sea days does your sailing include?** Some Disney cruises have none, while others include more than a week of at-sea time. If you're participating in land-based activities every day, then the view from your stateroom might not be that important.

- **Will you be getting off the ship at every port?** This is related to the point above. While most DCL Bahamian cruises stop in Nassau, many guests prefer not to get off the ship there (see page 354). Still, it can be fun to sit on your verandah and watch the hustle and bustle in port.

- **Are you a good sleeper?** A stateroom with no natural light may be the perfect solution for those who have trouble sleeping. It may also be a stateroom where it's hard to get out of bed before early afternoon.

- **Are your kids good sleepers?** Most Verandah Staterooms are configured so the verandah is on what would naturally be the kids' side of the room. You may have visions of enjoying a glass of bubbly on the verandah while your kids are snoozing, but if they're light sleepers, you may not be able to do this without disturbing them. In that case, why pay for a verandah if you won't be able to truly enjoy it?

- **Does your ship offer virtual portholes?** Many (but not all) Inside Staterooms on the *Dream* and *Fantasy* have porthole-shaped video screens that broadcast what you'd be seeing if your stateroom had an actual porthole. The illusion is highly effective—so much so that you may not even notice that it's an illusion after a while. As a bonus for Disney fans, there are often surprises such as Nemo swimming by or Tinker Bell soaring above the sea. Many kids enjoy a virtual porthole more than a real one.

- **Do you want to be on the port or starboard side of the ship?** This will affect your view when the ship is docked in port.

- **Do you need special accommodations?** The need for a specific type of stateroom that can accommodate a medical need or disability could trump all of the above. Accessible staterooms are available at a number of price points; if, however, you need to use a device like a walker inside your stateroom, this will be challenging in most of the smaller staterooms.

- **If you're planning to sail on the *Wish* or *Treasure*, do you strongly prefer that your stateroom be themed to a specific Disney character or movie?** Stateroom theming on the *Wish*, *Treasure*, and *Destiny* varies by deck. Options on the *Wish* include ***Cinderella, Frozen, Little Mermaid, The Princess and*** *the Frog, Moana, Sleeping Beauty,* and *Tangled* theming. On the *Treasure,* staterooms are themed to **Aladdin, Encanto, EPCOT, Finding Nemo, The Jungle Book, The Lion King, Pocahontas,** and **Up.** Themes on the *Destiny* will be **Big Hero 6, Brave, Fantasia, Hercules, The Incredibles, Mulan,** and **Raya and the Last Dragon.** (*Note:* Disney doesn't publish a map or a list of specific staterooms with specific themes, but you can call DCL or have your travel agent check.)

In addition to the macro decisions about your stateroom selection, here are some specifics to consider:

- Don't book connecting staterooms unless you absolutely need to, although this might be a challenge on the newer ships, which have many more connecting staterooms than the classic ships. The connecting doors are less soundproof than an actual wall.

- Rooms next to or across the hall from laundry rooms might be noisy because of the washers and dryers and the conversation among guests.

- Rooms directly above the theaters will be noisy during the evenings. We stayed in a stateroom directly above the Walt Disney Theatre on the *Magic* and heard music from the shows loud and clear.

- Some guests find that staterooms directly below the pool decks (Deck 10 Midship on the *Dream, Fantasy, Wish, Treasure,* and *Destiny* and Deck 8 Midship on the *Magic* and *Wonder*) are noisy during the day, with guests dragging deck chairs overhead.

- Mechanical noise from elevators is typically minimal, but there will be more foot traffic the closer you are to one.

- Guests with mobility issues may find it helpful to be close to an elevator; those hallways are long and narrow.

- Staterooms at the far-aft end of the ship will have the most panoramic ocean views. If staring at the sea is your priority, these staterooms are the ones to get. However, some guests find the far-aft staterooms on Deck 10 of the *Dream* and *Fantasy* (10158–10658) too noisy—the verandahs are directly below the outdoor seating for the Cabanas buffet. You'll also feel a good amount of ship vibrations back there when docking, especially on the *Fantasy.*

- The starboard side of your ship will face the island if you're docked at Castaway Cay, and the port side will usually face the island if you are visiting Lookout Cay. If you have a stateroom with a view, consider whether you'd prefer to gaze at the island or the water.

- Stateroom location may affect your comfort if you're prone to motion sickness.

- Some staterooms come pre-configured with enhanced communication for deaf and hard-of-hearing guests.

- Besides the stated stateroom capacity, consider the number of separate beds. Will the members of your party be comfortable sleeping together on the number of beds in the stateroom?

If particular features are important to you, then you may find it helpful to work with a DCL-savvy travel agent, who is likely well versed in the distinct characteristics of specific staterooms.

PART 5

The BOOKING PROCESS

KEY QUESTIONS ANSWERED IN THIS CHAPTER

- How do I book my cruise? *(see below)*
- Should I purchase travel insurance? *(see page 113)*
- What documents do I need to board a cruise? *(see page 115)*

PREP WORK

GETTING STARTED

ONCE YOU'VE SETTLED on a ship, an itinerary, and dates, it's time to book your trip. You have three ways to do this: Use the DCL website, call DCL at ☎ 800-951-3532, or use a travel agent.

Most guests will be happier if they book online or use a travel agent. The main advantage of booking online is that you can usually do it immediately. If you've booked a cruise before, have easy access to each traveler's information, don't have questions about the ship or itinerary, and want instant gratification, this may be your best option.

The main advantages of using a travel agent are that they can save you time by doing most of the tedious legwork for you, they bring product expertise, and they may also offer a discount in the form of onboard credit—money you can use to pay for items like adult beverages, port excursions, or photo services. Many agents have booked dozens, if not hundreds, of cruises and have a single-page form for you to fill out, where you provide your preferences for everything from what time you prefer to board the ship to when you prefer to eat.

Some travel agencies will also rebook your cruise automatically if a lower fare becomes available, and occasionally a travel agent might also be able to save you money because they have access to group space for a particular cruise. (You're not required to participate in group activities, but you get the price advantage of the group booking.) Finally, a seasoned travel agent may be able to help you find staterooms with special characteristics, such as an oversize verandah, a particular view, or one of the few "secret suites" on the *Wish*-class ships (see page 105).

When it comes to booking by phone or through big-box companies like Costco, we've heard countless reports of being put on hold for several hours. If you have questions that require a human response, you may want to have a travel agent handle them.

USING THE DISNEY CRUISE LINE WEBSITE TO FIND THE RIGHT CRUISE

IN ADDITION TO abundant information about the ships, onboard amenities, and port adventures, **disneycruise.disney.go.com** makes it easy to understand and compare prices for different sailings, party sizes, stateroom configurations, and more. By playing around with filter criteria, you can narrow down which cruises suit your budget, schedule, and destination preferences. Get started by clicking "Plan a Cruise" at the top of the homepage; then choose "Find a Cruise" from the pulldown menu. The options on the next page are as follows:

LEAVING (DATE) If you already know the month when you want to cruise, then narrowing down your search by date is a good first step because it eliminates a lot of unnecessary scrolling through lists that don't fit your needs.

SAILING TO Further narrow your search by checking the box(es) only for places you know you'd like to visit.

DEPARTING FROM If you strongly prefer a particular departure port (say, one near your home), select it here.

GUESTS The default search is for two adults. To get accurate pricing, adjust the party size and composition (children and adults) to reflect your travel group. You can also search for accessible staterooms or add additional staterooms for your party. Pay particular attention to "Add Another Stateroom" if you're traveling with more than two people—it could be worth your while to split your party between two staterooms. The price of two smaller staterooms is often equivalent to that of one larger stateroom, and you get an extra bathroom and more square footage. (See Part 4 for more on staterooms.)

MORE FILTERS This tab asks you for your preferences regarding the number of nights you want to sail, the ship you want to travel on, and whether you want to limit your search to voyages with themed events such as Marvel Day at Sea (see page 66). Again, check the boxes here according to your preferences. If you have a young child who's obsessed with Rapunzel, for example, you might want to choose the *Magic*, which has a *Tangled* stage show and a *Tangled*-themed restaurant. Or you might want to restrict your search to sailings on Disney's new *Wish*-class ships.

SPECIAL OFFERS Just below the "View Dates" button is a "Show Special Offers" button. Select any you might be interested in to see if there are any available dates.

DEPOSIT TERMS AND CANCELLATION POLICIES

MOST DISNEY CRUISE RESERVATIONS require a deposit equal to 20% of the cruise's price (before tax) for each passenger on a given reservation. Some DCL promotions, such as booking a follow-up cruise while on your current cruise (see "Repeat Cruiser Savings," page 30), require only a 10% deposit.

Before booking *any* cruise—on DCL or otherwise—make sure you understand the current cancellation policies and recheck them periodically before you sail. To do this, check the **DCL Terms and Conditions** page (theugseries.com/dcl-terms1), search for "cancellation" on the DCL website, and carefully read the **DCL Cruise Contract** (theugseries .com/cruise-contract). Note that slightly different terms and conditions apply based on your home country.

At press time, the cancellation policies were:

DCL CANCELLATION POLICIES	
IF YOU CANCEL	**THE FEE IS**
STANDARD: 1–5 NIGHTS *Full payment is required 90 days before sailing.*	
89–45 days before sailing	Deposit per guest
44–30 days before sailing	50% of vacation price per guest
29–15 days before sailing	75% of vacation price per guest
14 days or fewer before sailing	100% of vacation price per guest
STANDARD: 6 OR MORE NIGHTS *Full payment is required 120 days before sailing.*	
119–56 days before sailing	Deposit per guest
55–30 days before sailing	50% of vacation price per guest
29–15 days before sailing	75% of vacation price per guest
14 days or fewer before sailing	100% of vacation price per guest
CONCIERGE *Full payment is required 120 days before sailing (for trips of 1–5 nights) or 150 days before sailing (for trips of 6 or more nights).*	
90 days or more before sailing	Deposit per guest
89–56 days before sailing	50% of vacation price per guest
55–30 days before sailing	75% of vacation price per guest
29 days or fewer before sailing	100% of vacation price per guest

Cruises booked with a **restricted-rate** discount code (see page 100) are always nonrefundable.

Airfare and precruise hotels booked through Disney have their own cancellation policies. Check with DCL or your travel agent.

AGE REQUIREMENTS FOR BOOKING

DCL ALLOWS ADULTS age 18 and up to travel unaccompanied and book their own staterooms. However, **guests age 17 and younger must be booked into a stateroom with an adult age 21 or older.**

DCL's age requirement affords under-21 married couples, young military personnel, and most college students the ability to travel unchaperoned and unencumbered by extra paperwork.

Nevertheless, any group that includes minors needs to consider the implications of the age requirement when planning a Disney cruise. For example, a single parent who wants to travel with four minor children would have to book at least a Verandah Stateroom on the *Magic* or *Wonder*. That's often more expensive than booking two individual Inside or Oceanview Staterooms, but it's the only option in this case because DCL doesn't allow minors to be booked into a different stateroom, even if the staterooms are connected by an inside door.

For couples who want to book more than one stateroom but are traveling with just one minor child, Disney requires that one parent be booked into a stateroom with the child. Further, if the parent who is registered in a different stateroom wants to leave the ship with the child, that parent must first sign a waiver at the Guest Services desk.

A few situations would be a no-go or would need to be altered to meet the age requirement:

- Adults ages 18–20 who want to travel with younger siblings but without their parents
- Families traveling with an under-21 nanny whom they wish to book in the same stateroom as the child
- Guests wanting to travel with minors who aren't in their immediate family—say, a grandchild or a child's friend (whom you might not want sleeping in the same stateroom as you)

TRAVEL PROTECTION

WE RECOMMENDED TRAVEL INSURANCE for all Disney Cruise Line guests. There are risks associated with any kind of travel, but cruises are unique because they are all-or-nothing propositions. If your flight to Orlando is delayed and you miss the first day of your weeklong Disney World vacation, you'll be disappointed, but you'll still be able to have a great time for six of the seven days. Not so with a cruise: If your flight is delayed and you miss boarding the ship, your entire vacation is over before it starts.

Similarly, medical or weather issues that might be minor annoyances on land can completely derail a cruise. Tammy's flight to Vancouver was once delayed due to high winds at her departure airport, and she and her family missed their connection. The earliest they could arrive was 11 a.m. the next day. They would have missed their vacation had they not been flying in the day before the cruise. Her travel insurance paid for the unexpected hotel night.

The cruise lines themselves are becoming more stringent—and understandably so—about enforcing health and safety precautions, meaning cruisers now face a greater-than-ever chance of being denied boarding for illnesses of *any* sort. Illnesses on board can also happen, and medical care on board or in a foreign country can cost a fortune. Tammy's healthy mom contracted pneumonia on day 2 of a 12-night Mediterranean cruise, and her medical bills were several thousand dollars. If the ship's medical staff felt they couldn't safely treat her, she would have had to stay in a hospital in a port, and her medical and travel bills would have skyrocketed. Fortunately, her travel insurance paid her medical bills. For all these reasons, we strongly recommend buying trip insurance for your cruise, even if you wouldn't normally buy it for a land-based vacation.

US residents traveling internationally should contact their health insurance providers to check their coverage for emergencies outside the country. DCL offers its own trip insurance, called the **Vacation Protection Plan** (**VPP**). If you'd like to buy it, you must do so before you pay in full for your vacation or, if you are sailing Concierge, at the time of deposit (see theugseries.com/dcl-vpp for details). Note that many other reputable companies offer travel insurance at a variety of price points and coverage levels.

unofficial **TIP**
Some countries require travel insurance for visitors. If you plan to travel internationally before or after your cruise, check the requirements for these countries at theugseries.com/trav-ins-countries.

Providers reviewed in recent "best of" articles in *Forbes* magazine and at TheWirecutter.com (the *New York Times*'s product review website) include **AIG Travel Guard** (aig.com/travel-guard), **Allianz Global Assistance** (allianztravelinsurance.com), **American Express Travel Insurance** (americanexpress.com), **C&F Travel Insured** (travelinsured.com), **Seven Corners** (sevencorners.com), **Travelex** (travelexinsurance.com), and **Travel Guard** (www.travelguard.com). The websites **InsureMyTrip** (insuremytrip.com), **SquareMouth** (squaremouth.com), and **VisitorsCoverage** (visitorscoverage.com) can help you compare plans from many providers.

If you travel frequently, consider getting annual trip insurance, which provides coverage for multiple trips and is available from many of the aforementioned companies. In addition, find out if you already have some travel coverage through your credit cards, your regular insurance provider, or your employer. In general, when you're researching travel insurance, consider the following:

KINDS OF COVERAGE Plans are available that cover medical issues, with or without coverage for preexisting conditions; evacuation due to political unrest or weather; flight delays or cancellations (plus the cost of meals and/or hotels stemming from these); luggage replacement; trip cancellation due to unexpected events such as family emergencies; and various combinations of the above.

PRICE Trip insurance can be expensive, so compare quotes from different agencies to ensure you're getting the best price for the coverage you need. Disney's insurance does not consider age, which sometimes makes it one of the cheaper options.

TIMING OF PURCHASE Some companies offer discounts if you buy insurance within a week or two of placing a deposit on a trip. Some will cover preexisting conditions if you purchase at the time of your deposit.

REIMBURSEMENT LIMITS If a policy caps your reimbursement, consider whether the maximum amount would be sufficient to cover the cost of your vacation or your medical care in an emergency.

FINE PRINT Make sure you understand *all* the details of the policy you're purchasing, including your deadline for submitting a claim.

CANCEL FOR ANY REASON Cancel-for-any-reason coverage is harder to come by and is expensive. One benefit of DCL's insurance is that it does offer a cancel-for-any-reason option of sorts. If you cancel for any reason that is *not* covered, you will receive a 75% Future Cruise Credit for DCL, to be used within 12 months. We think it's the best thing about DCL's insurance.

How Much Will Travel Insurance Cost?

unofficial **TIP**
MedJet (medjetassist.com) provides insurance specifically for medical evacuation when overseas. Short-term and annual memberships are available.

You can expect to pay 4%–8% of your total prepaid, nonrefundable trip expenses for a travel insurance policy. That range reflects a wide variety of coverage options: You'll find some basic plans that cost even less than 4% of your trip expenses but provide only limited coverage, as well as deluxe plans, costing as much as 12% of your trip, that cover anything and everything you can think of. Reputable insurance companies will offer a brief trial period during which you can review the policy you've selected, then return it for any reason within the trial period for a full refund, minus a small administrative fee.

If you've purchased DCL's VPP trip insurance (see opposite page), you're entitled to 24-7 global assistance during your trip. Services include medical assistance and emergency services. To access this feature, call ☎ 877-303-5909 within the United States and Canada or ☎ 516-342-4594 outside the United States and Canada.

Before your cruise, create a document with critical medical information and share it with others in your travel party. Include contact information for your doctors at home, your medications and their dosages, any allergies (for example, to medication or food), your insurance information, and any past surgeries or major illnesses. If you become incapacitated, having ready access to this information could save your life.

Also, consider installing an app like Life360 or Apple's Find My on the phones of everyone in your party—these can help you locate each other in an emergency.

PASSPORTS *and* TRAVEL DOCUMENTS

EVERYONE IN YOUR PARTY, including babies and children, must present proof of citizenship before boarding the ship. **A passport is your**

simplest, safest bet because it covers all your bases. Depending on the situation, it's either mandatory (see Unofficial Tip below) or good to have but not absolutely necessary.

unofficial **TIP**
You **must** have a passport book (not a passport card) if you're a US citizen flying from the United States to a foreign cruise port, or vice versa.

If you don't have a passport, you may be able to use alternative documentation if (1) you're a US citizen traveling from a US port; (2) you're traveling only within the Western Hemisphere (Canada, the Caribbean, Mexico, or the United States); and (3) you're on a closed-loop cruise—that is, you're embarking and debarking from the same US port on the same ship. According to US Customs and Border Protection (see theugseries.com/cbp-whti), adult cruisers meeting these conditions may present a government-issued photo ID *plus* proof of citizenship. Proof-of-citizenship documents include a state-issued birth certificate (the original; DCL no longer accepts copies), a Consular Report of Birth Abroad, *or* a Certificate of Naturalization.

US citizens under age 16 (or under age 19 if traveling with a school group, religious group, or other organized youth group) only need to present proof of citizenship.

Acceptable alternatives to a passport on a **closed-loop cruise** include the following:

- **A US Passport Card.** This limited-use document lets you enter the United States by land or sea from within the Western Hemisphere. At the time of this writing, a new (non-renewal) card costs $65 for adults age 16 and over, versus $165 for a first-time US Passport book. Expedited processing and shipping may be available for an extra fee.

- **An Enhanced Driver's License (EDL).** An EDL provides proof of both identity and citizenship in addition to certifying you to drive. Currently available only to US citizens in Michigan, Minnesota, New York, Vermont, and Washington, EDLs contain security features such as a radio frequency identification (RFID) chip.

- **A Trusted Traveler Program Card** (NEXUS, SENTRI, or FAST).

We recommend that all members of your party obtain passports, even for a closed-loop cruise. Let's say you're on a port adventure in Nassau and you learn of an urgent family emergency. If you have a passport, you can hop on a plane and be back home within hours. If you don't, you'll first have to go to the US Embassy, apply for an expedited passport, and wait for it to be processed.

Documentation requirements for Canadian citizens are similar: a Canada passport, EDL, or Trusted Traveler Program Card. Citizens of other countries may be required to present a passport or visa to enter a port even if US and Canadian citizens aren't.

As of May 7, 2025, all US citizens flying domestically must present either a **Real ID-compliant** driver's license/state ID card or an alternative, such as a passport, at their airport's Transportation Security Administration (TSA) checkpoint; see dhs.gov/real-id for details.

Converting a noncompliant license to the Real ID version can be a huge hassle—we've heard of waits at the DMV that are even more soul-crushing than those for routine license renewal—so get this done well before your cruise if it includes domestic air travel. **AAA** offers upgrading assistance for its members in Massachusetts, New York, and Rhode Island (see theugseries.com/aaa-real-id).

One particularly confusing issue regarding ID requirements applies to US citizens on DCL Alaskan cruises from Vancouver. The Western Hemisphere Travel Initiative specifies that you can drive from the United States to Vancouver with only an Enhanced Driver's License or a US Passport Card, but you may be required to present a full passport *book* to board the ship in Vancouver, depending on whether you're on a closed-loop cruise, a repositioning cruise, or a back-to-back sailing. Be sure to confirm your exact documentation needs well before your trip. When in doubt, a passport book will always work.

Check the specifics of your sailing when choosing excursions. Again, if you're an American citizen and you're flying to your embarkation point from a non-US port, you'll need a passport to get there. Also, note that some DCL port adventures on Alaskan cruises require a valid passport because you cross into Canada during the trip. Plus, some foreign ports require not only passports but also special visas for guests who plan to explore on their own versus with an approved excursion group or tour guide.

unofficial **TIP**
In most cases, you must book a cruise departing from the United States **at least three days in advance.** We have seen exceptions, however.

Whichever forms of identification you bring, be sure to secure them when traveling, either in your stateroom safe when you're not in port or on your person when you're out and about. Some guidebooks recommend leaving your passport on board at all times, but we've seen too many instances of people being left behind because of a taxi breakdown or other unforeseen mishap on a port adventure. If you have your passport and a credit card, you can fly to the next port to meet the ship if you need to. That beats searching for an embassy, possibly having to wait for it to open after a weekend or holiday, and then paying for and waiting on an expedited replacement.

unofficial **TIP**
We recommend uploading everyone's birth certificates to the cloud. That way, you'll have access to copies if you left them in your stateroom while ashore.

Also be sure to prepare for the unlikely event that your ID is lost or stolen. Make photocopies of your passport or other documents; keep one set of copies in your luggage and another set at home with a trusted friend or relative.

GETTING A PASSPORT US citizens may obtain passports themselves by following the steps at theugseries.com/apply -passport. Passports typically take about six to eight weeks to process. If you need one, plan to get it far in advance of your trip. If you already have one, be sure to check the expiration date to make sure you have time to renew it if needed. You may be able to get a passport more quickly by applying in person at an official passport office. See theug series.com/passport-agencies for locations. Note, however, that there may still be delays even with expedited passports.

While Disney offers no additional passport advice beyond working directly with the U.S. Department of State, many other major cruise lines (including Royal Caribbean, Holland America, and Norwegian) refer guests needing passport assistance to **Visa Central** (☎ 877-535-0688, visacentral.com). This reputable, fee-based service can help with passport processing and offers a one-day turnaround on passport renewals. If you find the application process too complicated to tackle on your own, Visa Central may be worth the cost.

PASSPORT EXPIRATION Many countries (and cruise lines) require your passport to be valid for six months after your cruise. To avoid complications, make sure yours meets that requirement.

EXPEDITING YOUR AIRPORT SECURITY CHECK If you fly at least a couple of times per year, consider registering for **TSA PreCheck** (tsa.gov /precheck). This service can greatly shorten your waits in line and lets you skip removing your shoes and unpacking electronic devices from your carry-ons. Membership costs $85 for five years (renewals are $70 online and $78 in person). In our opinion, it's money well spent.

We are also fans of **Global Entry** (theugseries.com/global-entry), a fee-based adjunct to TSA PreCheck (and includes TSA Precheck) that will reduce the time you spend in line as you reenter the Unites States. Approved travelers use automated kiosks to proceed through US Customs stations at some airports. We have found Global Entry to be a massive time-saver in Vancouver in particular.

The free **CBP Mobile Passport Control App** (theugseries.com/cbp -app) also makes processing more efficient by letting you fill out some of the necessary paperwork ahead of time.

unofficial **TIP**
Join the U.S. Department of State's **Smart Traveler Enrollment Program** (**STEP**) (step.state.gov/step) to get updates on safety conditions abroad and to facilitate contact with US Embassies in an emergency.

If you don't mind tinkering with credit card or mileage points, you may be able to obtain TSA PreCheck and/or Global Entry membership at no cost. While offers vary, there are currently nearly 50 credit card, airline, or hotel loyalty programs that offer credits or reimbursements for TSA PreCheck fees. Other programs let you pay for PreCheck access with points or miles instead of cash. See tsa.gov/precheck/credit-cards-offer.

If you fly often, consider **Clear** (clearme.com), a higher-fee service that provides even faster screening at some airports, letting you skip to the front of the TSA PreCheck line if you have PreCheck or the regular line if you don't. Rates are currently $189 per year, $60 for each additional adult family member, and free for children under age 18 who are flying with an adult member.

Frequent travelers may want to download the **MyTSA** app, which provides estimates of security-line waits at US airports, as well as information about packing rules and ID requirements. Visit tsa.gov/mobile.

EUROPEAN TRAVEL UPDATE Beginning in mid-2025, US citizens visiting Europe, as well as passport-holding citizens of several other nations, will need a **European Travel Information and Authorization System** (**ETIAS**) visa waiver to enter countries in the European Union (EU). For DCL passengers, this includes almost everyone sailing on the *Fantasy* during the summer.

An ETIAS waiver is *not* a tourist visa; rather, it's a prescreening registration for travelers visiting the EU from countries that don't require a visa. It's very similar to the US Electronic System for Travel Authorization, which most EU nationals must obtain to travel to the United States.

Valid for three years, an ETIAS waiver costs €7 (less than $10) for adults and is free for children under age 18. For more information, see schengenvisainfo.com/etias; to apply online, go to etiasvisa.com /etias-form-application.

TRAVELING WITH MINORS

IF YOU'RE AN ADULT age 21 or older traveling with someone else's minor child, DCL requires written permission from the child's parent or legal guardian in addition to proof of the child's citizenship. DCL's **Minor Authorization Form** is available as a PDF at theugseries.com/dcl-minors. Present a signed printout at check-in at the cruise terminal.

If you're cruising outside the United States with your own minor child but without the child's other parent—whether you're a single parent or your spouse/partner couldn't make the trip—US Customs and Border Protection strongly recommends that you also bring along a signed, notarized permission letter in addition to proof of the child's citizenship. (See theugseries.com/cbp-child-travel for details.) Adults traveling with someone else's minor child are advised to do the same in addition to filling out DCL's Minor Authorization Form.

The permission letter isn't legally required, and many cruisers, including Tammy, report that they've never been asked for it. That said, customs reserves the right to investigate situations it deems suspicious, so it's better to be safe than sorry.

The letter should include (1) the child's full name and birth date; (2) both parents' full names, your address, and your phone number; (3) a description of the entire trip (dates, countries, and cruise information); (4) the purpose of the trip; (5) the other parent's original signature, in ink; and (6) the date of the signing.

Don't wait until the last minute to get the letter notarized. Banks and post offices often have notaries on staff, and some will come to you (Google "mobile notaries" in your area). The notary will have to witness the other parent signing the form, so it's best to have the other parent present the form to the notary. DCL doesn't require that the Minor Authorization Form be notarized, but if you're already getting a permission letter notarized, it can't hurt to get this form notarized while you're at it.

Also be aware that other cruise lines may have different requirements for a child traveling with just one parent. Other lines may require parents who do not have the same last name as a child to travel with both a passport and the child's birth certificate as proof of relation. If a child is adopted or in your guardianship, if your child's other parent is deceased, or if you are legally separated or divorced, it never hurts to bring legal documentation of these situations. To be clear, Disney does not require these extra items, but you never know what you might encounter in a foreign country.

If you're traveling with any child who is not your own, even a grandchild, also be sure to have a copy of their medical insurance information, a list of any medical conditions they have, and contact information for the child's medical providers. These items may facilitate care in an emergency.

PAYMENT METHODS *for your* CRUISE

YOU CAN PAY for your initial cruise package in US dollars, British pounds, or euros. The DCL website will display cruise and transportation prices in one of these three currencies, depending on where you access the site. To change currencies, use the selector at the top of the home page, next to the "Sign In" button.

On the DCL website, all other purchases, such as spa services, port adventures, and adult dining, are priced in US dollars. Charges will be billed to your **folio,** or stateroom account.

ADDING FLIGHTS *and* HOTELS

WITH MANY GUESTS FLYING to their embarkation point, airline issues may have a significant impact on your cruise vacation. There have been several times in the last few years when air travel was, well, a mess, with tens of thousands of flights canceled over multiple days. Sometimes the problems were due to weather, but there were also other problems. According to the US Bureau of Transportation Statistics, nearly 20% of flights in the United States are delayed or canceled.

We've said it elsewhere, but it bears repeating multiple times: **Do not plan to fly to your embarkation port on the morning of your cruise departure.** Always give yourself at least one extra day to arrive before your sailing if you are flying to your destination. The ship will not wait for you. Arriving early will add a hotel stay and extra meals to your trip, but consider that a necessary expense.

At the first whiff of imminent air travel problems, you should begin researching alternative arrangements, such as switching carriers or flying to a nearby state and driving part of the way. A good travel agent will be able to help you with this process. You can also make your own life easier by doing the following:

- Booking your air reservations directly with your carrier rather than via a travel aggregator or code-sharing agreement.

- Making sure your party's reservations are linked in the airline's system (so that you're all rerouted on the same itinerary, should that become necessary).

- Packing all necessities (including medications, paperwork, and two changes of clothing per person) in carry-on bags.

- Choosing larger airports that are likely to be put back in service more quickly if there are delays.

- Having your airline's app (and the apps of other airlines that service your destination and nearby airports) downloaded onto your phone or tablet.

- Familiarizing yourself with alternative airports within a few hours' drive of your embarkation point.

We don't usually recommend letting Disney book your flights—it will rarely save you money, not to mention you'll lose control over your flight details. We've been told by both Disney-specialist travel agents and a Disney cast member that the booking agents generally don't pay attention to things like layovers, departure times, airports, the type of plane, or other particulars that can turn a good trip into a logistical headache. You may also find that refunds are more difficult to obtain if you arrange your flight through Disney.

If you're looking for bargains on airfare, your first stop should be a website such as **Expedia, Google Flights, Kayak, Orbitz, Priceline,** or **Travelocity;** many of these sites will also find you discounts on hotels and rental cars. Sites like **Airfare Watchdog** can send you alerts about airfare discounts. That said, if things go sideways with the flight, it can be easier to switch it or get rerouted in a timely manner if you've booked directly with the airline. Before you purchase airfare with one of these websites, see if you can get the same deal directly with the airline.

If you would like to add a hotel to your reservation, Disney has options at every departure port. You will often pay more than if you book directly with the hotel, but it can be worth it for convenience. If you book through Disney, a Disney rep will usually be on-site the day before and/or the day of your sailing who can help with luggage tags, transfers, and more. Disney will also usually pick up your luggage from your room on the morning of the cruise. You can also book Disney transfers to the port from the hotel if you book through Disney. We will book our precruise hotels directly through Disney if the price difference isn't a big one. We discuss more about how to get to the port and where to stay the night before in Part 8.

MANAGING *your* CRUISE ONLINE

ONCE YOU'VE BOOKED your cruise, either directly with Disney or through a travel agent, you'll frequent the "Already Booked" tab at the top of the DCL homepage. The following items appear under this tab:

MY RESERVATIONS This includes all the vital information: dates, stateroom numbers, reservation numbers, members of your party, ports of call, and so on. The **Cruise Details** subtab provides a diagram of where your stateroom is on the ship, as well as your assigned dinner seating and the ability to request a seating-time change. This is also where you'll find information about the **Vacation Protection Plan** (see page 114) and about reserving Disney transportation to or from your port to another destination, such as an airport or Disney hotel. The **My Plans** subtab is a list of the reservations you've made for port adventures, adult dining, spa treatments, and other activities and experiences.

YOUR GUIDE TO UPDATED EXPERIENCES Here you'll find the latest information about health and safety requirements and protocols. There are separate pages for sailings departing from the United States, Canada, Europe, New Zealand, and Australia.

MAKE A PAYMENT Here, not surprisingly, is where you pay for your cruise. If you've booked through a travel agent, you'll get a message here stating that you need to contact your agent to arrange payment.

BOOK/MANAGE CRUISE ACTIVITIES Click here to make reservations for adult dining, port adventures, spa treatments, and so on. You won't be able to book activities until after you've paid in full and your booking window, based on your Castaway Club status, opens (see page 6).

AIR AND GROUND TRANSPORTATION Find information on booking pre- or postcruise air travel and hotel/airport shuttle service through DCL.

ONLINE CHECK-IN This becomes available after you've paid in full *and* your booking window opens (see page 6).

DOWNLOAD THE NAVIGATOR APP Here you'll find download links to the DCL Navigator app (see page 124). The app is invaluable for communicating with your party, staying abreast of what's going on aboard the ship, and keeping informed about the ports you'll be visiting. It offers much the same functionality as the "Already Booked" section of the website, allowing you to manage the details of your cruise, including making payments and booking activities.

ONBOARD GIFTS Buy flowers, gift baskets, and other goodies and have them delivered to your stateroom (see page 153).

PHOTOGRAPHY This page provides information about photo purchasing opportunities (see page 271).

GETTING TO THE PORT Click on this for GPS addresses and driving directions to all DCL embarkation ports. (See pages 175–177 for individual port instructions.)

TRAVEL DOCUMENTATION This outlines the citizenship documentation, passports, and/or visas required for each DCL embarkation location.

PACKING CHECKLIST Here you'll find basic suggestions for various DCL destinations. (See page 137 for more packing tips.)

SPECIAL REQUESTS This section encompasses **Table Requests, Dietary Preferences, Celebrations,** and **Child Amenities** (all detailed below). You may select only one of these online, though we've heard of guests calling DCL to note preferences for more than one. Also note that you are not required to make any of these requests.

TABLE REQUESTS Options include the following:

- **Near a window.** Make this selection if you enjoy looking at the sea during dinner or find that being near a window helps with motion sickness. (Note that not all dining rooms have windows.)

- **In a quieter location.** Select this option if you prefer quiet conversation with your companions.

- **Near a screen for entertainment.** Several of the DCL dining rooms include large video screens that are part of the dinner entertainment. These include **Worlds of Marvel** on the *Wish* and *Treasure* and **Animator's Palate** on the *Magic, Wonder, Dream,* and *Fantasy.* Select this option if you want to have a good view of the screens. Pay particular attention to this option if you're sailing on the *Dream* or *Fantasy.* The Animator's Palate show on the *Dream* has an interactive element in which an animated Crush (from *Finding Nemo*) speaks with guests at dinner. You are unlikely to interact with Crush if you're not seated near a screen.

- **At a private table.** DCL sometimes seats unrelated parties at the same table. This is particularly common if you're sailing alone or with a party of two, three, or four. If you prefer not to dine with strangers, select this option.

- **Near the center of the dining room.** Choose this option if you want to be in the middle of the action. This choice is particularly important if you're sailing on the *Wish.* The dinner show at **Arendelle: A *Frozen* Dining Adventure** is much harder to see and enjoy from the far corners of the dining room. Other restaurants where this might be important are **Rapunzel's Royal Table** on the *Magic* and **Tiana's Place** on the *Wonder.*

Additionally, you may indicate here whether you'll need a booster seat or high chair at your table.

DIETARY PREFERENCES DCL can accommodate guests with many allergies, as well as those needing lactose-free, vegetarian, vegan, low-fat, low-sodium, halal, or kosher meals. If you need any of these dietary modifications, you should check the appropriate box on the Special Requests section *and* complete the Food Allergy section of the DCL Request Special Services form (see page 163).

CELEBRATIONS Make a selection here if you're celebrating an anniversary, an engagement, a honeymoon, a birthday, a reunion, a graduation, or a retirement. If you're celebrating something else (like beating cancer or getting a new job), you or your travel agent can call to note this in your file. You are welcome to purchase gifts or stateroom decor to enhance your celebration, but be aware that DCL does not allow open flames on board (they're a safety hazard), so you won't be able to have candles on your cake.

CHILD AMENITIES This section allows you to tell DCL if you'll need a crib or bed rails for a child staying in your stateroom. There are a limited number of these items on each ship, so be sure to let Disney know in advance if you need them.

The DISNEY CRUISE LINE APP

A SMARTPHONE AND the **DCL Navigator app** have become essential to life on board. Unless you purchase a Wi-Fi package, communicating with family and friends on different parts of the ship requires the use of this free app. Your dining rotation and the ship's activity schedule are listed on it, as are reservations and instructions for port excursions. Onboard booking of some activities is done via the app. And so on.

There are some workarounds. You could stop by Guest Services to ask about your dining rotation. The activity schedule is listed on your stateroom TV, or you could beg Guest Services for a printout (we've had about 50/50 luck with this). But in general, you'll have a much smoother experience if you have access to a smartphone or tablet.

The app consists of five main categories: dining information (including menus); deck plans (maps showing each floor of the ship); hours for various services (shops, gym, and so on); activity schedules; debarkation information (what you need to do at the end of your vacation); and onboard chat. It works through the ships' onboard Wi-Fi, so you can keep your device in airplane mode while using it; you won't be charged for Wi-Fi if you're using it only with the app. To avoid unnecessary data charges, however, be sure to download the app to all of your family's mobile devices before you depart.

Onboard chat, our favorite feature, allows you to text other passengers at no charge over Wi-Fi. It's as easy and intuitive to use as any other messaging app. Choose from DCL-specific emojis featuring Disney, Marvel, and *Star Wars* characters to spice up your messages. Guest Services will also send reminders and informational messages through this feature.

unofficial **TIP**
When using the chat feature, make sure to turn notifications on. Be aware that the time stamps in the chat are not always accurate.

Complete menus are available for every restaurant on the ship, usually several days in advance. Of course, you could wait until you sit down at your table to see what's cooking, but in scenarios such as those below, it helps to know what's being served ahead of time:

1. If you or others in your party are picky eaters and the dinner menu on a particular night is a hard pass, you can adjust your dining plans accordingly.

2. If, on the other hand, your assigned dining room will be serving something you really like on a night when you have reservations at one of the adult-dining restaurants, you can try rebooking those for another night.

3. If you see something delish on the menu of a different dining room for the same night, you can sometimes have it brought to your dining room. (Yes, you can order anything served at any of the three main dining rooms—not just the one you're assigned to!) *Note:* This is more difficult on the *Wish*-class ships.

Other nice features of the app include the ability to mark favorites to remind you when your favorite activities are starting, plus real-time updates to the ship's schedule. It's also helpful to be able to look ahead to see if a favorite activity will be repeated, so you can plan accordingly.

PRECRUISE FEATURES In addition to keeping you in the loop during your cruise, the app functions much like the DCL website does for pre-trip planning. You can link existing reservations, track your cruise countdown, change your stateroom, make payments on your cruise, and complete online check-in. You can also modify your dinner seatings, make special dining requests, add Disney's trip insurance, add ground transportation, and access details about your air transportation. (*Note:* Anything that involves a payment will not be available if you've booked your cruise through a travel agent.)

MAKING CHANGES *to* *your* RESERVATION

GETTING THE BEST RATE for your cruise often means booking more than a year in advance (see "Saving Money," page 20). But a lot can change in a year, including little things (school and work schedules) and big things (pregnancy, marriage, divorce). Sometimes these changes mean you have to cancel the cruise (see page 112 for more on how to do that), but at other times you'll still want to go on the cruise but travel with different people.

Don't worry: DCL lets you change the names on a reservation until close to sailing time, assuming one of the originally booked guests remains on the reservation. Tammy's husband has a much harder time getting away than she does, so while she often adds him as the second guest on a reservation when booking, more often than not she's switching him out for her daughter or a friend at some point. There's a fee for a name change within 45 days, but otherwise it's not a problem.

You may also make changes to the number of guests in your stateroom until your paid-in-full date. If you're unsure about exactly which friends or family members you'll be traveling with, you should make the reservation for the larger of the possible party sizes (unless you are sailing Concierge, in which case each person's deposit is non-refundable). Here's why: In some cases, your stateroom can physically accommodate more people but DCL won't let you add them to the stateroom; this typically happens when there is a higher-than-average number of guests on your part of the ship. This has to do with lifeboat capacity and other safety issues beyond individual stateroom capacity—it's nothing personal.

Another good reason to book your maximum party size and then pare it down if necessary is that it locks in your booking rate. If you don't lock it in and want to add someone else later, that person will be charged a higher price if the prices have gone up. As long as you make party deletions before your paid-in-full date, and unless you are sailing Concierge, you'll always be able to reduce the number of guests in your stateroom.

BOOKING ONBOARD ACTIVITIES

WHEN YOUR ACTIVITIES WINDOW OPENS

NON-CONCIERGE GUESTS may start booking cruise activities online based on their **Castaway Club** status (see page 6) after they've paid in full. Booking windows open at midnight Eastern time, and many eager guests go online at exactly that moment in an attempt to snap up their preferred activities before all the spots are claimed. If there's a particular activity that you consider a must-do, then plan to be on the DCL website at the appointed hour. If you've booked through a travel agent, they may offer to do this for you.

unofficial **TIP**
Reserve bikes, floats, or snorkels for Castaway Cay or Lookout Cay once you're on the island. DCL has enough of these on hand that they hardly ever run out. You'll have a better idea of whether you need them when you are actually there.

If you've booked a Concierge Stateroom, you or your travel agent can email your activity requests to the DCL shoreside Concierge 130 days before you sail. Activities are automatically added to your account at the 123-day mark, and the shoreside Concierge team may contact you beforehand to clarify your requests. Whether you're a Concierge guest or a Pearl Castaway Club member, we recommend first trying for **cabana reservations** on Castaway Cay or Lookout Cay. We also recommend booking the following as early as possible:

- **Adult-dining reservations,** as well as **spa reservations,** on sea days
- **Nursery reservations** during dinnertimes
- **Bibbidi Bobbidi Boutique** appointments
- **Port adventures** to major tourist sites on European cruises

If you are interested in meeting several princesses at once, you can also book the **Royal Gathering** 30 days before you sail. The Royal Gathering is a meet and greet with five princesses: one line, one

WHEN YOUR BOOKING WINDOW OPENS FOR ONLINE CHECK-IN
Concierge guests: 40 days before sailing
Pearl Castaway Club members: 40 days before sailing
Platinum Castaway Club members: 38 days before sailing
Gold Castaway Club members: 35 days before sailing
Silver Castaway Club members: 33 days before sailing
First-Time Guests: 30 days before sailing
All guests must check in **at least 3 days** before sailing.

meetup with each princess. We aren't sure why Disney does this booking separately from everything else.

If you can't get what you want on the first try, keep checking back, both online before your trip and at the Guest Services desk once on board—often there are cancellations.

ONLINE CHECK-IN

ONLINE CHECK-IN opens according to your Castaway Club status or stateroom level (see table above). Many guests choose to complete their online check-in at the exact moment it opens, which can result in site crashes and slow upload speeds, although this has been somewhat alleviated by the return to staggered check-in dates. The advantage to being among the first to check in for your sailing is that you may have the opportunity to snag an earlier port-arrival time (see page 186). If early arrival is not important to you, then save yourself a headache and wait until later in the day to check in. You'll need to provide the following for each guest:

- Photos of your proof-of-citizenship documents
- Headshot-type photos of all members of your party
- Your contact information
- Emergency contact information
- Payment method for onboard spending
- Travel plans to and from the port
- Acceptance of the cruise contract

*un*official **TIP**
Be sure to bring all your travel documents with you to the port and upload them to the DCL website.

PHOTOS OF PROOF-OF-CITIZENSHIP DOCUMENTS For most people, this will be an image of the passport pages that include your signature, photo, legal name, and passport number. Other folks on closed-loop cruises from the United States may be able to use alternate documentation (see page 115). See the DCL website for the complete list of acceptable citizenship documentation (theugseries.com/dcl-travels-docs).

Note: Your required identification documents may vary depending on your citizenship and the destinations you're visiting. **It is your**

responsibility to check with your travel agent, government agency, embassy, or consulate to ensure you have the proper documentation to board the ship and enter each of the countries on your cruise. US travelers can visit the **Department of State**'s travel resources website (state .gov/travelers) or call the **National Passport Center** at ☎ 877-4-USA-PPT (877-487-2778) for more information.

Whichever documents you're using, the photos/scans of these items should be in focus and free of shadows, glare, and other distractions. Don't be surprised if your documents are rejected at first. It happens a decent percentage of the time. If your documents are valid and the photo is clear and glare-free, also don't be surprised if it's accepted the second time.

PHOTOS OF EVERYONE IN YOUR PARTY, including children. These must be head-and-shoulders color pictures with no filters, one person per photo, with a neutral background. You cannot wear a hat, sunglasses, or any glasses that obscure your eyes. You cannot use the same picture that is on your passport. If you follow these guidelines, you'll find that a selfie or a child's school photo often works.

Your check-in photo is used by the crew as identification while you're on board and when you exit and enter the ship during port stops. Your picture doesn't need to be perfect or glamorous; it just needs to allow the crew to accurately identify you. Simpler is better.

We've had some rare instances where the system does not accept clear documents or headshots, no matter how many times we submit them. Don't stress about it—just bring them to the port with you.

EMERGENCY CONTACT INFORMATION The odds of your emergency person being contacted are extremely small. Pick any competent close friend or family member who's not traveling with you.

TRAVEL PLANS TO/FROM THE PORT If you say you're flying to or from your cruise port, DCL will ask for details such as your flight number and arrival times. If you don't have this information handy or haven't made reservations yet, just choose "no"; you can (and should) update this section later.

PORT-ARRIVAL TIME Concierge guests and Pearl Castaway Club members may arrive anytime; everyone else must select a time. Typically, options are available in 15-minute increments beginning at about 10:30 a.m. and ending at about 3:30 p.m., but there are variations depending on the port and itinerary. Most guests will select the earliest time available, but there may be circumstances where you'd prefer to have a later arrival window—perhaps if you have a work call you must complete before boarding or if you want your children to nap before heading to the port.

YOUTH ACTIVITY REGISTRATION If you have guests in your party under age 18, you'll have an additional section to register them for the kids' clubs. Don't let this part slow you down. You can skip it for now and register them when you're at the port or aboard the ship.

THE CRUISE CONTRACT The cruise contract is the official document that outlines the rights and responsibilities, both yours and DCL's, regarding your cruise. There are different versions for cruises in different locations. You'll have the opportunity to print the contract or have an electronic version emailed to you. There's a lot of technical, legal info in the contract, but it makes sense to give it a read, particularly if you're a first-time guest or haven't sailed in many years. **To complete check-in, you must scroll to the bottom of the contract and accept it.**

You'll know you're finished with online check-in when you are issued a port-arrival form. You can download this immediately or have it emailed to you. The form will include your arrival time and ship-boarding group number, along with QR codes for your party members. **You will need this form at the port,** so be sure to bring it with you (both print and electronic versions are accepted). We like to screenshot the QR code and keep it handy on our phones.

Your check-in status will likely remain as "pending" even after you've been issued an arrival form. DCL uses humans to review all identification documents and photos—this takes time, often a few weeks. You will receive an email notification when your documents have been successfully reviewed.

PART 6

PREPARING *for* LIFE ON BOARD

KEY QUESTIONS ANSWERED IN THIS CHAPTER

- How do I pay for things on board and in port? *(see below)*
- What is the Wi-Fi service like? *(see page 134)*
- What should I pack? *(see page 137)*
- How much can I expect to spend on gratuities? *(see page 144)*

PAYING *for* THINGS ON BOARD *and* IN PORT

PAYMENT METHODS ACCEPTED on DCL ships are cash (as detailed in the next paragraph), American Express (credit cards and Travelers Cheques in US dollars), Discover, JCB, MasterCard, and Visa. They also accept Disney gift cards, Disney Rewards Dollars (available to Disney Chase Visa holders), and Disney Dollars (which were officially discontinued in 2016 but are still redeemable). When you complete online check-in (see page 127), you'll choose your preferred method of paying for incidentals on the ship: cash or credit card.

unofficial **TIP**
If you're traveling in the same stateroom with friends, you can arrange to have your respective onboard charges go to your individual credit cards or other payment methods. Arrange this during online check-in or at Guest Services at the beginning of your trip.

If you prefer cash, note that you can't use it to pay directly for beverages, spa or salon services, photos, laundry, or retail purchases. You'll first need to stop by the Guest Services desk to set up a **cash account**—you'll use this to fund onboard charges made with your Key to the World (KTTW) Card or DisneyBand+, which functions somewhat like a credit card on the ship (see page 152).

With a cash account, you'll be asked to sign an agreement that lets you charge up to a specific amount on your KTTW Card or Disney-Band+ before you can make additional charges. For a three-night sailing, you'll likely hit a $300 limit before being asked to deposit more cash into your account. You can also top up your account using Disney gift cards. But even if you'll be using a credit card to fund your folio and pay for stuff in port, you'll still want to keep some cash on hand for gratuity envelopes or on-the-spot tipping (for things like luggage assistance, port excursions, and room service). You can cash checks and get change from Guest Services; you can also use other credit cards on board.

Be aware that Disney ships have no ATMs, but you can sometimes exchange small amounts of money (bills only, not coins) at the Guest Services desk, at prevailing exchange rates. DCL takes no commission on these transactions.

MAKING PURCHASES ABROAD

US DOLLARS ARE WIDELY ACCEPTED in most of the **Caribbean** and the **Bahamas,** and most prices are quoted in dollars. Credit cards from US-based banks are also accepted at many shops and stores, but don't count on smaller stores, bodegas, markets, and taxis taking them.

> *unofficial* **TIP**
> When using a credit card abroad, you will often be asked if you would like to pay in US dollars or the local currency. Always choose the **local currency.** There are usually hefty fees if you choose dollars.

The US dollar is unofficially accepted by many markets, bodegas, and taxis throughout **Mexico,** but you'll rarely get a good deal that way. You'll probably be offered a simple exchange rate of 10 pesos per dollar, whereas at press time the actual exchange rate was about 18 pesos per dollar, a significant difference.

Not all countries in **Europe** use the euro as legal tender. DCL European ports that don't use it include those in **Denmark, Iceland, Norway,** the **United Kingdom.** In the **British Isles,** the UK (including Northern Ireland) uses pounds, but the Republic of Ireland uses euros.

If you're traveling to **Canada, Europe,** or **Mexico,** you have a few options for obtaining the appropriate currency:

- **Have your bank convert your US dollars before you leave home.** Many banks will do this at a reasonable exchange rate; some charge a small fee. Give your bank about a week to obtain the currency you need because many branches don't keep euros, pesos, or Canadian dollars on hand. Your bank will also likely convert any unspent currency back to dollars when you return.

- **Use a local bank ATM.** If you are traveling in Europe and are not sure how much cash to bring along, you can usually get a fair exchange rate by withdrawing money at a local cash machine. Visa's website has a handy worldwide ATM locator (visa.com/atmlocator), and in our experience there are usually many more ATMs available than those listed online. Keep in mind that the bank may add a withdrawal fee and a foreign-transaction fee, so it's better to make a few large withdrawals than lots of small ones. If you plan to use ATMs abroad, be sure to review **"The Overseas Traveler's Guide to ATM Skimmers & Fraud,"** published by the U.S. Department of State. Download a PDF of this document at theugseries.com/atm-skimmers.

- **Exchange traveler's checks for local currency when you debark.** Traveler's checks are safer than cash because they can be replaced if lost or stolen. The downside is that converting them to local currency takes more time than using an ATM or obtaining local currency before you leave home. Personally, we use credit cards with no foreign-transaction fees as much as possible and get cash from local ATMs when necessary.

If you want to convert traveler's checks to cash, do it at a reputable local bank—*not* a currency-exchange stand—and do the math yourself on-site to verify you're getting the correct exchange rate. We've heard from readers who were promised one rate but got another (lower) one when the conversion was done.

AVOIDING THE INCONVENIENCE OF LOST OR STOLEN CARDS

HAVING A CREDIT CARD LOST or stolen is an annoyance at any time, but it can be particularly upsetting when you're traveling and relying on your card for food and lodging or for paying off your onboard bingo and bar bills. We've had to cancel cards while on vacation more than once due to suspected identity theft. Replacing a compromised card on the road (or in the middle of the ocean) is much more complicated and stressful than simply having a new card delivered to your home or office. For this reason, we strongly suggest that you or members of your party travel with at least two kinds of credit and/or debit cards, with enough access to funds to pay for several days of your trip. Keep one card with you and the other tucked in your stateroom or hotel-room safe.

unofficial TIP

To prevent any sudden stops on your accounts, let your bank and credit card companies know you're traveling abroad before you leave home.

DISNEY VISA CARD DISCOUNTS

DCL CRUISERS WHO USE a Disney Visa card to fund onboard purchases are entitled to various discounts on the ship; register your card during online check-in or at the cruise terminal. Your Key to the World Card will then indicate that you're eligible for discounts such as 10% off select photo packages, 10% off most merchandise purchases over $50, 10% off some Castaway Cay rentals, and 20% off some spa treatments. Offers are subject to change, and they can't be combined with other discounts. For more information, see disneyrewards.com /vacation-perks/disney-cruise-line-savings.

HEALTH CONCERNS

MOTION SICKNESS

THE DISNEY SHIPS are large vessels with sophisticated stabilizers and other technology that keep motion to a minimum, and the navigation staff does as much as possible to minimize the impact of weather on ship motion. Often, you'll feel no different on the ship than you would if you were strolling across your own front yard; nonetheless, there may be times when you feel the motion of the ocean. Depending on your level of sensitivity, the ship's route, the conditions at sea, and other factors, your perception of this situation might range from mild amusement to abject misery.

If you know you're prone to motion sickness in other situations (such as on long car rides and roller coasters), speak to a healthcare provider before you sail. A variety of remedies are available, including:

- **Acupressure tools** (such as Seabands)
- **Electrical-stimulation tools** (such as ReliefBands)
- **Ginger supplements**
- **Over-the-counter medicines** such as Bonine, Dramamine (available in regular and nondrowsy versions), or Emetrol
- **Motion-sickness eyeglasses** (such as Seetroën)
- **Peppermint capsules** (such as IBgard) or peppermint tea
- **Probiotic capsules**
- **Queasy Pops** (drug-free lollipops made with essentials oils and botanicals)
- **Prescription remedies,** such as scopolamine patches (for severe cases)

Regular and children's versions of Dramamine are available for sale in the ships' gift shops, as well as in single-dose form at Guest Services and at the onboard Health Center, but you'll likely save a few dollars if you buy it at home. We're not doctors, but in our experience it can be more effective to stave off motion sickness before it starts rather than waiting until it sets in to treat it. You may have to experiment to find the best solution for you.

Another aspect of motion sickness may be the location of your stateroom. Midship staterooms generally experience the least rocking, followed by aft and then forward staterooms. Lower decks are more stable than high decks. If you're prone to motion sickness, a Deck 2 Midship stateroom may be more comfortable than a Deck 9 Forward stateroom. The exception would be if you find that fresh air helps you; in this case, a midship stateroom with a verandah on Deck 6 might be your best bet.

GASTRIC DISTRESS

WHILE MOTION-SICKNESS MEDICATIONS are sold at the onboard shops, you'll have to head to the ship's Health Center to get remedies for gastric distress, such as Imodium or Pepto-Bismol. DCL wants to reassure guests that they're on top of possible contagions, so if you have unexpected stomach or intestinal issues, do the responsible thing and go to the Health Center. But if you typically experience minor GI upsets in any travel situation and know that you don't need a doctor, bring your own over-the-counter meds.

unofficial **TIP**
News of a guest's GI distress will result in a report to the onboard medical staff and a likely 24-hour quarantine.

As with motion sickness, preventing "traveler's tummy" is preferable to fighting it once it has started. Here are a few suggestions:

- **Take it easy on your first day aboard.** If you traveled from home the same day you boarded the ship, chances are you got up several hours before normal, packed yourself onto a plane or into a car, may have skipped breakfast, and headed to the cruise terminal. What are you going to do first? Start stuffing your face with the all-inclusive food, of course! It's great to start your cruise off with a bang, but remember that you can always get more food if you're still hungry later.

- **Stay hydrated.** Carry a water bottle and keep it filled throughout the day. Then refill it at night and keep it in your stateroom's beverage chiller for morning.
- **Take a walk.** Stretch your legs on the outside decks and enjoy the sea air.
- **Take an antacid.** Tums and Zantac are typically stocked on board, or you can bring your own.
- **Lay off the soda if it doesn't help, or keep it up if it does.** Free or not, if bubbly beverages aren't your norm at home and make you feel worse on the high seas, don't drink them. On the other hand, Tammy lives on Coke Zero, and going off it on a cruise would be horrendous for all involved. You know yourself; make good choices.
- **Pack some loose-fitting clothes.** Bring along at least one dinner-appropriate outfit that will fit no matter what's going on in your gut. Maybe that's a caftan or pants with a drawstring or elastic waistband.
- **Make safer choices in port.** Stick with bottled water and cooked foods. (Drinking from a water fountain in Mexico is playing with fire.) Additionally, if you're prone to motion sickness or GI issues, avoid port adventures involving things like rides on small boats or Jeep trips down bumpy roads.
- **Wash/sanitize your hands.** The disinfecting wipes handed out every time you come within 20 feet of food are only a start. The best way to avoid major and minor bugs is to wash your hands at every opportunity.
- **Chat with your doctor.** Before your cruise, ask your healthcare provider for advice about prescription and over-the-counter remedies.

PHONES *and* INTERNET

PHONE SERVICE

WHEN IT COMES to staying connected to the outside world during your cruise, first figure out exactly *how* connected you want to be. Do you want to be accessible only in an emergency? Do you want to check email once or twice a day? Do you want to post on social media? Do you want to listen to music or watch videos using Wi-Fi? Are you willing to put in the effort to search for Wi-Fi in port, or do you want to always be connected? *Note:* Connectivity on the ship and in port are two entirely different animals. You may have to set up two separate phone/data plans: one for use at sea and another for use on land.

unofficial **TIP**
The phone number for incoming calls to your stateroom is ☎ **888-322-8732** in the US or **732-335-3281** outside the US; callers must provide a credit card number, along with the name of your ship and your stateroom number.

ON BOARD Every stateroom has a landline-style phone with voicemail that you can use to call other staterooms and onboard services such as Room Service and Guest Relations. You can also use this phone for ship-to-shore calls, but that costs an outrageous $7–$9.50 per minute, charged to your stateroom.

Cellular service is available through DCL's **Cellular@Sea** satellite wireless network. The rates for pay-as-you-go talk, text, and data roaming on board vary depending on your carrier, but they're expensive compared to a standard phone plan. **Turn off roaming** when you don't need it.

Most cellular carriers offer special cruise-ship packages. While these are more expensive than a regular wireless plan, they've become more affordable over the past few years, and they're cheaper than Cellular@Sea. For example, **AT&T** offers two versions:

1. Thirty days of unlimited shipboard and ship-to-shore talk and text, with 1GB of data included, for a $100 one-time charge (data overage is charged at $10 per 100MB).

2. Thirty days of unlimited shipboard and ship-to-shore texting with 100MB of data and an overage charge of $10 for 100MB, with 100 minutes of talk time included, for a $60 one-time charge (talk time over the first 60 minutes is charged at $1 per minute).

unofficial **TIP**
If you have a smartphone you don't use anymore, give it to your kids to use during your cruise. Having access to texting via the Navigator app will greatly increase your ability to communicate with them.

If you have pressing work issues or might need to reach family members while you're at sea, then buying at least the cheaper of these two packages would make sense for your peace of mind. And it would be far less expensive than using your stateroom phone to call from ship to shore.

IN PORT Most wireless carriers in the United States offer international talk, text, and data at rates far more reasonable than paying roaming charges. Note that if you purchase a cruise package from your wireless carrier (see previous page), it won't cover the use of your mobile phone while you're in port—that's an entirely different set of charges.

International plans vary slightly from carrier to carrier, but **AT&T**'s **International Day Pass** is typical: It includes unlimited talk and text in most countries for $10 per day (plus $5 per day for each additional family member on your plan, used on the same day); data availability is based on your regular AT&T plan. **Verizon**'s international plans are similar to AT&T's, while **T-Mobile** includes limited "buckets" of international text and/or data in some standard plans.

Our general advice is to thoroughly research your carrier's options, paying particular attention to differences in rates and coverage aboard the ship versus on land. Again, international phone plans used in port are nearly always a better value than special shipboard plans, and they're definitely a better value than just letting your cell phone roam indiscriminately.

unofficial **TIP**
If you have a tablet or smartwatch that has cell-signal or calling capabilities, make sure you also put these devices in airplane mode while at sea or abroad to avoid incurring unwanted charges.

If you've chosen either a land package or a sea package but not both, pay attention to what type of service your phone is actually using. When the ship's cellular network is on, the display on your device will show **Cellular@Sea, 901-18,** or **NOR-18,** which indicates that you're roaming on Cellular@Sea. When you start roaming on a land carrier, your device will display that carrier's network information.

The easiest ways to keep your wireless bill from spiraling out of control both on and off the ship are as follows:

1. **Keep your phone turned off when you're not using it.** If you don't have the patience or tech savvy to tinker with settings, this is the simplest way to ensure that your phone doesn't connect to a cellular network without your consent, possibly leaving you with a whopper of a phone bill later.

2. **Put your phone in airplane mode.** This shuts off voice, text, and data but still lets you take pictures, listen to downloaded music, and connect to Wi-Fi.

3. **Turn off data when you don't need it.** Look for an icon or button called "Settings" on your phone. From there look for "Cellular," "Wireless and Networks," or the like. Under that, look for "Data Usage," "Cellular Data," "Data Roaming," "Mobile Data," or something similar and **make sure that's unchecked or turned off.** As mentioned above, airplane mode also disables data.

unofficial **TIP**
Wi-fi calling may be available on board if you select DCL's Premium Surf plan (see below).

4. **Use Wi-Fi calling.** The three major US wireless carriers (AT&T, T-Mobile, and Verizon) offer free Wi-Fi calling to the United States from international locations, depending on your plan. You need a phone that supports Wi-Fi calling; check with your carrier for details. The catches, of course, are finding a hotspot with a strong signal and deciding whether you want to pay for Wi-Fi versus scrounging around for free access (try Googling "free Wi-Fi in cruise ports"). If you do find a free hotspot—say, at a restaurant or shop—keep in mind that you may be expected to buy something in return. We've also had good luck with Wi-Fi calling through DCL's internet if we buy the highest package.

Depending on your cruise destination, you may not need to make any changes to your cell service when calling in port. Some US carriers include land-based calling to and from Mexico and Canada in their standard plans; again, confirm with your carrier.

Finally, in Alaska, Hawaii, Puerto Rico, and the US Virgin Islands, you won't need to make changes to your cell service just for a cruise, but your signal quality may fluctuate compared with your service at home. For example, our AT&T service in Skagway, Alaska, was OK, but our travel companion's Verizon service in the same area was spotty at best.

ONBOARD WI-FI

FOR MANY OF US, being offline for the duration of a cruise simply isn't an option. You can sign up for an at-sea wireless plan with your mobile carrier (see page 135), or you can purchase DCL's onboard Wi-Fi. DCL has transitioned to a tiered pricing structure. Packages are available by the day or for the length of your cruise; the prices below are *per device*. Here are the options at press time:

STAY CONNECTED ($16 per day when purchased for the full voyage, $18 when purchased for 24 hours). This package lets you post text and pictures on social media, but you can't browse the web or check email.

BASIC SURF ($24 per day when purchased for the full voyage, $28 when purchased for 24 hours). Adds full web and email access to the Stay Connected package.

PREMIUM SURF ($34 per day when purchased for the full voyage, $42 when purchased for 24 hours). This plan gives you faster speeds than Stay Connected and Basic Surf. Premium Surf lets you do everything you can do using your phone's data plan or your home internet, *except* stream movies and TV shows. (Music and short videos, like Instagram stories and YouTube clips, stream just fine.)

You get a price break of about 20% for multiple devices or for purchasing a length-of-cruise package versus buying by the day. Some guests choose to purchase onboard internet only on sea days (relying on their phone's cell service when in port) or only on the last day of their trip (to check in for their flight or confirm other travel arrangements), while others opt to have service throughout their sailing.

Tammy usually purchases the Premium Surf plan and has had acceptable service with most online activities. Texting, checking email, posting to Instagram and Facebook, and reading most websites were fine, if a little slow. Short videos were fine, but longer videos were usually not.

Scott Sanders of *The Disney Cruise Line Blog* regularly tests Wi-Fi speeds on board. He had this to say:

I often need to connect to a remote computer for work-related purposes. My experience is somewhat of a roller coaster, but it also depends on where the ship is sailing. There are times when it just works, while other times there is significant lag, resulting in simple tasks taking five times as long to complete. Working like this on board is doable with the internet packages, but just be prepared to allocate more time to complete tasks. One other aspect of DCL's internet plans is the ability to use cellular over Wi-Fi, which allows you to make and receive regular phone calls while connected to your data plan. After needing to make a couple of borderline emergency phone calls during the course of a sea day, I am grateful this service was available.

Bottom line: The Wi-Fi is getting better. We've even noticed some of the ships have upgraded to Starlink.

Here are a few tips for using DCL's onboard Wi-Fi:

1. Update your apps (including Navigator) and download movies, music, and such **before** you board the ship. To do otherwise is a waste of time and money.

2. If you have a job-critical need for email, set up an autoresponder on your account so that people will know your replies may be delayed. (You may or may not choose to state that the reason is that you're being slathered with exotic beauty products at the spa.)

3. If you're having technical issues, check with Guest Services.

PACKING

unofficial **TIP**
If you're not absolutely sure you're going to use something, **leave it at home.**

HAVING TRAVELED WITH lots of people over many years, we realize that asking "What do I need to pack?" is like asking "What is art?" Everyone has their own preferences. Some people consider checking a bag akin to a criminal act and may plan to do laundry on the ship, while others would rather pay for an extra suitcase to carry more options. *Bottom line:* It's up to you. We don't judge.

Knowing what to pack is equally important, and the range of opinions regarding packing essentials varies wildly. The DCL website has a helpful page (theugseries.com/dcl-pack-list) with suggestions on appropriate clothing for the ship's restaurants and ports of call, along with a short, reasonable list of incidentals to pack (as well as items you can't bring aboard), and the Centers for Disease Control and Prevention (CDC) has a good list of items to pack for healthy travel (wwwnc.cdc.gov/travel/page/pack-smart).

When you're looking at the packing tips on the DCL website, be sure to consult the list for your destination—not surprisingly, you'll need to pack a bit differently for Alaska than you would for the Caribbean. In addition to general packing lists, consider the port adventures you've selected. For example, if you're touring in Rome, you may want to dress more stylishly than you would if you were just hanging out at the beach. If you're planning to visit churches and cathedrals, you'll want to take a moment to research their dress codes; many do not allow bare shoulders or knees.

unofficial **TIP**
No matter where you're headed, we suggest that every member of your group bring at least one light sweater or jacket that can be worn on board—the dining rooms can get downright chilly.

Beyond that, just type "Disney Cruise Line packing list" into your favorite search engine, and you'll see myriad lists with a wide range of items. Some of these read more like an Amazon jungle–trek prep list (yes, mosquito netting appears on more than one of them). It's useful to read through a couple of lists to see if they mention anything you can't live without.

Our most important packing advice is this: Don't drive yourself crazy trying to pack for every scenario. You're going to be lugging those bags a lot farther than you might think.

You can buy many personal-care products and over-the-counter medicines on board (see page 267). You may not find your preferred brands at the best prices, but if, say, you run out of ibuprofen or you forgot to pack anti-itch cream, you'll appreciate the convenience. Notably, however, remedies for gastric distress *aren't* sold on the ships—see page 133 for more about that.

Besides appropriate clothing, our packing list includes the following essentials:

- **Chewing gum.** As is the case at the Disney parks and the Orlando airport, gum is not sold on DCL ships (though mints and other candies are). If you need to chew gum to relieve ear pressure during air travel, whether for your flight home or a port excursion that involves a seaplane or helicopter, bring your own.

- **Baby powder.** Baby powder is amazing for getting wet sand off your legs and feet before getting back on the ship or into a taxi.

- **Games and diversions.** The DCL lounges have a limited selection of games available, but if you have a favorite that you like to play, bring it. We've been known to find an empty table to play a game of cards with our family on long cruises. Other relaxing diversions for kids and adults might include paperback novels, magazines, coloring books, puzzle books, sticker books, or yarn crafts like knitting.

- **Large ziplock bags.** Store damp, sandy swimsuits, shoes, and such in these to keep the rest of your packed luggage clean and dry.
- **Packing cubes** (especially if sailing on the *Wish*-class ships). The *Wish*-class stateroom storage consists of a few deep shelves rather than the numerous drawers available on other DCL ships. We've found that packing cubes help you keep some sense of order.
- **Portable phone-battery charger.** Your phone is your lifeline when you're traveling abroad. You don't want to run out of juice.
- **Prescription medications.** Pack these in carry-on luggage in their original containers. (Also see pages 141 and 196.)
- **Sun hats and sunglasses.** Sunscreen is reasonably priced on the ships if you don't want to pack it.
- **Tablet computer.** DCL's Wi-Fi speed and pricing make video streaming all but impossible, so load enough books, music, movies, TV shows, and games for the cruise and for the trip to and from the port. If your child must have access to particular content, download it *before* you set sail.
- **Water shoes or flip-flops.** You'll need these for the pool and beach.
- **White-noise mobile app.** This is useful for drowning out noise from hallways, next-door staterooms, and ship machinery.

If you're traveling with young children or someone with disabilities, you may also want to pack the following items:

- **Diapers (regular and swim).** The onboard shops carry these in a couple of sizes at most.
- **Earplugs or noise-canceling headphones.** The ship's horn can be *loud,* and some of the music played during the deck parties may be too intense for sensitive ears. If you or anyone in your party has auditory sensitivities, bring ear protection.
- **Favorite snacks.** Yes, the Mickey-shaped cheese crackers sold on the ships *look* a bit like Pepperidge Farm Goldfish, but they don't *taste* exactly the same—and that could trigger a tantrum in a persnickety toddler. (*Note:* Any food you bring on the ship must be factory-sealed in its original packaging.) To cut down on open bags and boxes, stock up on single-serving snacks. A great place to get them online is **Minimus.biz,** which also sells travel-size toiletries, easy-to-pack games and toys, and small travel accessories.
- **Night-light.** There are no night-lights in the bathrooms on the *Magic* or the *Wonder,* nor do most DCL staterooms have night-lights elsewhere to soothe children who may not be accustomed to sleeping in total darkness. Battery-operated tea lights or fluorescent glow sticks cost less than a dollar and will keep outlets free for phone charging, prevent stubbed toes on the way to the bathroom, and help anxious kids sleep better in an unfamiliar place.
- **Sippy cups and/or drinking straws.** Disney Cruise Line has largely transitioned away from serving beverages with lids and straws, and during our most recent sailings, we couldn't find sippy cups for sale on board. If you're cruising with toddlers or anyone who needs assistance with drinking liquids, you should bring your own supplies.

COMMON EXTRAS

THESE ITEMS ARE not imperative, but enough guests swear by them that we think they're worth mentioning.

- **Bluetooth trackers,** such as the Apple AirTag. Put them in or on anything you want to keep track of while traveling: luggage, rental cars, and even your kids. Tammy was able to recover a lost suitcase in Europe only because of an AirTag.

- **Costumes.** Most DCL cruises have a Pirate Night, and there are themed sailings and holiday sailings for which many guests choose to wear coordinating outfits (see page 66). Costumes are not at all required, but some guests consider them an absolute must, for both children and adults.

- **Magnetic hooks.** The walls of a cruise ship are metal. Strong magnetic hooks can give you extra spots to hang a jacket, hat, or toiletry case.

- **Sleep headphones** or **SoniSleep Sleepbar.** The staterooms are small. If you need music or a podcast to fall asleep, you'll need a means to listen without disturbing your companions.

- **Travel mugs.** The poolside paper cups are small and not insulated. If you want to keep a larger beverage with you, bring a travel mug.

- **Waterproof camera** and/or **waterproof phone case.** Castaway Cay and Lookout Cay are great places to get underwater photos of sea life.

SOLUTIONS FOR LOTS OF STUFF

SOME GUESTS FIND that they have more luggage than they can reasonably transport to the ship on their own; this often happens to guests with small children sailing on longer voyages with bulky items such as diapers and wipes. If you need to bring bulky items onto the ship but don't want to incur excess-baggage fees by flying with them, you have a few alternatives, particularly if you're going to Walt Disney World before your cruise (see page 75):

- **Drive a rental car to the port instead of flying** or use a car service that allows stops. On the way to the port, stop at a grocery store to stock up.

- **Ask if your precruise hotel accepts packages.** If it does, ship your items there. (All Walt Disney World hotels accept packages for a small fee.)

- **Amazon Prime members** can have groceries and baby-care products delivered same-day to Orlando-area hotels. Also, **Garden Grocer** (gardengrocer.com) and **Turner Drugs** (turnerdrug.com) offer delivery in the Orlando area.

ALCOHOLIC BEVERAGES

SOME GUESTS CHOOSE to economize on booze by bringing their own. Guests age 21 or older may bring aboard a maximum of two bottles (no larger than 750 milliliters) of unopened wine or Champagne or a six-pack of beer (bottles or cans no larger than 12 ounces each) at the beginning of the trip *and* at each port of call. These beverages must be packed in carry-on bags. Any alcohol packed in your checked luggage will be removed and stored—the next time you'll see it will be when you're getting ready to head home.

unofficial **TIP**
You can bring sealed nonalcoholic beverages, such as bottled water and canned soda, onto the ship in any reasonable quantity that you can carry yourself.

If you bring hard liquor, powdered alcohol, or beer or wine on board in excess of the allowed quantity, it will likewise be stored until the end of your cruise. If you plan to buy the local hooch while in port, ask to have it packaged for travel (for example, in bubble wrap).

Be aware that if you bring alcohol on board, you can't drink it in a bar or other public area. The one exception is beer, wine, or Champagne that you want to drink with a meal (the dining rooms charge a corkage fee of $29 per bottle for wine or Champagne).

Note: Many readers have asked us if it's OK to bring aboard single-serving "hard" beverages like hard cider, hard seltzer, and malt beverages like Mike's Hard Lemonade. Technically, they're not allowed, but cast members may not bother to confiscate them.

BANNED ITEMS

WHILE YOU'RE PACKING, it also makes sense to review the extensive list of items that are prohibited aboard DCL ships. Not surprisingly, you can't bring fireworks, illegal drugs, or weapons, but did you know you also can't bring extension cords, fishing gear, kites, musical instruments, power strips, or pool noodles? Other prohibited items include balloons, candles, clothing irons and steamers, fresh flowers or fruit, air mattresses, medical or recreational marijuana, drones, skateboards, string lights, toy guns (including Disney-themed guns such as *Star Wars* blasters), and TV-streaming devices (such as Apple TV, Roku, Amazon Fire TV Stick, and Google Chromecast).

unofficial **TIP**
For a complete list of items banned on DCL ships, see theugseries.com/dcl-banned.

Even if you've cruised with DCL before, make sure to review the banned-items list, which is updated fairly regularly. We've seen posts on social media that advise packing seemingly mundane items that are against the rules. A common example is over-the-door shoe racks.

Likewise, exercise common sense and leave at home anything that would be difficult or impossible to replace, such as expensive or sentimental jewelry or your young child's one and only "lovey." We had a daughter's beloved plush bunny, Pinky, go missing on a cruise, much to the distress of the entire family. If items such as these must make the trip, label them with your contact information and stow them in your safe when not in use. This applies to favorite toys as well as jewelry: Pinky vanished when a housekeeper inadvertently carried her away with the sheets after stripping the bed.

unofficial **TIP**
If you lose something on board, stop by Guest Services and have them check the lost-and-found box. If you realize you've left something on the ship after your cruise is over, file a report with **Chargerback,** Disney's third-party lost-and-found service (chargerback.com/dcl).

Also note that several Caribbean countries, including the Bahamas, have a ban on wearing camouflage clothing. If you're on a Caribbean sailing, it's best to leave all these items at home.

TRAVELING WITH PRESCRIPTION MEDICATIONS

A HOT TOPIC on many online discussion boards is whether prescription medicines must be transported in their original containers or can be transferred to handy daily-dose containers. Some guests with complex medical conditions say they'd need an additional suitcase to pack all their bottles and claim they've never been questioned about their meds. We've never been questioned either, but we also realize that it just takes one challenge to derail your otherwise relaxing vacation.

DCL recommends keeping medicines in their original bottles, as do the FDA and US Customs. If, like most cruisers, you'll be visiting countries other than your own, be aware that they have their own regulations and that foreign airlines may also have restrictions. If you choose not to transport your medications in their original containers, bring copies of your prescriptions and/or a note from your doctor listing the meds you take. In short, err on the side of caution.

If you'll be taking your medicines with you into port, also make sure to check the policies of the countries you'll be visiting. For example, some over-the-counter medicines commonly used in the United States, including Actifed, Sudafed, and Vicks inhalers, aren't allowed into Mexico, nor are medications that contain codeine. See theug series.com/mexico-meds for links to additional information. In addition, be aware that your ship's onboard Health Center may not be able to refill prescriptions (especially those for controlled substances), so get them refilled before you leave home.

During our travels, we've had transportation or weather issues delay our arrival home by as many as four days. If you take medication that's critical to your health and well-being, we strongly encourage you to bring several days of extra doses whenever you travel, particularly when traveling to countries where medical protocols may be different from what you're used to at home.

LAUNDRY SERVICES

SELF-SERVICE LAUNDRY FACILITIES are available on Decks 2, 6, and 7 of the *Magic* and *Wonder;* Decks 2 and 5–10 of the *Dream* and *Fantasy;* and Deck 8 of the *Wish, Treasure,* and *Destiny.* The laundry rooms are furnished with washers, dryers, irons, and detergent for purchase. It costs $3 to wash a load of clothes and another $3 to dry them; detergent costs another $1 per load.

In general, you'll find the laundry rooms less crowded on non–sea days, as well as after 11 p.m. and before 7 a.m. You will also likely find them easier to access on three- and four-night cruises originating in the United States than on longer sailings.

Competition for washers and dryers often reaches *Hunger Games* levels of intensity during the dinner hour on most sailings, and on long European voyages, guests who traveled before their cruises or plan to do so afterward tend to make heavy use of the laundry facilities to keep their packing manageable.

In addition to do-it-yourself laundry, each ship offers **full-service laundry and dry-cleaning,** with pickup from and delivery to your stateroom. Just drop your clothes in the laundry/dry-cleaning bag hanging in your closet, and complete the attached paper form with any special cleaning instructions. Laundry service usually takes 24 hours, but we've had simple requests, such as laundering and pressing a couple of shirts, turned around the same day. There may be an additional charge for rush service.

Prices are subject to change, but for full-service laundry you can expect to pay about $4 for a men's dress shirt and about $2.50 for a T-shirt. Dry-cleaning is available for about $9 for a men's suit and $10 for an evening dress. Pressing is available for half the cost of laundry and dry-cleaning. We think having someone else press our clothes for our sailing is a splurge that's well worth it.

ELECTRICAL OUTLETS

OUTLETS ON DCL SHIPS conform to the North American 110V/60Hz standard. If you live in the United States or Canada, any electrical device that operates normally at home should work on board. *Note:* Some guests on the *Wish* have experienced glitches with hair appliances, including high-wattage items like flat irons and the Dyson AirWrap in particular. Tammy has one curling iron that will not work aboard the *Wish* in any stateroom, a random plug in the hall that she tried, or the spa. She has started bringing a cheap curling iron that works fine. Ironically, it's the expensive brands that don't seem to work.

unofficial **TIP**
We recommend bringing one converter or adapter (see below) per person, two if you're traveling alone.

All staterooms have hair dryers, so if you're tight on space and not overly attached to your own dryer, you may not need to pack one. Look for the dryer in a drawer at your stateroom desk. If it's missing, ask your stateroom host to bring you one. In addition to these dryers, which are newer models with plenty of power, the *Magic* and *Wonder* have older dryers (attached to some bathroom walls) that may not do much if you have a lot of hair to dry, so don't overlook that newer-model dryer in the desk drawer.

If you're visiting from outside the States, you may need an **adapter** or a **converter** for your electrical gadgets. What's the difference? An adapter ensures that the plug on your device will fit into the receptacle in the wall, but it doesn't change the voltage. A converter does both (and costs more).

unofficial **TIP**
If you are traveling to somewhere like Europe and expect to rely on the US plugs on board, don't forget about your precruise hotel stay. You'll likely need converters and/or adapters there as well.

There is a significant scarcity of outlets in most DCL staterooms, and the introduction of the DisneyBand+, which requires daily charging (see page 152), only worsened the problem. If two people in your party over age 8 will be sharing a stateroom, you'll almost certainly need to bring along some means of adding outlet access; unfortunately, power strips and extension cords are on DCL's list of prohibited items. A good workaround is a **plug-in USB hub**. Many inexpensive models allow four or five USB devices (phones, tablets, and the like) to charge on one outlet. A **laptop** can also be used as a charging hub.

Another possible workaround is an international electrical converter, even if your cruise takes place in the United States. Most staterooms have a 220-volt outlet near the desk, which is intended for the provided hair dryer. If you have a converter, you can use this outlet for your 120-volt US devices.

GRATUITIES

YOU'LL ENCOUNTER CREW MEMBERS throughout your cruise, many of whom you'll see several times per day, and they will have a direct impact on the quality of your trip. You can prepay your basic gratuities on the DCL website in the Special Requests section (see page 123). If you choose to pay on board, unless you request otherwise at Guest Services, a daily gratuity will be added to your stateroom bill for the four crew members most directly responsible for your well-being: your **stateroom host,** your **dining room server** (in charge of your food), your **assistant server** (in charge of your drinks), and the **head server** (or dining room manager). *Note:* Concierge Staterooms also have an **assistant stateroom host.** (See page 147 for our tipping recommendations for Concierge guests.)

The table below shows the basic daily tip amounts for these crew members, for each member of your party. Thus, if you have four people in your party and you're taking a seven-night cruise in a non-Concierge Stateroom, you should budget **$406** (**$101.50 × 4**) for the personnel listed. (See the sidebar on the opposite page for details on specific tipping procedures.)

SUGGESTED GRATUITIES BY CREW MEMBER				
CREW MEMBER	SUGGESTED GRATUITY PER DAY	SUGGESTED GRATUITY, 3 NIGHTS	SUGGESTED GRATUITY, 4 NIGHTS	SUGGESTED GRATUITY, 7 NIGHTS
Stateroom Host	$4.75	$14.25	$19.00	$33.25
Dining Room Server	$4.75	$14.25	$19.00	$33.25
Assistant Dining Room Server	$3.75	$11.25	$15.00	$26.25
Head Dining Room Server	$1.25	$3.75	$5.00	$8.75
TOTAL (PER GUEST)	$14.50	$43.50	$58.00	$101.50

Concierge guests: *Add $1 per person, per night, for your assistant stateroom host and at least $8 per person, per night, for your Concierge host (but see page 149).*

These suggested amounts are the amounts you will be charged if you prepay or the amount that will be automatically added to your folio (stateroom account) based on the number of people in your cabin and your cruise length. Once on board, you can adjust these amounts or pay in cash by contacting Guest Services (open 24 hours a day). Lines at Guest Services will be long on the last night of your cruise, so plan to make any adjustments sooner rather than later to avoid a wait.

HOW TO TIP ON A DISNEY CRUISE

ON THE LAST FULL DAY OF YOUR CRUISE, you'll find a tip summary sheet in your stateroom, along with four small envelopes labeled **Server, Assistant Server, Head Server,** and **Stateroom Host.** If you are staying Concierge, you will also have one labeled **Assistant Stateroom Host.** The summary sheet shows the gratuity amounts billed to your onboard account—or amounts that you've prepaid—for each of these crew members, plus four perforated strips showing individual gratuity amounts, one for each crew member.

If you're satisfied with the gratuity amounts, there's nothing more you need to do—your crew members will automatically receive your tip along with their regular pay; you can throw out the envelopes and keep the summary for your records. The following advice covers what to do in specific tipping situations.

- **If you plan to give your crew members the standard gratuities** but think it feels weird to leave on the last day without handing them anything, place the perforated strip from the summary sheet in the designated envelope, and hand it to the crew member on the last night of your voyage.

- **If you want to give one or more of your crew members an additional gratuity,** you can **(1)** place cash in the envelope and hand it to them on the last night of your voyage; **(2)** place both the perforated strip and the cash in the envelope and hand it to them on the last night of your voyage; **(3)** go to Guest Services and have additional gratuities added to your account; or **(4)** go to Guest Services, have additional gratuities added to your account, and ask for a new summary form; then remove the perforated strips from the new form, place them in the envelopes, and hand the envelopes out on the last night of your voyage.

- **If you're uncomfortable carrying cash but want to give something of financial value** (and don't want to deal with lines at Guest Services), you can place a gift card in the designated envelope instead. Although cash is the best thing to give a crew member—it's easy to use in ports and send to family back home—Visa or American Express gift cards or store cards from Walmart or Target are also appreciated.

- **Do any of the above** and add a personal note of gratitude to the envelope.

Here are our suggestions for tipping other DCL crew:

PORTERS People who handle your luggage at the port before or after your cruise should get **$1–$3 per bag.**

BARTENDERS AND DRINK SERVERS An **18%** gratuity is automatically added to all onboard purchases of alcohol, such as in the bars and dining rooms and by the pool deck. You may add an additional tip when you sign your receipt.

CAFÉS An **18%** gratuity is automatically added to specialty coffees purchased in the onboard cafés. Again, you may add an additional tip when you sign your receipt.

ROOM SERVICE Most room-service food is free, but it's customary to tip the crew member who brings your food **$1–$2 per item** or a minimum of **$5.** If you don't have cash, ask the crew member for a receipt to sign; you can add a gratuity there.

SPAS An **18%** gratuity is automatically added to your spa treatments. You can add an additional tip to your bill at the time of purchase.

CABANA HOSTS If you are lucky enough to snag a cabana at Castaway Cay or Lookout Cay, it will be attended by the Concierge host, who will check on you all day, bring you extra towels and snacks, and possibly give you a golf-cart ride to or from the ship. Tips aren't mandatory but are always appreciated. Tip in cash at a level that feels right to you.

PORT EXCURSIONS Shore trips are typically run by outside companies, not Disney. Nearly all excursion guides appreciate a cash tip, given at your discretion. It's also customary to tip the drivers.

KIDS' CLUB STAFF Gratuities aren't required for nursery or club staff, although you may want to reward a counselor who goes above and beyond for your child. Cash and gift cards are accepted, though not expected. Personal notes from your child are a thoughtful touch.

IS TIPPING NECESSARY?

A FEW DCL GUESTS have asked us whether they have to tip at all; these guests are usually from countries outside of the United States and Canada, where tipping isn't the norm (usually because restaurant wait-staff in these countries are paid standard wages).

While it's not mandatory, tipping your crew absolutely *is* the right thing to do: Gratuities are an expected part of cruise travel and an important component of crew members' income.

unofficial **TIP**

If you really care about your stateroom and dining room teams, the best thing you can do to reward them, in addition to tipping, is to give them rave reviews on your postcruise comment card.

Guests have also asked us whether they should tip the servers in the main dining rooms if they don't eat there. (Some cruisers on three-nighters on the *Wish*, for example, often prefer to skip the dining rooms and dine once at Palo, once at Enchanté, and once from Room Service.) We recommend tipping at least the baseline amount whether you eat in the main dining rooms at night or not—these same servers not only work in the same dining rooms during the day, but they also work at the buffet restaurants and the food stations on Castaway Cay and Lookout Cay.

TIPPING EXTRA

WHEN IT COMES TO tipping more than baseline amounts, it's not mandatory, but many people do give additional tips to the crew who attend to them most closely.

We have found the crew on board to be amazing. They know our drink orders, they cut meat for our kids, and they keep ice in our staterooms. We usually tip extra in cash, especially whenever we feel like they have gone above the standard.

The next question you'll undoubtedly ask is, "How much extra should I tip?" To that we say, *it's up to you*. For some guests, an extra $10 is a meaningful gesture. We've also heard of guests handing several hundred dollars in cash to beloved crew members. For most, it's somewhere in between.

Some guests bring candy, magazines, or other personal items as crew gifts. This is a nice thought but probably not the best practice:

Crew quarters are shared spaces, and your crew's tastes may not be the same as yours. We also still see social media posts saying that cast members "love" getting long-distance calling cards as tips. While there may be the individual cast member who would love getting one of these, those days are over for the vast majority of people, given the ubiquity of smartphones and all the ways to easily connect with someone overseas. Again, cash is best, and gift cards are second best. If you really want to give something else, make sure it's in addition to (not instead of) the tip.

TIPPING FOR ADULT DINING

AT PALO, PALO STEAKHOUSE, REMY, AND ENCHANTÉ, a gratuity is automatically added for alcohol only; an additional gratuity for dining service is left to your discretion. Because the service at these restaurants is typically impeccable, we tend to tip as if we had eaten at an onshore restaurant of their caliber. If you are looking for a clear amount, we spoke with a former Palo server who told us that $25 per person for brunch and $50 for dinner was a good amount. (That works out to 25% of a $100 brunch or a $200 dinner.) That being said, it's up to you if that feels like too little or too much.

TIPPING GUIDELINES FOR CONCIERGE GUESTS

THE SUGGESTED MINIMUM gratuity in this case is **$15.50 per person, per night,** broken down as follows: **$4.75** for your dining room server, **$3.75** for your assistant server, **$1.25** for the head server, **$4.75** for your stateroom host, and **$1** for your assistant stateroom host.

You'll notice the only suggested tip that's added for Concierge is $1 per person, per night, for the assistant stateroom host. The reality, however, is that some of those staterooms are huge, and an extra $1 doesn't feel like enough. Go with your instinct.

Concierge guests will also be given an envelope for the Concierge hosts, and Disney recommends a gratuity of **$8** per person, per night. We have found that the Concierge hosts are some of our favorite people on board, and we didn't feel like that was quite enough. We do want to tip them appropriately, so we asked a former Concierge host for guidance. The Concierge hosts are hard-wired never to give specific amounts and to assure you that any amount you choose is appropriate, so it's like pulling teeth to get them to name a dollar figure. So, we suggested an amount to get their reaction. We asked if $100 per night (total per stateroom) was a good tip and were met with an enthusiastic yes! So that's our baseline. If we request a lot from the Concierge hosts or feel like they are spending a lot of time helping and getting to know us, we try to get as close to that $100 as possible. If, on the other hand, we didn't need any help with reservations or anything else on board, we may go a little lower. Again, it's up to you.

We have also found that if we spend a lot of time in the lounge, we usually get to know some of the bartenders and serving team, and they take great care of us and our children. In that case, we will often hand cash directly to them.

WEATHER

AS MUCH AS WE'RE SURE they'd love to, Disney can't control the weather. You're probably envisioning spending your Caribbean cruise sipping piña coladas on the pool deck, but the reality is that you may encounter inclement weather during your sailing. Don't worry if it rains; there are plenty of indoor activities for children and adults. Disney also does a terrific job of providing extra indoor programming if conditions warrant. Check the **DCL Navigator app** (see page 124) for up-to-the-minute changes in the schedule.

In extreme-weather situations, DCL will alter plans more substantially than just running a few more games of bingo. On rare occasions, sailings have left their embarkation port a day or two late, returned to port a day or two early, returned to port a day or two late, cut or substituted a port stop, ended a voyage at a port other than the one planned, or even canceled a sailing, all in the interest of guest safety.

While Walt Disney World has an official hurricane policy (disney world.disney.go.com/faq/hurricane-policy), Disney Cruise Line has no such policy. It does, however, have an admirable record of assisting guests with refunds and remediation for missed sailing days and fees at skipped ports. For example, in the case of Hurricane Irma in 2017, DCL offered refunds on missed days for sailings that returned early and offered a 25% discount on future sailings in 2017 or 2018. Those on the canceled sailings were given a full refund and the same 25% discount on future sailings.

If your itinerary changes, it may be easier to get refunds for excursions booked through Disney rather than for those booked on your own (see page 347). Also keep in mind that if you're flying to your sailing, weather can also affect your airline, and guests with pre- or postcruise hotel reservations may also see those plans affected.

If you encounter a storm, rest assured that the chance of any real danger at sea due to a hurricane is virtually zero. Weather tracking is such that cruise lines typically know about impending severe weather at least three days before it hits, giving the captain and crew plenty of time to change course. Captains also have great latitude when rerouting ships to avoid areas of concern. Large ships, such as DCL's, can even outpace the danger zone of a storm: Most hurricanes travel at a speed of about 10 knots, and the ships are able to sail at more than 20 knots.

If you want to delve into the minutiae of maritime weather tracking, check out **PassageWeather** (passageweather.com), a terrific source of information about phenomena that affect ships, such as surface winds, wave height and direction, and sea-surface temperatures. The **National Weather Service** also offers detailed current information at its **Ocean Prediction Center** (ocean.weather.gov).

Whenever possible, build in a day or two on both sides of your sailing to account for unexpected weather situations. This is one reason we highly recommend **trip insurance** (see page 113). Depending on the policy, it may cover flight-change fees and/or unexpected hotel stays. Be sure to read the fine print on any trip-insurance contract to understand exactly what it covers before you purchase.

On the other end of the spectrum, some guests, equating cruising with the tropics, are wary of booking a sailing to colder-weather regions such as Alaska, Canada, and Northern Europe. We've sailed itineraries to these areas and rank them among our favorites. During a Norwegian Fjords cruise on the *Magic*, we often heard the maxim, "There's no bad weather, only bad clothing." In other words, if you're dressed appropriately, touring in a cooler climate can be a fabulous experience, with more variety in the sights than you're likely to find on a beach-intensive voyage in the Caribbean. Plus, the ships feel particularly cozy on cold-weather routes. For example, on the glacier-viewing days of Alaskan sailings, the DCL staff places piles of fleece blankets on deck and rolls around a cart stocked with hot cocoa, Irish coffee, and hot toddies. Cuddling up with your honey, sipping a warm beverage, and watching seals and whales swim by makes for a truly memorable day. We're with Elsa on this one: "The cold never bothered us anyway."

WEATHER IN PORT

KNOWING APPROXIMATELY what the weather will be like at your cruise destinations can help you fine-tune many aspects of planning your trip, including packing, the port adventures you choose, and the type of stateroom you select.

Starting about 10 days before your cruise and then again 2 or 3 days before, check the current short-term weather forecasts for the ports you're scheduled to visit. Sites such as **Weather Spark** (weatherspark.com) and **Holiday Weather** (holiday-weather.com) list the averages for cities around the globe; look not only at daytime and nighttime temperatures but also at typical rainfall and the number of days with clouds or sun.

PREPARING YOURSELF *and your* CHILDREN

PREPARING YOURSELF AND YOUR HOME FOR TRAVEL

IN ADDITION TO cruise-specific preparations, you should also be aware of general guidelines for international travel. If you want to be comprehensive, **Pinterest** is filled with hundreds of travel-prep hint lists, but a few of our favorite tips are as follows:

- Consult with your doctor about whether you're up-to-date on vaccinations.
- Confirm all travel and transportation arrangements, and double-check that the names match on all documents.
- Consider adding the numbers of foreign embassies or consulates to your phone contacts. (If you lose your passport, you'll need this information.)
- Make sure your credit/debit cards will work in a chip-style reader (the standard outside the United States).
- Download maps of your destination cities to your phone.
- Line up pet sitters or housesitters.
- Arrange to stop mail and newspaper delivery if you won't have a housesitter.
- Unplug electrical appliances such as coffee makers and toasters. If you need reassurance that everything is safe and sound, take photographs of these appliances just before you leave home.
- Hire someone to maintain your yard or remove snow so that your absence isn't immediately apparent to strangers.
- Empty your refrigerator of perishable items and arrange grocery delivery for the day of your return.
- Turn off (or adjust) the thermostat before you leave.
- Load your mobile devices with plenty of content for your flight or drive, and for poolside lounging on board.
- Make sure you have plenty of any prescribed medications you'll need.
- Give a trusted friend or family member your itinerary information and a way to contact you in an emergency. You may also want to give them the ship-to-shore phone number (see page 134) in case they can't reach you easily by phone, text, or email.

MAKING SURE YOUR CHILD IS READY TO CRUISE

IT'S NO SECRET that many Disney Cruise Line guests are families with young children. Most of these guests have a fabulous time; the small number who don't are typically those whose expectations aren't in line with the reality of traveling on a cruise ship.

When you're considering a Disney cruise with kids, know first that travel with children under 6 is almost always more challenging than travel with older kids or grown-ups. Adults who are used to traveling solo or with other adults may be surprised at the difficulties they experience when traveling with young children.

Rest assured, however, that whatever issues you encounter aren't specific to Disney or cruising but rather par for the course when it comes to travel in general. Whenever you travel with young kids, you're carrying their stuff, making sure they eat what they're supposed to, hovering over them at the pool, and making sure they get something approximating sleep. This always-on feeling can be hard to reconcile with the "cruise as ultimate relaxation" ethos that many expect.

To figure out if you and your child are ready for a cruise vacation, ask yourself these questions:

- **Is my child a good sleeper?** Or are there certain situations in which they *don't* sleep well? For example, will they be frightened by the motion of the ship? Will they feel anxious about sleeping in an unfamiliar room or bed? Will sleeping in the same room as your child affect their (or your) ability to sleep?

- **How does my child react to changes in their schedule?** Many younger children have trouble coping with changes in their nap or eating schedule, particularly if that schedule is disrupted for several days in a row. Most activities on the ship take place at set times—times that may not align with your child's usual schedule. Can your child deal with the disruption, or are tears and tantrums inevitable? Are you willing to forgo eating in the main dining rooms if your child's schedule requires it?

- **Do we have any claustrophobia issues?** On any cruise ship, spaces are more compact than those in most land-based locations. Staterooms are smaller than many typical hotel rooms; stateroom bathrooms may be smaller still than what you're used to.

- **Does my child have issues with characters?** By elementary school, most kids will have outgrown any reticence about meeting Santa or the Easter Bunny. But quite a few toddlers and preschoolers find such encounters terrifying. Characters are difficult to avoid completely on Disney ships. Many character greetings take place in public areas such as the atrium or the theater exit, and characters sometimes make surprise appearances in the kids' clubs. Given the closed-in nature of a cruise ship, you'll likely run into characters at some point during your trip. If your young child has a serious character phobia, you may want to hold off on booking until they're older.

- **Is my child easily overwhelmed in new situations?** On a ship, there are new foods, new people, new activities, loud ship horns—the list goes on and on. (I've heard several stories about children becoming upset upon seeing the yellow lifeboats.) It may be difficult to predict what exactly will unsettle a 3-year-old, but chances are you already know if your child becomes easily upset or overstimulated. Additionally, you may want to consider that on sea days, there may be few options for separating your child from other people, other than staying in your stateroom.

- **Will childcare eat into my vacation budget?** DCL's kids' clubs are included in your cruise price for potty-trained children age 3 and up. The nurseries (for infants–age 3) charge a fee—currently $9 per hour for the first child and $8 per hour for each additional child in the same family. It may be relatively easy to leave your 10-month-old in the nursery while you enjoy the sunshine, but those fees can sneak up on you over the course of a long sailing.

- **Will I be able to find childcare?** Children ages 3–17 have unlimited use of the kids' clubs whenever they want, with no reservations necessary. The nurseries, however, accept only a limited number of children per hour, and reservations are required. Depending on how crowded your cruise is and your Castaway Club status, which will determine when you can book nursery times (see page 240), you may not be able to arrange babysitting when you want it.

- **Is my child in a particularly active phase?** Given the constraints of the ship, space is limited for large motor activities like ball play, climbing, and running. The kids' clubs offer some physical activities, but they may not be exactly the type of activity your child is used to, and opportunities for young children besides the clubs are fairly limited. Additionally, there are many expectations for restrained behavior (sitting still in a restaurant, for example). If you have a child with separation issues who also needs lots of physical activity, or a child with separation issues with an aversion to water play, then you may want to think hard about whether this is the right time to book a cruise.

- **Does my child require lots of gear?** Staterooms are small. Boxes of diapers, strollers, play mats, and the like may seem quite large in a confined space.

- **Traveling with my child means I wouldn't get to experience everything the ship has to offer. Would I be wasting my money by booking a cruise?** *Absolutely not.* Some of our most memorable cruise experiences haven't involved a specific activity or event. However, factors such as a child's sleep schedule may make most adult activities—and even many family activities—inaccessible to you. If you're in for the night because your child is asleep at 8 p.m., then you'll miss the stage shows, family game shows, and other experiences that take place later in the evening. There are some partial workarounds, though. For example, the main stage shows are available on closed-circuit TV in your stateroom (though not currently on the *Wish*-class ships).

- **What are the needs of those traveling with us?** Many folks with young children cruise with extended family. This can be a boon for the parents if Grandma offers to babysit while they enjoy Palo or the margarita-mixing class. On the other hand, it can be a struggle if Grandma expects the entire clan to sit still for a 3-hour dinner every evening or if Grandpa needs physical assistance or has medical needs of his own.

- **Are there appropriate excursions or other activities in port?** If you want to leave the ship while it's in port, review your shore-excursion options carefully. At some stops, there may be limited offerings for children under age 5 or even under age 8. At other ports, excursions may technically be available to younger children but aren't practical. For example, a 5-hour bike tour probably isn't appropriate for a 4-year-old. You may want to consider arranging your own excursions or just going for a leisurely walk near the dock area. The counterpoint to this is that some families find cruising to be one of the easiest ways for a young child to experience a distant land.

unofficial **TIP**
See our thoughts about food issues with young kids on page 207.

By age 6 or 7, most children have developed strong enough coping skills to deal with meeting new people, waiting their turn, sitting still for extended periods, and being separated from their family while in the kids' clubs. Additionally, a school-age child likely has a broader palate, little need for special equipment, and enough language skills to effectively communicate. Each of these capabilities will make cruising, or any travel, more relaxing for the entire family.

KEY TO THE WORLD CARDS *and* DISNEYBAND+

DCL OFFERS TWO options for onboard transactions and identification: the Key to the World Card and the DisneyBand+. All guests will be issued the credit card–like **Key to the World (KTTW) Card.** You can use it for onboard transactions, unlocking the door to your stateroom, and identification. Your KTTW Card also contains helpful information about your cruise. The first line just beneath the DCL logo lists the dates of your cruise. The second line lists the name of your ship, and next to that is either **A** for "adult" or **M** for "minor," indicating whether you're old enough to drink. The rest of that line may be blank or, if you've purchased land transfers from Disney, will list a letter indicating what type of transfer you've paid for: **P** means "port," **R** means "resort" (if you've booked a combination cruise/WDW vacation), and **A** means "airport." Sometimes combinations of letters are used: For example, **PA** indicates a port-to-airport transfer. The next two lines display your name, Castaway Club status, and Castaway Club number. A large single letter in the lower-left corner indicates your lifeboat station, which you'll find during the embarkation-day assembly drill. If you are a Disney Visa cardmember, you'll also see **DV** in the bottom right corner so the applicable discounts will be applied when shopping on board. You'll find your KTTW Card in a sealed envelope on a small shelf located next to your stateroom door the first time you go to your stateroom.

During summer 2023, DCL introduced the **DisneyBand+,** which is similar to the MagicBand+ at Walt Disney World theme parks and resorts. Indeed, the DisneyBand+ can be used both on the DCL ships and at Disney World. DisneyBand+ is not mandatory (with a few exceptions), and you'll still need to use your KTTW Card to identify yourself to port and ship personnel when you reboard the ship after debarking at port stops, but many guests find them helpful.

A word of caution: Children in some of the kids' clubs may be issued wristbands for identification, but they don't have the same functionality as a DisneyBand+, and you must return them at the end of your voyage or be subject to a $13 fee per unreturned band (it's $25 on the *Wish*). If children have a DisneyBand+, they can use it instead of the kids' club wristband to enter and exit the clubs.

DisneyBand+ is waterproof and can be prepurchased 11–45 days before your sailing for around $35–$45. There are a limited number of styles available on board for $50. It can be used to enter your stateroom, pay for merchandise and specialty food, and check into the kids' clubs. There are also times when the band will light up or vibrate around the ship or during shows.

So, should you purchase DisneyBand+? It's not necessary, but it is convenient. Many guests find wearing something around their wrist more desirable than wearing a lanyard with their KTTW Card or carrying a card in their pocket. Children, in particular, will enjoy the interactive elements of fireworks and shows.

If you have a MagicBand+ from the parks, you can use that on board. Standard MagicBands do not work, but the MagicBand+ does. MagicBand+ and DisneyBand+ have to be charged, which is the biggest drawback for us. The good news is that a dead battery only means it won't light up or vibrate; you can still access your stateroom.

STATEROOM GIFTS *and* GOODIES

ONCE YOU'VE PAID IN FULL for your Disney cruise, you'll have access to the **Onboard Gifts** section of the DCL website: At the top of the homepage, go to the "Already Booked" tab and choose "Onboard Gifts" from the pull-down menu. This is where you can arrange to have treats and surprises waiting for you when you arrive at your stateroom; you can also have gifts delivered to someone else's stateroom if you have their reservation number.

The options include stateroom decorations for birthdays and holidays (about $70–$82), floral bouquets (about $90–$100), Champagne and chocolates (about $55–$130), and a platter of tropical fruits or sweet snacks (about $30). Tammy discovered Cloudem (a premium nonalcoholic beverage perfect for occasions when Champagne is served) aboard a Disney ship in 2021 and has unsuccessfully searched for it Stateside ever since. She stocks up when on board and preorders a few bottles (around $20 each). You can also preorder a birthday cake (regular or food-allergy-friendly; about $55), along with more-prosaic items like eco-friendly cans of bottled water ($14 for 6, $28 for 12, or $55 for 24) or a six-pack of Bud Light (about $34). Note, however, that you may bring aboard as much bottled water as you like and up to a six-pack of beer per adult in your carry-on luggage (see page 140 for more on the alcohol policy), making that a much more economical option.

> **_un_official TIP**
> You need a reservation number to buy but not to browse. To see what's available, choose "Browse by Departure Port" on the Onboard Gifts landing page of the DCL website.

You can also add an onboard credit to your account. This can be a fun surprise for someone in your stateroom or a way to "prepay" for things on board that will be charged to your account, like excursions and specialty dining.

Cake orders must be placed no later than seven days before you sail; all other orders must be placed no later than three days before. For more information, call ☎ 800-601-8455, Monday–Friday, 8 a.m.–10 p.m. Eastern time, or Saturday and Sunday, 9 a.m.–8 p.m. Note that cake orders have a strict cancellation policy, so read the fine print.

SHOP DCL AT HOME

MANY DISNEY-BRANDED items sold in the shipboard gift shops are also available at **shopDisney** (shopdisney.com); to find DCL merchandise, type "cruise" into the search bar. This is the place to order personalized DCL family T-shirts before your trip (about $30 each) or pick up that souvenir you forgot to buy. The sale prices at shopDisney are sometimes lower than those on the ships, and they almost always list a free-shipping code for orders over $75.

PART 7

INSIDE SCOOP *for* DIFFERENT GROUPS

KEY QUESTIONS ANSWERED IN THIS CHAPTER

- Will I enjoy cruising by myself? *(see below)*
- How does Disney accommodate guests with disabilities? *(see page 163)*
- How does Disney handle dietary restrictions? *(see page 167)*

WITH ALL THE VARIOUS travel needs, party makeups, and preferences out there, you may be wondering what cruising will be like for you. We have some tips for all kinds of circumstances.

DCL *for* SOLO TRAVELERS

BECAUSE DCL IS TARGETED to families, roughly 90% of its guests are couples or parents and children. That's about 10 points higher than the cruise industry's average, and it means that there are around 200 solo travelers per cruise on the *Magic* and *Wonder* and around 400 on the *Dream, Fantasy, Wish, Treasure,* and *Destiny.*

Like the Disney theme parks, Disney Cruise Line is great for solo travelers. The bars, lounges, and nightclubs are clean, friendly, and interesting; the restaurants are welcoming; and the spas are excellent places for grabbing some solo time in public. One aspect you do have to be vigilant about when traveling alone is shore excursions in foreign countries—more on that later.

If you're interested in meeting other singles, Disney sometimes runs get-togethers for solo travelers, usually with a catchy name like **Singles Mingle** on one of the first few days of each cruise. These informal get-togethers last about an hour and are typically held at the **Cove Café** in the adults-only part of the ship. We've also seen lunchtime gatherings called **Cruisin' Solo.**

CRUISE FARES Whereas some cruise lines have staterooms designed especially for solo travelers, staterooms on Disney's ships are designed to hold at least two people. Disney also adds a 100% surcharge (or

single supplement, in cruise-industry lingo) to most solo-traveler fares, making the cost equivalent to two people taking the same trip.

DINING Unless you request otherwise, single travelers will almost certainly be paired with other groups for dinner in the main dining rooms. When we cruised solo, our dinner companions were usually one or two couples and several singles. Our dinners with these new friends have gone well—we've met people from many different places, never run out of things to talk about, and even kept in touch with a few folks after returning home. That said, not everyone enjoys dining with strangers, and you can request a table alone, although that may be hard to come by on a full ship. You can also order room service or eat by the pool deck if you'd rather not eat with others at dinner.

Solo travelers are also welcome at the adult-dining venues, and we've had many fine dinners and brunches there when cruising solo.

PORT ADVENTURES As with dining, there's a good chance that you'll be paired with other guests for shore excursions. We've experienced everything from cooking demonstrations to snorkeling to city tours as solo travelers, and the Port Adventures staff did a great job of making us feel welcome.

unofficial **TIP**
If your port adventure involves boating, snorkeling, or any other water-based activity, you'll almost certainly be assigned another traveler or couple as a buddy for safety.

As Len discovered, however, you could be the odd person out if you're doing an excursion with a third-party company and there's not enough room for you on the shuttle vehicle:

I was once the only solo traveler in a group of nine for an excursion in Mexico that involved a 30-minute bus ride. When we got to the departure point, we saw that not all of us were going to fit on the eight-person bus, so the tour company hurriedly arranged an unmarked, nondescript "taxi" for me.

As I got in this random car on a random street in a random Mexican town, my last words to the others were, "Take a good look—this is what I was wearing the last time you saw me." Of course, I made it to the excursion just fine, and we all had a good laugh once we were reunited. But I wouldn't recommend that others do this, especially women traveling alone.

In the unlikely event that you're asked to travel alone on an excursion, politely request to be accompanied by a staff member or escorted back to the ship.

ONBOARD ACTIVITIES Solo adults are welcome to participate in virtually all onboard activities: trivia sessions, cooking classes, shows and movies, and so on. Given that most of the other guests are paired up with partners or family members, the odds of anyone bothering you at a bar are virtually zero. The only onboard activities that are incompatible with solo travel are onstage participation in the few game shows where a known partner is required (Match Your Mate is the prime example), though of course you're welcome to watch from the audience with everyone else.

DCL *for* SINGLE PARENTS

CRUISES ARE A TERRIFIC OPTION for single parents or parents looking to get some one-on-one time with a subset of their children.

CRUISE FARES Not having a second adult in the party often means that a larger stateroom is unnecessary, making less expensive staterooms easily workable.

ONBOARD ACTIVITIES The ample hours of the kids' clubs mean that there are built-in opportunities for children and adults to get a break from each other from time to time. The parent can get an hour of relaxation at the lounge or pool, knowing the child is perfectly taken care of nearby. Time in the clubs means that kids get a chance to bond with peers and get a break from constant time with their parent. It's a win for everyone.

DCL *for* LARGER GUESTS

AS WITH ITS THEME PARK GUESTS, Disney acknowledges that its cruise guests come in all shapes and sizes and makes many accommodations to ensure they're treated well. Your stateroom's personal flotation devices (PFDs, or life jackets) are designed to fit most body sizes. Chest size, not weight, is the measurement that determines proper fit. Disney's PFDs include a nylon strap that wraps around your body to keep the jacket snug against your chest. Try on your PFD when you first get to your stateroom to ensure that the strap fits around your body. If it doesn't, ask your stateroom attendant to find you a larger PFD.

STATEROOM SELECTION We have heard that some larger guests prefer the bathrooms that are not split because they have a little more space inside a singular bathroom. If that sounds good to you and you don't mind an Inside Stateroom, look for a "Standard Inside Stateroom" not a "Deluxe Inside Stateroom."

DINING Ask for bench seating or chairs without arms. If you don't see any, a cast member may be able to locate them for you.

PORT ADVENTURES If an activity or port adventure has a weight limit, it will be printed in the details describing the activity; look for phrases such as "Guests must weigh" or "Weight must be" in the activity's listing. Some shore excursions, including kayaking and some scuba and snorkeling trips, have weight limits of 240 or 300 pounds per person. Segway tours generally accommodate riders weighing up to 250 pounds.

Many Alaskan excursions involving helicopters or seaplanes have a weight limit of 250 pounds, including all gear (clothing, cameras, and such), but it may be possible to modify this requirement by offering to pay an excess-weight fee. Other activities have weight limits of up to 350 pounds per person. Again, check the activity's details for more information, or check with the Port Adventures desk on board.

ONBOARD ACTIVITIES The **AquaDuck** waterslides on the *Dream* and *Fantasy* and the **AquaMouse** slide on the *Wish*-class ships all seem to be able to accommodate guests of virtually every body size and shape; we've heard success stories from individuals weighing more than 300 pounds and couples weighing more than 400. The **AquaDunk** slide on the *Magic* has a weight limit of 300 pounds.

DCL *for* INTROVERTS

AS A QUICK GLANCE at the Navigator app shows, a Disney cruise includes lots of activities for people with a social bent: karaoke, dance parties, and so on. But all that hustle and bustle could be overwhelming for an introvert or someone with sensory-processing issues. If that's you, here are a few suggestions for a more enjoyable cruise.

STATEROOM SELECTION Spend a little more and choose the right stateroom. A stateroom with a verandah lets you take in the ocean views without having to venture out to the public decks.

DINING Request your own dinner table. DCL sometimes seats small parties with other guests in the main dining rooms. If eating with strangers isn't your cup of tea, indicate this when you complete the Special Requests section of your online check-in (see page 123) or call DCL to request your own table. Alternatively, you can order room service or eat at one of the restaurants on the pool deck.

DCL tends to make a fuss about special occasions, especially at dinners. If that's not your thing and you'll be celebrating your birthday on board, don't let the cruise staff know. If you're traveling with a group, make sure they are aware of your wishes.

PORT ADVENTURES Book your own port excursions, explore ports on your own, or just stay on the ship. Because port adventures are group events, a self-guided tour may be more your speed. Likewise, staying on board when others are in port can feel like having the ship to yourself.

ONBOARD ACTIVITIES Use the adults-only areas as much as possible. The adult pool areas on board and Serenity Bay at Castaway Cay and Lookout Cay are much less raucous than the comparable family areas on both ship and shore.

We also suggest communicating your needs to your stateroom host. If you need quiet time in your stateroom during certain hours, let your attendant know.

DCL *if* YOU'RE EXPECTING

DISNEY CRUISE LINE prohibits guests who are **24 or more weeks pregnant** on the date of sailing or who would reach the end of their second trimester during their trip. If you'll be 23 weeks pregnant on embarkation day, a 12-night transatlantic cruise would be a no-go.

Here are some specific concerns to be aware of on board and in port; be sure to discuss these with your doctor before your cruise.

PORT ADVENTURES Excursions such as scuba diving, off-road driving, and parasailing prohibit pregnant guests from participating. And some tour operators have restrictions on snorkeling and dolphin encounters. But even if all you have planned is a day of sightseeing or lying on the beach, be aware that the trip to your destination could involve a lengthy trip in a rattletrap vehicle on a bumpy road.

ONBOARD ACTIVITIES The waterslides, both on the ships and on Castaway Cay and Lookout Cay, are off-limits to pregnant guests.

Certain treatments at the onboard **Senses Spas** are also restricted, but the wording on the DCL website is vague and confusing:

We are unable to provide massage services to pregnant Guests in their first trimester. After the first trimester, Guests may partake of massage treatments, although aromatherapy is not recommended.

When it comes to massages, we assume you're on the honor system if you're in your first trimester but not visibly pregnant. Otherwise, we're not sure how this policy is supposed to be enforced.

DCL *with* YOUNGER CHILDREN

DISNEY CRUISE LINE requires that infants be at **least 6 months old** to cruise on most sailings from the United States and **at least 1 year old** on some longer voyages. Here are some key topics to think about if you're traveling with kids age 5 and younger.

DINING The Disney ships serve a wide variety of foods, but naturally they're not going to have *everything* your child likes to eat. Depending on how picky your little one is, that could lead to a tantrum or two. ("*Orange* mac and cheese? I wanted white!") If you have a truly limited eater, you'll need to strategize in advance.

If your child is still learning to drink from a cup, be sure to bring your own lids and straws. As part of its environmental efforts, DCL has banished plastic straws and cup lids.

In general, the younger the child, the closer you'll want to stick to their typical eating and sleeping schedules. In most cases, that will mean choosing the early dinner seating, but depending on where you sail, you could be competing with lots of other families for that early seating. And if you'll be cruising far from home, be aware that adjusting to a different time zone could play havoc with your child's sleep schedule.

unofficial **TIP**
If your preferred dinner seating is fully booked before your cruise, get on the waitlist. If you don't make it off the waitlist, you may be able to switch your seating after you're on board.

ONBOARD ACTIVITIES DCL furnishes portable cribs free of charge to families who need them, along with supplies such as bed rails, bottle warmers, and diaper pails. Request these during your online check-in process (see page 127), call DCL at ☎ 800-951-3532 before your sailing, or check with Guest Services on board.

Families traveling with young children should think about sleeping arrangements before their trip. A crib could make a small stateroom feel even smaller, so think carefully about whether you absolutely need one. If you have a toddler who's still sleeping in a crib at home, consider helping them make the switch to a bed before your cruise. *Note:* DCL may limit the number of cribs per stateroom to one.

A kindergartner in a clingy phase may not deal well with going to the kids' club. In this case, it can help to adjust your expectations: If you assume that most of your cruise will consist of family time rather than "parents at the spa" time, then you'll be pleasantly surprised if your preschooler ends up loving the kids' club. See page 237 for more considerations for cruising with young children.

You're welcome to nurse anywhere on board, including the dining rooms, theaters, and pool decks. When it comes to breastfeeding in port, however, it's a good idea to research the cultural norms in the countries you'll be visiting.

DCL *with* OLDER CHILDREN

CRUISING WITH 17- TO 18-YEAR-OLDS

SOME FAMILIES WITH 17- and 18-year-olds may encounter frustration during their trip due to Disney's strict enforcement of age restrictions on teen and adult activities.

DINING A few years ago, we traveled with a teen just days away from her 18th birthday, and even though she was a high school graduate, she wasn't allowed to dine at Palo—yes, we tried bribery, and no, it didn't work—or go to some of the adults-only cooking demonstrations.

PORT ADVENTURES Over the years, Disney has offered port adventures exclusively for teenagers. We've seen them on Castaway Cay and in Alaska, for example. If you're interested, keep an eye on the port adventures options and check with Vibe (the teen club) once on board.

ONBOARD ACTIVITIES We've also seen 17- and 18-year-old cousins unable to do virtually anything together because the older teen wasn't allowed into Vibe and the younger one wasn't allowed into any of the grown-up activities. We've even met teens who turned 18 during their cruise and were allowed into Vibe for the first part of the trip but were denied entry after their birthday.

Bottom line: If you have an older teen, consider whether a slightly different travel date would improve your family's experience.

CRUISING WITH 18- TO 20-YEAR-OLDS

SOMETIME IN THE LAST FEW YEARS, Disney realized that 18- to 20-year-olds needed a little more on board. They are in that in-between age where they can enjoy all the adult activities but may still want a gathering space where they can meet other travelers their age.

ONBOARD ACTIVITIES To fill this need, Disney created the **1820 Society.** Gatherings are listed in the Navigator app and range from meeting for coffee to playing games in the atrium. Depending on the sailing, several guests may participate or just one or two. The crew members often join in if the numbers are low. The *Wish*-class ships have also created a special area on the ship called **The Hideaway,** where the 1820 Society holds some of its meetups when the younger teens aren't using it.

CRUISING *without* KIDS

DISNEY CRUISE LINE was obviously created with families in mind, but over the years, we've seen more and more adults-only groups choosing Disney over other lines.

CRUISE FARES Because many parents are hesitant to take their kids out of school, you'll find the lowest cruise prices when school is in session. If your group has the flexibility to travel when schools are in session, do it.

unofficial **TIP**
Longer sailings during the school year tend to have fewer children.

DINING When we travel without kids, we choose adult-dining restaurants as often as possible. There's an upcharge, but the food is delicious, the servers are top-notch, and the atmosphere is wonderful.

PORT ADVENTURES If your sailing is stopping at Castaway Cay or Lookout Cay, you may want to beeline to the adult beaches. They both have dining, bars, and even a few cabanas that you may be able to reserve in advance (see pages 327 and 334). Cabana or not, we love the adult beach areas at Disney's island destinations.

There are also some adult-exclusive port adventures (though not many) at ports around the world. We recommend them if you are cruising without kids.

ONBOARD ACTIVITIES All the ships have adults-only pools and coffeehouses. During the day, you'll see several activities for adults like trivia and tastings (tastings must be reserved in advance). In the evenings, the nightclubs become adults-only spaces, and one features games, shows, and other entertainment every night for adults.

You can easily find adult-specific activities each day by checking the Navigator app and turning on the "18 and above" filter at the top of the screen.

DCL *for* LARGE GROUPS

A CRUISE CAN BE a great travel choice for family or class reunions, bachelorette parties, or large groups of friends. Nobody has to cook or clean, so everybody gets to relax.

We have found it's important to have a guiding ethic to make large-group cruises successful: Every family or solo traveler is responsible for their vacation. That means every family or solo traveler gets to pick the activities that will make them happy. We find that allowing this kind of freedom, rather than trying to mandate that everyone participate in the same activities, increases the chances of having an enjoyable large-group cruise.

unofficial TIP

We highly recommend sailing Concierge with large groups when possible. Getting everyone into Palo or all on the same excursion is problem-solving at which the Concierge team excels.

CRUISE FARES Disney has official groups that you or your travel agent can set up through its Group Reservations department (☎ 407-939-1942). Groups are set up as one party with one form of payment and the potential for small discounts if you have a group of 14 staterooms or more.

If your large party doesn't meet that minimum or isn't comfortable with the contract and possible financial risk of booking as an official group, you can still form an unofficial group. Disney will link several staterooms together for dining purposes, and you can always plan the same excursions and meetup times.

DINING If your group is linked together, you will be sitting near each other in the dining room. Depending on how large your party is, you could be at one big table, or you could be at a few tables grouped together. If your group is extra large, you may even be split among dining teams, but if that happens, you'll be near each other.

PORT ADVENTURES We've found traveling with extended family across several staterooms to be a great way to travel, and we do it frequently. We split up during the day when Grandpa wants to watch movies in the theaters and the teenagers want to snorkel with turtles in the crystal-clear waters of the Caribbean. Then we meet back up for dinner to share tales of our day before taking in the nightly show together. At the end of the cruise, we all feel like we get the vacation we want and still have a memorable time as a family.

Note that if you have more than four staterooms linked together, you probably will not be able to book activities for everyone at once, even if everyone's booking window is open. Disney's system sometimes doesn't play nicely with large groups booked together. When we are traveling with a large group, we usually link in groups of four until after port adventures and the like are booked; then we relink.

ONBOARD ACTIVITIES One thing to note about activities is that guests with different Castaway Club levels can book excursions and adult dining at different times, which may make some things hard for the group to do if a particular port adventure or dining time fills up. Once on board, the adult-dining team can usually help get everyone together, and there's a chance you will find availability for a port adventure if they have cancellations, although the latter is much less common. If you happen to all be sailing Concierge, the Concierge team will help you get everyone together.

DCL *for* GUESTS *with* DISABILITIES

DCL STRIVES TO make its ships accessible to everyone. Virtually the entire ship, from staterooms to restaurants to nightclubs and pools, is accessible to guests using wheelchairs and electric conveyance vehicles (ECVs, or scooters).

Your first step in getting the help you need is to fill out DCL's **Request Special Services** form, available online at theugseries.com /dcl-req-services (a printable PDF is available at theugseries.com/dcl -services-pdf). This form must be submitted online **at least 60 days before sailing.** You may also contact **DCL Special Services** with specific questions by phone (☎ 407-566-3602 [voice] or 407-566-7455 [TTY]; email (specialservices@disneycruise.com); or mail (PO Box 10210, Lake Buena Vista, FL 32830).

Overall, guests with mobility issues can expect that their needs will be met with courtesy and good design. Roberta from Florida writes:

As a disabled individual, I have been fortunate to be fairly well traveled. Cruise travel, in particular, is well suited to disabled travelers. Personally, I have found DCL to be superior to other cruise lines in regards to how well disabled travelers are cared for. The ship's design is taken into consideration with such items as wider door passageways, swimming pools with specialized entrance accommodations, and bathrooms with all the necessary physical appointments. Besides the numerous design adjustments, Disney ensures that all cast members are thoroughly versed on how to assist disabled individuals with any and all of their particular needs. As I like to say, no stone goes unturned, even for disabled travelers, while traveling on a Disney cruise.

STATEROOM FURNISHINGS In addition to the standard stateroom amenities, DCL offers a number of features for guests with disabilities, as noted below:

• Closed-captioned TV (most stations)	• Portable toilet	• Shower stool
	• Raised toilet seat	• Transfer benches
• Bed boards and rails	• Rubber bed pads	• Sharps container
• A Stateroom Communication Kit, including an alarm clock, door-knock and phone alerts, a phone amplifier, a bed-shaker notification, a strobe-light smoke detector, and a text typewriter (TTY)		

WHEELCHAIR AND ECV USERS DCL suggests that guests using a wheelchair or ECV request an accessible stateroom or suite. Found on every Disney ship, accessible staterooms include the following:

• Doorways at least 32 inches wide	• Fold-down shower seating and handheld showerheads	• Open bed frame for easier entry and exit
• Bathroom and shower handrails	• Lowered towel and closet bars	• Ramped bathroom thresholds
• Emergency call buttons and additional phones in the bath and bedroom		

One advantage to having an accessible stateroom is that its wider door lets you store your wheelchair or ECV inside your stateroom when it's not in use. This also makes it easier to recharge the equipment when needed. If you find yourself in a standard stateroom whose door isn't wide enough to accommodate your vehicle, you may be asked to park it in a designated area elsewhere on the ship, even at night. In practice, we've seen many ECVs parked in a corner of each deck's elevator-landing areas. Chances are that yours will be stored within a short distance of your stateroom.

Outside your stateroom, most ship activities have designated areas for guests in wheelchairs. At the Walt Disney Theatre, for example, cast members direct guests in wheelchairs to a reserved seating area. Shops, restaurants, bars, and nightclubs are all accessible, and accessible restrooms are available throughout the ship's public areas. A limited number of sand wheelchairs are available on Castaway Cay and Lookout Cay, too, on a first-come, first-served basis.

unofficial **TIP**
Service animals are welcome on all Disney ships, and each ship has a designated animal-relief area on an outside deck.

Note that you must transfer from your wheelchair to use DCL's pools. For this reason, Disney recommends that guests in wheelchairs travel with someone who can help transfer them to and from the wheelchair.

PORT ADVENTURES Many DCL port adventures have mobility requirements. For more information, check at the onboard Port Adventures desk, see disneycruise.disney.go.com/port -adventures, or see "Finding Port Adventures" on page 345.

Guests with mobility issues should be aware of Disney's partnership with **Accessible Travel Solutions** (accessibletravelsolutions.com). Through this partnership, DCL now offers port adventures specifically designed for ease of access for wheelchair users. To check availability, submit your request to **DCL Special Services** (see previous page) when your cruise reservation is paid in full and you have access to your Castaway Club booking window. A minimum number of participants are required; if the minimum is not met, guests may book the port adventure as a private experience at an additional cost.

Another area to be aware of is tendering from ship to shore. The water at some ports, such as Grand Cayman, isn't deep enough to accommodate large cruise ships like Disney's. At those ports, smaller boats, or tenders, pull up next to the ship, and guests board them for travel to and from land.

Some tenders use steps instead of ramps to get guests on board. In those cases, wheelchair passengers must use the steps. Also keep in mind that the Disney ship and tender craft both float freely in the ocean. It's not uncommon for the stairs to move 2 or 3 feet up and down during a transfer. If the seas are too rough, wheelchair guests may be denied transfer.

ONBOARD ACTIVITIES While we are fans of the *Wish*-class ships, we do feel like accessibility was a miss in some areas. Some of the criticisms:

- **The elevators are narrow and long,** which may make getting inside a crowded one more difficult for wider wheelchairs. (Midship elevators on the *Magic* and *Wonder* are also narrow.)

- **Not all elevators go to the top decks,** and you can't summon specific elevators. That may mean having to change elevators during the same journey up. While the other ships also have elevators that do not go all the way up, on the *Wish* class, those elevators go to popular locations like the adult section and Palo.

- **The adult pool is accessible only via the stairs.** The pool has a lift for wheelchair users, but it must be booked in advance through DCL Special Services (see page 163).

Considering these accessibility issues, wheelchair users should carefully consider whether to book a cruise on DCL's newest ships, particularly if pool use is an important part of their vacation.

GUESTS WITH VISION AND/OR HEARING LOSS For guests with vision loss, DCL provides accessibility aids such as Braille signage and audio descriptions for movies. For guests with hearing loss, in addition to closed-captioned TVs, assistive listening devices and printed scripts are available for shows at the ships' main theaters and show stages; contact Guest Services to pick those up.

American Sign Language (ASL) interpreters are also available for live performances on some cruise dates. They typically work a schedule aligned with the second (later) live performance at the **Walt Disney Theatre,** following the first dinner seating. To request an interpreter for a cruise originating in the United States, contact **DCL Special Services** (see page 163) at least 60 days before you sail. For guests interested in ASL services on international sailings, requests must be made at least 120 days in advance. At press time Disney had confirmed that the following 2025 sailings would have ASL interpreters:

- **May 17–May 24:** 7-Night Mediterranean Cruise from Barcelona
- **June 30–July 12:** 12-Night Mediterranean with Greek Isles Cruise from Civitavecchia
- **July 24–July 31:** 7-Night Western Europe Cruise from Barcelona ending in Southampton
- **August 10–18:** 8-Night Norwegian Fjords Cruise from Southampton
- **September 8–15:** 7-Night British Isles Cruise from Southampton

CHILDREN WITH DISABILITIES Disney's youth programs are open to all children ages 3–17. Participants must be potty-trained and able to play well with other kids who are about the same age and size.

The number of disabled children who can participate is limited and is based on the number of available counselors, the total number of other children in the programs, the number of children with disabilities already enrolled, and the specific needs of the children to be enrolled. Check with the Youth Activities team for more information when you get on board.

Youth club counselors are unable to provide one-on-one care or specialized medical assistance. Children who can address their own medical needs may store their supplies at the Youth Activities desk.

GUESTS WITH CANCER An advisory at the onboard **Senses Spas** states, "Guests diagnosed with cancer must obtain medical clearance from an oncologist (in the form of a doctor's note) to partake of massage treatments." We've never heard of anyone being turned away at the spa because of a cancer diagnosis, but if you have concerns, ask your home medical provider for advice. If you're planning to get a massage treatment, bring the doctor's note to be safe.

OTHER CONSIDERATIONS Guests who use electronic devices (insulin pumps or pacemakers, for example) to wirelessly transmit information to medical providers should know that connectivity on board can be intermittently spotty and potentially expensive. If you must constantly monitor these devices, you'll need to make well-informed decisions when planning your cruise.

Additionally, guests with a specific medical condition or care regimen should carry documentation about the nature of care and the contact information of their medical providers. The location of this information should be known to the guest's travel companions.

As noted earlier, DCL no longer stocks plastic straws and cup lids for drinks. Straws, however, can be crucial aids for guests with mobility, eating, and sensory-processing issues, so bring your own if you or someone in your group needs them.

Other amenities, such as accessible parking at the Port Canaveral cruise terminal, are also available. See DCL's **Guests with Disabilities FAQs** (theugseries.com/dcl-disabilities-faqs) for more information.

EQUIPMENT RENTALS Guests who need medical equipment on board may find it convenient to rent from **Special Needs at Sea** (specialneeds atsea.com), which delivers to the DCL ships at most embarkation ports, including Barcelona, Fort Lauderdale, Galveston, Port Canaveral, San Diego, San Juan, and Vancouver. The available equipment includes wheelchairs, ECVs, walkers, oxygen and respiratory aids, and audiovisual aids.

Another option for mobility rentals is **Scootaround** (☎ 888-441-7575, scootaround.com), which can deliver equipment to hotels or cruise ships at a number of US and international destinations, including Barcelona, New York, Port Canaveral, and Vancouver.

COMPLAINT RESOLUTION To submit complaints, including those regarding disability accommodations, use the following contacts:

- **Before your cruise** DCL Special Services, ☎ 407-566-3602, 407-566-3760 (fax), or 407-566-7455 (TTY); specialservices@disneycruise.com; PO Box 10210, Lake Buena Vista, FL 32830-0210.

- **At the cruise terminal** Ask for the supervisor at the check-in desk.

- **On the ship** Call or visit Guest Services.

- **After your cruise** Email guest.communications@disneycruise.com, or write to Disney Cruise Line Guest Communications, PO 10238, Lake Buena Vista, FL 32830.

ADDITIONAL RESOURCES Two sites provide information that can help disabled travelers plan the noncruise parts of their trip, such as flights to and from DCL port cities and pre- and postcruise hotel stays. **AccessibleGo** (accessiblego.com/home) is a clearinghouse for information on travel with all types of disabilities, and **Wheelchair Travel** (wheelchairtravel.org) is geared to travelers with mobility issues.

DCL *for* GUESTS *with* DIETARY RESTRICTIONS

DINING All of DCL's table-service menus include vegetarian, gluten-free, no-sugar-added, dairy-free, and Lighter Note (lower-calorie) offerings. (See the next page for our vegan and vegetarian dining tips.) With advance notice, the restaurants can also accommodate low-sodium, kosher, and halal diets, as well as diets that omit food allergens such as eggs, nuts, and shellfish, all at no additional cost. Counter-service restaurants and room service may have fewer options for those with dietary restrictions. Notify DCL of your needs at least 60 days in advance using the **Request Special Services** form (see page 163).

unofficial **TIP**
Pizza with gluten-free crust is available by request on the pool deck.

As a company, Disney has a pretty good reputation for handling special diets, but guests should nonetheless be prepared and proactive in their dealings with the DCL dining staff. Although DCL makes every reasonable effort to accommodate its guests' dietary needs, **they don't maintain separate kitchen facilities** for the preparation of special meals. Most cruisers with food allergies give DCL high marks, but you eat at your own risk.

On most sailings, an informational session for guests with food allergies is held on embarkation day, typically at 1 p.m. Call ☎ 800-951-3532 to find out whether this is happening during your cruise.

Your best resource for food issues during your sailing may be your dining-service team. At the beginning of your cruise, your servers will ask you about any allergies or special diets. Take advantage of this opportunity to discuss your needs with them. Some guests have found they are most comfortable if they stick with the same serving team for all meals, and even on Castaway Cay. Feel free to ask your team about their daytime restaurant assignments.

If you have a specific brand preference—for instance, a type of soy milk or gluten-free waffle—you'll find that there isn't much in the way of choice. If you or your child eats only one brand of something, your best bet is to bring it with you.

PORT ADVENTURES Most port adventures are run by independent contractors, not Disney. Your food requests and accommodations will *not* be automatically transferred to excursion contractors, and some providers may not be equipped to work with certain dietary issues. What's more, in many ports you won't be able to bring certain types of food off the ship due to legal and agricultural restrictions. Check with Guest Services for advice on how best to handle your dietary needs in port.

VEGETARIAN AND VEGAN DINING STRATEGIES

VETERAN DISNEY CRUISER **Laurel Stewart** sticks to a vegan diet at home. Here are her tips for guests who don't eat meat:

- **Breakfast** Your best bet is the buffet—you can see exactly what you're getting. Ask a server for nondairy milk.

- **Lunch** Again, you'll rarely go wrong with the buffet. Also, the pool deck's counter-service eateries have options like cheeseless pizzas, yummy wraps, veggie burgers (vegans, skip the buns), and fries.

- **Dinner** Vegetarian entrées are often vegan as well, but egg- and dairy-free appetizers and sweets can be harder to find. Fresh fruit or sorbet is always a good choice for dessert, though.

- **Adult dining** If you're traveling with an omnivore who wants to dine at one of the adults-only restaurants, be prepared to miss out; ovo-lacto vegetarians have more and better choices. Unfortunately, due to the specialized nature of the offerings, vegans cannot be accommodated at the Remy and Enchanté dessert tasting events.

unofficial **TIP**
For more tips on vegan dining in the Disney theme parks and on DCL, check out **Vegan Disney Food** (vegandisneyfood.com).

- **Castaway Cay and Lookout Cay** You can ask ahead for veggie burgers; plus, many of the sides are vegan, and there's lots and lots of fresh fruit.

- **Miscellaneous** Room service doesn't have a lot to offer right off the menu, but ask when you call if there's anything that can be modified. The evening antipasti at Cove Café and Vista Café are a good choice (just skip the cheeses). Finally, ask if off-menu options are available. During one sailing, we learned that we could order Indian food even though it wasn't on any of the menus. After a chat with our servers, they brought us huge bowls of delicious veggie curries and masalas, which were even tastier than many of the regular entrées.

DCL *for* LGBTQ+ TRAVELERS

DCL IS VERY WELCOMING to LGBTQ+ guests. Many cruisers have good luck finding like-minded cruisers while out and about, but if you're traveling solo, it may be worth joining the Facebook group for your cruise or posting to a Disney discussion board to make connections before your trip, assuming you want to interact with other guests.

PORT ADVENTURES The experiences of LGBTQ+ travelers in non-US ports will depend largely on the itinerary. Most places won't present a problem, but there are a few where it may pay to be cautious, such as parts of the Caribbean. The **U.S. Department of State**'s resource page for LGBTQ+ travelers includes a wealth of information: see theugseries .com/state-dept-lgbtq. Another good resource is **Equaldex** (equaldex .com). You can also Google "LGBTQ+ travel advice" as a starting point for additional research.

Transgender people and parents of transgender youth may encounter additional hiccups when arranging cruise travel or any international travel. DCL is legally required to ensure that cruise-booking documentation matches legal identification information—meaning that your passport or birth certificate must match your boarding documents exactly. This may mean you'll be required to use your previous name upon embarkation and when reboarding the ship after port adventures. Once you're on board, you can stop by Guest Relations and ask them to add a preferred name to your account for staff use.

SMOKING *on* BOARD

SMOKING, INCLUDING CIGARETTES, cigars, pipes, and electronic cigarettes, is prohibited in your stateroom, on your verandah (if your stateroom has one), and in any indoor space on the ship.

unofficial **TIP**
Guests caught smoking in their stateroom or on their verandah will be charged a $250 cleaning fee.

On the *Magic* and *Wonder*, outdoor smoking is permitted on the starboard side of Deck 4 (6 p.m.–6 a.m.) and on the port side of Deck 9 Forward, excluding the AquaLab area on the *Magic* and the Mickey's Pool area on the *Wonder*. On the *Dream* and *Fantasy*, smoking areas are on the port side of Deck 4 Aft (6 p.m.–6 a.m.); the port side of Deck 12 Aft, accessed by walking through the Meridian lounge; and near Currents bar on the port side of Deck 13 Forward. On the *Wish*, *Treasure*, and *Destiny*, the smoking areas are on the port side of Deck 4 (6 p.m.–6 a.m.) and on the port side of Deck 14 Forward and Aft.

FRIENDS *of* BILL W.

BEER, WINE, AND SPIRITS flow freely on cruise ships, even the relatively tame ones run by Disney. Daily **Alcoholics Anonymous** meetings are held on all cruises; check the specifics for your sailing on the Navigator app. Note that some meetings are held in bars and lounges, but no bottles are out in the open during meetings.

That said, you will almost certainly be confronted with alcohol from time to time on a DCL cruise. If you're in recovery and need a more fully alcohol-free environment, we encourage you to consider booking a trip with a company such as **Travel Sober** (travelsober.com), **We Love Lucid** (welovelucid.com), or **Sober Vacations International** (sobervacations.com). Some of these trips take place on cruise ships (Travel Sober, for example, uses Norwegian Cruise Line); others offer experiences similar to Adventures by Disney trips.

GETTING *to* *and from* YOUR CRUISE

The NIGHT BEFORE *your* CRUISE

STAYING AT A LOCAL HOTEL THE NIGHT BEFORE

WE'VE SAID IT BEFORE, and we'll say it again: If you choose to fly, we wholeheartedly recommend flying at least a day before you sail. Even the smallest of airline delays, missed connections, or bad weather can cause you to miss your vacation. You don't need that cushion if everything goes well, but that cushion may save your vacation if it doesn't. You can book your pre- or postcruise hotel stay through Disney as part of your vacation package, no matter which port you're sailing from. This has its advantages and disadvantages:

THE PROS Disney has vetted the property, so you're unlikely to end up in a dump. Plus, transportation to and from the port will be seamless if you've also purchased ground transfers (see page 177).

THE CONS Your choices are limited, and you will often pay more when booking through Disney.

For the type A trip planner, booking a hotel through Disney can feel (to use a travel metaphor) like flying blind. Before one DCL Alaskan cruise, for instance, we had Disney book our pretrip accommodations at the Fairmont Vancouver Airport Hotel. Because we booked through DCL, we received no direct information about our room reservation—not even a confirmation number. Then, about six weeks before our trip, we called the Fairmont to find out what type of room we were booked in, only to be told that they didn't know. As it turns out, Disney doesn't send your hotel your room preferences—or even your name—until about two weeks before you check in.

If you're driving to the port, most hotels near cruise terminals offer inexpensive parking and shuttle transportation. There are exceptions, of course, but parking rates are often substantially less than what you'd pay at the terminal. In Port Canaveral, for example, parking at many hotels costs less than $10 per day, compared with $17 per day to park at the terminal.

If You're Cruising out of Barcelona

Barcelona is an iconic city, full of great hotels. **The Renaissance Barcelona Hotel** (Pau Claris 122, ☎ +34-932-723-810, theugseries.com/ren -bcn) is a gorgeous property in a great location with rooms and suites that sleep up to four. **The Hilton Diagonal Mar** (Passeig del Taulat 262– 264, ☎ +34-935-070-707, theugseries.com/hilton-diag-mar) is a nice property about 2 miles from the Basílica de la Sagrada Família and offers guaranteed connecting rooms when available. If you would like to be in the heart of La Rambla, a wonderful walking street in Barcelona, **Le Méridien Barcelona** (La Rambla 111, Pintor Fortuny 4–6; ☎ +34-933-186-200; theugseries.com/meridien-bcn) is one of our favorite places to stay; the rooms and suites sleep up to four.

If You're Cruising out of Civitavecchia

Because Civitavecchia is an hour-plus train ride from Rome, you may prefer to stay in Rome. If you choose to stay in **Rome,** there are many good options. **The Westin Excelsior** (Via Vittorio Veneto 125, ☎ +39- 06-47081, theugseries.com/westin-excelsior) is a beautiful hotel near the US Embassy and within easy walking distance of several popular sites. **Hotel Scalinata di Spagna** (Piazza Trinità dei Monti 17, ☎ +39- 06-45686150, hotelscalinata.com) is located near the top of the Spanish Steps, which is a fun location.

If you would like to go ahead and get to the port, there are some options in **Civitavecchia. Hotel San Giorgio** (Viale Garibaldi 34, ☎ +39- 0766-5991, theugseries.com/hotel-san-giorgio) is a lovely hotel with sea-view rooms available, as well as rooms that sleep up to four. If you are looking for more of a guesthouse experience, **La Casa Sul Mare** (Galleria Giuseppe Garibaldi 32, ☎ +39-3282496603, lacasa sulmare.net) is a great place to stay. All the guest rooms have private terraces and views of the sea. Some rooms sleep up to four.

If You're Cruising out of Fort Lauderdale

If you want a swanky beach resort, try **The Ritz-Carlton** (1 N. Fort Lauderdale Beach Blvd., ☎ 954-465-2300, theugseries.com/ritz-ftl). We enjoy the **Fort Lauderdale Marriott Harbor Beach Resort & Spa** (3030 Holiday Drive, ☎ 954-525-4000, theugseries.com/marriott-ftl-harbor) when we want to be right on the beach and have a great view of the ships sailing out of the port in the evenings. The **Hilton Fort Lauderdale Marina** (1881 SE 17th St., ☎ 954-463-4000, theugseries.com/hilton-ftl -marina) has a great location with ship views, but some of the rooms are run-down, so make sure you book a room in the tower. If you book through DCL, you will usually get a tower room on a higher floor. There is also an inexpensive shuttle to the port that you can book on-site. The **Renaissance Fort Lauderdale Marina Hotel** (1617 SE 17th St., ☎ 954-626-1700, theugseries.com/ren-ftl-marina) has a great location near the port, but the rooms are a bit more dated than we've come to expect from a Renaissance property. And don't forget that **Miami** is about an hour's drive from Fort Lauderdale if you want to explore the sights there before your cruise.

If You're Cruising out of Galveston

Located on a narrow strip of land in the Gulf of Mexico about 50 miles southeast of Houston, Galveston offers beaches, historic charm, excellent dining and shopping, and family fun at the Galveston Island Pleasure Pier. The century-old **Grand Galvez** (2024 Seawall Blvd., ☎ 409-765-7721, grandgalvez.com) has tastefully appointed rooms, a spa, a heated pool, and free shuttle service to the port, which is less than 2 miles away. Open off and on since 1839, **The Tremont House** (2300 Ship Mechanic Row St., ☎ 409-763-0300, thetremonthouse.com) is located in the Strand Historic District, just a few blocks from the port. Like the Grand Galvez, The Tremont House is historic and luxurious. Although it doesn't have a pool or spa, its location near downtown is better than the Grand Galvez's for people who want to explore the area on foot. Both hotels offer AAA, AARP, and other discounts.

If You're Cruising out of Honolulu

Aulani, A Disney Resort & Spa (92-1185 Ali'inui Drive, Kapolei; ☎ 866-443-4763; disneyaulani.com) is the obvious choice when you are sailing out of Honolulu. Aulani is an absolutely gorgeous oceanside Hawaiian resort with subtle Disney touches throughout. There are several room categories, including stunning three-bedroom villas that sleep up to 12, and the views are stunning, with prices to match. If you would like to be closer to downtown Honolulu, the **Hilton Hawaiian Village Waikiki Beach Resort** (2005 Kalia Road, ☎ 808-949-4321, theugseries.com /hilton-hawaiian-village) is a popular place to stay right on the beach. There are suites available that sleep up to six. **Waikiki Beach Marriott Resort & Spa** (2552 Kalakaua Ave., ☎ 808-922-6611, theugseries.com /marriott-waikiki-beach) is another nice hotel downtown on the beach.

If You're Cruising out of Port Canaveral

There are advantages to spending the night in either Cape Canaveral or Orlando. Staying in Cape Canaveral means you're just minutes from the terminal. You can enjoy a relaxed breakfast on the morning of your cruise, take a swim in the pool, and pick up any last-minute items. The main downside of staying here is that there's not as much to do as there is in Orlando. Plus, the attractions may not be convenient to your hotel or may require reservations.

Our favorite hotel in **Cape Canaveral** is the **Residence Inn Cape Canaveral Cocoa Beach** (8959 Astronaut Blvd., ☎ 321-323-1100, theugseries.com/res-inn-canaveral). Its studio, one-bedroom, and two-bedroom suites sleep up to six people. There's a free breakfast buffet, along with plenty of nearby dining options; other amenities include a fitness center and free Wi-Fi. Due to its location and pool, the **Radisson Resort at the Port** (8701 Astronaut Blvd., ☎ 321-406-5615, theugseries.com/radisson-canaveral) is still a popular option for cruisers, even though parts of it have become dated. There are many dining options nearby, as well as a shuttle to the port and parking packages.

The advantage of staying in **Orlando,** of course, is its proximity to Walt Disney World. You can add any Disney resort to your cruise reservation, although we recommend booking them separately for the best pricing and flexibility. It's always fun to enjoy some time in the parks before your cruise. If we are not visiting Disney World before our cruise, we enjoy staying at the **Hyatt Regency Orlando International Airport** (9300 Jeff Fuqua Blvd., ☎ 407-825-1234, theugseries.com/hyatt-mco), which is located inside the Orlando International Airport (MCO). It's incredibly convenient, especially for later flights, and the airport is full of good options for dinner and breakfast. If you book Disney transfers, your luggage will be picked up from your room on the morning of your sailing, and you won't see it again until it appears in your stateroom later that afternoon. You will be given times to meet the shuttle to Port Canaveral, which is just downstairs.

If You're Cruising out of San Diego

Disney fans, you're in luck—you can stay at **Disneyland** before your trip. Getting from **Anaheim** to the San Diego cruise terminal typically takes less than 3 hours (with traffic). We love the rooms at the **Disneyland Hotel** (1150 W. Magic Way; ☎ 714-778-6600; disneylandhotel.com), while Disney's newly redone **Pixar Place Hotel** (1717 S. Disneyland Drive, ☎ 714-999-0990, theugseries.com/disney-pixar-place) is usually the least expensive choice. The luxurious **Grand Californian Hotel & Spa** (1600 S. Disneyland Drive, ☎ 714-635-2300, theugseries.com/disney -grand-californian) is one of our favorite hotels anywhere and is attached to the **Disney California Adventure Park.**

In **San Diego,** try the iconic **Hotel del Coronado** (1500 Orange Ave., ☎ 619-435-6611, hoteldel.com). Its red-gabled roof and white walls provided architectural inspiration for the Grand Floridian Resort & Spa at Walt Disney World, and the exterior was featured in the 1959 comedy classic *Some Like It Hot.*

If You're Cruising out of San Juan

San Juan is easy to get around with Uber and taxis. The **Sheraton Puerto Rico Resort & Casino** (200 Convention Blvd., ☎ 787-993-3500, theug series.com/sheraton-pr) is a good hotel option from a familiar brand.

Rooms sleep up to four, and a Presidential Suite sleeps up to six. **Hotel El Convento** (100 Calle del Cristo, ☎ 787-723-9020, elconvento.com) is located right in the heart of Old San Juan, with rooms that sleep up to four. It's a great location. The **Caribe Hilton** (1 San Gerónimo St., ☎ 787-721-0303, caribehilton.com) is a beautiful beachfront resort with rooms that sleep up to six.

If You're Cruising out of Southampton

Southampton is a train ride away from London, one of the world's greatest cities. If you stay in London before your cruise, you have hundreds of options. One of our favorites is the **London Marriott Hotel County Hall** (London County Hall, Westminster Bridge Road; ☎ +44-207-928-5200; theugseries.com/marriott-london-county-hall), located right next to the London Eye and across the Thames River from Big Ben. **St. Ermin's Hotel** (Caxton Street, ☎ +44-207-222-7888, sterminshotel .co.uk) is a deluxe hotel located between Buckingham Palace and Westminster Abbey. If you are looking for a more reasonable price, there are several Premier Inn properties in London that fill the bill. **Premier Inn London County Hall Hotel** (County Hall, Belvedere Road; ☎ +44-333-321-1246; theugseries.com/premier-london-county-hall) is very close to the London Marriott above and all the nearby attractions.

If you choose to stay closer to the port in the quieter town of **Southampton,** the boutique **Moxy Southampton** (Harbour Parade, ☎ +44-23-81680269, theugseries.com/moxy-southampton) has rooms that sleep up to four. **The White Star Tavern** (28 Oxford St., ☎ +44-2380-821990, whitestartavern.co.uk) is a historic boutique hotel with rooms that sleep up to two, along with award-winning food.

If You're Cruising out of Sydney

Among Sydney's countless hotel options, we have a few to recommend. **Four Points by Sheraton Sydney, Central Park** (88 Broadway, ☎ +61-2-8288-8888, theugseries.com/sheraton-4-points-sydney) is a reasonably priced option downtown with easy access to trains. The rooms sleep up to four. **The Grace Sydney** (77 York St., ☎ +61-2-9272-6888, gracehotel.com.au) is a beautiful historic hotel just a few blocks from the water and a mile or so from the Sydney Opera House. The rooms sleep up to four. **The InterContinental Sydney** (117 Macquarie St., ☎ +61-2-9253-9000, sydney.intercontinental.com) has views of the opera house and the harbor from the rooms on higher floors and the rooftop bar—one of the most famous vistas in the world. The rooms sleep up to four.

If You're Cruising out of Vancouver

The **Pan Pacific Vancouver** (999 Canada Place, Ste. 300; ☎ 604 662-8111; panpacificvancouver.com) is posh and pricey but also incredibly convenient to the port. The **Fairmont Waterfront** (900 Canada Place Way, ☎ 604-691-1991, fairmont.com/waterfront-vancouver) is also expensive and located right across the street from the port. Another high-end (and fabulous) option is the **Shangri-La Vancouver** (1128 W. Georgia St., ☎ 604-689-1120, www.shangri-la.com/en/vancouver/shangrila), which has huge marble baths, friendly staff, and spectacular views of the ocean and mountains. A more economical option is the **Metropolitan Hotel Vancouver** (645 Howe St., ☎ 604-687-1122, metropolitan.com/vanc), near the Granville Station Expo Line stop.

DEPARTURE PORT HIGHLIGHTS

BARCELONA

BARCELONA IS AN AMAZING CITY, and we always add time there when possible. We like to stay near **La Rambla** or at least make our way over there for a day. It's a wonderful walking street full of shops, La Boqueria (an open-air food market), cafés, street performers, and more. The **Basílica de la Sagrada Família** is a stunning cathedral that's been under construction for more than 140 years and is considered one of the greatest buildings to visit in the world. **Park Güell** is a UNESCO World Heritage Site with stunning architectural elements designed by Antoni Gaudí (who designed Sagrada Família) and great views. Soccer fans can tour **Camp Nou** (home of FC Barcelona), and chocolate lovers won't want to miss **Museu de la Xocolata de Barcelona**.

CIVITAVECCHIA

IN THE TOWN OF Civitavecchia, the most popular local attraction is **Fort Michelangelo,** which was built in 1503 to protect the village from invaders. The **Terme Taurine** are ancient baths built around hot springs located about 4 miles east of the city. **Rome,** where you'll probably want to spend most of your time, is about an hour and a half away by train or an hour by taxi or car. The historic sites are abundant and popular. It's unlikely you can see them all in a day, so see what you can and plan to return. **Vatican City** is home to the **Sistine Chapel** and **Saint Peter's Basilica.** The **Colosseum** is a must-see for most visitors, as well as other stops like the **Spanish Steps,** the **Pantheon,** the **Trevi Fountain,** and countless museums. Don't leave Italy without having gelato. It's a must.

FORT LAUDERDALE

IT'S KNOWN FOR its beaches, but there are other things to do too. **Las Olas Boulevard** is a walkable beachfront street full of restaurants and shops. If airboat rides to see gators or kayaking with manatees appeal to you, **Everglades National Park** is about an hour away.

GALVESTON

THE GALVESTON PORT is about two blocks from a bustling tourist area with shops, restaurants, and more. **Pleasure Pier** on the seawall is a low-key carnival area, but for real fun, head to **Schlitterbahn** water park. A few small museums are in the area, including the **Galveston Railroad Museum,** the **Texas Seaport Museum,** and the **Ocean Star Offshore Drilling Rig & Museum.** We're pretty sure there's a law somewhere that you can't leave Texas without trying the local barbecue, and while you're at it, head to **La King's Confectionery** for ice cream and taffy.

HONOLULU

HONOLULU IS FULL OF wonderful spots to visit, and we highly recommend adding time there. The biggest draw for many American visitors is the **Pearl Harbor National Memorial,** which includes the USS *Arizona* Memorial. Make sure to buy tickets in advance. The **Polynesian Cultural Center** is a great way to spend a day (but know it's on the other side of Oahu from Waikiki), and we also enjoy hiking up **Diamond Head** for views of the island. We have also enjoyed our visits to the **Dole Plantation,** which will be a hit with Dole Whip fans.

PORT CANAVERAL

THIS IS ONE of the busiest cruise ports in the world. We always recommend a stop at **Walt Disney World** (about an hour away) before or after you sail, but there are several local attractions too. We highly recommend the **Kennedy Space Center,** a spectacular stop for anyone interested in space travel. **Jetty Park** is a fun place to visit in the evenings to watch the ships full of excited guests embarking on their vacations. We also enjoy watching the ships from one of the waterside restaurants the night before we sail. **Fishlips Waterfront Bar & Grill** is a favorite for both tourists and locals. The town of **Cocoa Beach** (about 15 minutes south) is great for beach lovers. Don't miss the flagship location of **Ron Jon Surf Shop,** which claims to be the world's largest surf shop.

SAN DIEGO

SAN DIEGO IS about an hour and a half south of **Disneyland,** so it's possible to add days there. **Balboa Park** is home to gorgeous gardens and 18 museums, including **The San Diego Museum of Art** and the **San Diego Natural History Museum.** The **San Diego Zoo** is one of the best zoos in the world and one of the few places in the United States where you can see giant pandas. **SeaWorld** and **Legoland** are also nearby.

SAN JUAN

DISNEY SHIPS DOCK in Old San Juan, which is very close to the main city. History buffs will want to visit **Castillo San Felipe del Morro** (known as El Morro), a fortress built to protect the island from attack by sea. The **Museo de Arte Contemporáneo** (Museum of Contemporary Art) showcases modern artists from Latin America and the Caribbean. The **Casa Bacardí** distillery (aka the Cathedral of Rum) is a popular spot for a tour. We highly recommend sampling the local cuisine while in town. We've never been disappointed.

SOUTHAMPTON

ABOUT A 90-MINUTE train ride from London, Southampton is home to museums like the aviation museum **Solent Sky** and the **SeaCity Museum,** which tells the tales of locals who were part of the *Titanic* story. If you're staying in London before your cruise, you could entertain yourself for days with things like **West End shows,** a tour of **Buckingham Palace, The British Museum, Westminster Abbey,** the **Tower of London,** and the **London Eye** for sweeping views of the city. And that barely scratches the surface.

SYDNEY

IF TRAVELING FROM the United States, you should probably make that long flight worth it and spend some extra time in this world-class city. Take in a performance at the **Sydney Opera House** or arrange a backstage tour. The **Queen Victoria Building** is a five-level shopping center that occupies an entire block. **The Sydney Tower Eye** is more than 1,000 feet high, with 360-degree views. The **Sydney Zoo** is home to more than 4,000 animals and includes an aquarium, and there are numerous beautiful parks to stroll through around the city.

VANCOUVER

VANCOUVER IS ONE of our favorite port cities. There is so much to do and see there that we recommend coming in a day early or departing a day later to give yourself time to explore. Disney sails from the Canada Place cruise ship terminal in downtown Vancouver. The **Vancouver Lookout** is nearby and has a glass elevator that will take you up 553 feet for panoramic views of the city and surrounding areas. The **Vancouver Aquarium** is a fun way to spend the day, as is a trip to **Stanley Park,** where you can ride a train, ride bikes, dine, swim, and more. For great views and fun activities like a wildlife refuge, a ropes course, and a zipline, take the **Skyride** up **Grouse Mountain**. Be sure to try the local seafood while in town as well.

DISNEY TRANSFERS *to and from* YOUR CRUISE

USING DISNEY TRANSPORTATION FROM THE AIRPORT OR A DISNEY-CONTRACTED HOTEL

TO ARRANGE A DISNEY TRANSFER, ask your travel agent, call ☎ 800-951-3532, or go to theugseries.com/dcl-my-reservations. If you have arranged a Disney transfer and are flying in on the day of your cruise, unless told otherwise, assume that a uniformed greeter will be stationed near the airport baggage-claim area holding either a DCL sign or a sign with your party's name on it.

If you fly in on the day before your cruise and are staying at a Disney-contracted hotel, there will be a desk set up in the hotel lobby where you will check in for your transfer the morning of your cruise. You should receive an email the day before you sail letting you know what time you will meet the transfer the next morning.

A Disney transfer is convenient, particularly if you're in an unfamiliar country, but understand that the convenience comes at a cost. For a family of four, you can almost certainly find cheaper private options. Children under age 3 are free.

The prices and ports below are for 2025 and are correct at press time, but be aware that Disney changes contractors, and prices change or may not be available to purchase until closer to sailing dates.

BARCELONA If you are flying into Barcelona International Airport (BCN), private transfers are available to purchase from Disney. **On embarkation day,** Disney recommends that your flight into BCN arrive no later than 12:45 p.m. If you're sailing on a **round-trip cruise from Barcelona,** your flight should depart out of BCN after 12:30 p.m. on debarkation day. If you are sailing **from Barcelona to Civitavecchia,** your flight out of Leonardo Da Vinci Airport-Fiumicino (FCO) should depart after 1 p.m. on debarkation day. If you are sailing **from Barcelona to Southampton,** your flight out of London Heathrow International Airport (LHR) or London Gatwick International Airport (LGW) should depart after 2:15 p.m. on debarkation day.

CIVITAVECCHIA If you are flying into FCO in Rome, private transfers are available to purchase from Disney. **On embarkation day,** Disney recommends that your flight into FCO arrive no later than noon. If you are sailing **round-trip from Civitavecchia,** your flight out of FCO should depart after 1 p.m. on debarkation day. If sailing **from Civitavecchia to Barcelona,** your flight out of BCN should depart after 12:30 p.m. on debarkation day.

FORT LAUDERDALE If you are flying into the Fort Lauderdale area, you can use Disney shuttles to get to Port Everglades for $29 per person, each way, from Fort Lauderdale–Hollywood International Airport (FLL) and $35 per guest, each way, from Miami International Airport (MIA). **On embarkation day,** Disney recommends that your flight arrive no later than 1 p.m. if flying into Fort Lauderdale (noon if flying into Miami) and that your flight out **on debarkation day** depart after 11 a.m. if flying out of Fort Lauderdale (noon if flying out of Miami).

GALVESTON If you are flying into the Houston area, private transfers are available to purchase from Disney. **On embarkation day,** Disney recommends that your flight arrive at IAH no later than noon and that your flight out **on debarkation day** depart after 1:30 p.m. If you happen to be on the **Galveston to San Juan sailing,** your flight should depart from Luis Muñoz Marín International Airport (SJU) after 11:15 a.m.

HONOLULU If you are flying into Honolulu, private transfers from Daniel K. Inouye International Airport (HNL) are available for purchase through Disney. If you are on the **Hawaii to Vancouver sailing,** Disney recommends that your flight arrive no later than 1 p.m. on embarkation day. On debarkation day, your flight out of Vancouver International Airport (YVR) should depart after 1 p.m. If you are on the **Vancouver to Hawaii sailing,** your flight should arrive at YVR no later than 1 p.m. on embarkation day. On debarkation day, your flight out of HNL should depart after 1 p.m. If you are on the **Honolulu to Sydney sailing,** your flight should arrive at HNL no later than 2 p.m. on embarkation day. On debarkation day, your flight should depart out of Sydney Airport (SYD) after 12:30 p.m.

PORT CANAVERAL If you're flying to Orlando International Airport (MCO), you can use DCL's shuttle service to get to Port Canaveral for $45 per person, each way. DCL recommends that your flight into MCO arrive by 1 p.m. **on embarkation day** (by noon if flying in from an international destination) and that your flight out **on debarkation day** depart after 11:15 a.m.

SAN DIEGO If you are flying into San Diego, private transfers are available to purchase from Disney. For **round-trip sailings out of San Diego,** Disney recommends that your flight arrive by 2 p.m. and that your flight out on debarkation day depart after 11:15 a.m. If you are sailing **from San Diego to Vancouver,** your flight should arrive at SAN no later than 2 p.m. Your departure flight out of YVR should be no earlier than 1 p.m.

SAN JUAN If you are flying into San Juan, private transfers are available to purchase from Disney. Disney recommends that your flight arrive no later than 12:30 p.m. **on embarkation day.** If you are sailing **from San Juan to Fort Lauderdale,** your flight out of FLL on debarkation day should depart no earlier than 11 a.m. If you are sailing **from San Juan to Galveston,** your flight into SJU on embarkation day should arrive no later than 2:45 p.m., and your flight out of IAH should depart no earlier than 12:30 on debarkation day.

SOUTHAMPTON If you are sailing from Southampton, you will be flying into and out of LHR or LGW. Private transfers are available to purchase from Disney. **On embarkation day,** Disney recommends that your flight arrive no later than 10 a.m., and **on debarkation day,** your flight should depart no earlier than 11 a.m.

SYDNEY If you are flying into SYD, private transfers are available to purchase through Disney. **On embarkation day,** Disney recommends that your flight arrive no later than 1 p.m. If you are sailing **from Sydney to Melbourne,** your flight out of Brisbane Airport should depart after noon. If you are sailing **from Sydney to Honolulu,** your flight out of HNL should depart after 11:30 a.m.

VANCOUVER If you are flying into YVR, private transfers are available to purchase from Disney. **On embarkation day,** Disney recommends that your flight arrive no later than 11:45 a.m. If you are sailing **round-trip from Vancouver,** your flight should depart after 1 p.m. on debarkation day. If you are sailing **from Vancouver to San Diego,** your flight should depart from SAN after 11:15 p.m. on debarkation day.

USING DISNEY TRANSPORTATION FROM WALT DISNEY WORLD TO PORT CANAVERAL

DCL ALSO PROVIDES SHUTTLE SERVICE from on-property hotels at Walt Disney World. Per-person prices are the same as for the airport shuttle ($45 each way).

LUGGAGE TRANSFER If you're taking a DCL cruise after staying at a Disney World hotel *and* you've booked your transportation to the port through Disney, cruise representatives can transfer your luggage directly from your hotel room to your ship's stateroom.

In the past, pickup times and luggage transfers have not always been clear, but DCL has improved greatly in this area, and we are optimistic. When staying at Riviera Resort before a recent cruise, we received an email from Disney Cruise Line giving us both the times our luggage would be picked up and the time to meet our shuttle bus. If you do not receive that email, there is also a phone number you can call for details on your pickup time: Call the **Embarkation Information Line** at ☎ 407-566-4040 and enter your resort information.

THIRD-PARTY TRANSFERS

IF YOU HAVE A PREFERRED AIRPORT (for budget reasons, convenience to where you live, or the like) that isn't served by Disney, you'll have to arrange your own ground transportation to the port. For sailings out of Galveston, for example, you can arrange Disney transfers from Houston's **George Bush Intercontinental Airport** but not from its other major airport, **William P. Hobby Airport.** From Houston Hobby, you will be on your own to get to the Galveston port.

Depending on your port, the easiest, cheapest way to get from the airport to your hotel or to the terminal may be **Uber** or **Lyft.** Prices are typically for up to four people in a single car rather than the per-person rate that Disney charges. If, however, you have more than four in your cruise group or you have a lot of luggage, you may want to use a third-party shuttle service instead (not all Uber or Lyft cars have room for lots of luggage). *Note:* Ride-sharing apps are likely to be the best option in places like Fort Lauderdale or San Diego, where the port and airport are close together and there is a relatively large local population. These apps are less likely to work well in places like Port Canaveral, where the port is distant from the airport and the population is too small to support a large pool of regular drivers.

FORT LAUDERDALE SuperShuttle serves Fort Lauderdale; download its mobile app at supershuttle.com/app. **Mears Transportation** does as well; see Port Canaveral on the opposite page for more information.

GALVESTON Galveston Express (☎ 409-762-4397, galvestonexpress
.com) offers both shared and private transfers, with the former being
less expensive. From Houston Hobby airport to the Port of Galveston,
transfers are about $65 per person, round-trip. **Galveston Limousine**
(☎ 409-744-5466, galvestonlimo.com/airport-shuttle) has coach bus
service from both Houston Hobby and George Bush airports several
times per day. Round-trip fares are $60–$120 per person, with discounts available for booking online.

PORT CANAVERAL If you have a large party, a third-party service like
Mears Transportation (☎ 407-423-5566, mearstransportation.com)
offers cost savings and the ability to schedule your departure at your
convenience. Round-trip prices between Orlando and Port Canaveral
are about $320 for up to four people in a town car, $380 for up to five
people in an SUV, or $410 for up to eight people in a luxury van. The
Mears mobile app lets you track your driver's location and may also
offer discount codes or coupons. Another well-regarded car service in
the area, **Park Avenue Limousines** (☎ 407-668-0850, parkavenuelimou
sines.com) can provide service from the airport or Walt Disney World
to the port in a range of vehicle types.

SAN DIEGO Blacklane (blacklane.com/en/cities-san-diego) offers one-
way and round-trip transfers, with up to an hour of complimentary wait
time and flight tracking.

INTERNATIONAL CITIES We are more hesitant to recommend third-
party shuttles in international cities because the reviews vary so wildly,
but we have had good luck with Uber.

DRIVING *or* RENTING *a* CAR

THE FOLLOWING SECTION provides driving directions to DCL
ports in California, Florida, Louisiana, New York, Texas, and Canada,
along with information on parking rates at the various cruise terminals.
See theugseries.com/dcl-departure-ports for additional port addresses
and customizable driving directions that incorporate Google Maps.

DRIVING YOURSELF

TO PORT CANAVERAL It takes about an hour to drive from Orlando
to Port Canaveral under normal conditions. Traffic and road construction on the Beachline Expressway (FL 528), a toll road, can
turn that trip into a 3-hour ordeal. And because Port Canaveral and
Orlando are linked by just three main roads with only limited connections between them, there are a couple of points along the Beachline
Expressway where you have no way of taking an alternative route if
traffic is delayed. Our advice is to allow at least 2 hours for this trip.

If you're using GPS, enter this address as your destination: **Port
Canaveral Terminal 8, 9155 Charles M. Rowland Drive, Port Canaveral,**

FL. If your GPS doesn't recognize Port Canaveral as a city, substitute Cape Canaveral.

If you're driving from Walt Disney World, the most direct route uses eastbound FL 536 to the Central Florida GreeneWay (FL 417) and then to the Beachline Expressway. The GreeneWay and Beachline are toll roads; you'll encounter fees of about **$10.** Be aware that many of the toll plazas in Central Florida are unmanned or do not accept cash. You may want to consider purchasing an E-PASS if you'll be doing lots of driving in Florida. See theugseries.com/fl-tolls for more information.

You'll be on the Beachline almost all the way to Port Canaveral. Once you arrive, you'll find that the port's terminals function almost exactly like an airport's. The same kinds of signs for airline terminals are posted for cruise terminals. In 2025, DCL ships are using both **Terminal 8** and **Terminal 10,** so look for road signs to that effect. If you want to see what the drive looks like, YouTube has videos showing the exits, terminal, and parking options from a car passenger's perspective (search "driving to Port Canaveral").

unofficial **TIP**

Take a picture of your parking spot with your smartphone before you leave the lot. This will help you remember where you parked when you return from your cruise.

Once you arrive at the terminal, you'll drop your luggage at the curb, where baggage handlers are waiting for you (have cash ready to tip them). After that's done, park and walk to the security checkpoint. Parking at Port Canaveral costs $17 per day, including the days of your arrival and departure. See portcanaveral.com/cruise/directions-parking for details.

TO FORT LAUDERDALE (PORT EVERGLADES) If you are driving to Fort Lauderdale from North Central Florida, you will likely be traveling on I-95. The port is just south of Fort Lauderdale and north of Dania Beach. You can also take the Florida Turnpike toll road, which may be faster and quieter. It runs from Ocala in North Central Florida through Orlando to Miami.

The GPS address is **1800 SE 20th St., Fort Lauderdale, FL.** Upon arriving at the port, follow the signs to the Disney Cruise Line ship and **Terminal 4,** where you can drop off luggage. From there, you'll be directed to the parking garage to park your car.

Parking operated by Port Everglades is available adjacent to Terminal 4. The garage opens at 10:45 a.m. The daily maximum rates are $15 for standard-size vehicles and $19 for oversize vehicles.

There are several off-site parking options available for even less. Investigate bookparkngo.com, goldcoastcruiseandflyparking.com, or parkbytheports.com.

TO GALVESTON The port is about 71 miles from Houston's George Bush Intercontinental Airport—roughly a 90-minute drive with traffic. If you're being dropped off, the GPS address to use for **Terminal 1** is **2502 Harborside Drive, Galveston, TX; Terminal 2** is at **2702 Harborside Drive, Galveston, TX.**

If you're parking, the GPS address is **Port of Galveston Parking, 33rd Street and Harborside Drive, Galveston, TX.** Parking fees range from $18 to $22 per day (including tax and local surcharges), with discounts for prepaying. Other discount or promo codes may be posted on the port's Facebook page or other sites such as visitgalveston.com. Book your spot at portofgalveston.com.

TO SAN DIEGO There is no parking directly at the terminal, but several lots are located nearby; some are within walking distance, while others offer shuttle service. See theugseries.com/san-diego-parking.

TO VANCOUVER The port is about a 30-minute drive from the airport: **Cruise Terminal, 999 Canada Place, Vancouver, BC, Canada.** Traffic in the several blocks surrounding Canada Place can be quite congested on cruise-departure mornings, so budget an extra 20 minutes or so if you're planning to arrive at the port during the late morning of your sail date.

The cruise terminal has over 750 parking spaces, which cost $32 CDN (about $25 US) per day. Reservations are recommended and can be made online at canadaplace.westpark.com/reserve-a-space.html.

If you're a group of able-bodied adults with a reasonable amount of luggage, the easiest, cheapest way to get from the airport to the terminal is Vancouver's clean and efficient **subway-light rail service.** A one-way trip costs $10 CDN (about $7 US) and takes about half an hour, with no transfers needed. Visit translink.ca for more information. (Input **YVR** as your start point and **Canada Place** as your end point.)

Electric Vehicles

Although electric vehicles (EVs) are becoming ever more popular, the charging infrastructure is still developing, and charging may not be available where you plan to spend the night or park for your cruise. If you are driving an EV, contact the individual hotels and parking locations to find out if there will be somewhere to charge it. When we parked a Tesla at the Port Canaveral parking garage shortly before press time for this book, we did not see any EV chargers at the parking garage, but there is a new Tesla Supercharger in Cape Canaveral, a mere 3 miles away. Almost every car company is now switching to the North American Charging Standard (i.e., the Tesla charging standard) for EV charging; go to tesla.com/findus and enter your destination to find all the nearby Supercharger locations. You can also go to Google Maps and enter "EV charging" to find additional charging options.

RENTING A CAR

WE OFTEN DRIVE OURSELVES in our own vehicles, but we've also rented vehicles several times. Sometimes that's your least expensive option for a family of four, plus it gives you more flexibility. In US ports, it's often nice to have a car to go to dinner the night before and to depart for the port on your own schedule the next morning. Most of the big rental car companies have locations near the ports and shuttles that run back and forth.

A WORD ABOUT THE TRAIN FROM ORLANDO TO FORT LAUDERDALE

IN LATE 2023, Brightline began a high-speed rail service between Orlando, Fort Lauderdale, and Miami, making it even easier to get from Orlando to the terminal in Fort Lauderdale. In Orlando, the train station is right next to the airport, while in Fort Lauderdale, it's approximately 10–15 minutes from the port.

The trains are comfortable, include Wi-Fi, and run frequently. The terminals themselves are bright and modern. There are places to store luggage on board, or you can pay to check a bag if you don't want to drag it around yourself.

Both standard and premium tickets are available. Premium tickets include a small meal (at certain times of day), drinks, snacks, and a lounge with a small selection of food and drinks in the terminal. In theory, Premium tickets also include a checked bag. In practice, Brightline will happily sell the luggage space on the day of, and once the baggage car is full, no more bags can be checked, whether you've purchased premium tickets or not. Tammy found this out the hard way in 2024 when the baggage car was full almost 2 hours before her train was scheduled to depart.

Between the two classes of tickets and the frequent special offers we've seen, pricing varies greatly. If you are interested, keep an eye out for a discount.

AFTER *your* CRUISE

FLYING OUT LATE ON DEPARTURE DAY FROM ORLANDO INTERNATIONAL AIRPORT (MCO)

AS MENTIONED, DCL asks that guests flying out of **Orlando International Airport** (**MCO**) from Port Canaveral not schedule flights home before 11:15 a.m. If you can fly out in the early afternoon, you're golden: Grab some lunch at the airport and you're good to go. But there may be times when you can't or don't want to fly home until later in the day. So how do you occupy your time if you debark at 8 a.m. but aren't getting on the plane until 8 p.m. or later? Here are a few suggestions.

- **Rent a hotel room just for the day.** The **Hyatt Regency Orlando International Airport** (inside MCO) has day-use rooms available from 10 a.m. to 6 p.m.; to check availability, call ☎ 407-825-1234.

    You could also rent the cheapest on-property room at **Walt Disney World.** Take the DCL shuttle or a rental car to the hotel. (The room might not be ready until 3 p.m., but if you have a reservation, you can use the pool and other hotel facilities in the meantime.) Then take a third-party shuttle, taxi, or ride-sharing service to MCO just before your flight.

- **Purchase a day pass for an executive lounge at the airport,** and get some work done in peace and quiet.

- **Visit other Orlando-area attractions.** You have plenty of recreation choices that don't absolutely require booking in advance (but do check availability before you go). Visit **Universal Orlando, SeaWorld, Madame Tussauds,** or the **Kennedy Space**

Center (in Cape Canaveral); go **horseback riding** at Disney's Fort Wilderness Resort; or experience **iFly indoor skydiving** (iflyworld.com). If needed, rent a car big enough for you and your luggage at the cruise terminal.

- **Go shopping!** We like **Lake Buena Vista Factory Stores Outlet Mall** (15657 S. Apopka–Vineland Road). The mall also has an outpost of **Orlando Baggage Storage** (☎ 407-539-4742, orlandobaggagestorage.com), which will hold your luggage for the day for a nominal fee.

FLYING OUT LATE ON DEPARTURE DAY FROM OTHER PORTS

AS WITH PORT CANAVERAL and Orlando, most ports have plenty of interesting things to see and do if you're not flying home until late in the day. If you want somewhere to park your luggage while you're off enjoying the attractions, try **Vertoe Luggage Storage** (vertoe.com) or **Luggage Hero** (luggagehero.com). These services have outposts in dozens of cities worldwide, including Barcelona, Galveston, San Diego, San Juan, and Vancouver, and will keep your bags safe for several hours for a fee.

If you need a place to rest before a long flight home, **Dayuse** (dayuse.com) offers partial-day hotel rentals in cities around the globe.

TRANSFERS TO WALT DISNEY WORLD HOTELS

IN RECENT YEARS, DCL has been tinkering with departure procedures for guests who have purchased transfers from the ship to a Walt Disney World resort. In years past, buses started running from Port Canaveral to Disney World as soon as the ship cleared customs, usually around 7 or 7:30 a.m., but there are times it's later. If you're an early riser, this can feel like a lot of unnecessary waiting around, so you may want to consider arranging your own transportation to the hotel.

You may also want to arrange your own transportation to the airport if time is tight on the last day of your trip. If, for instance, you really want to squeeze in a couple of extra hours in the parks but don't want to cut things too close for your flight home, a town car, cab, or rideshare may be a better choice than the Disney shuttle that morning.

PART 9

ARRIVAL *and* DEPARTURE DAYS

KEY QUESTIONS ANSWERED IN THIS CHAPTER

- What time should I arrive? *(see below)*
- What happens on embarkation day? *(see page 189)*
- What happens on debarkation day? *(see page 194)*

ARRIVAL PROCEDURES

CHOOSING A PORT-ARRIVAL TIME

DURING ONLINE CHECK-IN, you'll select the time you anticipate arriving at the port. When you arrive at your assigned time, you should be able to board the ship not long after your party completes the port security screenings.

Port-arrival times are tightly regulated at certain times of the day. If you arrive too early, you may have to wait for a long time outside the terminal. Your port-arrival time is not the same as your boarding time. Port-arrival times begin as early as 10:30 a.m., and boarding will usually begin between 11:30 a.m. and noon. You will be assigned a boarding group number based on your selected port-arrival time.

Concierge guests and Pearl Castaway Club members do not select a port-arrival time and may arrive anytime after the terminal opens and before boarding ends. Concierge guests will be in boarding group 1, and Pearl members are automatically assigned boarding group 2.

HEALTH QUESTIONNAIRE

BEFORE BOARDING, adults are asked to complete a mandatory questionnaire. This form will be emailed to you on embarkation day, typically between 5 and 6 a.m. The questions you'll be asked vary depending on prevailing world health conditions and your ship's destination. In 2024, there were only three items on the health questionnaire:

- Within the last three days, have you or any occupant of your stateroom developed symptoms of vomiting or diarrhea?

- Are you or any occupant of your stateroom experiencing a fever *and* any one of the following symptoms: cough, sore throat, runny nose, muscle aches, or headache?
- Will anyone in your travel party be pregnant 24 weeks or more at any point during your sailing?

Answering yes to any of Disney's questions will trigger an interview at the cruise terminal and may prevent you from boarding—so be sure that everyone in your party is in excellent health. Disney states the following in the contract that you were required to sign when you booked your trip:

The Carrier [DCL] reserves the right, without liability whatsoever, to refuse passage . . . to any Guest whose physical or mental condition . . . is considered a risk to the Guest's own well-being or that of any other Guest, crew member, or person.

The person completing the health form for their stateroom (who must be at least 18 years old) will be asked to affirm that:

On behalf of myself and all Guests occupying the stateroom listed above, I certify that all answers are complete and accurate, and I understand that any dishonest or misleading answers may have serious public health implications. The information in this Online Health Questionnaire may be reported to the relevant public health authorities.

I/we attest that all the Guests occupying this stateroom: (1) are knowledgeable about their individual risk of developing severe illness if infected with COVID-19; (2) have made an informed decision about cruising based on their individual risk; (3) have decided whether to consult with a health care provider based on their individual risk; and (4) agree to follow all health and safety measures during this cruise to minimize the spread of disease, such as wearing face coverings, proper hand washing, coughing etiquette, and appropriate physical distancing.

If you get sick in port, the **International Society of Travel Medicine** has an online directory of clinics that specialize in treating travelers: see istm.org/clinic-directory. The **International Association for Medical Assistance to Travellers** (iamat.org) also maintains a list of clinics and English-speaking doctors worldwide. **InternationalSOS** (internationalsos .com/personal-travel) is a fee-based service (sign up for it before your trip) that provides medical and security assistance for international travelers. If you work for a large corporation, check with your human resources department to see if they have a contract with a similar service.

unofficial **TIP**
If you receive medical treatment on your cruise, save any records, such as prescriptions, lab reports, and X-rays, and share them with your regular doctor once you're back home.

CHECKING IN AT THE TERMINAL

HAVE ALL YOUR TRAVEL DOCUMENTS, including your port-arrival QR code and your government-issued ID, ready as soon as you arrive. At Port Canaveral and Fort Lauderdale, drop large luggage pieces with a nearby porter (make sure your items are tagged with your name and stateroom number), park your car if needed, and then proceed to the terminal's entrance. You'll see lots of cast members there who can help direct you to the proper line.

After your initial boarding documents are scanned, you'll be sent to the passport/ID checkpoint just inside the terminal's entrance; then you'll pass through a metal detector while your luggage undergoes X-ray scanning. Security screening at the terminal is somewhat like that at the airport, but here they're looking for slightly different things. Not surprisingly, weapons of any sort are forbidden, but you can bring liquids like shampoo or cosmetics in any quantity you like, within reason. You may also bring nonalcoholic beverages (say, a case of water or soda) as long as they're factory-sealed. You can't, however, bring homemade food or fresh produce onto the ship due to the potential for contamination, which could make you *and* others sick. See page 141 for information about other prohibited items.

After you've passed the security screenings, your party will be directed to a lounge to wait until your boarding group is called. If you are a Concierge guest, you'll have a separate waiting area or lounge. Make yourself comfortable and don't crowd the waiting area; the lines move quickly once your group is announced. Have your boarding QR codes available—you'll need them again as you step onto the ship.

Disney's cruise terminals, particularly the ones at Port Canaveral and Fort Lauderdale, are spacious, clean, and comfortable. Foreign terminals vary. Barcelona offers Spain's finest folding chairs for you to sit on while you wait. If you have to wait a few minutes for your group to be called, restrooms are available, and most terminals have vending machines. When your group is called, head to the gangway, present the cast member with your QR codes, and proceed onto the ship.

After the ship clears and is ready for guests, anyone doing a back-to-back cruise (see page 74) will board first, followed by the Family of the Day and Concierge guests. After those groups are on board, the boarding group numbers will be called, starting with group 1. Each boarding group usually takes 5 minutes or so to board.

BABY, YOU'VE ARRIVED!

JUST BEFORE YOU STEP ABOARD, photographers will offer to take a photo of your party. If this is important to you, it's a good idea to dress in something you'd like recorded for posterity and do a quick mirror check in the restroom. Otherwise, politely decline and keep moving.

When you reach the atrium, a cast member will ask for your party's last name and then announce your arrival over the PA system. Some cruisers get a kick out of the pomp and ceremony of being announced, while others find it intrusive. It could also be awkward when there are people with different last names in the same party (blended families, for instance). If you don't feel comfortable giving out your last name, you can provide just your first names or even make something

SCOTT'S ARRIVAL ADVICE
by Scott Sanders of The Disney Cruise Line Blog

1. If you're not driving yourself to the port, arrange your pre- and post-cruise transportation yourself in advance. Although arriving a day ahead adds to the cost of your trip, it also creates a safety buffer in the event of a delayed flight or the like.

2. Before your port-arrival time, assign someone in your party to be in charge of the check-in process and have each person's government-issued ID in hand to present, along with the port-arrival form or mobile wallet with everyone's QR codes. The check-in and embarkation process is much quicker if you arrive on time and have all your documents ready to present to the awaiting cast member.

3. While you wait to board the ship inside the terminal, see if you can connect to your ship's Wi-Fi network (**DCL-GUEST**). If you can, launch the **DCL Navigator app** to browse the embarkation-day activities or see if there are openings for popular onboard activities or port adventures that may not have been available prior to arrival.

4. Need to change a dinner seating or don't like your assigned rotation? Check the schedule in the Navigator app for "Dining Reservation Changes" and arrive early to increase your chances of having your request granted. This is also the time to check for adult-dining reservations if the times were sold out online previously.

5. Last but not least, take time to study the deck plan for your ship before your sail date. Learning the layout will make it easier to get around, including the best route to your stateroom.

up—it's all in good fun. "Thurston and Lovey Howell" are the preferred aliases of Len and his partner, Laurel; we've also heard of parties calling themselves "The Addams Family," "The Von Trapp Family," and "The Three Amigas." (We don't think "The Seymour Butts Family" would fly, however.)

YOUR FIRST AFTERNOON
on BOARD

WHILE YOU STILL have access to your phone's regular data plan, download the latest version of the **DCL Navigator app** (see page 124). For practical purposes, not having the app installed isn't an option.

If you need to make last-minute reservations or finesse aspects of your trip that you couldn't get exactly right earlier, you might be able to do this via the app while waiting to board. Otherwise, immediately after boarding is a good time to take care of that. The app will tell you where to go to change dining rotations, seating times, and

YOUR DCL ARRIVAL TIMELINE

THE FOLLOWING ASSUMES that you'll arrive at your embarkation point a day before you sail and that you're sailing out of the United States.

3 DAYS BEFORE YOUR TRIP

- **Be sure you want to commit to any port adventures you've previously reserved.** This is your last chance to cancel without a penalty.

2 DAYS BEFORE YOUR TRIP

- **Check in for your flight.**
- **Make sure everyone's passports, port-arrival forms,** and other necessary documents are packed in your carry-on bags.
- **Confirm your transportation to the port.**

1 DAY BEFORE YOUR TRIP

- **Make sure to have some small bills handy** for tipping the porters at the terminal.
- **Download the DCL Navigator app** if you haven't done so already. **Don't put this off until you're already on the ship.**

EMBARKATION DAY

- **Put the DCL luggage tags** (the ones you received in the mail) on your bags.
- **Take the health questionnaire** either on the Navigator app or at the link you received.

AT THE CRUISE TERMINAL

- **Show up at your designated arrival time,** with port-arrival forms, passports and ID, QR codes, and all other important documents ready. *Remember:* Showing up early means you'll just have to wait to be admitted.
- **Give your large pieces of luggage**—including anything unlikely to fit through the X-ray scanner—to the porters. You can also give them any carry-ons you don't want to be stuck with until the staterooms are ready; just make sure you don't give them your identification documents or any beverages you're bringing.
- **Make your way inside the terminal** for the ID and security screenings. Have your documentation ready *before* you reach the first checkpoint. Be prepared to present your documents at any point—or at several points—before you board.
- **While waiting to board,** request any stateroom upgrades that you might be interested in. If you're able to connect to your ship's Wi-Fi in the terminal, fire up the Navigator app and start making tentative plans for on board.

ON THE SHIP

- **Make any last-minute changes to your nightly dinner seating,** check for any late-breaking openings at the adult-dining venues, and note any onboard activities you might be interested in (check the Navigator app for details).
- **Grab some lunch.** It's one of our favorite meals on board.
- **Complete the mandatory assembly drill.**

adult dining. You can also ask **Guest Services** where to go. Get there quickly—the lines get long, and activities fill up.

Many guests make a beeline for **Senses Spa** soon after boarding to check availability for treatments that weren't available earlier online or to make reservations for the **Rainforest** (see page 264).

There's a good chance you'll be hungry at this point. If you're in the mood for a buffet, head to **Marceline Market** (*Wish*-class ships) or **Cabanas** (all other ships) or grab a pick-me-up at the adults-only coffee bar or one of the pool deck's quick-service eateries. Alternatively, check the Navigator app to see which one of the dining rooms is open.

Once guests have been cleared to go to their staterooms (usually between 1:30 and 2 p.m.), you can head to yours, pick up your party's Key to the World Cards (see page 152), and drop off any bags you carried on. You may see your stateroom host sprucing up your stateroom for the evening; this is a great time to introduce yourself and let them know if you have any special requests related to your stateroom, such as more hangers or not to be disturbed during your child's nap time.

If you're sailing from a warm-weather location, the **pool deck** will be full of guests swimming and lounging. And when we say *full,* we mean packed—if you want to relax, don't go there. But feel free to pick up a drink at the beverage station or grab a burger or slice of pizza to tide you over until dinner.

*un*official **TIP**
On embarkation day, you'll likely see servers walking around the pool deck with big trays, passing out fruity cocktails. Though refreshing, these drinks aren't free.

The chaos comes to a head with the **Sail-Away Celebration** deck party. Think Champagne and confetti, Captain Stubing and Julie, Charo and Carol Channing. It's a fun way to start your cruise, but it's certainly not a must. (If these references don't ring a bell, we encourage you to check out reruns of *The Love Boat* on Paramount+. The theme song alone may or may not be the reason Len is a cruise junkie today.)

WHERE'S MY LUGGAGE?

IF YOU'RE CRUISING with anything more than hand luggage—and if you aren't, mad respect—you'll be asked to leave your suitcases for screening when you arrive at the terminal. The next time you see them, they will be in the hallway in front of your stateroom door. Suitcases are delivered throughout the afternoon and into the early evening, and it's quite likely that some in your party will receive their bags earlier than others. On almost every cruise, we've experienced an hour or so of controlled panic as everyone's bags trickle in. Just in case, we keep at least one change of clothes, along with must-have items like medications, in a small bag that we carry onto the ship ourselves.

STATEROOM GIFTS

MANY CRUISERS ARRIVE to find gifts in their staterooms (typically left on the bed by cast members). If you're a **Castaway Club** member, welcome-aboard stateroom gifts will await you. Gifts change every couple of years or so, but most recently we've seen things like beach bags, beach towels, insulated tumblers, and wet/dry bags emblazoned with the Castaway Club logo and/or the recipient's membership status. After they board, Pearl and Platinum Castaway Club members may choose an additional gift, such as a box of chocolates, a bottle of sparkling wine, or a fruit plate, to be delivered to their stateroom. **Concierge** guests get exclusive items as well.

On some **special sailings,** such as Marvel cruises, new itineraries, and sailings that coincide with Christmas and New Year's Day, you'll receive additional holiday-themed stateroom gifts midcruise—say, a commemorative lithograph or a themed box of candy.

Disney Vacation Club (**DVC**) members can expect to find a gift magnet on their door. DVC members booked on members-only sailings also receive swag such as travel mugs or Disney-themed board games.

If you booked your cruise through a **travel agent,** you may find that they've sent you a token of appreciation, such as an onboard credit, a bottle of wine, or a cheese plate.

If you don't have a particular special status with DCL but you'd like to give someone in your party a nice surprise—or if you'd like to treat yourself—you can order your own goodies in advance through the **Onboard Gifts** section of the DCL website (see page 122).

ROCKET LAUNCHES

PORT CANAVERAL IS less than 10 miles from the launchpads at **Kennedy Space Center** and **Cape Canaveral Space Force Station,** so cruising out of Florida means you may have the opportunity to see a rocket

launch. Launches get rescheduled for all kinds of reasons, so while we wouldn't recommend planning a vacation around a projected date, we do recommend checking the calendar to see if anything happens to coincide. We've seen launches from the ship and launches from the terminal, all of which we may have missed had we not known to be looking at the sky. Check this website via the QR code at left, and make sure the launch site listed is Cape Canaveral or Kennedy Space Center to see if anything is coming. Eagle-eyed space aficionados may see SpaceX's drone ships and recently flown rockets docked on the north side of the port as your cruise ship exits and enters.

ASSEMBLY DRILL

ALSO CALLED THE MUSTER or lifeboat drill, the mandatory assembly drill is typically held at 4 or 4:30 p.m. and, by law, must happen before the ship leaves port. Every member of your group needs to attend, and you must bring your KTTW Card or DisneyBand+ to register your

attendance. During the drill, you'll learn how to put on a life jacket, what the ship's emergency sirens sound like, and where to gather on the ship to board the emergency lifeboats.

unofficial **TIP**
Your KTTW Card lists your assigned lifeboat station; you'll also find it listed on the DCL Navigator app.

If a member of your party has autism or experiences sensory issues, you may qualify for a modified muster experience. See the DCL information form for guests with autism spectrum disorder (theugseries.com/dcl-autism).

ONBOARD SERVICES

EACH SHIP HAS a 24-hour **Guest Services** desk just off the lobby to answer questions, make reservations, and provide other help. You can contact the desk from your stateroom by pressing the Guest Services button on your stateroom phone.

The crew member you'll likely get to know best is your **stateroom attendant** (also called a stateroom host), who will tidy your stateroom after you depart in the morning and turn down your beds each night. You'll almost certainly interact with this person more than you will any other crew member.

Given the nature of a cruise, you'll find that your stateroom attendant is in and out of your stateroom much more often than a typical hotel housekeeper would be. This makes it particularly important to make ample use of your STATEROOM OCCUPIED sign if you plan to sleep late or nap for a couple of hours, or if you just don't want to be disturbed for a while.

Port Adventures

In addition to Guest Services, a **Port Adventures desk** (on Deck 3 of the *Magic* and *Wonder;* Deck 5 of the *Dream* and *Fantasy;* and Deck 4 of the *Wish, Treasure,* and *Destiny*) handles booking for shore excursions. The staff are usually knowledgeable about the most popular excursions at each port. In addition to providing information about cost and time, they can typically answer questions regarding the appropriateness of a particular activity for the members of your family; they can also help you reschedule an activity if possible. (See Part 15 for details.)

Health Services

Every DCL ship has a **Health Center** on Deck 1. The center is staffed by a doctor and nurse who attend to medical issues for the crew and passengers. There are regular office hours daily (see your Navigator app), and the medical team is also on call 24/7 and is experienced in emergency and critical care. The most common shipboard medical complaints are motion sickness and sunburn, although the staff has also seen its share of broken bones over the years.

*un*official **TIP**

EpiPens are available on a case-by-case basis at the Health Center on board and at First Aid on Castaway Cay. If you urgently need an EpiPen, tell the nearest cast member right away, or dial ☎ **7-3000** from any ship phone.

The Health Center offers three tiers of service:

- **Emergency medical services** would be used in a life-threatening emergency. In severe cases, particularly those involving surgery, the individual would be evacuated from the ship and taken to the nearest hospital.

- **Urgent care** refers to visiting the Health Center without an appointment to get something treated right away. This is the most expensive version of non-emergency care.

- **Standard care** refers to making an appointment with the doctor during regular operating hours. There is a charge, but in many cases guests can get reimbursed by their insurance carriers.

The Health Center is equipped with many common over-the-counter and prescription medications, basic laboratory equipment, bandages, sutures, oxygen, wheelchairs, stretchers, immobilization for back and neck injuries, automated external defibrillators, ventilation equipment, and ECG and X-ray machines.

DEPARTURE PROCEDURES

YOUR LAST NIGHT ON THE SHIP

A DAY OR TWO before your departure, in addition to the tipping-related information discussed on page 144, you'll receive debarkation information, including luggage tags, instructions on what to do with your bags, information on where to get breakfast on your last morning, and what time you need to be off the ship.

What To Do with Your Luggage

You'll be given a set of small, colorful, oval luggage tags decorated with Disney characters: green Tinker Bell, orange Goofy, blue Donald Duck, and so on. If you want Disney porters to carry your luggage for you from the ship into the port terminal upon docking, fill out the information requested on the tag (name, address, stateroom number), attach the tag to your bag, and follow the instructions on your departure-information sheet. (Snap a picture of your tags or make a note of which characters were on them—you'll need this information later.) If you're sailing into Port Canaveral or Fort Lauderdale, you'll typically be asked to leave your luggage outside your stateroom door between 8:30 and 10:30 p.m. Other ports may have slightly different instructions.

You may be asking, "Why do I need Disney to take my bags off the ship?" If you're on a three-night cruise with only a small rolling suitcase, you probably don't need any assistance. But if you have large suitcases or small children, or if anyone in your party has a disability, you probably do. On your departure morning, the same group of 4,000 people who boarded the ship over the course of about 5 hours will be trying to get off the ship in 2 hours. The hallways are narrow, and if you want to avoid the same small, slow elevators that everyone else is using, you'll need to navigate many stairs. In short, it's a logistical nightmare if everyone tries to take their bags off the ship themselves. If you have large luggage, avail yourself of this **free** service. Someone else is going to lug our suitcases off the ship? Sign. Us. Up.

Packing

As you pack your bags in preparation for setting them outside your stateroom door, pay attention to the following:

- Set aside clothes to wear off the ship the last morning. We know first-hand how easy it is to pack *everything* without thinking.
- **Don't** pack passports, birth certificates, KTTW Cards, and any other travel documents in your checked bags. You'll need these as you debark the ship and pass through customs, so keep them in a carry-on bag. Let us emphasize that you must have your KTTW Card when you debark the ship.
- If you're flying home, you must pack any alcohol and any liquids measuring more than 3.4 ounces in your checked bags.
- Remove any old airline or cruise tags from your luggage.
- Keep any bags you'll carry off the ship yourself inside your stateroom.

DEPARTURE TIMELINE

2 DAYS BEFORE DEPARTURE

- **Check your current stateroom charges on the Navigator app** to make sure you understand them, and make payments as needed. Guest Services gets very busy on the last day, so doing this two days ahead can save you lots of time. *Note:* You will not receive a hard copy of your final bill. If you want a hard copy for your records before leaving the ship, stop by Guest Services. After debarkation, you can download a copy of your bill in your Castaway Club account online.
- **Adjust your gratuity payments** if desired (see page 144).

1 DAY BEFORE DEPARTURE

- **Check in for your flight** if you're heading straight home upon debarkation.
- **Give tip envelopes** to your dining room servers and stateroom host (see page 145).
- **Complete your cruise survey** (see page 196).
- **Check with Lost and Found** if you are missing any belongings.
- **Leave large luggage outside your stateroom** in the evening unless you're using Express Walk-Off (see below). **Do not pack** your KTTW Card, ID, electronics, or medications.
- **Return your child's kids' club wristband** to the club before 11 p.m. to avoid incurring a stateroom charge.

DEPARTURE DAY

- **If you're eating breakfast on board,** go to your assigned dining room; **Cabanas** on the *Dream, Fantasy, Magic,* and *Wonder;* or **Marceline Market** on the *Wish, Treasure,* and *Destiny*) or grab a coffee at an open café.
- **Check your final bill** and make sure your account is in order.
- **Make sure you understand how to access/download any photos you've purchased.**
- **Double-check that you are not carrying any prohibited items off the ship** (fresh fruit is a commonly overlooked no-no).
- **Have your KTTW Card in hand** as you leave the ship. Also have your passport ready if you are not debarking in Fort Lauderdale or Port Canaveral.
- **Complete the US Customs Declaration Form** if you've made any purchases that require it (see page 196).

DEPARTURE DAY

Express Walk-Off

For guests who wish to be among the very first off the ship—those who need to get straight to the airport or who have other time-dependent plans that day—DCL offers Express Walk-Off. As soon as the ship clears customs, you may leave the ship.

You must carry your own luggage to take advantage of this service; you may not set it out the night before. Please be considerate and let your stateroom host know that you'll be doing this well ahead of time so that they aren't waiting for you to put your luggage out the night before. (*Note:* Express Walk-Off may not be available on some sailings, so check the specifics for your cruise.)

Breakfast on the Morning of Your Departure

You'll have the chance to eat one more sit-down meal on debarkation morning. Breakfast will be provided at the restaurants, with assigned, staggered seating times. Typically, you will be assigned the same restaurant where you ate dinner on the last night of your sailing. Additionally, **Cove Café** will be open for coffee from 6:30 to 8:30 a.m., and the buffet restaurant will serve a limited menu of breakfast basics.

Be warned: These are very early breakfast times. While it is always fun to see your servers one last time, feel free to skip this breakfast if the time doesn't work for you (you can always grab breakfast in **Cabanas** (*Dream, Fantasy, Magic,* and *Wonder*) or **Marceline Market** (*Wish, Treasure,* and *Destiny*).

Retrieving Your Luggage in the Morning

If you put oval-tagged luggage outside your stateroom the night before debarkation, the next time you'll see it is inside the cruise terminal, back on land. Walk off the ship into the terminal, and you'll immediately see many rows of suitcases on the floor and nearby tables, sorted by the character and color on the oval tags—all the green Tinker Bells will be grouped together, along with all the tan Plutos, and so on.

Theoretically your luggage should be grouped together by stateroom, but if it's not, do a quick scan to check a few bags up and down your section. You should find your bag in the same general area, if not the exact same area, as the other bags with your tag(s). If you still can't find your luggage, speak to one of the many crew members stationed in the terminal.

Once you have all of your luggage back in your possession, follow the signs and instructions to the customs area, where your identification will be checked and you will then be allowed back into your debarkation country. In Fort Lauderdale and Port Canaveral, if you use your passport to embark on the cruise, getting off will be a breeze with their facial recognition system.

Clearing Customs

If your sailing ends in the United States and you have purchased large quantities of alcohol or cigarettes; are bringing home agricultural products or prescription medications purchased outside the United States (Mexico, for instance); have made total purchases of more than $1,600; and/or have more than $10,000 in cash on you, then you may need to fill out a customs form. The forms are available in the terminal if you need to pay duty on your vacation purchases.

If you're not sure whether you'll need to fill out a form, Customs and Border Patrol has extensive information about customs duty at theugseries.com/uscbp-duty-info.

Comment Cards

On the last night of your cruise, you'll either be given a link or a physical brochure that contains a comprehensive survey asking for your evaluation of the ship's cleanliness, the entertainment offerings, the condition of your stateroom, the children's programming, your dining service team, and other aspects of your cruise.

Note that the dining staff's performance reviews and pay are often strongly affected by guest input on these comment cards. Because of this, some servers may give guests a high-pressure sell for Excellent ratings, basically begging for high marks. If you really do love your servers, then by all means rate them as Excellent, but don't feel strong-armed into doing so if the service wasn't *truly* outstanding.

The survey also asks you to name any cast members "who made your cruise experience particularly magical." In addition to the obvious dining, stateroom, and entertainment cast members, we like to be on the lookout for cast in minimally guest-facing roles—maintenance crew, for example—and note when we see them doing a great job. Don't forget to place the survey in one of the collection boxes that morning—don't leave it in your stateroom.

KEY QUESTIONS ANSWERED IN THIS CHAPTER

- Should I choose early or late dining? *(see below)*
- Is the adults-only dining worth it? *(see page 203)*
- What's the dress code for meals? *(see page 210)*

OVERVIEW

THE FIRST THING many cruisers discover when exploring the ships on embarkation day is the near-endless displays of food at the pool-deck restaurants. In the way that some people remember the birth of their first child, we remember our first glimpse of the food stations stretching out as far as the eye can see. (Sorry, kids, it's eatin' time.) On one table sat a pile of crab legs that almost reached eye level, and next to this sat a trawler's worth of peel-and-eat shrimp. Surrounding all this delicious-ness was enough cocktail sauce to float the ship itself. On the other side of the aisle, a chef was flash-cooking a steak, the spices, sizzle, and flame making the air smell savory. It was *heavenly.*

You'll never go hungry on a DCL cruise. The variety of dining options is staggering, with everything from coffee shops and pizza stands to Vegas-style buffets and ritzy French and Italian restaurants. That said, there are a few ways to increase your chances of enjoying memorable meals on board. This section describes your dining options in detail and includes our advice on how to make the most of them.

ROTATIONAL DINING

ONE OF THE INNOVATIONS that DCL brought to the cruise indus-try is the concept of rotational dining, in which you visit one of three main dining rooms on each night of your cruise. As you change from restaurant to restaurant, your dining room server, assistant (beverage) server, and head server (dining room manager) all move with you. Your server team will quickly learn your dining preferences, including favorite drinks and desserts, and make menu suggestions. Along with

10 WAYS TO GET THE MOST FROM DCL DINING

1. **Communication is key.** If, say, you want your meal served faster or slower, or you don't want your kids eating dessert, let your serving team know.

2. **You can order from any part of the menu, in any combination.** If you want two main courses or two soups, no problem. If all you want is two appetizers and a salad or just bread and dessert, that's fine too.

3. **The main dining rooms are "all you care to eat."** If you want more of any dish, let your servers know and they'll bring it to you at no extra charge.

4. **Try it—you may like it!** Not sure you like scallops? Order some with your favorite steak. Whether you hate the scallops or love them, you'll have learned something.

5. **Don't be afraid to say "when."** If you're full, say so politely but firmly.

6. **You can order from a main dining room besides the one where you're eating.** A full list of menus is available on the DCL Navigator app. If another dining room is serving something you like on the same evening, just ask. *Note:* You may get pushback if attempting to do this on the *Wish*-class ships because the restaurant kitchens are not connected behind the scenes. Order in advance for best results.

7. **Ask your server if anything is available off-menu.** Did you know you can order Mickey ice-cream bars for dessert? French fries for an appetizer? You can also order some things for free in the main dining rooms that would cost extra elsewhere on board— for example, kiddie "cocktails" like Shirley Temples and "No-Hitos" that you'd have to pay for at an onboard bar.

8. **It's OK to skip the main dining room.** Honest. You may want to take advantage of the low crowds at the pool slide, your tablemates are getting on your last nerve, or you have an insatiable craving for chicken nuggets from the pool deck. Whatever the case, remember: It's *your* cruise. Don't feel obligated to do what doesn't work for you.

9. **Servers love helping you celebrate (safely).** They'll gladly bring you an extra dessert (or extra, *extra* desserts) and a birthday button. (What they *can't* do, however, is put candles on your cake: open flames aren't allowed on the ship.)

10. **You can have fancy ice-cream desserts delivered to your main dining room** (for an extra charge). Early in the day, stop by **Vanellope's** (*Dream*), **Sweet on You** (*Fantasy*), **Inside Out** (*Wish*), **Jumbeaux's Sweets** (*Treasure*), or **Edna À La Mode** (*Destiny*) to place an order, tell them your dining time and table number, and they'll make your child's wildest dreams come true.

your stateroom attendant, you'll almost certainly rely on your dining team more than any other members of the crew during your trip.

The main dining rooms have two dinner seatings, typically around **5:45 p.m.** and **8:15 p.m.** (For sailings originating in Europe, seatings are typically at **6 p.m.** and **8:30 p.m.**) The live stage shows in the theaters are timed to coordinate with the dinner hours: If you have the 5:45 dinner seating, you'll be able to watch the 8:30 show, and vice versa.

Because Disney sets your schedule, there's no need to make reservations each night. You can request either the main (early) or second (late) seating when booking your trip. If you can't get the seating you want before you sail, you can join a waiting list in the My Reservations section of the DCL website. If you don't make it off the list before you sail, check for an opening immediately after you board at the location noted in the Navigator app.

On cruises of four nights or longer, you'll repeat at least one of the three main dining rooms (the menus change each night). Rather than visit the same restaurant twice on a four-night cruise, we recommend trying one of the adult-dining venues: **Palo** on the *Magic, Wonder,*

Dream, and *Fantasy;* **Remy** on the *Dream* and *Fantasy;* or **Palo Steakhouse** or **Enchanté** on the *Wish*, *Treasure,* and *Destiny.* The food is stellar, the crowds are small, and the service is impeccable.

REQUESTING A ROTATION You may have your travel agent request a specific dining rotation by calling DCL directly at ☎ 800-951-3532. This way, you can choose which restaurant you're assigned to visit twice on a four-night cruise, for example, or three times on a seven-night cruise. Requests aren't guaranteed but are honored whenever possible.

ALTERNATIVES TO THE MAIN DINING ROOMS If you'd rather skip the main dining room, you can order room service, eat at one of the counter-service restaurants, or book dinner at one of the adult-dining venues. If you're in the mood for something light and snacky, the ships' sports bars typically offer items like sliders and wings, for an additional charge. On the *Magic, Wonder, Dream,* and *Fantasy,* you'll find a free version of light bites at **Cove Café,** which offers things like tiny cheese plates during dinner hours.

On days when the ship has an unusually late port departure or an overnight in port (for example, in Bermuda or in Reykjavík, Iceland), you may find that the pool-deck buffet is open or the quick-service restaurants have extended hours. Check the Navigator app for details.

Also note that if you're not in the mood to fight the crowds at **Cabanas** or **Marceline Market** during breakfast and lunch, at least one of the main dining rooms will be open during the day. Again, check the Navigator app for more information.

DINNER SHOWS Several of the main dining rooms feature live entertainment. In most cases, you'll have it on only one night, even if you're assigned to that restaurant more than once. If, for example, you're on a four-night sailing of the *Wish* and are assigned to eat at **Arendelle** twice, you'll experience the *Frozen* show only once, with regular dinner service on the other visit. If Anna and Elsa aren't your thing, you can always eat somewhere else on show night.

Some restaurants have two shows. For instance, **Animator's Palate** (*Magic, Wonder, Dream,* and *Fantasy*) offers *Drawn to Magic* on the *Magic* and *Wonder,* **Undersea Magic** on the *Dream* and *Fantasy,* and *Animation Magic* on the *Fantasy* and on longer cruises on the *Magic.*

DINING WITH STRANGERS DCL often seats different families together in the main dining rooms. Couples and solo travelers are almost always seated with others. Some cruisers love this—but if, say, you're an introvert (see page 158) or you're on your honeymoon, you may find it awkward and intrusive.

If you'd rather not eat with strangers during your rotational-dining seatings, let DCL know before you sail or check with your head server once you're on board. Again, though, keep in mind that seating changes aren't guaranteed.

SHOULD I CHOOSE THE EARLY OR LATE SEATING? The following factors, among others, may influence your decision:

TIPS FOR DINING ON DISNEY CRUISE LINE
by Scott Sanders of The Disney Cruise Line Blog

IF YOU'RE NEW TO DCL, I suggest experiencing the main-dining-room menus first. If brunch at the adult-dining venues is offered, use that as an opportunity to experience these elevated offerings. Then, on your next cruise, explore the adults-only dinner options. Or, if your designated main dining room is featuring a dinner show or menu you're not interested in, use that night to try one of the other dining options.

Cruising is also a great opportunity to try new foods outside your comfort zone. If nothing on the dinner menu strikes your fancy, ask your server if there are any other options. For example, the menu for guests with food allergies sometimes includes delicious dishes.

- **Culture and customs** Early seatings tend to fill up more quickly on US sailings, while late seatings tend to be preferred on European ones.
- **Cruise length** You may be able to more easily cope with a less-than-optimal dining time on a 3-night sailing. Conversely, a 12-night voyage would give you ample time to adapt to either seating.
- **Time zone** If you live on the West Coast and you're sailing from Port Canaveral or Fort Lauderdale, you may find that the early seating feels more like lunch than dinner. On the other hand, East Coast guests sailing out of San Diego or Vancouver may initially have a hard time staying awake during the late seating.
- **Health concerns** Guests with GI issues such as acid reflux often need to eat their last meal of the day several hours before bedtime. Other guests may be on medications that must be taken on a full (or empty) stomach at a particular time.
- **Kids' sleep schedules** Many young children simply can't stay awake past 7:30 or 8 p.m. If you want them to eat dinner with you in the main dining rooms, then the late seating may be a no-go. If you want to see the early stage show with your kids, skip the main dining room and grab a quick bite from a counter-service restaurant instead.
- **Seating for stage shows** If you're picky about where you sit, a late dinner seating will help you beat the crowds to the early show.
- **Eating habits** Some guests may need a snack in the late afternoon to ward off the "hangries" before a late seating. (Cheese and crackers, anyone?) Conversely, slow eaters may find the second seating less rushed.
- **Plans in port** If a shore excursion will have you returning to the ship close to or after the early seating, and that stresses you out, then choose the late seating.
- **Noise tolerance** While there will be children at both seatings, there are likely to be fewer of them at the late seating, making for a quieter dining experience.
- **Brunch plans** Brunch at the adult-dining restaurants is a lavish, multicourse affair featuring dishes that are often rich and heavy. A late dinner seating would allow extra time for your meal to digest.
- **Your schedule on your last day on board** The time of your last breakfast is tied to your dinner seating: Early diners eat breakfast earlier than late diners. If you don't have an early flight and want to grab a bit of extra sleep, choose the late seating.

RESTAURANT CATEGORIES

Counter Service (aka Quick Service)

Found on the pool deck of each ship, the counter-service restaurants used to be a level below McDonald's and Taco Bell in food quality, but we think they've gotten better. The ones on the *Wish*-class ships are real standouts. We've had some excellent meals there. Counter-service restaurants for each ship are listed starting on page 213.

Cafés and Lounges

Each ship has a dedicated adults-only coffee bar called **Cove Café** that serves espresso, cappuccino, teas, and smoothies, along with wine, mixed drinks, and spirits. On the *Magic, Wonder, Dream,* and *Fantasy,* Cove Café also serves snacks and sweets all day long. A good alternative to a heavy dinner is Cove Café's small selection of complimentary cold appetizers, available each evening. (There is no food available in Cove Café on the *Wish*-class ships.)

Besides Cove Café, a few of the ships' bars and lounges set out food in the late evenings and serve a small selection of food for purchase during the day.

Buffet Dining

Each ship has a large pick-what-you-want buffet on the main pool deck. On the *Magic, Wonder, Dream,* and *Fantasy,* it's called **Cabanas;** on the *Wish*-class ships, it's **Marceline Market.** Both offer a wide array of foods, typically representing a number of themes or cultures. Cabanas is self-service: Grab a tray and help yourself. At Marceline Market, most of your picks are dished up by a cast member. In either case, you may go back as often as you like and eat as much as you desire. Open for breakfast and lunch on most days, the buffets are an easy way to satisfy a group with diverging preferences or appetites; plus, they let picky kids (and adults) see what the food looks like before taking the plunge.

> *un*official **TIP**
> On some days, **Cabanas** and **Marceline Market** serve a special treat that we highly recommend: **Mickey Churro Waffles.** Check with the servers to see when they will be offered on your sailing.

Main Dining Rooms

Each ship has three restaurants offering full table service for all ages. They are part of the standard rotational dinner schedule. Virtually all the food served here will be familiar to American palates. Most dishes, especially at dinner, feature steak, pork, chicken, and fish entrées similar to those you'd find at an upscale chain restaurant. DCL's chefs will add some sort of flavor twist to these, such as soy and sesame if it's an Asian-themed menu, but the basic ingredients will be recognizable to almost everyone. If you want your entrée mild and largely unadorned, look for the **Lighter Note** menu offerings—you'll see here that you can always get plain steak or chicken served with plain rice or a baked potato.

Although fresher and of higher quality than counter-service food, most food served in the main dining rooms is prepared ahead of time. On the upside, this means you get your meal faster. On the downside, not all requests are doable: Ordering a different side dish or getting your sauce on the side shouldn't present a problem, but asking the kitchen staff to scrape off a baked-on glaze definitely would.

Along with the dining-survey ratings and comments we get, we closely monitor comments about DCL food on social media. A representative sample of recent feedback includes the following:

I absolutely love the food on DCL. I've been on four Disney ships, the Dream, Fantasy, Magic, *and* Wish, *and everything I've had, from room service to quick service to Cabanas to the main dining room to adult dining, has been delicious. The service is impeccable, and the servers go out of their way to make sure you're enjoying your meal. Once, when I couldn't decide what I wanted for dinner, my server brought me three different entrées to try! Plus, any food I didn't have to cook served on dishes I don't have to wash is #1 in my book!*

—Sherry from Pennsylvania

The presentation and taste of the food on my Disney cruise was fabulous, and I loved the variety offered on the menu.

—Katie from Idaho

When dining in the main dining rooms, they will make sure you are always satisfied, whether that means letting you order from the kids' menu or altering a dish to your liking. This is the type of service that brings me back.

—Jess J. from Louisiana

The food I have had on Disney ships is not the best in the cruise industry; however, it still always exceeds my expectations. There is usually one dish that I love from each menu.

—Jess F. from Massachusetts

Overall, DCL guests' impressions of the food are highly subjective, but most people like it just fine. Our advice: Keep your expectations realistic, and if you aren't enjoying your meal, speak up—your server will be happy to bring you something you might like better.

Adult Dining

Each ship features an upscale Italian restaurant, serving only adults (age 18 and up). On the *Magic, Wonder, Dream,* and *Fantasy,* it's called **Palo;** on the *Wish*-class ships, it's **Palo Steakhouse.** The *Dream* and *Fantasy* have a second adult-dining restaurant, **Remy,** that serves French cuisine. On the *Wish*-class ships, the equivalent venue is **Enchanté,** with a menu created by French chef Arnaud Lallement.

These restaurants have both prix fixe and à la carte menus. Regardless of which menu you order from, you will be charged a minimum of $50 (the prix fixe at Palo and Palo Steakhouse) or $135 (the prix fixe at Remy and Enchanté), which includes a four-course menu with limited choices. At Palo and Palo Steakhouse, the starters are a calamari-and-shrimp cocktail or a buffalo mozzarella salad; second-course choices are a mesclun or baby arugula salad; main-course options are penne with tomato sauce, pan-seared salmon, roast chicken, or beef tenderloin; and for dessert you can choose from chocolate soufflé or limoncello tart. That's it.

You aren't limited to the prix fixe menu, however. You may choose to order other dishes à la carte instead of or in addition to the prix fixe menu. Some of the most popular à la carte options can really add up. The antipasti platter ($22), ciuppin (seafood soup, $14), Dover sole ($32), grilled asparagus ($4), and amaretto soufflé ($10) total $82.

Theoretically, you *could* order à la carte instead of prix fixe for a total cost of less than $50, particularly if you're a light eater and/or a vegetarian, but that would be an unusual circumstance. (See page 168 for adult-dining suggestions for vegetarians and vegans.)

unofficial **TIP**
If they aren't offered to you, make sure you ask for the almond croissants at Palo brunch. Trust us.

In addition to dinner, these restaurants usually serve (adults-only) **brunch** on select days. Enchanté and Remy sometimes offer a **dessert experience.** Palo's brunch ($50) includes everything on the menu (sans adult beverages), and you can eat as much as you want. You will also be offered a complimentary sparkling alcoholic or nonalcoholic starter beverage. This makes brunch a *much* better value than dinner.

Palo and Palo Steakhouse have also added **Prima Notte** on the first night; this small-plates and wine-pairing experience is $85 per person. These dining options can be tough to get into, so be sure to make a reservation at your earliest opportunity (see opposite page).

Diane from Massachusetts enjoyed her Prima Notte experience:

We did the Prima Notte at Palo on embarkation day. I am not much of a wine drinker, but I enjoyed the five different types of Italian wines they served, with an explanation for each by the sommelier. I also wasn't sure on a couple of the bite-size delicacies from Palo, but they were good—nice to try something out of my comfort zone. It was a perfect way to start our cruise.

In addition to serving food that's superior to what's served in the main dining rooms, the adult-dining restaurants also have a higher level of service. Audrey from Texas reports:

Dining at Palo is one of our favorite Disney cruise experiences! My husband and I prefer the quiet and elegant atmosphere of the evening dining at Palo. We have enjoyed the prix fixe menu, which includes our favorites, as well as the à la carte menu. The chef goes above and beyond to accommodate those with dietary restrictions, and the level of service and attention to detail are outstanding and make us feel very special.

Disney often tinkers with its adult-dining offerings, testing special events for specific sailings or individual ships. For example, some sailings of the *Fantasy* have offered an experience at Palo called **Be Our Chef,** which provides the opportunity to learn how to prepare four Palo dishes and take home a keepsake. If you're interested in enhanced adult-dining experiences, check your My Reservations page on DCL's website or call DCL at ☎ 800-951-3532.

On some sailings, you're limited to one adult-dining reservation, or one reservation per adult-dining venue. If a sailing isn't full or you elect to dine at one of the adult restaurants on your first night, you may be able to make more than one reservation in advance; check My Reservations online for the specifics of your cruise. Or stop by the restaurant in person and ask if you can make another reservation—by doing this, we've been able to eat at the adult restaurants on multiple nights on a single cruise.

> *unofficial* **TIP**
> Meals at the adult-dining restaurants are not short—we have had both brunch and dinner run 3-4 hours. For that reason, we recommend not planning anything immediately afterward. If you must, tell your serving team up front so they can manage the time appropriately.

ADULT-DINING CREDIT Platinum (and above) Castaway Club members and other adults in their staterooms will be offered one free prix fixe dinner at Palo or Palo Steakhouse or a $50 credit on their bill at dinner. Brunch may be substituted for dinner.

MAKING RESERVATIONS FOR ADULT DINING While reservations are not required at the main dining rooms, they *are* required for adult dining and can be made up to 130 days in advance, as noted in the table below, after you've paid for your cruise in full. Make reservations online or in the Navigator app.

PRIVATE ADULT DINING Each ship's adult-dining venues have an adjacent private dining room. When not reserved by DCL for onboard activities, these can be reserved by guests with larger groups. To request a private room, download and fill out the request form at theugseries.com/dcl-private-dining. Then email the completed form to dcl.cruise.activities@disney.com at least 30 days in advance. To request a reservation beforehand, your party size must be as follows:

- **Enchanté** 6–8 guests (*Wish/Treasure/Destiny*)
- **Palo** 10–14 guests (*Dream/Fantasy*); 8–14 guests (*Magic/Wonder*)
- **Palo Steakhouse** 8–10 guests (*Wish/Treasure/Destiny*)
- **Remy** 8–10 guests (*Dream/Fantasy*)

WHEN YOUR BOOKING WINDOW OPENS FOR ADULT-DINING RESERVATIONS
Concierge guests: **130 days** before sailing
Pearl Castaway Club members: **123 days** before sailing
Platinum Castaway Club members: **120 days** before sailing
Gold Castaway Club members: **105 days** before sailing
Silver Castaway Club members: **90 days** before sailing
All other guests: **75 days** before sailing

THEME NIGHTS

ON CRUISES LONGER than three nights, Disney gets festive with themed dinners. These may include a **Pirates' Menu,** which is somewhat Caribbean-influenced, on Pirate Night; **Till We Meet Again,** on the final night of your cruise; the **Captain's Gala;** and **Prince and Princess Menus.** The menus will depend on your itinerary. For example, Alaskan voyages typically include a seafood-focused night featuring local salmon and king crab.

*un**official* TIP

On theme nights, each main dining area serves the same menu, so no one misses out.

Beginning in late 2017, **Marvel Days** were added to some *Magic* sailings. Menu selections include Black Widow's Sliced Smoked Salmon, Dr. Banner's Greens and Lobster Salad, Bounty Hunter's Pastry, and Ravager's Devil's Food Cake.

ROOM SERVICE

ROOM SERVICE IS GREAT if you want to eat fast before heading out on a port excursion, dine on your verandah, or enjoy a movie on your stateroom TV while you eat. Our kids have loved it over the years, as it made them feel quite grown up to order a snack, tip the server, and then watch a Disney movie of their choosing.

Room service is available 24 hours a day (except the last morning of your cruise). Look for the menu on the Navigator app. To place an order, press the ROOM SERVICE button on your stateroom phone. To preorder breakfast, use the order form in the desk drawer. Except for some packaged snacks and bottled beverages, there's no charge for room service, other than a tip ($1–$2 per person or item ordered, with a $5 minimum, is appropriate).

*un**official* TIP

Need a caffeine hit immediately after you wake up? Order a carafe of coffee at bedtime and it'll still be warm in the morning.

Lunch and dinner offerings include burgers, pizza, sandwiches, chicken fingers, salads, soups, and fresh fruit. The cheese-and-crackers plate is particularly popular with guests who need something to tide them over before the late dinner seating. Continental breakfast items are offered in the morning.

The menu always has a selection of warm cookies, usually chocolate chip and oatmeal raisin. If you want to be a hero to your kids (or your spouse), surprise them with cookies and milk as a bedtime snack. Even better, dive into the unadvertised menu offerings and order a round of Mickey ice-cream bars for the room. All you have to do is ask.

You can also call ahead to schedule room service deliveries. For example, if you want dessert delivered right after the evening show, call in advance and it'll show up at the appointed time. If you've brought your own wine (see page 140 for guidelines), Room Service can bring you glasses and a bucket of ice so you can enjoy your beverage in your stateroom in style.

DINING *with* KIDS

ON DISNEY CRUISE LINE, kids are people, too, when it comes to dining. While there are kids' menus with standard fare like corn dogs and mac and cheese, kids of all ages are welcome to eat from any part of the upper-deck buffet and order any item in the main dining rooms. If *you* want chicken nuggets for dinner and your 6-year-old wants escargots and prime rib, DCL has you covered.

Your serving team should be your partner in planning a strategy for how to best meet your family's dining needs. Do you want your kids' food brought to the table first so they're not ravenous? Do you want the bread basket left off the table so your kids fill up on more protein and veggies than carbs? Do you want only milk and water offered to your kids, not soda? Tell your serving team those things on the first night, and they'll make notes about your preferences.

There's no rule that your kids must sit through an entire lengthy meal. If they've eaten their fill and their patience has worn thin, feel free to have one adult member of your party take 5 minutes to take them to the kids' club and then return to the restaurant to enjoy a more leisurely meal. (Be sure to share your plan with your serving team so they know what's happening.) This strategy is particularly popular for guests who have been assigned the second dinner seating. Be aware, however, that there are some special experiences that occur toward the end of the usual dinner hour, some of which your children might not want to miss. For example, at the end of dinner on one night at **Animator's Palate** on the *Fantasy* and *Magic,* guests are treated to a short animated film created from diners' drawings. Most kids get a real kick out of seeing their artwork on-screen.

In the realm of healthy eating, Disney is taking ongoing steps toward offering healthful options at its theme parks and on its ships. **Disney Check** meals are available on the kids' menus at the main dining rooms and on the menus posted on the Navigator app. (Visit citizenship.disney .com/disney-check for details.) The Disney Check symbol indicates that the meal falls within specific dietary guidelines for calorie count; percentages of sugar, sodium, and fat; and recommended amounts of vitamins and other nutrients.

Baby food is sold in gift shops, near the over-the-counter medications. The selection is typically limited, however, to two to four flavors of jarred baby food and one brand of single-serving baby formula. If you want to bring your own baby food on board, it must be prepackaged and sealed (homemade foods and open containers of any type are prohibited), and you must pack it in your carry-on luggage, not your checked bags.

DCL chefs will also puree any food available on the ship for you. For instance, they can whip up something like pureed peas, carrots, or chicken quite easily. Also keep in mind that many of the soft foods already available on the ship—like soft-scrambled eggs, mashed potatoes, oatmeal, and soups—may be fine for older babies and toddlers.

If you're planning to bring your own baby food on board, be aware that your child will likely have to eat it cold unless you can improvise; see the Unofficial Tip below. (At Walt Disney World, by contrast, guests have free use of microwave ovens in the resort food courts and in the theme park Baby Care Centers.) Additionally, you may not bring any cooking appliances on board with you: no electric kettles, rice cookers, hot plates, chafing fuel cans, or anything else that could be a fire hazard. Further complicating matters, DCL kitchens won't heat any food you've brought onto the ship, nor will they heat baby food that you've purchased in the onboard gift shop.

unofficial **TIP**

If you want to feed your baby something warm, ask the kitchen staff to puree food that they've prepared. Or you can heat a jar of baby food in very hot water for a few minutes. (A cereal bowl from the buffet and hot water from the coffee/tea dispenser will do the trick.)

Children are welcome to eat in the main dining rooms on their own or with young siblings, cousins, or friends in their party. If the grown-ups are having dinner at an adults-only restaurant, the kids can have a nice meal of their own in the main dining room. Parents will have to assess whether their kids are ready for this, but we've seen many 8- and 9-year-olds dining together while their parents were having a date-night meal elsewhere. Our own children have done this and said they felt like royalty with all the attention they received. Let your server know you're planning to do this, and they'll be sure to take special care of your child's dining needs. Of course, if you'd rather not have your children eat a full restaurant dinner on their own, you could feed them room service or grab them something from the pool-deck quick-service venues.

On longer sailings, Disney sometimes serves a character breakfast in one of the main dining rooms, with Mickey, Goofy, or other Disney favorites stopping by to add merriment to your meal. While kids are the biggest fans of character meals, parties consisting of adults only are also welcome to partake. There is no additional charge for these meals. Your server will let you know if and when they are happening.

Kids' Menus 101

As noted earlier, youngsters are welcome to order anything on the main menu at the main dining rooms, but each dining room also has a separate kids' menu. Unless you request otherwise, it will be offered to kids under age 10. Adults can order from this menu as well.

Each kids' menu consists of four sections: **starters, entrées, desserts,** and complete **Disney Check meals.** Each section offers two or three choices in kid-size portions. (*Note:* You can always get french fries by request.) Here's a sampling:

APPETIZERS Soup (chicken noodle, sweet corn, tomato), garden salad

ENTRÉES Mini burger, breaded fish nuggets, mini pizza, corn dog, breaded turkey breast with tomato sauce, mac and cheese

DESSERTS Mickey ice-cream bar, scoop of ice cream, apple pie, cheese-cake with strawberry compote, strawberry shortcake, caramel custard

DISNEY CHECK MEALS Baked salmon with broccoli and rice, strawberry yogurt parfait for dessert; whole-wheat pasta with tomato sauce and broccoli, apple slices for dessert; grilled beef tenderloin with green beans and smashed potatoes, fruit cup for dessert; grilled chicken breast with steamed carrots, fresh watermelon for dessert; turkey Bolognese over fettuccine served with steamed carrots, apple slices for dessert; grilled pork tenderloin with brown rice and green beans, applesauce for dessert

Beyond the Kids' Menu: Options for Adventurous Dining

If, on the other hand, your kids are open to more than just munching on nuggets and fries, we suggest the following:

- **Trying new foods.** Because most of the menu items available to children are included in the price of your cruise, kids can feel free to order something they're not sure about, with no repercussions if they don't like it.

- **Practicing restaurant manners.** The main dining rooms are a terrific place for kids to practice proper table etiquette. At home, teach your children to look waitstaff in the eye while speaking, order in a clear voice, make polite dinner-table conversation, and use napkins and utensils properly. If your kids fumble a bit, rest assured that DCL's servers are exceptionally patient and kind. Be sure to tip them well at the end of your cruise.

- **Learning a new vocabulary.** A restaurant can be a terrific place to teach your kids new words: *Bisque, brioche, confit, fennel, gravlax, harissa, marjoram, poached, satay, strudel, tamarind,* and *turbot* all appear on the menus in DCL's main dining rooms. Depending on your cultural background, some of these terms may be unfamiliar. Clue your children in on what these words mean or have them practice their manners by asking the server (politely).

- **Dining alone for the first time.** This can be a great way to give older kids a taste of independence. If your tweens or younger teens have aced their manners prep, book a meal for the grown-ups at an adult-dining venue and send the kids to your regular dining rotation alone. We recommend doing this toward the end of your sailing, by which time your kids should know the lay of the ship. (Be sure to let your server know what you're doing ahead of time.)

- **Discovering the wonders of room service.** Sometimes being lazy and eating grilled cheese in your PJs on vacation is where it's at.

- **Breaking all the rules!** Mealtimes at home call for sensible stuff like eating your vegetables and watching your portions. But who wants to be sensible on a cruise? Eat nothing but ice-cream sundaes for lunch! Order your growing tween a second steak as dessert! Stir some soft-serve into your pool-deck Coke! Wolf down piles of chicken nuggets three times in a single afternoon!

DRINKING AGE

IN GENERAL, DCL REQUIRES that guests be 21 or older to drink alcohol. On some European cruises and repositioning cruises between Hawaii and Australia, guests ages 18–20 may drink with a parent or guardian's written consent, provided the adult is present when the alcohol is purchased and consumed. For round-trip cruises from Auckland, Brisbane, Melbourne, and Sydney, guests as young as 18 may purchase and consume alcoholic beverages without parental consent.

WHAT TO WEAR

SHORTS AND T-SHIRTS are acceptable at the standard restaurants, even for adults. We think most adults will feel more appropriately dressed in pants or dresses at dinner; Bermuda shorts paired with a nice button-down shirt and shoes would also work. Disney refers to this as "cruise casual." Swimwear and tank tops are prohibited at all times (and, frankly, you'd be freezing for most of your meal).

Heidi from Kentucky praises Disney's shorts-tolerant policy:

> *My husband was thrilled to find out he could wear shorts to dinner! It doesn't feel like a vacation for him if he has to wear "work" clothes. While some passengers prefer to dress up for dinner, he felt completely comfortable wearing shorts and a nice shirt.*

On one night of your cruise, most itineraries will also have **Pirate Night.** On three-night sailings, that involves a deck party (or two) in the evening, and on sailings of four or more nights, it will include a deck party plus a pirate-themed menu in the main dining rooms. A surprisingly large number of guests dress up in pirate attire for Pirate Night, but cruise casual will suffice if you don't want to dress up.

Cruises of three or four nights will have an **Optional Dress-Up Night,** and many longer cruises have a designated **Formal Night** and sometimes a **Semiformal Night.** The food served in the main dining rooms is essentially the same as on any other night. But while dressy clothing isn't required, you will find that many people enjoy upping their dinnerwear game for the occasion. The definition of *formal* is fluid: If you own a tux or evening gown, go ahead and bring it, but you'll also see guys in khakis and golf shirts. Kids should wear whatever nice clothes seem comfortable and appropriate. For girls, a sundress is fine; boys may wear a button-down shirt or a tie to look dapper. Formal night is also the perfect time to break out those princess dresses, especially if your little one has been Bibbidi Bobbidied that day.

If you don't have any fancy duds handy, you can always rent some. We are fans of **Rent the Runway** (renttherunway.com) for women's wear; good bets for men include **Men's Wearhouse** (menswearhouse .com), **Jos. A. Bank** (josbank.com), and **The Black Tux** (theblacktux .com). If you need to get professionally measured, check at a clothing store in your hometown that does prom and wedding rentals.

The dress code for dinner in the adult-dining restaurants falls just short of semiformal: The minimum requirement might be described as "business casual" or "smart casual," but some people are more comfortable in cocktail attire. Dress slacks and collared shirts are recommended for men, and a dress, a skirt and blouse, or pants and a blouse are recommended for women. Jeans are fine, provided they're in good condition (no holes, intentional or not). Not allowed are tank tops, swimsuits and cover-ups, shorts (see exception below), hats, cutoffs, torn clothing, flip-flops, athletic shoes, and T-shirts with offensive language and/or graphics. The dress code for brunch at Palo and Palo Steakhouse gets a

DRESSING FOR DINNER

SOME OF THE MOST frequently asked questions we get from new cruisers have to do with what to wear to dinner. There's just something about seeing zillions of movies and TV shows with cruisers gliding around in tuxes and glamorous gowns that makes the average traveler question their sartorial IQ. We're here to help, so read on.

- **What is *cruise casual?*** This is DCL's term for acceptable casual attire in the **main dining rooms**—in short, anything but swimwear and tank tops. We've never seen anyone turned away from these restaurants because of how they were dressed, although we have seen requests to change. On some specific nights, the main dining rooms have additional dress suggestions depending on the specifics of your sailing—these might include formal, semiformal, dress-up, pirate, tropical, *Frozen,* or Marvel attire. **All of these are completely optional.**

- **What does *formal attire* mean?** In the strictest sense, it means tuxedos for men and evening gowns for women. Again, though, it's completely optional. Many guests choose to wear something nicer than cruise casual on Formal Night, but the range of dress is broad. *Very* broad.

- **What do *semiformal* and *optional dress-up* mean?** For men this often means a suit, with or without a tie. For women it typically means a cocktail dress of approximately knee length. But as with Formal Night, you're likely to see a wide range of styles.

- **Will I get the side-eye if I don't dress up?** If you feel self-conscious, you could grab something from the pool deck or order room service, but if you want to wear shorts in the main dining room on Semiformal Night, don't worry about being judged. *You do you.*

- **What's the scoop with princess gowns?** As in the Disney theme parks, many girls under age 10 enjoy rocking princess attire while cruising. You can buy dresses on the ship, but we've observed that some of the most charming princess wear is homemade.

- **What do I need to know about themed events?** The most common themed event is **Pirate Night,** which takes place on almost all DCL sailings in the Caribbean and Bahamas, plus a few other destinations. Guests may be given a pirate-themed bandanna to wear, and the onboard shops have kids' pirate costumes for sale along with related accoutrements, such as faux hook hands and eye patches. During **Marvel sailings** (see page 66), about half the ship dresses up to an extent, even if it's just a themed T-shirt.

- **When are the Formal, Semiformal, and themed nights on my cruise?** To find out what will be happening on your sailing, call ☎ 800-951-3532. In general, however:
  - **Three-night cruises** typically have one standard cruise-casual night, one Pirate Night, and one Optional Dress-Up Night.
  - **Four-night cruises** typically have two standard cruise-casual nights, one Pirate Night, and one Optional Dress-Up Night.
  - **Seven-night cruises** typically have four standard cruise-casual nights, one themed night (Pirate Night or other depending on the destination), one Semiformal Night, and one Formal Night.
  - **Cruises of seven-plus nights** typically have additional cruise-casual dinners.

- **Are there times when the dress code isn't just a suggestion?** Yes. The **adult-dining venues** strictly enforce their respective dress codes, and we *have* seen guests be asked to change in these more upscale restaurants.

little more casual, and dress shorts are acceptable, although you won't see many of them.

Many guests are confused by the "no tank tops" language in DCL's dress codes. This is meant to prevent athletic and undershirt-style tanks, particularly on men. We've seen many women in the main and adult dining rooms wearing dressy sleeveless tops, sundresses, and the like. If your outfit doesn't look like swimwear or athletic wear, then you're probably OK.

We have personally seen a dining room server bring a sport coat to a man in a tank top at dinner, and we've also seen Palo offer pants to a man in shorts at dinner and Remy offer shoes to someone in flip-flops. If the thought of that makes you never want to leave your stateroom again, don't walk the line of "Is this too casual?" These are nice restaurants and should be treated as such. There are plenty of other options for anyone who wants to live in athletic shorts on board.

DCL's official word on dressing for these venues now reads:

Adult-exclusive restaurants aboard Disney Cruise Line ships are elegant dining experiences. Guests are requested to dress in a manner consistent with the restaurant's sophistication. Formal or semi-formal attire is recommended. Also permitted is dress-casual attire with a polished look, such as dress pants, jeans in good condition, collared shirts, dressy tops, and lifestyle shoes. For brunch at Palo and Palo Steakhouse, dress shorts are acceptable. Clothing such as T-shirts, swimwear, and sports attire is not permitted.

Do with that what you will.

COSTUME DRESS RULES

THOUGH COSTUMES ARE never required on board, DCL invites guests to dress in costume for themed events such as Halloween, Pirate Night, or Marvel sailings.

The 2022 debut of the *Disney Wish* saw a completely guest-generated fancy-dress phenomenon. Many guests choose to dress up in 1920s attire when dining at **1923**. You may see women in flapper dresses and long strands of faux pearls and men wearing *Great Gatsby* or *Boardwalk Empire*–style suits and hats. This trend was not instigated by Disney and is not required, but if you like playing dress-up, feel free to participate.

If you'd like to wear a costume, there are a few rules. Per Disney:

Masks that completely cover a person's face may only be worn when standing still at character photo locations and must be carried when moving around the ship. We also ask that you choose costumes that are not obstructive or offensive. To avoid any disappointment or delay in the boarding process, please refrain from bringing toys or props that resemble guns, knives, or other related implements, as these items will not be allowed on board.

RESTAURANT PROFILES

TO HELP YOU make your dining choices, we've developed profiles of DCL's counter-service and table-service restaurants, grouped by ship and then listed alphabetically. To keep things simple, buffets are included with the table-service restaurants.

RATINGS We typically receive around 150,000 dining surveys per year for Walt Disney World, and we've received over 1 million since 2018. Because DCL serves far fewer guests, we get fewer surveys—in most cases (and especially in 2020–23), not enough to provide a reasonable assurance of data accuracy for any single restaurant. Thus, the ratings here are based on a combination of reader surveys, conversations with other travel professionals, and our own experience.

For table-service restaurants, the **overall star rating** represents the entire dining experience: style, service, and ambience, in addition to the taste, presentation, and quality of the food. Five stars is the highest possible rating; four stars is above average; and three stars indicates good, though not necessarily memorable, meals. (No table-service restaurant was rated below three stars for this edition.)

Quality ratings, on the other hand, focus on the food. The quality of counter-service food is measured on a scale of **A (excellent) to F (poor).** (No counter-service restaurant was rated below a C for this edition.) For table-service restaurants, food quality is measured on a scale of **one to five stars,** with five stars being the best. Here, the star ratings take into account flavor, freshness of ingredients, preparation, presentation, and creativity.

For the adult-dining venues, where you pay extra to eat, price is not considered in the quality rating. But if you're looking for both quality *and* a good deal, check the **value rating,** also expressed as stars.

A REMINDER ABOUT ALCOHOL Wine, beer, and mixed drinks cost extra in the main dining rooms. They are also not included in the cost of meals at the adult-dining venues, except for one sparkling drink at brunch.

Note: At press time, it was too early to review the restaurants on the *Treasure* and *Destiny,* but in some cases we were able to make some assumptions based on their counterparts on the *Wish*.

Disney Magic

COUNTER-SERVICE RESTAURANTS

Daisy's De-Lites

QUALITY B   LOCATION DECK 9 AFT

OPEN Morning–midday.

SELECTIONS Breakfast includes pastries and fruit, as well as build-your-own yogurt parfaits and oatmeal or granola bowls. Lunch includes sandwiches, soups, and a build-your-own-bowl station with a base of rice or quinoa and toppings such as shredded pork or chicken and fresh veggies.

COMMENTS Daisy's De-Lites is our favorite quick-service restaurant on the *Magic* and *Wonder.* It's a good alternative to the breakfast buffet if you want something light. The customizable bowls are terrific for vegetarians.

Duck-In Diner

QUALITY B   LOCATION DECK 9 AFT

TABLE-SERVICE RESTAURANTS BY CUISINE

RESTAURANT	SHIP	OVERALL RATING	QUALITY RATING
AMERICAN/ASIAN			
Animator's Palate	Magic, Wonder, Dream, Fantasy	★★★	★★★
AMERICAN/BUFFET			
Cabanas	Magic, Wonder, Dream, Fantasy	★★★	★★★
Marceline Market	Wish, Treasure, Destiny	★★★	★★★
AMERICAN/CALIFORNIAN			
1923	Wish, Treasure, Destiny	★★★★	★★★★½
AMERICAN/CONTINENTAL			
Enchanted Garden	Dream, Fantasy	★★★	★★★
AMERICAN/ECLECTIC			
Worlds of Marvel	Wish, Treasure, Destiny	★★★	★★★
AMERICAN/GERMAN			
Rapunzel's Royal Table	Magic	★★★	★★★
AMERICAN/FRENCH			
Lumiere's	Magic	★★★	★★★
Royal Court	Fantasy	★★★	★★★
Royal Palace	Dream	★★★	★★★
Triton's	Wonder	★★★	★★★
AMERICAN/MEXICAN			
Plaza de Coco	Treasure	Too new to rate	Too new to rate
AMERICAN/SCANDINAVIAN			
Arendelle	Wish	★★★	★★★
AMERICAN/SOUTHERN			
Tiana's Place	Wonder	★★★	★★★
AMERICAN/TBD			
Pride Lands: Feast of the Lion King	Destiny	Too new to rate	Too new to rate

ADULT-DINING RESTAURANTS

RESTAURANT/CUISINE	SHIP	OVERALL RATING	QUALITY RATING	VALUE RATING
Enchanté French	Wish, Treasure, Destiny	★★★★½	★★★★½	★★★★½
Palo Italian	Magic, Wonder, Dream, Fantasy	★★★½* ★★★★**	★★★½* ★★★★**	★★★½* ★★★★**
Palo Steakhouse Italian/Steak	Wish, Treasure, Destiny	★★★★	★★★★½	★★★★½
Remy French	Dream, Fantasy	★★★★½	★★★★½	★★★★½

* Magic, Wonder   ** Dream, Fantasy

OPEN Midday–late evening.

SELECTIONS Middle Eastern meats such as chicken and lamb shawarma, served on your choice of pita or a tortilla. Daily specials, burgers, and french fries are also available.

COMMENTS There are lots of creative toppings and condiments, such as hummus, pickled veggies, baba ghanoush, chile mayonnaise, garlic-mustard aioli, sambal, tzatziki, or mint-cilantro sauce.

Pinocchio's Pizzeria

QUALITY C   LOCATION DECK 9 AFT

OPEN Midday–late evening.

SELECTIONS Cheese, pepperoni, and specialty pizzas (including veggie); cheeseless or gluten-free pizza is available upon request. If you're in the mood for fancy pizza, go for the flatbreads, which are often topped with mushrooms, pancetta, or other items of adult appeal.

COMMENTS It's about the same quality as store-bought frozen pizza—but hey, there are plenty of times when that's just what you want.

TABLE-SERVICE RESTAURANTS

Animator's Palate ★★★ DECK 4 AFT

AMERICAN/ASIAN   QUALITY ★★★   SERVICE ★★★★

Reservations Not accepted. **Meals served** Dinner. **Alcohol** Red, white, and sparkling wines, plus mixed drinks and spirits.

SETTING AND ATMOSPHERE The *Magic, Wonder, Dream,* and *Fantasy* all have an Animator's Palate, with different shows, technology, and decor on the *Magic* and *Wonder* vs. the *Dream* and *Fantasy*. All four serve the same food. On the *Magic* and *Wonder,* the main dinner show is **Drawn to Magic.** The idea is that you're in an old-fashioned black-and-white animated film that slowly colorizes as you dine. The entrance's walls are decorated with black charcoal sketches of various Disney characters. Inside, the entire color scheme starts out in black, white, and gray from floor to ceiling, including checkerboard-tile floor, black chairs, white tablecloths with black napkins, and black-and-white uniforms for the waitstaff. Even the support columns are dressed up as paintbrushes. Along the outside wall are video monitors that display images and "how to draw" sketches from Disney films. As the evening progresses, you'll notice bits of color being added to the walls and artwork, which become fully saturated by the end of your meal.

A second show, **Animation Magic,** typically takes place on your second evening at Animator's Palate on cruises of seven nights or longer. At the beginning of the evening, you're given a sheet of paper and a marker and instructed to draw a self-portrait. (There are guidelines on how to do this.) At the end of the evening, all the self-portraits are shown in a cartoon similar to Disney's 1929 short *The Skeleton Dance.*

HOUSE SPECIALTIES Pennette Bolognese, grilled tuna steak, ginger-teriyaki beef, sesame-Halloumi parcels (a vegetarian entrée of goat-and-sheep-milk cheese in puff pastry), roasted-garlic dip with bread.

COMMENTS Disney characterizes the cuisine as Pacific Rim/American, but it's really just your standard chain-restaurant fare, with probably as many Italian selections as Asian.

Cabanas ★★★ DECK 9 AFT

AMERICAN/BUFFET   QUALITY ★★★   SERVICE ★★★★

Reservations Not accepted. **Meals served** Breakfast and lunch. **Alcohol** Red, white, and sparkling wines, plus mixed drinks and spirits.

SETTING AND ATMOSPHERE Cabanas consists of two identical food-service areas, accessible from twin entrances on Deck 9. There are both indoor and outdoor seating options. Indoor seating is air-conditioned and features floor-to-ceiling windows with excellent ocean views. Outdoor seating is great on mornings when the ship is docking because you're sometimes able to watch the port come into view. Self-service soda fountains are located around the restaurant.

HOUSE SPECIALTIES Made-to-order omelets for breakfast. For lunch, there is a seafood bar with oysters, clams, crab legs. The peel-and-eat shrimp served on embarkation day is a big draw.

COMMENTS The buffets are easily comparable to those at upscale Las Vegas resorts and serve about as wide a variety of items. Breakfast includes everything from fruit, yogurt, and oatmeal to doughnuts and lox. Even cold cereal has options: Besides the usual cornflakes and granola, there's a build-your-own-muesli bar where you can add ingredients ranging from brown sugar to exotic dried fruits. Don't worry if you skipped dessert last night—you can get several at breakfast here.

Lunch is similarly lavish, with everything from chicken tenders, sandwiches, and burgers to salmon steaks and pasta.

Lumiere's ★★★ DECK 3 MIDSHIP

AMERICAN/FRENCH   QUALITY ★★★   SERVICE ★★★★

Reservations Not accepted. **Meals served** Dinner; breakfast and lunch on select days. **Alcohol** Spirits; mixed drinks; and a limited selection of red, white, and sparkling wines.

SETTING AND ATMOSPHERE Despite the name, there are only a few references to *Beauty and the Beast* here. The most notable are the light fixtures, which contain a single red rose, and a mural on the back wall that depicts characters from the movie. Besides that, most of the decor is Art Deco, which makes sense given the restaurant's location, just off the ship's atrium.

HOUSE SPECIALTIES Deep-fried Brie cheese, iced lobster and jumbo shrimp, crispy roasted duck breast, rack of lamb.

COMMENTS With a 95% thumbs-up rating among the *Unofficial Guide* readers we've surveyed, Lumiere's is the highest-rated main dining room on any Disney cruise ship.

DCL puts escargots and French onion soup on the menus of its French-themed standard dining rooms. Besides these dishes, however, most of the rest of the menu is decidedly un-français and would be equally at home at a so-called neighborhood bistro: grilled meats and chicken, a vegetarian tofu selection, and pasta. A couple of entrées, such as the herb-crusted rack of lamb and the crispy duck breast, stand out. The excellent Grand Marnier soufflé is the most popular dessert, but unlike the authentic soufflé served at Palo (see below), this is more of an airy cake.

Palo ★★★½ (adult dining) DECK 10 AFT

ITALIAN   QUALITY ★★★½   VALUE ★★★½   SERVICE ★★★★½

Reservations Required. **Meals served** Dinner; brunch on select days. **Alcohol** Large list of Italian wines, plus select wines from around the world; mixed drinks and spirits; limoncello; grappa; ice wine. **Comments** Palo's base dinner service is a four-course, prix fixe menu priced at $50. The dinner specialties described below—apart from the chocolate soufflé—are offered à la carte (typical full meals ordered à la carte also cost $50 or more per person). *Note:* If you need to cancel a reservation, you must do so 24 hours in advance, or you may incur a $50-per-person charge. Also note that Palo's brunch transitioned from a serve-yourself buffet to table service post-pandemic, with courses served family-style. Guests must be 18 or older to dine at Palo.

SETTING AND ATMOSPHERE Palo spans the entire aft section of Deck 10, which means that almost every seat has a spectacular view of the sunset over the ocean during dinner. Palo has contemporary decor, with decorative wood panels, round leather benches, and deep-purple fabric on the wood chairs. A small bar is available for guests waiting for their tables to become available, and part of the kitchen is open, in view of guests seated in the middle of the restaurant. Red-and-white-striped poles near the bar, evocative of those used to steer gondolas, call to mind Palo's roots in Venice (*palo* means "pole").

Because Palo is adults-only, it's much quieter than DCL's main dining rooms. The quietest tables of all are on the port side, aft. If you're looking to do some people-watching with dinner, request a table on the starboard side of the ship, near Palo's entrance. Background music is mostly Italian and ranges from Vivaldi to Sinatra.

HOUSE SPECIALTIES For a first course at dinner, try the ciuppin, a soup of fish, mussels, clams, and lobster in a tomato broth. The antipasto freddo, a selection of familiar cheeses and cured meats, is a little more adventurous. Our favorite entrées are the pasta in lobster and tarragon sauce, the Dover sole, and the rack of lamb. The chocolate soufflé, by far the most popular dessert, is served with both dark- and white-chocolate sauces. If you're not in the mood for chocolate, there may be other versions of the soufflé available—it never hurts to ask.

Palo's brunch is excellent. It's served family-style: You can have as much or as little as you like. Starters may include ahi tuna, crab legs, or prosciutto. Main courses include eggs Benedict for breakfast and wild mushroom ravioli and made-to-order pizza for lunch. Small cups of tiramisu or berries with cream will satisfy your sweet tooth.

COMMENTS Palo, the *Magic*'s one upscale restaurant, is its own little island of adult serenity and food. Service is very good, and don't be surprised if the maître d' and your server are from Italy.

Dinners are tasty and relaxing, especially with a glass or two of wine. That being said, we think Palo is better for brunch: Besides offering the best selection of midday food anywhere on the ship, the view is much better during the day; once the sun sets at dinner, the spectacular windows just reflect the inside of the restaurant. And considering the pricing structure at dinner—in which many favorite dishes can only be ordered à la carte—we consider brunch a much bigger bang for your buck. Even though both meals now cost at least $50, brunch pricing still includes anything you want (except alcohol), in any amount.

If we could improve one thing at Palo, it would be the coffee, which is Joffrey's (read: barely drinkable). A restaurant this good can do better.

Note that we rate Palo on the *Dream* and *Fantasy* slightly higher than the versions on the *Magic* and the *Wonder*: The decor is more sophisticated, and the kitchens are larger, allowing for more efficient food preparation. Nevertheless, on both the *Magic* and the *Wonder,* Palo is outstanding and definitely worth the extra cost.

Disney sometimes adds special adult-dining experiences to specific sailings; see page 206 for more information.

Rapunzel's Royal Table ★★★ DECK 3 AFT
AMERICAN/GERMAN   QUALITY ★★★   SERVICE ★★★★

Reservations Not accepted. **Meals served** Dinner. **Alcohol** A decent selection of reds, whites, and sparkling wines, plus mixed drinks and spirits.

SETTING AND ATMOSPHERE During the *Magic*'s 2018 dry dock, Carioca's restaurant was transformed into Rapunzel's Royal Table, a nod to the popularity of the 2010 Disney film *Tangled*. Characters such as Rapunzel and Flynn Rider make appearances. Encourage your kids to stick around until the end of the meal to see the procession of floating lanterns.

HOUSE SPECIALTIES Many dishes have a *Tangled* theme, such as the Snuggly Duckling Platter (sliced meats with pumpernickel and mustard); Maximus Salad (potatoes, carrots, and greens); Flynn Rider Platter (smoked pork loin with braised cabbage); and the pièce de résistance, Tangled Pasta (angel hair tossed with basil pesto and scallops). Gimmicks aside, the food is quite good.

OTHER RECOMMENDATIONS On longer sailings, Rapunzel's serves German-style dishes in honor of the Brothers Grimm (who popularized Rapunzel and other characters in their best-selling *Children's and Household Tales*). These may include pretzel bread, a grilled-knockwurst appetizer, a green-and-white asparagus salad, a trio of veal (tenderloin, pulled shank, and pasta with veal sauce), and a Sacher torte for dessert.

COMMENTS The kids' menu is full of safe bets—mac and cheese, mini burgers, baked salmon, whole-wheat pasta—and much of the adult fare successfully straddles the line between kid-friendly and grown-up, making it a great way to introduce your children to more-sophisticated dishes that aren't totally weird or unfamiliar. (At Lumiere's, on the other hand, we've heard a few kids cry with dismay when they learn what escargots are.)

Disney Wonder

COUNTER-SERVICE RESTAURANTS

Daisy's De-Lites
QUALITY B   LOCATION DECK 9 AFT

COMMENTS See the profile of Daisy's De-Lites on the *Magic* (page 213).

Pete's Boiler Bites
QUALITY B   LOCATION DECK 9 AFT

OPEN Midday–early evening.
SELECTIONS Hamburgers, fish burgers, veggie burgers, hot dogs, chicken tenders, fries. The shawarma station offers carved chicken or lamb with

toppings such as hummus, pickled veggies, baba ghanoush, chile mayo, and mint-cilantro sauce. Watch for daily specials like Philly cheesesteaks.

COMMENTS A nearby fixin's bar provides standard burger toppings, but if you want to mix things up, ask for a plateful of shawarma toppings instead.

Pinocchio's Pizzeria

QUALITY C   LOCATION DECK 9 AFT

COMMENTS See profile of Pinocchio's Pizzeria on the *Magic* (page 215).

TABLE-SERVICE RESTAURANTS

Animator's Palate ★★★ DECK 4 AFT

AMERICAN/ASIAN   QUALITY ★★★   SERVICE ★★★★

COMMENTS See the profile of Animator's Palate on the *Magic* (page 215).

Cabanas ★★★ DECK 9 AFT

AMERICAN/BUFFET   QUALITY ★★★   SERVICE ★★★★

COMMENTS See the profile of Cabanas on the *Magic* (page 216).

Palo ★★★½ (adult dining) DECK 10 AFT

ITALIAN   QUALITY ★★★½   VALUE ★★★½   SERVICE ★★★★½

COMMENTS See the profile of Palo on the *Magic* (page 216).

Tiana's Place ★★★ DECK 3 AFT

AMERICAN/SOUTHERN   QUALITY ★★½   SERVICE ★★★★

Reservations Not accepted. **Meals served** Breakfast, lunch, and dinner. **Alcohol** Limited selection of red, white, and sparkling wines, plus mixed drinks and spirits.

SETTING AND ATMOSPHERE An homage to the restaurant in *The Princess and the Frog,* Tiana's Place evokes a New Orleans supper club, with rustic elements interspersed with purple-and-green fabrics and polished-gold fixtures (think upscale Mardi Gras). Live music is performed on the main stage and features the jazz, swing, and blues sounds of Louisiana. While the music is fun and usually performed well, it can sometimes overwhelm dinner-table conversation. If you have a child with sensory issues and you want to enjoy the performances, you may want to consider noise-canceling headphones for them to wear during sets.

HOUSE SPECIALTIES Look for respectable approximations of NOLA specialties, including boudin sausage fritters, shrimp and grits, Cajun-spiced sea bass, and roasted Creole chicken. The white-chocolate bread pudding is delicious, and you can't go wrong with the bananas Foster sundae.

COMMENTS When Tiana's first opened, there were a few complaints about the food, but it has improved since then. As for us, it's a toss-up: While Tammy enjoys the beignets in particular, Len wishes there were a secret door leading to a quieter restaurant with more-authentic flavor.

Triton's ★★★ DECK 3 MIDSHIP

AMERICAN/FRENCH   QUALITY ★★★   SERVICE ★★★★

Reservations Not accepted. **Meals served** Breakfast, lunch, and dinner. **Alcohol** Limited selection of red, white, and sparkling wines, plus mixed drinks and spirits.

SETTING AND ATMOSPHERE In case you've forgotten that King Triton is Ariel's father in *The Little Mermaid,* a large tile mosaic of Triton and Ariel at the back of the restaurant is there to remind you. The blue, beige, and gray color scheme also lends a vaguely seaworthy theme to the decor.

HOUSE SPECIALTIES Breakfast features the usual suspects: fruit, cereal, eggs, waffles, bacon, sausage, and pastries. Lunch includes soups, salads, sandwiches, and burgers, plus a couple of alternative offerings such as pasta or fish. Dinner appetizers include escargots and French onion soup; order a crispy duck breast for the table if no one is adventurous enough to try it themselves. The Grand Marnier soufflé is the most popular dessert, but unlike the chocolate soufflé served at **Palo** (page 216), this one is more of an airy cake.

COMMENTS Triton's serves essentially the same menu as **Lumiere's** on the *Magic* (page 216). It has a decent selection of French-inspired entrées, plus vegetarian, chicken, beef, and pork dishes.

Disney Dream

COUNTER-SERVICE RESTAURANTS

Fillmore's Favorites

QUALITY C   LOCATION DECK 11 MIDSHIP

OPEN Midday–early evening.

SELECTIONS Sandwiches, wraps, salads, fruit, cookies.

COMMENTS Although the menu changes from time to time, it usually includes a roast-beef-and-cheddar sandwich, a Greek-salad veggie wrap, and a chicken Caesar wrap. Fresh fruit, such as whole bananas, grapes, and oranges, is also available.

Luigi's Pizza

QUALITY C   LOCATION DECK 11 MIDSHIP

OPEN Midday–late evening.

SELECTIONS Cheese, pepperoni, and specialty pizzas (including veggie); cheeseless or gluten-free pizza is available upon request. If you're in the mood for fancy pizza, look for offerings labeled "flatbread."

COMMENTS You'd never mistake Luigi's for authentic pizza, but it's fine if you need a quick bite. It's occasionally open after dinner, offering a convenient alternative to room service or restaurant dining.

Senses Juice Bar

QUALITY B   LOCATION SENSES SPA, DECK 11 FORWARD

OPEN Morning–midday; midafternoon–late afternoon.

SELECTIONS Fresh-squeezed juices in inventive combinations; fruit smoothies customized with ingredients like spinach; ginger; avocado; basil; protein powder; chia seeds; yogurt; and soy, almond, or coconut milk.

COMMENTS Prices range from about $6 to about $10, depending on which ingredients you select. Suggested smoothie blends are listed on the menu, but feel free to try whatever combination strikes your fancy. A small selection of Champagnes and cordials is also available.

Tow Mater's Grill

QUALITY C   LOCATION DECK 11 MIDSHIP

OPEN Midday–late evening.

SELECTIONS Grilled hot dogs, sausages, burgers, chicken sandwiches, fried chicken strips, french fries.

COMMENTS The burgers and fries are sustenance for chlorine-addled kids (that is, if they can be pried out of the pool long enough to eat). The chicken strips and hot dogs are the best things on the menu. A nearby fixin's bar provides toppings for burgers and sandwiches.

Vanellope's Sweets & Treats

QUALITY B   LOCATION DECK 11 MIDSHIP

OPEN Midday–late evening, with a 1-hour closure during the late afternoon.

SELECTIONS Named for Vanellope Von Schweetz, the sugar-fueled game character from *Wreck-It Ralph,* Vanellope's Sweets & Treats serves ice cream and house-made gelato with an extensive array of toppings, along with cupcakes, cookies, candy apples, chocolate truffles, and bulk and packaged candies. Ice-cream and gelato flavors vary seasonally. Kick your sugar buzz into high gear with espresso-based drinks.

COMMENTS You can get free soft-serve at the **Eye Scream** self-service machine and smoothies for an extra charge at **Frozone Treats,** both around the corner. The more upscale treats at Vanellope's start at about $3.50 for a single scoop; toppings and waffle cones cost extra. Sundae selections are imaginative, and the serving sizes are generous—even the smallest sundaes, starting at about $5.75, are big enough to serve two. If you have a large group, indulge in Ralph's Family Challenge: an eight-scoop, eight-topping sundae served in a souvenir trophy cup.

Like **Sweet on You** on the *Fantasy* (page 225), **Inside Out: Joyful Sweets** on the *Wish* (page 228), **Jumbeaux's Sweets** on the *Treasure* (page 228), and **Edna À La Mode** on the *Destiny* (page 228), Vanellope's delivers to the main dining rooms.

TABLE-SERVICE RESTAURANTS

Animator's Palate   ★★★   Deck 3 Aft

AMERICAN/ASIAN   QUALITY ★★★   SERVICE ★★★★

Reservations Not accepted. **Meals served** Dinner. **Alcohol** Spirits; mixed drinks; and red, white, and sparkling wines.

SETTING AND ATMOSPHERE The *Magic, Wonder, Dream,* and *Fantasy* all have an Animator's Palate, with different shows, technology, and decor on the *Magic* and *Wonder* (see page 215) vs. the *Dream* and *Fantasy*. All serve the same food. On the *Dream* and *Fantasy,* the space has caramel-colored walls and red carpeting with silver, gold, and blue stars. The dining room chairs mimic Mickey Mouse's pants, with red backs, yellow buttons, and a black "belt." Shelves along the walls hold toy versions of Disney and Pixar icons in between video screens displaying animation sketches from popular Disney movies. The more interesting ones will show how a complete animated cel (short for celluloid) is drawn, from sketches of the main characters to the finished art. The art changes throughout the evening, keeping the view fresh.

The **Undersea Magic** dinner show is unique to the *Dream* and *Fantasy*. At certain points during your dinner, some of the screens will switch from sketches to an interactive video featuring surfer-dude turtle Crush from *Finding Nemo*. When we say *interactive*, we mean it—Crush will ask you questions and react to your responses. Based on the same real-time computer graphics found in the *Turtle Talk with Crush* theme park attraction, the technology allows Crush's mouth to move as it would if he were actually speaking the words. Parents may be more amazed than kids.

A second show, **Animation Magic**, typically takes place on your second evening at Animator's Palate on cruises of seven nights or longer. At the beginning, you're given a sheet of paper and a marker and instructed to draw a self-portrait. (There are guidelines on how to do this.) At the end of the evening, all the diners' self-portraits are shown in an animated cartoon similar to Disney's 1929 short *The Skeleton Dance*.

HOUSE SPECIALTIES Pennette Bolognese, grilled tuna steak, ginger-teriyaki beef, sesame Halloumi parcels (a vegetarian entrée of goat-and-sheep-milk cheese in puff pastry), and roasted-garlic dip with bread.

COMMENTS Disney characterizes the cuisine as Pacific Rim/American, but it's really just standard chain-restaurant fare.

Cabanas ★★★ DECK 11 AFT

AMERICAN/BUFFET   QUALITY ★★★   SERVICE ★★★★

COMMENTS See the profile of Cabanas on the *Magic* (page 216).

Enchanted Garden ★★★ DECK 2 MIDSHIP

AMERICAN/CONTINENTAL   QUALITY ★★★   SERVICE ★★★★

Reservations Not accepted. **Meals served** Dinner; breakfast and lunch on select days.
Alcohol Spirits; mixed drinks; and a limited selection of red, white, and sparkling wines.

SETTING AND ATMOSPHERE Designed to resemble a 19th-century French greenhouse, with patinaed cast-iron arches supporting a spectacular ceiling display of plants, sun, and sky, Enchanted Garden is the prettiest of the *Dream*'s main dining rooms. During lunch, lights in the ceiling simulate the midday sun, and diners see what appears to be ivy climbing up the side of the ironworks; as the sun sets, the "sky" turns to dusk and eventually to dark. Chandeliers in the shape of flowers open their "petals" as night falls.

The centerpiece is a 7-foot-tall concrete fountain topped by Mickey Mouse. Look for framed Hermès scarves outside the restaurant—a posh touch of France. (Disney says Enchanted Garden is inspired by the gardens at Versailles, but we think it looks more like the hothouse at Paris's Jardin des Plantes.)

HOUSE SPECIALTIES Caramelized sea scallops with roasted asparagus; pan-seared sea bass with fava beans and pea risotto; marjoram-scented roast chicken; roast prime rib.

COMMENTS Despite the French setting, the menu is more American bistro than Parisian brasserie. Besides the brioche, the most French thing on the menu is the word *julienne*. There's usually at least one pork dish, such as pork tenderloin; one chicken dish (baked or roasted); and steak or prime rib, along with several seafood and vegetarian options. Honestly, you could serve these dishes at Animator's Palate or Royal Court without anyone noticing, but maybe the scenery here makes the food taste a bit better.

Palo ★★★★ (adult dining) DECK 12 AFT AND STARBOARD

ITALIAN QUALITY ★★★★ VALUE ★★★★ SERVICE ★★★★

Reservations Required. **Meals served** Dinner; brunch on select days. **Alcohol** Large list of Italian wines, plus select wines from around the world; mixed drinks and spirits; limoncello; grappa; ice wine. **Special comments** Palo's base dinner service is a four-course, prix fixe menu priced at $50. The dinner specialties described below—except the chocolate soufflé—are offered à la carte (typical full meals ordered à la carte also cost $50 or more per person). *Note:* If you need to cancel a reservation, you must do so 24 hours in advance, or you may incur a $50-per-person charge. Also note that Palo's brunch transitioned from a serve-yourself buffet to table service post-pandemic, with courses served family-style. Guests must be 18 or older to dine at Palo.

SETTING AND ATMOSPHERE Palo is on the starboard side at the back of Deck 12, opposite the adults-only French restaurant **Remy** (see next profile) and adjacent to **Meridian** bar. We think Palo on the *Dream* and *Fantasy* has nicer furnishings than the versions on the *Magic* and *Wonder*. The entrance to Palo on the *Dream* has a pretty, gold-and-ruby-colored glass chandelier, surely one of the most photographed parts of the restaurant. Guests walk past a glass-enclosed wine closet to the main dining room, decorated with deep-mahogany paneled walls and columns and rich burgundy carpet. One half of the room features deep-green patterned fabric on the booths and chairs, with paintings of the Italian countryside and seashore along the walls. The other half of Palo uses a saturated red fabric for its seating, and illustrations of Italian villas hang on the walls.

Naturally, tables next to Palo's floor-to-ceiling windows afford the best views, but tables near the back wall sit on an elevated platform, allowing diners to see over the tables nearest the windows. Our favorite table is on the left side of the second room, tucked by itself in a rounded corner along the inside wall and surrounded by a mural depicting Venice from the water. It's a bit high-profile, though; quieter seats are available at the far ends of either side of the restaurant.

HOUSE SPECIALTIES Start your dinner with the ciuppin, a soup of fish, mussels, clams, and lobster in a tomato broth, or the white-bean soup, with prosciutto and perfectly al dente beans. A large selection of pastas is available, including potato gnocchi with roasted tomatoes, lobster pappardelle, and butternut squash agnolotti. Our favorite entrée is the rack of lamb, which comes in a crispy crust of Parmesan cheese and oregano. For seafood, we like the grilled tuna with potato risotto a bit more than the grilled scallops, and you can't go wrong with Dover sole. The chocolate soufflé, with dark- and white-chocolate sauces, is by far the most popular dessert.

As on the other ships, Palo's brunch menu is excellent. It's served family-style, and your server will bring you as much or as little of each offering as you like. Starters may include ahi tuna, crab legs, or prosciutto. The main course includes breakfast options such as eggs Benedict and lunch options such as artichoke ravioli and made-to-order pizza. If there's any room left for dessert, small cups of tiramisu or berries with cream will take care of your sweet tooth.

COMMENTS Considering Palo's pricing structure, with many favorite menu items à la carte, we think brunch is a much bigger bang for your buck than dinner. Even though both meals cost at least $50, brunch includes anything you want (except alcohol), in any amount.

Remy   ★★★★½   (adult dining)   DECK 12 AFT

FRENCH   QUALITY ★★★★½   VALUE ★★★★½   SERVICE ★★★★

Reservations Required. **Meals served** Dinner; brunch on select days. **Alcohol** An extensive selection of French wines and Champagnes. **Special comments** An $80-per-person charge will be added to your cruise bill for each brunch at Remy ($135 per person for each dinner), with à la carte offerings available at an additional charge. See "House Specialties," below, for information about special dining experiences. If you need to cancel a reservation, you must do so 24 hours in advance, or the full per-person charge will be applied to your bill. Guests must be age 18 or older to dine at Remy.

SETTING AND ATMOSPHERE Remy is remarkably elegant and understated for a Disney restaurant—and one named after a cartoon rat at that. The most prominent features are the floor-to-ceiling windows, which look out over the ocean on the port side of the ship from high on Deck 12, and the Art Nouveau lights, which seem to spring from the floor as thick vines, branching out into yellow lights as they reach the ceiling. Besides those touches, and perhaps the oval mirrors along the wall opposite the windows, the rest is simple and elegant: oval, round, and square tables, all with white-linen tablecloths, and round-backed wood chairs with white upholstery. The olive-green carpet pattern matches the Art Nouveau decor without being distracting. A small teak deck wraps around Remy, allowing you to walk out for a breath of fresh air between courses.

HOUSE SPECIALTIES Entrées such as Australian Wagyu beef and pork from central France are divine. The tasting menu may be one of the best 3-hour dining experiences you'll ever have, but if that sounds like too much food, you can't go wrong with the regular menu.

Remy also offers an extensive brunch on select days. Like Palo's brunch, Remy's has an extensive selection, including fruit, pastries, seafood, beef, pork, pasta, and fish. A Champagne pairing is available for an additional $30 per person. We prefer the dinner experience, but spending the morning at Remy is a lovely way to start a day at sea.

Remy sometimes offers special dining experiences. Recent ones have included **Pompidou's Patisseries Dessert Experience**, which featured a sampling of six premium desserts for $60 per person ($85 per person with a supplementary wine pairing), and **Petites Assiettes de Remy** (**Remy's Small Plates**), a six-course tasting menu for $50 per person. If you're interested in these or similar experiences, check the **My Reservations** section on DCL's website or call DCL at ☎ 800-951-3532 to see if they'll be offered during your sailing.

COMMENTS What makes a great restaurant such as Remy different from restaurants that are simply very good is that, while the latter usually have a few signature dishes they do very well, virtually *everything* at Remy is nothing short of exceptional. An appetizer of carrots—yes, the humble root vegetable—will be the most extraordinary carrots you've ever had, probably in varieties and colors you didn't know existed, and with a flavor that is the pure essence of carrot-ness. Now imagine a meal of three to eight courses, all equally good. That's your average evening at Remy.

If you have the time and inclination, order the tasting menu, which allows you to savor every bit of creativity and technical mastery that Remy's kitchen can muster.

Pro tip: If you order a wine pairing, be aware that you get a *lot* of wine. Len's first evening at Remy was preceded by a martini at **Meridian** (page 301) and continued with a wine pairing at dinner. The first few courses were memorable—both in the sense that they were delicious and in the sense that Len remembered them—but as the meal wore on and the wine kept flowing, he was observed applauding a cheese cart as it rolled by for dessert service. That called for another dinner at Remy, minus the booze.

Royal Palace ★★★ DECK 3 MIDSHIP

AMERICAN/FRENCH   QUALITY ★★★   SERVICE ★★★★

Reservations Not accepted. **Meals served** Breakfast, lunch, and dinner. **Alcohol** Limited selection of red, white, and sparkling wines, plus mixed drinks and spirits.

SETTING AND ATMOSPHERE The most attractive part of Royal Palace may be its entrance, done in gold-and-white marble tile with a pretty flower-shaped chandelier accented with blue-glass "diamonds" and red "rubies." Inside the doors, gold-and-white faux-marble columns form a circle just inside one ring of tables; royal-blue carpet with gold trim lines the inner part of the restaurant. Curtains cover the windows lining one side of the room, and tile mosaics of Disney princesses line another.

HOUSE SPECIALTIES Breakfast is standard fare: fruit, cereal, eggs, waffles, bacon, sausage, and pastries. Lunch includes soups, salads, sandwiches, and burgers, plus a couple of other offerings like pasta or fish. Dinner appetizers include escargots and French onion soup; the crispy roasted duck breast is tasty. The Grand Marnier soufflé is the most popular dessert, but unlike the chocolate soufflé at **Palo** (page 223), it's more of an airy cake.

COMMENTS You know Disney is serious about the French theme when it puts snails on the appetizer menu. There are other Gallic influences too—many entrées have sauces made with butter, wine, or spirits, plus enough standard vegetarian, chicken, beef, and pork dishes to please everyone.

Disney Fantasy

COUNTER-SERVICE RESTAURANTS

Fillmore's Favorites

QUALITY C   LOCATION DECK 11 MIDSHIP

COMMENTS See profile of Fillmore's Favorites on the *Dream* (page 220).

Luigi's Pizza

QUALITY C   LOCATION DECK 11 MIDSHIP

COMMENTS See profile of Luigi's Pizza on the *Dream* (page 220).

Senses Juice Bar

QUALITY B   LOCATION SENSES SPA, DECK 11 FORWARD

COMMENTS See profile of Senses Juice Bar on the *Dream* (page 220).

Sweet on You Ice Cream & Sweets

QUALITY B   LOCATION DECK 11 MIDSHIP

OPEN Midday–late evening, with a 1-hour closure during the late afternoon.

SELECTIONS Choose from chocolate truffles (about $2 each), macarons (about $2.25 each), fancy cupcakes (about $4.50 each), wrapped candy by the pound, and an array of Mickey-themed pastries. The star attraction is the freezer case, stocked with ice cream, house-made gelato, and toppings aplenty. Kick your sugar buzz into high gear with espresso-based drinks.

COMMENTS You can get free soft-serve at the machine by the pool and free ice cream at dinner in the main dining rooms. If you need a fancier fix, single scoops start at about $3.50; toppings and waffle cones are available for a small upcharge. Sundae selections are imaginative, and portions are generous; even the smallest sundaes, starting at about $5.75, can likely serve two. For a special indulgence, try the create-your-own ice-cream sandwich (about $5): pick any two cookies (white-chocolate macadamia, chocolate chip fudge, M&M's, chocolate chunk, or peanut butter) and any flavor of ice cream or gelato. Like **Vanellope's Sweets & Treats** on the *Dream* (page 221), **Inside Out: Joyful Sweets** on the *Wish* (page 228), **Jumbeaux's Sweets** on the *Treasure* (page 228), and **Edna À La Mode** on the *Destiny* (page 228), Sweet on You delivers to the main dining rooms.

Tow Mater's Grill

QUALITY C   **LOCATION** DECK 11 MIDSHIP

COMMENTS See profile of Tow Mater's Grill on the *Dream* (page 221).

TABLE-SERVICE RESTAURANTS

Animator's Palate ★★★ DECK 3 AFT

AMERICAN/ASIAN   **QUALITY ★★★**   **SERVICE ★★★★**

COMMENTS See profile of Animator's Palate on the *Dream* (page 221).

Cabanas ★★★ DECK 11 AFT

AMERICAN/BUFFET **QUALITY ★★★** **SERVICE ★★★★**

COMMENTS See profile of Cabanas on the *Magic* (page 216).

Enchanted Garden ★★★ DECK 2 MIDSHIP

AMERICAN/CONTINENTAL **QUALITY ★★★** **SERVICE ★★★★**

COMMENTS See profile of Enchanted Garden on the *Dream* (page 222).

Palo ★★★★ DECK 12 AFT AND STARBOARD (adult dining)

ITALIAN   **QUALITY ★★★★**   **VALUE ★★★★**   **SERVICE ★★★★**

COMMENTS See profile of Palo on the *Dream* (page 223).

Remy ★★★★½ DECK 12 AFT (adult dining)

FRENCH   **QUALITY ★★★★½**   **VALUE ★★★★½**   **SERVICE ★★★★**

COMMENTS See profile of Remy on the *Dream* (page 224).

Royal Court ★★★ DECK 3 MIDSHIP

AMERICAN/FRENCH **QUALITY ★★★** **SERVICE ★★★★**

Reservations Not accepted. **Meals served** Breakfast, lunch, and dinner. **Alcohol** Limited selection of red, white, and sparkling wines, plus mixed drinks and spirits.

SETTING AND ATMOSPHERE Royal Court's most distinctive design elements are the gold-painted columns topped with large frosted-glass "flowers" decorated with gold stems and leaves. Along with these, white marble columns and a carpet designed to look like fancy rugs give Royal Court a formal feel, even when it's half full of kids. Small round lamps placed around the room look like Cinderella's pumpkin coach, and some of the walls feature tile mosaics depicting scenes from *Cinderella* and other Disney princess films. Tables near the starboard wall sit under portholes offering ocean views, although these are partially blocked by a privacy wall.

HOUSE SPECIALTIES Breakfast is standard fare: fruit, cereal, eggs, waffles, bacon, sausage, and pastries. Lunch includes soups, salads, sandwiches, and burgers, plus a couple of alternative offerings such as pasta or fish. Dinner appetizers include escargots and French onion soup; the crispy roasted duck breast is tasty. The Grand Marnier soufflé is probably the most popular dessert.

COMMENTS Only differences in decor distinguish this restaurant from **Royal Palace** on the *Dream* (see page 225).

Disney Wish, Disney Treasure, *and* Disney Destiny

NOTE: At press time, it was too early to review the restaurants on the *Treasure* and *Destiny*, but in some cases, we were able to make some assumptions based on their counterparts on the *Wish*.

COUNTER-SERVICE RESTAURANTS

THE *WISH, TREASURE,* AND *DESTINY*'S quick-service eateries are housed in a food court called **Mickey and Friends Festival of Foods.** The food is a substantial step up from what you get at the comparable pool-deck venues on the other four ships.

Daisy's Pizza Pies

QUALITY B   **LOCATION DECK 11 AFT**

OPEN Early afternoon–late evening.

SELECTIONS Pizza in various permutations: prosciutto, pepperoni and sausage, four-cheese, and Margherita.

COMMENTS Plant-based and gluten-free options are also available. We find Daisy's to be superior to the pizza locations on other ships.

Donald's Cantina

QUALITY B   **LOCATION DECK 11 AFT**

OPEN Early afternoon–early evening.

SELECTIONS Mexican favorites such as burritos, tacos, and build-your-own bowls similar to what you might get at Chipotle. Start your bowl with a base of rice or lettuce, then add any combination of fajita beef, chicken, pork carnitas, beans, veggies, guacamole, salsa, sour cream, or queso.

COMMENTS We're *obsessed* with the hot-sauce bar.

Goofy's Grill

QUALITY C   LOCATION DECK 11 AFT

OPEN Early afternoon–early evening.
SELECTIONS Grilled burgers, Impossible burgers, bratwurst, hot dogs, and plant-based sausages, plus DCL's famous chicken nuggets.
COMMENTS Fries are available with any entrée—or on their own.

Mickey's Smokestack Barbecue

QUALITY B   LOCATION DECK 11 AFT

OPEN Early afternoon–early evening.
SELECTIONS Smoked brisket, chicken, and sausage; St. Louis pork (cuts of smoked pork butt—think a barbecue "steak"); pulled pork. Sides include mac and cheese, collard greens, sweet potato fries, and cornbread.
COMMENTS This is one of our favorite pool-deck restaurants. There are several barbecue sauces to choose from. Have a family taste test to see which everyone prefers.

Inside Out: Joyful Sweets (*Wish* only)

QUALITY B   LOCATION DECK 11 AFT

OPEN Early afternoon–late evening.
SELECTIONS The signature dessert is the colorful Memory Orb cupcake—a chocolate sphere filled with gummy candies, marshmallows, and other goodies ($4.50)—but most folks are here for the house-made ice cream and gelato. Prices for one to three scoops are $3.50–$6 for ice cream and $3.75–$6.25 for gelato. Packaged treats and fresh pastries round out the offerings.
COMMENTS Inside Out is the *Wish*'s equivalent of **Vanellope's** on the *Dream* (page 221), **Sweet on You** on the *Fantasy* (page 225), **Jumbeaux's** on the *Treasure,* and **Edna À La Mode** on the *Destiny*. (Free soft-serve is available at **Sweet Minnie's Ice Cream.**) The theme, if you hadn't guessed, is Disney's *Inside Out*: Memory Orbs decorate the space, and statues of Anger, Disgust, Fear, Joy, and Sadness make for fun photo ops.

Jumbeaux's Sweets (*Treasure* only)

QUALITY B   LOCATION DECK 11 AFT

OPEN Early afternoon–late evening.
SELECTIONS Most folks come for the house-made ice cream and gelato, but there are carrot cupcakes made with spiced carrot cake, raspberry-and-crème cupcakes with red velvet cake, and paw-shaped shortbread sandwiches too. Packaged treats and fresh pastries round out the offerings.
COMMENTS This is the *Treasure*'s equivalent of **Inside Out** on the *Wish*, **Vanellope's** on the *Dream* (page 221), **Sweet on You** on the *Fantasy* (page 225), and **Edna À La Mode** on the *Destiny*. Themed after Jumbeaux's Café from *Zootopia*, there are sculptures of Judy Hopps and Nick Wilde.

Edna À La Mode (*Destiny* only)

QUALITY TOO NEW TO RATE   LOCATION DECK 11 AFT

OPEN Early afternoon–late evening.
SELECTIONS We expect the offerings here to be similar to those at **Jumbeaux's** on the *Treasure* and **Inside Out** on the *Wish*.

COMMENTS Named for Edna Mode from *The Incredibles,* this confectionery will be themed after the fashion designer's costume-making "lab," with sculptures of Edna and Jack-Jack.

TABLE-SERVICE RESTAURANTS

Arendelle: A *Frozen* Dining Adventure (*Wish* only)
★★★   DECK 5 AFT

AMERICAN/SCANDINAVIAN	QUALITY ★★★	SERVICE ★★★★

Reservations Not accepted. **Meals served** Dinner. **Alcohol** Modest wine selection, plus mixed drinks and spirits.

SETTING AND ATMOSPHERE The theming begins before you even enter the dining room—the jewel-toned Nordic decor in the extra-long entry corridor extends into the restaurant. Not surprisingly, the draw here is not the food but the entertainment, provided by *Frozen* characters. Elsa and Olaf host a wedding celebration for Anna and Kristoff, with Oaken (of Wandering Oaken's) doing the catering. The characters sing, accompanied by a small band of troubadours.

HOUSE SPECIALTIES Arendelle serves a mix of standard-issue American fare and Scandinavian-inspired dishes. Appetizers include a smoked-fish plate, baked scallops, asparagus and field-greens salads, a ham-and-cheese tart, and carrot soup (definitely *not* made from Olaf's nose). Entrées include sea bass, roasted rib eye, pork tenderloin, and chicken breast. If, like us, you're a fan of the IKEA food court, you'll love the meatballs with rosemary cream and lingonberry chutney.

For a sweet ending to your meal, try the Norwegian pancake roulade, layered with lingonberry jam and white-chocolate cheesecake, or the Troll Family's Rock Chocolate Bar, made with chocolate cake, pistachio-cookie pieces, and elderflower meringue.

COMMENTS Musical performances take place during more than half of your meal. You'll hear the hits from both *Frozen* films, although they're sometimes performed by characters other than the ones who performed them in the movies, which upsets some kids. Also note that the default embodiment of Olaf is a small animatronic wheeled in on a cart by one of the troubadours. If tiny Olaf is glitching, he'll be replaced by a human-size, walking version. Occasionally, he does not appear at all.

We think the entertainment is charming—the performers are talented, and their comic banter is delivered with a light touch. As fans of the films, however, we'll admit to a little bias: Some guests we've talked to who don't share our enthusiasm for the *Frozen* franchise think the show runs too long and find the volume level intrusive. If you want to be sure to see the show, or if you want to be sure to see less of the show, indicate this in the Special Requests section of your online check-in preferences (see page 123).

Enchanté   ★★★★½   (adult dining)   DECK 5 AFT

FRENCH	QUALITY ★★★★½	VALUE ★★★★½	SERVICE ★★★★

Reservations Required. **Meals served** Dinner. **Alcohol** A wide selection of French wines and Champagnes. **Special comments** An additional $80-per-person charge will be added to your cruise bill for each brunch and $135-per-person for each dinner, with à la carte offerings available for an additional charge. If you need to cancel a reservation, you must do so 24 hours in advance, or the full per-person charge will be applied to your bill. Guests must be 18 or older to dine. Menus are subject to change.

SETTING AND ATMOSPHERE The decor reminds us of a spa. The carpet is ocean blue, with dabs of white and gold, while nearly everything else is bedecked in shades of cream and gold. The overall effect is so clean and lovely that we would be nervous about ordering red wine, lest we spill it. Each table is decorated with a dark-blue dried rose—which we find slightly macabre. The centerpiece of the dining room is a floor-to-ceiling chandelier made of gold-toned, bubble-shaped orbs. The entryway walls are decorated with clever candelabras (Lumiere from *Beauty and the Beast* makes an appearance) and showcase a selection of the ship's finest wines.

HOUSE SPECIALTIES At dinner, Enchanté offers both à la carte and prix fixe options. **Passion,** the prix fixe dinner, consists of six courses: an appetizer of tomatoes prepared three ways, John Dory (white fish) with sea urchin and plankton, halibut with onion confit and vermouth sauce, and squab fermière (pigeon in puff pastry) with turnip relish, along with a cheese cart and dessert. The pricier **Collection** menu ($195) includes some of the prix fixe offerings, along with à la carte options such as Waygu beef, langoustines, caviar, Maine lobster, and assorted seasonal specialties. The lemon dessert is a standout.

Brunch features tomato pie, braised pork with salad, halibut with creamy scrambled eggs, chicken with gnocchi, and an incredible lemon dessert. Wine and Champagne pairings are available for all meals.

COMMENTS We think Enchanté offers one of the finest culinary experiences you can have at sea—it's as much about the ambience, service, and presentation as it is the incredible food. If you eat here, we'd love to hear from you.

Marceline Market   ★★★   DECK 11 AFT

AMERICAN/BUFFET   QUALITY ★★★   SERVICE ★★★★

Reservations Not accepted. **Meals served** Breakfast and lunch. **Alcohol** The adjacent **Marceline Market Café** has bar service. **Special comments** This is very similar to Cabanas on the other ships—so much so that we just call it Cabanas among ourselves ("Marceline Market" is a mouthful).

SETTING AND ATMOSPHERE Marceline Market consists of two identical buffet lines, accessible from twin entrances on Deck 11. (During slower hours of the day, only one line may be open.) There are both indoor and outdoor seating options. Inside you'll find warm-toned wood tables appropriate for various party sizes, as well as high-top bar-style seating for individuals. Self-service soda fountains are located around the restaurant.

HOUSE SPECIALTIES Breakfast stations include bacon and sausage, made-to-order eggs and omelets, pancakes and waffles, grits and oatmeal, cold cereals and yogurt, pastries, and the like. We're particularly fond of the Asian breakfast station, which features a rotating selection of congees (porridges) and a savory-toppings bar.

Lunch options vary daily and include both hot and cold selections such as pasta, rice and veggie dishes, carved meats, soups, curries, fish, salads, sandwich fixings, and peel-and-eat shrimp. The kiddie station (available to adults as well) includes faves like mac and cheese, fries, and chicken nuggets. We're fans of the mini charcuterie board, which has a small selection of cheeses, meats, and antipasti.

COMMENTS Although Marceline Market is similar to **Cabanas** (page 216), getting your food isn't as straightforward here. Instead of serving yourself, you tell cast members what you want; then they dish it up for you and hand you a plate. But unlike a cafeteria, Marceline Market doesn't provide trays, so transporting your plates to your table could get complicated. Chances are your family will want to eat from several different stations, each of which will give you a plate. At breakfast you may end up with an egg plate, a waffle plate, *and* a fruit plate. And with no trays to put them on, this means you'll have to either make several trips to the service line, dropping off a plate at your table after each trip, or ask a cast member to help you carry your plates. If you're a single parent or helping care for someone with a mobility issue, we recommend flagging down a cast member for assistance *before* you get in line.

1923 ★★★★ DECK 3 AFT

AMERICAN/CALIFORNIAN   QUALITY ★★★★½   SERVICE ★★★★

Reservations Not accepted. **Meals served** Breakfast, lunch, dinner. **Alcohol** Impressive selection of wines for a rotational dining room, along with mixed drinks and spirits.

SETTING AND ATMOSPHERE The dining room is divided into two areas: the Roy Disney Room and the Walt Disney Room. (The restaurant's name refers to the year the brothers opened their first animation studio in Los Angeles.) The partitioning cuts down on the cavernous feeling—and the accompanying noise—that's endemic to DCL's other main dining rooms. The overall vibe is Old Hollywood glamour: if you're familiar with Carthay Circle at Disneyland, you're in the ballpark, but 1923 is sleeker and more refined. The decor includes more than 1,000 drawings and props illustrating Walt and Roy's early days in California.

HOUSE SPECIALTIES Breakfast is standard fare: pancakes, eggs, bacon, and Mickey waffles cooked to order. Lunch includes burgers pennette pasta, Caesar salad, and salmon. For dinner, starters include duck confit, guinea hen corn chowder, Napa baby romaine salad with Caesar dressing and grape tomatoes, and fennel-and-pear salad with Manchego cheese. The entrées are several steps up from the ones in the other main dining rooms: peppered filet mignon; salmon fillet with parsnip purée; rosemary-crusted rack of lamb; and roasted chicken with Brussels sprouts, potatoes, and apple chutney. Vegetarians will love the soft-shell tacos stuffed with quinoa, salsa fresca, peppers, and onions. The signature dessert is the blueberry-lemon Bavarian cream; other options include flourless orange-almond cake, Fuji apple cheesecake, spicy churros, and a hot-fudge sundae.

COMMENTS You won't find a better main dining room on the *Wish*—or any other DCL ship. Every dish we've tried has been delicious. *Note:* Some guests choose to wear 1920s-era attire when dining here (see page 212).

Palo Steakhouse ★★★★ (adult dining) DECK 12 AFT

ITALIAN/STEAK   QUALITY ★★★★   VALUE ★★★★½   SERVICE ★★★★

Reservations Required. **Meals served** Dinner; brunch on select days. **Alcohol** Large list of Italian wines, plus select wines from around the world; mixed drinks and spirits; limoncello; grappa; ice wine. **Special comments** A $50-per-person charge will be added to your cruise bill for each prix fixe meal at Palo Steakhouse, with additional charges for à la carte menu items. If you need to cancel a reservation, you must do so

24 hours in advance, or the full per-person charge may be applied to your bill. Guests must be 18 or older to dine.

SETTING AND ATMOSPHERE The dining room is divided into two main seating areas. The first features booth and banquette seating with plush red-velvet upholstery. The second has tables, mostly for groups of two or four, with beige armchairs. Carpets are a muted rust color, and both rooms have floor-to-ceiling panoramic views of the ocean.

HOUSE SPECIALTIES The Italian portion of the dinner menu is similar to that of Palo on the other four ships. At Palo Steakhouse, however, the bill of fare is beefed up (see what we did there?) with a plethora of proteins. Choose from bone-in cowboy rib eye, Angus tenderloin, New York sirloin, porterhouse, veal rib chops, Parmesan-crusted rack of lamb, and Wagyu tenderloin (*tender* being the operative word—you can cut it with a fork).

Brunch is likewise similar to what you'll find at Palo on the other ships—in other words, divine. Choose from seafood or meat antipasti, then move on to frittatas and omelets. The breakfast entrées are variations on waffles and pancakes (we're partial to the blueberry pancakes with whipped cream). The lunch part of the menu includes lasagna, veal saltimbocca, chicken Parmesan, red snapper, mushroom ravioli, and sirloin. The desserts are tempting—chocolate-raspberry tart, limoncello torte, amaretto chocolate cake, and panna cotta—but don't sleep on the warm apple-cinnamon sticky buns, a brunch staple at the other four Palos. We're not ashamed to admit that we've booked cruises solely to sate our cravings for these.

COMMENTS The food is great at dinner, but we prefer brunch for the more economical pricing and the daytime views of the ocean.

Plaza de Coco   DECK 5 AFT

MEXICAN   TOO NEW TO RATE

Reservations Not accepted. **Meals served** Dinner. **Alcohol** Spirits; mixed drinks; and a limited selection of red, white, and sparkling wines.

SETTING AND ATMOSPHERE Dinner includes two different shows on two nights. On the first night, Miguel from *Coco* performs with a live mariachi band. On the second night, the plaza is transformed into a fun-filled celebration with Mamá Coco, Abuelita, and the rest of the Rivera family.

HOUSE SPECIALTIES The appetizers include Shrimp Diabla, with chipotle sauce, cilantro, pickled red onion, and toasted birotes, and Chorizo Street Croquettes, with chile-lime crema, cotija cheese, and cilantro. Entrées include Luisa's Pollo Asado, which features Michoacán citrus chicken, cilantro rice, and serrano-tomatillo salsa; port-braised beef short rib with crispy shallots, cheddar-and-green-onion mashed red potatoes, and green beans; pan-seared adobo-spiced sea bass with seared scallops, rainbow carrots, spinach, Romanesco, peas, and chimichurri sauce; a blistered poblano stuffed with Oaxaca cheese and green rice; and red-capsicum and parsley grilled snapper with fried yucca, refried beans, baby spinach and pico de gallo. Desserts include Margarita Lime Cheesecake, with sea salt shortbread and raspberry-agave margarita coulis; Mexican Chocolate Tart, with spiced chocolate crème, caramel pecan nuts, and chocolate glaze; and Warm Coconut Tres Leches, featuring milk-soaked coconut cake, caramel sauce, and dulce de leche ice cream.

COMMENTS We've been waiting for a delicious Mexican restaurant on board!

Worlds of Marvel ★★★ DECK 4 AFT

AMERICAN/ECLECTIC   QUALITY ★★★   SERVICE ★★★★

Reservations Not accepted. **Meals served** Dinner. **Alcohol** Limited selection of wines, plus mixed drinks and spirits.

SETTING AND ATMOSPHERE Worlds of Marvel has two shows: *Avengers: Quantum Encounter* and *Marvel Celebration of Heroes: Groot Remix.* Here, you're in the world of Pym Tech, with decor coming from the mind of Tony Stark—it's superhero chic bathed in blue light. Even the silverware is marked with the Avengers logo. The dining room is encircled by video screens, as are the newer versions of Animator's Palate on the other DCL ships. In this case, however, you're not talking to Crush from *Finding Nemo* but gazing upon the eternally boyish face of Paul Rudd as Ant-Man; everyone's favorite sentient tree, Groot; and Rocket the raccoon. The "Quantum Core" gadget sitting on your table is nominally interactive: You'll be asked to press some buttons on it to help the superheroes save the world.

HOUSE SPECIALTIES Disney describes the food as "American, Sokovian, and Wakandan," which translates to American with a smattering of cuisines from around the world.

For *Quantum Encounter,* you can begin your meal with an heirloom-tomato or iceberg-wedge salad (both classified as Wakandan) or appetizers such as steamed bao buns, shrimp marinated with dill and Meyer lemon, and hearts of palm with cilantro and lime. Entrées include beef tenderloin, grilled tuna steak, pork chops, and chicken schnitzel. For dessert, the "signature" Cheesecake Byte (basic cheesecake) pales in comparison to the showstopping Pym Doughnut Sundae: dulce de leche ice cream topped with a pecan brownie, caramel fudge sauce, whipped cream, and a chocolate-glazed mini doughnut. This indulgence is on the order of the extra-cost treats at **Inside Out** (see page 228), so skip those during the day if you'll be eating dinner here. Rounding out the offerings are sticky date pudding, Key lime pie, Dobos torte (a Hungarian-style cake with chocolate filling), and flourless chocolate-beetroot cake.

The food for *Marvel Celebration of Heroes* was too new to review at press time.

COMMENTS The video presentation is cute (as is Rudd), but like the live show at Arendelle, it's very loud and hard to ignore—you won't be having much family conversation while it's going on.

Also keep in mind that the wow moments of the show take place at the very end of your meal, much like the revelatory moments during the end credits of a Marvel movie. If your kids grow tired and cranky during late dinner seatings, getting them to bed may be a higher priority than waiting around to be wowed.

The video presentation during *Celebration of Heroes* involves Groot planning the ultimate surprise party for Rocket, all while diners enjoy Marvel trivia and awesome mix-tape music. You may want to brush up on your Marvel trivia before your dinner.

The entertainment is prerecorded, meaning it will be exactly the same at every seating. If you've seen the show before and don't care to see it again, you may want to consider springing for dinner at **Palo Steakhouse** (see 231) or **Enchanté** (see page 229) on one of your assigned Worlds of Marvel nights.

PART 11

NURSERY *and* KIDS' CLUBS

KEY QUESTIONS ANSWERED IN THIS CHAPTER

- Which club will my child spend time in? *(see opposite page)*
- What goes on in the kids' clubs? *(see page 238)*

OVERVIEW

WHEN IT COMES TO entertaining children, Disney Cruise Line has no equal. The kids' clubs (Disney officially calls them **youth clubs**), for infants to 17-year-olds, open as early as 7:30 a.m. for babies and close as late as 2 a.m. for teens. Kids can participate in organized activities ranging from crafting to trivia contests and dance parties, or they can play individually with computer games, board games, books, and craft materials. Most of the organized activities last 30–60 minutes, so a new event will likely start soon after your child arrives; this means kids become part of the group quickly.

Much like the Disney theme parks, the ships offer a contained environment that gives tweens and teens some autonomy to roam on their own. The texting function of the **DCL Navigator app** (see page 124) means you'll always be able to reach your children, and the food on the pool deck and at the buffet, which are included in your cruise fare, means there's no worrying about finding something to eat or how to pay for it, not to mention the fact that free food may make it even easier to find them. When Tammy's kids were tweens, she could camp out by the pizza on the pool deck and pretty much count on seeing them at some point.

Children with separation anxiety may resist going to the clubs (see page 237 for our advice), but based on our reader surveys, most kids love them and don't want to leave. That said, there's plenty for children and families to do outside of the clubs. Activities from karaoke to character appearances are scheduled throughout the day (see Part 12). Other recreational opportunities include minigolf (*Dream* and *Fantasy*) and the sports areas, all topside.

KIDS' CLUBS IN BRIEF

"IT'S A SMALL WORLD" NURSERY!

- **LOCATION** Deck 5 Aft (*Magic, Wonder, Dream, Fantasy*), Deck 2 Midship (*Wish, Treasure, Destiny*)   • **AGES** 6 or 12 months (depending on itinerary)–3 years
- **FEE** $9/hour for first child, $8/hour for each additional child
- **MEALS** Bring your own food, milk, and formula.

OCEANEER CLUB/OCEANEER LAB

- **LOCATION** Deck 5 Midship (*Magic, Wonder, Dream, Fantasy*). On the *Wish, Treasure,* and *Destiny,* the Oceaneer Club is on Deck 2 Midship; the check-in desk is on Deck 3 Midship, where kids can access the main club via a "secret" slide.
- **AGES** 3-10 years   • **FEE** None   • **MEALS** None

EDGE

- **LOCATION** Deck 9 Midship (*Magic, Wonder*), Deck 13 Forward (*Dream, Fantasy*), Deck 5 Aft (*Wish, Treasure, Destiny*)
- **AGES** 11-14 years   • **FEE** None   • **MEALS** None

VIBE

- **LOCATION** Deck 11 Midship (*Magic, Wonder*), Deck 5 Forward (*Dream, Fantasy*), Deck 12 Aft (*Wish, Treasure, Destiny*)
- **AGES** 14-17 years   • **FEE** None
- **REFRESHMENTS** Sodas (free), smoothies (extra charge)
- **EXTRAS** Sundeck with splash pools (*Dream, Fantasy*)

We provide in-depth profiles of DCL's nurseries and kids' clubs starting on page 242, organized by ship and ordered from the youngest to oldest age groups. See table above for the basics.

KIDS' CLUB OPEN HOUSES

ON EACH SAILING, the kids' clubs hold several open houses, during which families may use the clubs' facilities together, making this the perfect time to, say, dance on the Magic Floor or play some PS5 Mario Kart with your child.

unofficial **TIP**
Parents aren't allowed in the kids' clubs during regular hours.

Open houses are especially good for kids who aren't ready to separate from their parents, kids who are slightly too young or too old for a particular club, and children with disabilities who cannot go to the clubs alone (see page 163).

CHOOSING A CLUB

CHILDREN IN THE FOLLOWING age groups may choose which club they wish to participate in: Three-year-olds may choose the nursery or (if potty-trained) the Oceaneer Club/Lab, and 14-year-olds may choose between Edge and Vibe. This flexibility is helpful when siblings who are close in age want to be in the same club.

Once a choice is made, however, it may not be changed. Disney is also strict about making sure that kids stick to the club for their age group—that means, for example, no sneaking into Vibe if they're not old enough or if they're even slightly too old.

REGISTERING

PARENTS CAN SIGN their children up for the kids' clubs during the online check-in process or on embarkation day during one of the open houses. While reservations are required at the nursery, they're not needed at the kids' clubs for children age 3 and up—once you've registered your kids, you can drop them off at the club as often as you like for the duration of your cruise, with no need to let anyone know in advance. It's an incredibly flexible system that allows for a great deal of vacation spontaneity.

SPECIAL CONSIDERATIONS

INFANTS Babies must be 6 months of age or older to sail on most Alaskan, Bahamian, Caribbean, and other cruises of seven nights or fewer. On some longer cruises, often those with multiple consecutive sea days (such as the transatlantic crossings), DCL requires that children be at least 1 year old to sail.

TWEENS AND TEENS We know from our own experiences and those of other parents that teens will practically forget you exist once they get a feel for the clubs and activities. In fact, before you even set foot on the ship, you should set some ground rules for how often your teen needs to check in with you. Our rule is that everyone has to have dinner together each night and stay together during shore excursions. At Castaway Cay and Lookout Cay, we reserve morning activities for family time, and the teens are allowed to explore the island on their own after lunch.

ONLY-CHILD SITUATIONS The clubs are seamless for tweens and teens who are traveling with similarly aged siblings, cousins, or friends: They have built-in companions for activities and can sample the club offerings at will, with no fear of being the odd kid out. But for a middle schooler or teen who's an only child—or the only sibling on the cruise—the clubs can be more challenging. Many teens who've sailed on DCL observe that the so-called single kids who do best at Vibe are the ones who take the initiative to participate in as many activities as possible, increasing their opportunities for bonding with the group.

ACTIVE KIDS As a parent, you're the best judge of how much physical activity your child needs. We've rarely seen truly bad behavior on the DCL ships, but when we have, it's usually been an active child running wild after sitting in passive activities all day.

To ensure that your kids burn off their excess energy in a positive way, keep an eye out for ways to add physical activity to their day, particularly if you're spending several consecutive days at sea. The pool and sports deck are obvious solutions, but these may sometimes be unavailable due to weather or temporary maintenance issues. Ask the kids' club counselors about which activities have the most opportunity for movement—for example, onboard dance parties that are happening during your sailing.

WHAT IF MY YOUNG CHILDREN DON'T WANT TO GO TO THE KIDS' CLUB?

UNOFFICIAL GUIDE AUTHOR AND BLOGGER **Becky Gandillon** has two young daughters who are veterans of several Disney cruises.

CLINGY KID? Reluctant socializer? Been there, done that, raised those. We always look forward to dropping our kids off in the kids' club so we can enjoy the adult spaces and activities on the ship. But that doesn't always work out. Thankfully, there are still lots of ways to keep young kids entertained even if they are averse to the clubs.

The first thing we do is look for any activities in the **Navigator app** that have the word *family* in them. There are usually several family crafts offered throughout the day, as well as many family-specific trivia, animation, or game-playing events in spaces like the D Lounge. Occasionally you'll find something even more exciting like a family Silent DJ party, where you can all wear headphones and listen to curated music stations while dancing like maniacs. If an activity has *family* in the title, you can bet that there will be lots of kids there and that it will generally be appropriate for even your youngest family members.

The next strategy is attending any and all **kids' club open houses,** even after embarkation day. This serves two purposes: (1) It allows for family fun in a space built for kids—they can run, play, draw, and explore without being as concerned about bumping into people in tight hallways. (2) It offers them an opportunity to fall in love with the clubs while still in the safe company of their parents. Maybe they'll eventually opt to go back on their own.

Besides family-oriented versions of activities, we've had success in bringing our young kids to almost any activity listed in the Navigator that isn't specifically designated as adults-only. **Trivia** is always fun even if they know zero answers, **drawing classes** can work for even the scribbliest of beginners, and **games** are hilarious to watch.

Finally, we default to the **pool** or even our **stateroom.** The pool and splash pad can get crowded and crazy—often bringing anxiety to the same kids who are opting out of the kids' clubs because of the chaos. But if having a parent around makes everything better, the pool is a great way to spend a lot of time together. Additionally, our girls would probably call the cruise a success if they could sit in the stateroom and watch Mickey cartoons all day. We limit screen time at home and try to stick to that on vacation too. But if they want to watch something for 30 minutes, we can go out and read on the verandah. Or we can all catch a movie together in the theater or on the pool deck. I'm happy as long as I can feel the sea breeze.

USING THE KIDS' CLUBS WHEN YOU'RE OFF THE SHIP

GUESTS ARE WELCOME to use the kids' clubs whenever they're open, including when the ship is in port. Using the clubs in this situation can play out in a number of ways. You might, for example, choose to leave your sand-phobic 6-year-old on the ship for an hour while you're a 10-minute walk away on Castaway Cay. We've also met cruisers who didn't hesitate to leave their tweens on board while they toured a port for several hours. The tweens got to enjoy the ship, and the parents got to tour at their own pace.

unofficial **TIP**

Keep your passport with you at all times. In the unlikely event that you get left behind at the port, having your passport handy will help expedite your reunion with your child.

If you do decide to leave your child on the ship for an extended period of time, communicate your plans to the counselors at the club. Let them know where you'll be, when you'll return, your phone number, and any pertinent medical information, along with contact information for the child's home medical providers and other emergency contacts.

Keep in mind that to ensure you make it back to the ship as scheduled, you may be better off taking a Disney port adventure than booking your own shore excursion (see Part 15). In the event that you encounter delays in getting back to the ship, the crew is more likely to wait a few extra minutes for a large group on a DCL port adventure than they would be for a lone guest on a third-party excursion.

WHAT GOES ON IN THE KIDS' CLUBS?

SOME ACTIVITIES, such as video games and crafts, are generally available anytime. In addition to free play, the kids' clubs offer a range of age-appropriate structured activities, from the creative to the competitive. If your kids prefer directed activity over self-initiated play, keep a careful eye on the Navigator app, which lists the times and short descriptions of planned activities. Most of the listings are self-explanatory; others are more cryptic, with unadvertised character appearances. See the table on the opposite page for a sampling of what may be available on your sailing.

Amy from Florida clued us in on some of her child's favorites:

Minnie's Captain Academy: *Minnie is recruiting new kids to be on her crew. You spell your name with nautical flags, learn to tie knots, and do other activities. Captain Minnie appears at the end for a dance party.*

Experience the Force: *Jedis teach you how to use the Force, and a stormtrooper comes looking for rebels. The Force is used to move objects and then make the stormtrooper leave.*

Pathfinders: *There are two teams. A youth counselor writes a path on a piece of paper to get through the Hula-Hoops or stars on the floor. The different teams try to guess the path that was written on the paper by going through the Hula-Hoops or stars.*

SAMPLE ACTIVITIES IN THE KIDS' CLUBS

OCEANEER CLUB/LAB (AGES 3-10)

- **Animation Antics** Discover the history of animation, draw Disney characters, and create a flipbook to take home.
- **Anyone Can Cook: Cookies** Inspired by the film *Ratatouille,* kids will learn how to mix and measure ingredients before baking up a batch of chocolate chip cookies.
- **Craft Corner** It's time to get creative and put your crafty skills to use!
- **Get the Hook!** Join Detective Clue for a search that leads kids from one "crime scene" to the next—catch the culprit and collect a reward from the captain.
- **Monsters, Inc. Open "Mike" Night** Kids can help Mike and the gang rescue Monstropolis by putting on a comedy show and collecting enough laughter to power the town.
- **Piston Cup Challenge** Build race cars from bars of soap (based on Disney's *Cars*).
- **Super Sloppy Science** Join Professor Make-O-Mess in some of the most extreme experiments you'll ever see.
- **Wacky Relays** Show off your wacky skills in some of the wackiest races at sea.

EDGE (AGES 11-14)

- **Animation Cels** Learn what it takes to be a Disney animator, then put your skills to the test as you create your very own animation cel.
- **Crowning of the Couch Potato** Do you think you know your movies, TV, and commercials? Well, it's time to test your knowledge.
- **Foosball Tournament** Show us your Foosball skills and see who's the best of the best.
- **Heroes and Villains** Put your athleticism and intellect to the test. Teams compete to solve clues, complete challenges, and win a final prize.
- **Pathfinders** A path has been chosen for you. Can you find it?
- **A Pirate's Life for Me** Compete in physical challenges and answer trivia questions about scalawags and buccaneers of yore.
- **Scattergories** See who can think of the most creative answers.
- **That's Hilarious** Ever wanted to show off your comedy skills? Then be a part of the cast for this crazy improv show.

VIBE (AGES 14-17)

- **Dream Now! Sea How!: Animal, Science, and Environment** In an interactive session, you'll dive into the background, education, and mentors that brought animal-care workers into their profession.
- **Gotcha!** Armed with a code name and an arsenal of "gotcha" methods, teens spend the day tagging out their competition on the ship in creative and cunning ways.
- **Ice Cream Social** Make your own frosty treat with your counselors.
- **Teen Download** Using media technology, interact with other teens and counselors to design your dream vacation filled with activities, games, port adventures, and downtime.
- **Vibe Movie Makers** Learn moviemaking skills to create a film to show your family at the end of the cruise.

The Power of Pym Particles: *Ant-Man gets shrunk into the Quantum Realm and almost gets eaten by a creature there. The kids need to make Pym Particles to help him. You learn about ants, and at the end, Ant-Man and the Wasp come for a meet and greet.*

Search for the Snuggly Duckling: *There is a new sign going up at the Snuggly Duckling, and someone breaks it and hides the sign. The kids need to look for clues to find all the pieces before Rapunzel and Flynn return. Rapunzel and Flynn appear at the end.*

Additionally, counselors at Edge and Vibe may take kids in groups to the all-ages performances, game shows, or other events on board.

PERFORMANCE OPPORTUNITIES

KIDS WITH A REAL YEN to perform can check out karaoke on most sailings or talent show opportunities on many longer sailings (see "Family Nightclub Activities," page 291). There may also be a few performance opportunities for teens and preteens enrolled in Edge and Vibe.

"IT'S *a* SMALL WORLD" NURSERY!

THIS IS THE ONBOARD NURSERY for infants and toddlers ages 6 months–3 years. (On some longer sailings, DCL requires children to be 12 months old or older.) Trained staff care for and play with the children throughout the day. Unlike the activities at the clubs for older children, tweens, and teens, activities at the nursery are unstructured but may include movies, story time, crafts, and occasional visits from Disney characters.

The nursery requires reservations and charges an hourly rate for services. Rates are $9 an hour for the first child and $8 an hour for each additional child in the same family, with a 1-hour minimum. Parents should bring their own milk, formula, and baby food, along with diapers and wipes, a change of clothes, and a blanket and pacifier (if their child needs those to nap).

Space is typically limited; reservations are first come, first served, as detailed in the table below. If you haven't made reservations by the time you board the ship or would like to make additional reservations, you can either stop by before dinner or call from your stateroom.

Hours vary, especially when the ship is in port, but on most sea days the nursery is open 9 a.m.–11 p.m.; it sometimes opens during late afternoon/early evening on embarkation day.

Note that the nurseries take the children's health seriously. Kids who show signs of a contagious illness—fever, runny nose, or the like—must be picked up by their parents immediately and may not return to the nursery unless cleared to do so by the ship's medical staff.

WHEN YOUR BOOKING WINDOW OPENS FOR THE NURSERY
Concierge guests: **130 days** before sailing
Pearl Castaway Club members: **123 days** before sailing
Platinum Castaway Club members: **120 days** before sailing
Gold Castaway Club members: **105 days** before sailing
Silver Castaway Club members: **90 days** before sailing
All other guests: **75 days** before sailing

Amanda from Texas had this to say about the nursery:

Prior to the cruise, our baby had never been to any type of daycare before, had never been left with a stranger, and had barely been left with family members, so my husband and I were anxious about how things would go. The crew members were exceedingly kind and gentle, and the baby seemed to love his time there. They were cognizant of his severe allergies and kept his EpiPen in a special container at their front reception desk. They were able to get him to sleep for nap time, and when we came to pick him up, the crew member was able to successfully transfer the baby to my husband's arms without waking him. I was very impressed by that!

On the *Magic* and *Wonder*   LOCATION DECK 5 AFT

DESCRIPTION AND COMMENTS Too cute. Decorated with brilliantly colored murals inspired by the art of Mary Blair, the Disney animator who designed the It's a Small World ride at Disneyland and Walt Disney World, the nursery is cleverly divided into three sections. At the front is the "acclimation zone," a welcome area where kids can get used to their surroundings; this leads to a long, narrow, rectangular, brightly lit play area. Off of that is a darkened, quiet room for naps. The play area is stocked with pint-size activities, including a playground slide on a padded floor, a small basketball hoop, plenty of leg-powered riding vehicles, play mats with large toys, and adorable miniature craft tables that you'd swear came from the Lilliput IKEA. A one-way mirror lets parents check up on their tots discreetly.

> *unofficial* TIP
> If your little one has a known fear of costumed characters, alert the nursery staff so they can take your child to a different room in case any characters stop by.

At the far end of the nursery is the resting room, with several cribs and glider chairs. Murals in soothing blue and gold adorn the walls. This room is kept dark most of the day, and the staff ensures that activities in the main room happen far enough away that noise isn't a problem. A sink and changing area are just outside.

On the *Dream* and *Fantasy*   LOCATION DECK 5 MIDSHIP

DESCRIPTION AND COMMENTS Much like its counterparts on other ships, this adorable space is decorated in brilliant colors, murals, and furniture inspired by the art of Mary Blair. There are play mats, changing stations, tiny high chairs, and comfy seating for tiny people. The play areas are large, with interactive toys and Disney movies playing. The resting room is full of cribs and glider rockers.

On the *Wish, Treasure,* and *Destiny*
LOCATION DECK 2 MIDSHIP

DESCRIPTION AND COMMENTS The nursery on the *Wish* is also bright and colorful and full of artwork clearly inspired by Mary Blair, as well as modern Disney movies, including *Tangled, Aladdin, Brave, Lion King, Coco,* and even *The Black Panther.* There's an adorable train that travels along the ceiling and some very clever interactive elements built into the artwork. There are also plenty of cribs and rockers for nap time.

OCEANEER CLUB *and* OCEANEER LAB *(ages 3–10)*

THESE CONNECTED SPACES host the 3- to 10-year-old set. Activities for older kids usually take place in the Lab and are often educational or participatory in nature (think cooking demonstrations or science experiments). Younger children's programs are generally held in the Club and include story time, character appearances, and movement activities. Children ages 3–4 have dedicated counselors and their own set of activities in the club.

*un*official **TIP**

A fee of 50% of the cost of your nursery booking applies if you cancel a reservation less than 4 hours before your scheduled time to drop off your child. No-showing or arriving more than 30 minutes late will result in both a cancellation charge and losing the reservation.

Disney designates 7 as the border age for the Club and Lab and provides details in the Navigator app about each area's different activity tracks. During open houses, one side remains open for activities, while the other side is open to the public.

Parents must check kids ages 3–7 in and out of the club. With a parent's permission, 8- to 12-year-olds may check themselves in and out—just designate your preference when you register them.

Kids in the Oceaneer Club and Oceaneer Lab are required to wear a wristband while they're on the premises, and their parents' contact information is recorded. When a child enters the club, the band is secured to their wrist or ankle. The fastener mechanism, easily visible to the staff, is color-coded: Red, for instance, alerts counselors to a food or other allergy. *Note:* The kids' club wristbands are *not* the same as the DisneyBand+ (see page 152), but kids can use a DisneyBand+ instead of the kids' club wristbands.

Door sensors at each club trigger an alarm if a child tries to leave without a parent on hand to deactivate the wristband. If the cast members need to contact you, they'll text you on the Navigator app.

On the *Magic* and *Wonder*   LOCATION DECK 5 MIDSHIP

DESCRIPTION AND COMMENTS The Oceaneer Club and Lab are separate areas connected by a short private hallway, allowing children to go from Lab to Club and vice versa. Besides providing kids twice as much space, this arrangement separates younger and older children while giving siblings of different ages the ability to stay in contact.

The Oceaneer Club consists of four distinct sections branching off from a central "library" decorated with oversize children's books and outfitted with a huge high-definition TV for movie screenings. **Andy's Room** is *Toy Story*–themed and is for smaller children. Its main feature is a tall, circular, gentle playground slide in the shape of Slinky Dog. There's also a large pink Hamm (the piggy bank) sitting in the middle of the play floor and a giant Mr. Potato Head with equally large plug-in pieces scattered about.

Club Disney Junior, the second themed room, serves as the Oceaneer Club's primary activity center. The grass-green carpet is surrounded by

SETTING YOUR CHILDREN UP FOR SUCCESS IN THE KIDS' CLUBS

UNOFFICIAL GUIDE AUTHOR AND BLOGGER **Becky Gandillon** has two young daughters who are veterans of several Disney cruises.

WE LOVE TRAVELING WITH OUR CHILDREN, and Disney Cruise Line makes family time so much fun! But sometimes we all need our space. That means a little adult time and a little kids-only time. The best place for that kids-only time is in the kids' club! But if your little ones are hesitant among larger crowds of kids or in new situations with new people, then convincing them to go—and ensuring they have a good time—could be surprisingly difficult. We've figured out some ways to help them make the most of their kids' club time.

The number one thing we do is attend open hours (typically around noon–4:30 p.m.) in the kids' club as a family on embarkation day. During this time, you can set up your kids' profiles at the check-in desk. But more important, you can explore the club, sample activities, and help your children feel more comfortable while you're still around. We typically head to the kids' clubs immediately after lunch and stay as long as our kids want. The more they discover during this playtime with Mom and Dad, the more they'll want to come back later. Plus it keeps them busy until our stateroom is ready.

Next, when we're planning our days, we involve the kids in selecting activities from the app. I'll cleverly point out kids' club activities that I know will intrigue them. If your kid loves characters, look for activities like princess story time, Avengers Academy, or puzzles and games with Mickey. Most young kids love creating things they can take home. There will be plenty of guided crafts, such as making slime, pillowcases, or superhero outfits. Those sessions are always big winners.

We try to avoid taking our kids to the kids' club during unstructured play or when the scheduled activity is something they're not interested in. Outside of the guided activity, things tend to get a little more loud and chaotic.

Finally, we try to remove barriers and disappointments. This may include little things like checking them in 15–20 minutes before what we expect to be a popular activity, to avoid a long line. Or we check them in at the Oceaneer Lab if the activity is scheduled for the Oceaneer Club, or vice versa; the areas connect, and most parents default to the one listed in the Navigator—might as well avoid that line. We also *always* ask at checkout if the kids created anything they want to take with them. There are just too many kids and crafts for the cast members to be able to keep track of everything, and asking the kids as we check them out usually jogs a memory and allows them or a cast member to go back and grab the paper-plate superhero shield they would otherwise forget and throw a tantrum about later.

sky-blue walls painted with clouds. The room has a large video screen on one wall and sturdy kid-size furniture in bold colors.

Club Disney Junior connects to both Andy's Room and **Marvel Super Hero Academy,** where you'll find Thor's hammer, Captain America's shield, and a life-size Iron Man suit on the *Magic,* and Captain America's World War II shield, Iron Man's helmet, Spider-Man's web-shooters, and Black Widow's gauntlets on the *Wonder.* In the Super Hero Academy, kids can play high-tech video games, do arts and crafts, and visit superheroes who drop by for surprise visits.

Opposite Marvel Super Hero Academy on the *Magic* is **Pixie Hollow,** a Tinker Bell–themed dress-up and play area with costumes, an activity table, and a few computer terminals with themed games. On the *Wonder,* it's the **Frozen Adventures** area for creative and interactive play. A key feature of the *Frozen* zone is a digital screen where an animated Olaf leads games and songs; character experiences include the requisite visits by Anna and Elsa.

The Oceaneer Lab is decorated in a 19th-century nautical theme, with lots of exposed wood, red leather chairs, navigation maps, and sailors' tools. More than a third of the space consists of one long room filled with kid-size tables and stools that serves as the primary area for arts and crafts. At the far end of this space is a set of computer terminals.

Next to the craft space, in the middle of the Lab, is a large screen for watching movies. Facing the screen is a collection of comfortable bean-bags. Finally, the left side of the Lab is a set of small rooms. A couple have computer terminals or video-game consoles; one is a smaller crafts room, and another is an animation studio where kids can learn to draw Disney characters and create their own computer animations.

On the *Dream* and *Fantasy* LOCATION DECK 5 MIDSHIP

DESCRIPTION AND COMMENTS Like their counterparts on the *Magic* and *Wonder,* the *Dream*'s and *Fantasy*'s Oceaneer Lab and Club are separate areas connected by a short private hallway, allowing children to go from Lab to Club and vice versa. Besides providing kids twice as much space, this arrangement separates younger and older children while giving siblings of different ages the ability to stay in contact.

The Oceaneer Club consists of four distinct sections branching off from a central rotunda painted royal blue; on the ceiling are "constellations" of Disney characters made up of small, twinkling electric lights. **Andy's Room** is *Toy Story*–themed and intended for smaller children. There's a crawl-through tube in the shape of Slinky Dog, along with a giant pink Hamm (the piggy bank) in the middle of the play floor, and a giant Mr. Potato Head with equally large plug-in pieces scattered about.

The next area is **Pixie Hollow,** a Tinker Bell–themed dress-up and play area with costumes, an activity table, and a few computer terminals with themed games. The *Dream* and *Fantasy* Oceaneer Clubs both have **Star Wars–themed immersive play areas;** on the *Dream* it's a life-size *Millennium Falcon,* and on the *Fantasy* it's a "Command Post" holo-table where kids can train with X-Wing pilots. The *Falcon* on the *Dream* lets kids pilot a remarkably well-done simulator (yep, it jumps into hyperspace) and participate in a shipboard version of the **Jedi Training** audience-participation show many will remember from Walt Disney World's Hollywood Studios. Adults can take a turn in the captain's seat of the *Falcon* during club open houses (check the Navigator app for details). Wearing a black vest and knee-high boots is completely optional.

The *Dream* has a **Disney Infinity** gameplay area, while the *Fantasy* has a **Marvel Super Hero Academy** with guests like Doctor Strange stopping by.

The Oceaneer Lab is decorated in a 19th-century nautical theme, with lots of exposed wood, red leather chairs, navigation maps, sailors' tools, and inlaid images of sea horses and compasses on the floor. The main hall features a celestial map on the ceiling and a huge **Magic Floor,** which is composed of 16 HD video screens surrounded by foot-powered touch pads and is used to play interactive games. (If you remember the giant piano from the movie *Big,* you get the idea.)

Surrounding the main hall are the **Media Lounge,** for relaxing and watching movies; the **Animator's Studio,** where kids can learn to draw Disney characters and create digital animations; **The Wheelhouse,** with computer stations and interactive games; the **Explorer's Room,** where kids can learn about ships and the sea; and the **Craft Studio.**

On the *Wish, Treasure,* and *Destiny*
LOCATION DECK 2 MIDSHIP *(club)*, **DECK 3 MIDSHIP** *(check-in)*

OVERVIEW Disney calls the largest youth space on the *Wish*-class ships Oceaneer Club rather than breaking it out into a Club and a Lab. The fun starts right at the entrance: Kids access the club via a "secret" slide located in the Grand Hall atrium. (Adults can use the slide during open-house hours. Be careful, though: The trip down is faster than it looks.)

The Oceaneer Club is the crown jewel of the kids' spaces. Its massive size and attention to detail are breathtaking. Our only criticism is that a significant number of the interactive elements involve complicated technology that could be prone to downtime. The roller-coaster simulator, for example, has had some glitches here and there.

DESCRIPTION AND COMMENTS The Oceaneer Club on the *Wish*-class ships consists of five areas. At **Marvel Super Hero Academy,** young "recruits" will train to be the next generation of superheroes with help from Marvel favorites like Spider-Man, Black Panther, Ant-Man, and The Wasp. **Fairytale Hall** is a trio of Disney princess–themed activity rooms. Kids can explore their creativity in Rapunzel's Art Studio, read and act out stories at Belle's Library, or test their icy princess powers at Anna & Elsa's Sommerhus. **Walt Disney Imagineering Lab** is a first-of-its-kind opportunity where kids can discover the secrets of world-renowned Disney Imagineers—the creative masterminds behind Disney's theme parks, resorts, and cruise ships—with hands-on activities and experiments.

Star Wars: **Cargo Bay** teaches kids to be "creature handlers" as they manage and care for exotic beings from all corners of the galaxy, including Porgs, Loth-cats, and Worrts. During this experience, kids use augmented-reality datapads and participate in a mission involving Rey and Chewbacca. The fifth area, **Mickey & Minnie Captain's Deck,** is a playground-like area designed for the youngest Oceaneer Club guests. The space includes nautically themed slides, crawl-throughs, busy boxes, and other interactive and physical activities. **Minnie's Captain Academy,** offered here on some days, includes a series of age-appropriate STEAM learning challenges and visits from Captain Minnie.

Cast members have the ability to open up and close off any room to segregate groups by age or interest as needed. In addition, some adult character greetings take place in the Marvel and *Star Wars* rooms when these spaces aren't being used by kids.

EDGE *(ages 11–14)*

TWEENS AND EARLY TEENS RULE at Edge. Unlike at the Oceaneer Club/Lab, kids can come and go as they please. If your kids get bored, they may leave to visit a character greeting, go to the pool, grab a snack, go back to the stateroom, or just roam around. (They *won't* be allowed to leave the ship without a supervising adult, unless you've completed a special form allowing them to do so.)

Activities range from drawing and cooking classes to scavenger hunts and computer games. Parents may be surprised to see things scheduled past midnight on some nights.

Edge is likely to be the first of the kids' clubs in which the staff will treat your kids as peers to interact with rather than as children to be supervised. The staff generally does a great job of getting to know each child and will even compete in games alongside the kids. If you ever want to feel old and slow, watch the cup-stacking competition, where the object is to stack and unstack a pyramid of 15 plastic cups as quickly as possible. Some kids can do both in less than 10 seconds total!

For some kids, this club offers an unprecedented amount of freedom that may cause discomfort for the parent or child. Other children relish the opportunity to have a little more ownership of their time on the ship. In either circumstance, it's a good idea to set ground rules for your kids about notifying you where they are. This might mean periodic texts or leaving a note in your stateroom.

On the *Magic* and *Wonder*   LOCATION DECK 9 MIDSHIP

DESCRIPTION AND COMMENTS Edge is the rec room of your kids' dreams. There are sections for electronic gaming, active play, and lounging. You'll see both a high-tech zone and comfy couches. Kids can move freely between both.

On the *Dream*   LOCATION DECK 5 FORWARD

DESCRIPTION AND COMMENTS Edge on the *Dream* was moved to Deck 5 Forward, right next to Vibe. It now has an outdoor deck with a ball pit and games exclusively for Edge and Vibe. There is also a lounge and dance floor.

On the *Fantasy*   LOCATION DECK 13 FORWARD

DESCRIPTION AND COMMENTS Built into the *Fantasy*'s forward (nonfunctioning) smokestack, Edge has an open layout and a clean, 21st-century feel. The walls are papered in a geometric Mickey-head design. The centerpiece of the space is a huge video wall that's more than 18 feet wide and nearly 5 feet tall. Across from it are tables with built-in screens for playing interactive games, surrounded by bright-red seating that looks like something out of *The Jetsons.* Behind those are cubbyholes outfitted with flat-screen TVs and Wii consoles. Next to the game tables are an illuminated dance floor (think *Saturday Night Fever*) and a lounge area with beanbags arranged next to floor-to-ceiling windows. On the other side of the video wall are laptop stations loaded with video games and an onboard social media app. When the *Fantasy* undergoes a dry dock in the fall of 2025, we expect it to replicate the new design on the *Dream.*

On the *Wish, Treasure,* and *Destiny* LOCATION DECK 5 AFT

DESCRIPTION AND COMMENTS Edge's design aesthetic on the *Wish*-class ships is "trendy urban loft." Finishes on the walls simulate exposed brick, weathered steel, and poured concrete—sometimes within the space of a few feet. Side tables are built to resemble tree trunks; carpets feature neon checkerboards and fields of daisies.

One side room is dedicated to video games; the central area has a soda and smoothie bar and a giant movie screen; and the far end of the room has more game consoles, as well as tables for crafts and board games. The bookshelves are stocked with books on the art behind Disney and Pixar films, such as *The Art of Encanto.* Tchotchkes on the shelves include vintage Disney Pez dispensers and an assortment of 9-inch Vinylmation figurines.

VIBE *(ages 14-17)*

VIBE IS ONE OF THE COOLEST SPOTS on board. Counselors lead the activities—dance parties, karaoke, group games, and the like—but teens are given plenty of autonomy. Parents should note that the only curfew for teens on board is the one they impose themselves. One rule of note that's strictly enforced: No public displays of affection.

On the *Magic* and *Wonder* LOCATION DECK 11 MIDSHIP

DESCRIPTION AND COMMENTS Vibe sits up a flight of stairs in the ship's forward smokestack, but your teens probably won't mind the climb. Inside is a two-story-tall lounge with exposed-brick walls, leather furniture, and a smoothie bar. We think there should be a Vibe for adults.

On the *Dream* and *Fantasy* LOCATION DECK 5 FORWARD

DESCRIPTION AND COMMENTS Up a flight of stairs from Deck 4 to Deck 5 Forward and accessed through a neon-lit hallway, Vibe has a decidedly adult look and feel on the *Dream* and *Fantasy*—if you didn't know better, you'd think you were in a trendy urban nightspot. The central indoor gathering area is the theater/TV lounge, accented with soft-pink neon lighting and featuring a 103-inch TV. Two rows of couches are arranged in a semicircle in front of the screen, and giant throw pillows scattered on the floor make for additional places to lounge. Behind the couches and built into the rear wall are a row of podlike, porthole-shaped nooks for playing video games, watching videos, or hooking up an electronic device. Just off the row of pods is a smoothie bar; ultramodern stools with low, curved backs; and white banquette seating.

Off the TV lounge is another sleek space for socializing. The walls are covered in alternating black-and-silver horizontal bars. Black faux-leather benches line the walls; next to those are retro-mod tables and chairs arranged nightclub-style. Video-game booths stand nearby. Across from the seating area are a dance floor and DJ booth, a karaoke stage, and another large video screen.

The main attraction, though, lies outside. The **Vibe Splash Zone** is a private deck with two splash pools, lounge chairs, sets of tables and chairs, and recessed seating. Furnishings and decor share the same ultramod style as the indoor spaces.

On the *Wish, Treasure,* and *Destiny*   LOCATION DECK 12 AFT

DESCRIPTION AND COMMENTS Here, Vibe evokes a modern-art collective. Pillars are decorated with posters of Parisian landmarks and splashes of dripping paint. Several walls are adorned with graphic art or painted in bold colors that make excellent backdrops for selfies. Much like Edge, Vibe has areas for video games, movies, board games, crafts, and snacking. One-third of the room can be closed off to become **The Hideaway** (see below).

The HIDEAWAY *(ages 18-20)*

THE HIDEAWAY IS AN AREA of Vibe that can be configured just for young adults.

On the *Wish, Treasure,* and *Destiny*   LOCATION DECK 12 AFT

DESCRIPTION AND COMMENTS This hangout offers a place for young people to relax, listen to music, and more in a stylish setting, complete with a dance floor and DJ booth. It's decorated in a vibrant color palette with retro-inspired design details. Configured as a multipurpose space, this flexible venue can be opened to expand the footprint of Vibe, closed off for tween activities, or reserved exclusively for use by guests ages 18–20.

PART 12

ACTIVITIES, RECREATION, *and* SHOPPING

KEY QUESTIONS ANSWERED IN THIS CHAPTER

- What are the pools like on board? *(see below)*
- What other recreational opportunities are available? *(see page 258)*
- How do you get the photos taken by DCL's photographers? *(see page 271)*
- Will I get bored on a sea day? *(see page 279)*

POOLS *and* WATER-PLAY AREAS

EACH SHIP HAS separate freshwater pools designed for small children, families, and adults. All are heated to a minimum temperature of 75°F. If you've never been on a cruise ship before, you may have been duped by creative photography into thinking you'll be able to swim laps in the pools on cruise ships. In reality, not only is it impossible to exercise in the pools, but you can barely even splash in them. One of our dear friends calls the kiddie pools "people soup."

No DCL pool has a capacity of more than 80 guests (and most pools' capacities are much smaller than this), even on the *Dream, Fantasy,* and *Wish*-class ships, which carry about 4,000 guests each. In a highly unscientific study, we've shown photos of the pools, with varying numbers of guests in the water, to several noncruising acquaintances. The consensus seems to be that the pools start to look uncomfortably crowded when they're filled to about half capacity.

Rachel from Tennessee had this to say about the crowded pool:

Saw it. Walked by it. Went to play trivia instead.

Beth from Pennsylvania has some tips to avoid the crowds:

My family loves to watch movies at the pool. We stay away from the pools on sea days and take part in all the other amazing activities occurring on the ship. The best time to enjoy movies at the pool is on port days or at night after dinner, if it's open. Want a VIP pool experience? Go to the pool while the ship is docked at one of Disney's island destinations!

The good news for grown-ups is that the adult pools are rarely raucous. In general, all of the pools are more relaxed during cold-weather itineraries. You can also find less competition for pool space if you visit on port days or during evening showtimes.

RULES ABOUT POOLS

DCL HAS A FEW strict regulations designed to protect the health and safety of guests using its pools.

- Anyone under age 16 must be supervised at the pools at all times, and height and weight restrictions for the waterslides are strictly observed.
- Swim goggles that fit only over the eyes are permitted at all pools, hot tubs, and waterslides on DCL ships, except the AquaDunk on the *Magic,* where goggles are not allowed. *Note:* You can wear eyeglasses on any of the water features that allow goggles, though you may want to purchase retainer cords to keep them from falling off. These are available on the ships, at Castaway Cay and Lookout Cay, and through many non-cruise vendors.
- Swim masks that cover the eyes and nose are permitted at all pools. They are not allowed on any slides, including the AquaDuck.
- Snorkels are not permitted in pools, in hot tubs, or on waterslides.
- Goggles, masks, and snorkels are all welcome at Disney's island destinations.
- US Coast Guard–approved flotation devices (life jackets), water wings, and flotation bathing suits are permitted in all pools and waterslides except the AquaDunk, but rafts, floats, and foam noodles are not. Complimentary flotation vests are provided.
- Swim diapers are *not permitted* in hot tubs, spas, or pools or on waterslides. This includes the AquaDuck, AquaDunk, AquaLab, and AquaMouse. Little ones wearing swim diapers *are* permitted at **Nemo's Reef** on the *Dream* and *Fantasy,* **Nephews' Splash Zone** on the *Magic,* **Dory's Reef** on the *Wonder,* and **Toy Story Splash Zone** on the *Wish, Treasure,* and *Destiny.* DCL's swim-diaper policy states: "The United States Public Health Service requires that only children who are toilet-trained are permitted to enter swimming pools and spas aboard cruise ships."

If poop happens in the pool, all guests must evacuate, and the pool must then be drained, cleaned, refilled, and tested for bacteria and chemical balance. The entire procedure takes about 4–5 hours depending on the size of the pool—so don't be *that* parent who let your almost-but-not-quite-potty-trained child into the water and ended up spoiling an afternoon for hundreds of other families. Keep in mind that on a cruise, even potty-trained kids may get distracted or overwhelmed and that unfamiliar foods may result in new digestive demands.

POOLS ON THE *MAGIC* AND *WONDER*

A VARIATION ON the AquaDuck coaster found on the *Dream* and *Fantasy,* the *Magic*'s **AquaDunk** is short and mildly fast, with a vertical

POOLS FROM A KID'S PERSPECTIVE

THIRTEEN-YEAR-OLD veteran cruiser **Wes Fry** offers his take on DCL's water activities.

ABOARD A DISNEY CRUISE, there are many water areas for both kids and adults to enjoy. If you're looking to cool off or lounge in the refreshing water, then you will love the different choices of pools, hot tubs, and even waterslides. Let's explore some of these areas.

On the *Magic* and *Wonder,* both kids and adults can enjoy **Goofy's** large pool located on Deck 9 Midship. On the *Dream* and *Fantasy,* everyone can have a great time in **Donald's** and **Mickey's Pools,** both located on Deck 11 Midship. On the *Wish,* there are several pools to enjoy, named after the Fab 5 and Daisy. **Pluto's, Minnie's, Daisy's,** and **Mickey's** are on the main pool deck, and there are stairs leading up to the two top pools from **Donald's** and **Goofy's.** Don't forget that adults need their time away from the kids! Adults have a special area with a pool and lounge area on all DCL ships. Each ship also has a large **Funnel Vision** screen that plays movies and does some trivia all day long.

Do you enjoy the thrill of the water slides? Disney has many options for you aboard its ships. I highly recommend the **AquaMouse** (*Wish, Treasure, Destiny*), **AquaDuck** (*Dream, Fantasy*), and **AquaDunk** (*Magic*). All three slides bring a fun and magical experience for all who may ride. If you or any of your kids are not interested in the thrill part of the previously mentioned slides, you may enjoy the **Twist 'n' Spout** (*Magic, Wonder*), **Mickey's Slide** (*Dream, Fantasy*), or the **Slide-a-saurus Rex** (*Wish, Treasure, Destiny*).

For our younger cruisers, there are additional areas where you can splash and play. On the *Magic, Wonder,* and *Fantasy,* you can experiment in a water playground called **Aqua Lab,** giving great fun to each family member. On the *Dream* and *Fantasy,* you can join Nemo and his friends in a crazy water-play area. Lastly, on the *Wish,* you can become a toy yourself and splash around in the *Toy Story* and friends splash zone.

Now that we have talked about the pool sections on the cruise ships, there are still more activities on Disney's island destinations. The first island Disney cruises may visit is **Castaway Cay.** The second is the brand-new **Lookout Cay at Lighthouse Point,** which started to welcome guests in June 2024. At Castaway Cay, you can visit **Spring-a-Leak,** where kids can splash around in dripping pipes and water misters. Along the family beaches, there are two different activities to enjoy. **Pelican Plunge** has two slides, one enclosed and one open. They both drop you right into the ocean! There is also a **water playground** that has monkey bars and rope activities right over the water. At Lookout Cay, there are many beaches and pavilions around the island offering small games to enjoy. There is also one large splash pad and jungle gym for kids to play and splash around in.

start. You start by entering a vertical tube. You then lean against one side of the tube while a clear plexiglass door closes opposite you to seal the tube. Suddenly, the floor drops away and you plunge nearly vertically down the tube, through a quick 270-degree turn and into a braking pool. The entire experience takes perhaps 7–8 seconds, but the initial sensation of falling is fun enough to make it worth repeating. Depending on when you sail, the AquaDunk opens at around 9 a.m. and closes at around 11 p.m.

Because the AquaDunk has an hourly capacity of only around 120 riders, long lines develop quickly; we've seen 80-minute waits posted. If you're not there first thing in the morning, try during lunchtime or the first dinner seating.

As a reminder, goggles and face masks are not permitted on the AquaDunk—the force of the drop all but guarantees you'll lose them.

*un*official **TIP**
Pools and feature slides may close in adverse weather conditions.

AquaLab, the *Magic*'s and *Wonder*'s water-play area for children age 3 and up, is on Deck 9 Aft. It consists of four areas: AquaLab proper, the **Twist 'n' Spout** slide (age 4 and up and over 38 inches tall; children under 16 need adult supervision to ride), **Nephews' Pool,** and **Nephews' Splash Zone** on the *Magic,* and **Dory's Reef** on the *Wonder.*

Every inch of AquaLab is covered in water, which comes out from both vertical and horizontal surfaces. Overhead buckets, slowly filling with water, will dump their contents periodically on anyone standing below, while sprays from faux ship plumbing will drench anyone walking within 10 feet. Your kids will probably want to spend hours here, so it's a good thing that both covered seating and refreshments are available nearby.

Next to the main AquaLab area on the *Magic* is **Nephews' Splash Zone,** a water-play area for children up to 3 years old. This plexiglass-enclosed area has water spouting from pint-size figures of Donald Duck's three nephews, Huey, Dewey, and Louie. Padding on the ground allows kids to jump and run around safely, and you'll find parents sitting and relaxing nearby while their little ones get soaked. The equivalent area on the *Wonder* is **Dory's Reef.**

A three-story spiral waterslide, **Twist 'n' Spout** is a lot longer and slower than the AquaDunk, making it perfect for kids who are not quite tall enough for the big slide. Twist 'n' Spout starts above Deck 11 and ends on Deck 9 next to AquaLab. The top part of the slide isn't usually staffed, but a camera system there allows the attendant at the bottom of the slide to monitor both the start and the end simultaneously. Kids must be 4–14 years old and 38–64 inches tall to ride; children under 16 need adult supervision to ride. There's plenty of nearby seating for parents to get some sun while watching the little ones splash around.

Nephews' Pool is a shallow, circular pool in the middle of the deck, touching both AquaLab and Nephews' Splash Zone (*Magic*) or Dory's Reef (*Wonder*). Small children can splash around to their heart's content while parents sit on ledge seating. Adjacent to AquaLab are three counter-service eateries: Just past the forward end is **Pete's Boiler Bites** (*Wonder*) or **Duck-in Diner** (*Magic*), and just past the aft end is **Daisy's De-Lites.**

Goofy's Pool, the *Magic*'s and *Wonder*'s family pool, is on Deck 9 Midship. It's the focal point of outdoor activity on the ship. The pool is 4 feet deep at every point, and deck chairs and lounges are arranged on both sides along its length. At the forward end of the pool is the **Funnel Vision** LED screen, which plays movies, TV shows, and videos almost constantly. At the aft end are **Pinocchio's Pizzeria** and two covered hot tubs. Both Goofy's and Nephews' Pools are typically open daily, 8 a.m.–10 p.m.; check the Navigator app to confirm hours.

The adults-only **Quiet Cove Pool** is on Deck 9 Forward. Like Goofy's Pool, it's 4 feet deep throughout, and two adults-only hot tubs are nearby. Teak lounge chairs are provided for relaxing. Just past the aft end of the pool are **Signals** bar and **Cove Café.**

While the *Wonder* lacks a thrill-style feature slide, the ship does have the spiral **Twist 'n' Spout** waterslide. As on the *Magic,* the slide starts above Deck 11; it ends next to a new **AquaLab** children's play area on Deck 9.

unofficial **TIP**
Unlike the other ships, the *Wonder* doesn't have a headliner water attraction.

Children who don't meet the requirements for Goofy's Pool on the *Wonder* can play in nearby **Dory's Reef,** on the port side of the pool. Surrounded by short walls and themed to *Finding Nemo,* this water-play area for kids age 3 and under features gurgling sprays, jets, and sprinkles of water bubbling up from fountains on the floor. Best of all, there's plenty of covered seating nearby. Kids playing in Dory's Reef must be supervised.

POOLS ON THE *DREAM* AND *FANTASY*

THE *DREAM* AND *FANTASY* have **Mickey's Pool** for children age 3 and up, roughly midship on Deck 11. Divided into three smaller pools corresponding to Mickey's face and ears, the pool has a maximum depth of 2 feet, and the bright-yellow spiral **Mickey's Slide** rises about one deck high. Kids must be 4–14 years old and 38–64 inches tall to use the slide. There's plenty of nearby seating where parents can get some sun while watching the little ones splash around.

Children who don't meet the requirements for Mickey's Pool can play in nearby **Nemo's Reef,** toward the aft end of the pool. Larger and wetter than Nephews' Splash Zone on the *Magic* and Dory's Reef on the *Wonder,* this *Finding Nemo*–themed water-play area for kids age 3 and under features gurgling sprays, jets, and sprinkles of water bubbling up from fountains in the floor and from kid-size replicas of some of the movie's characters. A set of restrooms is just behind Nemo's Reef.

Found on Deck 11 Midship is the family pool, **Donald's Pool.** Like Goofy's Pool on the *Magic* and *Wonder,* it's the center of outdoor activity on the ships. The rectangular pool is about a foot deep close to its edges; in the middle is a roughly circular section that drops to a maximum depth of around 5 feet. The different depths allow younger swimmers to relax in the shallows without having to get out of the pool.

Deck and lounge chairs line both sides of Donald's Pool. At the forward end is the **Funnel Vision** LED screen, which plays movies, TV shows, and videos almost constantly. At the aft end is Mickey's Pool. Just beyond the Funnel Vision stage are the counter-service restaurants: **Fillmore's Favorites, Luigi's Pizza,** and **Tow Mater's Grill** on the starboard side and the **Eye Scream** ice-cream station and **Frozone Treats** smoothie station on the port side. Both Donald's and Mickey's Pools are typically open daily, 8 a.m.–10 p.m.; check the Navigator app to confirm hours.

Like the *Magic* and *Wonder,* the *Fantasy* (but not the *Dream*) has an **AquaLab** water-play area. On Deck 12 Aft, it's similar to Nemo's Reef in that its entertainment is provided by splashing water, but whereas the water comes up from the floor at Nemo's Reef, it comes down from above at AquaLab. High above your head are pipes filling buckets and buckets of water, which are counterbalanced so that they spill down on unsuspecting (and suspecting) kids below. In fact, water comes at you from every angle in AquaLab, and that's exactly the appeal. AquaLab is for kids too old to play in Nemo's Reef.

The adults-only **Quiet Cove Pool** is on Deck 11 Forward on both the *Dream* and the *Fantasy.* This pool is 4 feet deep at its deepest spot. There's a hot tub nearby, and the *Dream*'s designers wisely placed an outdoor bar, **Cove Bar,** at one end of the Quiet Cove Pool. The area around the bar is a splash-friendly, nonslip surface, with white bench seating and a round, ottoman-like seat in the middle; there are also a few seats directly at the bar. Behind the pool is the lovely **Cove Café;** on either side is covered seating with deck and lounge chairs.

Both the *Dream* and the *Fantasy* have an **AquaDuck** waterslide, a 765-foot-long, clear acrylic tube that's almost as popular as the Disney princesses. Riders board an inflatable plastic raft at the aft end of Deck 12. The raft is shot forward through the tube by high-pressure water faucets below and to the sides, making the AquaDuck a water-powered miniature roller coaster. There's enough water pressure here to propel your raft up two full decks' worth of height, followed by a descent of four decks into a landing pool. Guests must be at least 42 inches tall to ride, and children under age 7 must ride with someone age 14 or older who also meets the height requirement.

unofficial **TIP**
The best time to visit the AquaDuck is between 5 and 7 p.m., when most families are either at dinner or getting ready to go (check hours during your sailing). You'll also find smaller crowds on days when the ship is in port.

The AquaDuck's track sits at the outside edge of Deck 12 and goes as high as one of the ship's smokestacks. If you can keep your eyes open (and your wits about you), it offers some awesome views of the ocean and any nearby islands.

The *Dream* and *Fantasy* also have **Satellite Falls,** an adults-only splash pool and sundeck on Deck 13 Forward. Covered with long, vertical tiles in shades of blue and green, the pool looks great at night. In the center, a structure that looks like a giant Doppler radar receiver (and mimics a pair of actual satellite receivers on either side of the pool) pours a gentle stream of water into the pool below. It's one of our favorite places on board.

Concierge guests can enjoy a large hot tub on the Concierge sundeck on Deck 13.

POOLS ON THE *WISH, TREASURE,* AND *DESTINY*

UNLIKE THE POOLS on the other ships, which are all on one level, most of the pools on the *Wish*-class ships are staggered on several levels, stadium-style, between Decks 11 and 12. Stairs connect the various tiers; guests with mobility issues may need to head back indoors and take the elevator to access some of the water areas. All of the main deck's pools can be covered to become stages for outdoor events, such as the **Sail-Away Celebration** (see page 287) and **Pirate Night** (see page 288).

unofficial **TIP**
The pool deck gets super hot on sunny days. Keep your water shoes or flip-flops handy.

The six family pools vary in size and depth. **Mickey's Pool,** closest to the **Funnel Vision** screen, is most similar in size and design to the main pools on the other DCL ships. The nearby **Minnie's Pool** is just 2 feet deep; you'd think this would be the perfect spot for toddlers to splash, but children in diapers are not allowed here. What's more, we stepped into this pool a few times to cool our feet on an exceptionally hot day, but we found that the water had become uncomfortably warm in the sun.

One level up from these larger pools are **Daisy's** and **Pluto's Pools.** These are just 6 inches deep, ideal for smaller (and potty-trained) children and their caregivers. On the highest tier are **Donald's** and **Goofy's Pools,** the deepest of the family pools at 4 feet 6 inches. They're nowhere near large enough for laps, but they're the only places where adults can fully submerge themselves on the main pool deck.

The many pools could be an issue for single adults monitoring multiple children. If you think your kids will want to sample lots of pools and water-play areas, set some ground rules about whether they need to stick together or how they'll let you know which pool they're visiting.

Toy Story Splash Zone (Deck 12 Forward) is a splash pad for toddlers. Two small slides and several waterspouts squirt gentle sprays from the floor or from giant *Toy Story* character heads.

There is one entrance/exit to the Splash Zone. **Trixie's Falls,** located near this entrance, is just 6 inches deep, but a waterfall-style shower spans the length of the pool's back wall, adding entertainment and an extra element of cooling.

The **AquaMouse** slide, with its 42-inch height requirement to ride (54 inches to ride alone), is similar to the AquaDuck on the *Dream* and

Fantasy. You experience the slide on a double raft, which you're welcome to use solo. During the first half of the ride, you're in an enclosed tunnel. The tunnel walls are fitted with video screens showing one of two cartoons in the same style as Mickey & Minnie's Runaway Railway at Walt Disney World. Disney's promotional materials made a big deal about watching movies on a slide, but we were too distracted by the water nozzles spraying us to pay much attention. Overall, we prefer the non-movie-themed versions on the other ships because they provide more-panoramic views of the ocean.

The bright-yellow **Slide-a-saurus Rex** slide is for guests 38 inches tall or taller. It's a quick ride, but it's fun for elementary school kids who might be intimidated by the AquaMouse.

Chip 'n Dale's Pool, on Deck 14, is a shallow wading pool with views of the bow (front) of the ship. This pool is away from the noise and frenetic activity on the main pool deck, making it the best water spot for guests with sensory-processing issues.

Concierge guests have two hot tubs on the Concierge sundeck. There's also a water feature with a bench between the two hot tubs. It's a great space.

On the other hand, the **Quiet Cove** adults-only pool area on Deck 13 is one of our biggest disappointments regarding these ships. On the plus side, the location is far removed from the rest of the ship, so you won't find noisy kids accidentally walking through. On the minus side:

1. **No food is available in the adult pool area.** Cove **Café** on the other DCL ships has a refrigerated case stocked with goodies, but the version on the *Wish* (and presumably the *Treasure* and *Destiny*) does not. If you're hungry, you'll have to walk downstairs and wait in line at Mickey's Festival of Foods to grab a bite.

2. **Some of the lounge seating is directly under the AquaMouse loading zone,** meaning the slide's music is omnipresent. This is not ideal if you want a quiet adult space to read or nap.

3. **Some of the adult pool area is adjacent to the ship's main smoking areas,** so you may catch whiffs of cigarette smoke, depending on the prevailing winds.

4. **The infinity pool—DCL's first—is beautiful but small.** It's so small, in fact, that it feels crowded when occupied by even half a dozen guests. It's also accessible only via steep stairs, which could be a problem for guests with mobility issues.

The only public hot tub on board is located just as you enter the adult area on Deck 13. There are no hot tubs for kids other than the two in the Concierge lounge and the ones located on the private verandahs of the Royal Suites.

ONBOARD SEMINARS

LED BY CREW MEMBERS and attended by a limited number of passengers, these seminars are 30- to 60-minute interactive talks. Topics vary, but most involve food, wine, shopping, fitness activities, or how the ship is run. A fee is charged for seminars involving alcohol (see next page) and some fitness activities.

Several wine, liquor, and beer **tasting sessions,** led by sommeliers or experienced bartenders, are usually held on most cruises, especially those of more than four nights. There are also mixology classes, where you may get to help make the drinks. Most tastings serve four to five drinks in 2- or 3-ounce pours. These sessions vary in price but usually run between $40 and $70 per person.

The **cooking demonstrations** are some of the best presentations on board and are free! Cooking demos often follow a theme: The first day, for example, may show how to prepare an appetizer; the second involves an entrée; and the third will be dessert. Each demo is led by a member of the kitchen staff, usually a chef. These presentations are typically held in one of the ship's nightclubs so that more people can attend. To make it easy for everyone to see what the chef is doing, several video cameras are often mounted above the chef's worktable, providing a view of the preparations.

Cooking demos where wine is served, along with fitness activities, are restricted to guests age 18 and up. Wine and spirits tastings are for guests age 21 and up only, except during cruises that sail solely in Europe or the South Pacific, where participants may be 18 if a parent or guardian (1) is traveling with them, (2) has provided written permission for them to drink, and (3) is present when they do so.

We also enjoy the **towel or napkin folding classes** on longer sailings. There is no cost, and they are usually entertaining and practical. Plus, who doesn't like to create towel monkeys and hang them from the ceiling to scare—we mean delight—your houseguests?

If you're looking for exercise and information instead of food, the **walking tours** of the ships are a great way to keep moving and see the inner workings of your vessel. Most tours begin somewhere in the atrium and wind their way around the ship. The cast members who lead these tours are fonts of knowledge about the ships and can answer most questions you may have. If you want to know what it takes to prepare 800 appetizers at the same time, your tour leader can tell you.

Shopping seminars are usually held on sea days when the ship will be docked at a port the following day. (The seminars are also videotaped and available on your stateroom's television 24 hours a day.) Most seminars last 60–90 minutes, with multiple sessions held per day. Each session usually covers one kind of item, such as watches or a particular kind of gemstone sold at an upcoming port stop.

Frankly, shopping seminars aren't our bag (pardon the pun). You won't hear much—if anything—negative about the products being shilled: The seminar leaders are nearly always representatives of local retail associations, *not* Disney cast members, so they have a personal stake in persuading you to buy stuff.

If you're considering splashing out big bucks on, say, expensive jewelry, you're almost certainly better off postponing your purchase until you're back at home and can do your own research. Not to mention, most items you'll find for sale in port can easily be found online for much less money. (See "Shopping," page 266, for more information.)

Senses Spa and the ship's Fitness Center host **wellness seminars** most mornings. Activities include everything from stretching exercises and acupuncture to group cycling and Pilates. Many of the sessions, such as stretching and cycling, are free, although space is limited and you're strongly encouraged to sign up well in advance to guarantee a spot. Personal-training sessions cost about $100 per hour, before tip; nutritional consultations are also about $100 per hour; and an hour-long body-composition analysis is about $50.

The **Disney Vacation Club** (**DVC**) also hosts presentations about its time-share program. They're peppy affairs that frequently involve free booze, giveaways of swag like DVC baseball caps, and the opportunity to win a $200 stateroom credit. If you have time to kill and you want a free cocktail, head on over—you don't even have to pay attention to the presentation. (Canadian residents should be aware that there may be legal restrictions that prevent them from winning onboard credit.)

SPORTS *and* FITNESS

FITNESS CENTERS

DCL'S SHIPS OFFER an array of indoor and outdoor sports and fitness options. While it's no substitute for your local mega-gym, there's enough cardio and weight-training equipment on board for almost everyone to stay in shape during the cruise. Each ship's **Fitness Center** is outfitted with weight machines, free weights, treadmills, stair climbers, elliptical machines, stationary bikes, and more. Virtually all the electric cardio machines have video monitors, along with headphone jacks, allowing you to watch the ship's TV programming while you work out. The gyms also provide yoga mats, step benches, exercise balls, and exercise bands.

unofficial **TIP**
If guests in your stateroom are struggling to make one bathroom work as you are all getting ready, one or more of the adults might try going to the Fitness Center locker rooms to use their showers. However, some guests have reported not being permitted to do this on the *Wish*-class ships.

Also provided are a water fountain, complimentary fresh fruit, towels, paper towels, and spray bottles of sanitizer to clean the equipment when you're done. Locker rooms have showers, a sauna, sinks, robes, towels, grooming items, and lockers with electric locks. There is no extra charge to use these facilities. Guests ages 14–17 are welcome to use the Fitness Center if accompanied by a parent; the exception is guests on sailings originating in the UK, who must be 18 or older. The facilities are generally open from around 6 a.m. to 11 p.m.; check the Navigator app for exact hours. They tend to be most crowded in the morning between 8 and 11 a.m. and least crowded between 5 and 11 p.m.

Group- and personal-training sessions, including weight training and Pilates, are available for an additional fee. Individual sessions cost about $100 (plus tip) for a 1-hour session. To arrange personal training, stop by the Fitness Center on embarkation day.

One thing we find disconcerting in the gyms is that the treadmills on the *Dream, Fantasy,* and *Wish*-class ships face the port (left) side of the ship, not the bow. If the ship is moving while you're running on one of these treadmills, the scenery in front of you will be passing from left to right, but your brain expects to see the scenery moving toward you. Some people—including coauthor Len—instinctively twist their bodies left in an attempt to line up the scenery with the way their mind thinks they should be going. This makes for awkward running (walking doesn't seem to be much of an issue). If you find yourself unable to run correctly on the treadmill and you're not on a *Wish*-class ship, try the outdoor course described below.

WALKING/RUNNING ON THE SHIPS

RUNNERS AND WALKERS will appreciate the **0.3-mile track** circling Deck 4 of the *Magic* and *Wonder* and the **0.4-mile track** on Deck 4 of the *Dream* and *Fantasy.* One of the great things about running laps on the ship is the amazing scenery, which (almost) makes you forget that you're exercising. We've run laps on four of the ships, and the track is certainly good enough to get in a few miles to start your day. Some sections take you through some relatively narrow corridors, and there's a good chance you'll be running past groups of other guests who are out enjoying the deck. Finally, keep an eye out for water on the deck, which can make the track slick.

unofficial **TIP**
If you wear an Apple Watch, Fitbit, or similar device when you exercise, it may get confused by the ship's motion. In this case, you may want to keep a mental note of your distance and enter it into your device manually.

Of our quibbles with the *Wish*-class ships, one of the biggest is that they lack a deck that fully circles the ship. Color us disappointed that one of the great joys of a cruise—a leisurely stroll around the deck after dinner—is not available on this vessel. Sets of steep stairs ostensibly take you around the ship via multiple levels, but we found that these were often blocked by locked gates. Runners trying to train would find the steps to be treacherous on rolling seas; plus, the stairs present an obstacle to wheelchair users. The lack of a walking deck is pretty normal for other cruise lines, but it's something many guests have come to love (and expect) on Disney ships.

GAMES AND SPORTS COURTS

IF RUNNING ISN'T YOUR THING, every ship has **basketball courts.** These are popular with kids and parents looking to shoot a few hoops—we've never seen a competitive game played at one. A basketball court can also be converted into a miniature soccer field or volleyball court if you can find enough people to play. (See "Hero Zone," on the next page, for information about basketball on the *Wish*-class ships.)

Each ship also has **shuffleboard courts,** located near Deck 4 Midship. Because the only time we ever play shuffleboard is on a cruise, we tend to forget the rules between sailings, and then we make them up as we go along while we're on the ship. There are brief official rules posted near the courts, but if you're a competitive family and want to make sure you are prepared for every possible rule challenge, take a peek here before you sail: theugseries.com/shuffleboard-rules.

If you're up for a challenge, **table tennis** is available on Deck 9 Forward on the *Magic* and *Wonder* and Deck 13 Aft on the *Dream* and *Fantasy*. Readers report that the wind makes it difficult to play, but perhaps your game will benefit from a bit of unpredictability. On the *Wish*-class ships, table tennis is indoors in the Hero Zone (see below).

The *Dream* and *Fantasy* both have Disney-themed **minigolf courses** outdoors on Deck 13 Aft. These are a lot of fun for the entire family. The *Dream* and *Fantasy* also have outdoor **Foosball** tables; the *Wish*-class ships have Foosball in the Hero Zone and in the Vibe teen club.

SPORTS SIMULATORS

IF YOU'RE LOOKING to get in some individual practice time on the *Dream* and *Fantasy*, **virtual sports simulators** are available on Deck 13 Aft for golf, basketball, soccer, football, hockey, and baseball. These indoor facilities have a large movie screen set up in a dedicated room; a computer projects a simulated soccer field, basketball court, or other appropriate venue on the screen, and you're given actual sports equipment to kick, throw, or swing. Your movements, and the movements of the ball, are tracked by computers and displayed on-screen—there's a slight lag in the display but not enough to be distracting. Half-hour sessions cost about $28 for golf and about $13 for other sports; hour-long sessions are about $49 for golf and about $22 for other sports. A penalty charge (50% of your session fee) applies if you cancel on the day of your session; you may cancel without a penalty up to the day before.

Guests age 13 and younger must be accompanied by an adult (age 18 or older) when playing at the simulator; guests ages 14–17 must be accompanied by at least one other guest who's the same age or older.

HERO ZONE (*WISH*, *TREASURE*, AND *DESTINY*)

THIS MULTIPURPOSE INDOOR SPACE on Deck 12 Aft of the *Wish*-class ships is sports central. The top level has games like table tennis, air hockey, and Foosball and serves as a viewing loft for activities taking place on the main floor below. The large, open space can be configured for free play; half-court basketball; chip-it golf; or **Jack-Jack's Incredible Diaper Dash**, an *Incredibles*-themed variation on a popular event for babies old enough to crawl (see page 288). There's also a side room that can be opened, which is full of table-tennis tables during the day.

unofficial **TIP**
You must wear socks to use the Incredi-Games course—no bare feet or shoes are allowed. To avoid a trip back to your stateroom, bring a pair of socks with you.

The showcase element of the Hero Zone is an inflatable obstacle course called **Incredi-Games** (you must be at least 40 inches tall to participate).

The course will be inflated for 5–6 hours during some sea days (or Nassau day on cruises with no sea days), with various time slots open for free use, teens only, or timed family competitions.

We think the Hero Zone is a wonderful addition to DCL ships. It's a great space, and Disney uses it well.

SPAS

*un*official **TIP**
The best time to visit the spa is during dinner or when the ship is in port.

THIS SECTION SUMMARIZES the major spa and salon services offered on each ship, but note that many more are available. We recommend visiting the spa on your first afternoon on board to sign up for any last-minute treatments and check for specials. *Note:* Prices listed are approximate and do not include a tip, which is typically 18% of the cost of your treatment and is automatically added to your bill. There's a 50% cancellation charge if you cancel within 24 hours of your appointment time.

Some salon services, such as manicures and massages, may be booked on the **My Reservations** section of the DCL website before you sail. If you want to book a hair appointment online, you can reserve a time, but you'll have to stop by the spa after you board to specify what kind of service you want (styling, coloring, etc).

If you're trying to book spa services before your cruise, Disney's website may not let you book some services, such as facials, for two people at the same time of day. (We think the website assumes that only one person per ship is qualified to do these tasks and that this person will be unavailable once the first service is booked.) If you run into this problem, try booking the services online one after the other, then visit the spa in person when you board to explain what you want.

One thing that's different about spa treatments on Disney ships versus on land is that the same person is likely to be your masseuse, facialist, and manicurist—on a confined space like a cruise ship, roles have to be combined. Some readers like the familiarity, but others think a jack of all beauty trades can't provide the same level of service as a team of individuals with particular expertise in one area.

NOT-SO-RELAXING STUFF We've found two aspects of the DCL spa experience to be less than serene. First, you have to fill out a lengthy intake form and medical waiver before any service. This makes sense if you're getting Restylane injections, but not if you're getting your hair cut. (We exaggerate only slightly when we say we were asked about our latest bloodwork before we sat down for a manicure.)

Second, the spa staff will invariably rope you into a post-treatment upsell spiel: You can never *possibly* look or feel your best unless you buy this $75 bottle of shampoo or that $125 bottle of aromatherapy oil. Be prepared to just say no—often and sometimes emphatically. We've sometimes been able to avoid the hard sell by requesting "No Upselling" when we check in.

SERVICES AVAILABLE AT SENSES SPA AND SALON

THE DCL SHIPS OFFER an extensive array of spa services for men, women, teens, and couples. On the *Magic, Wonder, Dream,* and *Fantasy,* the spas look like their counterparts at a high-end resort, with no Disney theming to speak of.

unofficial **TIP**
An 18% gratuity is added to all spa services.

On the *Wish*-class ships, some of these areas do have a subtle Disney theme. The women's hair salon is called **Untangled,** with design elements inspired by Rapunzel and *Tangled,* including purple-and-gold floating-lantern light fixtures and cut-metal privacy screens that replicate Rapunzel's paintings. For the guys, there's **Hook's Barbery.** The dark wood-and-leather decor features narrative details inspired by Captain Hook. In addition to offering styling and barbering services, the Barbery has a hidden bar specializing in vintage whiskeys, ports, and aged rums. (Who says hard liquor and sharp objects don't mix?)

Men's salon services include basic haircuts ($39) and facials, such as the **Biotec Supercharger for Men** ($199) and the tongue-twisty **Elemis Pro-Collagen Grooming Treatment with Shave** ($115). Touted as "the shave of all shaves," the almost hour-long treatment includes a shave; a hot-towel wrap; a mini facial; and face, scalp, and hand massages. (If you normally use an electric shaver, be aware that a straight razor shaves much closer than an electric blade and can cause razor burn. Your face will be as smooth as a baby's bottom, though.)

Women can get a literal head-to-toe makeover, starting with hairstyling. A basic shampoo and blowout starts at $39, depending on the length and thickness of your hair. A shampoo, cut, and style starts at $79; a formal updo starts at $59. If you want deep conditioning, the **Kérastase Elixir Ultime 24-Carat Treatment** ($59) entails a scalp massage and the application of "precious oils" to your hair.

Manicures ($69) and pedicures ($79) include a heated-stone massage of your various digits. *Note:* You have to book these separately—you can't get a mani–pedi. We've had onboard manicures and pedicures several times. The hand massage is nice, but we've found that the polish invariably chips within hours. *Every time.*

Facials and massages for guests of any gender are administered in private treatment rooms or in one of the dedicated Spa Villas for singles or couples. Facials include the **Biotec Radiance Renew Facial** ($189; includes an ultrasonic peel), the **Biotec Skin Resurfacer** ($199; includes an ultrasonic peel and light therapy), the **Biotec Firm-a-Lift Facial** ($199; includes facial massage and treatment with galvanic technology), and several others. Most facial treatments last 50 or 55 minutes.

Body massages include the traditional deep-tissue kind ($179 for 50 minutes, $209 for 75 minutes), as well as those featuring aromatherapy and seaweed wraps ($299), aromatherapy and hot stones ($179 or $209), or bamboo shoots ($189 or $229). The **Elemis Couture Touch** treatment combines a facial with a Swedish massage ($299). Most of these can be done as couples' massages, which start at $259 for a basic 50-minute Swedish massage. *Couple* need not mean "romantic"—it can also mean siblings, friends, or even a parent and adult child.

The *Wish*-class ships advertise spa experiences in a **Zero Gravity Suite** and a **Hydration Suite** (both $499 for 130 minutes or $599 for 155 minutes), but we haven't had a chance to try them yet. If you book a treatment in one of the suites, please let us know what you think.

Massages can also be arranged at Castaway Cay and Lookout Cay. On **Castaway Cay,** the massage hut is located on the adult beach, Serenity Bay. At **Lookout Cay,** guests in the cabanas can arrange an in-cabana massage.

SPA VILLA SERVICES AND TREATMENTS Each Senses Spa has a handful of private Spa Villa rooms. Amenities include special treatments, a private verandah, an in-room whirlpool tub, an open-air shower, a Roman bed with canopy, a tea ceremony, a foot-cleansing ceremony, and the bathing ritual of your choice.

A Spa Villa reservation is typically about 2 hours long and includes your choice of couples' massage, plus private time in the room. Expect to pay about $450–$500, depending on the options you select.

OUTDOOR OASIS (*WISH, TREASURE,* AND *DESTINY*) The only fully outdoor adult spa area in the DCL fleet, the Outdoor Oasis features canopy-covered hot tubs, plush lounge chairs, swing-style lounge beds, and spaces for open-air yoga. The only thing that would make it better would be if you could actually see the ocean: though open overhead, the Oasis is enclosed on the sides, blocking all views of the sea.

REJUVENATION SPA This is DCL's umbrella term for medically supervised beauty treatments (some of which aren't offered on the *Magic* or *Wonder.*) If you book an appointment, you'll be required to participate in a 30-minute consultation with the doctor beforehand. Pricing information is revealed only after the consultation. (To paraphrase that quote attributed to J. P. Morgan: If you have to ask, you can't afford it.)

Some Rejuvenation services, such as Thermage (a radio-frequency skin-tightening treatment), are noninvasive. Some, like GoSmile teeth whitening and acupuncture, are semi-invasive. The most invasive treatments of all are Dysport and Restylane, prescription injectables that temporarily smooth wrinkles and plump lips. Speaking for ourselves, if we were going to have anything injected into our faces, it wouldn't be with an unfamiliar practitioner in the middle of the ocean, with no possibility of follow-up down the road.

Another Rejuvenation offering, **CoolSculpting** (which uses cryolipolysis, or the process of freezing fat deposits in order to reduce them), was the subject of an April 2023 *New York Times* report that uncovered a relatively high incidence of severe disfigurement. Again, this is not something we'd feel comfortable doing on an ocean liner, but if you're considering the procedure, please do advance research and consult with your own medical provider.

CHILL SPA This is DCL's spa for teens ages 13–17. (Eighteen-year-olds have access to all the adult spa services.) On the *Dream* and *Fantasy,* Chill Spa is a dedicated spa-within-a-spa, with several teen-only rooms. On the *Magic* and *Wonder,* it's a single room tucked behind the beauty salon. There is no designated Chill area on the *Wish*-class ships, though teens might be able to book some of the spa experiences if they have a parent's permission.

Spa services for teens must be booked on board; you can't reserve them in advance, as you can most spa services for adults. If you have a stressed-out teenager who needs a massage, you'll probably incur a bit of stress yourself hightailing it to the spa to score a reservation before they all get snapped up.

Some Chill Spa services have cutesy names like **Me! Bath Ice Cream Manicure, Fabulously Fruity Facial, Hot Chocolate Wrap,** and **Truth or Hair.** The **Acne Attack** facial costs about $100 and is more practical than fanciful.

Chill Spa also offers mother/daughter and father/son side-by-side massages lasting either 25 minutes (half body) or 50 minutes (full body). While your teen may cringe at the thought of getting oiled up next to Mom or Dad, officially a parent or guardian must be present during all Chill Spa appointments. In practice, however, this varies depending on the ship. During one cruise on the *Dream,* coauthor Erin was asked to stay in the treatment room with her teen daughter while she was getting a massage. When the same daughter got a massage on the *Magic* a few months later, Erin was told to wait in the nearby spa lounge because the *Magic*'s treatment room was too small. If you have a strong preference for staying in the same room with your child at all times, inquire about the spa's policy when you book the appointment.

Finally, if you don't want your teen to be offered additional services or extra-cost lotions and potions, also note that at the time of booking. You may also find it useful to coach your teen on how to politely but firmly say no to aggressive sales techniques. We've had to go back downstairs to the spa to cancel a follow-up appointment our teenager felt pressured to book.

THE RAINFOREST Each ship has a Rainforest, a suite of saunas, specialty showers, and relaxation areas. The Rainforests on the *Dream* and the *Fantasy* are significantly larger and better appointed than those on the *Magic* and *Wonder;* the version on the *Wish*-class ships is a significant step up from the other four. The newer ships have outdoor hot tubs (available to guests with a Rainforest pass), while the older ships' hot tubs are indoors.

unofficial **TIP**
Bring a towel to sit on in the saunas, and wear sandals—the seats and floors are very hot.

Sauna selections include the **Laconium,** which has mild heat and low humidity; the **Caldarium,** with moderate heat and humidity; and the **Hamam,** a full-on steam bath with the hottest temperatures. Unique to the *Wish* is the **Frigidarium,** an ice lounge that allows guests to combine cold therapies with warm therapies. Each sauna zone also has its own scent and music.

Tanya from Pennsylvania had this to say about the Rainforest:

The Rainforest is a hidden paradise with various scents, steam rooms, cold rooms, and the ultimate relaxation. It's the perfect place to chill after a massage or just get some alone time. Sit in a lounger and breathe in the cleansing air while you read a book.

We enjoy hopping between these saunas and the nearby Rainforest showers—tiled circular cutouts hidden behind the walls along the path leading to the saunas. Each shower has different options for water temperature, pressure, and spray pattern, each of which you select by pushing a button. For example, one option might be a light, cool mist, perfect for when you've just come out of the sauna. Another is like a warm, steady downpour in a tropical jungle. Shower scrubs in various scents (we like orange) are offered for an additional fee, though sometimes we skip those because it seems like washing money down the drain (literally).

The best thing about the Rainforest is that DCL sells only a limited number of passes per cruise. We hear that number can be as low as 40—on the entire ship—on the *Dream* and *Fantasy*. While Disney doesn't usually offer up those numbers so that we can fact-check that claim, we can tell you that we never see very many people in there. Port days are especially empty. It's the single most relaxing thing you can do on board.

On the *Magic, Wonder, Dream,* and *Fantasy,* it costs about $40 per day to use the Rainforest, with possible discounts for length-of-sail/multiday passes or couples' passes.

Pricing on the *Wish*-class ships is significantly higher: about $80 for a one-day pass, or $180 per person or $300 per couple for a three-night sailing. Bump each of those rates up by $20 for a four-night sailing. Granted, these ships' Rainforests are larger than those on the other four and have an outdoor lounge and hot tub area, but we're not sure these upgrades are worth paying twice as much.

When it comes to booking the Rainforest, you may be able to make a reservation during your pretrip activity booking window, or you may have to call (☎ 800-951-3532); passes can also be purchased at the spa once you're on the ship, depending on availability. If you weren't able to snag a reservation before your sailing, we encourage you to buy your passes as soon as you set foot on the ship because they go quickly.

SENSES JUICE BAR Senses on the *Dream* and *Fantasy* offers freshly blended juices and smoothies for about $7–$10. See the profile on page 220 for more information. Note that you don't have to use the spa to order from the juice bar. Also keep an eye out for special juice-tasting menus, typically offered on embarkation day. The same types of juices are available at several of the coffee bars on the *Wish*-class ships.

SHOPPING

SHOPPING DOESN'T HAVE TO BE part of your cruise experience, but, like most cruise lines, DCL makes it hard to avoid. Shops on the ships sell everything from infant T-shirts to engagement rings; there are also shops in every port, both reputable and sketchy, along with opportunities to shop for DCL merchandise before and after your cruise.

ONBOARD SHOPS

EACH DCL SHIP has several shops that stock everything from diapers to designer watches. Most shops are located on **Deck 4** of the *Magic* and *Wonder,* **Deck 3** of the *Dream* and *Fantasy,* and **Decks 3 and 5** of the *Wish*-class ships. If you think you're going to run out of something critical, stock up while the shops are open (for hours, check the Navigator app); note that the shops close whenever the ship is in port.

Souvenirs

Expect to see many of the same items you'd find in the Disney theme parks, such as T-shirts, trading pins (see Unofficial Tip), picture frames, baseball caps, and plush toys. Some of our favorite DCL-specific souvenirs are paintbrush-shaped butter knives like the ones at Animator's Palate and trading pins with a specific sailing or year.

unofficial **TIP**
The onboard shops sell colorful pins themed to Disney characters or elements of the ships (most are priced in the $12–$15 range). You can trade these pins with crew members and other guests.

The souvenir shops may also stock location-specific items. During an Alaskan cruise, for example, the shops may carry mittens, knit caps, binoculars, and books about local wildlife. In case you forgot to pack your eye patch for Pirate Night (see page 288), the shops can outfit your entire family from head to toe.

Disney-branded merchandise sold through DCL is priced the same as the equivalent souvenirs sold at Disney's US theme parks—a Mickey Mouse T-shirt sold on the *Dream* or *Fantasy* costs the same as at EPCOT. See the table below for approximate prices of some typical Disney souvenirs sold on the ships.

Note: Intermittent supply-chain issues have resulted in problems keeping merchandise in stock on the ships. If you see something you want, buy it immediately; they're unlikely to have extra stock. If you change your mind, you can always return items later in your sailing.

COST OF DISNEY SOUVENIRS			
PRODUCT	**PRICE**	**PRODUCT**	**PRICE**
Adult T-shirt	$30	Disney coffee mug	$17
Autograph book	$18	Disney trading pin	$13–$17
Baseball cap	$30	Plush Mickey or Minnie	$25
Beach towel	$30	Spirit jersey	$90

Drugstore Items

Each ship also has a sundries section in one of the onboard shops that stocks basics similar to those you'd find at your local CVS or Target. The selection is consistent across the ships, with only minor variations (different flavors of baby food, for example). Here's a sampling of what's typically available:

BABY CARE PRODUCTS Baby food and formula; baby oil, body wash, powder, and shampoo; bottles and pacifiers; diapers (including swim diapers), diaper rash cream, and wipes; nursing pads

FIRST AID SUPPLIES Adhesive bandages, antibiotic ointment, anti-itch creams and sticks, jellyfish-sting-relief lotion, aloe spray and gel

FIX-IT GEAR Eyeglass-repair kits, sewing kits

ITEMS FOR THE POOL DECK AND IN PORT Cooling towels, ear and nose plugs, insect repellent, sunscreen, swim goggles

OVER-THE-COUNTER MEDICATIONS Antacids, cold and flu remedies, antihistamines, eye drops, laxatives, pain relievers (aspirin and nonaspirin), anti-motion-sickness tablets and bands, sleep aids, thermometers.

unofficial **TIP**
You won't find OTC remedies for gastrointestinal woes, such as Imodium or Pepto-Bismol. (See page 133 for more on treating gastric distress.)

PERSONAL CARE PRODUCTS Antiperspirant; body lotion; body wash; contact lens cases; cotton swabs; razors and shaving cream; menstrual products; hair-care products (brushes and combs, hair bands and clips, shampoo, conditioner, hair spray/gel); hand sanitizer; lip balm; nail-care products (clippers and files, polish remover); oral-care products (breath strips, dental floss, mouthwash, toothbrushes, toothpaste); petroleum jelly; tissues; tweezers

TRAVEL NEEDS Electrical adapters, luggage locks

MISCELLANEOUS ITEMS Condoms, stain-remover pens, dish soap

When it comes to selection, what's on the shelves is all there is. If you insist on a particular brand, particularly for baby supplies, you should bring your own.

You also won't find much in the way of cosmetics. Depending on the sailing, the duty-free fragrance section in one of the other onboard shops (see next page) may also stock a few high-end beauty products. But if you forgot to pack eyeliner, you're probably out of luck until you can buy more in port.

COST OF SUNDRIES ON BOARD VS. OFF-SHIP		
PRODUCT	DCL PRICE	AMAZON PRICE
Benadryl Liqui-Gels (24 gel caps)	$7.50	$7
Coppertone UltraGuard Sunscreen Lotion SPF 70 (8 oz.)	$14	$10
Gillette Foamy Shave Foam (2 oz.)	$3	$1.30

Sundries on board are sold at a moderate to considerable markup. See the table on the previous page for a few products whose prices we spot-checked aboard DCL and on Amazon.

If you have a sudden personal-care need when the sundries shop is closed, stop by **Guest Services,** which is always open and has a stash of many "single serving" basics, free of charge. On rough sea days, we've also seen a basket of free motion-sickness meds placed just outside the **Health Center** (see page 193).

Accessories, Clothing, Fragrances, and Jewelry

In addition to the souvenir and sundries shops, each DCL ship also has a few stores that sell prestige fragrances (such as Chanel, Hermès, and Prada), along with name-brand clothing (such as Tommy Bahama and Vineyard Vines); handbags (such as Dooney & Bourke and Kate Spade); sunglasses (such as Michael Kors, Prada, Ray-Ban); jewelry (such as Gucci and Pandora); and wristwatches (such as Citizen, TAG Heuer, and Tissot). Aside from a few shipboard exclusives, most of these items can be found at any nice mall or reputable online store.

The full prices for brand-name clothing, accessories, and the like on the ships generally square up with the full prices on land, but you can generally get better deals online. For example, a Vineyard Vines blouse we found on the *Dream* cost $88, the same as on the Vineyard Vines website, but it was eventually marked down to $63 during an end-of-season sale online. On the ship, a Platinum Castaway Club discount, along with a lack of onboard sales tax, would bring the price down some, but not as much as if you bought directly from Vineyard Vines.

You'll also find pricey skin- and hair-care products (such as Bliss, Elemis, and Phyto) for sale at **Senses Spa** (see page 261).

Disney-Themed Art

Some DCL ships have a **Vista Gallery** that sells Disney-themed prints and original art. The prices are the same as what you'd pay at, for instance, the Art of Disney store at EPCOT. The pieces are nice enough if Disney art is your thing—but if you decide to buy a sofa-size painting, have a plan for getting it home before you commit to the purchase. Some items can be shipped directly to your home.

On other Disney ships, art sales take place at a stand-alone kiosk near the atrium. The kiosk offers the same **Disney Art On Demand** service that's available at several locations in the theme parks. Select an artwork, the size you'd like it to be, whether you want the print on paper or canvas, and if you want it framed or matted. Your piece will be delivered to your home within a few weeks.

CASTAWAY CAY AND LOOKOUT CAY

THE SHOPS AT Castaway Cay and Lookout Cay sell some items that are exclusive to those locations, such as T-shirts and beach towels. We've

IDEAS FOR BETTER SOUVENIR SHOPPING

BEFORE YOU SPEND money on things that will make you go "What? Why?" when you're back home, consider these ideas.

1. **Look for place-of-origin labels.** Whether you're shopping for hand-carved figures or hand-knit woolens in Norway, always inspect your item for place-of-origin markings to ensure that your Irish sweater, say, wasn't loomed in China.

2. **Consider whether photos are enough of a souvenir.** There's no rule that says you have to buy any souvenirs. You can turn your photos into mugs, textiles, and wall art.

3. **Are you breaking any rules?** Fresh fruits, cheeses, and meats may not be allowed on board or into your home country. Also note that Disney Cruise Line has limits on the amount and type of alcohol you can have in your stateroom (see page 140). You may purchase other types of liquor, but the ship will have to hold it for you until you disembark. Also note that some foreign over-the-counter medications are illegal in the United States and vice versa.

4. **Google your item before purchasing.** Brand-name jewelry, handbags, clothing, and the like may be searched online. Make sure the price you're paying makes sense.

5. **Look beyond port-side souvenir shops for ideas.** Some of our favorite places to buy souvenirs are
   - **Bookstores** Look for coffee table books with pictures of your destination or copies of a beloved children's fairy tale in a different language.
   - **Museum shops** Postcards, prints, and gallery guides are great ways to remember a significant exhibit.
   - **Sports shops** Caps and jerseys featuring the logos of the local pro, amateur, or university teams are fun reminders of your travels.
   - **Grocery stores** Look for packaged items that are unusual or hard to find at home. Tammy believes the best way to get a true feel for a country is by trying their version of a Kit Kat bar.
   - **Post offices** Buy a few beautiful stamps at each of your port stops and create a hangable artwork.

6. **Stick to a theme.** With so many options to choose from, souvenir shopping in port can quickly become overwhelming. Some travelers find it helpful to limit their choices to just one type of item, such as holiday ornaments, decorative housewares, trading pins, puzzles, or even the stereotypical snow globe.

7. **Consider whether the price is the final price.** The cultures of some port cities allow for haggling or price negotiation. It never hurts to ask a vendor if lower prices are available.

DOING YOUR DUTY

YOU'LL LIKELY ENCOUNTER the words *duty* and *duty-free* when you shop on your cruise, but many international travelers have no idea what they mean. Simply put, duty is a customs tax or tariff that's levied when you bring certain purchases across international borders.

Under certain conditions, US residents may bring back up to $800 in merchandise bought outside the country without having to pay duty on it. In general, these conditions are as follows: (1) Your trip outside the United States lasted at least 48 hours, (2) you haven't traveled outside the US more than once within a 30-day period, and (3) the merchandise in question is in your possession and is either for your personal use or a gift for someone else.

You may bring up to 1 liter (33.8 ounces) of alcohol, 200 cigarettes, and/or 100 non-Cuban cigars into the US without having to pay duty on them.

Found primarily in airports, **duty-free shops** sell products to international travelers (you'll be asked for proof of travel, such as an airline boarding pass), but you could still have to pay duty in the US on such purchases if they fall outside of your exemption allowance. For instance, if you were to buy 2 liters of wine at the duty-free shop at Charles de Gaulle Airport in Paris, the 1-liter exemption limit on alcohol means you'd still have to pay duty on 1 of those 2 liters even if your overall purchases totaled less than $800.

If your purchases total more than $800 but less than $1,800, you'll be charged a flat 3% rate on the portion in excess of your $800 exemption, up to $1,000. Thus, if you're bringing $1,500 worth of merchandise into the US, you'll pay 3% duty on $700 of your total purchases, or $21. Again, the previously listed limits on alcohol and tobacco apply.

If your purchases exceed $1,800, the remaining duty is calculated based on US tariff rates for the country from which you're importing the goods and the types of goods you're importing.

Note: You must pay duty before you clear customs. US currency, checks drawn on US banks, and US money orders are accepted; some (but not all) customs checkpoints also take credit and debit cards.

A great resource for information on duty-free shopping is the **US Customs and Border Protection**'s website: theugseries.com/uscbp -duty-info. For more on clearing customs, see page 196.

purchased cords for our sunglasses, water-resistant pouches for our phones, and other beach supplies here.

IN PORT

MANY TRAVELERS FIND shopping in port as essential to cruising as gambling is to Las Vegas. If you approach buying things with this attitude, you won't be disappointed. You'll be surrounded by shopping opportunities at each port from the moment you step off the ship;

bargaining is expected, so assume that the first price you're quoted isn't the final one. If you need cheap souvenirs, you'll have no trouble finding T-shirts and tchotchkes within a few hundred yards of the ship.

Northern European ports are the exception to the schlock-shopping onslaught. As in every port, though, you need to ask pointed questions about the things you want to buy to make sure you're getting what you're paying for. If it's mittens in Norway, for instance, ask not only if they're made from local wool but also whether they were hand- or machine-knit, as well as whether they were knit in Norway (versus a factory in China).

JEWELRY Buying jewelry in port can be tricky. Because fair prices vary greatly with the quality of gems available for sale, you need to be an informed shopper to know just what a fair price is. Our recommendation is to pre-shop online—**Amazon** and **Blue Nile** (bluenile.com) are great places to start—to know the going rates for gems of the weight and quality you're interested in. One common brand, **Effy,** is sold on Amazon and its own website (effyjewelry.com); **Diamonds International,** which is ubiquitous in the Caribbean, has an online presence as well (diamondsinternational.com).

ALCOHOL Duty-free alcohol is available in most ports. If you're thinking about purchasing spirits during your cruise, be sure to do a little pricing research before you travel. Depending on your place of residence and its tax situation, the duty-free pricing may not differ much from what you'd pay at home. Look at the *per-ounce* price to make sure you're comparing apples to apples, or rather, tequila to tequila. Further, be aware of price differences between grades of liquor (*añejo* versus *reposado* tequila, for example).

unofficial **TIP**
If you decide to buy alcohol during your trip, remember to review DCL's rules for bringing it aboard (see page 140). In many cases, you won't have access to your purchase until the last night of your cruise.

On the other hand, cost may not be a major concern if you're considering a sentimental purchase (like that bottle of wine you learned about during a port-adventure vineyard tour) or you want to buy something that you can't get anywhere else (say, a liqueur made from a flower that grows only in the part of the world you're visiting on your cruise).

ONBOARD PHOTOGRAPHY

MANY DISNEY CRUISERS consider the pictures taken by shipboard photographers to be an integral part of their experience (although you're certainly under no obligation to buy photos or have your picture taken). We have had some of our favorite family pictures taken aboard the ships. You can buy an all-inclusive onboard photo package before your trip by visiting the **My Reservations** section of the DCL website (see page 122) and selecting "Onboard Fun." To purchase, your cruise must be paid in full, and you must be within your window for booking activities (see page 6). Advance purchases may be completed up to three days before you sail. The photos are provided to you via digital download.

Prepurchasing a photo package is often less expensive than buying one on the ship. For example, on a three-night, summer 2024 sailing of the *Magic,* the onboard price for an unlimited photo package was $230, while the precruise price was $195. The main disadvantages of prepurchasing photos are that (1) you may not be happy with the photos or (2) something unforeseen may happen—onboard quarantine, for example—that prevents you from taking as many photos as you might otherwise.

Because there's no limit to the number of pictures in an all-inclusive package, you want to put your face in front of the cameras as often as you can to get the biggest bang for your buck. You can also buy smaller quantities of photos, but you can do this only on board, and smaller packages aren't discounted. Typically, if you think you'll want more than 15 onboard photos, it makes better economic sense to buy the unlimited package in advance.

unofficial **TIP**
To prepurchase a photo package, you must select a specific day and time. It does not matter when you pick; your package remains in effect from the moment you board the ship until the photographers stop taking pictures on the last day of your cruise.

Photo packages are sold by stateroom, not by passenger or party. If you prepurchase a package, you'll need to designate one person in your stateroom as the purchaser—all guests in your stateroom may use the package, but the transaction won't go through if you select more than one purchaser. If your party includes more than one stateroom, check with DCL regarding discounts or bulk rates. The one exception to this rule is that if a family occupies more than one stateroom, and the second stateroom includes the family's minor children, they may have some of the photos from both staterooms included in one package. Stop by the Shutters photo desk on board to arrange this and to get specifics.

Photos taken on board come with a decorative custom border that includes such details as the ship's name—this border can't be removed. The photos are also usually taken in nonstandard aspect ratios, so if you want to get them printed on your own, you may need to crop or resize to print them on standard 4-by-6, 5-by-7, or 8-by-10 paper.

While on board, you can view your photos at kiosks in Shutters or on your phone via a QR code link. After signing in, you can see all your photos. We recommend checking your photos periodically while on board to make sure you see them all. They do sometimes get erroneously assigned to the wrong stateroom account.

Photo packages and individual photos *cannot* be purchased after debarking, so make sure you purchase them before your cruise ends. After debarking, any photos you purchased will be available online. Wait 48 hours after debarking and then visit disneycruise.disney.go .com/photos and log in. Click the "Link" option at the top right of the screen, enter your Castaway Club ID, and click the "Link Photos" button. If you have any problems, email dcl.photo@disneycruise.com.

Finally, all the ships have **Shutters Portrait Studio,** which is separate from the main onboard photo system. The pictures taken here are artistic black-and-white shots that aren't included in the price of regular onboard photography. Packages range from $550 for 5 digital images to $2,500 for a USB drive containing up to 100. If you're also vacationing at Walt Disney World, we think Disney's **Capture Your Moment** portrait sessions (theugseries.com/capture-moment) are a much better value.

BIBBIDI BOBBIDI *Boutique*

LIKE THE DISNEY PARKS, all DCL ships have varying incarnations of this wildly popular makeover spot for kids ages 3–12. Makeovers take about 45 minutes and start at about $100 for the **Deluxe Carriage Package,** which includes hairstyling (but not shampooing or cutting), nail polish, makeup, a princess sash, and a BBB-branded T-shirt. The *Frozen* **Package** (about $180) includes your princess's choice of Anna or Elsa hairstyling and costume, snowflake hair accessories, and an Olaf plush. The **Castle Package** (about $200) includes the same services as the Deluxe Carriage Package but swaps the T-shirt for a choice of princess gown, plus some coordinating accessories.

For the princess who has everything, BBB offers luxury options— with prices to match. The **Princess Signature Package** (about $450) starts with the standard hair, makeup, and nail treatments but adds a crystal tiara in a keepsake box, along with an heirloom-quality princess gown (complete with an organza garment bag and satin hanger to keep it pristine on the way home). The **Royal Sea Package,** priced at about $500–$1,100 (yes, you read that right) depending on the options you choose, includes multiple variations on the Castle or Princess Signature Package, plus a rolling trunk, a fancy picture frame, a ribbon necklace, and a glass slipper.

Pirates' League packages are available for both kids and adults on Pirate Night (see page 287). The basic **Swashbuckle** package for grown-ups (about $70) includes pirate makeup plus a bandanna, an eye patch, an earring, a vest, and a sash. The deluxe **Pirate Costume** for kids (about $200) adds a full outfit, a drawstring bag for holding plundered booty, a telescope, a coin necklace, and a parrot (not a real one!) for your little buccaneer's shoulder.

Parents of 2-year-olds should note that the Bibbidi Bobbidi Boutique age requirement on the ship is nonnegotiable. While a kind Fairy Godmother at Walt Disney World might look the other way and agree to do a makeover on a child who's not quite in the stated age range, the cast members on the ships won't cut you a break because they know exactly how old your child is.

But while BBB holds a hard line regarding the minimum age for makeovers, all of the makeovers are available for girls and boys alike.

MEETING *the* CHARACTERS

DISNEY CHARACTERS ARE available for photos and autographs several times a day at various locations on the ships; they also make occasional visits to the "It's a Small World" Nursery! and the kids' clubs. A complete schedule is usually posted on the **Character Information Board** in your ship's atrium. It's also listed in the Character Appearances section of the DCL Navigator app and is available by calling ☎ **7-PALS** (7257) from your stateroom phone.

unofficial **TIP**

You'll have better interactions with face characters (that is, those who can speak) if you're familiar with their film franchises and the things they're known for. Ask Thor about shawarma, Elsa about chocolate, Captain Jack Sparrow about sailing, and so on.

Disney may offer reservation times for meeting the hugely popular *Frozen* characters Anna, Elsa, and Olaf; a selection of Marvel superheroes; and what we call the Princess Palooza: a group of four or five Disney princesses who appear in the atrium at once. (Disney officially calls this the **Royal Gathering,** but we like our moniker better.)

If your sailing offers advance character greetings (and character-dining experiences), they'll appear in the **My Reservations** section for your sailing at the DCL website. Character encounters may not become available until days or weeks after your standard port-adventure and adult-dining selections appear, so if you're interested in these, keep checking back. If your specific cruise doesn't offer pre-booking, check the Navigator app to find out if character-greeting reservations are in effect for your sailing.

If reservations *are* being used on your voyage, it's essential that you get them. Some princesses may greet guests on the spur of the moment, with no ticket required, but be aware that the A-list stars—namely Anna, Elsa, Olaf, and the Marvel gang—are unlikely to make such impromptu appearances.

For some character greetings, guests will start lining up well before the posted start time. Unique characters will have long lines—we once had quite a wait to see the White Rabbit from *Alice in Wonderland,* who was serving as the Easter Bunny on the *Fantasy.* Likewise, Captain Jack Sparrow is a big draw on Pirate Night.

Most onboard character greetings are limited to 15 minutes or half an hour; the line will be closed once it has been determined that no more guests can be accommodated in the allotted time. If your child is intent on meeting a specific character, your best bet is to get in line **15–30 minutes** before that character is scheduled to appear. (We've arrived as much as 45 minutes ahead to get a spot for our kids to meet Belle, and we weren't even the first in line.)

You can also expect longer waits for common characters in unusual costumes, like Mickey Mouse wearing red, white, and blue on the Fourth of July or Goofy wearing a parka during an Alaskan voyage.

On longer cruises, classic Disney characters such as Mickey, Minnie, Donald, Goofy, and Pluto may make onboard appearances many times throughout the voyage. The lines for these favorites are typically shorter later in the trip, when most folks have already had their fill of photos with Mickey and company.

On **Castaway Cay,** photo ops featuring the Disney gang in beach attire take place near the ship's dock, weather permitting.

In 2019, Disney added character greetings with **Minnie Mouse** dressed in a ship captain's uniform, with the intent of inspiring girls to pursue maritime careers. Concurrent with Captain Minnie's addition to the meet-and-greet lineup, DCL has begun funding scholarships to **LJM Maritime Academy** in the Bahamas for female cadets seeking to become ship captains and other onboard leaders. Scholarships include tuition to the three-year program: two years at the academy and one year working on a Disney ship.

For some cruisers, meeting the characters is a highlight of their cruise. Joanna from Florida wrote:

One of my favorite things to do on a Disney cruise is meeting the characters. I love seeing the VIPs in their different outfits (be it pirate outfits on Pirate Night or Halloween costumes during Halloween on the High Seas). It's fun trying to see how many different outfits one can see throughout the cruise. I also love the variety of characters—from princesses to Marvel characters, there's a character for everyone.

ROYAL COURT ROYAL TEA PARTY (*DISNEY MAGIC, WONDER, DREAM, AND FANTASY*) This character experience allows kids and their adults to meet Lady Chamomile (the hostess), Chef Bule (the pastry chef), and a cadre of Disney princesses for lavish attention and a teatime meal of savory and sweet courses. Reserve in advance on the DCL website. The cost is $220 per child and $69 per adult. Kids leave with a plethora of gifts: a doll, jewelry, an autograph book, and a tiara for girls, and a plush Duffy bear, a sword and shield, and an autograph book for boys.

The tea party is expensive and gets mixed reviews from readers who have done it. If you're concerned about the cost, skip it. If your children would love some extra time with the princesses and some fun swag, it's probably worth it.

OLAF'S ROYAL PICNIC (*DISNEY WISH*) Priced at the same $220 per child and $69 per adult as the Royal Court Royal Tea Party, Olaf's Royal Picnic features appearances by Olaf, Anna, Elsa, and Kristoff, who will lead guests in celebrating a fictional Nordic midsummer festival, including songs and stories. Kids in attendance receive an assortment of gifts, including Olaf headwear, a cinch bag, a mandolin, a plush troll doll, a water bottle, a picnic blanket, a troll necklace, and an activity book.

A Note About Autographs

A significant subset of guests at the Disney parks and on Disney cruises collect character autographs as souvenirs. Items that characters may sign include those listed below.

ITEMS DISNEY CHARACTERS MAY SIGN
• Autograph books
• Disney-branded items, provided they're appropriate to the character doing the signing. For example, Cinderella would be unable to sign a Buzz Lightyear item.
• A Disney-approved photo. Only the characters in the photo can sign it.
• Disney note cards
• Disney Dollars—once signed, however, they can no longer be used as currency. (*Note:* Disney Dollars were discontinued in 2016 but are still redeemable.)
• Clothing (but it may not be worn while being signed)

Guests often have characters sign things other than autograph books, such as photo mats, pillowcases, and T-shirts. (One of Tammy's favorite signature-collecting mediums was a white baseball cap purchased in the parks.) After waiting in line, you present the character with whatever you want signed, then pose for a photo if you like. Be aware, however, that DCL imposes a number of restrictions on the kinds of items that characters may sign. Prohibited items include those listed below.

ITEMS DISNEY CHARACTERS MAY NOT SIGN	
• Flags of any nation	• Receipts or banking slips
• Money other than Disney Dollars	• Skin
• Non-Disney merchandise	• Non-family-friendly or sexually explicit items

BINGO

DCL IS ONE OF THE FEW CRUISE LINES that have no casino gambling on board. What it does have is bingo, played most days on most ships, in one or two hour-long sessions per day, with four games played per hour. Prizes range from DCL swag to actual cash jackpots of several thousand dollars. On one sailing, we watched a young guy win nearly $9,000 at bingo—enough to pay for his entire vacation and then some.

With that much money potentially at stake, it's no surprise that many people take Disney bingo quite seriously. Games are fast-paced, and players are expected to keep up. Additionally, DCL interjects sound effects, music, dance, and random chatter into the number calling. (*Pro tip:* The reason the bingo crew members do a wacky dance every time the B-11 ball is called is that when the machine is in Spanish-language mode, *B-11* is pronounced *B once*, which sounds more or less like "Beyoncé.")

Children may play but must be accompanied at all times by a guest age 18 or older, who will officially be the winner of any cash prize. The cost to play varies; pricing is typically higher at the end of a sailing, when payouts are larger. Buy-ins start at around $30 for one set of paper bingo cards per session. Many guests, however, opt to rent electronic bingo machines, often priced at $40 or $50 for 24 cards per session. Because the machines keep track of which numbers have been called, you don't have to be on high alert every second.

If you think you're going to be playing frequently, be sure to stick around at the end of each session. The caller will often give out a special one-day-only password that's good for free bingo cards if you mention it at the next session. On longer sailings, the caller will sometimes offer free cards to guests who present personal items such as a child's drawing of the ship or a photo they took of a specific thing in port. Frequent-player discounts may also be available—be sure to ask. Platinum and Pearl Castaway Club members are also eligible for a free card with purchase.

IS THIS WORTH YOUR TIME? We aren't all big bingo players ourselves, but we've played with friends and had a great time. If you're OK with risking relatively small amounts of money, it could be worth the $30 buy-in just once to see if it's your cup of tea. But be aware that once you get hooked, costs can add up quickly.

 # INTERACTIVE GAMES

WHEN THE *DISNEY DREAM* BEGAN SAILING, Disney introduced interactive games and artwork to its ships. The artwork is fun to see, and the games give guests an activity that could stretch across several days of the sailing.

ON THE *DREAM* AND *FANTASY*

THE *DREAM-CLASS SHIPS* feature a self-guided interactive game called **Midship Detective Agency,** in which kids help Disney characters solve a mystery. You begin by signing up on Deck 5 Midship, where you'll be given a small, numbered cardboard game piece. One side of the game piece holds a bar code and your agent number, and the other side displays a detective's badge icon. There are three games: **The Case of the Missing Puppies** and **The Case of the Plundered Paintings** both feature Mickey and friends, and our favorite, **The Case of the Stolen Show,** stars the Muppets.

Along with your badge card, you'll receive a pamphlet describing each of the agency's suspects in the mystery. The pamphlet also includes a map of the ship that shows where to find clues to solve the mystery. Once you've signed up and obtained your game gear, you'll watch a short video that explains the mystery you're solving. You'll also be told where to go to find your first clue.

Each clue is presented on an **Enchanted Art** video screen somewhere on the ship. The screens look like ordinary wall art to anyone not playing the game—it's only when you hold up your badge that the screen comes alive with video and sound. To obtain the clue, you'll first have to solve a simple puzzle or win a simple game. You do this by using your badge as a sort of game controller while you're playing, tilting and moving the badge to guide the action on the screen. It takes a little practice, but you can repeat the action as often as needed. Once you've obtained the clue, you can eliminate one of the suspects from the mystery; then it's off to another section of the ship to get another clue.

Make no mistake: Playing this game involves climbing many stairs. However, you get to see a lot of the ship, and it's good exercise. You'll see kids playing at all times of the day and night, and lines often form in front of each video screen, especially on sea days.

ON THE *WISH, TREASURE,* AND *DESTINY*

THE *WISH*-CLASS SHIPS ALSO have an interactive ship-wide game: **Disney Uncharted Adventure.** Uncharted Adventure takes place via the **Play Disney Parks app,** which will transform your phone or tablet into an "enchanted spyglass" that allows you to wirelessly interact with artworks displayed on the walls of many of the ship's public walkways.

Using the spyglass, you'll unlock adventures, solve puzzles, and embark on quests. The experience culminates with an in-person event on the last day of the cruise. Families can play together on up to four devices at once or team up on one or two devices at a time.

RELIGIOUS SERVICES

CRUISES OF SEVEN NIGHTS or longer sometimes hold a nondenominational Christian service on Sunday mornings and a Shabbat service on Friday evenings. Worship times depend on when the ship is in port or, in the case of Jewish services, when sunset occurs.

There are no dedicated chapels on the ships, so services are typically held in a lounge or theater, depending on the number of guests on board and the ship's other offerings. **Guest Services** can recommend houses of worship in port. Additional services take place during religious holidays. Check the DCL Navigator app for details.

Many DCL ports have houses of worship as key points of interest. Tammy's family attended a service in the **Liverpool Cathedral** on a Sunday morning, and it was a highlight of their day. If you'd like to attend services while in port, check the institution's website in advance to view hours of operation or check whether a dress code applies (as is common in many European churches).

WHAT TO DO *on a* SEA DAY

SOME OF THE most frequently asked questions we hear from new cruisers are variations on, "What happens during a day at sea?" and "Won't I be bored staying on a ship all day?" To that we say, there are zillions of things to do for all ages and interests, and you'll only be bored if you want to be. Below is just a handful of the things we've done on sea days. Note that not all DCL-organized activities are available on all sailings—the longer your cruise and the more sea days you have, the more options you'll have.

ON A DAY AT SEA, YOU CAN . . .

- Meet characters.
- Get a manicure or pedicure.
- Sleep.
- Watch old or new Disney films.
- Play one of the interactive games.
- Read a novel.
- Write a short story.
- Shop for souvenirs.
- Play a round of minigolf.
- Play shuffleboard.
- Learn to mix drinks.
- Enjoy the drinks you mixed.
- Savor fine cuisine.
- Learn to draw Disney characters.
- Watch a stage show.
- Meet a Broadway performer.
- Learn the fine art of towel folding.
- Play cards.
- Take a cooking class.
- Lift weights.
- Go for a swim.
- Go for a run.
- Take a tour of the ship.
- Attend a religious service.
- Whoop it up at a deck party.
- Play Foosball.
- Play video games.
- Hang out at a piano bar.
- Get an acupuncture treatment.
- Stare at the sea.
- Attend a history class.
- Dance in a nightclub.
- Take a ballroom dance class.
- Sit in a sauna.
- Soak in a hot tub.
- Have a family portrait taken.
- Go on a waterslide.
- Order room service.
- Buy jewelry.
- Trade Disney pins.
- Watch for wildlife.
- Do karaoke.
- Get a massage.
- Sample a food you've never tried before.
- Do the entire *New York Times* Sunday crossword puzzle in one sitting.
- Play in a trivia competition.
- Chat with other guests.
- Chat with your family.

PART 13

ENTERTAINMENT *and* NIGHTLIFE

KEY QUESTIONS ANSWERED IN THIS CHAPTER

- What are the theater shows like on a Disney ship? *(see below)*
- What's the nightlife scene like? *(see page 291)*

◼ LIVE THEATER *on the* SHIPS

LIVE STAGE PERFORMANCES take place at the **Walt Disney Theatre.** The shows are generally either Disney-themed theatrical productions (typically musicals) or variety acts such as comedians, magicians, and ventriloquists. The theatrical presentations are usually of two types: (1) retellings of familiar Disney stories and (2) so-called jukebox musicals. (Note that not all productions are performed on every sailing.)

RETELLINGS *Disney's Aladdin: A Musical Spectacular,* on the *Fantasy* and the *Wish,* is an example of the retelling genre. This is DCL's interpretation of the *Aladdin* story: It's not the same *Aladdin* as the 1992 animated feature or the 2019 live-action film, nor is it exactly the same as the musical that's been playing on Broadway since 2011. The cruise version features live actors and multiple Arabian-themed sets reprising key scenes from the animated film, including the most popular songs, in about half the time of the original movie.

Frozen: A Musical Spectacular, on the *Wonder, Fantasy,* and *Destiny,* is the best of the retelling shows. The character puppets (Sven and Olaf) are charming, and the lighting, sets, and costumes are the best we've seen in any show at a Disney property, the theme parks included. We also like the *Magic's* **Tangled: The Musical,** with songs from beloved composer Alan Menken. **Beauty and the Beast,** on the *Dream* and *Treasure,* draws from both the 1991

> ✳ *unofficial* **TIP**
> If you're sailing on the *Wish,* the **Glass Slipper Kiss Goodnight**—a charming little music-and-light show that concludes the day—takes place at 10, 11, and midnight in the Grand Hall.

and 2017 films; while it breaks no new ground—yes, "Be Our Guest" is among the musical numbers—it's still entertaining. The *Magic*'s **Twice Charmed: An Original Twist on the Cinderella Story** is a fresh spin on the retelling genre, with surprises aplenty. The *Wish*'s new **Little Mermaid** show, on the other hand, is a letdown for some guests.

JUKEBOX MUSICALS DCL's jukebox musicals include **Disney Dreams, Disney's Believe, The Golden Mickeys,** and **Disney Seas the Adventure.** Each features songs and characters from a variety of Disney films, with the numbers linked by an original narrative. While we enjoy the jukebox shows for the most part, the weakest of these merely serve to string together unrelated songs. (*The Golden Mickeys,* we're looking at you.) And we'd be remiss if we didn't mention that these shows—even the ones we like—tend to recycle the same handful of characters and songs that permeate virtually every entertainment venue throughout the ship.

A BIT OF ADVICE

YOU'LL PROBABLY SEE at least one musical if you're taking small children on your cruise. Along with reading the show profiles that follow, we recommend watching a few minutes of each show on YouTube before your cruise. This will not only help you decide which shows are worth your time, but it will also let you know what you're missing in case another entertainment option is available.

Disney describes its theatrical offerings as "Broadway-style." This doesn't mean, however, that you're going to see the touring-company equivalent of a Broadway hit (like the versions of *Cats, Mamma Mia!,* and *Grease* staged on some Royal Caribbean sailings). As devotees of actual New York City theater, we confess that we used to scoff at the notion of "Broadway-style"—we thought it laughable to compare the stripped-down shows on the ships with real Broadway productions such as Disney's own stage version of *The Lion King.*

unofficial **TIP**
One of the perks for Concierge guests is early entry into the shows. Take advantage of it if you want to pick the best seats without racing other guests inside.

But in discussing our criticisms with Disney cast members, we've learned that, at least from a technical standpoint, DCL performances have much more in common with Times Square than Topeka: The stage mechanics, costuming, special effects, and lighting are as close to state of the art as is practical at sea. If you're watching a show with your kids and you find your eyes glazing over, try paying attention to the technological aspects of the production. They would be top-notch in most locales—and they're nothing less than remarkable given the constraints of a cruise ship. Check the **DCL Navigator app** for showtimes on your sailing.

We also want to highlight the entertainment crew. Even in the shows we give a lower rating to, we are always amazed by the talent.

Note: At press time, it was too early to rate the retellings **Disney The Tale of Moana** on the *Treasure* and **Disney Hercules** on the *Destiny.*

Disney Magic

Disney Dreams: An Enchanted Classic ★★★★
WALT DISNEY THEATRE DECK 4 FORWARD

IN A NUTSHELL: PETER PAN SAVES THE DAY

DURATION 55 minutes. **OUR TAKE** Not to be missed.

DESCRIPTION AND COMMENTS Peter Pan must help a girl named Anne Marie "find her own magic" before sunrise, whisking her through settings from *Aladdin, Beauty and the Beast, Cinderella, The Little Mermaid, The Lion King,* and *Frozen.* Each story's main characters appear in key scenes from their respective movies and sing their signature songs. The sets are attractive, the special effects are good (expect Elsa to unleash a minor blizzard in the Walt Disney Theatre), and the script is fast-paced and entertaining. The cast seems to enjoy it, too, and it shows.

Tangled: The Musical ★★★½
WALT DISNEY THEATRE DECK 4 FORWARD

IN A NUTSHELL: RAPUNZEL LETS DOWN HER HAIR AND SINGS UP A STORM

DURATION 50 minutes. **OUR TAKE** A fresh take on a classic fairy tale.

DESCRIPTION AND COMMENTS This faithful retelling of Disney's *Tangled* features songs by Broadway and film composer–demigod Alan Menken (*Aladdin, Beauty and the Beast, Hercules, Little Shop of Horrors, The Little Mermaid, Newsies, Pocahontas*). Actors, singers, and dancers—and miles and miles of synthetic hair—wend their way through intricate sets. The Snuggly Duckling tavern is particularly charming, the puppetry for the larger-than-life sidekick horse Maximus is good enough to make you believe its operator is actually equine, and the ending lantern scene is among the most appealing segments of any DCL production. Having seen this show several times, we think the lighting is more moving and affecting if you sit in the center of the theater rather than close to the stage.

Twice Charmed: An Original Twist on the Cinderella Story
★★★½ **WALT DISNEY THEATRE DECK 4 FORWARD**

IN A NUTSHELL: HAPPILY EVER AFTER? NOT SO FAST!

DURATION 55 minutes. **OUR TAKE** An engaging spin on a familiar story.

DESCRIPTION AND COMMENTS If you're familiar with Disney's animated film *Cinderella,* you'll recall that the wicked stepmother breaks the first glass slipper just as it's about to go on Cinderella's foot. But Cinderella produces the matching slipper, shows it fits, and goes on to marry the prince.

Twice Charmed begins where the original story ends. As the show opens, Cinderella's stepmother and stepsisters are bemoaning the fact that they didn't know Cinderella had the second slipper. A nefarious fairy godfather sends Cindy's evil kin back in time to destroy her slipper before the prince's foot-fitting team ever arrives. This means Cinderella must figure out a new way to show the prince that they're meant to be together.

As is the case with most Disney classics, you can guess in the first 5 minutes how everything is going to end, but *Twice Charmed* is interesting anyway because it has a new narrative. The sets are pretty, the songs aren't bad, and it's an enjoyable way to spend an evening.

Disney Wonder

Disney Dreams: An Enchanted Classic   ★★★★
WALT DISNEY THEATRE DECK 4 FORWARD

IN A NUTSHELL: PETER PAN SAVES THE DAY

COMMENTS See profile of this show on the *Magic* (opposite page).

Frozen: A Musical Spectacular   ★★★★½
WALT DISNEY THEATRE DECK 4 FORWARD

IN A NUTSHELL: WE DON'T MIND THE COLD . . . OR THE SAME OLD SONGS

DURATION 50 minutes. **OUR TAKE** *Brrr!* Not to be missed.

DESCRIPTION AND COMMENTS You know the music, but if you haven't seen DCL's take on this modern animated classic, you haven't seen the story performed with more heart or better artistry. The puppetry is critical to the storytelling, adding warmth to what could be a mere rehash. Life-size reindeer Sven and snowman Olaf are, of course, two of the characters portrayed as puppets, but there are several surprises too.

   Frozen's special effects provide a couple of genuine wow moments; we count them among our favorites in any Disney venue, and no, we're not talking about soap-bubble snow. The costumes are gorgeous too: If you are fascinated by theatrical costuming, try to sit up close so you can see the details in the fabrics; otherwise, a middle-of-the-theater view is the best vantage point from which to take it all in.

The Golden Mickeys   ★★
WALT DISNEY THEATRE DECK 4 FORWARD

IN A NUTSHELL: DISNEY DOES AN AWARDS SHOW

DURATION 45 minutes. **OUR TAKE** This is the weakest of DCL's live shows.

DESCRIPTION AND COMMENTS The premise is that you're at an Oscars-style ceremony (complete with a red carpet outside the theater) honoring Disney characters for their movie performances in various categories. As each winner is announced, live actors reenact key scenes, including the songs, as video clips from the movies play in the background.

   DCL does many things well, but *The Golden Mickeys* isn't one of them. The meager "plot" is just a device to tie the musical numbers together, and what little storyline there is doesn't always make sense. Cruella de Vil is a natural for Best Villain; on the other hand, the Salute to Friendship award was apparently the only way the writers could think of to get Woody, Buzz, and Jessie together onstage. Unless you just *have* to see yet another rehash of songs from *The Lion King* and *Beauty and the Beast,* skip this one.

Disney Dream

Beauty and the Beast
★★★½   **WALT DISNEY THEATRE DECK 3 FORWARD**

IN A NUTSHELL: I'M NOT CRYING, *YOU'RE* CRYING!

DURATION 50 minutes. **OUR TAKE** We love the score—really, we do—but even we think "Be Our Guest" is overplayed.

DESCRIPTION AND COMMENTS This is an abridged but otherwise faithful version of *Beauty and the Beast.* No, not *that* one, the other one: The set design and costuming are inspired by the 2017 live-action/CGI movie starring Emma Watson, not the 1991 animated classic.

DCL's *Beauty and the Beast* includes songs from both films. The actors who play the inanimate-object characters—Mrs. Potts, Cogsworth, and the like—wear regular (that is, human) period clothing rather than full-body character costumes, and they carry puppets of the household items they represent. (Example: Mrs. Potts carries a teapot with a painted face and lips that move.) Disney has made this concept work in other shows, such as *The Lion King* on Broadway; unfortunately, puppets *don't* work as well to convey the idea of nonsentient things that have been magically transformed into living beings. Nevertheless, the music soars; Gaston still wants to kill the beast; and true love prevails at the end—perhaps prompting a tear or two, depending on how much of a sentimental sort you are.

Disney's Believe ★★★
WALT DISNEY THEATRE DECK 3 FORWARD

IN A NUTSHELL: DISNEY MAGIC TRIUMPHS OVER CYNICISM

DURATION 50 minutes. **OUR TAKE** This is a nice change of pace.

DESCRIPTION AND COMMENTS A botanist father who doesn't believe in magic must learn to believe in order to reconnect with his daughter on her birthday. The father's guide is *Aladdin*'s wisecracking Genie, who takes Dad through time, space, and Disney music on his journey to acceptance.

Believe has one of the most sophisticated sets of any Disney stage show at sea, and there are enough visual elements to entertain almost any kid. Although it's not a holiday show, the plot seems like a loose adaptation of Charles Dickens's *A Christmas Carol,* with "ghosts" including Mary Poppins, Peter Pan, Baloo from *The Jungle Book,* and Rafiki from *The Lion King.* Other Disney stars make appearances, but, thankfully, *Believe* includes some less-familiar characters and songs. "Step in Time" is one of our favorites. The final stretch has a hit parade of other princesses and ends with performances by Mickey and Minnie.

The Golden Mickeys ★★
WALT DISNEY THEATRE DECK 3 FORWARD

IN A NUTSHELL: DISNEY DOES AN AWARDS SHOW

COMMENTS See profile of this show on the *Wonder* (previous page).

Disney Fantasy

Disney's Aladdin: A Musical Spectacular ★★★
WALT DISNEY THEATRE DECK 3 FORWARD

IN A NUTSHELL: CLASSIC SONGS AND A COMEDY CLUNKER

DURATION 45 minutes. **OUR TAKE** Genie needs better material.

DESCRIPTION AND COMMENTS A retelling of Disney's *Aladdin,* this show features stage sets depicting Agrabah, the Cave of Wonders, and the Sultan's palace. It also stars the film's main characters: Aladdin, Princess

Jasmine, Jafar, Iago, and Genie. All the big musical numbers are performed, including "Friend Like Me" and "A Whole New World."

This show is one of five variations on Disney's *Aladdin* story: the original animated film from 1992; a stage show (also called *Disney's Aladdin: A Musical Spectacular*) that ran at Disney California Adventure (DCA) from 2003 to 2016; the current Broadway show, which began its run in 2011; and the 2019 live-action film, starring Will Smith as Genie.

Aladdin is less sweet and sentimental than a show like *Believe.* Nevertheless, it has its shortcomings—take Genie, for instance. In the animated movie, he has the most important role: Besides providing narrative and background, he tells jokes to keep the action moving. In the DCA show, Genie likewise ad-libbed topical humor into the act, and he delivered so many fast-and-furious zingers that he inevitably got the biggest ovation at the end. On board, however, Genie's jokes are watered down so much that they don't provide the spark the rest of the script needs.

Disney's sixth ship, the *Treasure* (page 46) has an Aladdin statue in the Grand Hall but shows the *Beauty and the Beast* show rather than *Aladdin.* Color us confused.

Disney's Believe ★★★
WALT DISNEY THEATRE DECK 3 FORWARD

IN A NUTSHELL: DISNEY MAGIC TRIUMPHS OVER CYNICISM

COMMENTS See profile of this show on the *Dream* (opposite page).

Frozen: A Musical Spectacular ★★★★½
WALT DISNEY THEATRE DECK 3 FORWARD

IN A NUTSHELL: WE DON'T MIND THE COLD . . . OR THE SAME OLD SONGS

COMMENTS See profile of this show on the *Wonder* (page 283).

Disney Wish

Disney's Aladdin: A Musical Spectacular ★★★
WALT DISNEY THEATRE DECK 3 FORWARD

IN A NUTSHELL: CLASSIC SONGS AND A COMEDY CLUNKER

COMMENTS See profile of this show on the *Fantasy* (opposite page).

Disney Seas the Adventure ★★★
WALT DISNEY THEATRE DECK 3 FORWARD

IN A NUTSHELL: GOOFY TAKES THE HELM

DURATION 35 minutes. **OUR TAKE** A fun spin on the jukebox genre.

DESCRIPTION AND COMMENTS Minnie Mouse, here a ship's captain, hands over navigating duties to Goofy, and gentle chaos ensues. With an assist from Tinker Bell, Goofy sails through scenes that draw from the Disney canon. Among the songs you'll hear are "Go with the Flow" from the *Finding Nemo* stage show, "Into the Unknown" from *Frozen 2,* and "Almost There" from *The Princess and the Frog.* The overall feel is upbeat and silly instead of sentimental, as other DCL shows tend to be. We left the theater in a great mood.

The Little Mermaid ★★½

WALT DISNEY THEATRE DECK 3 FORWARD

IN A NUTSHELL: A DISAPPOINTING ADAPTATION OF A BELOVED STORY

DURATION 50 minutes. **OUR TAKE** This is the weakest of DCL's retelling musicals. Prepare to be underwhelmed.

DESCRIPTION AND COMMENTS This retelling of the *Little Mermaid* story bears little resemblance to Disney's 1989 animated classic, the Broadway musical that ran from 2007 to 2009, or the production that aired live on ABC in 2019. Cast members enter the stage clad in costumes that would have been equally at home in a 1970s community theater presentation of *Godspell*, and by that we mean lots of flowing harem pants and ombré silk scarves. The production has a kitschy "Let's put on a show!" vibe, with cast members pulling costume elements, props, and puppets out of a giant treasure chest.

In a puzzling costuming decision, the mermaid characters, including Ariel, wear dresses that stop midcalf, fully exposing their legs and feet. (This differs from the Broadway and TV productions, in which Ariel wore a floor-length skirt in scenes that required her to stand.) Willing suspension of disbelief is one thing, but we think this is a design choice that asks too much of the audience.

Also, while the performers are talented, the script has some weaknesses. The storyline has been modified to include messages about climate change, conservation, and consent in romantic relationships. While these messages are well intentioned, they feel forced and heavy-handed in this context.

There are some bright moments, however: Crabby Sebastian steals the show, and, as with Disney's other live renditions of this tale, bubbles inevitably fall from the sky. The ending is happily ever after—but you have to swim through some murky waters to get there.

Disney Treasure and *Disney Destiny*

Beauty and the Beast ★★★½ (*Treasure* only)
WALT DISNEY THEATRE DECK 3 FORWARD

IN A NUTSHELL: I'M NOT CRYING, YOU'RE CRYING!

COMMENTS See profile of this show on the *Dream* (page 283).

Disney Seas the Adventure ★★★ (*Treasure* and *Destiny*)
WALT DISNEY THEATRE DECK 3 FORWARD

IN A NUTSHELL: GOOFY TAKES THE HELM

COMMENTS See profile of this show on the *Wish* (page 285).

Frozen: A Musical Spectacular ★★★★½ (*Destiny* only)
WALT DISNEY THEATRE DECK 3 FORWARD

IN A NUTSHELL: WE DON'T MIND THE COLD . . . OR THE SAME OLD SONGS

COMMENTS See profile of this show on the *Wonder* (page 283).

OTHER LIVE PERFORMANCES

BESIDES LIVE STAGE SHOWS, the **Walt Disney Theatre** hosts variety acts, from magicians and comedians to jugglers and ventriloquists. Repositioning cruises, with their many sea days, sometimes host guest Broadway artists or other niche celebrities. Many of these acts will put on preview shows or short sets at various venues throughout the ship before their major engagement at the theater. We've seen some incredible acts on board (like the Beatles tribute band while we visited Liverpool) . . . and we've also seen a few for which *mediocre* would be putting it kindly. If your sailing offers preview performances, we suggest catching a few minutes to decide whether the act is worth your time. In our experience, the best live acts tend to be the magicians and the comics, who can adapt their material on the fly.

The pianists, singers, and other musicians around the ship are also high-caliber performers. We always enjoy listening to them while relaxing in a lounge in the evenings with friends and even have a few favorites that we try not to miss.

If you refresh the DCL Navigator app frequently throughout the day on a longer or specialty sailing (such as a holiday cruise), you may occasionally come across listings for **surprise special performances.** For instance, on a New Year's Eve sailing on the *Fantasy* not long after *Frozen 2* was released, Erin and her family got to attend a surprise performance/seminar by Bobby Lopez and Kristen Anderson-Lopez, the husband-and-wife team who wrote the songs for both of the *Frozen* movies. The pair described their creative process, played a few pieces that had been cut from the films, accompanied some of the ship's stage actors in song performances, and even passed a microphone around the audience so that selected guests could belt out verses of "Let It Go."

DECK PARTIES

FEATURING DISNEY CHARACTERS, deck parties are usually held several times per cruise, typically near the family pool or in the ship's main lobby. The first party, known as the **Sail-Away Celebration** or **Sail-A-Wave Party,** depending on the ship, happens as you leave port on embarkation day. Additional deck parties will happen anytime there is a themed day or evening on the ship (such as **Pirate Night,** *Frozen* **Celebration, Marvel Days,** and **New Year's Eve**).

Outdoor parties are high-energy affairs, with loud music, dancing, games, and other activities, plus videos displayed on the ship's giant Funnel Vision LED screen. The indoor versions of these parties are virtually identical, except for the giant video screen. Check the DCL Navigator app for the dates and times of these events.

ARE THESE WORTH YOUR TIME? If you're a fan of classic TV, and *The Love Boat* in particular, deck parties are a virtual must for the kitsch/

pop culture factor. Little kids typically love the show if they can see the stage. If you're an adult cruising for relaxation, feel free to skip it.

PIRATE NIGHT

THE VAST MAJORITY of itineraries have **Pirate Night,** when the crew, restaurants, and entertainment take on a buccaneer theme. The ship's transformation begins early in the day, when the usual background music is replaced by songs and audio from the theme parks' Pirates of the Caribbean ride and the spin-off film series. Afternoon craft sessions and family activities are pirate-themed as well. Sometime in the afternoon, your stateroom attendant may leave a pirate bandanna for each member of your group, along with booty such as chocolate "coins" covered in gold foil.

On cruises of four-plus nights, each ship's main restaurant will have a special menu for the evening, designed to look like a treasure map. Virtually all the crew, as well as the ship's officers, wear special pirate outfits, and families have an opportunity to pose for photos with them before dinner. Many guests pack their own outfits, including black knee-high boots, capri pants, white puffy shirts, and eyeliner (or guyliner, as the case may be).

Pirate Night concludes with a stage show and video on the family pool's Funnel Vision screen, accompanied by a short fireworks display. The fireworks are usually shot from the starboard side, so take that into account when you are finding somewhere to stand.

Pirate Night on the *Wish*-class ships is slightly different than on the other ships. The entertainment on deck takes the form of the **Pirate's Rockin' Parlay Party,** with a live rock band playing moderately Disneyfied covers of songs by Twisted Sister, the Rolling Stones, and KISS. Captain Jack Sparrow swings onto the stage instead of Mickey zip-lining over the deck. We think the live rock band was a brilliant addition to Pirate Night. If you're in the right age group to know the songs, we think you'll have an absolute blast at one of DCL's best live music performances; youngsters, however, may be baffled by the headbanging grown-ups around them.

JACK-JACK'S DIAPER DASH

WE ARE SUCH BIG FANS of this baby-racing (you read that right) event, we felt we needed to highlight it. **Jack-Jack's Diaper Dash** takes place on one day of just about every sailing in either the atrium on the first four ships or in Hero Zone on the *Wish*-class ships. It's a live entertainment event for the excited crowd that assembles and a serious competition for the under-2-year-old set.

Jack-Jack's invites all crawling babies on the sailing to participate in this race against their peers (crawling babies only; no walkers allowed). The babies are set loose on a long, slightly cushioned plastic mat with racing lanes. Parents or siblings are at the other end of the mat, encouraging the babies with everything from cell phones to toys to promises of big Mommy hugs on the other side. What happens next is never predictable, never the same two events in a row, and always ridiculously entertaining. We make a point to find it on the schedule the first day we're on board and clear our schedules for the appointed time. You won't regret it!

 MOVIES

RECENT DISNEY, PIXAR, *Star Wars,* and Marvel movies, including films released during the cruise, are shown on every DCL ship. On all ships except the *Wish*-class ships, films are shown primarily in the **Buena Vista Theatre,** on Deck 5 Aft on the *Magic* and *Wonder* and spanning Decks 4 and 5 Midship on the *Dream* and *Fantasy.* The *Wish*-class ships have two movie theaters, the **Wonderland Cinema** and **Never Land Cinema,** located across the hall from each other on Deck 4.

About half a dozen films (more on longer sailings) are shown almost continuously throughout the day, from about 9 a.m. to midnight. Admission is free. The movie schedule for your entire sailing is available on the DCL Navigator app. The same film may be shown three or four times during your cruise, at different times of day.

Each theater is outfitted with a digital film projector, a state-of-the-art sound system, and 3D equipment (plus glasses for guests). Padded, upholstered seats are arranged stadium-style behind the screen, allowing good views from almost anywhere in the theater. The aisles between the seats on the classic ships are especially narrow, however.

Popcorn and drinks are sold outside the theater before and during each presentation; you can also bring your own snacks and drinks. We've been known to make a quick dash up to the pool deck just before movie time to grab a free order of chicken nuggets and a soda to snack on during the film. Concierge guests can show their key card for free popcorn.

In the case of real blockbusters, films will be shown in the larger **Walt Disney Theatre** in addition to (or sometimes in place of) the live stage shows. We've been on board during the first week of release for several of the newer *Star Wars* films. In each case, the entire theater was packed more than once, and the concession stand was doing a brisk business in Darth Vader–helmet drink holders and popcorn buckets shaped like Han Solo in carbonite.

Classic Disney films are also shown on the giant 24-by-14-foot **Funnel Vision** LED screen perched high above each ship's family pool: **Goofy's Pool** on Deck 9 of the *Magic* and *Wonder,* **Donald's Pool** on Deck 11 of the *Dream* and *Fantasy,* and **Mickey's Pool** on Deck 11 of the *Wish*-class ships. Deeper cuts from the Disney catalog, including rarely seen films and documentaries, are shown on the stateroom televisions (see next page).

TELEVISION *and* NEWS

DCL STATEROOM TVS don't broadcast anything approaching the programming you're used to at home. You won't find HBO or Comedy Central, or even NBC or CBS.

unofficial **TIP**
You can't bring your own TV-streaming boxes or sticks on board.

Rather, the strength of DCL's television lineup is its film content. Cruisers have on-demand access to a giant library of films from Disney, Pixar, Disney-Nature, the Marvel and *Star Wars* franchises, and other Disney-owned companies.

The modest channel lineup includes the following:

- Channels airing clips of Disney TV shows or playing Radio Disney music
- Basic news and sports stations (BBC, CNBC, ESPN, ESPN 2, Fox, and MSNBC)
- Ship-information stations, including the weather forecast; a live broadcast of the view from the bridge; port, shopping, and shore-excursion information; and character-appearance schedules
- Infomercial-type stations advertising things like Disney Vacation Club time-shares

Live-news and sports stations usually come in fine when you're cruising in the Caribbean but may be available only sporadically—or not at all—in other locations due to international broadcasting rights or (more likely) poor satellite reception. To its credit, DCL is up-front about this on its website.

LIVE SPORTS *and* OTHER BROADCAST ENTERTAINMENT

THE DCL SPORTS BARS are **O'Gills Pub** on the *Magic* and *Fantasy*, **Crown & Fin Pub** on the *Wonder*, **Pub 687** on the *Dream*, **Keg & Compass** on the *Wish*, **Periscope Pub** on the *Treasure*, and **Cask and Cannon** on the *Destiny*. These are your primary venues for watching baseball, basketball, and soccer. NFL games are usually shown here too; some are also shown on the ships' **Funnel Vision** big screen on the pool deck.

Keep in mind that the ships get their TV programming from satellite feeds, which can be affected by weather. If you want to watch a specific game, show up at least 30 minutes beforehand and ask a crew member to find the right station.

If you happen to be sailing during a sporting event of national or worldwide interest, expect that it will be available for viewing in nearly every public space that has seating. During one *Wonder* sailing during the World Cup soccer finals, the Navigator app listed just two viewing venues, but we found screens pulled down from the ceiling in every bar, lounge, and café. And if you're interested in major live events other than sports, rest assured that Disney has you covered. We've been on board during the Oscars and saw the broadcast playing in several of the lounges and in the Buena Vista Theatre.

If you want to watch a big game without leaving your stateroom, try looking for **special-event channels** on your TV. Although the ships don't normally carry NBC, CBS, and Fox in the standard shipboard channel lineup, they sometimes turn these networks on during football season or during playoffs for other sports.

NIGHTCLUBS, BARS, CAFÉS, *and* LOUNGES

EACH SHIP HAS A COLLECTION of places to drink, dance, and listen to music; some are geared more toward quiet conversation than partying. Some clubs host family activities during the day but become adults-only at night, usually around 9 p.m. (Guests must generally be 21 or older to drink; see page 209 for an exception.)

FAMILY NIGHTCLUB ACTIVITIES

THE ACTIVITIES IN THE FAMILY NIGHTCLUBS (and sometimes in the lobby atrium) vary considerably depending on the length of the sailing, the itinerary, whether it's a special-events sailing (Marvel Days, holidays, and so on), and other factors. Days at sea will have a wider range of programming than days in port, when many guests will be off enjoying the sights on land.

There are, however, a number of activities that show up with some frequency. Among them are the following:

- **Trivia.** Trivia is big on board. Themes may include **Disney, cruises, sports, movies, pirates, holidays,** and **tunes.** It often helps to have team members from different generations because the questions could come from current topics or ancient times (like, you know, the 1980s). Though the prizes are typically things like plastic medals and keychains, the gameplay can get cutthroat. Watch out for Disney know-it-alls who study in advance with the specific aim of wiping the floor with their competition.

- **Game shows.** These may include **Who Wants to Be a Mouseketeer?,** a simplified version of *Who Wants To Be a Millionaire?*; **So You Think You Know Your Family,** a spin on *The Newlywed Game* in which parent–child pairs try to guess each other's answers to various questions; **The Feud** (think *Family Feud* with Disney-related questions); **The Inside Out Game—Playing with Your Memories,** in which kids and parents see what they remember about each other's lives; and **Mickey Mania,** in which four parent–child teams have to be quick on the buzzer for a chance to answer trivia questions.

- **Crafts.** These are usually low-mess, cut-and-paste projects geared to younger kids. Teens will likely find them boring.

- **Family karaoke.** Come prepared with a long list of possible song ideas, as you'll be able to sing only what they have on hand and there's no master database. Songs from Disney films are typically available, but you may find some outliers that are not. Other options include classic and contemporary pop and rock tunes, country hits, and American Songbook standards. As you might expect, any song with even a hint of profanity is a no-go. If you want to sing, arrive promptly at the starting time; available time slots often fill quickly.

- **Animation lessons.** If you're familiar with Animation Academy at Disneyland (or a similar experience that once took place at Disney's Hollywood Studios), then you have an idea of what to expect here. If you have a child who's a perfectionist, this could be a trouble spot—we once had a little one melt down when her drawing came out less than identical to the instructor's.

- **Dance lessons.** Longer sailings may offer instruction in some locally flavored dance—Irish step dancing on a Northern European cruise or tango on a Mediterranean cruise, for example.

- **Cooking lessons.** These are observational rather than hands-on—you'll be watching someone else do the cooking. Printed recipes are usually distributed at the end; we've had good luck re-creating dishes at home.

- **Art of the Ship tour.** DCL cast members lead guests around the ship, pointing out noteworthy construction and design elements along the way.

- **Family talent shows.** Some cruises of seven nights or longer will have one of these. If you're interested in performing, sign up at Guest Services early in your trip, and make sure to pack whatever costumes, recordings, or sheet music you might need to perform. While you're not allowed to bring your own musical instruments onto the ship, you can usually borrow a guitar or keyboard that's kept on hand.

ARE THESE WORTH YOUR TIME? Your enjoyment of any of these activities may be affected by your mood, the personalities of the other participants, and your perception of the people running the event. While the cast members who run the family activities are enthusiastic and engaging, it's always possible that someone could be having a bad day. Also, while it's usually good to arrive on time at the beginning of an activity (so you can hear the instructions for a game, for example), you're not required to stick around if you find it doesn't interest you.

ABOUT THOSE DRINK PRICES . . .

IF IT'S BEEN a while since you last cruised with Disney, you may notice that some signature cocktails cost significantly more than they used to. For example, the **Shipbuilder's Wife**—made with Absolut Pears vodka, limoncello, grappa, agave, and fresh lemon juice—was introduced on the *Fantasy* in 2012 for $5.75. By summer 2016 the price had increased by just a dollar, but by early 2017 the same cocktail showed up on the menu of the *Dream*'s Pub 687 sports bar for a notably higher $8.50. By mid-2019 it was sold at Pub 687 for $11.75, in mid-2022 it was priced at $12, and by mid-2023 it was $12.50—more than double its original price (on the *Fantasy*, the same drink is sold at the same price but under a different name: the **Mercutio**), though it's still a bargain relative to other onboard beverages. A few DCL specialty cocktails on the ships are now priced in the $20–$25 range, although most cost $4–$5 less. You may even find the same or similar drinks at different prices on the same ship. On one sailing of the *Dream,* for instance, we found Bloody Marys priced at both $4.75 (at the bar in Cabanas) and $10 (at Palo brunch).

unofficial **TIP**
Check your DCL Navigator app for **Happy Hours.** Drinks are often 30%–50% less during these events.

As a point of reference, you will be familiar with this type of pricing if you're used to drinking in a major city or at Walt Disney World; craft cocktails are priced at $16–$18 at Jaleo in Disney Springs and $19–$24 at the Gramercy Tavern in New York City.

If you enjoy wine with dinner, ask your server about a multibottle **Wine & Dine package,** available in the main dining rooms and at Palo. You can save as much as 25% compared with buying by the bottle. Likewise, a **beer package** may be a better deal than buying brews individually; choose from six-packs or a refillable mug (you present a token at the bar instead of carrying the mug around with you). You can also preorder these packages online in the **Onboard Gifts** section of the DCL website).

unofficial **TIP**
If you're trying to keep tabs on costs, stick with domestic beers, grab a **Drink of the Day** on deck, or BYOB (see page 140 for details on DCL's alcohol carry-on policy).

The poolside bars and roving waiters on the ships and Castaway Cay and Lookout Cay have menus listing fun-in-the-sun drinks like daiquiris and piña coladas. You'll probably order at least one of these, if only to post about it on Instagram, but be aware that the menus don't list prices—and that doesn't mean the drinks are free. They can pack a punch on your final bill if you're not careful, so check before you order.

Finally, keep an eye out for **Sommelier's Bin** wine and Champagne specials, which are offered in at least one bar or lounge on every ship. The price is right—$11 per glass at the time of this writing—but there's a catch: The bartender randomly pours from whatever bottles are already open and need to be finished. (Think of it as beverage roulette.) We've tried wines this way that ranged from average to extraordinary—including a Champagne that normally costs more than $40 a glass.

BAR *and* NIGHTCLUB PROFILES

unofficial **TIP**
On the *Wish,* Luna's Deck 5 space is fully open to passersby, who can hear everything going on inside. When adult-oriented games such as Match Your Mate take place, small children walking past with their parents may hear racy commentary from other guests.

THE FOLLOWING PAGES focus on the cafés, clubs, bars, and lounges found across the DCL fleet; we've included the **Cove Café** coffee bar as well, since it also serves alcohol. Check the **Navigator app** for exact hours, menus, and prices on your sailing.

While the primary bars on each ship feature signature cocktails available only at those venues, there's a fair amount of overlap among the other offerings. In particular, you'll find that the by-the-glass wine options are largely similar throughout each ship.

On the four oldest ships, specialty coffees are served in just one or two locations. Most bars on the *Wish,* on the other hand, have state-of-the-art espresso machines, so you can power up with caffeine almost anywhere.

Also, whereas the bars on the *Magic, Wonder, Dream,* and *Fantasy* are concentrated in so-called adult districts, the *Wish*'s watering holes are scattered around the ship. There are pros and cons to each setup, depending on your proclivities: You can find a drink wherever you are on the *Wish,* while on the other ships, it's easier to avoid alcohol if you're not in the mood to imbibe.

Disney Magic

Cove Café   LOCATION DECK 9 MIDSHIP

SETTING AND ATMOSPHERE Cove Café on the *Magic* received a complete design overhaul during the ship's 2018 dry dock. The decor now features neutral cushions on dark rattan seating, with green accents on the walls and bar and large potted palms in the corners. There are open areas for socializing, but you can still find nooks and crannies where you can curl up with a book or magazine and a latte.

SELECTIONS Cove Café serves just about every kind of java you can think of: espresso, cappuccino, latte, Americano, and cold brew. Cove also serves hot teas and has a good selection of wines, Champagnes, spirits, and mixed drinks. The service is excellent.

unofficial **TIP**
If you're one of those people who need a coffee or six every day, ask your server for a **Café Fanatic** rewards card; you'll get every sixth specialty coffee free.

In addition to beverages, Cove Café has a self-serve refrigerated case stocked with small bites. Breakfast items usually include plain and chocolate croissants, Danish pastries, and fresh fruit. Afternoon and evening snacks consist of assorted cookies, brownies, cakes, crackers, and fruit.

Served for a couple of hours, the nighttime appetizer selections are our favorite: prosciutto, dried sausages, marinated olives, cheeses, bread, and the like. You can make a light supper out of these, and because most families are either at dinner or preparing for it, you may have the café to yourself.

COMMENTS The Wi-Fi signal here is fairly strong, making it a good spot to catch up on email or the latest news. This is a big part of Cove Café's appeal: the ability to sit in a comfy chair, sip coffee, and read in blessed silence, surrounded by $350 million of luxury cruise ship.

ACROSS THE SHIPS All DCL ships have a Cove Café. The finishes are slightly different across the ships, but all are similarly cozy. Guests at Cove Café must be at least age 18 to enter and at least 21 to drink alcohol.

Soul Cat Lounge   LOCATION DECK 3 AFT

SETTING AND ATMOSPHERE The former Promenade Lounge became the Soul Cat Lounge during a 2023 dry dock. The new decor is meant to evoke a jazz club, with music posters and framed records on the walls. The furniture is a mix of café tables with classic bentwood hairpin side chairs and leather club chairs and banquettes. The flooring is a blonde-wood dance floor and areas of red carpeting with a piano key motif.

SELECTIONS The signature drink is the Half Note Smoked Old Fashioned. Also try the tableside presentation of custom Manhattans and martinis. Zero-proof options include the Lollipop Jar (Bodyarmor orange mango, Simply Smoothie mango pineapple, Aha sparkling lime + watermelon, and a Pop Rocks Dips strawberry rim) and the Maple Blast (Häagen-Dazs caramel cone ice cream with hazelnut chocolate and maple syrup). The featured sweet treat is a New York–style zeppole (a beignet-like fritter) with a very light dusting of powdered sugar and cinnamon.

COMMENTS Because the lounge is located between Lumiere's and Rapunzel's Royal Table, it's a high-traffic area; unfortunately, this means it can be noisy. Nighttime entertainment is usually provided by a musical duo, such as a pianist and vocalist, but it has to be like performing in Grand Central Station due to the din from outside. We recommend Soul Cat as a meeting place for groups to get a drink before dinner at **Lumiere's** (page 216) or to listen to live music with a nightcap.

ACROSS THE SHIPS The sister area on the *Wonder* is the **French Quarter Lounge** (page 298). The similar but much smaller lounge on the *Dream* and *Fantasy* is **Bon Voyage** (page 300). On the *Wish,* the most centrally located bar is **The Bayou** (page 311); it's **Skipper Society** (page 318) on the *Treasure* and **The Sanctum** (page 320) on the *Destiny*.

Signals LOCATION DECK 9 MIDSHIP

SETTING AND ATMOSPHERE Signals is an adults-only outdoor bar next to the adult pool. It has a few seats for those looking to get some shade, but most patrons take their drinks back to their deck chairs to sip in the sun.

SELECTIONS Much of Signals' menu is devoted to beers and frozen drinks, but the bartenders can whip up almost anything you can think of. Signals also serves coffee, juices, and bottled water. Soda machines are nearby.

COMMENTS Signals doesn't offer much atmosphere, but because it's near the Quiet Cove Pool, it's a little less hectic than other bars.

ACROSS THE SHIPS Only the *Magic* and *Wonder* have Signals. The *Dream* and *Fantasy* each have two poolside equivalents, **Currents** (page 301) and **Waves** (page 302). The *Wish*-class ships also have Currents, along with **The Lookout** (page 314). Drinks and service are comparable at all of these, but we think Currents has the best views. Of the poolside bars, Waves is the only one that permits guests under age 18.

AFTER HOURS

This is DCL's name for the collection of bars on the *Magic*'s Deck 3 Forward: **Fathoms,** a dance club; **Keys,** a piano bar; and **O'Gills Pub,** a sports bar. (These bars get higher reader-satisfaction ratings than those found elsewhere on the ship.) After Hours has an urban-nightclub theme, pulled together by a white-and-silver color scheme.

Some After Hours lounges, such as Fathoms, have family-oriented entertainment during the day, but after 9 p.m. all usually have an adults-only policy (age 18 and up to enter, 21 and up to drink).

After Hours' bars generally carry the same wines and beers, though each serves its own unique line of cocktails. O'Gills also serves a collection of Irish beers not found elsewhere.

Fathoms LOCATION DECK 3 FORWARD

SETTING AND ATMOSPHERE Fathoms has an undersea theme: fiber-optic light fixtures shaped like jellyfish, sand-art murals along the bar, and silver-and-black bench seating that evokes ocean waves. Six sets of couches are built into the back wall, providing an excellent semiprivate view of the entertainment stage. The middle of the club holds a dance floor and a stage with a professional sound system and lighting. Armchairs upholstered in silver fabric are arranged in groups of two or three around cocktail tables. These help control the echo in Fathoms' large, open floor plan.

SELECTIONS Sea-themed cocktails make up most of Fathoms' bar menu, with beer, wine, and spirits also available. Expect to find lots of fruity drinks made with blue curaçao, orange liqueur, and muddled citrus.

COMMENTS Like other DCL nightclubs, Fathoms does double duty during the day by hosting family-oriented activities, such as scavenger hunts, bingo, and talent shows. At night the stage hosts everything from live music and karaoke to performances by comedians and magicians.

ACROSS THE SHIPS Fathoms doesn't have an identical sibling on the other ships, but it's most similar to **Azure** on the *Wonder* (page 298), **Evolution** on the *Dream* (page 304), **The Tube** on the *Fantasy* (page 310), **Luna** on the *Wish* (page 314), **Sarabi** on the *Treasure* (page 318), and **Saga** on the *Destiny* (page 320).

Keys LOCATION DECK 3 FORWARD

SETTING AND ATMOSPHERE Keys features live piano music nightly. Six large porthole windows run along one of the rectangular room's long walls. The bar is in the middle of the opposite wall, and the pianist is between the two, at the far end of the room from the entrance doors.

Keys' theming is supposed to evoke nightspots of Hollywood's Golden Age, circa the late 1940s and early 1950s. The furnishings include midcentury-modern sofas and chairs with curved, radius-style arms and backs. Carpeting is a crisp silver with geometric sunbursts. Over the bar area is a columned pavilion topped with panels of stylized piano keys.

SELECTIONS The bar menu includes specialty drinks with musically themed names, such as the Moji-Do, a mojito, and the Bloody Mi-Re, a Bloody Mary with vodka, yellow-tomato juice, lime, and whiskey-flavored Worcestershire sauce. Cocktail prices are comparable to those at the other bars on the ship, but a specialty drink is typically offered for several dollars more, such as a Manhattan made with top-shelf liquors like Jack Daniel's Sinatra Select whiskey and Carpano Antica Formula vermouth. Coffee, cappuccino, and espresso are also available, but for those we recommend **Cove Café** (page 294).

COMMENTS Live entertainment usually begins with a show around 7:30 p.m.; a typical night's schedule will have more performances around 9:30, 10:30, and 11:30. The talented pianists play medleys of well-known songs by familiar artists. Some nights have themes, such as Elvis or Simon and Garfunkel, but you can always submit requests.

During the day, Keys is often used for group seminars on everything from wine and spirits to acupuncture. The bar typically opens anywhere from 5:30 to 6:30 p.m.; check the DCL Navigator app for hours on your sailing. Children are admitted to Keys until 9 p.m., when it becomes an adults-only venue until its midnight closing.

ACROSS THE SHIPS Keys is most similar to the **Cadillac Lounge** on the *Wonder* (page 299). The entertainment is the same, but Cadillac Lounge's decor is on the gimmicky side (albeit well done). **Nightingale's** on the *Wish* (page 314) is DCL's most elegant take on a piano bar.

O'Gills Pub   LOCATION DECK 3 FORWARD

SETTING AND ATMOSPHERE This bar's name is a nod to the Disney classic *Darby O'Gill and the Little People,* starring Sean Connery, which is set in Ireland. And while it sounds like it's an Irish pub, it's really a sports bar, with wall-mounted televisions providing live satellite coverage of whatever sports are being played around the world.

Comfortable burgundy leather banquettes and leather armchairs form cozy nooks along one wall. In the middle of the room, about a dozen bar-height tables and stools provide the best views of most TVs.

SELECTIONS The bar menu includes a beer flight of 5.5-ounce Irish brews. There's also a selection of Irish whiskeys (and cocktails made with them), as well as standard beers, wines, and a full bar. We like to sip an Irish coffee here after dinner when we're sailing in Northern Europe. Another nice choice is the Gin Tea Tonic (Hendrick's gin, cherry marzipan–flavored tea, and The King's Ginger liqueur), served from a pretty china teapot, with a macaron on the side. It's like you're drinking with royalty.

COMMENTS O'Gills is a comfy spot to sit, sip, and watch the game. Complimentary snacks like chips, crudités, small sandwiches, and pigs in a blanket are often available at night—enough for a light dinner. More-substantial items (bangers and mash, for example) are available at an extra cost, but we've found that ordering these could take up to an hour.

ACROSS THE SHIPS O'Gills is also located on the *Fantasy* (page 308), but the televisions are larger at this one. The other ships' upscale sports bars are the *Wonder*'s **Crown & Fin Pub** (page 299), the *Dream*'s **Pub 687** (page 305), the *Wish*'s **Keg & Compass** (page 313), the *Treasure*'s **Periscope Pub** (page 317), and the *Destiny*'s **Cask and Cannon** (page 319).

PALO Adults on the *Magic* and *Wonder* also have the option of grabbing a before- or after-dinner drink at Palo (see page 216 for information on the dress code and page 205 for booking information). When Palo is open for dinner, guests may sit at the bar, which is full service and offers a view of the open kitchen. Because many people don't realize they can do this, you could find yourself with the counter all to yourself. We love sitting there because it's quiet and you can talk to the waitstaff as they bring in drink orders for their tables. Because of the brunch setup during the day, bar service is available only during dinner.

Disney Wonder

Cove Café   LOCATION DECK 9 MIDSHIP

COMMENTS See the profile of Cove Café on the *Magic* (page 294).

French Quarter Lounge LOCATION DECK 3 AFT

SETTING AND ATMOSPHERE French Quarter Lounge complements **Tiana's Place,** the ship's *Princess and the Frog*-inspired dining room (page 219). Live music is performed on a gazebo stage, and there are themed activities for everyone in the family. The decor incorporates New Orleans–style design cues, such as wrought-iron balconies, lampposts evocative of those in the Vieux Carré, and a seating area inside a replica of one of the city's famed green-and-red streetcars.

SELECTIONS The soft drinks, coffees, cocktails, and snacks all have a decidedly New Orleans flavor. From Louisiana-based Abita Brewing Company, Purple Haze Lager, Strawberry Lager, and Big Easy IPA are available on tap, along with Andygator Doppelbock and Hop-On, Maison Blanc, and Turbodog bottled ales. For kids and teetotalers, there's root beer and vanilla cream soda. If you're in need of caffeine—and maybe some sugar—order a NOLA Café (that is, a regular cup of coffee) or café au lait (hot or frozen) in traditional, caramel, mocha, and vanilla variations. Get in a Mardi Gras mood with a Hurricane, Cajun Bloody Mary, Lillet Cocktail, or Sazerac.

The snack menu features beignets—the square, deep-fried, powdered sugar-dusted spin on a doughnut; they're not as good as the real New Orleans version, but they'll do in a pinch. Order them in single, double, or triple batches, or opt for La Bouff Favorite: a coffee of your choice with a shot of Evangeline praline liqueur on the side, plus two beignets, a chocolate truffle, a macaron, and a madeleine, along with chocolate or caramel dipping sauce.

COMMENTS If you're not into jazz, you'll probably have a better time over at **Cadillac Lounge** (page 299) or **Crown & Fin** (opposite page).

ACROSS THE SHIPS The approximate equivalent on the *Magic* is **Soul Cat Lounge** (page 294). The *Dream* and *Fantasy* have **Bon Voyage** (page 300) in a similar location, but they're much smaller. The menu at **The Bayou** on the *Wish* (page 311) is substantially similar to the French Quarter Lounge's, but the theme there is a New Orleans garden.

Signals LOCATION DECK 9 MIDSHIP

COMMENTS See the profile of Signals on the *Magic* (page 295).

AFTER HOURS

Like its counterpart on the *Magic* (see page 295), After Hours has a contemporary-nightclub theme. Some After Hours lounges are home to family-oriented entertainment during the day, but all usually have an adults-only policy (age 18 and up to enter, 21 and up to drink) after 9 p.m. After Hours' bars generally carry the same wines and beers, although each serves a unique line of cocktails.

Azure LOCATION DECK 3 FORWARD

SETTING AND ATMOSPHERE This is the *Wonder*'s dance club. The color palette of creams and blues is meant to evoke the sea.

SELECTIONS You'll find beer and wine along with some hard ciders and hard sodas. Cocktails are on the expensive side and include ingredients like sparkling sake, pomegranate puree, and elderflower liqueur.

COMMENTS The small stage will likely be the site of your bingo game during the day and some crew-facilitated partying and games in the evening.

ACROSS THE SHIPS Azure doesn't have an identical sibling on the other ships, but it's most similar to **Fathoms** on the *Magic* (page 296), **Evolution** on the *Dream* (page 304), **The Tube** on the *Fantasy* (page 310), **Luna** on the *Wish* (page 314), **Sarabi** on the *Treasure* (page 318), and **Saga** on the *Destiny* (page 320).

Cadillac Lounge LOCATION DECK 3 FORWARD

SETTING AND ATMOSPHERE This is the ship's piano bar. The decor pays tribute to 1950s-era Cadillac cars by way of leather-upholstered barstools and chairs, couches made to look like automobile rear seats, and a bar built into a replica of the front of a 1959 Cadillac Coupe de Ville.

"Designed by General Motors" isn't a concept that we normally associate with bar theming, but it works well in this case. The furnishings clearly call to mind a very specific time and place: dark woods; carpets in hues of burgundy, gold, and fuchsia; leather-covered walls; chrome accents; and those butter- and chocolate-colored leather barstools.

The best seats in the house are in the far corner, opposite the main entrance and to the right of the piano player. These include a comfortable leather couch and two leather armchairs, plus a side table to hold drinks. From here you can listen to music and watch some of the action at the bar, tucked away in your own discreet corner of the lounge.

SELECTIONS Cadillac Lounge serves beer, wine, spirits, and cocktails, and it's the only bar in After Hours that serves Champagne by the glass. The signature cocktails here are the Twenty One Rob Roy (Johnnie Walker XR 21 Scotch, Carpano Antica Formula vermouth, and bitters) and the Ketel One Experience for Two (Ketel One vodka, jasmine tea, and Cabernet Sauvignon ice wine). Coffee, cappuccino, and espresso are also available, but for those we recommend the **Cove Café** (see page 294).

COMMENTS Live entertainment usually begins with a show around 7:30 p.m.; a typical night's schedule will have more performances around 9:30, 10:30, and 11:30. The talented pianists play medleys of well-known songs by familiar artists. Some nights have themes, such as Elvis or Simon and Garfunkel. Plus, you can always make requests.

During the day, Cadillac Lounge is often used for group seminars on everything from wine and spirits to acupuncture. The bar typically opens anywhere from 5:30 to 6:30 p.m.; check the Navigator app for hours on your sailing. Children are admitted to Cadillac Lounge until 9 p.m., when it becomes an adults-only venue until its midnight closing.

ACROSS THE SHIPS Cadillac Lounge is most similar to the *Magic*'s **Keys** (page 296). The entertainment is interchangeable between the two, but Keys' retro-Hollywood decor is more restrained. **Nightingale's** on the *Wish* (page 314) is DCL's most elegant take on a piano bar.

Crown & Fin Pub LOCATION DECK 3 FORWARD

SETTING AND ATMOSPHERE Crown & Fin is the *Wonder*'s sports bar, modeled after an English tavern. The space is adorned with dark woods, plush leather furniture, and brass accents. Subtle nods to classic Disney films set in London can be found in the artwork and props.

SELECTIONS Cocktails and British craft beers are on tap, and a pub-grub menu is available for an extra charge. In a world with an abundance of free food, we're not sure why you'd want to pay for a German pretzel in a British bar, but sometimes the sea makes you do things you shouldn't.

COMMENTS Given that you're on a large cruise ship, the odds are good that you'll be able to find other fans of your favorite teams on board. In addition to televised sports, Crown & Fin hosts family-oriented and adult activities throughout the day, ranging from Disney-character-drawing classes for kids to trivia contests and afternoon beer tastings. Check the Navigator app for the schedule.

ACROSS THE SHIPS Crown & Fin is comparable to the clubby sports bars on the other ships: **O'Gills** on the *Magic* and *Fantasy* (pages 297 and 308, respectively), **Keg & Compass** on the *Wish* (page 313), **Periscope Pub** on the *Treasure* (page 317), and **Cask and Cannon** on the *Destiny* (page 319). We're pretty sure we'd be happy to watch the big game here or just while away a sea day nursing a pint of beer and playing checkers.

PALO As on the *Magic*, adults on the *Wonder* have the option of grabbing a before- or after-dinner drink at Palo (see page 216 for information on the dress code and page 205 for booking information). When Palo is open for dinner, guests may sit at the bar, which is full service and offers a view of the open kitchen. Because many people don't realize they can do this, you could find yourself with the counter all to yourself. We love it because it's quiet and you can talk to the waitstaff while they bring in drink orders for their tables. Because of the brunch setup during the day, bar service is available only during dinner.

Disney Dream

Bon Voyage   LOCATION DECK 3 MIDSHIP

SETTING AND ATMOSPHERE Sitting just off the atrium, Bon Voyage is one of the prettiest, and smallest, of the *Dream*'s (and *Fantasy*'s) bars, with just 10 seats at the counter plus 4 armchairs a few feet away. The two highlights here are the gorgeous Art Deco mural behind the bar and the swirled, maize-yellow, illuminated bar face, which reflects golden light off the beige-marble floors on the *Dream*. The *Fantasy*'s version has the same Art Nouveau style as the rest of the ship, and behind the bar are two gold-and-white peacocks etched in glass, while the bar's face is a translucent gold marble. Unfortunately, the lovely decor doesn't make up for the noisy location: the bar is in a heavily trafficked area that makes quiet conversation difficult.

SELECTIONS Bon Voyage's bar menu is similar to that in **The District** (page 303) and includes draft and bottled beer; wines by the glass and bottle; spirits; and mixed drinks, including a few special fruit-flavored martinis. Service is excellent.

COMMENTS Open from midday to late evening, Bon Voyage is a good place for groups to meet up before dinner. However, it's not conducive to much more than a quick cocktail due to the noise outside—which also makes live entertainment a no-go here.

ACROSS THE SHIPS The *Fantasy* also has a Bon Voyage just off the Deck 3 atrium. **Soul Cat Lounge** is the comparable bar on the *Magic* (page 294), and the approximate equivalent on the *Wonder* is the **French Quarter Lounge** (page 298). On the *Wish,* the most centrally located bar is **The Bayou** (page 311); it's **Skipper Society** on the *Treasure* (page 318), and **The Sanctum** on the *Destiny* (page 320)—the theming is different in each one.

Cove Café   LOCATION   DECK 11 FORWARD

COMMENTS See the profile of Cove Café on the *Magic* (page 294).

Currents   LOCATION   DECK 13 FORWARD

SETTING AND ATMOSPHERE This outdoor space has the best views of any bar on the *Dream.* Built behind and into the structure supporting the forward stairs and elevators, the curved, glossy-white face of the bar mimics the curve along the opposite deck rail and provides shade during the day. Currents is lovely at night, when a royal-blue neon sign with CURRENTS rendered in a retro-looking script (think a nameplate on a 1950s car) lights up the bar and bar shelves, accented with matching blue tile.

Stationary barstools are spaced far enough apart for easy access to walk-up traffic. Most guests take their drinks back to their lounge chairs, but there's also plenty of (unshaded) armchair seating.

SELECTIONS Currents serves standard-issue bottled and draft beer, cocktails, and frozen drinks.

COMMENTS The one downside to Currents is that it's next to a smoking section. Depending on the prevailing winds and your tolerance for smoke, this is either not an issue at all or a mild annoyance.

ACROSS THE SHIPS Currents is the same on the *Dream, Fantasy,* and *Wish*-class ships. **Signals** (page 295) on the *Magic* and *Wonder* is similar, but Currents' layout is more open, with much better views and nicer decor.

Meridian   LOCATION   DECK 12 AFT

SETTING AND ATMOSPHERE Situated between the adults-only restaurants Palo and Remy, Meridian is the *Dream*'s martini bar. It's also one of our favorite bars on the ship. Sitting high up on Deck 12 Aft, Meridian has windows on three sides of its relatively small, square room. Panoramic views of the sunset await early diners who stop in around dusk. Antique navigation maps and instruments adorn the walls and shelves. Furnishings include brown leather couches and armchairs, as well as cocoa-colored teak floors with brass inlays.

SELECTIONS Meridian's bar menu emphasizes mixed drinks and spirits over beer and wine, although those are also available, as are coffees. The best thing about Meridian is the bartending staff, who will often offer to make a custom martini for you on the spot. This usually starts with the bartender inquiring whether you like fruit- or herb-based drinks and what kinds of liquors you usually prefer. A couple of minutes of muddling, shaking, and stirring, and you have the first draft of your new drink. And if it's not quite what you expected, they'll be happy to start over.

Meridian also offers a cigar menu, with prices ranging from about $10 to about $45 for individual or small packages of cigars. The smoking area is nearby but outdoors (see page 169 for more information about smoking areas on the ships).

COMMENTS We recommend stopping by Meridian for its martini experience, even if you don't have reservations for Remy or Palo. If you're dining at Remy, though, beware of the one-two punch of Meridian's martinis and Remy's wine pairings.

Meridian usually opens around 5 p.m. and stays open until midnight. It's one of the few DCL nightspots with a dress code: Inside the lounge, men should wear dress shirts and pants, and women should wear dresses, skirts and blouses, or pantsuits. If you're just visiting the outdoor area, jeans and shorts are OK, but swimwear, T-shirts, and tank tops are no-nos.

ACROSS THE SHIPS The *Dream* and *Fantasy* have nearly identical Meridian lounges; the *Magic* and *Wonder* have no equivalent. Together with the two **Skyline** bars on the *Dream* (page 306) and *Fantasy,* the two Meridians rate at the top of reader-satisfaction polls across all DCL ships. **The Rose** (page 315) links the two adults-dining restaurants on the *Wish, Treasure,* and *Destiny* and is even more lush and lovely.

Vista Café   LOCATION DECK 4 MIDSHIP

SETTING AND ATMOSPHERE This small, Art Deco–themed nook is tucked into a corner of Deck 4.

SELECTIONS Vista Café serves everything from coffee and free pastries in the morning to beer, wine, cocktails, and light snacks at night.

COMMENTS With just four seats at the bar, this isn't the place for large groups. It's most useful as a place for a family to get a drink and a bite to eat on their way to one of the day's activities on Decks 3 or 4.

ACROSS THE SHIPS Vista Cafés can be found on the *Dream* and *Fantasy* (but not the *Magic* or *Wonder*). Both locations offer the same food and drink and are about the same size; the only significant difference is the decor—the Vista on the *Fantasy* has that ship's Art Nouveau theme rather than the Art Deco styling of the *Dream.*

Waves   LOCATION DECK 12 AFT

SETTING AND ATMOSPHERE Tucked behind the rear smokestack, Waves is an outdoor bar catering primarily to sunbathers on Deck 12. Its eight fixed barstools are arranged around an attractive bar with a white tile face, and the back of the bar is decorated with mosaic tiles in varying shades of blue. An overhang provides some shade for guests seated or standing at the bar, but most of the seating—glossy, curved-back teak booths with upholstered blue cushions, plus various sets of tables and chairs—is directly in the sun.

SELECTIONS The most popular drinks at Waves are bottled beers, frozen cocktails, and mixed drinks. Nonalcoholic smoothies and fruit juices are available for children and teetotalers.

COMMENTS Waves' hours vary, but it's usually open from late morning to late evening. Most visitors come from the lounge chairs or sports activities on Deck 13; some are just looking for a quiet spot away from the crowds.

ACROSS THE SHIPS The *Dream* and *Fantasy* have Waves. **Signals** (page 295) is the outdoor bar on the *Magic* and *Wonder*. Waves is quieter, has nicer decor, and welcomes kids, while Signals is for guests age 21 and up only. On the *Wish*-class ships, the closest equivalents are **Currents** (page 307) and **The Lookout** (page 314).

THE DISTRICT

This is the designation for the five bars and lounges on the *Dream*'s Deck 4 Aft: **District Lounge,** a piano bar in a hallway connecting the different venues; **Evolution,** a dance club; **Pink,** a Champagne bar; **Pub 687,** an upscale sports bar; and **Skyline,** a cosmopolitan watering hole.

The theming is meant to evoke images of exclusive urban nightlife. Along the faux-brick walls and behind velvet ropes are black-plastic silhouettes of couples "waiting" to get in.

Most of The District's bars open between 5 and 5:30 p.m. and stay open until midnight (check the Navigator app for hours on your sailing). District Lounge usually opens a little earlier; Evolution operates from around 10 p.m. to 2 a.m. Hot appetizers are usually served throughout the evening in one of The District's circular walkways.

Evolution, Pink, and Skyline admit guests age 18 and up only. Families are welcome at District Lounge and Pub 687 until 9 p.m., when the bars become adults-only.

District Lounge   LOCATION DECK 4 AFT

SETTING AND ATMOSPHERE A walkway connecting The District's bars runs between this attractive, contemporary bar and its seating area. The bar seats six along its curving, white-stone front. Lights hidden beneath the black-marble top point down, creating smoky gray shadows in the stone. Behind the bar is a bronze-colored wall; orange lighting illuminates the bottles and embues this side of the lounge with its most prominent color.

A lounge with couches and armchairs sits across the walkway from the bar; although it's not perfect, it's one of the more stylish places on the *Dream*. While the lounge is completely open to (and exposed to noise from) guests passing through, cocoa-colored carpeting, off-white leather couches, and Champagne-colored metal poles provide a visual boundary. Deeper inside are U-shaped armchairs, upholstered in the same off-white leather outside and in deep-brown leather inside, arranged in groups of four around small tables.

SELECTIONS A little bit of everything: draft and bottled beer, cocktails, frozen drinks, whiskeys and tequilas, and wine and Champagne by the glass. The signature drink takes its name from the bar: The District is hyped on the menu as "inspired by the Prohibition era" and "prepared in secret," but in a nutshell, you tell the bartender if you want dark or light alcohol and something fruity, herby, or plain, and they'll concoct a custom cocktail for you. A few nonalcoholic drinks and coffees are available as well.

COMMENTS The best seats are along the lounge's inside wall, where you can relax in those deep armchairs while you watch everyone else shuttle between clubs. The lounge is the best vantage point from which to watch District Lounge's entertainment, which includes live singers and pianists later at night, and it's also a good meeting place to start out the evening, especially for groups who haven't decided which of The District's bars they want to visit.

ACROSS THE SHIPS District Lounge roughly corresponds to the Venetian-themed **La Piazza** on the *Fantasy* (page 309) but has no relative on the *Magic, Wonder,* or *Wish*-class ships. We like District Lounge more than La Piazza: its recessed seating allows you to enjoy a drink away from the bustle of clubgoers walking to their next destination.

Evolution   LOCATION DECK 4 AFT

SETTING AND ATMOSPHERE According to Disney, Evolution is designed as "an artistic interpretation of the transformation of a butterfly . . . emerging from a chrysalis." What this entails is a lot of yellow, orange, and red lights arranged in the shape of butterfly wings and hung around the club. Pairs of wings also hang above the dance floor, and we'll forgive you for comparing slightly tipsy dancing tourists to wriggling pupae.

Fortunately, most of the butterfly business is concentrated around the dance floor and along a couple of back walls. Between the two, it's not as noticeable; plastic-shell chairs sit in the dimly lit sections, occasionally alongside high-backed couches. Short barstools line the edge of the room, surrounding small, round tables. The circular bar has gold-leather seats on one side, allowing guests a view of the dance floor while they drink; the other half of the bar is for walk-up traffic.

SELECTIONS Evolution's drink menu is similar to the District Lounge's, offering draft and bottled beer, cocktails, spirits, and wine and Champagne by the glass and bottle.

COMMENTS Because it's one of the largest venues on the *Dream,* Evolution is the site of family activities throughout the day, hosting everything from hands-on crafting seminars and tequila tastings to time-share presentations. Evolution's adults-only entertainment usually starts later than it does at other bars in The District, around 10 or 10:30 p.m.; check the Navigator app for the hours on your sailing.

Live entertainment includes magicians, comics, singers, and more. In addition to live acts, the dance club's DJs sometimes dedicate an entire night's music to a specific genre. Common themes include classic rock, disco, and something called urban country.

ACROSS THE SHIPS Evolution is most similar to **The Tube** on the *Fantasy* (page 310), **Fathoms** on the *Magic* (page 296), **Azure** on the *Wonder* (page 298), **Luna** on the *Wish* (page 314), **Sarabi** on the *Treasure* (page 318), and **Saga** on the *Destiny* (page 320), although there is no direct equivalent. We rate Evolution as the second-best dance club on DCL's ships, behind The Tube. Theming, lighting, and seating are nicer than at Fathoms and Azure, while The Tube's London Underground ambience is better executed than Evolution's more conceptual theme.

Pink   LOCATION DECK 4 AFT

SETTING AND ATMOSPHERE Pink, the *Dream*'s Champagne bar, is one of our favorite nightspots on the ship. Decorated in silver, white, and gold, the space is intended to make you think you're sitting inside a glass of Champagne. In the walls are embedded round lights of white and pink, tiny near the floor and larger near the ceiling, imitating the carbon dioxide fizz inside a flute of bubbly. The silver carpet's starburst pattern calls to mind bubbles rising from below, and the rounded, glossy-white ceiling is meant to represent the top of the glass. The light fixtures are upside-down Champagne flutes. Behind the bar are a multitude of glass "bubbles" that fan out as they rise from the bar to the ceiling.

Around the bar are half a dozen stools, with silver legs and clear, round plastic backs that continue the bubble theme. Beyond the bar, most of the seating is plush pink velvet, like you're living inside a bottle of rosé. The best seats in the house, though, are on the gold-toned sofa inside a dome-shaped cubby in the wall at one end of the lounge. Move a couple of those big chairs in front and you have a private little cocoon, or slide them away for a view of the entire room.

SELECTIONS Pink's Champagne menu includes many recognizable names: Cristal, Moët & Chandon, Taittinger, Veuve Clicquot, and the requisite Dom Pérignon. Champagne-based cocktails are also available; most include fruit juices, such as mango, pomegranate, and peach, while a few include other liquors—the Elderbubble, for example, contains raspberry vodka along with Champagne and elderflower syrup. A small selection of white, red, and dessert wines is available by the glass (more by the bottle), along with a dozen or so whiskeys and Cognacs.

COMMENTS If you love Champagne, Pink is a relative bargain. We estimate that its bottle markup is less than twice the average retail price—and often considerably less than what Disney charges at its theme park resorts.

ACROSS THE SHIPS You can get Champagne and Champagne cocktails on all the Disney ships; however, only the *Dream* and *Fantasy* have dedicated Champagne bars. We like Pink's understated theming better than the *très féminine* French-boudoir decor of **Ooh La La** on the *Fantasy* (page 308).

Pub 687 LOCATION DECK 4 AFT

SETTING AND ATMOSPHERE Anytime you see a venue with a dozen flat-screen TVs, chances are it's a sports bar. On the *Dream* it's called Pub 687, and screens are located above the bar, in a cluster at one end of the room, and individually in some seating areas.

Four porthole windows across from the bar let in light during the day, and moss-colored couches beneath them serve to partition the wall into seating areas. The scarlet, green, and gold carpet and burgundy-painted, wood-paneled walls give Pub 687 a more masculine feel than the sports bars on the *Fantasy, Magic,* and *Wonder.*

Besides the couches, barstools and tables are arranged around the room to provide good views of the televisions. A few leather-covered armchairs are also arranged around the screens and across from the couches. There's plenty of room to stand between these, too, in case you just want to catch up on some scores. Couches arranged in some of the corners provide quieter spots to unwind.

SELECTIONS The menu is similar to those at the sports bars on the other ships. There's a small wine and cocktail selection (though there's also a full bar and they'll make almost anything), but the focus is on beer, with more than a dozen varieties on tap and more available by the bottle.

The signature cocktail list consists of two drinks: the Shipbuilder's Wife (Absolut Pears vodka, limoncello, grappa, agave, and lemon juice) and the Keel (Maker's Mark bourbon, Campari liqueur, limoncello, orange juice, and fresh ginger, with a mint garnish). Among the beers are Lindemans Framboise Lambic and Trappist Ale.

The pub grub (available for an extra charge) includes sliders, wings, loaded potato tots, and chips and dip; you can also get free chicken fingers and fries from the pool deck and order a Bud Light if you want to watch some football the old-fashioned way (and we often do).

COMMENTS We've spent a few evenings watching games at Pub 687. The seating is comfortable, and it's easy to see and hear the action on the screens. Because of the way the seating is arranged, however, we've found it difficult to start conversations with other patrons. Try sitting at the bar if conviviality is important to you. Besides sporting events, Pub 687 hosts family activities during the day, including movie, music, and sports trivia.

ACROSS THE SHIPS We find Pub 687 more upscale than **Crown & Fin** on the *Wonder* (page 299) or **O'Gills** on the *Magic* (page 297) and *Fantasy* (page 308). While its seating isn't as open, it's a posh place to catch up on the day's highlights in relative quiet. The *Wish*'s **Keg & Compass** (page 313) is similar to the other sports bars but with more-nautical decor. The sports bar on the *Treasure* is **Periscope Pub** (page 317), and on the *Destiny* it's **Cask and Cannon** (page 319).

Skyline LOCATION DECK 4 AFT

SETTING AND ATMOSPHERE Along with Pink, Skyline is one of our two favorite bars on the *Dream*. The idea is that you're in a lounge high on the edge of some of the world's most famous cities. Behind the bar are seven "windows"—large HD video screens—depicting panoramic views of New York City, Chicago, Rio de Janeiro, Paris, and Hong Kong.

Each city is shown for about 15 minutes across all seven screens; then the scene changes to another locale. The foreground of each view includes close-ups of apartments and offices, while the middle and background show each city's iconic architecture and landscape.

That would be mildly interesting scenery on its own, but Disney has added special effects that make Skyline beautiful. Each view shows the city in motion: Cars move along streets, neon signs blink to illuminate sidewalks, and apartment lights go on and off as their residents come and go. (Look closely and you can even see Mickey Mouse waving to you from inside a tiny apartment in Paris.) Another interesting touch is that the scenery changes depending on the time of day you're there. In late afternoon, you'll see the sun setting on these towns. Stay long enough—and we have—and dusk turns to evening, then evening to night.

Lastly, Skyline has mirrors on the walls perpendicular to the video screens. The mirrors reflect the screens and make the bar look longer than it is. The rest of the decor is natural surfaces: wood panels, ceiling, and floors, in colors ranging from honey to mahogany; dark marble countertops; and leather chairs.

SELECTIONS The specialty is "around the world" cocktails themed to the featured cities. For example, the 1914, representing Chicago, pairs Absolut Vanilla and Absolut Kurant vodkas with fresh blackberries and raspberries; the Zen-Chanted, representing Hong Kong, is made with 3Vodka (distilled from soybeans), Zen green-tea liqueur, Cointreau orange liqueur, and guava and lime juices.

COMMENTS Adding movement to the scenery means the view at Skyline doesn't get boring. It also means that the club doesn't need a television to hold its patrons' attention.

ACROSS THE SHIPS Although there are Skylines on both the *Dream* and the *Fantasy,* their drink menus are mostly different. Drinks on the *Dream*'s version tend more toward the fruity, whereas drinks at the *Fantasy*'s **Skyline** (page 306) make more use of herbs and spices, such as basil, coriander, and cilantro.

Disney Fantasy

Bon Voyage   LOCATION DECK 3 MIDSHIP

COMMENTS See profile of Bon Voyage on the *Dream* (page 300).

Cove Café   LOCATION DECK 11 FORWARD

COMMENTS See profile of Cove Café on the *Magic* (page 294).

Currents   LOCATION DECK 13 FORWARD

COMMENTS See profile of Currents on the *Dream* (page 301).

Meridian   LOCATION DECK 12 AFT

COMMENTS See profile of Meridian on the *Dream* (page 301).

Vista Café   LOCATION DECK 4 MIDSHIP

COMMENTS See profile of Vista Café on the *Dream*. (page 302)

Waves   LOCATION DECK 12 AFT

COMMENTS See profile of Waves on the *Dream* (page 302).

EUROPA

THIS IS THE DESIGNATION for the five nightspots on the *Fantasy*'s Deck 4 Aft: **O'Gills Pub,** a sports bar; **Ooh La La,** a Champagne bar; **La Piazza,** an Italian-inspired lounge; **Skyline,** a cosmopolitan watering hole; and **The Tube,** a London subway–themed dance club.

While the nightlife districts on the *Magic, Wonder,* and *Dream* have distinctive theming, Europa has next to none. The ostensible theme is Europe, but the decor consists mostly of just shiny gold walls on which each club's name is illuminated and repeated. That said, one nice touch found only at Europa is the round black-and-white photos on the walls: The images, which feature European icons, including the Eiffel Tower, Big Ben, and the Leaning Tower of Pisa, turn into short animated videos.

Most of Europa's bars open between 5 and 5:30 p.m. and stay open until midnight (check the Navigator app for hours on your sailing). La Piazza usually opens a little earlier than that; The Tube operates from around 10 p.m. to 2 a.m. Hot appetizers are usually served throughout the evening in one of La Piazza's circular pedestrian walkways.

Ooh La La, Skyline, and The Tube admit guests age 18 and up only. Families are welcome at La Piazza and O'Gills Pub until 9 p.m., when they become adults-only.

O'Gills Pub LOCATION DECK 4 AFT

SETTING AND ATMOSPHERE O'Gills, the *Fantasy*'s sports bar, lies just off one side of La Piazza (see next page). It's supposed to be an Irish pub, but it's the least visually interesting bar in Europa. With some paint, antiques-store scavenging, and the right beer-of-the-month subscription, O'Gills would be right at home in Chicago, Dallas, or Green Bay.

A huge video screen in the back corner shows sporting events and sports news all day long. Several other smaller screens are distributed throughout the room, and there's plenty of seating and standing room.

SELECTIONS The bar menu features bottled and draft beer, including a house draft lager and several Irish brews. Wine is available by the glass and bottle, and the friendly bartenders can mix up virtually any cocktail you want. The specialty is Irish whiskey and Scotch; a private-label Irish cream liqueur is on the menu too.

COMMENTS You wouldn't come here for the Irish ambience, but as a generic sports bar, O'Gills isn't bad.

ACROSS THE SHIPS There's another O'Gills on the *Magic* (page 297). As a sports bar, however, it's similar to **Pub 687** on the *Dream* (page 305), **Crown & Fin** on the *Wonder* (page 299), and **Keg & Compass** on the *Wish* (page 313). We prefer Pub 687, the O'Gills on the *Magic,* and Crown & Fin over the *Fantasy*'s O'Gills because they have better sight lines to the TV screens from the seating areas. The *Treasure*'s sports bar is **Periscope Pub** (page 317), and the *Destiny*'s is **Cask and Cannon** (page 319).

Ooh La La LOCATION DECK 4 AFT

SETTING AND ATMOSPHERE This is the *Fantasy*'s Champagne bar. The French-boudoir theming—rose-colored fabric on the walls, purple carpet, and chairs lined with gold fabric—is enough to make you break out in "Lady Marmalade" as performed in *Moulin Rouge*. Along one wall is a series of couches in ivory and green. Gold-edged mirrors and fleurs-de-lis line the walls. A single red chair and a couple of small, red-topped side tables provide a touch of bold color.

The bar, at the far end of the lounge, seats six around its black marble top. In keeping with the boudoir theme, the mirror behind the bar looks like an oversize version of one you might find on the dressing table of a fashionable Frenchwoman at the *fin de siècle.* And because it's a Champagne bar, hundreds of small glass bubbles fill the mirrors.

SELECTIONS The menu here is virtually identical to the one at **Pink** on the *Dream.* Bubbly by the glass starts at about $9 and goes up to $60; bottles start at about $80 and go up to $500. If you're in the mood for something more indulgent—and you have the dough—have the staff call upstairs to Remy, which has a few truly special bottles that sell for about $3,000 each.

Several of Ooh La La's offerings are Champagne cocktails, combining bubbly with fruit juices or liqueurs, but remember the Second Law of Champagne: If it needs another ingredient, then you're drinking the wrong

Champagne. (The First Law: Champagne goes with everything!) Sparkling wines, along with reds and whites, are available by the glass and bottle, and the fully stocked bar can furnish virtually any cocktail you like.

COMMENTS The best seats in Ooh La La are on the L-shaped silver couch near the main entrance. It's the perfect private place to do some people-watching. Another nice touch is the use of area rugs to mark off sections of seats—it's possible to mingle within that small area, having individual conversations while still being part of the group. The club also has three porthole windows with ocean views and seating below them. If you visit during the late afternoon, the light from outside provides a gentle transition from day to dusk.

ACROSS THE SHIPS You can get Champagne and Champagne cocktails on all the Disney ships; however, only the *Dream* and *Fantasy* have dedicated Champagne bars. We like the relatively understated theming of **Pink** on the *Dream* (page 304) better than the frilly decor of Ooh La La.

La Piazza LOCATION DECK 4 AFT

SETTING AND ATMOSPHERE This Venetian-themed lounge sits near the front of Europa. Appropriately, La Piazza ("The Plaza") serves as the walkway to O'Gills and Ooh La La, whose entrances sit just off this venue; farther beyond are Skyline and The Tube, so you'll walk by La Piazza on the way to those as well.

The bar sits in the middle of a bright, circular room. It's themed to look like an Italian merry-go-round, its ceiling decorated with hundreds of carousel lights. Around the bar are rose-colored barstools; lining the wall are golden, high-backed, upholstered couches with small tables for drinks. The couches are separated, elevated, and set into niches in the walls, making them good vantage points from which to watch people walk between the clubs.

SELECTIONS La Piazza's bar menu features Peroni and Moretti, two Italian beers, as well as prosecco (Italian sparkling wine) and limoncello (an Italian lemon-flavored liqueur). These ingredients also make their way into La Piazza's five signature cocktails: the Mercutio, for example, features Absolut Pears vodka, limoncello, grappa, and fresh lemon juice, with the sweetness of the pear and grappa balancing out the tartness of the citrus.

COMMENTS The couches are good places to watch La Piazza's live entertainment, which has been an up-tempo jazz trio on our most recent cruises. Our favorite pastime at La Piazza, however, takes place starting at 11 p.m., when we start to wager a round of drinks on the number of couples who will stop to take photos on the lounge's Vespa motorcycle-and-sidecar prop in the next 10 minutes. The over–under on that bet is usually 2.5, and the rules prohibit shouting encouragement to the *ubriachi*.

ACROSS THE SHIPS Somewhat similar to **District Lounge** on the *Dream* (page 303), La Piazza has a better drink menu, while District Lounge has a better layout. The *Magic, Wonder,* and *Wish*-class ships have no comparable bar.

Skyline LOCATION DECK 4 AFT

SETTING AND ATMOSPHERE Skyline is our favorite bar on the *Fantasy*. The concept is that you're in a lounge high on the edge of some of the world's most famous cities. Behind the bar are seven "windows"—large HD screens—depicting panoramic views of seven cities: Athens, Barcelona, Budapest, Florence, London, Paris, and St. Petersburg.

Each city is shown for about 15 minutes across all seven screens; then the scene changes to another locale. The foreground of each view includes close-ups of apartments and offices, while the middle and background show each city's iconic architecture and landscape.

That would be mildly interesting scenery on its own, but Disney has added special effects that make Skyline beautiful. Each view shows the city in motion: Cars move along streets, neon signs blink to illuminate sidewalks, and apartment lights go on and off as their residents come and go. (Look closely and you can even see Mickey Mouse waving to you from inside a tiny apartment in Paris.) Another interesting touch is that the scenery changes depending on the time of day you're there. In late afternoon, you'll see the sun setting on these towns. Stay long enough—and we have—and dusk turns to evening, then evening to night.

Lastly, Skyline has mirrors on the walls perpendicular to the video screens. Because the mirrors are set at right angles to the screens, they reflect the videos and make the bar look longer than it is. It's a well-known decorating trick for making a small room seem larger, but it's still nice to see it included here.

The rest of the decor is natural surfaces: wood panels, ceiling, and floors; dark marble countertops; and leather chairs.

SELECTIONS The specialty is "around the world" cocktails themed to the featured cities. For example, El Conquistador, representing Barcelona, pairs Tanqueray gin and Absolut Peppar vodka with fresh muddled strawberries, basil, and cracked black pepper; the Aquincum, representing Budapest, is made with Casamigos Reposado tequila, Grand Marnier, paprika, and fresh lime juice.

COMMENTS Adding movement to the scenery means the view at Skyline doesn't get boring. It also means that the club doesn't need a television to hold its patrons' attention.

ACROSS THE SHIPS Although there are Skylines on both the *Dream* and the *Fantasy,* the latter version features two more cities in its "windows" than Skyline on the *Dream.* Also, the bars' drink menus are mostly different. Drinks at the *Dream's* Skyline tend to be flavored with fruits and fruit juices, such as cranberry, pomegranate, lemon, and lime; drinks at the *Fantasy's* Skyline are made with fruits, too, but also with herbs and spices, such as basil, thyme, coriander, cilantro, and paprika.

The Tube LOCATION DECK 4 AFT

SETTING AND ATMOSPHERE With its London subway-meets–*Austin Powers* theme, The Tube is the *Fantasy's* dance club and is terrifically themed, in our opinion. Its decor includes leather couches with prints that look like Underground tickets, 1960s-mod egg-shaped chairs, and a floor painted like a subway map. We especially like the upholstered leather couch set deep inside the lounge: It's under a set of lights in the shape of a crown and across from two shiny silver armchairs designed to look like thrones. A couple of red phone booths are set on either side of the dance floor. *Oh, behave!*

SELECTIONS The Tube's circular bar, set under Big Ben's clock face, serves a typical menu of bottled beer, mixed drinks, spirits, and wine and Champagne by the glass. The Tube also serves six signature drinks, our favorite of which is Mind the Gap, a mix of whiskey, Drambuie, and Coke.

COMMENTS The Tube usually opens around 10 p.m. and sometimes gets things going with a quick game of Match Your Mate (think *The Newlywed Game*, only groovier). Dancing usually gets started around 10:30 or 11. Most of the music is contemporary dance tunes, but there are also themed nights with disco and, of course, British hits. If you want a good view of the stage, particularly if you have a large party, plan to arrive a few minutes early for nondance activities.

ACROSS THE SHIPS The club's closest counterparts are **Fathoms** on the *Magic* (page 296), **Azure** on the *Wonder* (page 298), **Evolution** on the *Dream* (page 304), **Luna** on the *Wish* (page 314), **Sarabi** on the *Treasure* (page 318), and **Saga** on the *Destiny* (page 320), although there is no direct equivalent. The Tube, though, is our favorite dance club on any of the ships.

Disney Wish

THE BARS AND LOUNGES on all the *Wish*-class ships are distributed around the ship—there's no dedicated "adult district," as there is on the first four Disney ships. Adults have plenty of spaces for relaxing with a cocktail, listening to live music, or watching sports. Curiously, though, the *Wish* doesn't have a nightclub that's directly comparable to Azure on the *Wonder*, The Tube on the *Fantasy*, and so on.

Luna and **Triton Lounge** serve first and foremost as daytime hubs for family activities and group seminars, similar to **D Lounge** on the other ships. Both venues serve alcohol at night and host some evening events for adults, including karaoke, game shows, trivia, and dance parties (silent and otherwise), but they rarely offer the kind of dance events you'd normally associate with the word *nightclub*.

unofficial **TIP**
No DCL ship is a party barge. That said, some adults may find the nightlife on the *Wish* more sedate than on the other ships.

Unique to the *Wish* is **Star Wars: Hyperspace Lounge** (see page 315), a smaller version of a similar experience, Oga's Cantina, at Walt Disney World and Disneyland. The drinks are pricey—one costs a jaw-dropping $5,000, though most are more earthbound than that. If you've already experienced the *Star Wars* nightclub at the theme parks, DCL's rendition will probably seem redundant.

The Bayou   LOCATION DECK 3 MIDSHIP

SETTING AND ATMOSPHERE Here, the setting is a New Orleans garden with flower-laden trees above. The velvet upholstery, in shades of green and burgundy, is elegant and indulgent. The Bayou is centrally located and open to foot traffic on two sides, making it the best place on the ship for people-watching (meaning lots of people pass by) and one of our favorite spaces on the *Wish*.

SELECTIONS The cocktails here have a decidedly New Orleans bent. They include an Absinthe Frappe (Pernod absinthe, anisette, and vanilla cream soda); the Cajun Michelada (Abita Amber Lager beer, Clamato, and Cajun spices); and a take on the classic Hurricane (Bayou Reserve rum, passion fruit, and lime). Nonalcoholic choices include sodas from Louisiana–based Abita Brewing Company. The King Cake Soda, for example, recalls the flavors of the traditional Mardi Gras confection—think a coffee cake or a cinnamon roll. The specialty coffees and fresh juices sold here are also available at other locations around the ship.

Speaking of sweets, beignets (for an extra charge) are featured on the Bayou menu. They're more baked from frozen than freshly fried, but they still do the trick when you need a little treat. We like Mama's Special: three beignets served with Valrhona chocolate sauce. In the mood for a morning pick-me-up? The Bayou has carts serving custom Bloody Marys and mimosas made with freshly squeezed juices.

COMMENTS The bar stops serving beignets an hour or two before closing. If that's what your heart is after, make sure to ask when the latest time to order is. There is also a fun off-menu frozen, nonalcoholic hot chocolate drink—ask for Louie's Favorite.

ACROSS THE SHIPS From a theming perspective, The Bayou, with its *Princess and the Frog*–inspired decor and menu items, is most similar to the **French Quarter Lounge** on the *Wonder* (page 298), although the latter emphasizes the urban aspects of the Big Easy. From a location perspective, its closest equivalent is **Bon Voyage** on the *Dream* and *Fantasy* (page 300): Each has a prominent position adjacent to the main atrium of its respective ship. **Skipper Society** (page 318) and **The Sanctum** (page 320) are The Bayou's counterparts on the *Treasure* and *Destiny,* respectively.

Cove Bar   LOCATION   DECK 13 AFT

SETTING AND ATMOSPHERE Cove Bar serves the Quiet Cove adults-only pool area. Tables, deck chairs, and lounge chairs are located adjacent to the walk-up bar.

SELECTIONS The menu is heavy on tropical drinks, with updated riffs on the Mai Tai, piña colada, mojito, and Blue Hawaiian. The signature cocktail is the Amazonia Fizz: Hendrick's Amazonia gin, pineapple juice, lime, agave nectar, and Fever Tree tonic water. The Infinity Swirl (named after the nearby infinity pool) combines layers of SelvaRey white rum, strawberry puree, Dole Whip soft-serve, Dos Maderas PX 5+5 dark rum, and frozen piña colada.

COMMENTS The same drink menu is offered at **Currents** on the *Wish.* (See page 301 for our profile of Currents on the *Dream.*)

ACROSS THE SHIPS Aside from the Hawaiian-style theming, Cove Bar is more or less the same as the adult pool bars on the other ships.

Cove Café   LOCATION   DECK 13 AFT

SETTING AND ATMOSPHERE Seating areas for small groups have upholstery in muted shades of beige and seafoam green.

SELECTIONS This 18-and-up venue serves specialty coffee, hot and iced tea, cold-brew coffee cocktails, and wines by the glass. The talented baristas can decorate your latte's steamed milk with images of Disney characters. If you're not a coffee person, try the Hot Cocoa Magic or the Cornetto Caffé—a blend of milk chocolate, dark chocolate, and white chocolate.

COMMENTS Cove Café is an oasis of quiet on this bustling cruise ship.

ACROSS THE SHIPS All the ships have a Cove Café. Those on the *Wish*-class ships, however, don't serve food.

Currents   LOCATION **DECK 14 FORWARD**

COMMENTS See the profile of Currents on the *Dream* (page 301).

Enchanted Sword Café   LOCATION **DECK 5 MIDSHIP**

SETTING AND ATMOSPHERE This is a grab-and-go spot with a few stools to sit on while you wait for the barista to pull your brew.

SELECTIONS Like Cove Café, Enchanted Sword serves specialty coffees, teas, and wines by the glass. Also on offer are healthful juice blends such as the Booster (orange, carrot, lemon, and ginger), the Rejuvenate (beet, carrot, and apple), and the Detox (kale, spinach, cucumber, and spirulina). Add vanilla or chocolate protein powder for an extra hit of nutrition.

COMMENTS This is a great place to grab your morning latte if you don't feel like trekking all the way upstairs to Cove Café. A basically identical venue, the **Wishing Star Café** (page 316) is located on Deck 4 Midship.

ACROSS THE SHIPS When it comes to the beverages served, Enchanted Sword combines elements of **Cove Café** on all the ships (page 297), **Vista Café** on the *Dream* and *Fantasy* (page 302), and **Senses Juice Bar,** also on the *Dream* and *Fantasy* (page 220).

Keg & Compass   LOCATION **DECK 5 FORWARD**

SETTING AND ATMOSPHERE Eight large TV screens cover the walls. Tables with cozy leather chairs line the sides of the room, while the central area has two long common tables and stools that seat a few dozen guests. DCL uses this area for trivia games—seating is at a premium, so arrive early if you want to sit here. Be sure to check out the map artwork on the ceiling.

SELECTIONS This is primarily a brewpub, with menu selections divided into Lagers & Ales, Stouts & IPAs, Wheats & Ciders, Meads, and Specialty Beers. You'll also find wines by the glass and a few cocktails that pay homage to the bar's seafaring theme, including Northern Lights (aquavit, mead, Lillet Blanc aperitif, Cointreau orange liqueur, and Uncharted Lager) and Old-Fashioned Glogg (port, bourbon, and "Viking spices," whatever those are).

COMMENTS Like DCL's other sports bars, Keg & Compass serves late-night pub grub at an extra cost. Options include Buffalo wings, fish and chips, loaded potato tots, plant-based "chicken" nuggets, a charcuterie board, fried coconut shrimp, and a giant German soft pretzel served with mustard and beer cheese for dipping. For dessert, try the brioche bread-and-butter pudding with marmalade glaze and vanilla sauce.

ACROSS THE SHIPS Aside from differences in theming and menus, Keg & Compass is comparable to the other DCL sports bars: **O'Gills** on the *Magic* (page 297) and *Fantasy* (page 308), **Crown & Fin** on the *Wonder* (page 299), **Pub 687** on the *Dream* (page 305), **Periscope Pub** on the *Treasure* (page 317), and **Cask and Cannon** on the *Destiny* (page 319).

The Lookout   LOCATION DECK 11 FORWARD

SETTING AND ATMOSPHERE This is the bar window for **Mickey's Festival of Foods,** the quick-service food court on the main pool deck.

SELECTIONS A little bit of everything, including beer, wine by the glass, hard seltzer, iced tea, and tropical cocktails.

COMMENTS You're not going here for the ambience but to tank up before the kids make you ride the AquaMouse with them for the hundredth time.

ACROSS THE SHIPS All the ships have poolside bars. This one just happens to have a name.

Luna   LOCATION DECK 4 AND 5 MIDSHIP

SETTING AND ATMOSPHERE This two-story venue is the home to family activities and bingo during the day but turns into a bar and entertainment for the 18-and-up crowd at night. There's ample seating split between two decks, although you're more likely to feel more removed from the action if you choose the seating on Deck 5.

SELECTIONS The menu at Luna is along the lines of a full-service bar, offering draft and bottled beer, cocktails, spirits, hard seltzer, and wine and Champagne by the glass.

COMMENTS Luna is a great space. We've spent a lot of time camped out in the chairs here.

ACROSS THE SHIPS **Sarabi** (page 318) is the comparable space on the *Treasure,* and it's **Saga** on the *Destiny* (page 320).

Marceline Market Café   LOCATION DECK 11 AFT

SETTING AND ATMOSPHERE The café bridges the two halves of the Marceline Market buffet. The decor is upscale Starbucks, with plenty of seating for small groups.

SELECTIONS Similar to Cove Café, Marceline Market Café serves coffee, tea, and cocoa, as well as wines by the glass, cold-brew coffee cocktails, and a few of the tropical-themed drinks also available at Cove Bar.

COMMENTS This is another convenient place to grab a fancy coffee. Its proximity to Marceline Market, however, means it'll be hopping in the morning, so if you don't feel like waiting in line, swing by one of the cafés on Deck 4 or 5 before you head up to breakfast.

ACROSS THE SHIPS The *Treasure* and *Destiny* also have Marceline Market Café.

Nightingale's   LOCATION DECK 3 MIDSHIP

SETTING AND ATMOSPHERE Nightingale's gets its name from "Sing, Sweet Nightingale," a song performed by Cinderella in the Disney animated film from 1950. A grand piano and an ornate chandelier, featuring elements of a musical staff and glass-orb "bubbles," anchor the far end of the room. The walls are covered with dark upholstery that reads navy or gray depending on the light. The ceiling around the bar area is trimmed with a crystal border. The combined effect is elegant and intimate.

SELECTIONS The signature cocktail is the Sweet Nightingale (Hendrick's Amazonia gin, passion fruit juice, rosemary, and mint). Other featured drinks fall into three categories: Air Bubbles, Smoke Bubbles, and Frozen Bubbles. For the first two, the bartender uses an air gun to "blow" a large bubble—filled with smoke in the second case—on the surface of the liquid; the bubble pops within seconds. Frozen Bubble drinks contain ice spheres.

The Butterfly, a Smoke Bubble drink, is made with citrus juices, butterfly-pea flower tea, and Bombay Sapphire gin; Dreams Come True, an Air Bubble cocktail, combines Empress gin with elderflower liqueur, white cranberry juice, and rosé Champagne. Also available are wines by the glass and Champagne by the glass or bottle.

COMMENTS Evening entertainment consists of piano renditions of everything from classical music to Broadway to Elton John.

ACROSS THE SHIPS Nightingale's combines the piano-bar ambience of **Keys** on the *Magic* (page 296) and **Cadillac Lounge** on the *Wonder* (page 299) with the bubbly beverages and decor of **Pink** (page 304) and **Ooh La La** (page 308), the Champagne bars on the *Dream* and *Fantasy*.

The Rose   LOCATION DECK 12 AFT
(at the entrance to Enchanté and Palo Steakhouse)

SETTING AND ATMOSPHERE One entire wall of this space consists of floor-to-ceiling windows facing the sea. Mirrors on the opposite wall make the ocean feel even more present. The ceiling is dominated by a raised rose motif. The seating around the room is plush green and beige upholstered chairs and settees. The barstools are crimson velvet.

SELECTIONS Specialty concoctions here are named for aspects of the *Beauty and the Beast* story: The Rose (Komos Reposado Rosa tequila, Grand Marnier Cuvée Louis-Alexandre liqueur, and Perrier-Jouet Belle Époque Rosé Champagne); Mrs. Tea (SelvaRey white rum, Belvedere Pear & Ginger vodka, Pique Passion Fruit green tea, and Moët & Chandon Impérial Rosé Champagne); and the Royal Wedding (Buckingham Palace Dry Gin, Hangar One Fog Point vodka, and Lillet Blanc). There's also a full bar and a selection of wines by the glass and Champagne by the glass or bottle.

COMMENTS The Rose is restricted to guests age 18 and older. The dress code (page 210) for **Palo Steakhouse** and **Enchanté** applies here as well.

ACROSS THE SHIPS The Rose is similar to **Meridian** on the *Dream* and *Fantasy* (page 301), both in terms of location and atmosphere. You'll also find the atmosphere familiar if you've been to the **Enchanted Rose Lounge** at the Grand Floridian Hotel & Spa in Walt Disney World.

Star Wars: Hyperspace Lounge   LOCATION DECK 3 MIDSHIP

SETTING AND ATMOSPHERE You're in a bar, in space. The room itself—which seats just 60 people—is rather blandly industrial, with clean metallic lines and not much else in the way of embellishment. One side of the bar has a collection of drink dispensers that would be right at home in a science lab. The key theming element is the central giant screen that functions as a porthole on the "spaceship." Via the screen, hyperspace drive kicks in, and you're virtually transported to locations in the *Star Wars* universe. You may see familiar ships such as X-Wings and Star Destroyers, but you won't see any characters—for those, you'll have to visit ***Star Wars:* Cargo Bay** at the Oceaneer Club during open-house hours (see page 235).

The jump to hyperspace can be intense for guests who are prone to sensory overstimulation: The banquette seats vibrate, and the entire space becomes engulfed in noise for several seconds.

SELECTIONS The drinks are "exotic, otherworldly concoctions" made with ingredients that exist both in the *Star Wars* universe and on the earthly plane. The Golden One from the Moons of Endor is made with a mix of herbs and berries from the Forest Moon surface. Here on Earth, that translates to Belvedere Blackberry & Lemongrass vodka and Disaronno Velvet cream liqueur, with a floating glow-in-the-dark stamp. The Freetown Reserve from Tatooine is made of Bantha hides mashed with fermented grains (aka Woodford Reserve Double Oaked bourbon). And the Spire Sunset from Batuu is made from substances gathered from the sides of the planet's petrified spires (in other words, Saigon Bagur gin, kumquat, lychee, and coconut).

Nonalcoholic drinks include the Cloud City (oat milk, blue raspberry syrup, and ice cream) and the Temple Twist (apple, pineapple, and kiwi juices, with mint and ginger beer). For $12, you can add a souvenir Hyperspace Lounge glass to any of the primary cocktail offerings; for $17, you can have your mocktail served in a souvenir Porg-shaped glass. (After 9 p.m., guests must be 18 to enter and 21 to drink.)

The drink with the biggest buzz, however, is the **Kaiburr Crystal,** which costs an eye-popping **$5,000.** Disney is reluctant to disclose the ingredients, but travel blogger Arthur Levine and *Orlando Sentinel* reporter Scott Gustin verified them with Disney insiders. The Kaiburr Crystal is actually a flight consisting of a cocktail and three shots. The cocktail is made with Camus Cuvée 4.160 Cognac and Grand Marnier Grande Cuvée Quintessence liqueur, plus yuzu and kumquat juices. The shots are made with Pappy Van Winkle's Family Reserve 23-Year-Old bourbon, Taylor Fladgate Kingsman Edition Very Old Tawny Port, and Watenshi gin. The drinks are served in a multichambered cooler. The cups are silver-plated, and you get to keep them. You also get a *Star Wars* backpack and water bottle, plus a hyperspace-themed stateroom decoration. *But wait, there's more!* Also part of the package is a bottle of sparkling wine from George Lucas's Skywalker Ranch, along with a voucher for a visit to the ranch, which isn't open to the public otherwise.

unofficial **TIP**
The cooler used to serve the Kaiburr Crystal drink package—aka the **Camtono Safe**—isn't included in the $5,000 price. It has been sold for about $45 on shopDisney .com but is frequently out of stock; however, they pop up on eBay with some regularity.

COMMENTS According to Disney Imagineers, the Hyperspace Lounge isn't tied to any particular aspect of the franchise—rather, it's a celebration of all things *Star Wars*. We are big *Star Wars* fans and enjoy this space, but after experiencing other *Star Wars* spaces Disney has made, we feel like they could have done more with this one. *Note:* Your visit may be limited to 45 minutes due to the popularity of the bar.

ACROSS THE SHIPS There's nothing like the Hyperspace Lounge on the other DCL ships. The most similar watering hole in the Disney theme parks is **Oga's Cantina,** part of the *Star Wars:* Galaxy's Edge land at Walt Disney World and Disneyland. Oga's Cantina is a far more immersive experience than Hyperspace Lounge, however—if you've already been there, then you won't be missing much if you skip the lounge on board.

Wishing Star Café   LOCATION **DECK 4 MIDSHIP**

COMMENTS See profile for **Enchanted Sword Café** (page 313).

Disney Treasure

The Haunted Mansion Parlor   LOCATION   DECK 3 MIDSHIP

SETTING AND ATMOSPHERE This unique bar theme should appeal to Haunted Mansion fans everywhere with the deep purples, greens, and dark seating we've come to associate with the popular theme park attraction. Don't be surprised if some Grim Grinning Ghosts make an appearance. The setting is meant to evoke both nostalgia and a new nautical storyline.

The new storyline involves a sea captain who wasn't able to realize his dream of helming a luxurious ocean liner. He met his untimely demise right before he was to be wed to a beautiful survivor found in the wreckage of a doomed ship. A portrait of the captain, as well as clues about the couple's mysterious disappearance, can be found around the bar. The captain's hat can be seen in the aquarium full of ghost fish. There is also a portrait of the mysterious bride-to-be that flickers between her portrait and her true form.

SELECTIONS The libations take a walk on the spooky side, with several mocktail options. For those that imbibe, there's a twist on a margarita served with a swirl of flavored smoke and a tequila-based cocktail with a secret message that's revealed under a black light. Watch for glow-in-the-dark drinks to complement the atmosphere.

COMMENTS Expect this bar to be incredibly popular during the inaugural year of sailings. *Note:* Your visit may be limited to 45 minutes, and during peak times, you may need a reservation.

ACROSS THE SHIPS The *Destiny* also has a Haunted Mansion Parlor.

Hei Hei Café   LOCATION   DECK 4 MIDSHIP

SETTING AND ATMOSPHERE This is a grab-and-go spot with a few stools to sit on while you wait for the barista to pull your brew.

SELECTIONS Like **Cove Café** (page 297), Hei Hei Café serves specialty coffees, teas, wines by the glass, and healthful juice blends such as the Booster (orange, carrot, lemon, and ginger), the Rejuvenate (beet, carrot, and apple), and the Detox (kale, spinach, cucumber, and spirulina). Add vanilla or chocolate protein powder for an extra hit of nutrition.

COMMENTS This is a great place to grab your morning latte if you don't feel like trekking all the way upstairs to Cove Café.

ACROSS THE SHIPS A basically identical venue, the **Jade Cricket Café** (see below) is located on Deck 5 Midship.

Jade Cricket Café   LOCATION   DECK 5 MIDSHIP

COMMENTS See profile for **Hei Hei Café** (above).

Marceline Market Café   LOCATION   DECK 11 AFT

COMMENTS See profile for Marceline Market Café on the *Wish* (page 314).

Periscope Pub   LOCATION   DECK 5 FORWARD

SETTING AND ATMOSPHERE Periscope Pub is DCL's first venue inspired by the 1954 film *20,000 Leagues Under the Sea.* The interior is meant to resemble that of a submarine, and the ceilings look through "glass" at the ocean above. Some may say it's a bad idea to have a venue on a cruise ship that looks like it's underwater, but we're not superstitious. It's the *Treasure*'s sports bar, so come here to catch a game.

SELECTIONS There are light snacks on the menu to purchase, as well as craft brews and undersea-inspired drinks. It is a pub, after all.

COMMENTS The cozy atmosphere makes this pub a great place to sit back and enjoy a drink with friends.

ACROSS THE SHIPS Keg & Compass (page 313) is the comparable space on the *Wish*, and it's **Cask and Cannon** (page 319) on the *Destiny*.

The Rose   LOCATION DECK 12 AFT
(at the entrance to Enchanté and Palo Steakhouse)

COMMENTS See profile for The Rose on the *Wish* (page 315).

Sarabi   LOCATION DECKS 4 AND 5 MIDSHIP

SETTING AND ATMOSPHERE Much like Luna on the *Wish,* this two-story venue is home to family activities and bingo during the day and turns into a bar and entertainment for the 18-and-up crowd at night. There's ample seating split between two decks; if you want to watch rather than participate in the activities, you may want to make yourself at home on Deck 5.

SELECTIONS The menu is along the lines of a full-service bar, offering draft and bottled beer, cocktails, spirits, wine, hard seltzers, and Champagne by the glass and bottle.

COMMENTS It's named for the *Lion King* matriarch, and we are digging the *Lion King* theming.

ACROSS THE SHIPS Luna (page 314) is Sarabi's counterpart on the *Wish*, and it's **Saga** (page 320) on the *Destiny*.

Scat Cat Lounge   LOCATION DECK 3 MIDSHIP

SETTING AND ATMOSPHERE Scat Cat is themed after *The Aristocats* and has live entertainment on a piano covered in paw prints. Dark-colored walls and rich tones of red make for an elegant, upscale atmosphere.

SELECTIONS The headliner is The Cat Drink, a mix of bourbon, amaro, Aperol, and fresh lemon served in a handcrafted rocks glass with the image of a cat embossed on the bottom. The Créme de la Créme Martini, one of the signature cocktails, is made with rich chocolate and Cognac.

COMMENTS Live music and craft cocktails make for a fun evening.

ACROSS THE SHIPS Nightingale's (page 314) is the comparable space on the *Wish,* and it's **De Vil's** (page 319) on the *Destiny.*

Skipper Society   LOCATION DECK 3 MIDSHIP

SETTING AND ATMOSPHERE Themed after the Jungle Cruise theme park attraction, this bar is meant to appear like it's located on a smaller Jungle Cruise ship dubbed the *Ems Empress* (after Papenburg, Germany's Ems River, where the *Treasure* began its first voyage after construction was completed at Meyer Werft). The setting is surprisingly lush, with plants inspired by Disneyland foliage. In a particularly inspired touch, the background music includes Jungle Cruise skipper spiels from around the world.

SELECTIONS Jungle-inspired cocktails, wines, draft and bottled beer, and a waffle-themed dish.

COMMENTS While there are times we wish this lounge and its counterpart on the *Wish*, **The Bayou** (page 311), were a little more closed off from outside noise and passersby, we love this setting.

ACROSS THE SHIPS The comparable space on the *Destiny* is **The Sanctum** (page 320), and on the *Wish,* it's **The Bayou.**

Disney Destiny

Café Megara   LOCATION DECK 4 MIDSHIP

SETTING AND ATMOSPHERE This grab-and-go spot is super convenient to the Grand Hall.

SELECTIONS Specialty coffee, teas, and wines by the glass, along with juice blends such as the Booster (orange, carrot, lemon, and ginger), the Rejuvenate (beet, carrot, and apple), and the Detox (kale, spinach, cucumber, and spirulina). Add protein powder for an extra hit of nutrition.

COMMENTS This is a great place to grab your morning latte if you don't feel like trekking all the way upstairs to **Cove Café.**

ACROSS THE SHIPS **Café Merida** (below) is located on Deck 5 Midship and is virtually identical.

Café Merida   LOCATION DECK 5 MIDSHIP

COMMENTS See profile for **Café Megara** (above).

Cask and Cannon   LOCATION DECK 5 FORWARD

SETTING AND ATMOSPHERE Cask and Cannon is inspired by the *Pirates of the Caribbean* films.

SELECTIONS We're expecting rum bottles galore, and Disney says that some brews will be served straight from the barrel.

COMMENTS The surprising part of this lounge isn't that it's pirate-themed; it's the fact that it took Disney so long to do it.

ACROSS THE SHIPS The sports bar on the *Wish* is **Keg & Compass** (page 319), and it's **Periscope Pub** on the *Treasure* (page 317).

De Vil's   LOCATION DECK 3 MIDSHIP

SETTING AND ATMOSPHERE De Vil's looks to be a stylish lounge with dramatic black-and-white spots decorating everything from the carpet to the baby grand piano.

SELECTIONS Trendy martinis, high-end bubbles, and old-fashioned cocktails.

COMMENTS The concept art for De Vil's looks amazing, and we are crossing our fingers that it's as good as it looks.

ACROSS THE SHIPS **Nightingale's** (page 314) is De Vil's counterpart on the *Wish*, and it's **Scat Cat Lounge** (page 318) on the *Destiny.*

The Haunted Mansion Parlor   LOCATION DECK 3 MIDSHIP

COMMENTS See profile for The Haunted Mansion Parlor on the *Treasure* (page 317).

Marceline Market Café   LOCATION   DECK 11 AFT

COMMENTS See profile for Marceline Market Café on the *Wish* (page 314).

Saga   LOCATION   DECKS 4 AND 5 MIDSHIP

SETTING AND ATMOSPHERE Saga is a two-story venue that's home to family activities and bingo during the day and becomes a bar and entertainment space for adults at night.

SELECTIONS We expect Saga to be a full-service bar with draft and bottled beer, cocktails, spirits, wine, hard seltzers, and Champagne by the glass and bottle.

COMMENTS We are all in for a Wakanda-themed bar, but we are expecting very subtle theming here.

ACROSS THE SHIPS Saga is comparable to **Luna** on the *Wish* (page 314) and **Sarabi** on the *Treasure* (page 318).

The Sanctum   LOCATION   DECK 3 MIDSHIP

SETTING AND ATMOSPHERE You're in the mystical world of *Doctor Strange*.

SELECTIONS The menu will include cocktails, spirits, and coffee.

COMMENTS The Sanctum will be an interesting space on the *Destiny*. It's spectacularly themed, but with walls on only two sides, it's always open to passersby. While that may seem a little strange late at night when the adults are drinking, it means there's lots of overflow space for activities during the daytime hours.

ACROSS THE SHIPS Its counterparts on the *Wish*-class ships are **The Bayou** on the *Wish* (page 311) and **Skipper Society** on the *Treasure* (page 318).

PART 14

CASTAWAY CAY and LOOKOUT CAY

KEY QUESTIONS ANSWERED IN THIS CHAPTER

- Why are these ports so popular? *(see below)*
- What should I do on Castaway Cay? *(see page 325)*
- What should I do on Lookout Cay? *(see page 333)*

OVERVIEW

AT MOST PORTS OF CALL, it will cost you some amount of money to get to a beach, but Disney's **Castaway Cay** and **Lookout Cay at Lighthouse Point** (cay is pronounced "key" in both cases) are beautiful beach destinations that are included in the cost of your cruise, and the ship takes you right to them.

Castaway Cay, Disney's private island, has been part of Disney Cruise Line since its start and has long been a favorite port stop for guests of all ages. In mid-2024, DCL opened Lookout Cay on the Bahamian island of Eleuthera. Unlike Castaway Cay, however, Disney doesn't own the entire island, only a 758-acre parcel on the southern tip. Nor is Lookout Cay entirely private: As part of the purchasing agreement, residents of the Bahamas can visit the area and prepurchase food and beverage offerings. (They do not have unlimited access, though; they cannot, for example, use the kids' clubs.)

Like Castaway Cay, Lookout Cay has instantly become a desired destination for many repeat DCL cruisers. We've visited multiple times and have spoken to many others who've been as well. Whichever of Disney's cays you end up on, it's likely to be one of your favorite ports of call on your Bahamian or Caribbean cruise. The weather is almost always gorgeous; the shore excursions are reasonably priced (mostly); and, as is the case with Walt Disney World, there's little of

continued on page 324

Castaway Cay

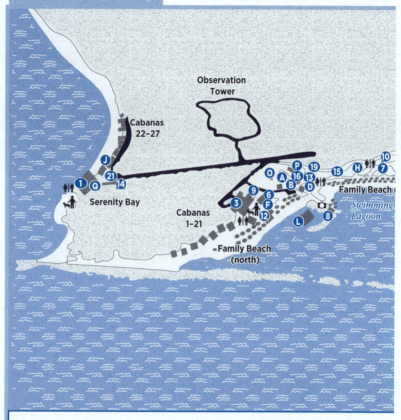

Observation Tower

Cabanas 22–27

J
21
Q
1
14

Serenity Bay

Cabanas 1–21

O
A
B
P
16
19
13
D
15
H
10
7

Family Beach

Swimming Lagoon

9
6
F
3
12
L
8

Family Beach (north)

ATTRACTIONS

A. Beach Sports
B. Bike Rentals
C. Castaway Ray's Stingray Adventure
D. Flippers and Floats
E. Gazebos (south)
F. Gazebos (north)
G. Gil's Fins and Boats
H. In-Da-Shade Games
I. Marge's Barges and Sea Charters Dock

 Service-Animal Relief Area
Bike/Nature Trail
First Aid

ATTRACTIONS (continued)

J. Massage Cabanas
K. Monstro Point
L. Pelican Plunge
M. Post Office
N. Scuttle's Cove
O. Spring-a-Leak
P. Teen Hideout (teens only)
Q. The Windsock Hut

Photo Opportunity
Restrooms and Outdoor Showers

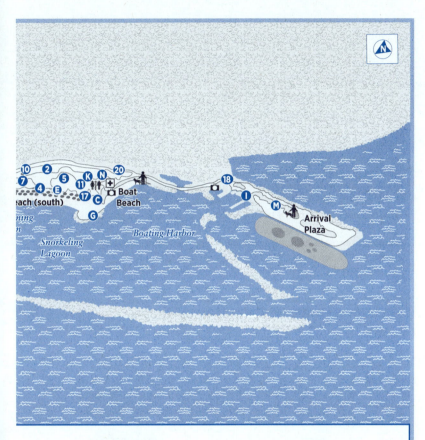

FOOD AND DRINK

1. Castaway Air Bar
2. Cookie's BBQ
3. Cookie's Too BBQ
4. Conched Out Bar
5. Dig In (covered seating)
6. Grouper (covered seating)
7. Gumbo Limbo (covered seating)
8. Heads Up Bar
9. Outdoor Seating (near Cookies Too)
10. Outdoor Seating (near Gumbo Limbo)
11. Pop's Props and Boat Repair
    (covered seating)
12. Sand Bar
13. Summertime Freeze (family area)
14. Serenity Bay BBQ

SHOPPING

15. Bahamian Retail
16. Buy the Seashore
17. She Sells Sea Shells ...
    and Everything Else

MISCELLANEOUS

18. Kargo Handling Tram Stop
19. Pelican Point Tram Stop
20. Scuttle's Cove Tram Stop
21. Serenity Bay Tram Stop

continued from page 321

the real world to get in the way of a relaxing day. And that's before the included food and (nonalcoholic) drinks. Keep reading for a comparison of Castaway Cay and Lookout Cay and what to expect at both.

WHAT *to* BRING

AT BOTH DESTINATIONS, Disney will provide you with medium-size towels after you debark the ship. You can get as many as you can carry. If you'd rather use a full-size beach towel, you can bring one of your own or buy one there. Disney also provides complimentary life jackets, as well as strollers, wagons, and a limited number of sand-capable wheelchairs (available on a first-come, first-served basis).

The sun and heat are intense, so bring plenty of **high-SPF sunscreen. Insulated sports bottles** that you can refill on the islands are also a great idea. Other sun protection you may need includes **light-colored, long-sleeved, lightweight shirts; swimsuit cover-ups; hats; lip balm;** and **sunglasses.** See below for additional items you may want to bring along.

- **Watch** or **cell phone** to check how long everyone has been in the sun and when it's time to reapply sunscreen. It's also useful for knowing whether the restaurants are open (usually 11 a.m.–2 p.m.).

- **Underwater/waterproof camera** or **waterproof case for your smartphone** for taking photos while swimming and/or snorkeling.

- **Small cooler** to keep medicine, baby formula, and other perishables cool. Fill it with ice on the ship and refill it from the restaurants' ice machines on the island. The cooler must be soft-sided and no larger than 12 by 12 by 12 inches.

- **Water shoes** to protect your feet from sharp rocks, coral pieces, and hot surfaces.

- **Small beach toys,** such as a shovel and pail (a collapsible pail makes for easier packing). Toys are also available for purchase on the island.

- **Your own snorkeling gear** if you already have it or if the idea of using a snorkel that someone else has used grosses you out.

- **Swim diapers** if you have little ones who like the water.

- **Hairbrush** or **comb.** It can get windy, and you'll want to look good (better?) in your vacation photos.

- **Insect repellent.** Disney does a good job of keeping bugs at bay, but it's still a good idea to bring something like Off!

- **Book** or **e-reader.** Be careful, however, about leaving expensive electronics unattended on the island.

- **Portable music player** and **headphones,** which are especially useful if you're planning to jog around the 5K course or the nature trails. Don't bring external speakers, though.

- **Athletic shoes and socks** if you want to play basketball on Castaway Cay.

- **Change of clothes.** While the sun will dry your swimsuit in a hurry, you may want dry clothes to wear while you're walking around the island, sitting down for meals, or riding bikes. You can return to the ship to change, but that does take some time.

OUR FAVORITE FUN STUFF ON CASTAWAY CAY

- **Castaway Ray's Stingray Adventure** affords you the opportunity to pet and feed small and medium-size stingrays in a dedicated lagoon.

- The **snorkeling lagoon** features underwater sights, such as a replica of the *Nautilus* submarine from *20,000 Leagues Under the Sea,* a statue of Prince Eric, a Dumbo ride vehicle, and more surprises. Common marine life seen in the lagoon includes stingrays, blue tang, and yellowtail snapper (plus the occasional barracuda).

- Rent **sailboats or paddleboats, personal watercraft,** or **inflatable floats and tubes.**

- Runners may want to start their day with the **Castaway Cay 5K,** a free (as in no-cost) jog through the developed parts of the island.

- Single-speed **bicycle rentals** allow you to fully explore the island, including its observation tower and trails, which can be accessed only on foot or bike.

GETTING FAMILIAR *with* CASTAWAY CAY

WHEN YOU SET FOOT on Castaway Cay, you'll be greeted by cast members handing out towels and offering water bottles to purchase. After passing the island post office, **Marge's Barges & Sea Charters Dock** for boat charters, and a photo op of the ship, you have the choice to either board a tram and ride to the beach or continue walking down a path to the beach.

The first stop the tram makes is **Scuttle's Cove Tram Stop,** which is the beginning of the first Family Beach. This is where you can rent personal watercraft, paddleboards, kayaks, floats, and snorkels; **Castaway Ray's Stingray Adventure** and the **Scuttle's Cove** kids' club area are also located here. Scuttle's Cove offers supervised activities, yet another water-play area, and a giant whale-bone excavation site.

Cookie's BBQ, the market-style dining spot, and **Conched Out Bar** are on the first Family Beach. **She Sells Sea Shells and Everything Else** is the merchandise shop on the first Family Beach. If you keep walking down the path behind the beach, you'll also pass some Bahamian retail shops and hair-braiding.

unofficial **TIP**

There are no Castaway Club discounts in the stores at Castaway Cay and Lookout Cay.

Pelican Point Tram Stop is the second stop, where everyone will debark. Guests age 18 and up heading to the adult beach will change trams here. This is also the check-in spot for the family cabanas. Bicycle rentals are right around the corner, as are **Flippers and Floats** for snorkel and float rentals and **Buy the Seashore,** the second merchandise location. The snorkeling lagoon and a second beach are short walks from there.

Located on the second Family Beach is **Pelican Plunge,** a floating platform with two waterslides and a water-play area. At Pelican Plunge, the waterslides begin on the platform's second story (accessed by stairs) and end with a splash back into the lagoon. Each slide offers a different experience: One is a long, open slide with moderate turns, while the other is a shorter, enclosed slide with plenty of tight

CASTAWAY CAY DONE RIGHT
by Scott Sanders of The Disney Cruise Line Blog

DISNEY'S ISLAND DESTINATIONS are an extension of the cruise ship experience, as the same crew works in various roles on the islands. On Castaway Cay, you may see your serving team barbecuing at Cookie's BBQ or your favorite bartender at Heads Up Bar on Pelican Point.

On the island, there are plenty of loungers and beach chairs for everyone, even if you sleep in and get a late start. Hammocks are more scarce, so arrive early (or look for one around 3 p.m.) if that's part of your island dream.

My favorite time to explore the snorkeling lagoon is in the morning before it gets crowded. As for seeing the rest of the island, the bike rental is a relatively inexpensive way to cover the trails and quickly get to the observation tower.

Not interested in going ashore? No problem. With most guests on the island, plenty of loungers are available around the pool and lines for the waterslides are much shorter—sometimes nonexistent.

turns and twists. Guests must be 38 inches tall to ride the slides, and 48 inches tall to ride without a life jacket.

Along with the slides, Pelican Plunge's water-play area includes pipes, nozzles, and plumes of water spraying out from every direction. The main feature is a giant overhead bucket, which is constantly being filled with water from the lagoon. The bucket is counterbalanced so that when the water reaches a certain level, the bucket tilts over suddenly, pouring gallons of water onto anything nearby.

Teens have their own dedicated area inland, near the second tram stop, called **Teen Hideout,** which includes volleyball, tetherball, and other activities. Some teens, however, may not like the fact that Teen Hideout is located away from the beach and has no water features or water-play areas.

The nearby **In da Shade Games** pavilion has fun games for all ages, including giant checkers, giant Connect Four, chess, table tennis, Foosball, and basketball. If you need some time out of the sun, In Da Shade is a fun place to spend it. We took shelter there during a rainstorm and ended up staying well after the sun came back out.

A small hook-shaped peninsula separates the Family Beaches. **Heads Up Bar** is located at the end.

If you choose to spend your day at the second Family Beach or are lucky enough to score a family cabana (see next page), **Cookie's Too BBQ** will be your closest lunch spot. On your way there, you'll pass **Spring-a-Leak,** an inland water-play area the little ones will love.

The adults-only beach is called **Serenity Bay.** It's a secluded beach with its own barbecue restaurant (this one has steaks!) and bar, **Castaway Air Bar.** The water on this side of the island is a brilliant, beautiful blue. Serenity Bay is located at the very end of a long runway that reaches temperatures approaching surface-of-the-sun levels during the summer. Although it's possible to walk to Serenity Bay, we recommend taking the tram.

The island **bike path** runs from the second tram stop out to a secluded observation tower for views of the island. Or you can keep going down to Serenity Bay and past it to an ocean lookout.

CABANAS ON CASTAWAY CAY

THE CABANAS ARE SO POPULAR that they're often fully booked in advance by Concierge guests and Pearl and Platinum Castaway Club members before the general public gets a crack at them. However, cancellations do happen. Don't get your hopes up too much, but if you're interested, ask at the **Port Adventures** desk as soon as you board the ship and periodically check back before the ship docks at Castaway Cay.

PRICING There are 20 private family cabanas on the **Family Beach** that can accommodate 10 guests ($880 for the first 6 guests, plus $56 for each additional guest), including a Grand Cabana that can accommodate up to 16 guests ($1,238 for the first 10, plus $56 for each additional guest).

At **Serenity Bay,** six cabanas are available that can accommodate 10 guests ($523 for the first 4 guests, plus $50 for each additional guest). There are no Grand Cabanas at Serenity Bay.

EXPERIENCE Imagine having a semiprivate place to yourself in the shade, with a stocked fridge of sodas and water, a bowl of fruit, a basket of chips, a plethora of lounge chairs, a hammock, floating mats or tubes, and a quiet beach on this gorgeous island. That's what the cabanas are.

On the Family Beach, the cabanas are in a private area just past Cookie's Too BBQ. No one else is allowed in the area or on the beach or in the water on that side of the beach. Because of the limited amount of guests, the quiet beach makes for a relaxing, peaceful day.

On Serenity Bay, the cabanas are set back from the water, with low-growing native vegetation separating the adult beach from the cabanas. Although there is no designated private beach area over here, we still find the cabanas to be very secluded.

RUNNING EVENTS ON CASTAWAY CAY

BELIEVE IT OR NOT, there is a free **5K** on Castaway Cay. You read that right—there is no entry fee. And you get a medal! It's a decidedly informal event started by crew members many years ago and eventually added by Disney to the schedule on the **DCL Navigator app** (see page 124). Originally, runners and walkers all debarked together and walked to the starting line near the Pelican Point tram stop, which felt approximately 10K from the ship. They were given running bibs and plastic medals at the finish line. The course route went up and down the airstrip, with a couple of loops to the viewpoint.

Over the years, the medal has been upgraded, and the run is more of a do-it-yourself event with no official start or finish time. (They stop giving medals out in late morning, so don't start too late.) You can pick up your medal in one of the shops near the finish line.

There is also sometimes an official event that goes along with the **Walt Disney World Marathon Weekend.** In January 2015, **runDisney** held the inaugural **Castaway Cay Challenge.** Guests were required to register and pay for the race in advance, as well as run at least one of the races happening on land at Disney World a few days prior. The event included an even nicer medal, and guests were able to get off the ship early in the morning and run before the temperature got too high. The Castaway Cay Challenge has been held sporadically since 2015. Check rundisney.com for upcoming events if you're interested.

FOOD AND BARS ON CASTAWAY CAY

Castaway Air Bar   LOCATION SERENITY BAY

SETTING AND ATMOSPHERE This is the bar at the adults-only beach. There are a few tables nearby, or you can take your drinks back to your seats. Bartenders also roam the beach selling the drinks.

SELECTIONS The menu is very similar to that at the bars on the Family Beach, serving Konk Koolers (dark and light rum in a blend of tropical juices) and other island favorites. The bartenders can make most of your usual drink orders as well.

COMMENTS Castaway Air Bar has a spectacular view of the beach.

Cookie's BBQ   LOCATION FAMILY BEACH

SETTING AND ATMOSPHERE This market-style lunch stop is the first one you come to when walking the island.

SELECTIONS Burgers, chicken sandwiches, ribs, potato salad, chips, cookies— all the things a barbecue restaurant should have! There are also some slightly healthier options like rotisserie chicken and salmon.

COMMENTS Maybe it's because we are starving when it's time for lunch on the island, but we think barbecue on Castaway Cay just tastes better. Don't miss the self-serve ice-cream stands. We also appreciate that they change up the menu slightly on double-dip cruises (itineraries that stop at Castaway twice on the same sailing).

Cookie's Too BBQ   LOCATION SERENITY BAY

SETTING AND ATMOSPHERE Cookie's Too is located at the far end of the Family Beach, near the family cabanas.

SELECTIONS The menu is identical to Cookie's (above).

COMMENTS Cookie's Too tends to be a little bit quieter than Cookie's.

Conched Out Bar   LOCATION FAMILY BEACH

SETTING AND ATMOSPHERE You'll almost certainly pass this bar, located on the main walkway across from Cookies BBQ, at some point during the day.

SELECTIONS Favorites are the Castaway Crush (mango, passion fruit, pineapple, mint, lime, and orange) and Castaway Sunset (coconut rum, peach and melon liqueurs, pineapple juice, and cranberry juice). Don't forget the souvenir coconut cups and bamboo sippers.

COMMENTS It can get a little loud with the DJ stand nearby, but what good island bar doesn't? Hot tip: Conched puts out baskets of potato chips early in the day if you can't make it until Cookies opens for lunch.

Heads Up Bar   LOCATION   FAMILY BEACH

SETTING AND ATMOSPHERE Located on a peninsula between the two Family Beaches, Heads Up has great views of the ship.

SELECTIONS The menu is similar to that at other bars on the island, with options like the Konk Kooler, Castaway Sunset, and Chukka.

COMMENTS We think this bar has the best location on the island.

Sand Bar   LOCATION   FAMILY BEACH

SETTING AND ATMOSPHERE Sand Bar is convenient for parents watching their kids at **Pelican Plunge** or lounging on the beach nearby.

SELECTIONS The menu is almost identical to that at other bars on the island.

COMMENTS What it lacks in originality, it makes up for in convenience.

Serenity Bay BBQ   LOCATION   SERENITY BAY

SETTING AND ATMOSPHERE Serenity Bay BBQ is a much smaller version of Cookie's, and it's only for adults.

SELECTIONS The barbecue at Serenity has an almost identical menu to that at Cookie's and Cookie's Too, with the addition of steaks.

COMMENTS We come for the peaceful atmosphere and stay for the steaks.

Summertime Freeze   LOCATION   FAMILY BEACH

SETTING AND ATMOSPHERE This is your bar for frozen drinks, many of which are nonalcoholic.

SELECTIONS This menu is different from that at other bars on the island, with several original combinations, all with cute names like Let it Go and Worth Melting For. We are fans of the Frozen Heart and the Ice Palace.

COMMENTS If you have *Frozen* fans in your party, you'll won't make it past Summertime without dropping some cash—the large collectible drink holders shaped like *Frozen* characters are on full display for passersby.

PORT ADVENTURES ON CASTAWAY CAY

CASTAWAY CAY OFFERS several excursions and activities, although if you're a beach person, you may be perfectly happy not doing a single one. Some things, like snorkeling-gear, float, and bike rentals, do not need to be booked in advance (unless you are bundling them together for savings), so you can wait and base your decision on the weather and your mood. If you are feeling active, you can prebook watercraft rentals or book on-site (availability is limited). These include paddleboards, kayaks, water bikes, and paddleboats. On the following pages, we've compiled a list of the more popular excursions.

Bicycle Rentals

MINIMUM AGE 3   **PRICE PER PERSON, PER HOUR** $15
DURATION 1+ HOURS   **ACTIVITY LEVEL** ATHLETIC

COMMENTS We enjoy renting bikes and going down to the observation tower. Men's and women's models are available, and the seats are designed for comfort and can be adjusted up and down to suit your leg length. The paths are never very crowded, so you can go at your own pace.

TOURING TIPS Pick up your bikes just past the Pelican Point tram stop, near the middle of the Family Beach. You can also rent bikes next to Serenity Bay, just behind the Castaway Air Bar. There are a limited number of bikes with toddler seats on the back, as well as some bikes with training wheels.

Years spent on the island have rusted many of the metal parts used to loosen the seats. Ask a cast member to help (they have wrenches) if yours won't budge.

We do not recommend riding in the afternoon when the heat is coming off the runway in waves. We've made that mistake and may have said some unkind words to each other on the way back.

Castaway Cay Fishing Adventure

MINIMUM AGE 8   PRICE PER PERSON $219   DURATION 2.5–3 HOURS ACTIVITY LEVEL MODERATE–ATHLETIC

COMMENTS This catch-and-release fishing excursion takes place in the waters around Castaway Cay, with DCL provided fishing rods and bait. Your boat's captain will take you into the waters around the island; the most caught species are yellow jack, grouper, various porgies, and snapper. It's not unheard of to hook a barracuda or a small shark.

TOURING TIPS Most charters leave around 9 a.m. and are back in time for lunch. Cruisers prone to seasickness should not take this excursion.

Castaway Ray's Stingray Adventure

MINIMUM AGE 5   PRICE PER PERSON $59 (AGE 10 AND UP), $48 (AGES 5–9)   DURATION 1 HOUR   ACTIVITY LEVEL MODERATE

COMMENTS If you have always wanted to pet and feed small- and medium-size stingrays in a supervised, structured setting, this is your chance. Disney keeps dozens of these stingrays in a sectioned-off part of Castaway Cay's snorkeling lagoon; the rays are trained to use a special feeding platform at mealtimes. There's plenty of food for the stingrays, and there are plenty to feed. Besides the feeding, you'll get a brief introduction to stingrays, skates, and sharks before you begin.

TOURING TIPS Holding a specially formulated pellet of food between two fingers, you'll place your hand, palm down, on the platform. A stingray will swim up to the platform, glide over your hand, and grab the food in its mouth. You'll also have the chance to pet the ray as it swims by.

Many children are worried about being bitten, and let's face it, the word *sting* in the name doesn't exactly help. But the stingrays don't have teeth, and the only thing that seems to get them excited is the prospect of feeding time. Calling them rays may help your kids find these animals more approachable. Fears might also be assuaged by a mention of the friendly Mr. Ray in *Finding Nemo*.

Float and Tube Rentals

MINIMUM AGE 5   PRICE PER PERSON $15 PER DAY OR $19 FOR TWO DAYS   DURATION ALL DAY   ACTIVITY LEVEL MILD

COMMENTS Inner tubes and floats are available. You can swap out one type for the other during the day.

Glass Bottom Boat Scenic Voyage

MINIMUM AGE NONE   **PRICE PER PERSON** $59 (AGE 10 AND UP), $39 (AGE 9 AND UNDER)   **DURATION** 1 HOUR   **ACTIVITY LEVEL** MILD

COMMENTS Board a small watercraft that holds about 25 people and ventures about 15 minutes out into the ocean. You can observe sea life below through several "windows" in the floor of the boat. During the trip, you're accompanied by a local guide who discusses the fish and other natural elements you'll encounter.

The highlight of the tour is the feeding portion, which takes place at approximately the midpoint of the journey. Guests are each given a cup filled with about 1 ounce of oatmeal, and when they toss the food overboard, several hundred tropical fish of various species surround the boat. The guide points out the characteristics of as many fish as possible. The feeding lasts about 5 minutes, after which the fish disappear quickly. Sightings of fish at other points of the tour are sporadic.

TOURING TIPS Guests must be able to climb five steps to board and debark, and they must stand for the duration of the excursion.

Parasailing

MINIMUM AGE 8   **PRICE PER PERSON** $140   **DURATION** 1 HOUR
ACTIVITY LEVEL ATHLETIC

COMMENTS The bird's-eye views of the island are the reason to take this excursion. Floating hundreds of feet in the air, you're the master of all you survey, or at least it seems that way for several minutes.

You board a speedboat and travel several hundred yards away from land. Then, in singles or pairs, you stand at the back of the boat and are harnessed to a line-bound parachute that is slowly let out until you and the parachute are 600–1,000 feet above the water, where you will enjoy panoramic views of your ship, Castaway Cay, and beyond.

TOURING TIPS Each excursion takes about 10 people onto the boat. There are no ride-alongs—every guest on the boat must pay. Your actual parasail event will last about 5–7 minutes. Parasailers must weigh between 90 and 375 pounds; those who weigh less than 90 pounds may be able to fly if they fly in tandem with another guest, but their combined weight may not exceed 375 pounds. Whether you fly solo or tandem is at the discretion of the staff.

Kids under age 13 must be accompanied by a paying adult age 18 or older. Guests ages 13–17 may go on the excursion unaccompanied but must be escorted to the Marge's Barges meeting area by an adult age 18 or older. All guests must sign a safety waiver.

You must leave your shoes on the dock and are strongly discouraged from wearing a hat or glasses during your sail; a storage area is provided on the boat for your personal belongings. Wheelchairs and other wheeled mobility devices cannot be accommodated.

No photography service is provided during the excursion. You're welcome to bring your phone or a camera along, but you assume all liability if you lose it in the ocean.

Snorkel Lagoon Equipment Rentals

MINIMUM AGE 5   PRICE PER PERSON $38 (AGE 10 AND UP), $22 (AGES 5-9)
DURATION ALL DAY   **ACTIVITY LEVEL** MODERATE-ATHLETIC

COMMENTS This is one of the least expensive, most rewarding shore excursions offered on a Disney cruise. We recommend it for every family. Fish species in the lagoon include yellowtail snapper, sergeant major, banded butterfly fish, blue tang, and barracuda.

TOURING TIPS Pick up your snorkeling gear at Gil's Fins and Boats, a short walk from Scuttle's Cove (the first tram stop), or Flippers and Floats at the second tram stop. You'll be given a mask, a snorkel, flippers, and an inflatable vest to make swimming easier. Also pick up a mesh gear bag, which makes it easier to haul your stuff back to your beach chairs.

Put on your vest before you get in the water, but don't inflate it just yet; wait until you're in hip-high water, which is also when you should put on your flippers because it's impossible to walk in them onshore (and they'll get sandy). Wait until you're in the water to put your mask on too.

If you're snorkeling with younger children, plan on spending 10–15 minutes adjusting the fit of masks and vests. Inflate a kid's vest by blowing into the vertical tube on the left side, adding just enough air to keep the top of the child's head above water. (If you overinflate it, they will have trouble getting their mask below the surface.) Also, practice using the flippers, which work best with slow, deliberate leg movements.

Once everyone's gear is working, take one last look at the lagoon to get your bearings. Disney has placed orange-and-white buoys above the underwater sites, so head for those. There usually aren't a lot of fish in the first 30–40 yards nearest the shore, though it's possible to see almost anything once you're in the water.

Walking and Kayak Nature Adventure

MINIMUM AGE 10   PRICE PER PERSON $79   DURATION 3-3.5 HOURS
ACTIVITY LEVEL ATHLETIC

COMMENTS This adventure begins at Marge's Barges, where everyone boards a tram to Serenity Bay. Next you walk behind the cabanas to a nature trail that leads to another beach. Your guide will point out interesting plants and animals and talk about the history of the Bahamas.

Upon reaching the beach, participants don their life jackets and head out in their kayaks. This is the part where you're at Mother Nature's whim. We took this tour after a friend raved about it. She headed out in the morning and was able to kayak to more places than we were later in the afternoon, when the tide was going out.

TOURING TIPS We wouldn't book this adventure in the afternoon again, even if it were the only time available. Even if you're able to book it in the morning, note that the tour is 3–3½ hours long, so you'll have much less time for snorkeling, biking, or lazing on the beach. Ideally, you would book this excursion on the morning of the second stop of a double-dip cruise.

Bring walking shoes, sunglasses, a hat, sunscreen, and a waterproof or water-resistant smartphone or camera; consider gloves for paddling to avoid blisters. Wear a swimsuit under your clothes for swimming. You must stow your belongings on the beach for the kayaking, so leave any valuables in your stateroom. Water is provided.

GETTING FAMILIAR *with* LOOKOUT CAY

LOOKOUT CAY IS LOCATED about 132 miles southeast of Castaway Cay on the Bahamian island of Eleuthera. Disney agreed to develop less than 16% of the 758 acres it purchased and to donate about 190 acres (25%) to the Bahamian government for use as parkland, maintaining much of the rest of the acreage in its pristine, undeveloped state. DCL also committed to using sustainable building practices and ensuring strict environmental standards.

You will see part of that agreement in effect when you first debark the ship. Rather than dredge up the ocean floor to dock alongside the island, as it did at Castaway Cay, Disney built an approximately 0.6-mile-long concrete pier out to the ship so as not to damage the coral. On the island itself, the buildings and walkways are built on raised structures to protect the flora and fauna.

The vibrant colors of the buildings, the Junkanoo dancers' costumes, and the Bahamian art located throughout Lookout Cay really do feel like a celebration of Bahamian culture.

The Family Beach is huge, and there are plenty of chairs available. Unfortunately, there are no hammocks, and some of the lounge chairs are behind a dune with no ocean view. The water is crystal clear and an absolutely stunning shade of blue.

For repeat cruisers who are used to Castaway Cay, Lookout Cay is a different experience, although you'll find many similarities. After debarking the ship at the former destination, guests can choose whether to take the tram or walk to the beach, while at Lookout Cay, guests must walk the long pier to the first tram stop. Guests with mobility issues can inquire with Guest Services on board about pre-arranging a golf cart, and Disney also runs golf carts back and forth periodically, picking up anyone who would like a ride. Unfortunately, there are only a few golf carts, so if you want a ride, you may have to wait a little while.

The first tram stop is called **Mabrika Cove.** There you'll find a bicycle rental stand, charter boat check-in, the family cabanas, and a small kiosk of merchandise called **First & Last Chance Stand.** There's also a small stand with specialty coffees and drinks to purchase called **Mangroves & Go.** Most guests will board the tram for a 10- to 12-minute ride to the family and adult beaches.

The **Family Beach** has two market-style dining restaurants with tongue-twister monikers: **True-True BBQ** and **True-True Too BBQ. Sebastian's Cove** (the kids' club area) and the **Play-Play Pavilion** are both on the south end of the beach (to your right if you're facing the water). **Triton's Trumpet Stage,** a gazebo where you can learn to build sand sculptures, is located on the south side as well.

Toward the middle of the Family Beach, you'll find the **Goombay Cultural Center,** where the excellent **Rush! A Junkanoo Celebration**

OUR FAVORITE FUN STUFF ON LOOKOUT CAY

- **Rush! A Junkanoo Celebration** at the Goombay Cultural Center is a wonderful musical party and parade. Don't miss it!

- There is no dedicated snorkeling lagoon, but guests can **snorkel** in the crystal-clear water right off the beach or book a snorkeling excursion.

- The family water-play area, **Rush Out Gush Out,** will be an instant hit with kids.

- **Disney Fun in the Sun Beach Bash** is a fun, interactive dance and game party with Pluto, Goofy, and friends.

- The **nature trail** leads to a small lighthouse and some beautiful rock formations down on the beach.

---

takes place. Nearby you'll also find a spectacular interactive family water-play area called **Rush Out Gush Out,** along with snorkeling-gear rentals and the main bicycle rental stop. There are two stores there, **Disney T'ings** and **Treasures of Eleuthera,** as well as **Plaits & Pleats** for hair braiding.

North of the Family Beach is the adult beach, called **Serenity Bay,** just like on Castaway Cay, along with **Serenity Bay BBQ.** The adult beach is also home to the **Blue Hole Bar.** Unlike at Castaway, where Serenity Bay is on the other side of the island from the Family Beach, on Lookout Cay it is adjacent to the Family Beach, which is convenient but perhaps not quite as peaceful.

South of the beaches you'll find a long **bike and nature trail,** as well as the namesake **lighthouse,** which is really more of a lighthouse station, not the large lighthouse you might have pictured when you heard "Lighthouse Point." The rock formations and beach near the nature trail are truly picturesque, and we recommend a trip out there.

The Gathering Tree is located near the second tram stop and is the meeting place for several excursions.

CABANAS ON LOOKOUT CAY

LIKE CASTAWAY CAY, Lookout Cay has family and adults-only cabanas to rent. And like Castaway Cay's, they are very popular and almost impossible to get if you are not a Concierge guest. Even then, it can be difficult, as there are more Concierge guests than cabanas.

PRICING There are 20 private cabanas for families at Mabrika Cove; 4 are Grand Cabanas and 2 are accessible. Standard cabanas accommodate up to 10 guests and cost $963 for up to 6 guests, plus $56 for each additional guest. The Grand Cabanas at Mabrika Cove can accommodate up to 16 guests and cost $1,375 for the first 10 guests, plus $56 for each additional guest.

At Serenity Bay, 6 cabanas are available, 2 of which are Grand Cabanas. Standard cabanas accommodate up to 10 guests and cost $523 for the first 4 guests, plus $56 for each additional guest. The Grand Cabanas can accommodate up to 16 guests and cost $963 for the first 10 guests, plus $56 for each additional guest.

EXPERIENCE On Lookout Cay, the family cabanas are removed from everything else, on the only beach with a view of the ship. Considering there are not many amenities (just a coffee shop, an unnamed food station serving lunch, a merchandise kiosk, and restrooms), it's pretty empty. While we are big fans of the cabanas on Castaway Cay, the family cabanas on Lookout Cay may not be the best for families with kids, as visiting the water-play areas on the Family Beach will mean a tram ride there and back. The water can also be a little rough here. All of this was fine for our party of all adults, but it would be trickier for children. Location aside, the cabanas themselves are beautiful structures, perfect for accommodating a family or group of friends. The beach is quiet and beautiful, and the water is clear.

The cabanas at Serenity Bay, like the adult cabanas on Castaway Cay, are set back from the beach, separated by vegetation. They are not nearly as private as the family cabanas, as all Serenity Bay traffic passes directly behind them.

All cabanas have cushioned chairs and loungers, plush beach towels, sunscreen, sand toys, a fridge stocked with sodas and water, a bowl of fruit, a basket of assorted chips and granola bars, and a safe to store your valuables. They also now have an ordering tablet to place drink orders, order more towels, request someone to pick up your food tray, and more. We love this addition!

Cabana guests can also arrange an in-cabana massage ($200 for an hour-long massage); the spa will bring a massage chair to your cabana.

Cabana rentals also include free use of snorkeling equipment and bikes. Those items total $53 per person when purchased separately. If you have six people in your cabana, that's a $318 value. If you'd normally spring for that equipment, the price of some private shade and comfort seems a lot more reasonable.

FOOD AND BARS ON LOOKOUT CAY

Blue Hole Bar   LOCATION SERENITY BAY

SETTING AND ATMOSPHERE It's the adults-only outdoor bar at Serenity Bay.

SELECTIONS The menu takes the standard drink options available at other bars and kicks it up a notch. We tried the zero-proof Aqua Tonic, with Brunswick Aces Spades Sapiir (nonalcoholic gin), Fever Tree tonic, elderflower, pineapple chunks, fresh mint, and lime, and found it a little bitter for our taste. The Island Colada has SelvaRey coconut rum, coconut water, pineapple, crème, and lime—a fun twist on a piña colada.

COMMENTS Servers also roam the beach if you don't want to go to the bar.

Bow & Ribbon Bar   LOCATION FAMILY BEACH

SETTING AND ATMOSPHERE This bar is centrally located on the Family Beach near The Gathering Tree.

SELECTIONS The menu consists of unique tropical cocktails, standard favorite canned hard seltzers, and bottles of bubbly. The Eleuthera Euphoria is

continued on page 338

Lookout Cay

AMENITIES	FOOD AND DRINK
A. Turbot Berth (charter boat check-in)	**1.** True-True BBQ
B. Mabrika Cove (cabana check-in and bike rental)	**2.** True-True Too BBQ
C. Mabrika Cove Cabanas	**3.** Serenity Bay BBQ
D. Serenity Bay Cabanas	**4.** Blue Hole Bar
E. The Gathering Tree	**5.** Bow & Ribbon Bar
F. Flippers & Fins	**6.** Watering Hole Bar
G. Rocky Point (bike rental)	**7.** Reef & Wreck Bar
	8. Sandsational Smoothies
	9. Mangroves & Go

ATTRACTIONS	MERCHANDISE
H. Goombay Cultural Center	**10.** First & Last Chance Stand
I. Rush Out Gush Out	**11.** Disney T'ings
J. Triton's Trumpet Stage	**12.** Treasures of Eleuthera
K. Play-Play Pavilion	**13.** Plaits & Pleats
L. Sebastian's Cove	

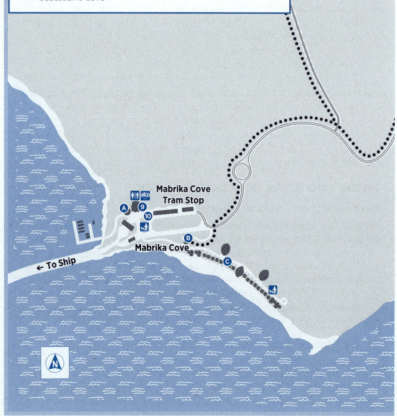

Mabrika Cove
Tram Stop

Mabrika Cove

← To Ship

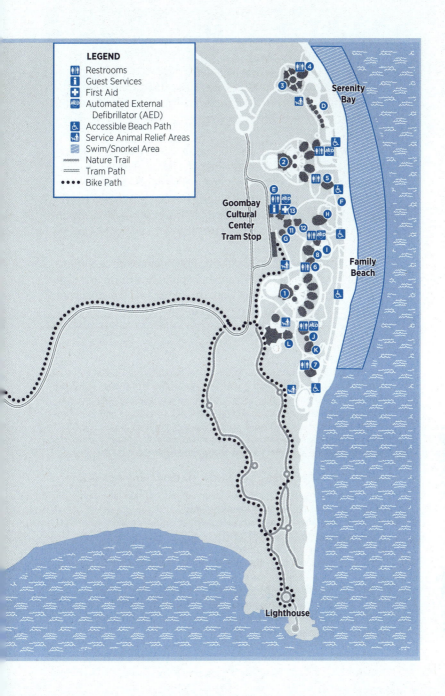

LEGEND
- Restrooms
- Guest Services
- First Aid
- Automated External Defibrillator (AED)
- Accessible Beach Path
- Service Animal Relief Areas
- Swim/Snorkel Area
- Nature Trail
- Tram Path
- Bike Path

Serenity Bay

Goombay Cultural Center Tram Stop

Family Beach

Lighthouse

INTRODUCING LOOKOUT CAY
by Scott Sanders of The Disney Cruise Line Blog

DISNEY LOOKOUT CAY AT LIGHTHOUSE POINT is not a copy of Castaway Cay; rather, the new destination complements Disney's original private island. Disney Cruise Line's agreement with the Bahamian government included a focus on environmental conservation, which was a driving force behind the development plans.

This will be as clear as the turquoise waters surrounding the destination when you first see the pier: To avoid having to tender guests ashore or dredge a channel through the reef so the ship could dock closer in, DCL built the 0.6-mile open-trestle pier, at the cost of requiring guests to traverse the distance on foot. In my opinion, it's a small price to pay to enjoy the beauty of the property.

By way of comparison, Castaway Cay reminds me of a World Showcase pavilion at EPCOT, and Lookout Cay is the actual destination that inspired the pavilion. Lookout Cay is the ideal spot to spend a day relaxing on the beach.

continued from page 335

served just about everywhere, and it features pineapple Dole Whip, so it's a pretty sweet drink; avoid it if you like your drinks less sweet. The Butterfly Switcha mocktail, made with lemonade, blue tea, and edible glitter, is eye-catching when served in a clear glass, but here it's served in the solid metal cups used on the island, so the visual element is lost.

COMMENTS Some of the same cold-brew and refresher options from **Mangroves & Go** are also served here if you didn't get them on the way in.

Mabrika Cove Cabanas   LOCATION MABRIKA COVE CABANAS

SETTING AND ATMOSPHERE This is an unnamed food station that serves lunch in the middle of the Mabrika Cove cabanas.

SELECTIONS The menu is very similar to that at True-True BBQ, with a great addition of cooked-to-order steak.

COMMENTS Our favorite menu item here is the ice cream, with several toppings and sauces to add—the perfect way to end a meal.

Mangroves & Go   LOCATION MABRIKA COVE TRAM STOP

SETTING AND ATMOSPHERE Mangroves & Co is located right at the first tram stop. It's your first chance to get a drink when you arrive, and the last chance to get one before you leave.

SELECTIONS The menu is full of specialty coffees and refreshers. Start the kids off on the right foot with a Dole Whip while the adults choose between specialty coffee or something with more of a punch. The Bahama

Brew (cold brew with coconut cream) is not a favorite with our group, but the Dole Whips sure are.

COMMENTS After the long walk down the pier, we appreciate having some refreshment options. This is also a good place to pick up a souvenir tumbler on your way back to the ship.

Reef & Wreck Bar LOCATION FAMILY BEACH

SETTING AND ATMOSPHERE Reef & Wreck Bar is located at the far end of the Family Beach, near the Play-Play Pavilion and Triton's Trumpet Stage.

SELECTIONS The menu here is exactly the same as at the Bow & Ribbon Bar and the Watering Hole Bar.

COMMENTS It's the most convenient bar location after dropping the little ones off at Sebastian's Cove.

Sandsational Smoothies LOCATION FAMILY BEACH

SETTING AND ATMOSPHERE A smoothie bar on the Family Beach.

SELECTIONS The menu contains favorites like pineapple Dole Whip in the Pineapple Pleaser and mango Dole Whip in the Mango Float. We absolutely love the Pineapple Pleaser, including the pineapple gummies inside. The Tropical Teaser with vanilla ice cream and Pop Rocks is also a hit with us. The Spicy Watermelon Limeade is a good lighter option and comes with a rock candy stick.

COMMENTS Cold smoothies on a hot day hit the spot. The Lighthouse Point Sierra tumblers are also a fun souvenir.

Serenity Bay BBQ LOCATION SERENITY BAY

SETTING AND ATMOSPHERE This all-adult restaurant is a quieter option than the other barbecue restaurants at Lookout Cay.

SELECTIONS The menu is identical to that at True-True BBQ and True-True Too BBQ, but with the addition of cooked-to-order steak—a huge plus for us!

COMMENTS If you are traveling without kiddos, this is where you will want to eat lunch.

True-True BBQ LOCATION FAMILY BEACH

SETTING AND ATMOSPHERE True-True is one of the two main family barbecue spots for lunch.

SELECTIONS In addition to standard barbecue favorites, like ribs, rotisserie chicken, burgers and hot dogs, you'll also find several fish dishes, as well as chicken and seafood rice bowls. There's fried okra, delicious coleslaw, cookies, and ice cream. There are also fries, which makes one of the authors of this book tremendously pleased!

COMMENTS We are fans of the new menu items and hope Disney keeps them.

True-True Too BBQ LOCATION FAMILY BEACH

SETTING AND ATMOSPHERE True-True Too is the second of the two main family BBQ locations.

SELECTIONS The menu is the same as that at True-True BBQ (above).

COMMENTS We have found True-True Too to be a little less crowded than True-True.

Watering Hole Bar   LOCATION FAMILY BEACH

SETTING AND ATMOSPHERE Conveniently located near the family water-play area and True-True BBQ.

SELECTIONS The menu here is the same as at Bow & Ribbon Bar and Reef & Wreck Bar.

COMMENTS Send one member of the group for something frozen at nearby Sandsational Smoothies (see previous page) while you pick up adult beverages here.

PORT ADVENTURES ON LOOKOUT CAY

IF YOU WANT TO just sit on a beach and do nothing all day, you don't need to book a thing at Lookout Cay. If think you will want to do more, there are several activities and excursions available. Some excursions stay in Lookout Cay, and some take you to other parts of the island. Here are some we recommend.

Bicycle Rental

MINIMUM AGE 3   **PRICE PER PERSON, PER HOUR** $15
DURATION 1+ HOURS   **ACTIVITY LEVEL** MODERATE-ATHLETIC

COMMENTS We are fans of renting bikes on Lookout Cay to see more of the island destinations.

TOURING TIPS Men's, women's, and children's bikes are available, and the seats are adjustable in height. There are bicycle rental locations at both tram stops.

Boiling Hole Reef Snorkel

MINIMUM AGE 8   **PRICE PER PERSON** $109 (AGE 10 AND UP),
$79 (AGES 8-9)   **DURATION** 3 HOURS   **ACTIVITY LEVEL** ATHLETIC

COMMENTS The Boiling Hole Reef is a popular snorkeling location about a 20- to 30-minute sail from Lookout Cay. It's a great option for snorkelers who want to go beyond the beach.

TOURING TIPS Your destination could change based on weather.

Ebike, Sand, Snorkel and History Tour

AGES 16-75   **PRICE PER PERSON** $139   **DURATION** 2 HOURS
ACTIVITY LEVEL MODERATE-ATHLETIC

COMMENTS We are suckers for e-bikes. You'll ride out of Lookout Cay into southern Eleuthera, stopping at a few historical sites before arriving at Miller's Beach, where you can soak or snorkel.

Snorkel Rental

MINIMUM AGE 10   **PRICE PER PERSON** $38   **DURATION** ALL DAY
ACTIVITY LEVEL ATHLETIC

COMMENTS We love snorkeling in the crystal-clear waters of the Bahamas, and we think renting gear from Disney is reasonably priced. The coral right off the beach is full of sea life. We heard one snorkeler compare it to sticking your face in an aquarium.

TOURING TIPS Pick up your snorkeling gear at Flippers & Fins on the Family Beach. You'll be given a mask, a snorkel, flippers, and an inflatable buoyancy vest to make swimming easier. Also pick up a mesh gear bag to carry it all in. Note that due to the commitment to protecting the environment, diving down while snorkeling is not permitted at Lookout Cay.

South Eleuthera Eco and Cultural Tour

MINIMUM AGE NONE   **PRICE PER PERSON** $149 (AGE 10 AND UP), $119 (AGES 3-9), FREE (AGE 2 AND UNDER)   **DURATION** 3-4 HOURS **ACTIVITY LEVEL** MILD

COMMENTS This tour begins with a 35-minute scenic drive through the island. You'll make your way to several amazing sites on Eleuthera, such as the Boiling Hole, Cathedral Cave, and Ocean Hole.

TOURING TIPS At press time, this tour was new and had some kinks to be worked out, but we are confident they will be, and we think it's worth a try for the sites you'll see.

OUR THOUGHTS ON LOOKOUT CAY

WE WERE AT LOOKOUT CAY on opening day when it was still being fine-tuned. Even though we dealt with a long walk down a hot pier in the bright Bahamian sun and a biblical swarm of flies at lunch, we still had a great day. We've been back several times since and were happy to see that the flies have been dealt with and drinking water has been added to the pier, making the walk more tolerable. Also, wagons and strollers are now available for the walk to the tram, and the plants are growing, making it feel lusher and more established every time we visit. This destination is only getting better.

The vibrant colors on the buildings and elevated walkways make Lookout Cay feel like a nice beach resort. The food is good and goes beyond standard beach-barbecue offerings. The cabanas are gorgeous, and their new amenities make them feel like even more of a treat.

Disney did a great job adding Disney touches while still appreciating and respecting the Bahamian culture. The Junkanoo Celebration is led by Mickey and Minnie in their adorable Bahamian outfits. We loved meeting and talking to the local artists who display and sell their creations in Treasures of Eleuthera.

The areas for kids and families are particularly well done, with Rush Out Gush Out being a favorite. It's more accessible than some of the family slides and water areas on Castaway.

The gorgeous blue water will entice even the most reluctant of beach bums. It's some of the most beautiful water we have seen, and pictures do not do it justice.

We are huge fans of Castaway Cay and didn't know what exactly to expect from Lookout Cay, but we were pleasantly surprised. Lookout is not a carbon copy of Castaway, and ultimately that's not what we wanted. We think Lookout Cay is going to be a very popular stop for many years to come.

COMPARING LOOKOUT CAY *and* CASTAWAY CAY

WHILE WE ARE FANS OF BOTH, Lookout Cay and Castaway Cay are different experiences. You may find yourself wondering which is right for you. The answer may be both, but if you have to choose, these questions may help.

- **Are you a beach person?** Castaway Cay has great beaches, but the Family Beach at Lookout Cay feels more expansive. The sand is powder soft, and the ocean is crystal clear.

- **Is your travel party made up of only adults?** Serenity Bay on Castaway Cay is completely removed from the Family Beach and completely removed from children playing on the Family Beach and in the ocean. Serenity Bay on Lookout Cay is adjacent to the Family Beach, with no real barrier between.

- **Do you want to swim?** Castaway Cay is a protected cove, and the water is very calm. At Lookout, the waves are a little more energetic.

- **Do you want to snorkel?** Castaway Cay has a dedicated snorkeling lagoon with sunken objects to see and a somewhat protected environment. On Lookout Cay, guests snorkel in the ocean mixed in with the swimmers. You'll probably see more exotic sea life because Lookout's swim area is not a cove but open ocean. Also note that on Lookout Cay, because of environmental concerns, guests cannot dive down and must remain at the surface of the water.

- **Do you like to exercise on vacation?** At press time, only Castaway Cay has a 5K. Both have nature trails with water stops along the way.

- **Are there teens in your party?** There is no dedicated teen space on Lookout Cay.

- **Would you like food beyond typical barbecue?** Castaway Cay has all the standard favorites, but Lookout Cay has added a few things to the expected barbecue fare.

- **Do you want to play sports?** Castaway Cay has sand volleyball courts, soccer fields, tetherball, and table tennis.

- **Do your kids love the clubs?** Sebastian's Cove on Lookout Cay is a great space for kids, with a wonderful water-play area. It even serves lunch.

- **Does anyone in your party have mobility issues?** The walk down Lookout Cay's pier seems especially long on a hot day, and some guests will have problems with it. Golf carts are available, but you may have to wait longer.

- **Do your kids love waterslides?** Rush Out Gush Out at Lookout Cay is a wonderful play area for families, and it's on land, so it's much easier to get to than the waterslides at Castaway Cay, which require a short swim to reach.

PORTS *and* ADVENTURES

OVERVIEW

DISNEY CRUISE LINE offers more than 600 shore excursions—or **port adventures,** in Disney-speak. While it's impossible for us to have tried them all, we have embarked on quite a few. We've also interviewed scores of families and DCL employees to learn which are the most popular and which ones they'd recommend to friends.

Beyond Disney's island destinations, **Lookout Cay at Lighthouse Point** and **Castaway Cay,** most port adventures last about 3–6 hours, including transportation time, and all are designed to fit comfortably into the ship's schedule. Third-party companies based near the port run virtually all the port adventures.

DOING MORE THAN ONE EXCURSION PER DAY

SOME GUESTS MAY consider booking more than one port excursion in a single day, one in the morning and one in the afternoon, hoping to pack in as much guided activity as possible. While this is technically possible in some ports, it's not something we recommend. We've seen enough port adventure hiccups to know that the possibility of an excursion running long is real. It may also be exhausting. You'll likely have a more relaxed experience if you have only one planned activity per day and use any additional time in port to explore on your own.

BALANCE YOUR EXCURSIONS THROUGHOUT YOUR SAILING

IF YOU'RE ON a quick three- or four-night sailing, you may have only one or two opportunities to explore a port. However, if you're on a sailing of seven nights or longer, you'll likely be able to undertake a variety of port experiences.

Port adventures fall into several categories, such as animal encounters, water sports, land sports, culinary exploration, historic-site visits, city tours, beach days, and shopping days. Many people, particularly children, have a more memorable and less overwhelming vacation if they schedule an assortment of these activities rather than focusing on just one. For example, while you may love museums, visiting them four days in a row may cause them to blur together. If you were to break up those visits with a cooking lesson or a visit to an animal sanctuary, the contrast would allow you to enjoy both types of experiences more fully. "All things in moderation" is a good rule of thumb.

READ THE FINE PRINT

OFTEN WHEN GUESTS have been dissatisfied with a port excursion, the disappointment can be traced to a misunderstanding of the excursion offering. When booking a port adventure, with Disney or on your own, pay particular attention to the fine print: Exactly how long is the excursion? What is the cancellation policy? (There are some variations even within DCL.) What transportation is used to get to the excursion site? Will there be additional fees? Is there challenging terrain? Is any food included? Forewarned is forearmed.

DEBARKING THE SHIP

ANY PORT ADVENTURE you've booked through DCL will be noted in your **Navigator app** under **"My Plans."** If you don't see it there, stop by Guest Relations or the Port Adventures Desk on board to confirm your booking. The app will provide instructions on when and where to gather on the ship, usually a restaurant or lounge, and whether you'll need to bring anything with you. At a minimum, you'll need to carry your Key to the World Card (or sometimes your Disneyband+) and a photo ID with you, as you do anytime you debark. Make sure you know where your meeting place is; DCL won't delay a port adventure for stragglers, and you're unlikely to get a refund if you don't show up for a reserved excursion.

Other than Lookout Cay and Castaway Cay, your meeting point will probably be on board. Once there, a Disney cast member will ensure that you have the correct port adventure documents and photo ID to reboard the ship. Additionally, some excursions may require that you carry your passport as well. You may also be asked to sign a liability waiver to participate in a particular activity. When those tasks are complete, everyone signed up for the activity will be escorted by cast members off the ship to a meeting point on the port's docks. There, representatives of the third-party company running the port adventure will meet you. You'll be in their care until you're returned to the port after your activity.

GOING WITHOUT AN EXCURSION

WHILE EXCURSIONS ARE a great way to experience a port, there are times when we just want to walk around on our own. Disney often docks right in the middle of town, so it's easy to get off on your own, and in ports that are not downtown, there is usually a shuttle into town. Some ports, like Skagway in Alaska, have plenty of things to do and see within walking distance. Others, like Falmouth, Jamaica, have built up a shopping area for cruisers, but there's not much to do without taking an excursion away from the port area.

FINDING PORT ADVENTURES

ONCE YOU'VE BOOKED a cruise, you can see your port-adventure options on the DCL website (disneycruise.disney.go.com) in the **My Reservations** section for your voyage.

Before you book, you can also see full lists of options that may help you choose a specific itinerary. At the top of the DCL homepage, click "Destinations," then choose "Port Adventures" from the pull-down menu. On the next page, scroll down until you see "Port Adventures by Destination." From there, select a region, such as "Caribbean Port Adventures." From here you can further sort excursions by port and by using the tabs for Experience Type (active, cultural, nature, and so on); Activity Level (athletic, moderate, or mild); Accessibility (wheelchair accessible and the like); and Price Range.

Clicking on a port adventure lets you drill down to specifics like price, age and clothing requirements, and duration. Some ports offer dozens of choices in a wide range of activity levels and price points.

You can also check out specialized port adventures in the "Premium Experiences" section, in the center of the main port adventures page. Options here include **Private Adventures,** which are typically expensive but may be appealing if you're interested in an off-the-beaten-path experience or you want to tour with a bit of luxury; **Accessible Port Adventures,** designed for guests who use wheelchairs or have other mobility issues; and **Culinary Adventures,** featuring cooking classes or wine and dessert tastings.

Of course, you're not limited to Disney's offerings: you can explore on your own, or you can book an excursion through another vendor. If you don't see something that strikes your fancy on the DCL website, your travel agent or fellow cruisers in the Facebook group for your cruise may have suggestions. You can choose to organize it all yourself or book through an outside company like **Project Expeditions** (projectexpeditions.com), which offers excursions all over the world.

If you're not up for a full port adventure but don't want to hang out on the ship all day, you can also book a day pass to a hotel or resort in port. A safe and convenient alternative to finding a beach on your own, a resort pass gives you access to amenities such as pools, beaches, and spas; some packages include transfers and meal vouchers

20 QUESTIONS TO ASK WHEN CHOOSING A PORT ADVENTURE

1. Have I looked at all the physical requirements of the excursion?

2. Does the price make sense to me?

3. Are there hidden fees that increase the cost—for example, add-on photo packages, tips for drivers and/or guides, or meals?

4. How does the price of this excursion fit into my overall excursion budget?

5. What percentage of the excursion will be spent on transportation?

6. What percentage of the excursion will be spent with a guide versus on my own?

7. Is there an adults-only or teens-only version that would make more sense for me?

8. What is the mode of transportation? If you are prone to motion sickness or afraid of heights, for example, then you'll probably want to avoid helicopter trips.

9. Is a meal or snack provided?

10. Will adverse weather conditions drastically affect my enjoyment of the excursion?

11. Does the excursion take place in a port where guests tender to shore? (Tender excursions are more likely to be canceled.)

12. Are there similar excursions at other ports? For example, numerous ports have dolphin encounters—is this particular port the best for such an excursion?

13. Are there similar excursions at the same port? For example, several dogsledding variations are available in Juneau—consider which one appeals to you the most.

14. What percentage of my day will it take up? Are there other things I'd rather do in port?

15. Is a similar experience available close to home or at another frequently visited vacation spot? (Think zip-line and go-kart experiences.)

16. Does this excursion appeal to everyone in my party, or might we be better off choosing different excursions on different port days?

17. Is this excursion too similar to something I'm doing in another port?

18. Will the timing of the excursion interfere with my child's eating or nap schedule?

19. Can I bring a stroller?

20. Are there elements of the excursion specifically designed with children in mind?

as well. Good sources for partial-day hotel access are **Resort for a Day** (resortforaday.com) and **Daycation** (daycationapp.com).

Finally, remember that you're under no obligation to participate in *any* organized activities. Feel free to hang out on the ship or just amble aimlessly around the port city. Your vacation, your call.

EVALUATING A PORT ADVENTURE

THE PORT ADVENTURES offered through Disney Cruise Line have all been vetted for quality and reliability. When you book your excursion through DCL, it's unlikely that you'll end up with an experience that's completely without merit. That said, just because an excursion is right for one person doesn't mean it's right for another. If you ask yourself the questions in the chart above, you should increase your odds of choosing the best option for your needs.

> ## PLANNING YOUR PORT ADVENTURE
> ### *by Scott Sanders of* The Disney Cruise Line Blog
>
> I'M A PROPONENT of putting together my own port adventures for just my family or a small group. It's easy to plan a walking tour using public transportation and not much more difficult to book a private tour. It's also significantly cheaper than private tours offered by Disney. When traveling with a group, it may be beneficial to book a third-party tour, as DCL's more popular offerings often sell out or may not have enough spots for your entire party.
>
> No matter how you explore a port, it's a good idea to take a portable USB battery charger, water, and snacks. (Pro tip: You can grab some boxed cereal from the breakfast buffet.) If you're traveling with kids and the tour involves a long ride, consider bringing an activity for them to do to help them pass the time. We've been on excursions where the total travel time was pushing 4 hours—and not all of it was scenic.
>
> Finally, take cash to tip your guides if appropriate for the excursion; US dollars are almost always welcome in the Bahamas and Caribbean, but I'd recommend carrying local currency across the globe in places such as Australia, Europe, and Singapore.

Our research shows that two of the most important factors that affect a guest's enjoyment of a shore excursion are the weather in port and the expertise of the guide. Even with the best planning, you may find that a sudden storm or an inexperienced guide dims the quality of the adventure. Of course, if the excursion turns out to be a total bust or the guide is lackluster, you should speak to the tour provider and to Disney, but try not to let normal ups and downs derail your enjoyment of the experience.

BOOKING ON YOUR OWN VS. BOOKING THROUGH DISNEY

AS WE'VE MENTIONED, you can book port adventures on your own or through Disney. Some advantages of booking through Disney include the following:

- **Time security.** In our eyes, the number one reason to book a port adventure through DCL is time security. Delays happen. Traffic jams, vehicle problems—you name it—a myriad of things could make you miss the ship-departure time. If you are on a DCL excursion, they'll do everything they can to make sure that doesn't happen, including holding the ship whenever possible. DCL does not hold the ship for guests who go out on their own.

- **Convenience of billing.** When you book through Disney, the fee appears on your stateroom bill, which you can pay using any of the acceptable DCL methods, and in US dollars, British pounds, or euros. As a bonus, you don't pay a deposit, and you're not charged until you sail. If you're booking an excursion in another country on your own, you may have to pay a large deposit, you may have to pay in another currency, or you may be limited to a particular credit card or other form of payment.

- **Safety.** Of course, you'll want to exercise an abundance of caution on any port adventure, but if you book a Disney-vetted excursion, you can rest assured that some of the work has been done for you. Disney verifies that the excursions it offers are through legitimate businesses. It makes sure that the transportation used is safe and that the guides are accountable for your whereabouts. If you book an excursion on your own, the onus is on you to do that research.

- **Communication with the ship.** When you book through Disney, your whereabouts are known. If something unforeseen happens, Disney representatives can contact your group and vice versa. If you book your own excursion, cast members on the ship will likely have no idea where you are.

- **Language issues.** Booking your excursion through Disney means that the transaction will take place in English. If you're booking an excursion on your own for a port in another country, the website or phone representative may use another language or speak limited English.

- **Cancellation policies.** DCL's port-adventure cancellation policy is clearly stated on its website. If you book on your own, you may be subject to an entirely different set of policies, which may or may not be clearly outlined—or fair.

- **Automatic refunds.** If DCL cancels your excursion for any reason (such as a missed port stop due to weather), you will automatically receive a refund for that excursion, no questions asked. But if you book on your own, refunds may not be available, even if your ship never docks at the port.

On the other hand, there are some advantages to booking your port adventures through an outside vendor:

- **Price.** Many guests have found they can save money by booking excursions similar to Disney's on their own.

- **More flexibility for kids.** Several outside vendors have a broader age range for excursions. We once booked Segways directly with the same company that Disney was using because the vendor would allow 14-year-olds when booking directly, while Disney's minimum age was 16. Obviously, Disney is trying to be extra safe, so make sure your child is mature enough to enjoy something and be safe.

- **More options.** While Disney offers a wide range of excursions at each port, the list of options is certainly finite. If you book on your own, there's no limit to the number of choices you might have.

- **Customization.** When you book on your own, you can often work with a vendor to put together an excursion custom-tailored to your interests or hobbies. You might be able to combine visits to two disparate sites in one excursion, skip part of a standard tour that doesn't interest you, linger longer at a favorite venue, or arrange for transportation that accommodates a physical need, such as wheelchair use.

- **Booking window.** On the DCL website, your ability to access excursion booking is based on your Castaway Club status (see page 5). First-time DCL cruisers might be locked out of some popular activities because they are already fully booked by Castaway Club members. When planning excursions on your own, your ability to book isn't tied to how many times you've cruised with DCL before.

CANCELING A DCL PORT ADVENTURE

DEPENDING ON YOUR CASTAWAY CLUB STATUS, you may make port-adventure reservations up to 123 days in advance (130 days if you are sailing in Concierge). Once you make a reservation, you may cancel it with no penalty up to three days before you sail—no refunds after that. Of course, you are not charged if Disney or the tour provider cancels the excursion due to inclement weather or other unforeseen circumstances.

The only other exception to the cancellation penalty occurs if you decide to upgrade your excursion. You can sometimes change a previously booked port adventure to one that's more expensive; you'll simply pay the difference in excursion fees, without any penalty. To upgrade on board, visit Guest Services or the Port Adventures Desk.

Note: A small number of DCL excursions using private transportation may have different cancellation windows. Always double-check.

MOST VISITED PORTS *of* CALL

SHORE EXCURSIONS TO A DISTILLERY may be popular, but popular doesn't necessarily mean good, or worth your time. Here we've included a few of our tried-and-true excursions in some of Disney's most visited ports of call, suggested a few to avoid, and offered our tips for going on your own. Ultimately, you know your family, and one excursion does not fit all. If we say snorkeling with turtles in St. John was the best thing we've ever done but your family hates swimming, move on to the next one. Note that prices and ports are subject to change.

Alaska

DISNEY BEGAN SAILING to Alaska in 2011 and has visited every summer since. It's one of the most popular itineraries Disney offers. Many cruisers consider Alaska a must-do at some point in their cruise career and don't want to miss a thing while there. You will be able to receive US cell service while in American ports, but given the proximity to Canada, watch your phone carefully (if you are a US resident) to avoid random roaming on Canadian cell service, which could come with surprise fees. Excursion options include zip-lining, kayaking, whale-watching, and dogsledding. Alaska gets a lot of rain in the summer, so be prepared.

PROS	CONS
• **Vancouver,** one of the most beautiful cities in North America, is a noteworthy destination in its own right, one that we recommend visiting for a few days before or after your cruise.	• The weather can range from chilly to downright cold—and it *will* rain at some point during your cruise.
• Breathtaking scenery.	• The length of the cruise plus travel time to and from Vancouver may be more than you can schedule (usually around 9 days total).
• If you've ever wanted to see a glacier from a hot tub, here's your chance!	• Only one DCL ship, the *Wonder,* cruises Alaska, and only during summer.
• West Coasters, this is an easy and convenient trip for you.	

CRUISES SAIL FROM Vancouver | **SHIP** *Wonder*

CRUISE LENGTHS Mostly 7 nights, occasionally 5, 8, or 9

SEASON Summer

SPECIAL TOUCHES A naturalist on board who talks about the glaciers and wildlife you'll see, mulled wine on the bar menu, blankets to keep warm on the upper decks, and more hot chocolate than any human should be allowed to drink.

WHAT TO PACK Warm clothing, including gloves, hats, and scarves; waterproof shoes (that you can hike in); binoculars; umbrellas

SIGNATURE PORT ADVENTURE **Dogsledding.** It's pricey, but you'll *love* it.

POSSIBLE PORT STOPS **Alaska:** Icy Strait Point, Juneau, Ketchikan, Sitka, Skagway, and glacier-viewing visits to Stikine Icecap. **Canada:** Victoria.

COMMENTS We realize that Caribbean-cruise fatigue is a trivial problem, so if you're rolling your eyes at us when we say that an Alaskan cruise is the cure for too many trips to Nassau, we hear you. That said, for the opposite of the Caribbean experience without leaving the Western Hemisphere, we heartily recommend seeing the 49th state by ship.

TOURIST HIGHLIGHTS **Glacier viewing** is an epic experience for many. Plan to bundle up and spend the day scanning the shoreline's massive cliffs for waterfalls, calving glaciers, and wildlife of every sort. Vary your location on the ship periodically from the top decks to the walking path on Deck 4 or your stateroom's verandah (if you have one); the perspective will be different from each location. Other popular site visits include the **Mendenhall Glacier** in Juneau, the **White Pass** and **Yukon Railroad** in Skagway, and the **Great Alaskan Lumberjack Show** in Ketchikan. In Vancouver, check out the **Dr. Sun Yat-Sen Classical Chinese Garden,** the **Vancouver Lookout,** or **Stanley Park.**

WHAT TO EAT No trip to Alaska would be complete without trying fresh salmon and king crab. **Tracy's King Crab Shack** in Juneau is a DCL guest favorite. For authentic Asian food, visit Vancouver's **Chinatown.**

WHAT TO BUY Look for carved Alaskan jade or crafts made by Indigenous people of wood, stone, or fur.

Wes Dauer from *The DCL Dude Podcast* had this to say about his Alaska cruise:

An Alaskan Disney cruise is an unforgettable experience that blends the magic of Disney with the untamed beauty of Alaska. As you navigate through the inside passage, each day offers breathtaking views of glaciers, fjords, and towering snow-capped mountains, with lots of opportunities to see wildlife from the comforts of your stateroom verandah. From taking a scenic train ride into the Yukon Territory in Skagway, to dogsledding on a glacier in Juneau, to salmon fishing in Ketchikan, Disney Cruise Line offered port adventures that gave my family authentic and immersive experiences in the Last Frontier.

On board, my family loved the local nature guides providing information about the landscape around us, and the Alaskan character costumes are some of the best you'll find on a Disney cruise. If you're looking for an adventure that offers you something different than sun and sand, I would HIGHLY recommend an Alaskan Disney cruise! In my opinion, it's one of the best products that Disney has to offer across its entire portfolio.

ALASKA EXCURSION RECOMMENDATIONS

HERE ARE SOME of our recommendations for the Alaska ports Disney visits most frequently.

GLACIER-VIEWING DAY While not technically a port because you never set foot on land, Disney offers a great excursion called **Glacier Explorer** on the days the ship visits a glacier. Disney visits one of the glaciers along the Stikine Icecap and may sail down Endicott Arm or Tracy Arm, depending on weather and ice conditions. Guests will choose a morning or afternoon time and board a smaller boat right from the cruise ship. The boat sails independently of the cruise ship and gets much closer to the glacier than a large ocean liner can. It's $309 (age 10 and up) and $209 (age 9 and under), but we think it's worth every penny, especially on sunny days. It does sell out quickly, however, so book as soon as your booking window opens.

GLACIER VIEWING WITHOUT A PORT ADVENTURE If you don't want to book the Glacier Explorer, you will still have beautiful views from the ship on glacier-viewing day (this is one of our favorite days aboard an Alaskan cruise).

Icy Strait Point

Icy Strait Point was built as a cruise port. The standard high temperatures range from 57°F to 64°F through the summer, with lows from 40°F to 51°F. Whales favor the area near Icy Strait Point, which makes

---

ICY STRAIT POINT PORT ADVENTURE RECOMMENDATIONS

TO DO

ADVENTURE PARK AND ROPES COURSE
If you want an active excursion, this large ropes course will keep you entertained. This excursion also includes the gondola, which is a great perk.
• **Minimum age** 5 • **Price per person** $74 (ages 10 and up), $54 (ages 5–9)
• **Duration** 2.5–3 hours • **Activity level** Athletic • **Transportation** Short transfer

ATV EXPEDITION
This excursion is a great way to see the scenery and explore Icy Strait Point.
• **Minimum age** 6 • **Price per person** $269 (ages 10 and up), $239 (ages 6–9)
• **Duration** 2.5–3 hours • **Activity level** Moderate • **Transportation** Short bus ride

WHALE WATCHING AND SEAFOOD FEAST COMBO
This combination whale-watching/seafood excursion offers a partial refund if you don't see whales, which we appreciate.
• **Minimum age** None • **Price per person** $349 (ages 10 and up), $269 (age 9 and under) • **Duration** 3.5–4 hours • **Activity level** Mild • **Transportation** Short walk

TO AVOID

SKYGLIDER TO SKYPEAK
We enjoy the gondola but don't think you should book it ahead of time. Wait and ensure that the weather is clear so you can appreciate the views—not to mention that several other excursions include a ticket to the gondola.
• **Price per person** $54 (age 10 and up), $44 (ages 3–9), free (age 2 and under)

IN ALASKA'S WILDEST KITCHEN
While we are fans of food excursions, this one does not get great reviews from cruisers, mainly because of the price.
• **Price per person** $119 (age 10 and up), $99 (ages 3–9), free (ages 2 and under)

JUNEAU PORT ADVENTURE RECOMMENDATIONS

TO DO

DOG SLEDDING ON THE MENDENHALL GLACIER

We think the title buries at least part of the lede: You take a helicopter to the glacier! Also, unlike many dogsledding excursions that are not on ice or snow and don't actually have you on a sled, this one is on a sled through the snow and ice on the glacier. Be aware that helicopter excursions are canceled more often than other excursions due to weather.

• **Minimum age** 2 • **Price per person** $859 • **Duration** 2.5–3 hours • **Activity level** Moderate • **Transportation** Short transport from pier

SLED DOG DISCOVERY AND MUSHER'S CAMP

If you are looking for an excursion involving sled dogs and don't want to break the bank with the previous excursion, this is a great option. This one is not on ice or snow, and the sled is more of a cart, but the dogs still pull you, and best of all, there are puppies—surely the highlight of any excursion.

• **Minimum age** None • **Price per person** $229 (age 10 and up), $199 (ages 3–9), free (age 2 and under) • **Duration** 2–2.5 hours • **Activity level** Mild • **Transportation** 30-minute bus ride

ALASKA WHALES & RAINFOREST TRAILS

There are myriad whale-watching excursions in Juneau, and we've been happy with several. Our general rule is that the smaller the boat, the better. This one uses smaller boats and involves some hiking and exploring on land as well.

• **Minimum age** 5 • **Price per person** $259 (age 10 and up), $159 (ages 5–9) • **Duration** 5–5.5 hours • **Activity level** Moderate • **Transportation** 30-minute bus ride

TO AVOID

MENDENHALL GLACIER FLOAT TRIP

We thought this was a perfectly fine way to spend the day, but the title and description are a bit misleading. You float near the glacier only for a short time before you head to the river. If you want to get closer to the glacier, try the **Mendenhall Lake Kayak Adventure**. Also, "whitewater rapids" should not be in the description for the float trip at all. These are the tamest of rapids we've ever seen!

• **Price per person** $269 (age 10 and up), $249 (ages 8–9)

it an excellent spot for whale-watching. Many excursion operators will guarantee a whale sighting or give you some percentage of your money back. Icy Strait also has the highest density of brown bears in Alaska. The ship docks within walking distance of almost everything. The **ZipRider** is the longest zip line in the world, and the wildlife-viewing is top-notch. The **Skyglider** gondola ride is beautiful on a clear day, and **Lil' Gen's Mini-Doughnuts** serves up tasty doughnuts in a couple dozen flavors. The waterfront restaurants serve local seafood, and there are several locally owned shops with local crafts.

Juneau

Juneau, the capital of Alaska, is unique in that it can only be reached by air or boat. The standard high temperatures range from 62°F to 64°F through the summer, with lows from 47°F to 50°F. The ship docks near downtown, with lots to see. Public transportation is easily accessible if you want to go to the **Mendenhall Glacier** or some other point of interest. The **Mount Roberts Tramway** is close to the port and affords some stunning views of the area. See our picks for excursions to do and to avoid in Juneau above.

KETCHIKAN PORT ADVENTURE RECOMMENDATIONS

TO DO

BLACK BEAR AND WILDLIFE EXPLORATION
This excursion operates only in certain seasons, but it was one of our favorites in Alaska. We could not believe how many bears we saw!
• **Minimum age** 12 • **Price per person** $319 • **Duration** 3–3.5 hours • **Activity level** Moderate • **Transportation** 30-minute bus ride

GREAT ALASKAN LUMBERJACK SHOW AND CRAB FEAST
The lumberjack show in Ketchikan is surprisingly popular. Cruisers give it high marks. It can be done on your own or on an excursion like this one with food.
• **Minimum age** None • **Price per person** $199 (age 10 and up), $139 (ages 3–9), free (age 2 and under) • **Duration** 3 hours • **Activity level** Mild • **Transportation** Short walk

RAINFOREST ZIP, SKYBRIDGE, AND RAPPEL ADVENTURE
Having zip-lined in a few places, we think Alaska is one of the best places to do it.
• **Minimum age** 10 • **Price per person** $289 • **Duration** 3 hours • **Activity level** Athletic • **Transportation** 30-minute bus ride

TO AVOID

KETCHIKAN DUCK TOUR
Cruisers have not been overly excited about this duck boat excursion.
• **Price per person** $91 (age 10 and up), $54 (age 9 and under)

Ketchikan

Ketchikan is one of the rainiest cities in the United States. It rains more than 200 days a year, so expect to be rained on. The standard highs range from 61°F to 64°F through the summer, with lows from 47°F to 52°F. We enjoy being on deck as the ship pulls into and out of the city, a bustling port with beautiful views. The ship docks right downtown, within walking distance of tourist sites like the **Salmon Ladder** and **Creek Street.** The **Great Alaskan Lumberjack Show** is very entertaining, and there are several small museums. The **Cape Fox Lodge Funicular** is a good way to get some great views of the port. We've been on some great kayaking trips in Ketchikan as well. See our picks for excursions to do and to avoid above.

SKAGWAY PORT ADVENTURE RECOMMENDATIONS

DOG SLEDDING AND GLACIER FLIGHTSEEING
As you can imagine, the views from a helicopter in Alaska are amazing. This one takes you to the top of the Denver Glacier for some dog mushing. • **Minimum age** 2 • **Price per person** $889 • **Duration** 2–2.5 hours • **Activity level** Moderate • **Transportation** Short transfer from pier

GOLD FEVER, ALASKAN SLED DOGS AND EXCLUSIVE SCENIC RAILWAY
We highly recommend the White Pass Railway, and we thoroughly enjoyed this excursion, which combines the train with gold panning and . . . puppies! All excursions are made better by puppies. We stand by this truth.
• **Minimum age** None • **Price per person** $289 (age 10 and up), $169 (ages 3–9), free (age 2 and under) • **Duration** 6–6.5 hours • **Activity level** Mild • **Transportation** Short walk

LIARSVILLE GOLD RUSH TRAIL CAMP & SALMON BAKE FEATURING EXCLUSIVE DISNEY CHARACTER EXPERIENCE
The kids love the gold panning, and the Disney characters that visit are a nice touch.
• **Minimum age** None • **Price per person** $144 (age 10 and up), $84 (ages 3–9), free (age 2 and under) • **Duration** 2.5–3 hours • **Activity level** Mild • **Transportation** 15-minute bus ride

---

VICTORIA PORT ADVENTURE RECOMMENDATIONS

BUTCHART GARDENS & SHORT CITY DRIVE
The Butchart Gardens is a National Historic Site of Canada and a popular place for tourists to visit. This tour will afford you scenic views as you journey to the garden, where you'll have about 2 hours to explore on your own.
• **Minimum age** None • **Price per person** $174 (age 10 and up), $114 (ages 3–9), free (age 2 and under) • **Duration** 3.5–4 hours • **Activity level** Mild • **Transportation** 30-minute scenic drive

MALAHAT SKYWALK & VICTORIA HIGHLIGHTS
This excursion includes a bus tour of Victoria and a trip to the Malahat Skywalk, which has some amazing views from the top—you can slide down if you don't want to walk.
• **Minimum age** None • **Price per person** $149 (age 10 and up), $119 (ages 3–9), free (age 2 and under) • **Duration** 4–4.5 hours • **Activity level** Mild • **Transportation** 50-minute bus ride

OCEAN WILDLIFE & WHALE WATCHING TOUR
We wish there were more port adventure options for whale-watching here because Victoria has some great wildlife-viewing, including whales.
• **Minimum age** None • **Price per person** $199 (age 10 and up), $129 (age 9 and under) • **Duration** 3–3.5 hours • **Activity level** Moderate • **Transportation** Short walk

---

Skagway

Skagway is a charming little town. Standard high temperatures range from 62°F to 64°F through the summer, with lows from 48°F to 51°F. The ship docks at the end of the main street. The town is so small and everything so convenient that you'll probably have enough time to walk around before or after any excursion. Don't miss the fry bread at **Klondike Doughboy.** The **White Pass and Yukon Railway** is right in town and takes guests on fun rides with great views. (*Note:* If your train enters Canada, you will need a passport.) **Gold panning** is another popular activity. See previous page for excursions we recommend in Skagway.

Victoria (British Columbia)

The port in Victoria is one of the busiest cruise ports in Canada. Standard high temperatures range from 61°F to 68°F through the summer, with lows from 50°F to 55°F. The ship is within walking distance of many tourist destinations like **Antique Row** and the **Royal B.C. Museum.** Victoria is also a popular city to explore via bicycle if you're up for it. **The Butchart Gardens** takes a little while to get to but is worth it; Walt Disney World fans may recognize this 55-acre display garden as the inspiration for the Canada Pavilion at EPCOT. **High tea** is also popular at locations like the dining room at The Butchart Gardens and the **Fairmont Empress.** See above for excursions we recommend.

Bahamas (Nassau)

NASSAU, ON NEW PROVIDENCE ISLAND in the Bahamas, is a regular port of call for all Bahamian cruises. Standard high temperatures range from 79°F to 90°F throughout the year, with lows ranging from 64°F to 76°F. The ship docks at **Prince George Wharf,** which was redone

PROS	CONS
• The ships dock in the heart of downtown.	• The port experience is *very* commercial.
• The US dollar is accepted, and English is spoken everywhere.	• Your ship will likely be one of many in port here.
• You have your choice of ships and many cruise lengths.	• The summer heat can be oppressive.

in 2023. The port area is a nice place to visit if you don't want to go far. Take some time to stop and watch the screen at the end of the dock; it's one of our favorite things about Nassau. While keeping safety in mind, there are a few sites within walking distance of the ship. If you don't mind street vendors and pushy cab drivers, you can easily walk to the **Straw Market** to shop, to **Señor Frogs** for a margarita, or to the **Queen's Staircase** up to **Fort Fincastle** for a great view of the city (be forewarned, it's likely you will be approached by someone trying to give you a "tour" of the steps who will then expect a tip). See our recommended Nassau excursions on the next page.

CRUISES SAIL FROM Fort Lauderdale, Galveston, Port Canaveral, San Juan

SHIPS The *Magic, Dream, Fantasy,* and *Wish* visit the Bahamas in 2025.

CRUISE LENGTHS 3–5 or 7 nights

SEASON Year-round | **WHAT TO PACK** Sunscreen, shorts, swimsuits, and shoes you don't mind getting sandy

SIGNATURE PORT ADVENTURE Swimming with dolphins

CLASSIC DISNEY ADD-ON Walt Disney World

COMMENTS With more than 200 annual DCL sailings to Nassau, the numbers are in your favor if you are looking for fun and sun. If you ever sail on the *Wish,* you will definitely go to Nassau.

   Note: The Bahamas bans the wearing of camouflage-print clothing. Leave all camo-print clothing items at home. This applies even to children and to obviously non-military items such as women's leggings or dresses.

TOURIST HIGHLIGHTS Nassau offers beautiful blue ocean waters with a variety of water sports, snorkeling, and stingray or dolphin encounters. The **Straw Market** feels like an obligatory stop, but you're unlikely to find anything compelling enough to purchase.

WHAT TO EAT Fresh seafood and rum cake can be found everywhere.

WHAT TO BUY Decorative conch shells make a nice reminder of the area. Also, look for local artwork and woven hats and bags.

Emily from Florida had this to say about Nassau:

Nassau is the default stop on the shorter Bahamian cruises, and while it has gotten a bad rap in years past, the recent port rejuvenation is really nice and is definitely worth some time off of the ship. The new port area houses gift shops, food and drink vendors, a museum, as well as clean bathrooms. Venturing out just past the port area, we enjoy conch fritters and both alcoholic and nonalcoholic

NASSAU PORT ADVENTURE RECOMMENDATIONS

TO DO

ATLANTIS AQUAVENTURE
We are fans of Atlantis and the water park. It's not cheap (and food is very expensive), but it's a fun way to spend a day. Between the casino, beach, and aquarium, there's plenty to fill a day.
• **Minimum height for waterslides** 48" • **Minimum age** None • **Price per person** $249 (age 10 and up), $149 (ages 4–9), free (age 3 and under) • **Duration** 4–6 hours
• **Activity level** Athletic • **Transportation** 25-minute bus ride

BAHA BAY DAY PASS AT BAHA MAR
Baha Mar is a beautiful new resort in Nassau. The water park is full of activities for all ages. The beach is beautiful, and there are lots of (expensive) options for food and activities for all ages.
• **Minimum height for most waterslides** 48" • **Minimum age** None • **Price per person** $199 (age 10 and up), $99 (ages 3–9), and free (age 2 and under) • **Duration** 6.5–7 hours • **Activity level** Moderate • **Transportation** 20-minute bus ride

BLUE LAGOON ISLAND BEACH DAY
Blue Lagoon is a beautiful resort with lots to do. Relax on the beach, have some lunch, and watch the dolphins and sea lions. If you want to swim or get in the water with dolphins, choose one of those excursions instead and explore the resort after. Choose the morning time for this excursion to spend more time at the resort before returning to the ship. Blue Lagoon can get fairly crowded if there are several ships in port, so you might want to check the port calendars before booking.
• **Minimum age** None • **Price per person** $85 (age 10 and up), $70 (ages 3–9), $29 (age 2 and under) • **Duration** 4.5–5.5 hours • **Activity level** Moderate
• **Transportation** 35-minute ferry ride

GRAYCLIFF CHOCOLATIER—THE ART OF CHOCOLATE MAKING AND FACTORY TOUR
Did someone say chocolate? After a short tour of the chocolate-making factory, get suited up in hypoallergenic gear and learn all about chocolate while making some of your own chocolate creations to take with you. We can say from experience that no matter how pretty your chocolate creations are (or are not), they are still delicious.
• **Minimum age** 5 • **Price per person** $74 (age 10 and up), $64 (ages 5–9)
• **Duration** 1.5–2 hours • **Activity level** Mild • **Transportation** 10-minute bus transfer

TO AVOID

ARDASTRA GARDENS AND WILDLIFE CONSERVATION CENTRE
A small, underwhelming "zoo." Avoid this tour if birds weird you out.
• **Price per person** $84 (age 10 and up), $59 (ages 3–9), free (age 2 and under)

SEAWORLD EXPLORER SEMI-SUBMARINE
The windows of the sub are often so dirty you can't see the animals.
• **Price per person** $74 (age 10 and up), $46 (age 3 and under)

beverages at the Pirate Republic Brewing Co. On a recent visit, we took the 10- to 15-minute walk over to Margaritaville, where we purchased day passes to enjoy the lazy river, hot tub, and water slides, which were enjoyed by our teenage daughter and the adults! If you are looking for a beach, just in front of Margaritaville is Junkanoo Beach, which provides you such pretty views of the cruise ships! We avoid the close quarters of the Straw Market, but we usually find something fun to do and enjoy in Nassau.

A NOTE ABOUT NASSAU SAFETY

WE'VE NEVER HAD a bad experience in Nassau. We acknowledge, however, that crime is a problem. In 2024, the U.S. Department of State urged travelers to exercise increased caution due to crime. It also noted that violent crimes happen both inside and outside the tourist areas.

Canada's official tourism website offers great travel safety tips. Although labeled **Advice for Women Travellers,** they are relevant for people of all genders and nationalities. See theugseries.com/canada-travel-advice.

If you're concerned, participating in an official Disney port adventure is a good idea. If you want to explore Nassau on your own, be aware of your surroundings and advise any family remaining on board of your onshore plans.

unofficial **TIP**
Don't book watercraft excursions in Nassau. Activities involving commercial recreational watercraft, including water tours, are not consistently regulated. Watercraft may be poorly maintained, and some operators may not have safety certifications.

Caribbean

AFTER THE BAHAMAS, the Caribbean is the most popular cruise destination. Visiting this tropical locale means you're going to find mostly warm-weather excursions. Think beaches and water excursions, for the most part. English is the norm, and US dollars are welcome practically everywhere.

PROS	CONS
• Ports are easy to get to.	• The port experience, except at Castaway Cay and Lookout Cay, is *very* commercial.
• The US dollar is accepted in all ports, and English is spoken nearly everywhere.	• Except at Castaway Cay and Lookout Cay, your ship will most likely be one of many in port.
• Castaway Cay or Lookout Cay is part of nearly every itinerary.	• If you're not at least a little creative, DCL's Caribbean port stops tend to blend into one big duty-free-jewelry/hair-braiding/frozen-cocktail blur.
• A cruise from Florida can be combined with a Walt Disney World vacation.	
• You have your choice of ships and many cruise lengths.	• The summer heat can be oppressive.

CRUISES SAIL FROM Fort Lauderdale, Galveston, Port Canaveral, San Juan

SHIPS The *Magic, Dream, Fantasy,* and *Treasure* make periodic visits to the Caribbean in 2025.

CRUISE LENGTHS 4–7 or 10 nights

SEASON Year-round | **WHAT TO PACK** Sunscreen, shorts, swimsuits, and shoes you don't mind getting sandy

SIGNATURE PORT ADVENTURE Snorkeling at Castaway Cay or Lookout Cay

CLASSIC DISNEY ADD-ON Walt Disney World

POSSIBLE PORT STOPS **Antigua:** St. John's. **Bahamas:** Castaway Cay, Lookout Cay. **British Virgin Islands:** Tortola. **Grand Cayman:** George Town. **Jamaica:** Falmouth. **Mexico:** Costa Maya, Cozumel, Progreso. **St. Kitts:** Basseterre. **US Virgin Islands:** St. Thomas.

COMMENTS With so many DCL sailings to these ports, the numbers are in your favor if you're looking for sun and fun. Note that several Caribbean countries have a ban on wearing camouflage-print clothing. If you're on a Caribbean sailing, leave all camo-print clothing items at home. This applies even to children and to obviously non-military items such as women's leggings or dresses.

TOURIST HIGHLIGHTS Nearly every port in this area offers pristine beaches with a variety of water sports, snorkeling, and stingray or dolphin encounters. Many islands also offer tours of the local distilleries or breweries. If you're sailing out of Galveston, **Pleasure Pier** is fun for the kids. Port Canaveral's must-do is the **Kennedy Space Center.**

WHAT TO EAT African, British, Creole, Cuban, French, Spanish, and West Indian cultures influence island cuisine. Look for stews such as callaloo and fish chowder, as well as every variety of seafood preparation. On Grand Cayman, you'll find turtle on many menus. Fresh fruit is plentiful on the islands, including bananas, coconut, guava, mango, passion fruit, pineapple, and soursop. Try these on their own or made into jams and sauces.

WHAT TO BUY Decorative conch shells make a nice reminder of the area. Also look for local artwork and woven hats and bags. Rum and rum cake are ubiquitous in local shops. In Mexico, authentic vanilla is a popular purchase. Many island shops offer packets of locally grown spices. Jewelry is sold everywhere, often aggressively. See page 268 for our thoughts on buying jewelry while cruising.

Unofficial Guide reader Cathy from Alabama said the following about her Caribbean cruise:

Disney's seven-night Eastern Caribbean cruise is the perfect itinerary for relaxation. With three glorious sea days and three beautiful beach destinations, you can have it all! On our most recent Eastern Caribbean cruise, we visited Tortola (BVI), St. Thomas (USVI), and Disney's private island, Castaway Cay. In Tortola, we boarded a catamaran to White Bay in Jost Van Dyke. We enjoyed the pristine beach and ate a delicious lunch at Ivan's Stress Free Bar. In St. Thomas, we took the Red Hook Ferry to St. John to spend the day at Trunk Bay. The unspoiled beauty of this beach is truly worth the journey! And last, but certainly not least, we enjoyed a blissful day at Castaway Cay. Our family loves the peaceful seclusion found at the adult beach, Serenity Bay. I would be remiss not to mention that a Disney cruise ship is a gorgeous destination in itself. You can always find something to do, or you can relax and do nothing.

CARIBBEAN EXCURSION RECOMMENDATIONS

Following are some of our excursion recommendations for the Caribbean ports Disney visits most frequently.

Cozumel, Mexico

Cozumel is a standard port stop for many Caribbean cruises. Standard high temperatures range from 81°F to 90°F throughout the year, and lows range from 69°F to 78°F. The ship docks at the end of a long pier with a sky bridge that leads to Punta Langosta Mall, where you'll find

COZUMEL PORT ADVENTURE RECOMMENDATIONS

TO DO

ALL TERRAIN BUGGY AND SNORKEL

This is a fun day with all-terrain vehicles to drive and a beautiful snorkeling stop. We also appreciate the chips-and-salsa stop. The **Buggy and Beach Snorkel Combo** is a good, similarly priced alternative that includes lunch.
- **Minimum age** 8 (18 to drive) • **Price per person** $104 (ages 10 to 70), $94 (ages 8-9) • **Duration** 4-4.5 hours • **Activity level** Athletic • **Transportation** 10-minute walk

DOLPHIN SWIM AT DOLPHINARIS

If you want to swim with dolphins, Dolphinaris offers a good price; similar experiences in Nassau are twice as much. You'll be in the water for approximately 40 minutes, and then you are free to enjoy the resort. Be aware that the resort will want to sell you expensive photos of your encounter, which is the norm for this type of excursion.
- **Minimum age** 5 • **Price per person** $139 (age 10 and up), $111 (ages 5-9)
- **Duration** 3.5-4 hours • **Activity level** Moderate • **Transportation** 5-minute taxi ride

FURY CATAMARAN SAIL SNORKEL AND BEACH PARTY

Catamarans are always a great way to spend a day. This one is a 20-minute sail to a snorkeling destination, where you'll swim for about 40 minutes before sailing to a beach for some beach time on a private beach with an aqua park, which you will enjoy for about 90 minutes. We think this excursion is a great price for multiple activities.
- **Minimum age** 5 • **Price per person** $89 (age 10 and up), $54 (ages 5-9)
- **Duration** 3.5-4 hours • **Activity level** Moderate • **Transportation** Short walk on pier

TO AVOID

COZUMEL BEACH BREAK

We did not love the Playa Mia resort. There are prettier resorts nearby, like **Paradise Beach,** which is right next door.
- **Price per person** $94 (age 10 and up), $74 (ages 3-9), free (age 2 and under)

FALMOUTH PORT ADVENTURE RECOMMENDATIONS

TO DO

DUNN'S RIVER FALLS EXPRESS

Dunn's River Falls is a very popular tourist attraction in Jamaica, and many people make the trek. The falls are beautiful, and while most cruisers say it's worth it, be aware that the climb to the top can be slippery and crowded. We don't recommend it if the sound of that makes you nervous.
- **Minimum age** 6 • **Price per person** $99 (age 10 and up), $74 (ages 6-9)
- **Duration** 4-4.5 hours • **Activity level** Athletic • **Transportation** 70-minute bus ride

SKY EXPLORER, BOBSLED & ZIPLINE

This is a three-in-one excursion: chairlift ride, bobsled ride, and zip line. The bobsled ride is the highlight—it makes the whole excursion worth the transport time.
- **Minimum age** 6 • **Price per person** $169 (age 10 and up), $129 (ages 6-9)
- **Duration** 6-6.5 hours • **Activity level** Athletic • **Transportation** 60-minute bus ride

ZIPLINE & BLUE HOLE

Despite the very long transit time, the Blue Hole is a treasure. After zip-lining through the lush landscape, enjoy the natural pools with crystal-clear waters.
- **Minimum age** 6 • **Price per person** $169 (ages 10-80), $129 (ages 6-9)
- **Duration** 7-7.5 hours • **Activity level** Athletic • **Transportation** 80-minute bus ride

TO AVOID

GREEN GROTTO CAVES EXPRESS

Cruisers described this excursion as boring, noting there are better caves elsewhere.
- **Price per person** $84 (age 10 and up), $59 (ages 6-9)

GEORGE TOWN PORT ADVENTURE RECOMMENDATIONS

TO DO

CORAL BEACH CLUB
We aren't normally fans of paying for a beach day when you can just catch a taxi to a beach, but it is sometimes nice to have a reserved chair and welcome drink. The Coral Beach Club is located on the beautiful Seven Mile Beach.
• **Minimum age** None • **Price per person** $84 (age 10 and up), $74 (ages 3–9), free (age 2 and under) • **Duration** 4–4.5 hours • **Activity level** Mild • **Transportation** 15-minute bus ride

MANGROVE KAYAK ADVENTURE
If you enjoy kayaking, this is a great way to do it. Kayakers are led through the mangroves before enjoying some time in the Camana Bay shopping district.
• **Minimum age** 5 • **Price per person** $69 (ages 10–60), $54 (ages 8–9)
• **Duration** 2–2.5 hours • **Activity level** Athletic • **Transportation** 15-minute bus ride

STINGRAY SANDBAR AND SNORKEL TRIP
The stingrays are amazing. If you aren't terrified of them like some of our family members, getting in the water and being surrounded by friendly creatures is a cool experience. Follow it up with snorkeling in the beautiful blue waters of Grand Cayman.
• **Minimum age** 5 • **Price per person** $139 (age 10 and up), $99 (ages 5–9)
• **Duration** 3–4 hours • **Activity level** Moderate • **Transportation** 15-minute bus ride

TO AVOID

INTIMATE TRIP TO STINGRAY CITY AND STARFISH BEACH WITH LUNCH
While we love Stingray City, this excursion often isn't as intimate as the description makes it sound. You are better off on a private charter for the cost.
• **Price per person** $169 (age 10 and up), $139 (ages 5–9)

some shops and restaurants and a Starbucks. You'll find taxis everywhere, waiting to take you all over the island—there are some good all-inclusive resorts with day passes that are a short taxi ride away. Snorkeling and scuba diving are the main draws to Cozumel. See our recommended excursions on the previous page.

Falmouth, Jamaica

Falmouth is a somewhat polarizing stop for cruisers. There are some great places to visit in Jamaica, but they aren't that close to Falmouth. Standard high temperatures range from 85°F to 91°F throughout the year, with lows from 70°F to 75°F. The ship docks in a small port with stores, local vendors, and restaurants that open for cruise ships. As we mentioned, most things you will want to see are not close to the port, and we don't necessarily recommend venturing very far outside the port without an excursion. **Mystic Mountain-Rainforest Adventures** is a popular destination for zip-lining, bobsledding, rock climbing, and other adventurous activities. **Dunn's River Falls** is a spectacular natural phenomenon that is a hit with most tourists. There are a few nearby beaches that are a short taxi ride away if you do want to go out on your own. Definitely try the jerk-style chicken and Jamaican patties. See our recommended Falmouth excursions on the previous page.

George Town, Grand Cayman

We really enjoy Grand Cayman, even though it's a tender port (meaning you have to board a smaller boat to get ashore), which can be a bit of a

PROGRESO PORT ADVENTURE RECOMMENDATIONS

TO DO

CHICHEN ITZA MAYAN RUINS AND CENOTE SWIM
While we really hate long transfers, most cruisers agree that these ruins are worth it, and cooling off with a swim and lunch is a good way to end the tour.
- **Minimum age** 3 • **Price per person** $179 (age 10 and up), $149 (ages 3–9)
- **Duration** 8–8.5 hours • **Activity level** Moderate • **Transportation** 130-minute bus ride

HOLY GUACAMOLE, SALSA AND MARGARITAS BEACH COOKING
If you're looking for something beyond a beach excursion, this is a fun one. Plus, it ends with some beach time. We are all for food-centric excursions.
- **Minimum age** None • **Price per person** $74 (age 10 and up), $49 (ages 3–9), free (age 2 and under) • **Duration** 5–5.5 hours • **Activity level** Moderate • **Transportation** 60-minute bus ride

MAYAPAN RUINS, LAZY RIVER TUBING AND CAVE SWIM
These are some great ruins, and the cave swimming is awesome.
- **Minimum age** 8 • **Price per person** $104 (age 10 and up), $89 (ages 8–9)
- **Duration** 7–7.5 hours • **Activity level** Moderate • **Transportation** 90-minute bus ride

TO AVOID

INCLUSIVE BEACH EXPERIENCE
We heard from a few cruisers who were disappointed in the beach on this excursion.
- **Price per person** $74 (age 10 and up), $44 (ages 3–9), free (under age 3)

hassle. Standard high temperatures range from 84°F to 90°F throughout the year, with lows from 73°F to 78°F. There are some restaurants and stores in the port area, and there are a few charter-boat companies if you want to customize your own excursion, which we have done. **Stingray City** is a highlight for us. We've been in some very choppy waters there, which wasn't as enjoyable, but when the water is calm, it's an amazing place. The snorkeling is also beautiful in Grand Cayman. Try the rock shrimp or conch while visiting. See our recommended excursions for George Town on the opposite page.

Progreso, Mexico

Progreso, located on the Yucatan Peninsula, is a relatively new port for Disney Cruise Line. Standard high temperatures there range from 82°F to 91°F throughout the year, with lows ranging from 67°F to 75°F. The pier is about 4 miles long and is one of the longest in the world. You can stroll along it or catch one of the frequent shuttles going back and forth between the ships and land. Cafés, shops, and a swimming beach are within walking distance of the pier. See our recommended excursions for Progreso above.

St. Thomas, US Virgin Islands

St. Thomas is longtime destination for Disney, and there's a reason it has stayed so popular. Despite the cars driving on the left side of the road like in the United Kingdom, you are fully in the United States when in St. Thomas. If you are a US resident, fire those phones up and enjoy sucking up that good old American cell service! Standard high temperatures range from 83°F to 89°F throughout the year, and lows range from 74°F to 80°F. There are some shops and cafés, a pharmacy,

ST. THOMAS PORT ADVENTURE RECOMMENDATIONS

TO DO

KAYAK, HIKE, AND SNORKEL OF CAS CAY
If you are looking for an active excursion beyond just beaches, this one is a three-in-one. Kayak through the mangroves, hike through this tropical ecosystem, and then snorkel through a marine sanctuary.
• **Minimum age** 8 • **Price per person** $109 (ages 10–76), $85 (ages 8–9)
• **Duration** 4–4.5 hours • **Activity level** Athletic • **Transportation** 20-minute bus ride

ST. JOHN CHAMPAGNE CATAMARAN SAIL & SNORKEL
Take a catamaran to St. John to relax on a beautiful beach and snorkel in the crystal-clear waters.
• **Minimum age** 5 • **Price per person** $99 (age 10 and up), $89 (ages 5–9)
• **Duration** 4.5–5 hours • **Activity level** Moderate • **Transportation** 20-minute bus ride

ST. JOHN TRUNK BAY BEACH & SNORKEL TOUR
Trunk Bay is beautiful. We highly recommend a visit. If snorkeling doesn't interest you or you have kids under age 5, opt for **St. John Trunk Bay Beach Getaway.**
• **Minimum age** 5 • **Price per person** $94 (age 10 and up), $79 (ages 5–9)
• **Duration** 4–4.5 hours • **Activity level** Moderate • **Transportation** Short walk to boat

TO AVOID

CORAL WORLD COMEBACK
In our opinion, Coral World is just OK. We don't recommend it if you are used to the huge aquariums we see in several US cities.
• **Price per person** $55 (age 10 and up), $49 (ages 3–9), free (under age 3)

SKYRIDE TO PARADISE POINT
We enjoy the Skyride; we just don't see the need to prebook through Disney. Walkups are welcome.
• **Price per person** $30 (age 12 and up), $20 (ages 6–11), free (under age 6)

and a bank near the port, and the **Paradise Point Skyride** is just steps away. At the top, you'll find gorgeous views and a restaurant and shop. It's just a 10-minute taxi ride (or 20-minute walk along the waterfront) to **Charlotte Amalie,** the main city on St. Thomas, with great walkable streets full of shops and restaurants. There are also some terrific beaches, like **Magens Bay,** just a taxi-ride away. Fresh seafood is abundant when you're ready to eat. See our recommended St. Thomas excursions above.

Tortola, British Virgin Islands

Tortola is the largest and most populated island in the British Virgin Islands (BVI), and it is quite beautiful. The BVI is a British Overseas Territory, but its official currency is the US Dollar (go figure). Standard high temperatures range from 79°F to 87°F throughout the year, with lows from 67°F to 73°F. The ship docks at Road Town Harbor which is about a 5-minute walk into town. Some of the best beaches around are in Tortola, including Cane Garden Bay, Smugglers Cove, and Apple Bay. We consider The Baths National Park a must when visiting Tortola and have chartered boats to get there. We have also visited via Disney excursions. The giant boulders at the Baths combined with the blue waters of Tortola make for a beautiful combination. See our recommended Tortola excursions on the opposite page.

TORTOLA PORT ADVENTURE RECOMMENDATIONS

TO DO

FAMILY BEACH ESCAPE TO JOST VAN DYKE
This motorized catamaran will take you to the absolutely gorgeous White Bay.
• **Minimum age** None • **Price per person** $179 (age 10 and up), $154 (ages 3–9),
$124 (age 2 and under) • **Duration** 5–5.5 hours • **Activity level** Moderate
• **Transportation** Short walk to catamaran

TOUR THE BATHS AT VIRGIN GORDA
The Baths are an incredibly popular destination, and you'll probably see several private
boats there. If you book a private option, you will likely have more time to explore the
caves and enjoy the baths, but this is a good option if you'd be more comfortable on
an official excursion.
• **Minimum age** 5 • **Price per person** $89 (age 10 and up), $69 (ages 5–9)
• **Duration** 4–4.5 hours • **Activity level** Athletic • **Transportation** 40-minute ferry

TREASURE ISLAND SWIM & SNORKEL
If you enjoy sailing, this is the excursion for you. Sail for approximately 1 hour to your
first snorkeling location, and then sail to a second location where you can relax on the
beach or snorkel from the beach.
• **Minimum age** 8 • **Price per person** $109 (age 10 and up), $89 (ages 8–9)
• **Duration** 4–4.5 hours • **Activity level** Moderate • **Transportation** Short walk to boat

TO AVOID

TOUR THE BATHS AT VIRGIN GORDA—WITH LUNCH
Unless you really want a lunch break at the Baths, which we don't necessarily object to,
we've heard that the lunch is not worth the increased price of this port adventure.
• **Price per person** $135 (age 10 and up), $115 (ages 5–9)

LESS VISITED PORTS *of* CALL

AS OF 2025 AND EARLY 2026, Disney Cruise Line sails to 11 different geographic locations. Here are some tips for the 8 that it doesn't visit quite as regularly.

Europe

PROS	CONS
• The scenery is spectacular.	• Food in port can be costly.
• This is a very family-friendly way to see Europe.	• These cruises are among DCL's most expensive, and the price doesn't include your airfare.
• Most of your meals are included in what are some expensive places to visit.	• Your budget could be affected by the currency exchange rates.

CRUISES SAIL FROM Barcelona, Civitavecchia, Southampton

SHIP *Fantasy*

CRUISE LENGTHS 3–12 nights | **SEASON** Summer

WHAT TO PACK Binoculars, warm clothing, good walking shoes

SIGNATURE PORT ADVENTURE Historic landmarks

CLASSIC DISNEY ADD-ON If you have any money left after your cruise, **Adventures by Disney** will gladly snap it up. **Disneyland Paris** is also fun.

2025 PORT STOPS Belgium: Zeebrugge (Brussels). **England:** Liverpool, Portland (Stonehenge), Southampton. **France:** Cherbourg, Marseilles, Toulon (Provence). **Greece:** Chania, Mykonos, Piraeus (Athens), Santorini. **Ireland:** Cobh (Cork). **Italy:** Civitavecchia (Rome), Genoa (Milan), Livorno (Florence, Pisa), Messina (Sicily), Naples (Pompeii), Palermo (Sicily). **Malta:** Valletta. **Portugal:** Lisbon. **Netherlands:** Amsterdam. **Norway:** Haugesund, Kristiansand, Stavanger, Nordfjordeid. **Scotland:** Greenock (Glasgow and Edinburgh). **Spain:** Barcelona, Bilbao, La Caruna, Palma de Mallorca, Vigo. **Sweden:** Gothenburg. **Turkey:** Kusadasi.

COMMENTS Mediterranean cruises are popular with families who want to see Southern Europe with minimal hassle. There was this movie called *Frozen* that was mildly popular a few years ago. We're not saying that Disney decided the best way for DCL to take advantage of this was to sail to Arendelle—sorry, *Norway*—but there are definitely a lot of tie-ins on the cruise. You'll also see scenery that can be appreciated only from a cruise ship. Dining has an international flair. In the summer of 2025, the *Fantasy* will sail to Europe.

TOURIST HIGHLIGHTS The Northern European ports also have many cultural and historical highlights: the **Van Gogh Museum** and **Anne Frank House** in Amsterdam, **Blarney Castle** in Cork, and the **Beatles tributes** in Liverpool. The more rural ports have striking natural wonders and wildlife. The **Blue Lagoon** hot springs in Reykjavík and the scenic vistas in the **Norwegian fjords** are magnificent.

WHAT TO EAT Fresh fish, fruits, and veggies are found in almost all port cities. You may have had the stereotypical cuisines of each country at home (pizza and pasta for Italy, tapas for Spain, souvlaki and baklava for Greece, bread and pastries for France, and so on), but having the real thing can be a real eye-opener. Bread in France really is better. Seafood is plentiful in Northern Europe, but you're more likely to find it here in salted, stewed, or preserved forms. Berries are the staple fruits; look for cloudberries and lingonberries, as well as blueberries and strawberries. In Norway, try School Bread, a sweet bun with a cream filling and toasted coconut topping. EPCOT's Norway Pavilion has a version of it, but you'll never see it in the same way after you've tried the real thing.

WHAT TO BUY Some of our favorite souvenirs have been books purchased at museum shops, jerseys or caps with the logos of the local sports clubs, and artifacts related to our own family history or religious background. Also look for products related to the local agriculture, such as a regional olive oil, jam made from local fruit, or a niche liqueur available only from one area. We also highly recommend handmade sandals from Greece. The price is great, and the leather is soft. In the Northern European ports, our favorite thing to buy is hand-knit woolen and felted items; they really understand how to make good mittens in colder climates. Many ports have shops dedicated to Christmas decor. If you celebrate, it's a great place to pick up fun and unique ornaments.

Heather from North Carolina said this about her European cruise:

European cruises provide a familiar and comfortable means of traveling to multiple countries over the course of the cruise. I loved my

11-night Norway/Iceland/Scotland and Mediterranean cruises with Disney. I highly recommend arriving a few days ahead of the cruise to allow time to get over jet lag and to explore the amazing port cities. Barcelona is a vibrant and fun city to visit, with so many amazing things to see, including La Sagrada Família, Las Ramblas, and Park Güell, and also venturing a little bit outside the city to Montserrat. Montserrat is an amazing place and a must-do, in my opinion! In Naples, an awesome port adventure is Pompeii and Mount Vesuvius. The history of Pompeii is honestly mind-blowing and chilling at the same time. Iceland is like being on another planet, and I can't recommend it enough. There's an adorable "Christmas House" in Akureyri that's a must-do if you have time. And naturally, doing the Golden Circle in Reykjavik is still one of my very favorite port adventures. Seeing the tectonic plates, the amazing waterfalls, the geysers, and the Blue Lagoon was life-changing! Europe is full of history and adventures for all ages.

Hawaii

PROS	CONS
• The cruises stop at multiple Hawaiian islands.	• Airfare can be pricey.
• Hawaii's natural beauty is unparalleled.	• You don't get much time in each port to get to know the islands in depth.
• The weather is mild.	• Your sailing may coincide with the rainy season.
• Sailing from the mainland West Coast eases you into the time difference.	• Food and activities on the islands can be expensive.
• United States residents have no issues with currency exchange or cellular roaming fees in port.	• Long cruises that include Hawaii require a substantial time commitment.
• The long sailings that include Hawaii give you plenty of time to bond with the crew.	• Disney's newer ships do not currently sail this route.

CRUISES SAIL FROM Vancouver or Honolulu (South Pacific Cruises also begin or end in Honolulu) | **SHIP** *Wonder*

CRUISE LENGTHS Typically 10 nights | **DATES** Spring and fall

WHAT TO PACK Clothing you can layer for warm and chilly weather. Suitable shoes for hiking if you're planning to explore beyond the beaches.

SIGNATURE PORT ADVENTURE Exploring a volcano

CLASSIC DISNEY ADD-ON A visit to Aulani, Disney's resort on Oahu

2025 PORT STOPS Hilo, Hawaii; Honolulu, Oahu; Kahului, Maui; Nawiliwili, Kauai

COMMENTS The 50th state is more than just sand and surf. If you have the time, stay for a few days before or after your sailing to more thoroughly explore the islands.

TOURIST HIGHLIGHTS Waterfalls and volcanoes are natural delights. The **Mauna Loa** macadamia nut factory and **Dole Plantation** offer tours and tastings. On Oahu, a main attraction is the **USS *Arizona* Memorial**; tours are a must, and tickets should be purchased in advance.

WHAT TO EAT Try fruits like durian, mangosteen, and rambutan. Spam musubi (Spam on rice) is a state favorite. "Shave ice" and Kona coffee are must-haves. The ubiquitous loco moco is a burger and fried egg over rice, and grilled fish is everywhere.

WHAT TO BUY Hawaiian shirts for the whole family, of course. There's no shortage of kitschy hula gear, if that's your thing. You'll almost certainly bring home a box of chocolate-covered macadamia nuts.

Jaason from California had this to say about his Hawaiian cruise:

I wanted to share our unforgettable experience on the Disney cruise to Hawaii. The natural beauty of the islands and the magic of Disney were a perfect match. Sailing from Vancouver, the anticipation grew as the weather gradually changed with each passing day. The sea days at the beginning were a perfect way to shift into vacation mode and relax before running around the islands. Cruises are a great fit for our family—my husband and I are able to enjoy the adults-only areas while our daughter makes friends from all over the world in the kids' club. The ship also transformed as we approached the islands, with Hawaiian music filling the air and tropical drinks served in pineapples. At each port, we were embraced by the aloha spirit and the warmth of Hawaiian hospitality. We chose to rent a car and explore at our own pace—if you're comfortable keeping an eye on the time, this is a great option to save money over the port adventures. The sights and experiences we discovered will be cherished for a lifetime, and we highly recommend this voyage!

Mexico

PROS	CONS
• These cruises can be especially afford-able if you live on the West Coast. • Short sailings are easy on your schedule.	• Although these cruises are marketed to families, they take place while school is in session, making scheduling an issue.

CRUISES SAIL FROM San Diego | **SHIP** *Wonder*

CRUISE LENGTH 3, 4, and 7 nights | **SEASONS** Spring

WHAT TO PACK Sun protection and sturdy walking shoes for excursions off the beach.

SIGNATURE PORT ADVENTURES The usual suspects: sightseeing, dolphin excursions, beach pursuits, shopping, partying

CLASSIC DISNEY ADD-ON Disneyland

2025 PORT STOPS Cabo San Lucas, Ensenada, and Puerto Vallarta, Mexico; Catalina Island and San Diego, California

COMMENTS These ports are standard stops for most cruise lines—the selling point for the autumn sail dates is Disney's onboard Halloween decor. For the spring sail dates, there's little to differentiate these cruises from those offered by other lines.

TOURIST HIGHLIGHTS The main draws for cruisers to Mexico are the stunning beaches.

WHAT TO EAT Try authentic versions of tacos, quesadillas, or tortas. Fare from a hole-in-the-wall stand or food truck may have mind-blowing flavors; wash it down with some Mexican beer. If there's a crowd, indicating rapid turnover, then you can assume the food is both delicious and safe to eat. For maximum safety, avoid consuming raw foods and avoid tap water.

WHAT TO BUY Unfortunately, much of the merchandise you'll encounter near the Mexican ports is mass-produced schlock. If you find a local craftsperson and admire their work, by all means support their business, but otherwise assume that many "Mexican" trinkets are made in China.

Cheryl from Texas had this to say about her cruise to Mexico:

Last year we realized our school district's winter break stretched longer into January than most, so we decided to check an item off our family's bucket list and sail Concierge for the first time out of San Diego on the beautiful Disney Wonder. *Pricing was very reasonable due to most kids being back in school by then, so we even upgraded to the two-bedroom suite. The Concierge staff was fantastic, attending to our every need, from supplying us with perpetual popcorn and cans of soda to immediately rebooking our port adventure in Ensenada when high seas canceled all the deep-sea fishing expeditions. Our artistic teens loved the alternate port adventure, learning about Mexican Day of the Dead traditions and painting their own sugar skulls. My favorite memory from this cruise was returning to the suite to find our kids and their cousins, who sailed with us, playing raucous Mexican card games at the dining room table in the spacious suite. We've sailed with Disney 16 times (and counting!), and this cruise, along with the European itineraries and Marvel Day at Sea, ranks near the top.*

New Zealand *and* Australia

PROS	CONS
• This is the best of both worlds for North American travelers! You get to visit the beautiful countries Down Under while also enjoying all that DCL offers.	• Getting to and from Australia is not easy or cheap for North American guests.

CRUISES SAIL FROM Aukland, Melbourne, Sydney

SHIP *Wonder* | **CRUISE LENGTHS** 2–7 or 10 nights | **DATES** Fall and winter (the US versions)

WHAT TO PACK Lots of layers.

SIGNATURE PORT ADVENTURE A tour of the Sydney Opera House.

COMMENTS Sandwiched between the long transatlantic crossings to New Zealand and Australia (see page 371) are a series of shorter sailings in and around Australia and New Zealand. There's also a 10-night sailing from Auckland to Sydney over Christmas in 2025.

2025 PORT STOPS Australia: Eden, Hobart, Melbourne, Sydney. **New Caledonia:** Nouméa.

TOURIST HIGHLIGHTS The **Sydney Opera House** is a must-see landmark, though many Australian guests will already be familiar with it.

WHAT TO EAT North American guests will want to sample things that are rare or impossible to find at home, such as kangaroo meat, Vegemite, or lamingtons (sponge cakes with shaved coconut). Australian barbecue is a classic main meal—"put another shrimp on the barbie" is for real.

WHAT TO BUY The Akubra hat was popularized by the *Crocodile Dundee* film franchise. Made from felted rabbit fur, they are great for keeping the sun off your face. Kangaroo leather goods, such as wallets or belts, are often inexpensive. Emu oil preparations are said to help with a variety of ailments. Boomerangs are a common souvenir, but be careful when learning how to use them. Ugg boots originated in Australia; you can buy them from the source here.

Ileen from Minnesota spent some days in Sydney before sailing:

Before leaving on a Disney cruise departing from Sydney, we spent a few days exploring the city. The Sydney Tower Eye has a great aerial view of Sydney, and the Sydney Opera House is a stunning building! The tour of the opera house was very informative. A ferry boat was our mode of transportation to get to the Taronga Zoo. I enjoyed seeing a lot of Australian animals up close. A day trip was on the schedule to the Blue Mountains outside of Sydney. Some of the highlights of our day tour were the Prince Henry Cliff Walk and riding on the Scenic Skyway and the Scenic Railway. At the Featherdale Wildlife Park, I was able to hand-feed the kangaroos. The Disney Wonder sailing under the Harbor Bridge was a great way to say goodbye to Sydney.

Pacific Coast

PROS	CONS
• Because these are among DCL's shortest cruises, they can be very affordable, particularly if you live on the West Coast. • Short cruises are easy on your schedule.	• Because they stop at only a few of the many worthwhile destinations along the Pacific Coast, these cruises aren't the best way to see California.

CRUISES SAIL FROM San Diego or Vancouver | **SHIP** *Wonder*

CRUISE LENGTHS 4 or 5 nights

SEASON Before and after the Alaskan runs

WHAT TO PACK Walking shoes, sunscreen

SIGNATURE PORT ADVENTURE City tour (but you're often better off exploring on your own).

CLASSIC DISNEY ADD-ON Disneyland

2025 PORT STOPS Astoria, Oregon; San Francisco; Seattle; Victoria, British Columbia.

COMMENTS Although recreational and/or medical marijuana is legal in many ports visited on these cruises, it is not allowed on the ships. Bringing marijuana aboard may result in expulsion from the ship or legal action.

TOURIST HIGHLIGHTS In San Diego, the zoo is a big draw for families. Also check out the **Hotel del Coronado,** a key inspiration for the Grand Floridian Resort & Spa at Walt Disney World.

WHAT TO EAT Many of the port stops are cities with vibrant Asian populations. Seek out the area's Chinatown or Koreatown for authentic dishes.

WHAT TO BUY Grab some gear representing the local sports teams.

Erika from Idaho loved her Pacific Coast cruise and had the following to say:

> *We were so impressed with the Disney cruise! First, the level of service is incomparable. The ship was clean, food outstanding, staff welcoming . . . We had been told about the magic of Disney cruises, but experiencing it really surpassed our expectations. We loved this cruise. We loved all of the days at sea to explore and enjoy the ship. Nothing felt hurried. We loved the spa and the restaurants. My husband and I are musicians and truly believe the singers in the evening shows on the cruise were better than the performers in the Broadway Disney shows. Victoria is breathtakingly beautiful, with great food and a quaint downtown. It was the perfect relaxing end to a relaxing week. We loved celebrating our 20th anniversary this way.*

Panama Canal

PROS	CONS
• On a per-night basis, longer cruises are less expensive than shorter ones.	• These sailings have become few and far between.
• Two weeks gives you lots of time to get to know the crew.	• Other than the canal itself and the city of Cartagena, Colombia, the ports are kind of a snooze—they're the same ones visited by every other line.
• This is a great way to experience the Panama Canal.	

CRUISES SAIL FROM Galveston | **SHIP** *Magic*

CRUISE LENGTH 14 nights | **SEASONS** The next sailing is in the spring of 2026 and will be westbound.

WHAT TO PACK Formal wear—14-night cruises give you lots of chances to dress up.

SIGNATURE PORT ADVENTURE It's all about going through the canal.

CLASSIC DISNEY ADD-ON Disneyland

2025 PORT STOPS **Colombia:** Cartagena. **Costa Rica:** Puntarenas. **Grand Cayman:** George Town. **Mexico:** Cabo San Lucas, Cozumel, Puerto Vallarta. **United States:** Galveston, San Diego.

COMMENTS Going through the Panama Canal is a classic itinerary for cruising, and you can let your friends and family know when they can see the ship in one of the great engineering achievements of the world by sending them to theugseries.com/panama-canal-cam (click on the "Web Cams" tab). Be sure to wave to the camera!

TOURIST HIGHLIGHTS The **Panama Canal** itself is the main attraction here. Plan to spend the canal-crossing day on the ship's outdoor decks or on your verandah if you have one.

WHAT TO EAT Try authentic tacos when in the Mexican ports.

WHAT TO BUY For the Mexican ports, see our section on cruising in Mexico (page 366). The ship will also likely carry some fun Disney-themed Panama Canal merchandise.

Kelly from Texas said this about her Panama Canal cruise:

The westbound Panama Canal cruise was easily the best cruise we ever sailed! The daily informational canal presentations leading up to the transit day were fantastic. They really prepared us to fully comprehend what we would be seeing. Having a retired canal pilot on the PA system the day of the canal transit was like having a guided tour all day. So informative! In Cartagena, be sure to get a tour of the old city. The monastery and numerous sanctuaries are absolutely gorgeous—such vibrant history and culture. In Cabo, we took a sailboat out to see Land's End and swim in the Pacific. We even spotted some late-season whales! With so many days on board (and not many port days), the crew went all out to keep the entertainment and food varied and interesting. We had a ball! Plenty of relaxation but also so much to do that was fresh to well-seasoned cruisers like us.

South Pacific

PROS	CONS
• South Pacific sailings are a nice way to experience the South Seas area without the shock of a massive time change.	• Whatever your departure port, your airfare to the port and/or home after the cruise will likely be expensive.

CRUISES SAIL FROM Sydney or Honolulu

SHIP *Wonder* | **CRUISE LENGTHS** 14 or 15 nights | **SEASONS** Fall and winter (the US version)

WHAT TO PACK Lots of layers. You will have summer temperatures in the South Seas, but the crossing will have a variety of climates.

SIGNATURE PORT ADVENTURE A tour of the Sydney Opera House.

COMMENTS These transpacific sailings are aimed at US/Canadian guests who want a long sea-based journey as transportation to Australia.

2025 PORT STOPS American Samoa: Pago Pago. **Fiji:** Lautoka, Suva. **Hawaii:** Honolulu. **New Caledonia:** Nouméa. **South Pacific:** International date line.

TOURIST HIGHLIGHTS There are worse things than beginning or ending your cruise in Hawaii, not to mention beginning or ending in Sydney on the other end. The gorgeous islands in between are the icing on the cake.

WHAT TO EAT Kokoda is a raw fish salad (similar to ceviche) that's very popular in Fiji. If you are a fan of poke bowls, you'll probably enjoy Kokoda as well. Fresh seafood is a good option at any of these ports.

WHAT TO BUY If you have enough room for a handmade basket in your luggage, it would make a great souvenir. There are also some exquisite pearls on the islands if you have a bigger budget.

Kris from Michigan had the following to say about her South Pacific cruise:

We absolutely loved our South Pacific cruise for many reasons: Sydney was fabulous to see before embarking; the long duration of the cruise (good mix of port and sea days); and the ports themselves (Fiji, New Caledonia, American Samoa, and Maui). On American Samoa, we even had dance troupes on the dock welcoming us and thanking us for visiting their island. I highly recommend a couple of excursions: in Fiji, the **Jewels of Fiji** *(longboat ride to swim in waterfalls, then back to the village for cultural ceremonies and lunch), and in American Samoa,* **The Village Way of Life** *(native demonstrations, dancing, and samples of food and drink). The people were so friendly, and we learned so much.*

Transatlantic

PROS	CONS
• A transatlantic cruise can be a cost-effective way to travel to Europe if you have the time to spare.	• You might not have 2 weeks to dedicate to a transatlantic cruise.
• Many cruisers have a transatlantic cruise on their bucket list.	• This is one-way transportation. Even if you end up getting a great deal on the cruise itself, remember that you'll have to make room in your budget for your airfare home.
• You can sometimes score excellent last-minute deals on these cruises.	

CRUISES SAIL FROM Southampton or Port Canaveral

SHIP *Fantasy* | **CRUISE LENGTHS** 13 nights

SEASONS Spring (eastbound) or fall (westbound)

WHAT TO PACK Formal wear—you'll have plenty of opportunities to dress up, if you want to—and a steamer trunk, if you have one.

SIGNATURE PORT ADVENTURE When it comes to transatlantic cruises, it's all about the journey rather than the destination.

CLASSIC DISNEY ADD-ON Disneyland Paris

POSSIBLE PORT STOPS Bahamas: Castaway Cay. **Portugal:** Lisbon, Ponta Delgada (Azores). **Spain:** Barcelona, Cadiz.

COMMENTS Want to travel to or from Europe without jet lag *and* pretend you've gone back in time? Crossing the Atlantic by ship is the old-school way to do it, harking back to the era of the grand ocean liner. This is the cruise on which you'll be able to read the entirety of the epic novel that's been sitting on your nightstand for months, or to write your own.

TOURIST HIGHLIGHTS The Cadiz Cathedral—once known as the Cathedral of the Americas because it was built with funds from the trade between Spain and America—is a popular stop. In Portugal, readers recommend a tuk-tuk (motorized rickshaw) tour.

WHAT TO EAT Fresh seafood is abundant in Cadiz. In Portugal, you'll want to try a pastel de nata (custard tart).

WHAT TO BUY If you can get it home without breaking it, the beautiful, colorful ceramics from Cadiz and Lisbon are nice souvenirs.

Misty from Virginia had the following to say about her transatlantic cruise:

We are big fans of Disney's westbound transatlantic cruise. Our most recent one was an 11-night cruise, so very heavy on the sea days, which we thoroughly enjoyed! Disney does an incredible job of offering special activities on the longer cruises (cooking demonstrations, lectures, dance lessons, etc.), so we found the perfect balance between complete relaxation and enjoying the activities. We took excursions in each port, which were fantastic! In Vigo, we took a group tour to the Cathedral of Santiago de Compostela, a UNESCO World Heritage Site and the end of the journey for many who walk the Camino de Santiago. And in Bermuda, we took a private driving tour that included the famous pink-sand beaches and Gibb's Hill Lighthouse. Bonus: The westbound transatlantic eases you back into Eastern time, so there's no jet lag when you get home.

OTHER WAYS *to* CRUISE

KEY QUESTIONS ANSWERED IN THIS CHAPTER

- What other cruise line may be right for me? *(see below)*
- How does a river cruise compare to ocean cruising? *(see page 378)*
- What's an expedition cruise? *(see page 380)*

OVERVIEW

ACCORDING TO THE Cruise Lines International Association (CLIA), the world's largest cruise industry trade association, 85% of travelers who have cruised will cruise again. Cruising is just that good.

With literally dozens of cruise lines to choose from, you might be wondering whether Disney is the right cruise line for you. Or maybe you have done Disney cruise and now want to try another line that offers a similar experience. Well, you've come to the right place! In this chapter, we take a deep dive (see what we did there?) into some of the other options that are available.

First, let's talk about the different types of cruising. There are lots of different ways to break down cruise types, but for our purposes, we will use the following: **ocean, luxury, river,** and **expedition.**

OCEAN CRUISES Disney Cruise Line obviously fits into this category. Ocean cruises are what most of us picture when we picture a cruise. Within the ocean category, you'll find ships with capacities ranging from 1,000 guests to 7,000 or more guests, and there is something that will appeal to just about everyone.

LUXURY CRUISES Luxury cruises include many more amenities than you would find on a typical ocean cruise line. If you are looking to travel the world in style and don't mind paying for it, a luxury cruise line may be just what you are looking for. There are also some small-ship lines that cruise the ocean and seas. They are similar to luxury ocean lines as far as what they include, but they also have the added benefit of being able to travel where the large ships can't.

RIVER CRUISING Thanks to some well-placed (and pervasive) ads by Viking, river cruising has really taken off in the last 10 years and has transitioned from a much older clientele to, well, a mostly older clientele. But the number of younger guests experiencing the joy of river cruising is certainly growing every year. Disney has dipped its toe into the river cruise market by chartering several AmaWaterways ships a year and broadening the appeal of river cruising to families with children as young as 5 years old.

EXPEDITION CRUISING is a hot, newer form of cruising. Several new and existing cruise lines have ships built to take you to new and exciting destinations in either the lap of luxury or a more standard experience. Expedition cruising is another type of travel where Disney saw the market growth and wanted a piece of it. It now has a few different options on chartered ships with Adventures by Disney.

So, which one is for you? Well, the truth is, there may be more than one. Keep reading to find out why.

OCEAN CRUISE LINES

THERE'S NO QUESTION that Disney charges a premium for its voyages. As fans of Disney Cruise Line, we believe there's a reason for that. Disney offers great service, has some of the most attractive ships sailing, and goes out of its way to make sure everyone has a great time with high-quality family experiences.

Disney isn't the only great cruise line out there, however, and there may be another that you will enjoy. We are also big believers that one cruise line does not fit all. Different lines target and appeal to different audiences. Let's look at some of them.

CARNIVAL CRUISE LINE Carnival is both one of the oldest mass-market ocean cruise lines and one of the most well-known. When it came on the scene, Carnival quickly became known for its inexpensive party cruises. Over the years, while it certainly couldn't be described as a luxury brand, it has improved its reputation somewhat. With more than 27 ships and some shockingly low prices, it still attracts a party crowd, especially over spring break. However, the newer ships—*Jubilee* and *Mardi Gras* in particular—are beautiful and filled with happy passengers. If you are looking to avoid the party boat atmosphere, we'd recommend avoiding traditional spring break times and sticking to longer cruises on the newer ships. If low prices are your only goal, find a great deal and go for it.

CELEBRITY CRUISE LINE Celebrity is one of Tammy's favorite (non-Disney) cruise lines, probably because of its similarities to Disney. Like Disney, Celebrity is a high-quality cruise line with excellent service.

While there are some upgraded dining options and add-ons, you aren't going to feel nickel-and-dimed on board, as you would on some other lines, and the service level is high. The ships are beautiful masterpieces, with the *Edge* class taking them to another level. The one area in which Celebrity may fall short of Disney would be its children's programming. There are some fun spaces for children ages 3–12 (especially on the newer ships), but they are nowhere near as elaborate as Disney's, and there will usually be a lot fewer children. Depending on your children's ages and how social they are, that may be a plus for your family.

HOLLAND AMERICA Holland America has some huge fans, but it is also not known as a line for children; it attracts an older, more laid-back crowd. There is some children's programming, but availability is not guaranteed if there is a particularly high number of children on board. One area of the world that Holland America does particularly well is Alaska. Interestingly enough, Alaska sailings also tend to have a younger demographic. Stick to the newer ships like MS *Nieuw Statendam* and MS *Rotterdam,* if you are interested.

MARGARITAVILLE AT SEA Calling all Jimmy Buffet fans! Well, maybe not all of them, but definitely anyone looking for an inexpensive cruise with an "It's five o'clock somewhere" mentality. The *Paradise* is an older ship that was purchased by Margaritaville and shows its age at times, but a brand-new ship, the *Islander,* launched in June 2024. Margaritaville at Sea does have some very generous discounts for military and first responders. There are kids' clubs, and often there's a surprising number of children on board, probably due to the low prices.

MSC MSC is an interesting cruise line. Although it started as a cruise line catering to a predominantly foreign market, it has worked hard to get more Americans on board and make them feel more welcome. Their newer ships, like the *Euribia, World Europa,* and *World America,* appeal more to the American market. The private island, Ocean Cay, is one of the best private islands in the Caribbean—and there are some spectacular ones out there, so that's saying a lot.

NORWEGIAN CRUISE LINE Norwegian pioneered the "freestyle cruising" concept that other cruise lines have adopted under different names. Freestyle dining is a break from strict dining times and lets the cruiser decide what time to eat each night. Norwegian has some great activities aboard its newer ships, like go-karts, ropes courses, waterslides, and more. (You'll encounter extra charges for many of those activities.) Norwegian also has solo staterooms on some of its ships, so if you are cruising alone, those are a great option. While not as inexpensive as lines like Carnival, Norwegian does tend to cost a little less than competitors like Royal Caribbean.

PRINCESS Princess made a name for itself in Alaska, and it touts itself as the number one cruise line in Alaska. We agree; it does Alaska very well. It's also a great option if you want to add time on land in Alaska, as Princess has a great system of lodges throughout the state. This cruise line, however, typically caters to an older crowd and may not be the best option for families. On Tammy's Alaskan cruise on Princess, there were exactly four children on board. Four. To be fair, those children did look pretty happy. Many of the Princess ships in Alaska are older; try the newest one, the *Discovery Princess*. The *Sun Princess* began sailing the Caribbean in 2024 to great reviews, and the *Star Princess* should follow in 2025. If you are a die-hard *Love Boat* fan, you will probably be happy with any of them.

ROYAL CARIBBEAN INTERNATIONAL Many consider Royal Caribbean to be Disney's closest competitor, and we wouldn't necessarily disagree. It is both marketed directly to and is very well suited for families. With the exception of its newest ships, Royal Caribbean easily beats Disney if price is your only consideration. If you look beyond price, however, it's a harder call. In our opinion, Royal Caribbean beats Disney in some areas, like onboard activities for teens (climbing walls, bumper cars, ice rink, surfing, indoor skydiving), the number of dining options, and the embarkation process, while Disney wins when you compare kids' clubs, theming, and nightclubs. More is included on Disney as well, like soda, room service, and real hair products (not that three-in-one stuff that's panned by women everywhere—or maybe just Tammy). Both lines have wonderful island destinations (we are huge fans of CocoCay), although Royal has several upcharges on its island, like the water park and adult beach area. Disney and Royal are not the same experience, and as we've said, there's a reason Disney charges more. We've done several Royal Caribbean cruises, however, and we think it's a great option for families with tweens and teens or families who don't want to pay Disney's prices. Shout-out to our friend Matt Hochberg, creator of *The Royal Caribbean Blog* (royalcaribbeanblog.com), who does a great job of keeping followers up-to-date on all things Royal Caribbean.

VIRGIN VOYAGES This Richard Branson–owned, adults-only cruise line entered the market in 2020. Or it tried to. We all know what happened to cruises in 2020. When the advertising first began, there was a lot of innuendo and some racy plans revolving around this adult-themed line. Perhaps the market for that type of cruise line wasn't quite as big as Sir Richard and company anticipated, and by the time the actual launch happened in August 2021, the ads (and plans) were much tamer. Virgin is still edgier than any other mainstream ocean cruise line, but we really enjoy it, and not just because of the lack of children. The ships are beautiful and, for the most part, well designed, with some unique spaces that we truly enjoy. There are no huge dining rooms, just a great collection of smaller specialty restaurants, all of which are included in your fare. We think Virgin may have the highest-quality food at its included restaurants of any ocean cruise line. Gratuities and basic Wi-Fi are also included in the cost of your cruise. There are some (tiny) solo cabins available, which will save solo travelers some money. If crazy-firm beds aren't your thing and some extra benefits are, we recommend upgrading to a RockStar suite.

LUXURY CRUISING

LUXURY CRUISING COMES at a luxury price tag, but it's about more than just the price. If you love sailing Concierge or end up paying for various upgrades and experiences on board, you might enjoy a luxury cruise line. There are several to choose from; some are large ships, and some are fairly small. Some include excursions, and some include things like alcohol. With a few exceptions, they generally range from about 400–1,200 passengers, and unlike most ocean cruise lines, almost all luxury lines offer low solo supplements (fees paid by solo cruisers to make up for the revenue lost when a cabin is not fully booked) from time to time. You won't find any megaships in the luxury category. We'll take a look at the differences in some popular options here.

AZAMARA CRUISES Azamara's four ships each accommodate around 700 guests and are small enough to get into smaller ports. Most specialty dining and alcohol are included, as is room service. Azamara prides itself on extended port stays. If you enjoy staying overnight in ports, Azamara may be for you. Children are allowed, but there is no programming of any kind for them. Select sailings have low solo supplements.

CRYSTAL This cruise line was recently purchased by the luxury group tour company Abercrombie & Kent. With only two ships that range from 600–700 guests each, every suite comes with butler service. Most dining and alcohol are included, and Crystal offers the only Nobu at sea, which is also included. Children are welcome, and there may be limited programming on some sailings. Select sailings also offer zero solo supplements.

EXPLORA JOURNEYS Explora is a new cruise line with two identical ships (more are on the way) with have a capacity of 900 guests. It offers specials for solo travelers, half-off fare for kids ages 2–17 (infants age 6 months to 2 years old sail free), and extensive inclusions, such as alcohol, almost all dining, gratuities, Wi-Fi, shuttles in port, a thermal spa, and some fitness programs. There is a dedicated space for kids ages 6–17, as well as adults-only spaces.

OCEANIA CRUISES Oceania's ships hold 680–1,250 guests and offer itineraries ranging from 7 nights to 200 nights. Cruise fares include all dining on board, gratuities, Wi-Fi, and nonalcoholic beverages. Alcohol packages are also available. Children are welcome, but there is no kids' programming. There are several solo staterooms available.

REGENT SEVEN SEAS CRUISES Regent touts itself as the world's most luxurious cruise line, and it does have some of the most inclusive fares in the industry; they include shore excursions, all dining, and alcoholic and nonalcoholic beverages. With marble floors and crystal chandeliers, the ships ooze luxury and hold around 700–750 guests. While children are welcome, not all ships and itineraries include programming. Regent offers zero-solo-supplement specials from time to time.

SEABOURN Seabourn likes to compare itself to a private yacht experience, and there are some similarities. Most of its ships hold 450–600 guests, and children are welcome. Although there is no formal kids' programming, children are free on shore excursions, which is nice. Seabourn includes alcohol, all dining, Wi-Fi, gratuities, some excursions, and even caviar. It offers special fares for solo travelers at times.

SILVERSEA Silversea has upped the all-inclusive idea by adding executive transfers from your house to the airport (provided you live within 50 miles), plus the same option in reverse when you return home. Fares generally include flights and precruise and postcruise hotels if they are needed, depending on the flight schedule. Every room is a suite, and every suite has a butler. Alcohol, Wi-Fi, gratuities, and some shore excursions are included, and select voyages have very low solo supplements. Children are permitted on only some itineraries, and there is no special programming. Ship capacity ranges from 200 to just over 700 guests.

VIKING OCEAN CRUISES To be honest, luxury doesn't always come to mind with Viking, and we stand by that for Viking River Cruises. Viking Ocean, however, is different. Viking Ocean ships hold around 900 guests and include a shore excursion in each port, Wi-Fi, and specialty dining. All rooms have verandahs. No one under 18 is allowed on board, so Viking might be a good choice for those looking for a more high-end vacation without children. It occasionally offers solo fares as well.

 # RIVER CRUISING

RIVER CRUISING IS a slower-paced vacation than ocean cruisers may be used to. These cruises are about the destination more than the journey. The ships are smaller, with less than 200 people on board, and the crowd tends to be a little older, although the median age is coming down slowly. There is one dinner seating, and usually there's not a lot happening late into the night. If that immediately sounds boring to you, let us assure you it is not. River cruise ships visit big and small towns and usually dock right in the cities. The time in ports, and there's a lot of it, is the real highlight. It's easy to walk on and off and explore on your own or take part in organized excursions, some or all of which are usually included in your cruise fare. The waters are calm, and seasickness won't be an issue on a river cruise. Guests need to be able to climb stairs, as elevators that reach the top deck are rare because everything on the top deck must be low-profile (or able to become low-profile) as the ship passes under low bridges. Tammy has done several river cruises and thinks they are a great vacation. There are several lines to choose from. Here's a little about the most popular ones.

ADVENTURES BY DISNEY Adventures by Disney (ABD) ventured into river cruising in 2016. While there are adults-only itineraries, ABD river cruises are targeted at families. Like all ABD vacations, these cruises are Disney lite. ABD emphasizes Disney quality and service over vacations with Mickey Mouse. Children age 5 and up can sail, and Disney has taken traditional river cruise excursions and added family-friendly elements, all of which are included in your price. Alcohol and sodas are included at meals. ABD has also added more activities on board to keep families entertained. If you've always dreamed of a group sing-along to *The Sound of Music* after a visit to Austria, look no further. ABD is the river cruise line for you.

Disney partners with AmaWaterways and charters several of its ships on rivers all over Europe. They follow the standard itineraries that other lines do, such as the Rhine and Danube, as well as some specialty cruises like Food & Wine and Oktoberfest. The Christmas Market itineraries are especially popular. We are fans of both Ama Waterways ships and ABD river cruises, so it's the perfect combination, but it comes at a premium cost. It's a great way to travel and a wonderful way to see Europe with your family. There are a lot of terrific river cruise lines, but if you want one that caters to families and includes excursions with children in mind, ABD is the option you want.

AMADEUS Amadeus has beautiful ships and appeals to guests who want a more à la carte experience. The base prices do not include excursions, but they can be added. The minimum age is 8, but the excursions aren't created with that age in mind.

AMAWATERWAYS AmaWaterways is the line that Disney partners with. Not surprisingly, Ama (as this cruise line is often called in the biz) has several ships with connecting rooms or rooms that sleep three. Both of these options are hard to find on other lines. Ama has multiple options for excursions each day, both for guests who want a vigorous activity and those who might be "gentle walkers"—and they are all included. The minimum age is 4, but there won't be excursions or activities that target younger kids unless you are booked on an Adventures by Disney charter (see above).

AVALON Avalon is very similar to AmaWaterways in terms of inclusions and pricing. The beds all face the water, which we think was a brilliant design choice. Who doesn't want to lie in bed and watch the beautiful countryside go by? The minimum age is 8.

EMERALD Emerald's ships are a little more bare-bones, and the minimum age is 12. If you aren't doing an ABD river cruise, 12 is about the age we think kids may start to enjoy a river cruise. Emerald has a lower price point, and only one excursion per day is included in the price.

NATIONAL GEOGRAPHIC Nat Geo also charters AmaWaterways ships and adds even more inclusions and experiences. Its river cruises have a minimum age of 5, but it doesn't cater to families like ABD. It does, however, have a similar price point. It also puts a regional expert on board for lectures and questions, and a photographer for lectures and photography tips. Tammy has done a Nat Geo river cruise and thought the additions to a standard AmaWaterways cruise were excellent.

RIVERSIDE Touting itself as a new luxury line, we were impressed with Riverside's ships and inclusions. There is no minimum age, but again, nothing is planned for smaller children. Excursions are not included but can be added.

RIVIERA Riviera has some great itinerary options, like shorter Christmas Market cruises for those who can't get away for seven or more days during the holidays. The prices are a little lower, and the ships are nice. The minimum age is 12. Fares include one excursion per port. We didn't have the smoothest cruise with Riviera, but it was the beginning of the season with a new (though very friendly) crew.

SCENIC Scenic is also more of a luxury line, and everything is included. It offers multiple excursions, beautiful ships, and an attentive crew. Alcohol and soda are available all day and are included. The minimum age is 12.

TAUCK Tauck, a luxury tour operator and a direct competitor of Adventures by Disney, has also moved into the river cruise market. Its ships have a luxury feel, and almost everything is included. If you get off the ship for an excursion at lunchtime, don't be surprised if you're handed cash to pay for lunch—that's how all-inclusive it is. Tauck also has some itineraries called Tauck Bridges, which are made for families (there's a minimum age of 3) and include activities and excursions made for families. We are big fans.

UNIWORLD UniWorld is a luxury line with everything included, and the ships are beautiful! The minimum age is 4, but it definitely isn't targeted to the kids.

VIKING Viking has the most recognizable name because of its incredible marketing, but it is not a luxury line. It does, however, offer a good river cruise, particularly for first-time river cruisers. There is only one excursion included per day, and the ships have the highest passenger counts with the smallest rooms. Viking's fans are very loyal, though, and the ships are nice. No one under 18 is permitted on board, so if you have little ones, this is not the line for you.

EXPEDITION CRUISING

WHAT EXACTLY IS EXPEDITION CRUISING? Expedition cruising is one of the hottest forms of travel right now. It's small-ship cruising not only to destinations that are hard to get to in traditional ways, like the polar regions and the Galapagos, but also to smaller cities and areas where larger ships can't go. While we've seen various levels of mobility among passengers on expedition cruises, they are generally targeted at a more active market. They are designed for adventurous travelers who want to see unique locations in, at a minimum, moderate style and perhaps even in luxury.

The size of the ship will greatly impact which destinations you'll visit. In Antarctica, for example, ships with more than 200 guests will not have as many opportunities to set foot on land, and ships with more than 500 guests will just sail through. Ships with more than 100 guests can't even visit the Galapagos.

Here are some popular expedition-cruise options, including some we've had incredible personal experiences with.

ADVENTURES BY DISNEY (**ABD**) As is the case with its river cruises, ABD doesn't have any of its own expedition ships but instead charters ships from other companies. Unlike river cruising, where ABD exclusively uses AmaWaterways ships, the ships it uses for expedition cruises vary greatly. Your travel agent or the ABD website can tell you exactly which ship it is using for your desired location.

In 2025, there are expedition cruises to the Adriatic and Galapagos, and we've seen them visit Antarctica and the Arctic as well. It's hard to predict where ABD will go and when it will add more options, so keep an eye out if you are interested. We love ABD, and it adds the same level of quality to its expedition cruises as it does to its traditional land or sea vacations (including the premium cost).

ATLAS OCEAN VOYAGES This luxury expedition line sailed onto the scene as the cruise industry began its recovery in 2021. It has three beautiful, nearly identical ships, all of which accommodate less than 200 guests, with two more ships on the way. Tammy sailed with Atlas to Antarctica and had one of the best and most unique vacations of her life. While the atmosphere on board is casual, the ship feels high-end all around. Gratuities, some Wi-Fi, and alcohol are included, and parkas are included on Polar expeditions. Our only real complaint was that Wi-Fi was not unlimited, although it was high-bandwidth via Starlink, even at the bottom of the world. Atlas is a great way to travel!

CELEBRITY Celebrity is more commonly known for its large ocean cruise ships, but it has a great offering for expedition cruising. It has a purpose-built ship in the Galapagos called the *Celebrity Flora*. The *Flora* is high-end all the way and holds 100 guests. We have sailed on the *Flora* and walked away wanting to drag every cruise lover we've ever known back on board to experience it.

NATIONAL GEOGRAPHIC National Geographic has partnered with Lindblad to visit the Galapagos, Antarctica, Japan, and more. It includes photographers and experts among the crew to enhance your vacation. It touts a flexible itinerary so it can take advantage of "wildlife opportunities or other spontaneous opportunities that arise." Two of its ships in Antarctica are new and even have glass igloos on the top deck that you can spend the night in at no additional cost on a first-come, first-served basis. We trust the National Geographic name and have had great experiences with this cruise line.

PONANT Ponant is a luxury line with luxury prices. The elegant ships sail to more than 450 ports on all seven continents. It has visited the poles longer than just about anyone else and is a self-proclaimed expert at it. You won't regret choosing it.

SEABOURN Seabourn entered the expedition market in 2021 with its first luxurious expedition ship. It now has two expedition ships that visit the poles during their respective summers and destinations all around the world during other times of the year. For an additional cost, there are submarines (!) on board, so you can get even more up close and personal with the underwater wildlife. The ships are stunning!

SCENIC Scenic describes its ships as "all-inclusive ultra-luxury," and that's not wrong. They're expensive and worth it. Scenic was one of the first cruise lines with expedition ships that realized there was a market for guests wanting to fly over the Drake Passage, the notoriously rough waterway guests must cross to get to Antarctica from South America. Anyone wanting to visit Antarctica and not have to deal with the "Drake Shake" appreciates that.

VIKING Viking dipped its toes into the expedition market in 2022 with two expedition ships. The ships are a little larger, with 378 passengers, but they are small enough to allow guests to set foot on land in Antarctica, although perhaps not as often as a smaller ship would allow. The ships are very nice, and we've had friends who loved their expedition cruises with Viking.

PART 17

WHAT'S NEXT *for* DISNEY CRUISE LINE?

KEY QUESTIONS ANSWERED IN THIS CHAPTER

- What do we think Disney's new ships will be like? *(see below)*
- What's coming up for Disney Cruise Line? *(see page 385)*

◗ THE *Disney Adventure*

HAS THERE EVER BEEN a more surprising announcement by Disney Cruise Line than that it was going to purchase a giant cruise ship commissioned by another cruise line? We don't think so. It makes sense on paper: DCL paid pennies on the dollar (maybe even fractions of a penny on the dollar) for what it would have cost to design and build a ship the size of the *Adventure*. But considering DCL's notorious attention to detail, buying a ship it did not design from the beginning was not on any of our bingo cards.

In our conversations with the crew aboard the current ships, their excitement for the *Adventure* has been palpable. We happened to be on board when the name was announced, and the crew couldn't stop talking about the ship. It's so different from anything we're used to, and we can't wait to experience it in person.

There are some things that will not change. Guests will still enjoy the Oceaneer Club, Edge, and Vibe for the kids, teens, and tweens. There will also be adults-only spaces and a luxurious spa. We will also see some familiar activities such as karaoke, bingo, silent DJ, and animation classes. Rotational dining will remain, as will some premium specialty dining (with regionally inspired food this time) at an additional cost. We can expect live stage shows featuring Disney songs and stories, as well as character encounters and both classic and recently released Disney movies on board.

THE FUTURE
by Scott Sanders of The Disney Cruise Line Blog

WE'VE REACHED INFINITY, and now Disney Cruise Line is taking it to the beyond with an unprecedented expansion on the horizon. It opened a brand-new port of call, **Disney Lookout Cay at Lighthouse Point,** in 2024, and two additional new cruise ships are scheduled to join the fleet in the coming years (with more on the horizon).

Disney's new year-round home port in Fort Lauderdale is now creating more opportunities to sail to the Caribbean and Bahamas. The additional year-round sailings from Florida will make regular use of Lookout Cay, which will complement Disney Castaway Cay.

The cruise line's rapid expansion started with the *Disney Wish* in 2022, and it is full steam ahead, with the recent launch of the *Disney Treasure* expanding the weekly offerings from Port Canaveral. The *Disney Adventure* will open the door to a whole new world, with sailings from Singapore, while the *Disney Destiny,* the third *Wish*-class ship, will expand offerings from Fort Lauderdale.

The fleet will continue to expand to 13 ships in 2031, including a partnership with Oriental Land Company that will bring a new *Wish*-class ship to Japan and launch 4 additional new builds between 2027 and 2031, creating opportunities for the cruise line to explore uncharted waters. With all this expansion, we may soon have the opportunity to book a voyage into the unknown..

The *Adventure* will feature seven uniquely themed lands:

- The **Disney Imagination Garden** is the central hub of the ship. Inspired by Disney stories from Mowgli to Moana, it's a gathering space with shopping, dining, and performances on an open-air stage. There will be some new quick-service restaurants here, including **Mowgli's Eatery,** which will serve Indian cuisine with a Disney twist, and **Gramma Tala's Kitchen,** a quick-service restaurant inspired by *Moana.* The concept art for this outdoor garden-type venue on the sea is absolutely beautiful.

- **Disney Discovery Reef** features ocean-themed stories such as *The Little Mermaid, Lilo & Stitch, Finding Nemo,* and *Luca* and will have themed shopping and dining options.

- Fans of *Big Hero 6* will be excited to see **San Fransokyo Street,** a family entertainment area featuring interactive games and activities, shops, cinemas, and more.

- **Wayfinder Bay** is a poolside retreat inspired by *Moana.*

- In **Town Square,** guests will find a fantastical forest filled with shops, lounges, cafés, restaurants, and entertainment venues inspired by the kingdoms of *Tangled, Cinderella, Frozen, Snow White and the Seven Dwarfs, The Princess and the Frog,* and others.

- Marvel fans will appreciate the new *Avengers* experience in **Marvel Landing.**

- **Toy Story Place** is for little ones and grown-ups alike, with friends from Andy's Room in a water-play zone and themed food venues.

The concept art for staterooms on board looks familiar (they'll still feature split bathrooms) but is updated with lighter woods and colors.

The *Adventure* is also the first Disney ship to feature staterooms with inward views of the ship. Concierge guests should have an upgraded experience with amenities not found on other DCL ships, such as an exclusive spa and fitness center.

Disney has confirmed that there will be a Marvel show on board, and Deadpool himself will even be aboard a Disney ship for the first time ever. (We have to assume that he will keep his irreverent brand of humor family-friendly for the cruise line.)

We are hopeful that Disney will strike the right balance between the things we love about Disney Cruise Line and new, unique experiences to keep North American and European cruisers excited enough to make the long journey to Singapore.

The FUTURE *of* DISNEY CRUISE LINE

IN THE SUMMER OF 2024, with two new ships (the *Disney Adventure* and *Disney Destiny*) still under construction and scheduled to begin sailing in 2025, Disney announced that an unprecedented five new ships were in the works.

In July, it announced that a new *Wish*-class ship would begin sailing year-round from Japan. Oriental Land Company, which owns and operates the spectacular Tokyo Disney Resort, entered a licensing agreement with Disney, and construction of the ship will begin in 2026 at Meyer Werft in Papenburg, Germany, where all its sister ships were built. It is expected to begin sailing in early 2029. Japan is one of our favorite destinations, and we are super excited about the prospect of sailing on a Disney ship from there. We're also looking forward to seeing what changes Oriental Land Company will bring to a *Wish*-class ship. If Tokyo Disney is any indication, the company has deep pockets and a big imagination. While the basic layout of the ship will remain the same, the interior possibilities are almost endless. We think they'll surprise us in the best of ways!

Then, in August, there was a lot of speculation at D23 (Disney's fan expo) that Disney would announce that two more ships were in the works. Well, it kicked it up a notch and announced not two but four more ships were coming between 2027 and 2031. Disney was sparse on the details, and we don't know what their destinations, names, or themes will be. We do know they will also be built at Meyer Werft. We expect Disney will give us the rest of the details like breadcrumbs over the next few years.

In the announcement, Disney did say the four new additions would bring the total number of ships to 13, which implies it will be keeping the *Magic* and *Wonder* until at least 2031. We love the two oldest ships (both more than 25 years old already), but at some point, no amount of refurbishment will keep them up to Disney's standards, and they will have to be retired (put out to sea?).

If we had to guess, we don't think these next four ships will be *Wish* class. The *Wish* class hasn't been wildly popular, and this is a great opportunity to either refresh the *Magic* class or start with a clean slate—a clean slate of red funnels, yellow lifeboats, and dark-blue hulls, of course.

Potential names and themes abound as well. Name ideas that have been discussed for years include *Believe, Discovery, Enchantment, Imagination, Inspiration,* and *Spirit.* As for possible themes, Disney's vault is a wealth of riches. With this many ships, it could do a ship fully themed to one franchise (*Star Wars,* anyone?) or keep mixing them up with something for everyone.

As for destinations, the world is Disney's oyster. Maybe New York City will finally get that year-round ship. We could see a ship spending all its time in Europe too. South America and Africa seem to be ripe for a ship, but this might call for an even smaller vessel to serve the expedition-cruise market.

Not even the most die-hard of Disney cruisers will be excited about everything that comes out. The great thing about having so many ships is that there should be enough variety in themes, ship sizes, and destinations to offer something that appeals to everyone.

The Cruise Lines International Association (CLIA) predicts the number of people cruising by 2027 will reach almost 40 million. The only thing holding that number back may be capacity. So, does Disney have even more ships in it? It's had great success in the river-cruise market with Adventures by Disney through its partnership with AmaWaterways. Could it be considering its own dedicated river cruise ships? What about the hot expedition-cruise market? Will Disney want to join in with its own take on expedition ships? We can't wait to find out!

DCL GLOSSARY

A CRUISE VACATION means you'll encounter a great deal of specialized lingo unique to the industry. That goes double for a Disney cruise, which has its own lexicon as well. Here are some general and Disney Cruise Line–specific terms you may encounter both in your planning and on the ship.

ADJACENT STATEROOMS Staterooms that are next to each other but aren't connected by an internal door. You must enter the hallway to travel between the staterooms. (Compare with **Connecting Staterooms.**)

ADULT DISTRICT The area on most DCL ships where the majority of the bars and lounges are located. The adult districts are typically restricted to guests age 18 and up after 9 p.m.

ADULT DINING The premium restaurants on the ship that require guests to be age 18 or older to attend and that charge an additional fee.

AFT The rear of the ship.

ALL ABOARD The time at which you're required to be back on the ship following a day in port. If you're not back at the ship by all-aboard time, you'll be left behind.

ALL ASHORE The time at which guests may disembark the ship for a day in port.

ASSISTANT SERVER The person on your serving team who is primarily responsible for your beverage orders and for making sure your plates are cleared between courses.

BACK TO BACK Booking two consecutive cruises on the same ship. This is most common on the *Disney Wish*, where guests with a fondness for Castaway Cay can book a three-day and four-day cruise one after the other. You can sometimes keep the same stateroom for such sailings.

BACKSTAGE Behind the scenes. Refers to any area of the ship that is not normally accessible to guests. (*Backstage* has the same meaning at the Disney parks.)

BLACKOUT DATES Specific sail dates for which onboard-booking (OBB) discounts (see page 28) are unavailable.

BOW The front of the ship.

BRIDGE The area at the front of the ship where the captain and his staff navigate the vessel.

BRIGHT STAR DCL's code for medical emergency. If you hear this over the ship's public address system, it will be paired with an onboard location, for example "Bright Star Animator's Palate" to direct trained staff where to go.

CAST MEMBER Disney-speak for "employee." Everyone who works for The Walt Disney Company is a cast member.

CASTAWAY CLUB DCL's "frequent cruiser" program. See page 5.

CLOSED-LOOP CRUISE A cruise that starts and ends at the same port. (Compare with **Repositioning Cruise**.)

CONNECTING STATEROOMS Staterooms that are next to each other and are connected by an internal door. (Compare with **Adjacent Staterooms**.)

CREW MEMBER Generally, the employees of a ship. On DCL, cruise staff (see below) are distinct from crew members.

CRUISE DIRECTOR The person responsible for onboard hospitality, entertainment, and social events; serves as the public face of the cruise line on their ship. On the DCL ships, you'll hear the cruise director make most onboard loudspeaker announcements. They'll also give opening remarks in the theater most evenings and record a fun morning show that will be available on the stateroom televisions in the mornings.

CRUISE STAFF You'd think this would mean all of the crew who work on the ship. On DCL, however, *cruise staff* refers to the dozen or so attractive, personable, and hyperenergetic cast members who run the onboard family and adult entertainment activities: bingo, karaoke, dance parties, and so on.

DECK The nautical term for "story," "floor," or "level." For example, your stateroom isn't on Floor 6 but Deck 6.

DISNEYBAND+ A plastic and rubber wristband equipped with an RFID chip. If purchased, it can serve as an onboard stateroom key, payment mechanism, and more (see page 152).

DOUBLE DIP Slang in the Disney-cruise community for an itinerary with two stops at Castaway Cay or Lookout Cay. Each year there are just a handful of double-dip cruises, making them particularly coveted.

DRAFT The distance from the waterline to the very bottom of the ship, or how much of the ship is underwater at any given time. The draft can vary depending on the weight of the ship, due to increased displacement. A ship's draft may affect which ports are available for docking.

FISH EXTENDER Next to each stateroom door is a shelflike metal sculpture (shaped like a fish on many staterooms) that functions like a mailbox. Some guests hang fabric pockets from the sculpture, extending the fish. This accessory is used to hold gifts from like-minded cruisers in a Secret Santa–type exchange. It is completely optional.

FOLIO Your stateroom account.

FORWARD The front part of the ship.

GALLEY The ship's kitchen.

GANGWAY The ramp or staircase that guests use to embark and disembark the ship. Depending on the specifics of a particular port, the location of the gangway may vary.

GTY Guarantee. This rate is used when a category is almost full and is *not* a discounted rate. You won't be able to select a specific stateroom, only a guarantee of a certain category (or, rarely, a better one). Compare to **IGT, OGT,** and **VGT** (also see page 24).

HEAD SERVER The waiter in charge of the entire dining room in Disney's rotational restaurants. You may not see your head server much, but that's because they're extremely busy making sure the entire dining operation runs smoothly. If you're having any trouble with your primary serving team, speak with the head server.

IGT Inside Guarantee. A discounted, nonrefundable fare typically booked at the last minute. You won't get to choose your exact stateroom, but you are guaranteed an Inside Stateroom. See page 24.

KEY TO THE WORLD (KTTW) CARD The card you receive upon check-in that functions as your room key, identification during photo opportunities, and charge card for merchandise and extra-cost food and beverage items on the ship. You will need your KTTW Card many times throughout your day on board, as well as to get on or off the ship. *Always* keep it with you during your cruise, even on debarkation day.

KNOT A unit of speed equal to 1 nautical mile (1.852 kilometers) per hour, or 1.151 miles per hour.

MDR Main dining room (aka **rotational dining room**). Each DCL ship has three MDRs.

MUSTER The required first-day safety drill.

NAUTICAL MILE See **Knot.**

OBB (aka **Placeholder**) **Onboard booking,** or booking your next Disney cruise while you're on your current cruise. If you book your next cruise on board, you receive a discount on the OBB sailing (typically 10%).

OFFICER A member of the leadership team of the ship. On DCL, officers typically wear white uniforms.

OGT Oceanview Guarantee. A discounted, nonrefundable fare typically booked at the last minute. You won't get to choose your exact stateroom, but you will get an Oceanview Stateroom. See page 24.

ONBOARD CREDIT "Gift" money that you can apply to your folio to pay for shore excursions, adult dining, shipboard merchandise, and so on.

Travel agents often give onboard credit to clients who book cruises through them. You can also win onboard credit at bingo on the ship and at promotional presentations for DVC, Senses Spa, and shopping.

PAT Port-arrival time. Often confused with boarding time, this actually refers to the time you can arrive at the port.

PLACEHOLDER See **OBB**.

PORT (ADJ.) The left side of the ship, as you face the front of it.

REPOSITIONING CRUISE Cruise on which the embarkation and debarkation ports are different (compare with **Closed-Loop Cruise**). Disney primarily uses this term to refer to its 10-plus-day transatlantic and Panama Canal sailings.

ROTATIONAL DINING ROOM See **MDR**.

SERVER Your dining room waiter. Your server will guide you through the menu each night, take your order, and ensure that it's delivered to your table properly and promptly.

SHIP A large oceangoing vessel—*don't call it a boat!* With a few exceptions, the general rule is that a ship can carry a boat but a boat can't carry a ship.

SOLO (OR SINGLE) SUPPLEMENT Fee paid by solo cruisers to make up for the revenue lost when a stateroom or cabin is not fully booked.

STARBOARD The right side of the ship, as you face the front of it.

STATEROOM Sleeping quarters on ships are traditionally called cabins; Disney calls theirs staterooms.

STATEROOM HOST/ATTENDANT The person who attends to your stateroom, turns down your bed at night, delivers messages, and generally assists with any aspect of your stateroom's functionality.

STERN The back of the ship.

TENDER A small boat that transfers guests from the cruise ship to land. Tenders are used when a port's waters are too shallow for a large ship to dock next to a pier.

TRANSFER The Disney-arranged method of getting you to the ship prior to sailing or to another form of transportation after sailing. For example, you can purchase transfers from a hotel at Walt Disney World to Port Canaveral or from Port Canaveral to Orlando International Airport. Transfers are available at all home ports.

VERANDAH Your private stateroom balcony.

VGT **Verandah Guarantee**. A discounted, nonrefundable fare typically booked at the last minute. You won't get to choose your exact stateroom, but you are guaranteed a Verandah Stateroom (see page 24).

VPP **Vacation Protection Plan,** or trip insurance (see page 114).

INDEX